Wasted

The Messy Story of Sanitation in India, A Manifesto for Change

Ankur Bisen

AF652200

MACMILLAN

First published in India 2019 by Macmillan

This paperback edition published in 2025 by Macmillan
an imprint of Pan Macmillan Publishing India Private Limited
707, Kailash Building
26, K. G. Marg, New Delhi – 110 001
www.panmacmillan.co.in

Pan Macmillan, The Smithson, 6 Briset Street, London EC1M 5NR
Associated companies throughout the world
www.panmacmillan.com

ISBN 978-93-61130-30-4

Copyright © Ankur Bisen 2019

All rights reserved. No part of this publication may be reproduced, stored in or introduced into a retrieval system, or transmitted, in any form, or by any means (electronic, mechanical, photocopying, recording or otherwise) without the prior written permission of the publisher. Any person who does any unauthorized act in relation to this publication may be liable to criminal prosecution and civil claims for damages.

1

This book is sold subject to the condition that it shall not, by way of trade or otherwise, be lent, re-sold, hired out, or otherwise circulated without the publisher's prior consent in any form of binding or cover other than that in which it is published and without a similar condition including this condition being imposed on the subsequent purchaser.

Typeset by Manmohan Kumar
Printed and bound in India by Repro India Ltd

FSC
www.fsc.org
MIX
Paper from responsible sources
FSC® C047271

CONTENTS

Praise for *Wasted*

'This book enhances our understanding of the historical issues that have plagued India's sanitation challenge. A must read for those who are interested in the important agenda of a clean environment for all.'

Naina Lal Kidwai, Chair, India-Sanitation Coalition

'Despite the clarion call by our Prime Minister, Indian society still lacks clarity on the nature of the desirable solution for sanitation. *Wasted* is a serious attempt at pointing out possibilities and solutions. Written lucidly and in a narrative style; it provides an inspiring peek of a clean future. A much-needed book for our times.'

Dr Rajiv Kumar, Vice Chairman, Niti Aayog

'*Wasted* advocates that the handling of waste in India requires the finest management and developmental architecture. The book remarkably delves into the depth and breadth of the problem of yesterday and today and presents it as a free-flowing story.'

Martin Macwan, Dalit human rights activist

'*Wasted* locates India's missed opportunities in sanitation in its complex civilizational legacy; its comfort with caste, informality and child labour; and in its appalling local governance systems. Necessary reading for every policy maker, town planner and engaged urban citizen.'

Harsh Mander, author and activist

'*Wasted* addresses India's complex caste-driven perception of waste. It traces the illogic of our constant discontent with modes of disposal, while being deliberately blind to socio-political processes behind its creation. This book must be read by all concerned Indians.'

Aruna Roy, socio-political activist and Magsaysay Award winner (2000)

'India is not working on the science needed towards the management of pollution that it emits in the name of development. Therefore, even well-intentioned projects do not yield results. This book can be an entry point to understanding the process to reduce use of nature and to rejuvenate nature for our sustainable future.'

Dr Rajendra Singh, environmentalist and Magsaysay Award winner (2001)

Wasted

Ankur Bisen is committed to his concerns about the environment and the accountability of citizens to improving conditions of sanitation in urban India. While growing up in India's quaint small towns, briefly leading an expat life and working in bustling Indian cities and towns, he developed an enquiring mind towards a cleaner and greener future.

In his years as a management consultant at Technopak Advisors and before that in the Tata Group and Lemon Tree hotels, he has thought and researched about India's sanitation problems and possible solutions while working in diverse fields such as affordable housing, food, retailing, urban and rural consumption clusters, resource recovery and consumer products with an India focus.

Ankur has written regularly for leading English dailies in the past. This is his first book.

INTRODUCTION

In 2017, two unrelated events, 7,000 kilometers apart, occurred revealing the chasm between the stance of two societies on a common issue – sanitation.

The Thames Water Plc., a public limited entity and the biggest water utility company in the UK, supplies water to nearly 15 million homes in London and in the Thames Valley region. In 2017, it was slapped with a penalty of GBP 20 million (₹200 crores) for allowing its operations to dump 1.4 billion liters of raw sewage into the River Thames in 2013–14. Thames Water admitted this gross misconduct after the prosecuting court found evidence that proved the offense beyond doubt. Since 2014, the UK has revised its sentencing and penalty guidelines for environmental offenses and has made them more severe than they had ever been in the past. This sealed the fate of Thames Water Plc.

Meanwhile, in India, the National Green Tribunal (NGT), the Indian judicial system formed in 2010 to expedite litigation matters that concern environmental protection, issued a verdict against four governance entities in 2017 – Uttar Pradesh State Pollution Control Board, Mathura Cantonment Board, District Magistrate Mathura, and Central Pollution Control Board: the matter being waste disposal at a garbage landfill site in the city of Mathura, which threatened to contaminate the river Yamuna due to its design and proximity. The verdict could only impose a penalty to the tune of ₹15 lakhs (GBP 20,000) for a sheer lack of specific rules and guidelines about waste disposal in landfills. Ironically, the verdict also directed these bodies to formulate proper rules for such waste disposal.

These two judicial interventions seemingly address the same issue, but bring out diametrically different approach by two different societies. In the UK case, the judicial order was a precise and severe judgment that clearly established the offense of a private entity found in breach of the law. The penalty imposed also reveals the country's clarity of jurisprudence regarding waste management. However, in India, the judicial verdict appears to be but an exasperated response that cries out of helplessness for the lack of laws on the issue. In common wisdom, the material evidence presented during the trial of the case suggests impropriety regarding waste disposal undertaken by the authorities. But, the verdict could not explicitly establish the guilt of the parties, and, on the contrary, was a pronouncement of the guilt of state actors – a mere rap on their knuckles – for inadequate legislation on waste disposal: the meager fine further highlights the frustration of the powerless judiciary to corner the executive and define 'proper' and 'improper' acts.

At present, India ranks among the top ten waste generators in the world, and is projected to be among the top four in the coming decade. At this stage, the judiciary pleading with the executive to accelerate legislation on the issue of waste management is catastrophic, while the state's lethargy to not pass a law on this issue is baffling. The arguments presented by the state actors in their defense during the trial of the Mathura landfill case hints at two reasons that explain their attitude.

The first is the government's sheer *ignorance* on the issue of waste disposal. The concerned bodies cited common dumping of biodegradable and non-biodegradable garbage, use of open landfills, and relying on ragpickers as acceptable methods of disposal, practices that have been banned in the First-World countries for decades now. The second reason is the *pretense* of the governance bodies, to knowingly accept non-conformity to the rule, arguing for lack of funds to take suitable action and passing the buck among each other.

It can be said that the Mathura landfill disposal case captures the Indian society's challenge on the issue in its entirety. It has taken seventy years since Independence for our prime minister to address the stinking issue of the country's garbage problem.

The silent acquiescence of the Indian society on toxic rivers that are unfit for any purpose, of simmering landfills that hold a towering presence in cities, of stinking littered garbage in neighborhoods, of choked sewers, contaminated soil, and polluted air, and of squalid hell holes that pack one quarter of urban Indians raises a pertinent question about the society's behavior on the issue of sanitation: Is this pretense or ignorance? Evidently, this surrender qualifies as an act of pretense. Why else would the prime minister acknowledge that India is dirty and needs to be cleaned? What are the reasons that compelled the Indian society to look the other way on the issue? The reasons are so illusive that they bring about a sense of helplessness to accept the status quo.

If we are to reject the pretense theory then the prime minister's speech is an acknowledgement of India's stance on the issue of sanitation as ignorance. It is also an acceptance that neither India's present generation nor its previous generations ever lived in a clean society. This pushes the issue of sanitation into the realm of philosophy: if a society has never experienced a desirable state of cleanliness then the entire notion becomes relative. My idea of hygiene may not pass your cleanliness standards, but I give two hoots to your standards. Perhaps I am fine with the toxic river because I have never seen it in any other color during my adult life. I am fine with the simmering landfill because I have spent my entire childhood absorbing its visuals and inhaling its presence. I am fine with littered garbage and choked sewers around my house because I am not aware of an alternate existence. It may baffle people who were raised in 'clean' surroundings, but I do not know what 'clean' means. If the Indian society is ignorant about the very notion of cleanliness then these are defendable arguments. But these arguments also raise other questions on human instincts and race.

Do humans have the instinct to appreciate a clean environment? How do they respond to dirty surrounding? How is this response similar to, or different from, that of threat on life or hunger or love? Literature offers some interesting points to ponder. *Perfume: The Story of a Murderer*, a literary classic written by the German writer Patrick Süskind in 1985, is an allegory for the human instinct of smell. Set in eighteenth-century France, a time when garbage and sanitation in the country were unresolved matters, the protagonist is an orphan whose mother, a poor young woman, brings him into the world on a pile of abject filth in the hope that he will not survive, as did all her previous stillborn children. But, miraculously, Jean-Baptiste Grenouille survives and grows up to possess an exceptional sense of smell. In his pursuit of superior fragrances, he becomes a perfumer, and when he becomes aware of the wondrous scent of the human body, he turns a murderer. When tried of the many killings, he hypnotizes the townsfolk by unleashing a soothing new scent, a welcome relief from the perpetual stink of their everyday surroundings. Perhaps the reason why Grenouille becomes a pursuer of good smells is to overcome the surrounding circumstances at the time of his birth.

People appreciate good smells and reject bad ones. Till the pre-industrialized period, the struggle with sanitation was largely driven by the pursuit of removing odor from the society. Are human species not the same across countries? Are Indians as a race different to interpret garbage than others? Then why does India continue to struggle with rubbish while many other countries sparkle?

Indian society displays remarkably contrasting evidence that makes it difficult to conclude whether its challenges on sanitation stem from an act of pretense or from an act of ignorance. Why are many Indian homes spotlessly clean, but the surroundings disgustingly dirty? Why are homemakers dogmatic about kitchen hygiene, but do not mind tossing waste from the windows on to the streets? Why are some automobile owners on a short fuse if their vehicles get dirty, but unabashedly throw litter on the street while driving? Why do we celebrate festivals with rituals that involve cleaning of homes? Why are cantonment or 'VIP' areas a picture of cleanliness and other areas of the same city a mess? Why do people not mind searching for god at places of worship that are perpetually surrounded by a sanitation hell? India, till now, has consistently used a sweeping stroke to seek solutions for its sanitation problems. Garbage is found littered on streets because there are hardly any bins. Why then are the streets equipped with an adequate number of garbage bins still strewn with garbage? To make a difference, India first needs to reconcile such contradictions, and see where it stands in the world order on sanitation vis-à-vis other developing and developed nations.

Corruption and population are cited as issues contributing toward India's poor sanitation. If so, how do many other equally corrupt countries have far better sanitation standards than India? Why is it then that cities like Tokyo and Hong Kong, two of the most densely populated clusters on the planet, have managed to keep themselves spotlessly clean while India struggles?

The Indian political system is also often accused for its chaotic structure that incentivizes stakeholders with divergent ideas that seemingly work at cross purposes for policymaking and governance. The Indian democracy is often blamed for its apparently low entry barrier or for allowing the existence of a multiparty representative system. But this too cannot be the reason for the sanitation mess or one needs to justify the existence of a nation like the Netherlands – an inspiration on waste management. For decades, the Netherlands has involved nearly a dozen parties to run the country. How does one then explain the emergence of the picturesque city of Amsterdam from such a seemingly 'messy' political system of the country?

It emerges that people have evolved their ideas about waste and sanitation management over centuries – a realization triggered by the constant onslaught of man-made inventions into daily life. Essentially a direct aftermath, progress, propelled by new inventions and advancements in science and technology, has taught humans a humbling lesson about sanitation, because every invention brought along its own sanitation mess. Horse carriages meant horse droppings on roads that need to be cleared. Printing press has led to a heap of newspapers as waste. Discarding smartphones has become an environmental hazard. Societies have been perpetually playing a catch-up game with waste management – by the time ways to manage waste from the previous invention have been figured, new challenges posed by the next invention come up. All societies therefore have had to struggle and create methods to handle the aftermath of progress. Biological reasons like race, instincts, or origins do not have any bearing on the issue of sanitation. But in the post–World War II order, the 'clean' countries of today found their way out of the maze of the urban sanitation problem. Concurrently, an interplay of geopolitics, ideology, social choices, and political priorities created a trajectory for India that pushed it into a quagmire of garbage.

***

The first chapter of the book deals with the devious impact this interplay had upon India's contradictions on sanitation and how it eventually pushed India into free fall on waste management. It served to wrongly partition the notion of sanitation in the Indian mind into cleanliness of private spaces versus public spaces. It further enabled the Indian society to interlink the sanitation of private spaces to a patriarchal mindset and to assign sanitation of public spaces to the caste system, thereby viewing waste management from the standpoint of entitlement, eventually fracturing the social contract between the Indian society and the Indian state on the issue. It suffocated the collective Indian mind and forced it to take a series of bad calls that landed us on the wrong side of the sanitation debate. Concurrently, many First-World countries succeeded in preventing their respective societies from taking such an entitled view and in creating the right social contract that helped them to conquer the sanitation challenge. Without learning from this lesson, any progress by India on this issue will merely remain an illusion.

A convoluted and vague understanding of the governance around waste also gave rise to a fractured social contract. The state, on behalf of its citizens, is entrusted with the responsibility of sanitation – an accepted norm of any modern human society. As an outcome of this responsibility, the state builds an apparatus to discharge it. Infrastructure for waste collection and disposal, enforcement, legislation are all organs of this apparatus and come under this purview. It so emerges that the Indian state, in its organizational design, never fully absorbed these responsibilities. How can such a state deliver the desired outcome if its responsibilities to manage sanitation were vaguely understood and with an absent apparatus? But, how was such a grave slip-up possible in the first place?

The backdrop at the time India became a republic was important. In a way, the sanitation mess represents the unfinished agenda of the creation of India as a democratic state, a process that started on 26 January 1950. Another folly of the Indian state was its failure to appreciate the issue of sanitation for its interdependencies and to appreciate its own role as an agent of change. Waste disposal and sanitation are a direct outcome of society's consumption behavior. The state actively shaped the consumption basket of the society and prioritized the pecking order of citizens' consumption choices. It formulated economic and agriculture policies, welfare and health programs, taxation, and controls that had a direct bearing on the society's disposition toward real estate, retail, education, healthcare, recreation, and other services. Then, why did the same state take a dormant stand on the issue of the waste generated as a result of this consumption? Why did the policy decisions of the Indian state stop short at anticipating the implications on waste management and sanitation of the consumption patterns of its citizens? How did the First-World countries succeed in avoiding this trap? What forced the Indian state to trivialize the issue of sanitation and not treat it with intellectual rigor or scientific temperament? The second and third chapters attempt to answer these questions.

The first half of the book explores reasons for India's twisted mindset (of both citizens and the state) on sanitation and the biases and prejudices that force it to oscillate between pretense and ignorance. Unfortunately, for India, this oscillation created a warped priority list with disastrous consequences, as argued in the second half of the book. These chapters highlight the extent of operational corrosion of the Indian waste and sanitation apparatus, and its extreme inadequacy in addressing the growing challenge of waste management. An isolated commentary on the extent of corrosion may be afflicted with the dangers of individual perception. Therefore, the narrative is layered with references to multi-country apparatus for a deeper understanding. Solutions needed to lubricate the corrosion are low-hanging fruits that can be easily reaped, and need to be pieced together for an easy roadmap. But a combination of circumstances and preconceived notions prevent the relevant stakeholders to see this roadmap, these chapters argue.

The book also squirts nervous energy for two reasons. Firstly, the clean countries of today were not blessed with a superior apparatus to manage sanitation and waste; it was created over a period that lasted more than a century. India, therefore, has no reasons to suffer from an inferiority complex yet. Secondly, the point-in-time when

India confronts this challenge with its antiquated apparatus offers hope that the challenge can be turned on its head at an accelerated pace rather than the linear pace that took over a century to bear fruit in the clean countries. If, for instance, today's clean countries were to address the sanitation challenge in the present time (and other things remained the same as they currently are), they would possibly not take the similar linear path they took to resolve the issue. Today, technology and the state of human evolution allow bypassing of many past solutions and to review solutions with a fresh pair of eyes. The relationship between waste management and ecological balance, for instance, was not established as clearly a century ago as it is today. Therefore, the thrust of solutions in these countries in the past were aimed toward the cleanliness of streets and neighborhoods and not so much from the perspective of ecology. Today, recycling and resource recovery ideas have become the mainstay of waste disposal in many of these clean countries. Wisdom, in retrospect, is allowing these countries to take another stab at reducing waste generation from the standpoint of relieving environmental stress. Therefore, some of these countries are increasingly pairing the subject of cleanliness with the agenda of resource conversation. This paradigm shift has propelled these countries to view cleanliness and circular economy in the same context. They are aspiring to stay clean while their biodegradable refuse safely integrates with the environment and the non-biodegradable is completely arrested from getting released into the biosphere. Circular economies like Sweden are recycling nearly everything that they consume – the target is to achieve harmony between ecology and clean living without blaming human progress. So much so that their recycling industry increasingly solicits refuse from other countries to scale up recycling as an independent economic activity. Thrust on multifaceted public transport, elevated walking trails that cover city centers and expressways, legislations like product liability for disposal and congestion taxes for automobiles, predictive and remote sensing surveillance to monitor waste generation and disposal in cities, plug-and-play urban solutions are all actions these countries have taken for a clean and environmentally sustainable living.

There is no reason for India to take a linear approach to improve its waste management apparatus like the First-World countries did a hundred years ago. Technology, economic stature, and demographic advantage present interesting possibilities for India to take a non-linear route and to significantly hasten this journey to clean itself. This will allow India to de-couple the issue of waste from prejudices and past baggage and to turn the sanitation challenge on its head. India has all the opportunity to repurpose sanitation challenge into a fulcrum of job creation, as a driver of social change, as a sustainable economic growth driver, and even as a tool for soft diplomacy to influence geopolitics. All these gains can turn waste management into an annual 15-billion-dollar industry or more for India.

There are no tables, graphs, or charts in this book because its purpose is not to find facts or to pinpoint villains. For there are no villains in this story, but there are biases and prejudices. There are no victims in the story, but there are actors. Everything from luck to circumstances, from geopolitics to faith, from needs to desire, from compulsions to choices has played a part in India's unfortunate struggle with sanitation. For these very reasons, solutions to a clean India lie in seemingly unrelated areas or in explicit places which require an altered perspective. Solutions do not lie in pleas and campaigns for clean living, in garbage bin installations on streets, in enrolment of more sanitation workers, or in the hunt for new landfills. India's approach to clean itself will not be one magic pill nor can it be one big-bang intervention. Instead, solutions lie in legislation, education policy, reforms in enforcement and policing, organic farming, policy for domesticated bovines, contract theory, cooperative movement, rental housing, resource recovery industry, and re-designed framework of state actors that strengthens local governance.

The last chapter stress tests this approach vis-à-vis one of the most visible sanitation challenges of modern India – the National Mission for Clean Ganga. The dirty river Ganga encapsulates all that is wrong and that is misplaced with the issue of sanitation in India. Therefore, if the approach succeeds to clean the river then it should pass the universality challenge of applicability to address all other sanitation challenges of the country. The book argues for encouraging results of this stress test.

It took nearly fifty years for the First World to figure out these solutions from their individual start points in the post-industrialized era and another fifty years to implement these solutions – they underwent trials by fire for decades before being nudged toward clean living. Rapid urbanization, triggered by industrialization, preceded the triumph of most of these countries on waste management and sanitation. Urbanization created immense pressure on political establishment of respective states and stressed their societies to seek comprehensive solutions on sanitation and waste. These clean countries teach us that urbanization and industrialization are preconditions for them to initiate their respective cleanliness drives. It was difficult for them to anticipate the implication of urbanization on sanitation and to proactively initiate cleanliness drives. Once urbanization hit these countries, trials and improvisations were hurriedly attempted to arrest the ensuing chaos, but offered no immediate respite.

If the theory that urbanization is a precondition to clean societies is true then does it mean that purely non-urban societies cannot exit as clean societies? This is a theoretical argument because sanitation in purely rural societies is a non-issue. Such societies naturally live a circular existence, which is balanced with the environment. If a village is not infringed upon by any industrial or urban trait then that village will not have any issue with sanitation. Its production and consumption cycles will work in perfect balance to square off production and consumption. Many tribes in the jungles of Amazon or in the islands of Bay of Bengal that still live an isolated existence, completely detached from the modern world, do not really struggle with the issue of sanitation precisely for this reason. A sanitation challenge emerges when foreign products infiltrate the consumption cycle of the village and disturb the natural recycling wheel, because it now needs to figure out a way to dispose its waste.

Let us consider the example of bathing in villages. The villagers rub mud on their bodies and clean themselves in the lake. The mud gets easily dissolved in the lake water and the water body is replenished during the rainy season. But with progress, soap replaces mud. Now the villagers have to figure out a way to dispose its packaging and to prevent contamination, and poisoning, of the lake with chemicals present in the soap. Consider another example of the practice of drinking beverages. Villagers produce and drink milk by rearing bovines at home. One day, however, they are introduced to aerated cola in a plastic bottle, and soon it replaces milk. How do they discard the empty plastic bottle? Do they burn it? Naively some of them do and in the process start to pollute the air. Some others dispose it off in the lake thereby choking the natural flow of the water body. Industrialization creates new markets for soap and cola, and it travels to the village in search of new consumers and creates a sanitation challenge. The cola example is also true in reverse. Milk, produced in the dairy, travels to the urban household in a plastic packet, and they are faced with the challenge to discard the packet.

Integrating human consumption with man-made modern marvels has disturbed the harmony of nature and has caused the sanitation problem we face today. The clean countries of today realized the futility of a counter-narrative to modernization as an effective remedy for the challenge of sanitation, and adopted society-wide abstinence of, detachment from, rejection of modern living. They also understood that cherry-picking 'good' modern-day marvels over the 'bad' ones to practice a middle-of-the-road existence was not an option. You cannot ignore the plastic bottle and accept the mobile phone: both require a process for safe disposal.

A counter-narrative for urbanization and industrialization was also not possible because modern human society had lost the right to proclaim such a resistance after the chest-thumping pursuit of industrialization as a symbol of human progress for centuries. Urbanization and industrialization are manifestations of humans' instinctive desire to change the status quo, while good or bad outcomes are fait accompli. Differently put, humans do not have the right to make an argument to resist industrialization because they are an outcome of it. Even pioneers of nineteenth-century industrialization were in no position to make an argument against it because they themselves were the modern and new-age thinkers of their time and were also a product of the pre-industrialized society that was 'industrialized' in its own way. The fact that these pioneers could print their ideas on a piece of paper was the result of the printing press invented a few centuries earlier. Even the society that gave rise to the printing press could not make that argument because it was a product of early man-made inventions that allowed them to travel and to smelt metal. This society was an outcome of the earlier invention of wheel and discovery of fire. The argument to resist industrialization, therefore, could have been made only by the inventor of the wheel, the cavemen. They should have thought, 'While we have invented the wheel and discovered fire, these inventions will pose a severe challenge of sanitation to our future generations and to the ecology of the world. So let's give it a pass.' That could have been a winning argument, but not one from us.

Clean countries of today understood this limitation and instead of resisting industrialization – and the accompanying urbanization – they worked relentlessly toward upgrading the apparatus to deal with the sanitation challenge that came as an essential addendum to industrialization. It meant that if a village had indeed migrated to drinking a beverage in a plastic bottle, these countries figured out the dangers of the discarded bottle and successfully installed an efficient system to collect and haul it for safe recycling or disposal.

Another reason for the long time it took these countries to surmount the challenge was that the problem of sanitation was a social issue in need of a technical response. Suddenly, these societies were exposed to modern scientific advancements, and allowed themselves to get packed into concentrated urban areas in hope for better a future. But such an arrangement put great stress on neighborhoods to haul sewage and solid waste. Back in the village, a septic tank in the backyard and garbage pit for biodegradable waste would suffice. Now the waste comprised a growing list of plastic bags, glass, metals, processed wood, electrical goods, and so on. Neither was there a septic tank for solid waste disposal, nor a backyard to put in such a pit. The society was bewildered about the new character of waste and the challenges that came with it. The collective mind was numbed and forced to act irrationally, compelling them to become immune to dirty surroundings. This was the crux of a social issue.

The technical response to the issue was the installation of a waste collection and disposal infrastructure that was supported by legislation and its enforcement. Another technical response was to improve the designs of neighborhoods so that their tendency to create dirty surroundings is curtailed. While logical, these responses meant disruption of livelihoods, displacement, and exasperation from the slow pace of change. Moreover, these responses were not executed as comprehensively as they are outlined. Here, the narrative has the advantage of wisdom in retrospect to be able to present it in a well-ordered manner. Responses in those times took decades to show results. Marrying the social issue with such technical responses needed strong-willed political sponsorship which was hard to achieve in these societies. Lack of previous experience on the issue played its part to delay political readiness. The sponsorship needed bold political bets that could pay dividends, but at the same time sponsors who were brave enough to stake their political careers. No past reference could be banked on for this purpose. Political sponsorship needed to stay the course to take tough calls and force the society to change its behavior toward sanitation, for instance, the practice of bagging garbage at home in standardized bins and to stop burning trash in the open. Such a resolve did not waiver for fear of a backlash.

This context offers hope for India, which is witnessing a similar wave of urbanization and an equally intense stress on the issue of sanitation as experienced by the First-World societies a hundred years ago. No society was conceived with all its sanitation woes addressed or parachuted into the lap of cleanliness. Intense misery, struggle, and suffering were hallmarks of the journey toward cleanliness for most of the clean countries of today.

Therefore, time is apt for India to craft a comprehensive response on the issue of waste management and sanitation because it took over seventy years for the enabling conditions to fall in place. Going forward, India's ambitions to compete on the world stage will ring hollow if it still struggles to offer a semblance of clarity on the issue. India cannot aspire for a world-class consumption story simultaneously with a medieval mindset to handle the aftermath of such consumption. More than a lesson in morality, this inference is rooted in the clinical nature of economic growth of a country.

In 2009, when India's gross domestic product (GDP) was 1,200 billion dollars, it consumed 1 billion dollar worth of packaging material (non-biodegradable waste such as pouches, sachets, glass bottles, cardboard boxes) for every 30 billion dollar worth of retail merchandise. By 2015, India's GDP grew to 1,800 billion dollar at a compound annual growth rate (CAGR) of 7 percent since 2009. But by this time, 1 billion dollar worth of packaging material was needed for every 18 billion dollar worth of retail merchandise. Within six years, the consistent and seemingly linear economic growth of 7 percent had a disruptive effect on India's consumption structure and propelled the packaging demand to grow at 15 percent during the same period. Linear economic growth created a non-linear rise of consumers' affordability, of disruptive investment in logistics, of accelerated growth in food processing that pushed the demand for packaging material in a non-linear manner. Take the growth of smartphones in India between 2009 and 2016 as a case in point. In 2009, 6 million smartphones were sold annually in India, which shot to 82 million annually in 2015. Every new smartphone meant a new packing box and an inescapable need to dispose it at the end of its lifecycle. Waste generated from this consumption is bound to overtake existing waste collection and disposal systems. Consequently, waste is bound to spill onto the streets or burn in the open. It is this disruptive effect of economic growth on waste management that has kept the First-World countries on their toes for a hundred years, and it is the implication of this disruptive effect that India is yet to fully grasp. India's consumption ambitions will need responsible handling of the aftermath of this consumption. Therefore, going forward, there will be villains in this story if India continues to ignore the treasure trove of lessons that our own unfortunate journey and past struggles of the clean countries have to offer.

Indian society lacks clarity on the nature of the desirable solution for sanitation and on the role of every stakeholder that is needed to solve the problem. Therefore, what better an icon than Gandhi's eyeglasses to symbolize this search for a Clean India. But we need to heed a warning before embarking on this search. India's journey on the issue till date carries a baggage of preconceived biases which have cracked the lenses and clouded the vision, threatening to misguide. Removing these biases will serve to rectify the cracks in the vision and significantly increase India's chances to find the right answers. Gandhi's eyeglasses finding a place on the new currency notes is an encouraging sign about the readiness of much-needed political sponsorship on the issue of sanitation. Though the circumstances seem overwhelming, the backdrop offers hope.

The illusive solution is not one magical formula. Many small initiatives will need to be stitched together to resemble a chimera – a Greek mythological fire-breathing monster with a lion's head, a goat's body, and serpent's tail. In the challenge of sanitation lies India's own Carpe Diem moment. There is no better time than now for this book.

1

WE THE PEOPLE

'Is India a dirty country?'

If you live in Mawlynnong, a village in the state of Meghalaya, considered one of the cleanest villages in Asia, your response will be but a baffled expression. Equally baffling will your response be if you are Niron Devi, a fifty-five-year-old landless laborer living in a *jhuggi* cluster on the floodplains of the river Yamuna in Delhi, who has relieved herself in the open for the last twenty-five years.

Residents of Citizen Nagar, on the outskirts of Ahmedabad, have woken up every morning for the last thirteen years to the sight of a 135-meter-tall landfill. Generations of children in Sipri Bazaar, Jhansi, have grown up flying kites and playing cricket alongside stinking garbage dumps and pigs lounging about in open sewage drains. Hartman de Souza expresses his anger at the now disfigured coastline of Goa. Mohan Lal, the Malayalam cine superstar, considers garbage the biggest threat to God's Own Country. Chances are such people will side more with Niron Devi than with the residents of Mawlynnong while answering if India is a dirty country. Why is Mawlynnong an exception while the other narratives become the default reality in India? How is it that within the same country there exists one of the cleanest human habitations and the dirtiest places on the planet?

What is it about sanitation that forces us to take such contrary stands? We invoke our cultural and philosophical heritage as logical arguments in debates on contemporary issues, but why do we still throw an empty food wrapper out of the car or burn trash outside our shops before the start of a business day? Are we conditioned to accept dirty surroundings as a state of equilibrium and not one of distress? It will be of little value to develop a critical commentary of any worth on the topic of sanitation without getting a hang of the Indian mindset on this subject. We need to deconstruct these questions and compare the Indian mind to the minds of those who live in the acceptably clean countries across the world.

During the time humans were cavemen, excreta was the only form of waste generated. Like any other animal, they would step out and relieve themselves in a place far away from their habitation. With their evolution into social animals, and with the knowledge of the importance of family as a cohesive, social unit, human colonies started to take shape. And with this they began to dump their waste in the outskirts of their settlements or in their own backyards, a simple extension of the waste disposal practice followed by their ancestors.

While every human invention created new and exciting consumption options, they brought with them the challenge of disposing the waste, a natural outcome. With the invention of the wheel arrived transportation. Horse-drawn carriages were made, which required a supporting ecosystem of stables and transit points to make them a viable mode of transport and tool of trade. But at the same time the horses dropped excreta on the streets, an inevitable side-effect. Until the invention of automobiles in the 1900s, horse droppings on the roads was of one of the biggest waste management challenges of human settlements in most cities in the world, from New York to Tokyo. The need to put mechanisms in place to clean the roads and make the surroundings safe and orderly was the primary concern.

Take also the invention of the printing press by Johannes Gutenberg in 1440. The printing press altered the cognitive ability of humans to assimilate and record knowledge. One direct outcome of this invention was the transition of paper-making from a niche cottage industry to a mass and industrial scale application. Nearly 170 years after the invention of the printing press, the first newspaper – a weekly publication called *Relations* – was published in Antwerp in 1605. But who thought about how to get rid of it once the weekly had served its utility of delivering news? Were they to store it, burn it, or simply discard it? One must note that the concept of public dustbins was another 250 years away.

Every invention gave rise to a new form of consumption, which preceded the way to dispose of its residue. Till the advent of the industrial age, the pace of human invention was slow. It took centuries to alter human behavior. This allowed time to create a response for waste disposal. Not always was the response appropriate; at times these were severely limited by the lack of resources and knowledge, such as burning of crop waste or dumping of garbage in the sea, which in today's context appear to be atrocious solutions.

Beyond the disposal of solid human waste away from the settlement, humans are not born with the natural instinct to manage waste. A toddler will figure out that wafers are meant to be eaten, but will not know what to do with its empty wrapper. He will toss it aside, which will lie around for hundreds of years if not properly disposed. On the other hand, with a mango, the discarded peel and stone may very well give rise to a new mango tree.

Clean countries of today learned early on that the toddler needs to be taught the process of correct disposal; however, this realization came through a painful struggle that lasted centuries, and not achieved until the onset of the twentieth century. Waste management and sanitation in the nineteenth century was a daunting task across the Western world. Human society then was unaware of the scientific relationship between dirty surroundings and the resultant diseases. That food garbage on the streets created ideal conditions for vector-borne diseases like cholera was not an obvious inference in those times. The subject of public health and medicine was under research, vaccines were some centuries away, and germ theory was not yet discovered. Prior to 'sanitation engineering', the New Yorker in 1903 captured this ignorance in a photograph of a dead horse lying next to children playing in the streets of New York City. Polluted rivers flowing through early towns of Europe were mentioned in the works of playwrights and poets of the Middle Ages. In August and September 1880, Paris struggled with the Great Stink, an odor so putrid that it sparked the fear of an epidemic, causing public outcry, outpouring of sentiments, political bickering, and journalistic badgering – a familiar scene in India today. However, people were sensitive to the bad odor their dirty surroundings emitted, and since they desired to live in a stench-free environment, any waste management approach that immediately took the odor away was acceptable, no matter how flawed the solution was for public health or environment. As a result in London in 1858, public latrines on the banks of the River Thames were acceptable because the flowing river took away untreated human waste and its odor in no time.

Nearly all the waste at that time was organic – food waste, animal carcasses, solid human waste – stored in deep cesspits located in the backyard. In London, these cesspits were called 'gongs,' or 'jakes,' or 'privies,' and men, called Gongfermours or Gongfarmers, were employed to empty these foul-smelling pits. They were allowed to work only at night and their job was to visit each house during their nightly beat plan, empty the cesspits into a carriage, and carry away the solid waste to dump it on the outskirts of the city – often described by historians as 'the worst job of the time.' They were restricted to live in a designated area and allowed to use only certain roads and bylanes to ferry the 'night soil.' While they faced isolation for the job they carried out, they were well compensated compared to other labor-intensive professions. This brings out an important aspect of social contract. Western societies recognized that the job of the Gongfermours was dirty and challenging, yet also recognized that it was critical for an odor-free living and thus compensated it with value. It is equally possible that given the challenging nature of the job, very few people were willing to take it up and therefore wages reflected the scarce availability of the labor. It was noticed that many Gongfermours were not socially pressured to undertake this job: they did it for the money. The exclusionist approach toward Gongfermours suggests a loosely defined caste system, based on the classification of profession, prevalent in Western societies. There was the royal class and then the commoners. Farmers were placed higher than tradesmen and others. However, this caste system had the option for people to enter and exit the professions. The quantum of wages earned by Gongfermours during that time indicates existence of free will. Perhaps, people who took up this profession of cesspit cleaning and waste disposal did it by choice and for the money it paid. While they were in the profession there were exclusionist rules for them such as designated areas to live in and an assigned time the for work and such others.

But these societies recognized that the human dependence on waste collection and disposal necessitated a better response. They started to adopt industrial approaches to manage waste at the early onset of Middle Ages. Paris for instance got its first underground sewer system in 1370.

By the end of the Middle Ages, many social changes started occurring in the backdrop of the Industrial Revolution in today's clean countries. The advent of this new era created possibilities of addressing many pressing and emerging challenges with liberal doses of scientific solutions. The invention of the first waste incinerator at the end of the nineteenth century in England eliminated the need to dump and burn waste in the open; people could now bag and segregate the garbage at source. WCs and sewer connections ended the need to ferry human waste manually. These interventions also eased the dependence on human hands and eventually eliminated the role of Gongfermours.

More importantly, these interventions helped societies put in place processes and policies that developed cognitive abilities in their inhabitants to manage a significant part of the chain. Societies were without bias toward waste and were genuinely hungry for sustainable solutions. Solutions of the past Gongfermours and slaves were taken away from the option list. Human labor to clean up waste eventually became expensive and hard to come by. Therefore, people abided by the rules and approaches of city administrators aimed at cleaning neighborhoods. Thus, these societies eventually succeeded in laying a strong foundation for a clean future.

Indian society in the preindustrial era was also influenced by factors similar to those of Western societies – growth of agrarian economy, influence of religion, wars and invasions, skills and crafts, monarchs and dynasties, human migration, and so on. But the scale of influence was significantly wider. Such was the contribution of these factors to the Indian economy that even by the eighteenth century undivided India's GDP was nearly 20 percent of that of the world, and was only behind China's.

However, India's concurrent journey to condition its society's attitude toward waste management is intriguing and unfortunate. A period of two centuries, beginning 320 AD with the establishment of the Gupta dynasty by Chandragupta I, is recorded in Indian history as the Golden Era. The dynasty with Magadha (in present-day Bihar) as its capital spread across a large part of north India. Samudragupta, Chandragupta's son, expanded the empire with a fine combination of military prowess and smart alliances. During his reign, geographical boundaries of the Gupta kingdom extended from some parts of present-day Afghanistan and Pakistan to the entire northern India, Gujarat, and northern regions of Maharashtra.

Culturally and intellectually, Indian civilization blossomed during this period. Nalanda University in Bihar and paintings in Ajanta and Ellora caves in Maharashtra are creations of this period. Two of India's greatest scholars Aryabhata and Kalidasa belonged to this period. The Gupta dynasty had a strong revenue-generation mechanism that relied on tax collection, state-owned mines, and cross-border trade. It is also believed that the period saw remarkable development in medical sciences, especially in defining early rules of vaccination and reconstructive surgeries. The dynasty also established a strong system of central government with a fair degree of local independence. Individual expression in the form of art and music was at its peak. Commerce with other countries flourished on the strength of artisans and ingenious skills. Loosely, the Gupta dynasty ruled this massive landmass for nearly three hundred years in its peak form, as against modern India's post-Independence journey, which is only seventy-one years old. The tenure of the dynasty and the vast geographical spread of its rule was one of the early instances of the idea of unified India.

All aspects that measure progress and development of society were at their zenith during this Golden Era, and there was a system that seemed adequate and rational at that time to tackle the issue of waste management. An organized system was in place to take care of carcasses of fallen animals, food waste, and solid human waste. However, the same system eventually became the reason for India's losing battle with waste management.

The Golden Era of the Gupta dynasty was also a period of a battle of religious supremacy between Hinduism and Buddhism. History is divided on the nature of this struggle. Whether it was a blood bath resulting in ethnic cleansing and persecution, or a soft war fought through ideologies and changes in the social order is still debated; historians, however, are tilted toward the latter. Buddhism blossomed and peaked across many parts of India during the Maurya dynasty that preceded the Gupta dynasty by 300 years. Monasteries, scriptures, and stupas proliferated across the subcontinent. This growth of Buddhism was perhaps at the cost of Hinduism because the then civilization did not experience a rapid expansion of population.

While, during the Gupta dynasty, Buddhism was still popular, Hinduism grew in complexity. It drew influence from astronomy and cross-pollinated ideas from Buddhism and Jainism. Much of Hinduism's popularity and ritualistic style of today owes its origins to this period. Temples grew across the empire and religious practices became more ritualistic. The Guptas were devout Hindus and Hinduism thus grew in stature and popularity under royal patronage, but the period also witnessed remarkable religious freedom for Buddhism to coexist and flourish, lending credence to the historians' tilt that the fight between Hinduism and Buddhism was more one for society's mindshare for a willing acceptance than to pressurize non-believers. If Buddhism and Hinduism fought a soft war of ideologies, how did Hinduism win this battle?

Reviving the Brahmanical order in the Hindu society was one of the most potent approaches used for the purpose during this era. The Brahmanical narrative strengthened social stratification of caste, class, and gender based on the Manusmriti. The Manusmriti, or the laws of Manu, laid the foundation for Hindu laws and jurisprudence, and defined the Brahmanical order of Hindu society. It defined the role of gender, profession-based stratification of society into hierarchical caste groups, and the codes that governed them. The correct dateline about its origin is still intensely debated. Various historical studies date it between 200 BC and second century AD.

The Brahmanical order used these codes defined in the Manusmriti to formalize social order during the Gupta period. This played a pivotal role in the resurgence of Hinduism during the Gupta dynasty. The Hindu lineage of the Gupta clan may have also provided a silent sponsorship to percolate this approach and to condition society's structure at that time. There is nothing to suggest that it was done with evil intentions or that it was done with any motive other than the dynasty's desire to condition its society in a manner that it deemed fit. It was well within its right as a monarchy to do so.

However, this social order classification strengthened the hold of Hinduism and perhaps played a major role in curtailing the spread of Buddhism within India. Buddhism was still prevalent during the era of King Harshavardhana during the seventh century AD that immediately followed the Gupta dynasty rule. But by then it was confined to a few pockets in India.

By the end of the Gupta period, caste system and Hinduism became synonymous with each other. Hinduism became the dominant religion and the caste system became the mainstay of Indian society. It can however be debated whether the same interdependency between the two existed before the Gupta dynasty period. The Brahmins, the custodians of knowledge, were assigned the top slot of the caste pyramid, followed by the warriors or the Kshatriyas, followed by traders and farmers, and then craftsmen. Those engaged in the job of cleaning and sanitation rested at the bottom.

Many social commentators have pointed out that the caste and class system was not as rigid as it sounds; some of the practices were more for practical reasons. The cultural and economic prosperity of the Gupta period also lends credence to this belief. People were learned, and had a high sense of self-worth and mutual respect for others. Bias in societies is inversely proportional to economic prosperity of all classes. If the Golden Era allowed groups belonging to all professions to experience a long period of stability and prosperity, there were no explicit reasons for caste discrimination and intercaste conflicts.

However, in its pursuit to triumph over Buddhism, the caste stratification approach of Hinduism laid an unintentional foundation for discrimination and bias to creep in the future. Herein lie reasons for the twisted mind of Indians regarding waste management. How did that happen?

During the Mauryan period, those littering the streets were penalized. Streets were equipped with underground drains; public bath areas were connected to water bodies; a cluster of homes had access to a water well – Chanakya's Arthashastra gives vivid details of this arrangement. It can thus be inferred that there was an administrative awareness toward virtues of clean public spaces and that individual households were responsible for keeping their surroundings clean.

However, the idea of cleaning public spaces and waste disposal outside the limits of homes significantly changed during the Golden Era. The caste system institutionalized manual scavenging of waste from homes, disposing it on the outskirts, cesspits, or dumping grounds, and cleaning public places, such as streets, drains, by the subcaste of Bhangis, similar to London's Gongfermours. It is difficult to imagine any operational or safety gear – machines, pulleys, or gloves – used to execute this job. Bare hands, wooden carts, and iron pails were possibly the only apparatus available to empty the night soil from homes. The nature of the job inspired a natural repulsion, which led to an instinctive discrimination and a secluded existence of this caste, a natural human reaction to dirt and unpleasant odor and sights. But this reaction was universal and not limited to only India.

There was, however, one big difference between the Gongfermours and Bhangis. The job of the Gongfermour was created to address the need of the society and the differential treatment was merely operational, to satisfy human instinct. The church, the custodian of religious doctrine in Europe, did not play any role in defining the job or the social structure around it. It did not issue any guidelines of acceptable and unacceptable behavior for them. Therefore, the Gongfermour had the option to exit the profession when he wished. The job of the Bhangis, on the contrary, was determined as part of the social structure that started to get defined with the lens of Hinduism during the Golden Era. It is difficult to imagine that the segregation began with the intent to exploit. Hinduism was interpreted as a way of life, and was viewed under an umbrella philosophy to define the existing society and encompass every aspect of daily living. Also, that this philosophical narrative was democratized under one giant kingdom which covered most of the subcontinent provided the necessary fire power of a unified state support to expand it to an almost noble form.

But, the basic construct of the caste system was flawed in its design. It created a natural organization of homogenous groups that started to stand out from other groups based on skill profile, appearance, recognition, importance, access to power centers, and so on, and became a potent tool for exploitation. Three hundred years of the Gupta dynasty rule is a very long time in human history to say that the design of the caste system did not reveal its vulnerabilities during this time.

More importantly, after the end of this period, the subcontinent became a conglomeration of many monarchs, dynasties, and kingdoms. Wars, alliances, invasions became the order of the day for the next 1,200 years. The Hindu philosophy driven by the Brahmanical order got divided into many forms, one for every monarch or dynasty that emerged after the collapse of the Gupta era. The caste system emerged as a common tool to softly exercise power for the kings to show political and social clout.

This had an acute implication on the way the issue of waste disposal was interpreted by the Indian society. The role of the Bhangi, the cleaning caste, changed from providing assistance in clearing to cleaning up the waste generated by the consuming class. In the earlier system, it is a shared responsibility where a household solicits the services of a Bhangi. The act of solicitation is voluntary for both parties: the Bhangi can accept or reject it. Later, however, the household has the right to ask the Bhangi to clean up the waste, but the Bhangi has no right to refuse, failing which he awaits punishment.

Religious dovetailing of the social order allowed the scope of this job to get reinterpreted in this fashion, and from here started India's downward spiral toward a waste management nightmare.

The reinterpreted narrative of Hinduism allowed the institutionalization of the contract of cleaning and waste disposal from merely being an economic understanding between the Bhangi and the household to being a dictum packaged under the guise of faith. This converted a simple practice of cleaning and waste disposal, which started as a social arrangement, into an activity guided by rigid codes. Insecurity about alternate ways to manage waste can also be a reason for the arrangement to have become a rigid system. Communities engaged in the job of cleaning and human waste disposal were nudged into a separate system of existence. Public spaces were segregated for those belonging to the cleaning castes, such as separate water wells, designated areas at river banks, even separate places of worship. These arrangements brought to surface the flawed design of the caste system. Behavior of those belonging to other castes that were consuming the services of the cleaning castes exerted biases and exploitative tendencies, injecting fear and ostracism among the cleaning castes. The system of outsourcing all aspects of cleaning, waste collection, and waste disposal to a section of society and of building social barriers to confine its members was India's answer to the issue of waste management.

Bhangis and Chamars became a convenient solution to a disgusting problem. Instead of a quid-pro-quo arrangement between supposedly equal parties of consuming class and cleaning castes as should have been the case, sanitation became the sole duty of the cleaning caste. Not only was the community burdened with the outcome of the job but were left to fend for themselves as regard the mechanics of cleaning and everything else that came along with it – tools, processes, working conditions. Only the outcome mattered to the consuming class. It didn't matter if the cleaning caste was hauling the waste and dumping it in the river or on the outskirts of the village. Nor, did it matter if the garbage was burned or buried in cesspits. Environmentally, it was all fine because the garbage was all organic and human footprints sparse. Getting the garbage out of sight and managing its bad odour were the only two expectations from the Bhangis and Chamars and if they did a bad job of it, the religious stick was used to flog them and make them fall in line.

In eighth century AD, about a few million people across the subcontinent generated primarily organic waste in their daily lives. While the exploitative arrangement of caste system to manage the cleaning job was abhorrent, it took care of the waste management issue with reasonable ease. The arrangement did not disturb the ecology, nor did it create any public health crises. It only helped clean public areas and pick garbage from households with reasonably good results.

The caste-system-based solution to waste management was discriminative and exploitative for a large section of the society, but, in the context of the world order of the eighth century, such notions of discrimination and exploitation were nebulous and viewed from a very different lens. Monarchies were the principled order of the state across the world. Society largely relied on practices and rituals passed from the previous generations as the source of wisdom and knowledge to solve problems of daily life. Security of communities and self-survival were primary motivators to evaluate choices of social contracts. People killed each other for valor, honor, and survival. Wars were bloody and life expectancy was low. Any solution that increased the probability of survival over the other was an acceptable norm on the moral compass. While in retrospect we can critique the caste arrangement for waste management with disdain and regret, this libertarian viewpoint was centuries away.

The caste system was an arrangement that started with the benign intention of organizing societies. The enshrined Vedic principles of karma, salvation, introspection, and rational thinking of Hinduism were overshadowed by ritualistic, symbolic, and rigid practices for reasons that were political and were passed on through centuries across the subcontinent and caste system paid the price. Then, the geopolitical landscape in the India of post ninth century AD started to change dramatically. Islam came to the subcontinent with invaders from the north and northwest frontiers. Though, the religion also entered the social order of South India through a relatively peaceful route of trade and commerce a few centuries earlier. The next five centuries witnessed numerous battles between Indian kingdoms and Turk, Afghan and Mongol rulers invaders and among Muslim monarchs. With the establishment of the Delhi Sultanate and the subsequent rule of the Mughal dynasty in much of the northern and central part of the subcontinent stabilized this power struggle. Though skirmishes for supremacy continued among various kingdoms in other parts of India, the Mughal and the Maratha dynasties became the lynch-pin of the subcontinent's political order till the eighteenth century AD when the baton was passed onto the British.

Starting from three centuries before the establishment of Mughal dynasty and three centuries after the coronation of Babur, Indian society witnessed pluralistic exposure to its religious order. Hinduism itself underwent a regional makeover. There was a Maratha way of Hindu living. The Rajput kings of Rajasthan placed Hindu living of valor and sacrifice at the heart of their political power. The Bhakti movement that started from present-day Tamil Naidu culminated into rich symbolic representation of temples in many parts of south India that bloomed under the Chola dynasty.

Islam manifested in India through many sects, namely, Deobandi, Sunni, Shia, Dawoodi Bohra, Sufism. With the landing of Vasco da Gama on the shores of Kerala in 1498, India also saw arrival of Christianity along with European explorers. Guru Nanak Dev laid the foundation of Sikhism with the sheer will to resist persecution, preserve individual freedom and identity. Amidst this churn of faith-exploration in the subcontinent, the concern of the custodians of faith was to bring new followers into their fold or to preserve existing followers. Messages of new faiths appealed to the Indian society out of fear, exclusion, or on the plank of resilience and escape.

But these multiple manifestations of religions in India hardly made a dent in the social order of the caste system. Out of fear of persecution or out of the sheer dejection from discrimination over centuries many people embraced Islam or Christianity. But, the caste hierarchy of the social order followed them in this journey. Therefore, a Hindu carpenter retained his tag of a carpenter and became a Muslim carpenter. A Hindu scavenger retained the caste tag of animal scavenging and became a Christian scavenger. Religious resurgence did not change the social order of the caste system during the medieval period, which has continued till today. In 2016, Catholic Bishops' Conference of India (CBCI), the apex decision making body of the Christian community in India, released a report that candidly admitted that Indian Christianity is not immune to caste discrimination. The report further admitted that while 63 percent of its members are Dalits, only twelve bishops out of a total of five thousand bishops in India are Dalits. This representation is less than 0.24 percent. In the India of the twenty-first century, the scourge of untouchability is alive and kicking among the Indian Muslims as well. A study published in 2015 researched this thesis in many Muslim households in north India and found widespread discrimination of 'Dalit' Muslims by the 'non-Dalit' in the community. It ranged from virtually no representation of Dalit Muslims in decision making bodies that concern the faith to separate seating of Dalit Muslims during feasts. The suicide of Manpreet Singh in Khai village in Punjab in 2017 highlights the deep tentacles of caste discrimination that confronts Sikhism as well. Manpreet, a twenty-two-year-old Sikh man consumed poison and ended his life in June 2017, when he found out that the parents of the girl he married a few days ago had an intercaste marriage and the girl's mother belonged to a 'lower caste' whereas he was a 'high' caste Sikh. This is the worst form of condemnation that could be bestowed on the girl's parents who decided to take a bold stand many years back to break the caste barrier. Sikhism in spite of being founded on the principle of brotherhood, inclusion and egalitarianism ended up marginalizing perceived lower caste groups who embraced it over time. The Jatt Sikhs by the virtue of their existing landholdings and social status became the perceived upper-caste group, whereas the Dalits of the region for their association as laborers tilling farmland or as owners of leather trade ended up as marginalized Dalits. The monopoly of Jatt Sikhs and the near non-existence of Dalits in the membership of SGPC (Shiromani Gurdwara Prabandhak Committee – the central governing body of Sikhs) were revealed in a research study in 2007 – a reality not very different from that of CBCI. The marginalization of Dalit Sikhs from the mainstream gave rise to separate gurudwaras for Dalits. The emergence of Ravidassia Dera (and many other deras subsequently) in Punjab (and in north India) as a sort of parallel sect to bring under its fold the perceived Dalit groups of the region was born out of this condemnation. Such was the brute power of the caste system that went much beyond the power of the myriad religious ideas being injected in the Indian society during the Middle Ages.

The monarchs irrespective of their faith, hardly prioritized social reforms in the towns, villages and communities they governed. They rarely interfered in the caste system, practices, and ritualism. The same village may have been governed by different rulers, but the villagers would have hardly felt the change of the monarchy in their daily lives. Everyday life continued with the same social order as long as the king's exchequer was able to extract the desired tax from the village. Unified jurisprudence codes that governed the civil laws of the land and defined social contracts within the society were patchy during that time. Verbal rules were passed as local laws of village panchayats primarily driven by the social order of the caste system. Therefore, it did not matter if a villager, whose father was a Hindu, embraced Islam. It did not allow him to escape from the caste order that defined his social standing in the village. Hamlets were largely left on their own to interpret caste system and define the social order. There were no checks and balance by way of the state's intervention in such matters of local governance. It was a free reign for the established custodians to interpret rules from their own vantage points. There was no scope of questioning rituals for the lack of any other recourse. Who will question whom? Can a Bhangi question the priest of the temple about his diktat to ostracize him from the village because the Bhangi dared to enter a temple? How will the Bhangi fend for himself and for his family if he is expelled from the village? It is not as if he could catch a bus and head to the city in search for a better life. A thousand years of reinterpretation of the caste system of social order progressively decayed, allowing the system to be interpreted in ways to suit the needs of the powerful. Practices became rituals. Rituals became rules. Rules became 'sacred' and 'rigid' codes that were insulated from questioning and rationale thinking. This insulation extended to the self-appointed custodians (nobility) of these rules. The state dared not get on the wrong side of the village head or the priest because they feared loss of loyalty to the king.

Within a thousand years from the sixth to the sixteenth century AD, the caste system that started as a simple 'Hindu' practice to organize the society for efficient and peaceful existence transformed into a rigid beast. So strong became its independent identity that it unshackled itself from the reigns of Hinduism and could not even be tamed by any other religious narrative. The situation needed cool heads who could take stock of the beast and whose words of wisdom the people would follow. It needed a spiritual cleansing and a philosophical re-assessment that could mellow its hardness and free up people's excessive dependence on it. Basavanna's (Kannada poet and social reformer) assertive and vocal revolt in the twelfth century against the caste system and his disdain toward the society's excessive drift toward idol worship needs to be interpreted in this backdrop. His assertion signifies that in the Middle Ages caste system in the subcontinent was a full-blown social evil that was a creation of apathy of the political order of the time and the potential of opportunistic use it served to its custodians. It is a different matter that nine centuries later the politics of this land turned on its head and packaged Basavanna's vision of a casteless society into a new caste altogether.

Unfortunately, this caste system also carried forward India's solution to waste management. By the nineteenth century, the cleaning community was the weakest, and most dejected and exploited section of the Indian society. They were assigned to live in seclusion, forced to carry out daily chores in a prescribed manner, expected to perform their duty with perfection, yet earned meager wages that just about managed sustenance living. The caste barriers ensured there was no way out. Perhaps caste barriers and meagre wage rates earned by cleaning castes served to strengthen the entrapment. They were not allowed to be within physical proximity of the consuming class, nor meet their gaze. The relationship between the two classes became that of master and servant, where the former felt entitled. A Bhangi was at the beck and call to pick up night soil, sweep streets, and remove other household or commercial waste. A Chamar was a call away to dispose of livestock carcass.

The destruction was complete in that the social order of the subcontinent ensured that waste management does not appeal to the psyche of Indian society as a shared responsibility. This social order also conditioned the Indian mind to separate the notion of waste management into private and public spaces. The idea of clean private spaces, namely, homes, shops, or equivalent comparable units, is a deep-rooted Indian custom for centuries. However, the patriarchal social order has primarily tasked the woman of the house with this and other household duties, while the bread-earning male spends most of his time outside the house to put food on the table. A homemaker's life in the Middle Ages was centered around executing this job for most part of her productive life. A clean home thus became the duty of the homemaker, rather than it being a shared responsibility among all family members. She would interface with the Bhangi to clean the toilet and pick up the night soil. The rest of the family, however, was oblivious to such activities related to waste management within the confines of the home. This baton was passed to the children of the house, upon attainting adulthood. The male child became a dutiful bread earning adult hardly concerned about what goes on inside the house as was the case with his father. The girl child would come under the wings of her mother for an informal apprenticeship, where she was prepped up for marriage before long.

Outside the boundaries of the home, a more formal caste system had its hold on society and cleaned public spaces. One could throw leftovers on the streets or defecate on the outskirts of the village because he knew a Bhangi would clean up after him and the Bhangi could not reprimand him for this un-civic behavior. A farmer need never worry about fallen livestock because a Chamar would come along and take care of the carcass, but the Chamar dare not dream to sit beside the farmer and share a meal. Cleaning thus became a compulsion for the homemaker or the cleaning community because the social norms had intimately tied it to their worth. This arrangement lacked an economic or a social contract between equal parties with a principle of reciprocity, as should have been the case, and as is evident in the Western societies.

This also created a false belief that waste management was not an issue in the Indian society and set it up for a giant failure in future. It seemed so legitimate and complete that even the noble and purists saw nothing wrong in it. Even, the 'smart' British fell in this trap. It is baffling because the British during their rapid colonization of India also suffered from myriad challenges to manage waste back home. For all the experimentation taking place in England back then to overcome the challenges of waste management, none of it touched the shores of the Indian subcontinent. The British hired on its rolls Bhangis and Chamars to take care of the waste disposal in British India, reinforcing a formal sponsorship of the state to the caste arrangement for waste disposal delivered through British municipalities. This was also part of the larger work of British rule that codified the caste system.

By the start of the nineteenth century, social reformers started to knock on the conscience of the Indian society, particularly about the Brahmanical order of the Hindu religion and its excessively ritualistic design and rigid codes. The rebellion of Raja Ram Mohan Roy resulted in the practice of Sati being banned under the Bengal Sati Regulation of 1829 and the establishment of Brahmo Samaj or a universal society without any discrimination based on caste and religion. In 1875, Dayanand Saraswati laid the foundation of Arya Samaj with the aim to reinterpret Hinduism into a spiritual and research-based religion rather than an overtly ritualistic one it had become. In 1886, Ramakrishna Paramahansa founded the Ramakrishna Math (re-christened Ramakrishna Mission by his disciple, Swami Vivekananda) with the aim to inject modernity, practicality, and universality into religious thinking. All these religious movements had one common theme: a voice against blind faith, ritualistic methodology, and discriminative tendencies of Hinduism, which perpetuated an exploitative social order and caste system. Within the span of sixty years, India saw three religious reform movements that critiqued the prevailing social order. Fundamental flaws of the social order in the Indian society had indeed started to become apparent to the rational mind.

However, two notable reasons hindered these movements from making severe dents in the mainstream narrative of the Indian caste order. First, the spiritual reformers heading these movements passed away prematurely, thus the influence of these movements remained confined to small groups or regions. Second was the emergence of a strong nationalist movement that started with the first war of independence in 1857, which later expanded into a full-blown independence movement by the start of the twentieth century. The movement overshadowed social reforms and prevented them from becoming a mainstream agenda. While we were struggling to attain freedom, the issue of managing waste did not seem a pressing matter. Surely it could be addressed once we had gained independence: this argument seemed defendable at the time, but it was not to be.

By the start of the twentieth century, migration from villages to towns, and the consequent population growth, had begun to put pressure on the approach of waste being exclusively managed by the cleaning caste. But the political scenario hardly afforded any space for this issue, except for Mahatma Gandhi, who severely critiqued the flawed design of the caste system to manage waste. He stands out as a lone warrior against Indian society's intellectual decay on the issue of sanitation. In 1903, when he first visited the famous Kashi Vishvanath Temple of Varanasi, he was unimpressed by what he saw. He wrote, 'The swarming flies and the noise made by the shopkeepers and pilgrims were perfectly insufferable.... Here one expected an atmosphere of meditation and communion, it was conspicuous by its absence.' Thirteen years later, when he visited the city a second time to be part of the stone-laying ceremony of the Banaras Hindu University, he found the temple just as dirty: he equated it to the state of the Indian society. In his speech at the foundation ceremony of the university, he said, 'If a stranger dropped from above on to this great temple and he had to consider what we as Hindus were, would he not be justified in condemning us? Is not this great temple a reflection of our own character?'

Gandhi's comments raised a hard-hitting question: how can one hope to commune with god in a so-called holy city amidst such dirty surroundings? It seemed no one saw the irony before it was questioned. Gandhi saw that the problem was chiefly behavioral, that waste management was being delegated instead of it being a shared responsibility. He recognized that a move toward a clean society had to begin at home, and championed the act of cleaning toilets by every member of the family, an act he felt would help open up the Indian minds toward a shared responsibility for cleanliness, and that it is at par with other skilled jobs. Yet Gandhi's voice against unhygienic and dirty surroundings through lectures, writings, actions, and self-criticism fell on deaf ears. The agenda of freedom, communal harmony, and national integration then were of critical importance. It might be a fair assumption that had Gandhi lived one more decade in independent India, his agenda of cleanliness would have taken center stage.

While the Western world rapped the masses on their knuckles to fall in line, India merely replicated its British colonizers' system of hiring cleaning-caste people on the rolls, which continued even after Independence. In 2011, various surveys, including the Census, pegged the number of people engaged in the job of manual scavenging at between 11,000 and 30,000. While urban homes gradually shifted to toilets connected to sewage system, they now employed a sewer cleaner instead of a manual scavenger. Statistics show, however, that in 2011 nearly a million Indian households still relied on manual scavengers to clean their toilets, while in 2016 India was still educating its citizens to stop open defecation and build wet toilets in homes.

In 1990, Delhi generated less than 2,000 metric tons of rubbish on a daily basis, much of which was dumped on the landfills outside the city. However, over the next twenty years, the city generated more than 10,000 metric tons of garbage daily and had exhausted all the available landfills for its disposal. Till the 1990s, waste in India was largely biodegradable in nature – food, human discharge, paper, leaves, and other such materials. The economic liberalization of 1991 is the tipping point when India's garbage composition changed rapidly. Since then the republic became younger, urban, and prosperous. Life expectancy grew, the average age of its population declined. A new crop of baby boomers, optimists, and restless people moved into new households with new dreams. Urbanization expanded its perimeter and metamorphosed sleepy towns into bustling centers of prosperity. It lifted many people out of poverty, created new references for bright futures, and set a new benchmark of aspirations. This progress directly translated into an explosion of household consumption. But it also accelerated India's descent into a sanitation nightmare. India hardly knew anything about waste management, while the quantum and nature of garbage inside and outside of the household changed rapidly. Electronics, batteries, plastic, construction waste became a sizeable part of its composition. The landfills were sucking up more and more garbage with each passing day, becoming more lethal and toxic. Unlike the benign food waste that would dry out in the sun, the cadmium and lead from discarded batteries were now getting discharged into the surroundings, setting the city on the path of a public health disaster by the decade of 2010s. Garbage landfills caught fire that refused to die down for weeks, smog blanket covered regions, and lakes frothed mysterious foam. These are just some of the ecological bombs that went off in 2016 exemplifying the challenge of new-age waste management.

The centuries-old conditioning of the Indian mind desensitized the entire society, rendering it unable to address this emerging challenge. Waste management and public hygiene were never taught as a subject in educational institutes. Moreover, the patriarchal set-up of Indian households left no scope for the homemaker to actively engage others in the chores of cleaning and waste management. Nor did any policy intervention of the Indian state make any attempt to reach out to this homemaker and teach her constructive practices of waste management as it did for immunization and family planning.

Concurrently, the developed economies made rapid advances to 'dumb down' the subject for those who did not understand, namely, bagging the waste or bins for segregation. It was only after centuries of ignorance and struggle that the clean countries of today overcame the challenges of waste management. They broke down the barrier of ignorance through self-criticism and constant learning. This helped them to shun any false need for conformity to the existing arrangements. The theme of bad sanitation featured in literature. Administrators treated it among the top challenges at work. Political leadership confronted the issue head on and made tough decisions and drafted hard-hitting regulations. The emerging scientific temperament in the backdrop of the Industrial Revolution in these societies prompted social scientists and technocrats to take a science-driven approach and design solutions to confront the challenge. These very societies were dependent on Gongfermours and slaves to haul their garbage till the twentieth century; today they have set the global benchmark of excellence in sanitation.

While the Western world was marching ahead in waste management, at start of the twentieth century Munshi Premchand, by way of his stories, was essaying the realities of the trials faced by the cleaning castes in India. In one such story, titled 'Sadgati', Dukhi – a frail Chamar knocks on the door of Ghasiram's (the priest in the village) home on a hot summer morning. Dukhi intends to get the 'auspicious' date for the marriage of his daughter – an exclusive domain of Ghasiram. Ghasi asks Dukhi to first clean his house and chop the wood before he can consider the matter. Dukhi had left his home on an empty stomach to catch Ghasi early at his home and get the task done. Dukhi curls up his hunger and gets down to completing these tasks in the fear that if he leaves them unfinished, Ghasi may leave his house and it will be difficult to get hold of him again or even worse Ghasi may get angry and not take up his matter at all. It is evening and Dukhi is dutifully chopping the wood but his body sapped of all the reserved stamina gives way and collapses. Ghasi and his wife looks at the lifeless body of Dukhi and curses the 'inauspicious' sight, while thinking of a way to remove Dukhi's body to restore the 'purity' of the passage at the earliest. The story is a severe criticism of the hypocritical caste arrangement that allows priest's job profile to instill fear and unquestioned subordination in the Chamar community, while it provides the priest a carte blanch for his scorn to a lifeless human body for the profession that the body engaged in while it was full of life.

This belief of the entire society created rigid boundaries around the issue of waste management and it did away with any desire to revisit it with changing times, thereby eradicating any scope for self-criticism or improvement. Every subsequent generation of the Indian society continued with the same arrangement because dismantling it not only required an alternative which was not present, but it also served the parochial interests of many stakeholders beyond the explicit issue of waste management.

If you think Premchand's story was a fictional account, think again. In 2016, Una, a small village in Gujarat, made national headlines for caste-related skirmishes. The conflict was between the upper-caste and the Chamar communities. The Chamars alleged that members of their community were falsely accused of cow slaughter and beaten up. They boycotted lifting an animal carcass from the village. A few days later, a fifteen-year-old Chamar boy was beaten up following his refusal to 'do his job.' Such was the backlash from this event that it launched the careers of new leaders in Dalit politics in the state. In 2017 a Reddy man in Andhra Pradesh killed his son-in-law and pushed his daughter to commit suicide because she had married a person from a 'lower' caste. In the same year, 'upper-caste' villagers in Mana Village of Madhya Pradesh allegedly poured kerosene in the water well used by Dalits to seek revenge for the latter's defiance.

These 'upper-caste' villagers were angry that the celebratory decibels of a wedding function in a Dalit family was 'way above'; and perhaps equated the decibels during their own wedding functions, signifying equality. How can Dalits' expression of happiness be equal to that of perceived upper castes? In 2018, Maruthi Rao – a 'successful' businessman in Miryalaguda town of Telangana hired two hardcore criminals and allegedly got his son-in-law – Pranay murdered solely for the fact that Maruthi's daughter – Amrutha chose Pranay – a Dalit as her life partner. The caste identity twisted Maruthi's moral compass to such an extent that he felt fine to reduce her young pregnant daughter into a widow than to accept a Dalit as his son-in-law. If Premchand were alive today, he would still be treated as a contemporary writer for his stories have not lost an iota of relevance even after a whole century.

While the Brahmanical order in the era of the Guptas had scored a victory for Hinduism over the spread of Buddhism, in the ensuing centuries it snuffed out philosophy and intellect from the narrative of Hinduism. Codes and practices that were defined under the order over time metamorphosed into superstition and occult, and laid the foundation for disastrous consequences on sanitation that India faces in the present day. The story of the Indian cow best portrays this descent into a quagmire that may have been unintended, but entirely avoidable. Apart from the caste system, the Brahmanical order also influenced food as a tool of silent onslaught over Buddhism. It successfully managed to reposition vegetarianism as symbol of superior 'Hindu' living, and the cow became the lynchpin of this philosophy. Historians have concluded that this positioning was diametrically different from the Vedic times, when Hindus used to slaughter cows and eat beef not only within the confines of their private spaces, but even in social gatherings.

In the post-Mauryan period, this functional view of the cow was suddenly replaced with the movement around vegetarianism and cow protection. There are two possible reasons for this change in stance. One, the Brahmanical order saw a leverage to build a counter-narrative to the Buddhist practice of eating beef to gain supremacy. Though, it is also argued that Buddhist virtue of ahinsa (non-violence) may have given birth to the concept of vegetarianism in the first place and that may have prompted Brahmanical narrative around cow protection to package its brand of vegetarianism as a superior alternative. Second, it is possible that excessive culling of cows for food may have caused an imbalance in the supply chain and compelled the political leadership to build a strong cow-protection agenda packaged with strong religious backing to ensure its success: the second reason was purely economic and survival-led.

However genuine the trigger for the change in stance around the cow be in the context of that time, the narrative that shaped up over the next sixteen centuries had an unintended consequence on India's struggle with waste management. By the end of the nineteenth century, the subject of the cow in India was disfigured beyond recognition, so much so that many social reformers and Hindu leaders took a stand on the issue with the objective of becoming the voice of reason in society. For instance, the cow as a functional subject finds support in the thinking of Swami Vivekananda. His stance sprang from his strong belief that Hinduism needed to regain the philosophical ground it had yielded to ritualism and eventually degenerated into superstition. To him, the prevailing thinking of Hindu society about the cow embodied this degeneration. Vinayak Savarkar also resented the excessively ritualistic association of the cow with Hinduism. His compassion for the cows was no different from the compassion he had for trees and other life forms that played an equally significant role in providing value to man's existence in Hindustan. For Savarkar, according religious identity and deity status to the cow was a superstition, and he abhorred the vulnerability displayed by the Hindus in defenselessly surrendering to such superstitions rather than to confront them with rational thinking. He believed that such superstitions destroyed a nation's intellect.

In the pre-industrial times, Indians reared cows for milk for self-consumption. A little extra milk was saved for offering to the deity in the local temple or gifted to peers in the social circle. Some may have even sold milk to the local sweet shop for an extra consideration. Primarily, it was consumed within the same ecosystem. When the call to protect the cow became the mainstream narrative of the Indian society, it was easy for such households to abide by it. Now, instead of killing them, they had to wait for the cows to die a natural death. Once the cow died Chamars were assigned the job to pick up the fallen animal and dispose of the carcass as they deemed fit. Chamars extracted economic value from the fallen animal by selling its meat and tanning its skin.

Wars, invasion, industrialization, and trade usurped the social order of Indian villages and triggered migration for survival or for better economic opportunities. Households stopped rearing cows at home, but that did not change their reliance on dairy products. Migration increased the distance from the villages to source milk to satiate this need. Milk became a much-needed, scarce commodity, and thus commerce around dairy kicked in. Commercial neighborhood dairies began to produce milk on a large scale to cater to this demand. While milk underwent this silent makeover, the symbol of the cow as a Hindu identity strengthened with every passing century.

But it was impossible for the cow (a deity) to coexist with milk (white gold). The moment milk entered the realm of commercial dairy business, economics forced the cow to become an industrial asset. The animal was strictly viewed by dairy operators as a trade off between its cost of ownership and the revenue it generated. In its lifetime, a cow goes through six lactation cycle. It is a cost head for the dairy operator in the period before and after lactation. No dairy owner minds bearing the cost of maintenance of the cow in the pre-lactation period because it is to prepare her for the forthcoming productive life. But the cost of her existence on the farm in the post-lactation period eats into the dairy farmer's earnings. In societies where the cow does not hold a symbolic position, it proceeds to the slaughterhouse once she has outlived her productive life. This timely transition from the dairy to the meat industry balances the commercial cycle of cow rearing in line with the economic need of the society.

In India, the protective status of the cow was defined when dairy was largely a domestic activity carried out in most village homes. For the economics of a commercial dairy business, it was not profitable to keep old cows in the corral. But the 'protectionist' dictate was never stress-tested for its effects on commercial dairies. The order meant extra cost and more infrastructure bandwidth, which yielded nothing in return. Unlike when cow rearing had not been commercialized, where one could wait for it to die a natural death and then have a Chamar dispose of the carcass, it now had to vacate the dairy after its lactating life was over, to make space for new animals. This compulsion was at loggerheads with the beliefs of the dairy owner. They had to view the cow as an industrial asset which depreciated over time and less as a deity to succeed in the business. Formal and informal contracts sprang up between these dairies and slaughterhouses to manage the onward movement of the animal. Dairy owners did not mind the arrangement because these slaughterhouses were managed either by Chamars or by Muslims, and therefore the perceived 'sinful' act of putting the cow to rest was 'outsourced' – a modified extension of the arrangement where cows were reared at home and a Chamar was entrusted to take care of dead animals. Some dairy owners conveniently reinterpreted the dictate to pass the test of religious conformity and reared buffaloes instead.

By the start of the twenty-first century, India became the second largest dairy producer in the world and consumed almost all the milk it produced. Old cows and buffaloes were dispatched to slaughterhouses, thereby supplying raw material to the meat and leather industries. The scale of this arrangement was widespread because it provided a convenient refuge to numerous small dairies all over the country that never owned more than a few dozen animals and could not afford to house non-productive cows. India thus emerged as the largest beef exporter in the world.

On the one hand, the arrangement provided valuable nutrition to its population and, on the other, it tested the Hindu beliefs propagated by the Brahmanical order. It was a fragile arrangement that had all the makings of a potent political conflict. But instead of initiating an objective debate to reconcile these contradictions, India, afflicted with pre-existing biases, merely ignored it. Consequently, the arrangement derailed into informality. Unregulated and informal dairies mushroomed on the fringes, which became a sanitation mess. Some dairy owners willingly gave the non-productive cows away for culling. Many other dairy operators or amateur bovine owners simply abandoned them to roam the streets. While they had to act righteous by not killing the cow, they paid no heed to abandoning it. Unregulated slaughterhouses also sprang up to facilitate the charade and they too became a sanitation and public health hazard. A better handling of the consequences of increased dairy consumption would have solved the sanitation problem, but this situation was entirely self-inflicted, one born out of deep caste divides, superstitions, and prejudices. The phrase *You don't like them, but you can't live without them* aptly defines the stance of various stakeholders in the dairy, slaughter, and meat business, where a fragile equilibrium for the sake of economics exists.

Till 2014, society's selective ignorance helped India to work around this fragility. The political narrative wisely shied away from testing the strength of the ideological boundary of those who believed in cow as a deity to withstand the pressures of cow as an economic asset. The assumption that there is a critical mass of politically relevant

Hindus for whom cow as a deity supersedes all other considerations was politically tested in India for the first time after 2014. The result was instant and in many boroughs, it was a landslide. Perhaps the assumption was not misplaced. Buoyed by this spectacular result, cow slaughter was banned in many states with immediate effect. Cow vigilantism made its debut as a popular tool to cull the 'culprits' and cow urine as a panacea for most of the ills in the society became a ubiquitous media byte. But, this euphoria was misplaced and short-lived. The ban on cow slaughter meant that farmers and dairy owners who were earlier able to trade their non-productive bovines and make way for the new stock were not able to do so. Consequently, they abandoned them instead to bear the cost of feeding them for the rest of their natural lives. Cows started to roam the motorways and farmlands. If the fast disappearing income from farming or failed crops because of drought were not big enough worries, farmers like Bishambhar and Mukesh in Deori village near Agra in Uttar Pradesh had to now stay awake all night and protect their standing crops from the graze of these abandoned cows. Farmers started to capture and lock these ownerless bovines in public buildings like schools and offices and posed confrontation challenges to the local governance on daily basis. Bureaucracy was suddenly expected to devise a policy for public funded gaushalas (sheds for abandoned cows) to fight this 'menace' and serve it like instant noodles, while the *babus* scratched their heads to figure out ways to fund this policy from an already starved government treasury.

The ideology that chased cow – the deity as a political currency wrongly premised that this ideology reigns supreme in people's mind at all costs. On the contrary, even in the minds of the believers, cow-the deity sits in tandem with cow – the economic asset. Cow-the economic asset may / may not supersede cow-the deity, but cow-the deity should never supersede cow-the economic asset. Farmer will be fine to bow his head in front of the cow till such time the deity does not graze his crops. The dairy owner will offer his daily ode to the cow only for the deity's productive life. 'Cow-the deity' ideology in its euphoria disturbed this harmony and offered nothing but losses for all the stakeholders to count. The bureaucracy lost the stamina to cook up solutions, the desperation quotient of farmers increased manifolds, owners of the onward supply chain became helpless victims, the society became a tad more vitriolic and divisive and the political fortunes of this ideology ran into troubled waters.

India is still bewildered about the cows and is yet to appreciate the inter-dependency of the problems with the beliefs we create around them. Solutions tend to be naïve and laced with emotional overtones, such as a ban on cow slaughter. The extremely intertwined arrangement among various stakeholders of the cow-related industries suggests that such a unidimensional solution will disrupt three sectors (dairy, meat, and leather) with disastrous consequences that will eventually spiral into a full-blown crisis. The food chain of the country will get distorted, not to mention jobs lost and trade imbalances arising out of a decline in exports, which may result in social unrest. It may have serious dietary and public health repercussions due to a shortfall in dairy supplies and cause food inflation. The complex interplay of the 'cow problem' necessitates a nuanced solution.

But, India as a liberal democracy will be morally wrong to question one's faith around cow. Beef eaters cannot be shunned to abdicate their habits and vegetarians cannot be coaxed into becoming non-vegetarians let alone eat beef, because if we do so then we are putting the idea of India under spotlight. Historical arguments cannot be used to question one's reverence or its absence around cow because this shall always remain a matter of personal choice. For the idea of a democratic India, it is of little consequence whether this choice is backed by historical facts or it is purely an emotive response.

A framework that can reconcile this contradiction for a cleaner nation is therefore a saner way to emerge unscathed from this quagmire rather than to engineer an attack of one point of view over the other. A better alternative would be to formalize dairy and meat industries and allow transparency for consumers, leading to implementation of food labeling standards that segment the output of dairy industry. The first segment of products would include regular dairy products using cows that were eventually put to rest in formal slaughterhouses. The second segment would include dairy products and milk produced by cows that were taken to care homes for the rest of their natural life after their productive cycles. These special products will obviously be priced at a premium due to the additional cost incurred toward protection and upkeep of the old cows. Such level-playing field will allow the language of economics to dictate the expression of different ideologies. Staunch Hindus with strong beliefs on cow protection would need to advocate the growth of these premium products. If consumers are willing to pay higher prices for such products, the gain in the market share of these products should satiate their aspirations. Hindus who do not think strongly about protecting the cow as a symbol of Hinduism, on the other hand, will, like the followers of other faiths, have the free will to patronize regular milk products. This war for market share will be more sane and intellectual, unlike the toxic war through vigilantism, which can eventually lead India to get a grip on the sanitation challenge that arises out of an unregulated economy around the cow. India's struggle with the cow problem depicts the deep fissures in the social order which are yet to be comprehended in their entirety. It also brings to surface baffling contradictions. India cannot clean itself and protect its cows at the same time. Swami Vivekananda and cow vigilantes cannot coexist, neither can Veer Savarkar and cow worship. If all cows are protected from slaughter, many will die a painful death out of disease, abandonment, and hunger, while India's neighborhoods will continue to be a living sanitation hell. If India wants to clean itself, it will have to willingly send many cows to slaughterhouses or entirely give up its dependence on dairy. How is that for a challenge?

The story of independent India's struggle to keep itself clean is incomplete without the mention of four individuals. They best capture the contradictions that exist in the Indian society regarding waste management and cleanliness.

The first is Lalit Bhanot, former secretary general of the Indian Olympic Association. The year was 2010, a few days before the opening of the Commonwealth Games in New Delhi. At the residential venue of the games, participants and accompanying officials were dismayed at the deplorable hygienic conditions. The media went into a frenzy and started to flash live images of dirty paan-stained toilets and filthy bedsheets. Some of the athletes walked out and checked-in to different hotels in the city. People across the board fumed with questions and embarrassment. How could we breech our long-held tradition of *Atithi Devo Bhava*, the guest is akin to God? Within a few hours, Bhanot addressed a press conference, and unabashedly announced 'while there were some rough edges and few areas that were found lacking in the games village, the issue of lack of hygiene and sanitation has been blown out of proportion.' He further claimed that 'Indian standards of hygiene and sanitation are different from those of other countries and that the issue should be viewed in the right context.' In other words, a paan-stained wall or a smeared bedsheet or a corridor strewn with construction debris will be treated as 'clean' by Indian standards: this was Bhanot's line of defense. Unwittingly, Bhanot entered the annals of history as the man who announced to the world that India is a far more tolerant country on cleanliness than any other country in the world. He eventually went on to win other laurels, but still remains the poster boy for India's status on hygiene. And he was right.

Public figures are not immune to such contradictions, as it happened with an incumbent union minister in the Government of

India since 2014 and a politician of stature. On an official road trip in 2017, he was caught relieving on the side walls of a building on the motorway that made national headlines. While the incident was briefly debated for its embarrassing visuals, the minister's behavior is exactly the claim that Bhanot made in the press conference. Our hygiene standards are different and therefore our subconscious wiring on the issue of sanitation yields actions that are contrary to 'Clean India' pleas. Bhanot brought to the surface a subconscious aspect of the Indian psyche that has caused unappetizing visuals for centuries.

Gurudas Kamat, the late politician from Maharashtra, is the second individual worth a mention. In 2009, his party led the winning alliance in the general assembly elections and was invited to form the government. Manmohan Singh was elected the prime minister, and the Ministry of Drinking Water and Sanitation was assigned to Kamat. Waste management and public sanitation come under its preview. It is also responsible for policymaking and legislation on these issues, conceiving projects that aim to make the process of urbanization smoother and cities cleaner, providing financial sponsorship to projects, and giving guidance to state governments. Anyone would be elated for having such faith reposed by the prime minister to hold such a position. On the contrary, Kamat was incensed on not being given a 'meatier' ministry or one with more clout or better rank, owing to his so-called high stature in life, and went into a political slumber. Here we have a country on the verge of drowning in its own filth and an elected public representative who fails to see the merits of his office which can play a pivotal role in helping the country. Kamat's abject denial of the job assigned to him brings out the widespread prejudice of the Indian society to discriminate amongst jobs that stemmed from the caste arrangement. During the British rule, jobs that brought Indians closer to the British Raj were considered to bring the holder a higher social stature. All other jobs were mostly skill-based and hardly received any attention in the colonial rule.

Farming was crippled with famine and poverty. Handicrafts and other skill-based self-employment opportunities dried up under the severe burden of imports from the British factories. This hangover continued even in the post-Independence India. Doctors, teachers, lawyers, soldiers, policemen, government officers, traders were perceived as 'symbols' of progress and upward social migration from lower-income group to middle-income group or higher. Cooks, plumbers, truck drivers, carpenters, housemaids, farmers, cleaning personnel were not perceived as representatives of the middle class, never mind their incomes may be many a times higher than that of middle-income households.

This widespread discrimination lowered the dignity of many skills-based jobs in India and undermined the role of such jobs in the economic and social progress of the country. The flawed notion of social progress twisted the Indian policy approach toward job creation. Wrong capital allocation and misplaced priorities for human development became the focal point of government interventions. Take, for instance, the proliferation of higher education institutions that proliferated from the growth of IT services. Many private colleges and universities obtained permissions to manufacture IT engineers, because an engineer was a symbol of upward class movement. In the initial years when demand outstripped supply, every kind of engineer produced in these education factories was absorbed by the industries, perpetuating a myth that the policy is right. Beginning 2015, the IT industry witnessed a slowdown because of advancements in robotics, machine learning, and artificial intelligence. Hiring became selective and the few jobs went to the best. Other branches of engineering studies were even worse hit and ended up with a large number of 'unemployable' workforce. Around the same time, other sectors of the Indian economy were faced with a peculiar challenge: the construction industry witnessed a shortage in skilled personnel for civil works, plumbing, and electrical works; the logistics sector faced a shortage of trained drivers for long body carriers; hospitality and facilities management companies faced a dearth of trained food service professionals, trained housekeepers, and others. Meanwhile, a farmer in a remote village readily mortgaged his land to raise money to send his son to one of the factories of higher education in the hope that he may eventually be able to secure a job in the IT sector and upgrade the social status of his family. But the son may end up as an unemployable youth who will either be idle at home or be forced to take up a job that does not justify his father's sacrifice of mortgaging the family land. For the farmer, an unemployable engineer is still more acceptable than he acquiring formal but the so-called less dignified skills of carpentry, plumbing, or food services, which are associated with those on a lower rung of the social ladder.

The urban migration that India witnessed in the guise of economic growth also saw mass abandonment of skills. Farmers left farming to become private security guards in cities. Pottery makers in small towns preferred selling tea at stalls in big cities. Consequently, informality continued with many skills-based jobs despite the explosive demand for such jobs. Informality keeps a job from becoming productive, efficient, and effective, and does not allow upgradation of human capabilities. Imagine if the car industry in India was not formalized as it is today. Many small car makers would informally engage the services of mechanics to manufacture a car. A dozen or so mechanics would have to work tirelessly for weeks to make one car, toiling away in unsafe working conditions. Would you bet your money and life on the safety or durability of such a car? Many skills in India that should have been organized under a formal structure ended up suffering such a fate, and delivering services or products in an inefficient and ineffective way.

Jobs related to all aspects of waste and garbage management sit at the bottom of this discrimination pyramid and have suffered the most collateral damage. Waste management requires enormous amount of skill, from collection to disposal. Yet the entire waste collection system in India rests on the shoulders of an army of bare-bodied people, armed with nothing more substantial than rusted wheelbarrows, pails, and brooms, who are barely paid minimum wages. This army is virtually set up to fail as it is tasked to lift 100,000 metric tons of garbage that India generates on a daily basis, the third largest in the world.

Why is it that we fail to take notice of the fact that clean countries systematically moved away from landfills in the 1980s toward greener, far more efficient methods? Why is it that the garbage littered on the streets is almost always blamed on the scarcity of cleaning staff to clean the area? Why do the local bodies not investigate the repeated littering and dirtying of the area in the first place? Perhaps unplanned human movement in the area, not budgeted for by urban design has a role to play in it.

This myopic view is an unconscious outcome of the set up of an Indian household and the neighborhood that house it. Governance comprises individuals who grow up in these households which are mostly dysfunctional units when it comes to waste management as we have witnessed so far. A representative subset of these individuals enter government jobs or public offices and end up managing the issue of waste management, applying the same prejudices that they imbibed at home. The same mandarins who never shied away from learning about renewable power generation from Germany, about drip irrigation from Israel, digital technology and defense from America, fail to learn anything about waste management and sanitation from the same countries. There is no other reason for this resistance other than a mental block stemming from skewered albeit deep rooted 'values' to pay no heed to the advancements in waste management in these countries. Consequently, the subject of waste management and sanitation is an under-researched area severely lacking critical thinking and starved of scientific temperament. Kamat was a victim of this mentality, and so he rejected the job offer.

The story of the third individual is a contrast to the picture of despair painted by the previous two stories. Pawan Kumar Chamling, till recently the chief minister of Sikkim, and the longest serving chief minister since 1994, represents the alternate reality of hope for India's fight for cleanliness and sanitation. He describes a path that India, the desperate republic, needs to take to become clean. We have seen that prevailing prejudices and caste systems are the major causes of India's challenges with waste management and can be extrapolated to a large geographical part of the country. But there are regions that have shunned this thinking and overcome such mental blocks and set their houses in order. Chamling and the state of Sikkim are proof of this alternate narrative.

In 2008, Sikkim was declared the only state in India to have achieved 100 percent sanitation. The state was completely free from open defecation, every person had access to toilets and they used them with discipline and pride. In 2003, Chamling passed a legislation to ban the use of pesticides and fertilizers for agriculture on the 600,000 hectares of land in the state, and by 2015, he succeeded to nudge the entire state toward organic farming. During implementation there were no protests, no loss of livelihoods, no decline in crop yields, and no counter-arguments against this move. In 2003, the state also passed a legislation for a complete ban on the use of plastic bags, and introduced heavy fines for spitting and urinating in the open and smoking in public places. Such political moves came at a time when the fight against waste and cleanliness was more than a decade away from mainstream thinking. Two key lessons, common to the journey of the clean countries of the Western world, can be learnt from Sikkim's journey.

The first lesson is the wisdom to appreciate that political sponsorship has to precede any other initiative in this fight. This sponsorship requires maturity to develop a vision, gumption to back the vision with political bets, and resolve to stay the course.

Chamling's conviction received wide political support that translated into legislation and supplied the ability to develop a grand vision to change the game on a state-wide basis, and not just confined to local village and town councils. The inability of local bodies, with their meager resources, to conceive the right vision is the key reason for the multiple false starts of India's sanitation journey. Take the case of fund utilization by local bodies who received grants from the central government under the Nirmal Bharat Abhiyan since 1986 (rebooted under the Swatch Bharat Mission in 2014) to build toilets in homes. The national average of funds utilized by local bodies for this purpose remained at approximately 50 percent, while local bodies in Sikkim achieved a utilization percentage of 99.2. A major reason for this difference was that local bodies in Sikkim had the blueprint to deploy funds as it had been worked out for the entire state by its legislative assembly. A clear vision such as this is absent in many Indian states. Although financial assistance is provided to tackle issues of waste and sanitation, decades of conforming to textbook responses has conditioned local bodies to think about these issues merely from the standpoint of troubleshooting and operational expenditure, and hence end up not utilizing the grants. Consider, for instance, the nine panchayats of Namthang Rateypani constituency in Sikkim. These panchayats received state grants and pooled together their resources to start a solid waste-management-cum-compost-preparation center in 2014 to collect all biodegradable waste to produce organic manure and sell it in the open market. All at once, the ban imposed on pesticides and fertilizers in 2003 by the Sikkim state assembly made sense. Sikkim recognized the strong interdependencies among the issues of waste, sanitation, and environment and reaped benefits from this wisdom.

The second lesson to be taken from Sikkim's journey is the virtue of specificity in the legislation on waste management and the power to harness young minds. Sikkim's legislation specifically outlined actions permitted and otherwise to citizens, and about keeping the legislation current with the changing times. For instance, Sikkim introduced a legislation to manage e-waste in 2014. But in 2003 when Sikkim first activated a set of legislations on waste management, it had remained silent because it was not a burning issue then. However, the progressive mindset of the political sponsorship allowed Sikkim to appreciate the growing generation of e-waste that led to the new set of legislations ten years later. Sikkim never assumed that legislation and vision development by local bodies alone can be the bedrock for success. It adopted an active engagement approach with children to get through to the adults. State-wide education programs actively involved children in live projects, demonstrations on sanitation and virtues of clean living, advantages of toilets at home, and many other tutorials, who, in turn, advocated clean living to their parents. This also ensured that these children would carry on a healthy legacy in their households.

Sikkim's story cannot be brushed aside merely because of any cultural and geographic advantages it may have: there are some inherent advantages of the egalitarian ethnic, hence lateral, segregation prevalent in the northeast region as opposed to a hierarchical caste order segregation in other parts of the country. Therefore, before Sikkim's accession to India in 1975, the king of Sikkim enshrined equality to all in the eyes of the state. This discouraged the tendency to discriminate between jobs on caste lines and accorded equal respect to all jobs. It also allowed communities to collectively preserve the wisdom of previous generations and lead an ecologically balanced life that naturally promotes clean surroundings.

Sikkim's success story is mirrored in that of Mawlynnong, a village in Meghalaya. A congregation of 95 houses and about 500 people, it has been voted as the 'cleanest village in Asia.' Everyone in this 100-per-cent-literate village is engaged in agriculture. Garbage is collected in bamboo bins and converted into manure and used for agriculture. Khonoma in Nagaland, called 'the green village,' has a similar story. Tamanth, a village in Maharashtra, has a strict policy for its habitants to follow civic rules regarding garbage disposal. Puzhakkal village in Thrissur district of Kerala overcame its challenge of solid waste management and became a role model for the entire state which struggles to remain clean under a rising wave of industrialization. The success of these remote villages lies in preserving the tenets of an egalitarian society and living that have been passed from generation to generation as well as on education toward better, cleaner living.

Many villages and towns across India are slowly waking up to bring about change, and countless, faceless committed souls – bureaucrats, social activists, sarpanchs, community leaders, block development officers, common people – are working tirelessly toward achieving this result. The city of Mysuru has consistently ranked as the top city in India on waste management practices and implementing modern techniques for waste collection and segregation, and is ironically located at a six-hour drive from Bengaluru, a city that rests on a ticking garbage time bomb. The city of Pune is home to SWaCH, India's first cooperative of self-employed waste-pickers, but the landfill at Deonar, Mumbai, rests just four hours away. Like Chamling, several unsung heroes are fighting for this cause; they understand that this journey will have to be infused with the conviction to stay the course.

The date 15 August 2014 should be recorded as a watershed moment in India's struggle with sanitation. In his first speech as prime minister, Narendra Modi acknowledged India's garbage and sanitation problem and made a call to address it. The issue finally received much-awaited political sponsorship and this makes Narendra Modi the fourth important individual in India's narrative on sanitation.

Slums, swamps, open drains, foul air, rancid rivers dotted the landscape of the First-World countries in the nineteenth century. In the backdrop of the Industrial Revolution, issues of urban infrastructure, housing, and sanitation came strongly into the political agenda and defined political leadership. The period between 1890 and 1920 is referred to as the Progressive Era in American politics, and was marked by intense social and political activism that was centered around the desire to root out corruption in public offices. However, the desire to remove corruption also resulted in a strong desire to reduce inefficiencies in the systems and incorporate scientific methods to improve existing processes of various organs of governments' service delivery. Champions of the era were avid modernizers who were convinced that past methods were not adequate to service the needs of the future. The era also witnessed major policy overhauls across all walks of American life, including unsafe working conditions, urban poverty, law enforcement, banking, universal suffrage, and municipal reforms. Proponents of this thought became the 'progressive' mayors of Los Angeles, New Jersey, Toledo, Kentucky, Louisville. The progressive era received widespread support from emerging middle class, professionals and administrators. 'Efficiency movement' and 'structural overhauls' were the primary tools for process owners. It invigorated the entire country with a strong desire to change the status quo for a better future. Issues of garbage and waste management were addressed with a scientific temperament to root out inefficiencies in its design under the broader umbrella of urban planning. New sewage and drainage systems were built and sanitation departments were instituted in cities. Garbage collection and sewage disposal systems were installed. Law enforcement was strengthened through human capability upgradation and infrastructure development. All these interventions had a direct impact on the waste and garbage challenges of America in the twentieth century.

Sweden's cleanliness is no accident either. Its beginnings lie in the political movement that started with the coming to power of the Social Democratic Party in 1932. It built a social narrative around Folkhemmet. Literally, People's Home, it is the concept of society as family, where every citizen contributes and everybody's needs are addressed. Housing was seen to play a vital role in promoting Folkhemmet that was built around inspiring designs. It took great effort in defining the concept of an ideal home based on honesty, responsibility, clean surroundings, and humility. It shunned the tendency to decorate homes with 'beyond necessary' installations – thick dark curtains were discouraged because they blocked natural light, and plain, light-colored ones were preferred. Housing was made accessible to the citizens, but great effort was also taken to prescribe these design philosophies to them, by way of distribution of design guideline brochures during disbursal of home loans, design classes for homeowners, among other initiatives. These interventions may sound a breach of the private space, but they played a vital role in shaping the attitudes of the Swedes toward green and sensible living, in turn promoting cleanliness. The larger purpose was to strongly associate democratic values with housing, cleanliness, and design. Eighty years later the Swedes were recycling and reusing nearly all the waste they generated.

Post Independence, the political establishment in India never had the time to think about these aspects for an effective political discourse. Issues such as urban housing, sanitation, and municipal reforms were deemed trivial and were thus consigned to the fringes, although it will be unfair to say that the policymakers had a choice in the matter and that they ended up cherry-picking other issues over those such as waste. Issues of poverty alleviation, national security, and agriculture took precedence over other issues given the infancy of the nation and the geopolitical scenario of that time. Moreover, how could the politics of a nation that was 90 percent agrarian look at an issue like waste which afflicts primarily cities and towns? Why should political capital be invested on the issue of waste that deals with the post-consumption human mess, when the more pressing need was to arrange two meals a day for majority of the citizens?

These seemingly compelling narratives for six decades in independent India took away opportunities for issues like sanitation to receive the political sponsorship they deserved. For instance, the drought in the 1960s prompted a strong political sponsorship for the Green Revolution that gained mass support. Similarly, tensions with neighboring countries translating into wars in quick succession created strong nationalist zeal that sponsored India's missile program and upgraded its defense policy. The scenario of the 1980s was a mixed bag of job security and affirmative action that transitioned to economic growth in the decade of 1990s. Where was the intellectual bandwidth to dissect the issue of sanitation and present it to the political establishment with a promise of winning votes?

The trajectory of clean countries of today suggests that for sanitation and public health to become politically relevant issues, there needs to be a trigger. Rewind to the sanitation problem caused by horse carriages at the turn of the twentieth century in cities like New York and Paris. Nearly 300,000 horse carriages roamed the city streets of New York, and the horse excreta and urine on the streets made it a public health hazard. Such was the magnitude of this waste hazard that horse excrement topped the agenda of the urban planners' conference in 1910, a sign of emerging political attention to the issue. It is a different matter though that Henry Ford's Model T changed the game forever, and by 1917 New York's streets were free from horse carriages.

In clean countries of today, the dual issue of sanitation and waste was almost always preceded by a strong wave of urbanization that saw vast voluntary displacement of people from villages to cities. The cities were not large enough to accommodate this sudden influx. People were forced to live in slums and breathe foul air and drink polluted water. Municipal bodies were either absent or not adequately equipped to handle the pressure. Concurrently, these societies were making rapid strides in scientific fields. At the beginning of the twentieth century, for instance, with the discovery of microbes, they understood for the first time the explicit link between unsanitary conditions and public health, and found that widespread human and animal waste is a carrier of various germs that cause diseases. These societies understood that dirty surroundings were not merely unsightly, but also a serious health hazard. The two-fold development of urbanization and of scientific discovery created a public view that promoted political sponsorship for sanitation-related ideas. In the backdrop of these developments, public housing in the UK, the progressive movement in America, and municipal reforms in Japan became the hallmark of advocacy for cleanliness in the earlier part of twentieth century. Does India need to go through the same cycle to gain political impetus for cleanliness? Do these countries not serve as case studies enough to accelerate our progress? After all, the germ theory that proves bad sanitation leads to poor health is a universal fact that need not be rediscovered by Indians. But, for the mainstream Indian politics, while the germ theory was a universal fact, the quantum of urbanization did not exert enough pressure in the first six decades of post-independence India for the issue of sanitation to garner political heft. Independent India failed to appreciate the interdependency of waste with other issues ahead of time for the lack of pressure points.

The case of Hindon river in Uttar Pradesh serves as a good reference to outline this. A tributary of Yamuna river, till 1980 it used to be a lifeline for settlements along 400 kilometers of its length. After 1980, the industrial policy doled out land to factories and manufacturing units in cities situated on the banks of the river, thus changing the character of many of these cities. However, the industrial policy did not frame guidelines or build supporting infrastructure to manage the industrial waste being dumped into the river. Within thirty-five years, the Hindon completely transformed into a stinking cesspool of industrial and human waste. In 2015, the river was accorded the status of a 'dead river' by the Central Pollution Control Board. The toxins from the river have reached the ground water, rendering it useless for irrigation or drinking. Caked up sludge formed a thick solid layer on the both sides of the river and that skirted a viscous black liquid underneath. Out of the 400 villages on the banks of this river, 150 have reported severe health problems.

Although the Hindon passes through seven Lok Sabha and thirty-seven assembly constituencies, and four hundred panchayats, this ticking time bomb has not yet qualified for any political sponsorship. Activists believe the problem requires a solution worth 500 crore rupees, but the state government in 2016 allocated only 2 crore rupees toward fixing the issue. There seem to be other far more important parameters of inconvenience, such as rural distress, the issue of the cow, caste alignments, job reservation, forced migration, than a foul-smelling, disgusting river. Are public representatives not within their right to respond with political apathy to the issue? Political representatives are not necessarily the culprits for the lack of political initiative. They merely reflect the society they represent in all its form. The grounds-up politics of today is a career actively pursued with high stakes and a competitive streak. Issues and actions are choreographed and coordinated. Therefore, it is reactive to the sentiments of the citizens, rather than being proactive to guide them. If citizens are conditioned to take a discriminatory stance toward waste from childhood, why should the political representative take up this issue and become a premature political martyr for the lack of groundswell support? Historically, for all issues that concern sanitation, waste, public health, and cleanliness political sponsorship in India had to be a top-down approach backed by intellectual rigor. It cannot be expected to become a bottom-up movement because it does not have the same romanticism of pride and honor for the 'haves' and the urgency of jobs, security, and food among the 'have-nots.'

Mainstream political narrative was laced with misplaced priorities on the issue of waste and sanitation, and also lacked literacy to comprehend the depth of the challenge and to take risks. But was mainstream politics the only missed opportunity for political sponsorship? What about the political representation of the Dalit castes that were engaged in the profession of waste management?

The roots for Dalit politics in India lie with Jyotiba Phule, who raised a strong voice of dissent in 1848 against the caste order and social arrangement in Maharashtra. He believed in overthrowing the social order that forced one section of the society to be economically and morally dependent on another, and thus founded the Satyashodhak Samaj (society of truth-seekers) in 1873. He championed initiatives like girl education and opened the first school for girls in 1848. His struggle and work served as a good reference point for Gandhi to develop a political narrative for the Dalits. The next direct uprising that laid the foundation for Dalit politics happened in 1916, when Sir P. Theagaraya Chetty presided over a meeting in Madras (now Chennai) and brought together prosperous non-Brahmins and started the Justice Party. This was also the start of the Dravidian movement that set the tone for Tamil politics for the next hundred years. Nine years later, Periyar E. V. Ramasamy also raised his voice against the caste order and founded the Self-Respect Movement, using a far more radical and candid approach to challenge the caste order. In 1937, Justice Party and Self-Respect Movement merged under the leadership of Periyar. This union formalized the Dravidian struggle and set the tone for an intolerant form of Dalit politics in Tamil Nadu and for the Dravidian faction to seek ruling right of the state in 1967, and since then being at the helm of the state in different avatars. The governing rights for Dravidian politics in Tamil Nadu saw many pathbreaking social programs aimed at breaking caste biases, namely, intercaste housing communities, legislation to remove caste barrier for pujaris, equal succession rights to women, and intercaste marriages. Today, Tamil Naidu scores high on inclusion and social development, an achievement that remains a pipe dream for many other Indian states and the credit goes to Dravidian politics. But this brand of politics also used a strong anti-Brahmin and anti-Hindi confrontationist plank that, on the one hand, achieved genuine inclusion of non-Brahmin castes in the state's order of things, but, on the other, witnessed mass migration of Brahmins from the state and set the stage for regional confrontation with others as well as with national politics. Perhaps strong regional identity was the glue that fused all non-Brahmanical castes with a common purpose. But this overtone that championed supremacy of regional identity blunted its potency for a genuine Dalit upliftment on many counts, and the state, like its other siblings, was still not free of caste-based skirmishes, biases, and discrimination that go way beyond the overly simplistic Brahmin versus non-Brahmin framework.

In 1927 Dr B. R. Ambedkar launched the Mahad Satyagraha, aimed to assert the rights of Dalits' access to water in public places. He abhorred the idea that while livestock and animals could access these water facilities, lower-caste people were prohibited to do so. This resistance marked Ambedkar's objective approach to Dalit politics, which injected the movement with rationality and economic thinking during that time. He took a broader view of the repressive caste system and viewed every social contract in the Indian society from the lens of equality. Therefore, every skewed arrangement that led to repression, exploitation, and inequality attracted his scorn. Ambedkar realized the importance of dovetailing the agenda of Dalit politics into policy and legislation. He raised the banner of Dalit rights by staying within the political mainstream that provided balance to the critical job of drafting the constitution and laid down a much-needed inclusive framework to protect India's pluralistic composition. The Indian constitution is one of the most forward-looking documents in modern human history on pluralism, affirmative action, and equality, and a fair share of this credit goes to him. Post Independence, he became the lone warrior of Dalit politics with a national appeal.

Ideally, his politics should have proliferated across India to become a strong force, but it failed because of his premature demise and a weak second line. The Republican Party of India, founded by Ambedkar after quitting the Congress, hardly remained a shadow of his vision after his passing. A new crop of Dalit leaders arose who fanned a sense of injustice among Dalits. This way, Ambedkar's idea of improving the system through intellectual assertion lost steam.

Kanshi Ram founded the All India Backward and Minority Communities Employees Federation (BAMCEF), a union of government employees from lower-caste section, and laid the ground for this confrontationist brand of Dalit politics in north India. He went on to found a full-fledged political party, the Bahujan Samaj Party (BSP) in 1984. His politics centered around the 'us versus them' debate that culminated in a caustic stance, in the hope of consolidating the vote of the 'lower' sections of the society. This brand of politics was more about the arithmetic of social engineering than about social change and saw stupendous success in soldering the Dalit votes. 'Miracle of democracy,' Ms Mayawati, emerged from the ascent of this stance and as a political heiress of Kanshi Ram. However, in 2017, the BSP suffered a near wipeout in the elections to the legislative assembly of Uttar Pradesh, the state that was central to its existence, while little more than one-fifth of the state's voters polled for the party. Mayawati was quick to raise doubts on the election process for the party's rout, ignoring the fact that the same process propelled her to a thumping victory nearly ten years earlier. In her heart, perhaps she knew that the social engineering brand that Kanshi Ram espoused had run its course and Dalit politics needed a new script.

These shortcomings notwithstanding, the rise of Dalit politics is a great validation for the Indian democratic set up. It created space for a perceived subaltern view to rise and assert itself. If we reference this achievement in the political order of the world, this is by no means an easy task. However, the predominant narrative of post-

Independence Dalit politics was premised on the fight for equality and for the upliftment of the Dalit class on a confrontationist ('us versus them') platform. It took a unidimensional approach to define the notions of 'equality' and 'upliftment.' This view was further premised on the notion that Dalits can only be uplifted if they can transition from their existing jobs to those of the upper-caste sections of the society because their present jobs are menial. Political representatives championed Dalits into becoming priests, teachers, clerks, engineers, doctors, accountants – jobs that symbolize 'upper-caste' professions. With this premise, Dalit politics ended up with only one lever for affirmative action (job reservations) to build the argument for the development of the Dalit class.

If the breadwinner of a Dalit family works as a garbage collector, his family cannot be uplifted until he or his next generation secures an upper-caste job. A boatman cannot be uplifted as long as he continues to be a boatman, same for a Chamar if he continues to dispose of dead animals. They can be uplifted only through a clerical office job, a sales job in a trade, a machine job in a factory, and such others. This unidimensional view unintentionally undermined the jobs of the Dalits. In the pursuit of upliftment, Dalit politics also ended up discriminating their jobs. It failed to take into account the importance of those jobs for the progress, economic development, and well being of the country. The biggest victim of this discrimination was waste collection and disposal, which Dalit politics took on face value of the job design, thus concluding that the job itself is so undesirable that the Dalits should aim to disown it.

The aspect that Dalit politics ignored was to build activism around correcting the job design of waste management, or, for that matter, any other job they were predominantly engaged in. This ignorance was perhaps an outcome of illiteracy about the economics of the profession of waste management. The major issue with such a job in India was the informal arrangement between the person who generated the waste and the person who disposed of it, the Dalits, which suppressed the wages, unlike in the Western societies where Gongfermours earned well. Dalits gained these job skills in an environment of oppression and exploitation of at least 1,400 years. Municipal bodies merely leveraged this skill and sponsored the arrangement. Therefore, the entire apparatus, infrastructure, and operational design of waste management in India is severely under-capitalized and mispriced, and continues to rely on the archaic practices of waste collection and waste disposal.

A job does not become less critical or less important if it is discharged in a wrong fashion. The job of guarding the border is not insignificant if the solider is meagerly paid or poorly equipped. The job of a doctor does not become less important if he is not given tools and facilities to examine patients. Dalit politics misinterpreted this important dimension. The inhuman working conditions for Dalits in waste management jobs made Dalit politics undermine the job itself. This discrimination squandered an economic opportunity that had all the potential for the Dalits to break free from the vicious cycle of condemnation and exploitation in a far more productive and successful manner. The caste segregation of jobs created an unintentional positive outcome for Dalits engaged in the waste management sector. The entire value chain of waste management that comprises the activities of collection, transportation, and disposal of waste was controlled and operated by a concentrated section of the Dalit society. Unintentionally, here Dalits faced no competition from any other class or group. To put this advantage in perspective, the Jewish people in Europe and in North America were deeply entrenched in the money lending business by the turn of the century. With the growth of the formal banks, the community's sway and presence in money lending allowed the community to benefit from many economic opportunities. It is common wisdom that the activity of waste disposal is an integral part of the economic cycle and consumption. Any disruption in the waste disposal regimen is bound to cause a blockage upstream which can clog the entire consumption cycle of an economy.

Let us imagine 6,000 metric tons of waste generated by Bengaluru everyday is not picked up for one month. At the end of the month, the city will be sitting on 180,000 metric tons of smelly, untreated garbage. With every percentage point added to our GDP, India was poised to add a significant quantum of generated waste, which was more complex and heterogeneous than at any earlier time in the recorded history of the country. Solving the quantum and complexity of waste, from the standpoint of economics, technology, and regulations, could have been an enormous opportunity for the sector. It needed a disposition to evaluate the sector for inefficiency, working conditions, and social contracts, and to design solutions which could nudge the sector toward formality. The only dominant social groups that had requisite skill and understanding to undertake these tasks were the Dalits.

The Dalits engaged in waste management only needed to organize themselves better, to view the profession with a scientific temperament and create enabling conditions for a transition toward formality. This backdrop would have enabled Dalit politics to create a policy approach for waste management that should have advocated better contracts with local governments on working conditions, safety, wages, citizens' duties; to build activism for country-wide legislation on enforcement, and to create an environment for the participation of private capital in the sector. It could have installed equitable quid pro quo across the entire value chain and re-organized activities into formal activities with strong contracts based on equality. The existing dominance of the Dalit caste in this sector would have spurred entrepreneurships prompting many Dalits to become entrepreneurs and promoters of formal enterprises that would have owned and operated large and efficiently run waste collection companies engaged by local bodies. These waste collection companies would have achieved high efficiency of waste segregation at source and promoted innovation in the next activity of the waste management chain, that is, disposal. Dalit entrepreneurship could have also given rise to specialized formal waste processing units that worked in niche areas of waste, namely, resource recovery units for electronic waste, safe disposal units for medical and hazardous waste, mechanized junkyards for automobiles, and recycling centers for plastic waste. The cooperative of SWaCH nurtured by the Municipal Cooperation of Pune is testimony to this possibility. All of this could have significantly altered the psyche of Dalit sanitation workers who were hitherto suppressed and conditioned to feel inferior, and helped them become formal workers who handled waste disposal with as much dignity and pride as workers assembling cars in a factory or miners excavating ore from the earth. Dalit politics could have spurred cooperative movements in the waste management sector and proliferated SWaCH-like models across India. Dalit politics was well positioned to play the role of a torchbearer and take the lead, instead it ended up playing the role of a Pied-Piper.

It was this dovetailing that was demanded from Dalit politics in India. Economics trumps prejudice, but Indian Dalit politics completely missed the potency of this insight while designing the blueprint of activism. Practices become biases out of information asymmetry and individual insecurity. The language of money (or equivalent incentives) breaks both these barriers that create prejudices in the first place. Take the example of the film industry that started its affair with India with Dadasaheb Phalke's first motion picture in 1913, *Raja Harishchandra*. The early crop of entrants in the film trade were largely those who worked in theater or traveling theater. There was a strong bias in society against female actors in the film industry in the early era, who were equated to concubines, so much so that Phalke had to rely on male actors to perform female roles. Then the prosperity and lavish lifestyle of successful Indian actors came to light and became a journalistic genre. Indian actors turned into symbols of all that was good and desirable. The earlier biases were replaced by a deeply aspirational admiration. By the 1990s, female actors, who by now were an integral part of Indian film industry, came from perceived 'respectable' backgrounds, irrespective of caste or religion. Commerce, which enabled individuals to accumulate wealth and capture the imagination of the masses, played a major role in overcoming the gender prejudices that had crippled an entire industry in its infancy.

The widely successful social experiment of K. Kamraj in Tamil Nadu in 1962–3, that conceived the free midday meals to children in schools, prompted families across the state to overcome deep-rooted prejudices against education and send their children to school. In one fell swoop, the program netted millions of children in the state to get educated. Impoverished families and low-income families saw a strong economic reason to send their children to a nearby school that provided nutrition to them, without any burden on the family's income. This reasoning was enough for families to wipe off any bias against education and to start on a clean slate.

The language of commerce and commercial contracts provides clarity and creates a strong base for equality in human interactions. It provides objectivity and has enormous power to trump biases, beliefs, and stereotypes. The Nobel Memorial Prize in Economic Sciences 2016 went to Professors Oliver Hart and Bengt Holmström for their contribution to propound this thought as a strong tool to remove vagueness and subjectivity in commercial and social agreements. The theory suggests an agreement between two human parties is an expectation of one party for a reward from the other party in lieu of an action. If this agreement between two human parties is vague, in which an action from one party does not yield specific outcome from the other or the outcome is subjected to more than one interpretation, it causes stress in the agreement. For these reasons agreements are translated into formal contracts with specificity of action and of a quid pro quo. The theory also extends to measure these formal contracts for different scenarios, and has seen wide application.

Waste management in India dearly missed the injection of contract theory. Championing the cause of improving the dignity of the job by building a strong contract with different stakeholders in the value chain should have better served the sincerity of Dalit politics for equality. Imagine if Dalit politics would have championed for wage rates, working conditions, access to capital for waste recyclers, and formal contracts for sanitation workers employed by different local bodies, it would have redesigned the waste management sector around formal structures and processes and steadily translated into social change. Society would have seen a gradual rise in the economic prosperity of sanitation workers, lifting both the worker and the job profile out of centuries of condemnation.

Sadly, the route adopted by Dalit politics to perceptively shun the existing professions of Dalits in lieu of jobs of the so-called upper caste as the only means to salvation not only lacked the economic fire power to make a widespread impact, but also smacked of a feeling of retribution, which was bound to cave in at some point in the future.

Dalit politics ignored the importance of injecting intellectual rigor while building arguments for activism to support Dalit upliftment. Waste management was the primary sector of employment for the Dalits. Their politics took a confrontationist route to develop the argument that excluded the massively positive potential it presented. This exclusionist argument seemed to have worked at first because it gave instant results in terms of populist appreciation and support. Centuries of condemnation naturally translated into anger and support for the voice of dissent. However, problem starts when the activism ends up winning the mandate to govern. It is here the paucity of intellectual thought leadership comes back to bite the activist. A similar outcome unfolded for

Dalit politics. Wherever Dalit politics ended up winning the governing mandate, be it local bodies, state assemblies, or national parliament, the best that Dalit politics could come up with for their upliftment was to juice out more from the policy of affirmative action via job reservations.

Dalit politics squandered away the chance to build a political narrative around the economic opportunity that the Dalit professions presented. To understand the unprecedented scale of this miss, take the instance of Marwari community that branched out from small hamlets in Rajasthan and built trading textile businesses across India during the British rule – the single biggest non-food merchandise category traded and retailed across India even today. The community developed expertise in cross-regional trade, learned about the factors that created value in the movement of goods, and encouraged members of the community to participate in the activities surrounding the business. The community's caste order did not require any political activism and thereby provided the natural power to hold sway on the textile business. Textile manufacturing underpinned the first wave of industrialization in the country. With it emerged a long lineage of successful Marwari businesses that dominated the textile industry – Singhanias, Birlas, Sakserias, Khaitans, and Khataus, to name a few.

The domineering presence of the Dalits in the waste management sector also had the potential for them to become the Marwaris of this sector, but they lacked in social stature. This is where Dalit politics should have stepped in to bridge this gap. It should have taken a scientific, objective, and fact-based constructive argument impacting the structure of the waste management sector, the job profile of the workers, and the necessary legislative and enforcement approach of the state to support the formalization and sustainable growth of the sector. Instead, it took the confrontationist approach that did more harm than good to the caste.

Using USA's generated waste to its waste management industry size ratio, if the Indian waste management sector was organized, it would today be worth more than US$ 15 billion in size annually. It is a sizeable economic potential for an impactful social change program and Dalit politics had a virgin field at its disposal to extract this value and divert it toward the upliftment of its community. Instead, they ended up with informal businesses processing waste and cleaning jobs that have not changed their stature for the last sixteen centuries.

Modi's speech, mentioned earlier, highlights many such missed political opportunities – it brings forward the intellectual illiteracy of the political class to appreciate the readiness of the issue for sponsorship. Modi has played a critical role in India's journey toward waste management by placing the issue in the mainstream national psyche.

Let us revisit the question raised earlier. 'Is India a dirty country?' The answer will depend on which individual the question is posed before: Bhanot, Kamat, Chamling, or Modi. A Bhanot will slyly agree that India is dirty, but will qualify his answer with a vague notion of how 'Indian culture' has birthed a different standard of cleanliness than the rest of the world. A Kamat will be incensed at your audacity to even ask a question about a subject which is below his stature. A Chamling will vehemently answer this question in the negative. And a Modi will accept that India is dirty and that something needs to be done about it.

These four individuals signify the inherent contradictions in the Indian psyche about the issues. They run so deep that most of us will find ourselves vacillating between these manifestations in our daily lives. Prejudices and social arrangements that evolved over centuries conditioned the Indian mind to the extent that the issue of waste and sanitation moved away from being an individual's duty to an entitlement for the consuming society. Bhanot and Kamat represent that consuming majority. By the virtue of being the majority, they also became the mainstream narrative of India that signifies condemnation, apathy, and mediocre standards toward waste management. On the other hand, Chamling represents a rarer viewpoint on the issue, acknowledging the ills of its mainstream counterpart and the will to right the wrongs.

The story of how the people of Mawlynnong made cleanliness a way of life lies in a cholera outbreak hundreds of years ago. The villagers learned from the visiting missionaries that to survive this outbreak they would need to keep their surroundings clean, and this triggered their inspiring journey toward cleanliness. Had it not happened, today Mawlynnong would likely have been just another Indian village struggling with filth. Another success factor is the egalitarian social structure that gives equal powers to women and is sans any caste bias. All community members are equal here and cleanliness is a shared responsibility. After the cholera outbreak, waste management practices became an integral part of the value system, diligently passed on to future generations. Also, with passing times the village embraced change and progress, such as generating solar power and banning the use of plastic.

The Mawlynnong story teaches us that the struggle with waste management is essentially a war of the human mind. The cholera outbreak created fear among the villagers – a state of mind. This resulted in series of actions that translated into a practice. Years of this practice became ingrained in the mind and became wisdom, one that could be passed on to future generations through rules, household training and enforcement. Systematic conditioning the minds of the generations to come led to the natural instinct that managing waste is a daily chore akin to having a bath or eating food. Deolali Pravara in Maharashtra also went the Mawlynnong way and installed vans fitted with 100 percent garbage collection GPS. As did Narnaul in Haryana, declared a model village. Mahabalipuram, a heritage site declared by the United Nations Educational, Scientific and Cultural Organization (UNESCO) and a town of 20,000 people in Tamil Nadu, went waste-free in two years when it joined hands with a non-governmental organization (NGO) and adopted integrated waste management techniques.

Unfortunately, though, these stories are but exceptions that have managed to survive the onslaught of mental biases and illiteracy of the mainstream through an incredible combination of circumstantial luck, individual grit, and the foresight to swallow the bitter pill of 'common wisdom.' Modi represents a bewildered and restless Indian, looking for ways to replace a Bhanot and a Kamat with a Chamling as India's mainstream discourse on waste management. He represents the search for an answer to simple questions: Why can India not become an extension of Mawlynnong? What should be done to make the mainstream psyche of India on waste mirror that of the villagers of Mawlynnong? Why has the Clean India campaign struggled to punch a decisive blow to India's sanitation challenge?

Reconditioning of the Indian mind on the notion of cleanliness and everything around it must become the lynchpin of any approach, be it a policy or an initiative. Its seriousness should not be underestimated for the inference's trite representation. Sixteen centuries of prejudice has given rise to this unproductive makeup of the Indian mind. It will be naive to believe that a few advertisements in the media that border on pleas will make any dent to these biases. No mass social change program anywhere in the world has ever worked that merely pleaded with the citizens for change. Take the instance of the advent of the insurance industry in North America. It faced stiff resistance from the church in its initial days and saw a sustained period of low adoption. Only when insurance was augmented with legislation was it adopted widely. Similarly, it took decades of persistent focus on infrastructure, regulation, and enforcement for people in the First World to observe traffic rules as a matter of habit. For any lasting solution to emerge for India's sanitation mess, the country will need to tunnel its way into the deep-seated biases of people and show them the light. If the approach required is akin to an earth-mover, the jingles, marathons, and advertisements being employed currently are no more than shovels.

The clean countries of today had three key weapons to make their societies toe the line on sanitation – legislation, enforcement, and education. India will need these with all guns blazing, given the unfortunate marriage of its sanitation issue with the caste system. Also, legislation plays an important role to convey the notion of right and wrong to bring civility and order in society. It is not sufficient to merely rely on established wisdom or on an individual's conscience to do so. Say, established wisdom is that killing a person is wrong. Let's assume that countries relied only on this wisdom and did not draft specific laws against the wrongful action of one person causing the death of another. There would be no deterrence in a person's mind apart from his own conscience. Let's say if a person is fired from his job and the manager asks him to leave the premises. The person is offended by this, interpreting the manager's act as wrongful, and so decides to kill him, even though he was only the messenger, not the decision maker. In the employee's mind, killing the manager is justified as a retaliatory action in lieu of the employer's perceived wrongful act, and his conscience on the matter is clear. In the absence of laws to define the right and wrong behavior human beings are capable of plunging society into total anarchy. From the middle of the twentieth century, clean countries of today figured out that legislation is the most effective tool to tell the society about acceptable and unacceptable behavior; any breach from these rules will attract a reprimand in the form of fines, jail time, etc.

In the 1850s, Sir William Chadwick submitted a detailed report in the English parliament on model civic behavior on litter, which was converted into a piece of legislation. It pronounced littering illegal, and also mandated to install garbage bins at homes; the first time the masses were told about such a thing. The wisdom to make acceptable alternatives go hand in hand with the prohibited actions started to condition the collective mind of the society toward compliance. In contrast, India's sanitation laws adopt a unidimensional view to merely prohibit undesirable actions, namely, burning of trash that was deemed illegal in the early 2000s. They do not replace such an action with acceptable alternatives, such as disposing trash. If trash burning is illegal what is the alternative and where is the mandate to abide to that alternative?

The challenges around waste management started to grow after World War II and the legislations of the previous era proved to be inadequate to address the evolving First-World consumerism. Composition of waste grew more complex; non-biodegradable materials in waste like plastic and polythene increased manifold. Clean countries of today went on a legislative overdrive to prepare for the new challenges posed to them. In countries like Sweden and Denmark, laws are so specific as regards segregation of garbage that citizens are now required to segregate their domestic waste in not two but seven different groups! In the 1980s, these countries banned the use of landfills as a method of waste disposal because they soon realized its harmful effects on the environment and public health.

In the context of sanitation, the role of legislation in these societies went well beyond its explicit purpose to define the right and wrong sets of actions. Establishment of an equitable social contract between the citizens and the state on all matters concerning sanitation was the legislation's pivotal role in the clean countries of today, allowing these societies to internalize the economic cost of sanitation delivery and witnessing the emergence of a formal sanitation and waste management sector. For instance, the improvement in waste segregation at source in the clean countries of today started in the 1960s, when in one fell sweep the legislation established the onus of waste collection on the citizens, a duty duly paid for by the citizens in the form of user fees or taxes for the service that concurrently saw the emergence of formal waste management enterprises to own and manage waste collection and disposal. Such specificity not only ensured uniformity in its interpretation among the masses, but also injected an economic argument. Today, in these countries bagging household waste in different containers is a normal and an accepted chore. Legislation was not only used as a tool to nudge the society to change its collective behavior, but also to transition the value chain of sanitation delivery toward economically sustainable formality.

Since the 1950s, Japan has either enacted a new law or amended an existing one that has a direct bearing on cleanliness once every two years to keep them relevant with the rapidly changing consumption profile of its society. India's legislative approach on waste management has not only been lethargic, but also vague. It drafted its first set of laws in 1985 under a generic platform of environment protection. So limited was the scope of the law that it constantly stressed the judiciary to seek creative interpretations of the law for its application to the rapidly changing reality of sanitation delivery India. India issued its first set of detailed guidelines on waste management in 2016, but the ban on the use of open landfills and collection of garbage continue to remain elusive. It is vague for the law to state that waste segregation is needed, which is precisely the language of India's laws on sanitation. It is specific to say that door-to-door collection of segregated waste in different bin types is mandated in lieu of user fees for all households in the city, which is the hallmark of the sanitation laws in the clean countries of today.

India needs to reboot its legislative approach on waste management and sanitation delivery with two objectives in mind. First, it should correct the social contract between the citizens and the state to reposition sanitation delivery as a shared responsibility, not as an entitlement. Second, in doing so it should evaluate the efficacy to these laws to build the economic argument for the challenges that concerns sanitation.

Many a times, the outstanding civic behavior regarding sanitation observed in clean countries overwhelms outsiders, especially us Indians. But, neither is this pristine visual a genetic advantage of these societies nor is this outcome delivered solely from the shoulders of dogmatic legislation. The wisdom of clean countries of today to appreciate enforcement as a twin sister of legislation is the architect of this outcome. Lessons must be learned from the clean countries of the world. Thomas Fresh was appointed the first sanitation inspector of Liverpool in 1844 to implement Chadwick's laws on sanitation. These inspectors would issue fines to the violators. The results were swift and local administrators quickly determined a strong linkage between strict enforcement and a change in civic behavior. From this commonsensical initiation of enforcement for sanitation emerged the profound wisdom in the clean countries of today that retribution as a tool of enforcement was an effective medium to communicate desirable civic behavior on sanitation. Over time these countries realized the cost benefit in investments to build enforcement capability, both human and infrastructure, to reduce unplanned litter in the first place, rather than investing in resource to get rid of that unplanned litter.

This bundling of legislation and enforcement yielded magic for sanitation delivery in these countries on many counts and that explains New York's superior approach to waste management in contrast to that of the approach adopted in New Delhi. New York and New Delhi produce nearly the same quantum of waste every day. While New York succeeds to keep its streets and neighborhoods clean with 20,000 workers employed in sanitation services, New Delhi struggles with its mounting waste while employing 60,000 sanitation workers on its rolls. Waste management laws and legislation helped New York to create a waste collection system that puts the onus on the citizens, thereby reducing the need for cleaning workers. Thus,

New York is able to keep its streets clean with one-third the human resources New Delhi employs.

The lesson that New York offers to New Delhi is that the purpose will be better served if the latter increases its sanitation inspectors on rolls and reduces the number of sweepers, or even better if a few sanitation workers are upgraded as sanitation inspectors armed with mobile devices and surveillance cameras than with brooms and mops. But it is easier said than done. The helplessness of New Delhi symbolizes the irony that confronted India on sanitation in that the sanitation-related laws were either absent or too vague to make any sense for any effective enforcement. Enforcement cannot precede legislation. Therefore, job design of health and sanitation inspectors was not revised to suit the changing times. Employment norms (number of inspectors needed for every thousand people) were never reviewed for efficacy with the rising population. Rarely did news of fines, punitive damages, or jail terms for bad sanitation practices give sleepless nights to perpetuators. This is just one part of the story. The other part is that India's political order has rarely looked at enforcement as an impact on social change and human development.

Take policing, for instance, that sits at the forefront of law enforcement in any civil society. In 2014, the United Nations ranked fifty countries in the world on their policing infrastructure; India stood at forty-nine. As per the report, the policing capacity of India measured in terms of the number of policemen per one lakh people is nearly half of the policing capacity of countries, like the UK, that employ 300 policemen per 100,000 citizens.

India last undertook its police reforms in 1978, something that needs to be updated with the changing nature of crime. An understaffed judiciary is another worry: India needs around 100,000 additional judges only to address the backlog of cases pending in courts. The instances of electronic detection of tax evasions far outpaced the installed human capability of tax authorities to follow these up with investigation and convictions. In the new normal, the city of New Delhi alone faced a shortfall of 40,000 tax inspectors in 2016. If mainstream enforcement organs, like policing, judiciary, and economic offenses, face all round apathy and wide chasm on human capability, it is difficult to imagine the incentive that India will need to build the enforcement apparatus for the socially discriminated issue of sanitation. Our struggles over sanitation are the collateral damage of India's overall apathy toward enforcement and, not surprisingly, local civic bodies consistently rue both the inadequacy of sanitation inspectors and the long gestation to onboard them.

India will need to shed its existing notion of enforcement and take a far more progressive view than it does today. Enforcement has a wider connotation and serves broader purposes. Explicitly, it acts as a deterrent that significantly reduces the cost of corrective action ex post facto. If counterterrorist force defuses a terrorist attack, in effect it reduces the cost of human tragedy. Similarly, if a sanitation inspector detects a case of gross neglect of food sanitation in an eatery, then he saves the healthcare cost arising out of food poisoning.

Enforcement is also a potent tool to drive society toward predictable outcomes. If, for instance, a waste inspector surveys an area regularly, it detracts the residents from disposing garbage there. Repeated survey drills by the sanitation inspector make the area clean. Recall the case of Liverpool that has seen this drill by a sanitation inspector for more than seventeen decades, since the deployment of the first sanitation inspector in the city in 1844. At an incremental cost of deploying a sanitation inspector, the local body saves the additional cost of picking up the waste out of turn. Luckily, India confronts the problem of waste management at a juncture when it has the luxury to use technology in myriad ways to its advantage. A hundred years ago, many of these challenges were responded to with linear thinking limited by operational and technical constraints. Today, technology allows us to think about lateral solutions to augment investigative research, to conduct scientific analysis, and enhance breach detection capabilities. For instance, technology can deploy digital surveillance systems to monitor areas for litter. Extraordinary human movement in an area can be detected and temporary waste collection and enforcement systems can be deployed to address the increased sanitation requirements. Such approaches will prove effective in dealing with the garbage mess in public places, especially during festivals, weddings, and other such gatherings. Moreover, predictive analytics and GPS monitoring can be used to detect instances of industrial pollutants from factories being dumped into the rivers by tagging the operating time of the factories. An active enforcement approach will ease the burden of the state's role from always discharging the function of waste management to the role of facilitating it, as we will see later in the book.

More than half of India will be in a pliable state of learning which will continue for decades to come. India needs to reflect on its approach to make its future generation wean off from the entitlement bias toward sanitation that possesses the Indian mind. We need to break the succession cycle that conditions the new generations with this bias because a biased society requires dogmatic legislation, an elaborate enforcement apparatus and costly infrastructure. You can legislate and impose fines on littering but this may not deter a parent from throwing the food wrappers from his car on an open stretch of the highway in full view of his children in the back seat. The children will register this action as a natural response. You can install surveillance systems to detect illegal discharge of industrial waste into the river but the owner of the factory may bribe his way out of the punishment, which his son will accept as the done thing and repeat when he takes over the reins in a few years. You can create a door to door waste collection system, but children in millions of homes may never see the act of garbage disposal beyond the eyes of their doted mother. These moments of truth happen across 250 million homes everyday. How should India prepare to protect its children from the adverse impact of such bias? How should good, safe practices related to waste be planted in their pristine minds? How should India prepare them to not mimic their parents' wrongful deeds and assert themselves?

If households are tainted on the issue of sanitation then the heavy lifting should be done by the classrooms of India. The country's formal education system must take responsibility to educate the young minds and break the succession cycle that has for centuries managed to effortlessly pass on biases and prejudices against sanitation. Indian students will need to be formally exposed to the practice and science of waste management from an early age. But, as obvious it may seem, India has struggled to get it right.

For the first time, Indian students were formally introduced to the concept of garbage management in 2005. In that year, Indian school education boards introduced the subject of Environmental Studies (EVS) in their curriculum that touches upon various aspects of waste management and sanitation. But, this step was not an outcome of an awakening but a response to a nudge from the judiciary. Due to this tame start that smacked of vapid intellectual capacity of the Indian education policy to connect the role of formal education with India's waste and environment challenges, the subject of EVS continues to remain on the fringes.

Only through education can one catch young minds before they fall into the trap of biases and prejudices – a challenge that is unique to India. Through the lessons learnt at school will children assert the virtues of cleanliness at home and in turn educate their parents and community at large. Curriculum design will need to image interesting tools to engage the students on this topic. For instance, children could be encouraged to collect e-waste at home, which can be given to approved recyclers for material recovery and environmentally safe processing, in exchange for credits or some other form of appreciation.

Formalized 'volunteering' in waste collection and waste disposal in higher school grades to earn credits or marks can be another way to create an army of unbiased minds to fight this challenge. Exposure to complex aspects of waste management should become agnostic to the field of study and apply to one and all studying to graduate from college. Minds of under-graduates can then be harnessed in a manner that allows them to treat their neighborhoods & communities as laboratories to conduct experiments and to undertake projects on various aspects of waste management before they pass college. They will then not shy away from becoming peaceful vigilantes against the burning of garbage in the vicinity. They will then feel inspired to undertake community work of collection and recycling projects with local bodies or conduct camps to teach better techniques to their elders in the community.

India will need such an orchestrated response through education for her youth to appreciate that garbage is an extension of one's existence on the planet. This youth will then feel responsible toward garbage rather than abhor its sight and appreciate different types of garbage and correct methods of disposing them. This youth will loath the visuals of vulnerable kids sorting garbage on a dump site. This youth will be brave enough to report an illegal act of dumping waste on the side of an open street and assertive enough to correct his elders on wrong practices. This youth will then learn the notion of sanitation without the lens of castes and entitlements and appreciate the gaps in the current system of sanitation management in India. India will reap rich dividends when such an aware crop of youth will grow up and occupy jobs as farmers, soldiers, sanitation workers, lorry drivers, tailors, judges, doctors, teachers, public servants, factory supervisors and confront the issue of waste in their private and public lives. The route of education may perhaps be the most inexpensive way to give rise to a rational and aware society on the issue of sanitation and waste management.

But, these tools may fall short of dismantling the calcified biases in the Indian mind about sanitation without the revival of the discourse that triggered various social reform movements in India more than a century ago. Had the independence movement not taken precedence, these social movements may have significantly softened the challenges of sanitation. In many respects, India's challenge with waste embodies the unfinished business of these movements which were all aimed at spiritually cleansing the society from the clutches of ritualistic conformance and bringing a semblance of rationality. The tenets of these movements need imbibition within the mainstream discourse to bring closure on many issues that today act as irritants in policymaking for sanitation. These irritants take away India's narrow bandwidth, giving rise to suboptimality and mediocrity. The incumbent deputy chief minister of the most populous Indian state in 2017 made a statement claiming that the cow protection laws are aimed at instilling fear among people who kill cows. The spirited emotion might be laudable if he could replace the phrase 'kill cows' with 'burning trash in the open,' 'illegal waste dumping,' 'cow abandonment,' or 'using a Dalit's bare hands for the cleaning of sewers' in his statement.

Sarvarkar's criticism of blind worship of the cow, Ambedkar's anger toward caste biases, and Gandhi's disdain for skewed social contract of Indian society toward sanitation make all three important figures of Indian modern history converge on the idea of clean India, while they may not have agreed on many other issues.

The choice is ours, which notion we should subscribe to, not its outcome.

2

STATE ACTORS

Suryadevara Ramachandra Rao is an Indian bureaucrat who was awarded the Padma Shri (the fourth highest civilian honor bestowed by the Indian state) in 1998 while in service. This was an acknowledgement of his exceptional leadership as the municipal commissioner of Surat, Gujarat, in 1994, when the city suffered the ignominy of a plague outbreak. Within the next three years, Rao took a series of exceptional steps to transform Surat, often called the city of 'floating sewage,' into one of the cleanest cities in India. This incident suggests that achieving cleanliness was so arduous a task that only a public health crisis could jolt the stakeholders out of their slumber and summon the brilliance of an individual to find a viable solution. No wonder then that Rao was found deserving of a rare honor for a serving bureaucrat to deliver sanitation to the city. Plague outbreaks were a regular feature in the clean countries of today in pre-industrial times. Every outbreak brought home their dilapidated state of sanitation delivery and contributed toward making improvements as it happened in the case of Surat. It is now more than two decades since the outbreak and the question remains if the Indian state actors have learned from it.

In 2018, Manish Grover, a minister in the Haryana government, chaired a grievance committee meeting and discovered that untreated sewage from Greater Faridabad (a new urban settlement in Faridabad city) was being dumped in the open. While the urban development body of the state – Haryana Urban Development Authority or HUDA – urbanized the area with full zeal, it did not consider the need for a sewage treatment plant in the area. The minister immediately issued orders to connect the area's sewage line with the nearest sewage treatment plant. But even this solution was a non-starter because the installed capacity of the treatment plant was exhausted with the current load. Consequently, the river Yamuna was pressed into services to absorb the untreated sewage from this new-age urban neighborhood. It seems that Greater Faridabad has all the makings of becoming the city of floating sewage and will demand the individual brilliance of the likes of Rao to clean itself.

In 2017, the local civic bodies of Delhi launched formal posts to receive grievances related to the city's sanitation; within six months they received nearly 20,000 complaints. Just when Delhi was grappling with a heap of garbage-related complaints, the NGT, in February 2017, passed a judicial order that concerned the pollution of the Mahananda River in Siliguri, West Bengal, through indiscriminate dumping of municipal solid waste. Notices were issued to the state, West Bengal State Pollution Control Board, Municipal Corporation of Siliguri, and the Deputy Commissioner of Siliguri. The NGT conveyed the illegality of the blatant dumping of municipal solid waste in the Mahananda to the errant executive and the bureaucracy. Fully aware that their arrangement could not stand upon any grounds, they waited for the judiciary's rap before reprioritizing their limited resources for sanitation. The judiciary loaded its order with extra rebukes aimed at the state actors for their 'ostrich-like approach.'

If there is any doubt that the judiciary's stance in Mahananda's case was too severe, then consider the case of Simran, a student in a state-owned school in Aya Nagar, Delhi, who filed a petition in the Delhi High Court in 2017 against the perpetual stench from a pond next to the school due to unauthorized garbage dumping. In her petition she pleaded that the garbage-engorged pond not only made it unbearable to study in the school, but also made many of her friends fall sick and created a mosquito menace. She further claimed that the issue was reported to concerned authorities for a redressal many times, all in vain. The court issued directions to the local civic body for urgent intervention and demanded a status report, making the 'concerned' authorities swing into action. Simran's plea will surely evoke a fist-tightening reaction from any sane mind. But for the Delhi state actors, merely appreciating this is of small consequence. Their unspoken pursuit is of a judicial stamp of 'illegality' to initiate any corrective measures. The local governance of Delhi appears more the victim than a culprit with vile intentions, with its inability to arrest the illegal dumping of garbage into the pond and its incapacity to clean it up thereafter. Its helplessness to not initiate action in the normal course compels it to rely on judicial rap as an overt tool to prioritize its limited bandwidth to deliver sanitation.

Grievance redressal systems and judicial activism give us comfort in the working nature of the Indian democracy. But implied in these mechanisms are the Indian state's recurring deviations from stated promises to deliver sanitation in the normal course – the garbage dump in the neighborhood that should get picked up in the normal course, a leaking sewage line that should be patched up in time, a sewage treatment plant while the city is being built, or a public hygiene outbreak.

Equally depressing is the fate of these grievances once they are inducted into the governance machinery for resolution. Responses may range from inaction to troubleshooting, depending upon the 'stature' of the complaint and complainant. If the reported sanitation issue is from a neighborhood that hosts VVIPs of the town, the troubleshooting team will promptly patch up the issue and file the documentation claiming; although within the next couple of months the situation would go back to what it was earlier. If the reported issue emerges from a neighborhood that lacks the heft of the public representative, then its redressal becomes a string of broken promises. If the constituency is lucky enough to be blessed with sufficient star power of the public representatives, the sanitation grievance will receive the sponsorship of the state's might for a speedy redressal. But the public representatives cannot do much beyond lifting their telephones and directing the civic machinery to look into the matter or issuing a rebuke or two for instant gratification. If they exercise their heft, they may occasionally have an overflowing sewer fixed. But the franchise seems to believe that these public representatives have a magic wand, why else would they persistently knock on their doors for resolution.

The explicit responsibility to deliver sanitation rests with the municipality, but even they wait for the judiciary's rebuke or surprise visits from their political masters: as does Rao Narbeer Singh, an elected member of the 13th Legislative Assembly of Haryana and a minister in the state government, when he witnesses blocked nallas and leaking sewers in his constituency. Lawmakers like Narbeer Singh helplessly fall back on their clout in the local administration to get quick fixes. As an elaborate demonstration of this clout, he gets the blocked sewer cleared or the garbage lifted, while delivering hope to the franchise and keeping his personal equity intact. Prospective councilors make great claims of delivering leakproof sewers and clean neighborhoods in lieu of votes, which turn out to be nothing more than a string of broken promises at the end of the tenure. Such theatrics, while they offer solace of recourse to the franchise, beg intriguing questions: are public representatives so insensitive that they wait for exceptional reminders from the franchise about dirty neighborhoods? Are their political ambitions so nefarious that they smell political opportunism in stinking neighborhoods? Why is it that the local civic bodies fail to deliver sanitation and force the franchise to adopt exceptional recourses repeatedly? Does the chief minister of an Indian state find the prospect of acting as a crisis manager to douse fires on the city's waste landfill exciting, or does he look forward to seeking investment for the state, hosting a foreign delegation or disbursing scholarships to meritorious girls in a school?

Arguably, this cacophony around local governance is a natural outcome of a maturing democracy, and one is left with no choice but to live in its din in hope for a better tomorrow. Infact, it is this hope to seek improvement in local governance that prompts people to seek solace in celluloid that delivers it in the fictional world and partially explains the roaring success of Telugu sociopolitical drama *Bharat Ane Nenu*. But what happens when the state becomes hardwired to deliver sanitation as a matter of exception rather than norm? What happens when the 'governance by exception' approach becomes the norm over a sustained period? Only when the neighborhood cries out aloud from the stink is the littered garbage picked up. Only when the judicial recourse stamps the immorality of the state are squatters removed from public spaces. Will the state clamor for better alternatives when people die from explosions in garbage landfills? The governance will not scramble for tools to improve public hygiene until hospitals are flooded with patients. When society starts to consistently seek remedies through exceptional grievance systems, both citizens and the state undermine the existing system that is in place or indicts it for inadequacy. Society begins to interpret the exceptional recourse as the norm. Public representatives attempt to resolve grievances in individual capacity and make the system work. The administration starts taking cues from judicial rebukes, reprimands from the executive, and outrage from the public to allocate its meager bandwidth to resolve grievances, leaving nothing in spare to engineer a better system to deliver the same service in regular course.

Between Surat's plague and Simran's plea is a timeline of over twenty years, and in this duration India's consumption profile, which has a direct bearing on sanitation, has changed drastically. But the habit of the Indian states to rely on exceptional remedies to deliver sanitation has largely remained unchanged. The fact that India is better equipped to successfully launch rockets in space than to deliver sanitation as a matter of routine is a spectacular failure of the Indian democracy. This failure incentivizes the governance to look up to exceptional recourses like pleas that test the boundaries of the judiciary where its role ends and that of the executive where its role begins for allocation, action, and troubleshooting.

If I cannot remember the name of the local councilor who represents my municipal ward or have never paid any importance to cast my vote in the elections of local bodies or cannot recall the name of my city's mayor or cannot dare to vote against the Pradhan (head/sarpanch) of my village then in these inadequacies lies India's inability to deliver sanitation as a matter of routine. Then it becomes imperative to revisit our history and grasp the full depth of this unfortunate story.

Indian local governance is principally tasked with delivering sanitation at the doorstep of its citizens. Local governance here should be understood as a formal arrangement of organization, processes, and resource that ensures the clean existence of a human settlement. Before colonization, India was a cluster of villages and kingdom towns: the city of Delhi came into existence in 1913, beyond its walled edifice; Kolkata owes its birth to the British who made it the seat of their power before shifting it to Delhi. A combination of unwritten laws, oral codes, and practices, handed down through traditions, managed the daily affairs of the villages through panchayat, while the affairs of the kingdom's capital cities were closely supervised by their respective seats of power. Monarchs changed from time to time, but panchayats remained intact. Monarchs rarely interfered with this model of local governance or sought to reform it; they were primarily concerned with the tax collected from these villages. Polygamy, wars, and internal squabbles for succession took up most of their bandwidths. Even if some noble monarchs showed genuine interest in the operational issues surrounding local governance, as was the case with Maharaja Bir Chandra Manikya of Tripura who was instrumental in setting up the Agartala Municipal Corporation in 1871, they had to confront the fear that their meddling might erode the mass support in villages and make them ripe for defection at the time of an external invasion.

India witnessed its first wave of disruptive growth of urbanization as new cities popped up during Western colonization. For instance, Mumbai came into existence in 1668 when the then area of Mumbai was handed over to the East India Company by the Portuguese. The city's population was then around 10,000, but in the next seven years it grew six times to nearly 60,000. Until then, India had no recorded precedence of such a phenomenon of a rapid rise of urban populace. Trade, administration, and defense needs played a key role in the boom of new cities across India. Without any existing reference to manage the daily affairs of these towns, colonizers installed a local governance system in their model. The first municipal corporation in India came into existence in 1687, the Madras Municipal Corporation (MMC). Incidentally, the MMC is the second oldest municipal corporation in the world after that of London, suggesting the colonizer's urgency to replicate the learnings from their home country on this form of local governance. Thirty-nine years after the MMC came into existence, municipal corporations of Calcutta (now Kolkata) and Bombay (now Mumbai) came into existence in 1726. By the end of the nineteenth century, municipalities became the norm to govern Indian towns under colonial rule and mirrored their counterparts in England in their administrative scope. They were responsible for providing essential services (to the extent relevant and possible at the time) like water, collection and disposal of city's sewage, cleanliness of public spaces, record-keeping and taxation of real estate, and so on. They supervised installation and the upkeep of infrastructure that concerned water pipes, sewage lines, and waste collection systems. However, office bearers in these local bodies were selected through appointments by the colonial administration. This was unlike the mayor of the local civic body of London who was elected by the Londoners of the day.

In 1882, Lord Ripon, the then viceroy of India, introduced democratic reforms in these municipal bodies and, in a sense, planted the first seeds of grass-root level democracy in India, enabling cities to elect their own representatives to the local bodies. Subsequently, Indian cities witnessed elected mayors for the first time in their existence. Fifty-three years later, in 1935 another resolution brought these local municipal bodies under the governance purview of the provinces of unified India. This journey from 1687 (first municipal corporation formed in India) to 1935 (municipal corporations becoming bodies of self-governance under respective provinces) spans 248 years. During this period, the colonial rule institutionalized the municipal system of local governance as an administrative set up (one that is appointed) for more than 200 years. The system catered to the immediate needs of Indian towns that touched no more than 10 percent of the Indian population that lived in these towns, but delivered a sound sleep to the British as to the daily affairs of these towns. Indians never self-discovered the rules of urban living because they were just getting inducted into these towns for the first time and were attuned to different rules of solid waste management, bathing, toilets, and public spaces. The structure of the city made many village practices of daily living untenable in the urban context. Though the municipal corporations created an infrastructure and service scope to manage sewer lines, waste disposal, roads, etc., they were primarily focused on addressing the immediate needs of the colonial masters – the administrative zones and residential neighborhoods that housed the families of the sahibs and their ecosystem. The scale of urbanization was minuscule when compared to that of Europe, Japan, and North America at that time. There was no pressing need for municipal bodies to address future needs of the cities or to devise mitigation plans for the same.

In the process, the caste system that took care of sanitation delivery of 90 percent of the subcontinent's rural population was improvised to meet the sanitation needs of the 10 percent urban folk. The extent of autonomy, resources, and human capability of this system was rationed to first address the comfort of the ruling class over the commoners. Who would protest if the sewage line of a working-class neighborhood of the town was not working? But surely all hell would break loose if a sewer were to overflow in the area where the sahibs live. The motion picture *The Life of Pi* vividly captures this contrast of the then Indian towns. The opening scene introduces the town of Pondicherry (now Puducherry), the beautiful, clean streets of the French part of town. The second frame shows the squalid neighborhoods of the commoners. The camera then captures the contrast between the two parts, with a road running between them, in a single frame. It is a different matter though that the vestige of the colonial past continued in independent India, but with an interesting twist. In the new reality, the Sahib neighborhoods were replaced with VVIP areas, the clean parts of the town with manicured pavements, clean streets well-lit with lamps, and functional public places that host the administration, governance, and the bulk of the town's architectural heritage. But the serenity of the Lutyens' Delhi, Kalidas Marg, Mantralaya, and Vidhan Soudha in various major Indian cities in the surrounding chaos of Indian urban living almost stands out like an eyesoar.

Local civic bodies were conceived without autonomy, groomed to survive on alms (funding and grants), and conditioned to serve the immediate needs of the colonial rule. These 'birth defects' laid out the pecking order of priorities for Indian local governance. This meant prioritizing Sahib areas with all available resources needed to keep them clean. The residual resources were then allotted to the neighborhoods for the commoners. But the colonial rule cannot be entirely blamed for this outcome. On the contrary, Lord Ripon deserves credit for codifying local governance for a unified India and introducing democratic reforms in it, although his primary motivation may have been to fill a lacuna that emerged from rapid urbanization and the administrative complexity it posed to the colonial rule. Besides, the colonial rulers were not elected representatives. They were conquerors, who were well within their 'rights' to view the system of local governance with a sense of exclusion. Therefore, it may not have struck the colonial rulers as odd that the appeal of the Indian local governance was restricted to the tiny urban populace of the subcontinent at the time. If not the colonial rule for three centuries, any alternate reality of local governance in India would have been equally vulnerable to this pitfall. Any other temperamental administrative system to govern towns that was primarily predisposed to the kingdom's needs may have emerged to be equally exclusionist. Panchayats laced with the caste system would have continued unabated, for instance, which it did even in the colonial times.

When the first local municipal body in the modern world came up in London in the seventeenth century, rapid urbanization in England was changing the character of its towns and throwing up new challenges in running their daily affairs. This backdrop acted as a trigger for the state actors to seek an effective governance tool. Municipal civic bodies showed promise in their modularity to govern individual towns and for people's representation. Swiftly, municipal bodies started to catch the imagination of the rapidly industrializing First World as a preferred model of local governance. They were not perfect institutions and many a times yielded atrocious outcomes. Local bodies could vote in a mayor of questionable credentials or vote against a tax reform. They could back an ill-conceived infrastructure project in the city and promulage laws that reeked of exclusion and biases. Pitfalls notwithstanding, the local bodies were conceived with a degree of autonomy that created space for people's voices irrespective of the outcome. People's representation in them allowed a groundswell support for the local civic bodies to evolve with time and respond rapidly to the changing needs of the towns they governed. As a result of the Great Seattle Fire of 1889, the local governing body unanimously voted to temporarily increase taxes on establishments to raise money to rebuild the city. But such a grass-root support should not be mistaken for a system that always delivered desirable outcome. People maneuvered the system to get disproportionate access to land rights, influenced the direction of the railway tracks, or colluded to dupe it for financial windfall. Yet the municipal governance framework afforded room for people's voices, which became saner with every passing year, to devise solutions to address the growing challenges of the town. At times such solutions were off the mark, like Seattle's sewage system made from lumber at the turn of the nineteenth century, but soon the representation of people in local governance converted the chaotic start of the municipal body into a refined and agile system of local governance in the First World. By the time these towns were confronted with the rapidly rising challenge of sanitation delivery in the post-industrialization era, their municipal civic bodies had soaked up 300 years of experience to make the participatory grass-root democracy-based local governance system work to overcome it.

In contrast, municipal bodies in India were an administrative response to govern day-to-day affairs of colonial towns. Though the reforms of 1882 and 1935 were aimed at improving local representation through people's choice in these local civic bodies, the political maturity toward elected representation was in its infancy in the subcontinent. The people who were expected to elect their representatives were themselves getting used to living in cities. Inhabitants lacked ideal reference to vote for a desired outcome or to even outline their stated expectation from the civic bodies. Lord Ripon's initiation of democratic reforms in local governance did set the stage for Indian municipal bodies to discover their independent footing, but it would be naive to ignore the presence of colonial rule that kept an eye on the extent of the 'people's expression' in these local bodies. By the time India gained independence, the Indian municipal bodies had been in the phase of self-discovery for nearly seven decades (1882–1947) under the strict supervision of the British rule.

The birth of the Indian Republic in 1950 was the calling card for the liberal order that emerged post World War II. The country succeeded in gifting itself a constitution that elegantly encapsulated the idea of democracy in its purest form. It granted universal suffrage, fundamental rights, equality and pluralism. In today's context, India's feat stands as a benchmark of sorts when many newly minted countries on much smaller scales of size and diversity struggle to etch out a constitution or install a half decent election process that could be called fair. The Indian Constitution established the guiding principles for the nation and demarcated the role of the union and its many states. It provided the foundation for the democratic structure that defined the sovereignty of the country and the individual identity of its incredibly diverse states. The national Parliament and state legislative assemblies demarcated between them responsibilities and duties. For an Indian citizen, it meant that the job of protecting the nation's borders was the sole responsibility of the national government, while subjects like land came under the purview of the respective state governments. However, at the time of Independence, Indian towns were managed through an existing system of local municipal bodies, which, in the case of Chennai, were as old as 250 years. The Indian Constitution did not prescribe an approach to reconcile the relationship between these existing municipal bodies and the newly minted state that hosted them, and left it open for the states to figure out.

In the earlier system, the local bodies had an explicit defined hierarchy that reported to the British government. But in the Republic of India, the formal space for the local body was left vague without any timelines for closure. It was fine if any state decided to keep the issue open ended (as many states did). Theoretically, it did not matter if any state scrapped the municipal bodies altogether. Local bodies or village panchayats were reduced to a voluntary existence, while the states planted their own administrative framework to give governance continuity from where the British left off.

The Indian Constitution's silence on this aspect is intriguing. Was it well intentioned, as a demonstration of empowerment for the states to custom-build their own local governance framework? Or was it out of a sense of doubt that viewed the local bodies as reminders of our colonial past? Sans direction to formalize this relationship, the states made a hash of integrating the existing local bodies (and their roles) within their newly found democratic identity. The states created a public works department to undertake public utility infrastructure development. They formed utility companies to manage water and power supplies. The job of building new cities or expanding existing ones fell on the shoulders of the urban development authorities of respective states. Housing and industrial development were handed over to the states' respective development corporations. In the pre-Republic days, the local bodies played an active role in these issues with the logic that their active ownership took a holistic view of infrastructure development, utility services, and financial sustainability. It increased the chance of crafting a balanced response toward the city's needs, no matter how limited its span of influence may be. Even though the local bodies existed to serve the immediate needs of the colonial masters, the ownership allowed these bodies to have an agile response mechanism.

Under the open-ended arrangement that emerged with the formation of the republic, Indian local bodies were suddenly ejected from centre stage. They were divested of active participation in many areas that had a direct bearing on the operations of the town. Their role in tax collection, tax rates, user charges, and legislation were curtailed, and had limited power to monetize assets and commit investments. Concurrently, states invested no effort to examine the residual remains of these local bodies after such divestures. Local bodies were quickly reduced to emaciated service providers that were expected to clean the streets, pick up garbage, and maintain gardens and other public areas, while following procedures and rules laid out during the colonial times. From the previous role of being at the forefront and addressing a town's growing needs, municipal bodies were reduced to managing the infrastructure of the cities and operating with archaic procedures using financial resources determined and supplied by their administrative masters. Indian states clipped the wings of the local civic bodies on most matters that concerned revenue generation from within their jurisdiction but burdened them with responsibilities that mostly demanded expenditure. The Indian local bodies were set up to fail. Unwittingly, India's early steps toward democracy created a skewed template of local governance which was replicated for all the new towns, cities, and villages that emerged in post-independence India.

Legislative state assemblies became like giant municipal bodies managing many cities and towns under their ambit, on matters that ranged from piped water to fumigation in towns, and from road repairs to fires in the landfill. Under this arrangement, the state's chief minister resembled a mayor who managed many administrative affairs of all cities, towns, and villages within the state. The state government he presided over essentially collected most of the taxes and user fees from its citizens, received grants from the union government, and disbursed them across different priorities as it 'deemed fit.' In a sense, it took on the dual role of an aggregator and allocator of financial resources. In this arrangement, there was tremendous scope for the state governments to politically leverage, influence, control, and supervise local municipal bodies. To add to all the excitement, these vagaries also oscillated with the political mood of the day and the extent of political convergence between the local governance and the state government.

Partly, such friction arising out of the constitution's silence was desirable for the Indian states to discover their autonomous ground in the new-found democratic freedom. But in this search for political autonomy, the administrative maneuverability of the local governance was squeezed and the agenda of sanitation delivery, which the local governance was solely responsible for, became a collateral damage. Imagine a city urgently in need of a waste incineration plant to dispose its waste. The citizens of the city have felt the need and the local municipal body is in approval of the idea. But the local body cannot do a jot as it does not have the wherewithal of its own to construct such a plant. Similarly, if an underground sewage system needs to be extended to a new residential settlement, the local governance will wait for the public works department of the state to design the project feasibility and commission its construction. The local body itself cannot do much beyond surrendering themselves to the mercy of the state government. The state government may decide on the fate of project after taking into consideration genuine paucity of resources, the economic leeway and perhaps the political urgency for such a project. If the priority order of the underground sewage project to receive resources is low, then the concerned citizens will have to bear their troubles for a few more years.

Such a vague arrangement manifested itself vividly in unfortunate forms. If the city or a town or a village was lucky to get influential political representation in the state assembly or the national parliament, it would witness a windfall of amenities, services, and infrastructure. The leader could muscle his way to his constituency receiving a disproportionate share of funds, focus, and execution, while other parts of the same state remained unfortunate. In return, the leader received the all-weather political loyalty of his franchise. When an aspiring prime minister of the country contests the election from the city on the plank that he will turn it into a world-class benchmark, the irony cannot be ignored. Would not that promise be more fitting coming from a prospective mayor who harbors ambitions to lead a local municipal body? Is it not then fair to assume that if one lives in a city that perpetually struggles with cleanliness, she would partially blame her fate for being born in a constituency that has failed to produce a star public representative in the legislative assembly or in the national parliament? Upstreaming issues that concern local governance to state government was per se not wrong, but the abandonment of local bodies on the agenda was. Local bodies instead should have been taken onboard to play the crucial role of gatekeeping the town's interest on all matters of local governance. They should have become active and assertive interlocutors with other organs of the government for their respective jurisdictions.

This was crucial because the newly minted states had limited wherewithal to ensure that an aggregated approach to legislation, policy, and welfare delivery has the teeth to protect the individual interests of towns and villages. If the local bodies were expected to become basic service providers of amenities to the citizens of the city, they needed more of a say in the development of the infrastructure which have a direct bearing on their delivery standards. But in such an opaque top-down system it was not to be. On the contrary, this organization design opened a huge window of opportunity for the political system to subvert the local governance in an individual capacity. Indian towns became regular recipients of whimsical changes in land use, misplaced priorities for infrastructure development, and populist strains in the delivery of utilities to satiate the thirst of the politics of the day.

The lack of space for local governance during the construction of the Indian democracy dealt a severe blow to the municipal bodies on two counts. The first major blow was that their autonomy to generate their own revenue was severely curtailed. Local bodies are supposed to be the custodians of the people's rights and duties in any human cluster. The gleaned wisdom from the clean countries tells us that they are not only responsible for delivering security and cleanliness to the citizens, but also for ensuring that the citizens perform their duties toward the human cluster, as an exchange. The local bodies facilitate the services (or rights) to the citizens and recover the financial cost to do so, by way of revenue earned from the citizens through taxes and fees that signify the citizens' compliance to their duties toward society. The success of the local bodies depends upon their ability to maintain this fine financial balance as a surrogate for their delivery of rights and the receipt of duties. This comprehensive supervision helps the local bodies to achieve collective responsibility among the communities they serve. If the services are not matched by the revenues collected, corrective action can be taken. If the revenue earned is not adequate for the desired service, they can re-evaluate and tweak the tax levers and/or fees and seek the people's mandate to do so.

However, Indian municipal bodies were kept from funding their role as essential service providers to their respective clusters through taxes, fines, asset monetization, and service fees, and were reduced to massive cost centers for recording births and deaths, collecting property taxes (the only revenue stream now left open to the local bodies), managing a few hospitals and schools, and the collection and disposal of waste. State governments took away from these local bodies all the scope that was essential for building a holistic and effective model of local governance. They wanted direction in the form of a policy, legislature, or guideline to help them evolve from their pre-Republic avatar. The processes, norms for employment, scope of work, guidelines, and responsibilities of these local bodies continued in the colonial template, while they were robbed of all their freedom. An excessive and prolonged dependence on fate makes institutions, much like people, lose desire and imagination for a self-sustaining existence. Indian local governance faced a similar fate and lost its intellectual capacity to behave as a proactive service provider of the towns or villages it served.

But the deformed birth of local governance is not the sole reason that undermined its financial autonomy. Two taxation levers – indirect taxation, that taxes consumption, and direct taxation, that taxes income – are constantly tweaked to make it work for the governance agenda of any country. The point in time in the economic journey of the nation usually determines which of these two levers should play the dominant role. A poor nation with low per capita income leans toward indirect taxes, while rich nations with high per capita income actively chase direct taxes to earn their revenue. Taxation, thus, is an incredibly nebulous issue and economists can hardly find convergence on it. But they all agree that the quantum of the share of taxation in a country's GDP reflects its installed collective psyche to fund its progress. In 2017, India's tax to GDP ratio stood at 18 percent, which ranks India far lower than the First-World countries, whose ratio stands at nearly 50 percent. India's ratio also ranks much lower than that of countries like South Africa, Malaysia, and Mexico, which hovers around 25 percent. A nation at the beginning of its economic journey predictably scores low on the metrics of tax to GDP ratio. But as its ambitions grow, a strong nation is expected to sync its society's aspirations (surrogate for consumption and economic development) with its responsibility to fund it (surrogate for the share of taxation in its GDP). It is difficult to miss the uncanny relationship between high tax share to GDP and the spotless profile of the First-World nations. For instance in the UK, while you can have access to superior healthcare or visit a world-class art gallery free of cost, you need to part with nearly half of your annual income at the end of the year. France can promise clean and well-appointed public places, but its citizens have to pay income tax that can go as high as 75 percent. On the contrary, the rich can get away with no income tax, but have to pay a premium to access decent healthcare.

India's taxation approach ends up with low tax base and a growing burden of welfare support. Our complex heterogeneity seduces the political narrative to drum-up a socialist fervor when convenient, all the while dreaming of India as a free market nation. Picture this: there are 50 million Indians whose consumption patterns mimic that of a First-World country, while 40 percent of India's children have stunted growth. In the income taxes returns filed in 2015, merely 1 million individuals declared their annual income to be more than ₹1 million, but in the same year 2.5 million automobiles were sold in India, which included 100,000 luxury cars priced at ₹2 million or more.

Conspicuous consumption of 50 million Indians is as much a reality of the country as are undernourished infants and farmers in distress. The former represents the nation's insatiable aspirational pursuits that find expression without wanting to share in the responsibility that comes with it, while the latter represent the residue of those aspirations. The lack of spine of the political narrative to increase the tax base inflicts the welfare delivery with weak arguments on financial sustainability, while giving unbridled exposure to aspirations that leads to disproportionate inequality. The Indian polity was seduced into maximizing welfare, but proved impotent when it came to funding it. It failed to take a moral high ground to connect the role of taxation with the nation's psyche. Therefore, at the first available opportunity it attempted to extract maximum taxation from whosoever got caught in the tax net. In the race for vote share, it continually lost the plot on the tax share which is essential to fund its welfare dreams. The Indian governance persistently overestimated its top-down prowess to fill its coffers that can concurrently put teachers in classrooms and doctors in hospitals, piped water in homes, nutritionally enrich children, pave roads, secure national borders, and of course provide sanitation. Under taxation was out of its depth to tick all these boxes. Sanitation was bound to lose out to other priorities in the pecking order because of the added bias of a flawed social contract that further exacerbated India's unique challenge on sanitation. India needed a back-to-back arrangement that could sync up the cost incurred to deliver sanitation with the revenue collected from the citizen as a quid pro quo. Furthermore, it was a dire need to reposition sanitation as a collective duty of its society. But the under-taxation psyche ended up perpetuating the bias instead of resolving it. The vagueness of the top-down tax collection approach and disbursal mechanism was thoroughly enjoyed by the union and state governments, and aggravated the stance of local governance. The convergence of political ideologies outlined one set of priorities to split the booty, while the political heft of public representatives held another strong sway in this allocation process. In this fight to get the lion's share of the government's limited treasury, local governance hardly had any say in the allocation. But there was no real urgency either: the franchise rarely complained about dirty neighborhoods or voted out public representatives from office due to bad sanitation.

The second blow was to curtail the powers of enforcement bestowed upon these local bodies. Enforcement, like the collected revenue, signifies the role of the local bodies as guardian of the citizens' duties toward their human cluster. Local bodies invest in capability (human and operational) to maintain a constant vigil to enforce rules among citizens. Enforcement allows the local bodies to supervise facilities, assets and areas it governs for breaches, damages, and deviations. They constantly keep a check on violations, issue penalties, and have the autonomy to decide on the quantum of punishment. Enforcement is viewed as a tool in the hands of local governance to maintain the harmonious cycle of rights and duties of the citizens. Citizens repose their faith in this promise when they vote for their local representatives and do not begrudge the presence of enforcement. When many generations of citizens see a predictability of enforcement, future generations follow the law more out of habit than fear of punishment. Undermining the local municipal bodies diluted their role as guardians of model citizen behavior in a human cluster. Civic sense, informal living, theft of utility services, destruction of public property, and improper garbage disposal are aspects of citizens' behavior in human cluster that need enforcement supervision. But in the new truncated role of local civic bodies these aspects of the enforcement agenda were consigned to anonymity.

Arguments against the discrimination meted out to Indian local governance are not to champion the idea that a local municipal body is the only viable form of local governance. From 1950 onwards, Indian states had sufficient time to ponder and interpret the silence of the Indian Constitution on local governance. Perhaps it was a window of opportunity to establish new benchmarks therein. For instance, it is immaterial if a state decided to position itself as one giant municipal body and deliver services across towns, villages, and cities through a purely administrative response. It could have done away with the facade of local civic bodies and the elected members of various legislative assemblies would then have doubled up as local councilors. For many smaller sized Indian states, such an interpretation of the Constitution would have made sense. The legislative assembly would have installed administrative machinery with technical and managerial experts to discharge services across the different towns and villages of the state. Therefore, it may not come as a surprise if the states tacitly supported the undermined residual status of the local bodies that India delivered in 1950.

It is the inaction of Indian states on the issue that needs to be criticized. They neither revamped the local governance framework, nor upgraded the roles and responsibilities of these local bodies or replaced them with competent operational alternatives. The responsibility of sanitation captures this oversight in its entirety. These local bodies were reduced to entities tasked with all the heavy lifting, or 'dirty' work, to manage waste and the city's crumbling infrastructure, while the state government reaped benefits of infrastructure, development, taxation, and revenue collection. If the streets were dirty and garbage piled up, the state leadership could always blame the local bodies. As we have seen, the caste system twisted the Indian mindset on sanitation. An institutional response was needed to rectify this societal defect, but instead the residual remains of the local bodies in post-republic India, who had limited intellectual and operational strength, perpetuated the bias.

In 1992, the silence of the Constitution was finally broken when India undertook the 74th Amendment and formally recognized nagar palikas, village panchayats, and municipal corporations across towns and villages. It became mandatory for cities and towns to install democratically elected local bodies and strengthen them for local governance. But nearly three decades since, the reforms in local governance that it yearned for remain elusive.

One good way to judge this is to measure the ability of local bodies to sustain their own existence. In 2015, the Janaagraha Centre for Citizenship and Democracy, a Bengaluru-based think-tank, conducted an annual survey of Indian cities, scoring them on four parameters: spatial planning within the city, capacities and resources, empowered and legitimate local representation; and transparency and participation – essentially, the key responsibilities and duties of self-sustaining local governance. All surveyed cities scored between two and four on a total score of ten. The assessment argued that cities like New York and London scored more than nine out of ten on a simulation of the same survey. The best cities in India are less than half the caliber of the global (and clean) cities, but the report card is hardly surprising. The four decades of constitutional silence that preceded the 74th Amendment gave rise to a political system that rather enjoyed the vagueness on local governance. Therefore, it is one thing to amend the Constitution in spirit and quite another to put it in action. The intention of keeping the relationship between the state and local bodies open-ended was perhaps a noble one in 1950. This demonstrated the Constitution's desire for the states to explore the relationship rather than to design a prescription, which could be interpreted as a case of union's overreach into the affairs of the newly formed states. Perhaps it did not want to convey a wrong picture for federal democracy right at the start, although it is equally possible that this vagueness was retained with rebellious intentions. Local bodies were perhaps viewed as representatives of the colonial rule.

In them (particularly the panchayats), Ambedkar saw formal custodians of the caste system that he so thoroughly despised and perhaps saw their continuation as formal sponsorship of this evil arrangement. His mistrust of the panchayats as perpetuators of the caste system was not misplaced if the incident that occurred in the summer of 2016 in Puchhikarguwan village, of Tikamgarh district of Madhya Pradesh, is anything to go by. Allegedly, the sarpanch of the village, a Dalit, shared the dais with the chief minister during a public function. The 'upper-caste' people were so incensed with his audacity that they publically beat him. Moreover, in 2014, a former sarpanch of Purawas Kalan village, in Morena district of Madhya Pradesh, and a Dalit staged a protest in Bhopal against the resistance she faced from the 'upper-caste' community in the village for her decision to build a school in a 'lower-caste' neighborhood. If the head of a village panchayat cannot protect himself from angry mob violence, or if she cannot build a school at a desired place decades after Independence, Ambedkar's disdain for this institution stands to reason.

But it is inconsequential to pursue the reasons for the Constitution's silence on the issue of local governance. It is possible that other priorities at hand prevented any intellectual exploration of the issue from the lens of concentrated economic units, which would, overtime, need empowerment and autonomy. It is the lack of effort to legitimize the role of local governance at that time that is objectionable. The oversight in assessing the implications of the stunted remains of local bodies on urban planning, sanitation, rural invigoration, waste management, and public health should be debated. The failure to anticipate the sheer inadequacy of the organizational design of the local body (or a competent alternative in lieu of its absence) to address the future needs of India that was poised to be more urban and heterogeneous was perhaps the biggest failure on the part of the founding fathers of the republic. Though this could be put down to good intentions back then, the failure to action the reforms in local governance after the 74th Amendment is more nefarious than noble. Till 1992, local governance was justified in playing the victim as a result of well-intentioned naivety. But afterwards, it became a pariah, masked with a reformed exterior, but retaining its pre-1992 avatar internally. The spirit of the Amendment was slyly overlooked in favor of the dividends the pre-1992 status quo of local governance earned for the stakeholders. By 1992, local governance was reduced to being merely a clearing house for commercial contracts and a leverage point to settle scores. They became outposts of sorts for their political masters in legislative assemblies and in the national parliament. They acted as the recipients of a top-down political ideology and less as bottom-up building block of politics, that should have ideally emerged from their role as a custodian of the duties and rights of citizens in a human cluster. This snuffed out any hope of turning them into the desired institutions that changing India so dearly needed to deliver sanitation.

The local bodies' subservience to 'higher public offices' for financial assistance provided a strong leverage to the political masters to dominate the narrative. Their financial incapacity became a conduit for political bravado by their mentors and to maneuver the sponsorship of non-aligned local bodies. Waivers of utility bills, regularization of informal living, and whimsical conversion of residential zones into commercial ones quelled any hope of the local bodies giving rise to progressive and independent grass-root leadership. Turf war and political alignment between state and national politics delivered mayors in cities and sarpanchs in villages. The municipal election of Gurugram in 2017 to elect public representatives and a mayor extended well beyond the election. The two warring factions within the winning majority, one backed by the incumbent minister in the state government and the other by the incumbent minister in the union government, fought for thirty days to elect a mayor to lead the civic body. If the arrangement compels the local bodies to seek their political legitimacy elsewhere, they cannot claim to be true custodians of the city's rights. If their political masters in legislative assemblies and the national parliament supply guidance, ideology, finances, operational capabilities, and career advancements local councilors cannot act as true elected representatives of the town. If the mayor of the city can never dream to match an MLA or an MP in political stature, he or she cannot provide progressive leadership to local governance. The disabled start of the Indian local governance during the colonial rule was never course-corrected when the Republic was formed. India, a beacon of democracy in the new world order forgot to nurture the virtues of grass-root level governance in its euphoria, and sanitation paid the price as we shall see.

Indian local governance was stripped of its capacities to effectively deliver sanitation, but at the same time was held responsible for non-compliance. Concurrently, union and state governments washed their hands off the duty of cleaning towns and villages. Occasionally, though, the chief minister of the state would intervene to douse fires on the city's landfills or direct the local authorities to take immediate and strict action to remove the garbage from any particular neighborhood. Local bodies were tasked with cleaning their respective jurisdictions, but without the right tools and capabilities. In this scheme to leave the local governance to fend for itself, the Indian state expected them to take care of the garbage, just like the cleaning class had done for centuries.

With this demobilization, Indian local governance was left with no choice but to deliver sanitation as a matter of exception, not a norm. For its under-trained human skills, depreciated assets, and medieval methods of waste management that the colonial rule laid down centuries ago, it could do no better, as evidenced from the story of the East Delhi Municipal Corporation (EDMC). The EDMC runs into annual losses of ₹600 crores (about US$ 100 million). While presenting its annual budget in 2015, the mayor acknowledged that it will continue to make losses for the next five years and only funding can help the situation. He further stated that the municipal body would explore ways to increase its revenues through taxes, user fees, and asset monetization. But his spirited arguments could not hide the crumbling edifice of India's local governance that is mandated to deliver sanitation. In December 2015, the EDMC decided to outsource the operational management of public toilets in twenty existing and sixteen new complexes under its purview for the lack of funds to manage their daily operations so much so that the water supply utility company stopped the water supply to these toilets for the non-payment of dues. But the decision to outsource operations of these toilets raised a monetary dilemma for the civic corporation – if the body had no money to run these toilets, how will it secure funds to pay the outsourced vendor. The EDMC countered that it would allow the service provider to charge a nominal service fees from the users of the facility. The local body could have done the same and contributed to its starved treasury. Severe financial crunch should have encouraged the municipal body to think of solutions like bio-toilets and monetizing external spaces through advertisements and publicity.

Institutions, which are essentially groups of people working together for a common goal, reflect the values of society. Bias in society seeps into these institutions, unless they are safeguarded during their inception. India was presented with an opportunity to course correct in 1950 and 1992, but local governance continued to perpetuate the bias of Indian society about sanitation. The processes designed to manage sanitation largely relied on sweepers. When the cities and towns grew, more sweepers were hired. This bias left the 'unsavoury' issue of sanitation at the hands of the local bodies. Societal biases percolated into the local governance. How could the elected councilors think differently about sanitation, when their own houses were perhaps cleaned by the segregated sweeper 'caste'?

The states formed institutions like the public works departments to build civil infrastructure, utility transmission companies to deliver electricity and water to homes, and upstreamed these issues as state or federal subjects. But the same state actors never explored the merits of a similar provincial infrastructure to collect and dispose waste. On the one hand, the states considered the local bodies incapable of creating an efficient local response for utilities like electricity and relived them of these responsibilities, but on the other they seemed convinced about the abilities of the same local bodies to handle sanitation, a fit case of personal bias leading to institutional casteism. The sole responsibility of delivering sanitation ended up on the shoulders of the weakest public institution, the local body, which was set up to fail on from the start.

The incapacity of Indian municipal bodies to address the growing problem of waste management and sanitation further ballooned because of their compulsory subservience to their political and administrative masters, who confronted the rapidly changing profile of the generated waste. This confrontation further reinforced the preexisting faulty social contract between the citizen and the state on sanitation delivery. Citizens felt entitled to sanitation services on the same lines as electricity and water. But, unlike these utilities, which are inputs for human living, waste is an output. When clean countries were confronted with such a challenge a century ago, administrators positioned waste management as a collective responsibility, not an individual right. This allowed the local bodies there to put elaborate guidelines that pinned down the responsibilities of the citizens in the effective delivery of sanitation and to realize the cost of waste management from the citizens as a service at actual cost, if not for a profit. Local bodies instituted waste-specific taxes and levies for breaches. All forms of human consumption that generated waste came under this ambit. User fees and taxes were used as an effective tool to establish this collective responsibility toward waste management and this allowed clean countries of today to accelerate their efforts toward clean living.

Indian local bodies, however, missed this point. They still attempted to solve the challenge of sanitation as an entitlement to be delivered without any monetary consideration from the franchise, and undertaken by the cleaning class. As a result, the Indian governance ended up not putting a price to the economic cost of delivering sanitation and did permanent damage to the efforts to evaluate sanitation delivery as an economic challenge.

The pricing of enforcement for sanitation by the Brihanmumbai Municipal Corporation (BMC) is a case in point. The BMC, the largest civic body in India and one of the better ones, took a bold step by instituting the practice of Clean-up Marshals in 2013. It penalized those who littered public places; the activity was outsourced to a contracted vendor, something many clean countries have successfully adopted. In Mumbai, the scheme faced a great deal of backlash from the start, ranging from harassment to extortion against the enforcement personnel. Citizens had hitherto not paid for keeping their neighborhoods clean, why now? was the argument of the biased mindset of society; the practice was eventually discontinued in 2014..

The demolition of the economic argument also robbed the local civic bodies of the ability to provide intellect on all issues that concerned sanitation. This crippled them to be able to appreciate the myriad challenges of sanitation presented by the quantum and pace of urbanization. Human settlement expanded and the nature of waste changed. Local bodies were expected to rise to the occasion and implement rules of living in these new urban neighborhoods.

Civic bodies in the clean countries made rules regarding sanitation and cleanliness and devised mechanisms to ensure their compliance. In Seattle, for instance, the pavement outside of homes should always be kept clean, failing which the civic inspector issues a penalty to the house which the pavement skirts, even though the pavement is a public space and does not belong to the home owner. It makes the homeowners responsible toward their surroundings, thereby reducing the burden to clean and collect rubbish from public spaces. The local bodies in India, however, were unable to appreciate such nuances, while their jurisdictions continued to expand at a rapid pace.

A herd of cows sitting in the middle of busy motorways is one of the most endearing stereotypical images of urban India and a proud badge of 'Indian-ness.' But to the logical mind, this picture reflects the failure of the local municipal bodies to demonstrate intellectual leadership on sanitation. Livestock rearing in rural homes is an essential source of additional income that provides a crucial stable income round the year in the backdrop of an erratic agriculture cycle. Cattle can be let loose to graze in the farmlands (even this poses grave threat to the rural economy) and nearby forests and are fed the post-harvest crop residue, free of cost. Households can also have the extra income from dairy produce and utilize the dung as fuel. When villages shunned agriculture and acquired an urban character, the daily lives of erstwhile rural folk were at cross purposes with the demands of a clean city. But the practice of bovine ownership in every home, as was the norm in the village, accompanied them in their transition to the cities. Forests or open fields for grazing were absent from the concrete jungle, as was the scope to use cow dung as a fuel source. Yet the migrants continued with this practice. Roads replaced open fields and open sewers replaced water bodies for their 'urban bovines.' Slowly, bovine rearing in homes grew into commercial dairy businesses that began supplying milk in the neighborhood. Before we knew it, this unregulated dairy industry in urban India became ground zero for adulteration and a nightmare for sanitation. Livestock roamed the streets unchecked. They would be left free to pick at the neighborhood garbage dump for food, even though it was toxic, but that saved the owner the cost of animal feed. Their owners dumped their droppings into sewage lines and these ended up getting choked, leading to foul-smelling neighborhoods. But it saved the dairies the cost of disposing this waste in a safe and secure manner. The unit economics made perfect sense for such dairies to thrive and prosper. It was of little consequent that the bovines produced toxin-laced milk from bruised intestines and diseased bodies, not to mention the public safety hazard they posed by being on the road during the day. But the dairy industry represented a powerful political symbolism of the cow, 'sons of the soil' migrants, and huge emotional franchise support, which tested the mettle of the local bodies to take a stand and provide progressive leadership, only to fail miserably. The issue is not per se with livestock rearing, but with carrying out this practice in spaces that are not designed for it. With right disposition it was easy for local bodies to pursue solutions that could balance the migrants' need for rearing livestocks with the sanitation needs of the city. A community dairy facility on a user fee model would have been an easy response. Livestock owners would have to pay the local body fees and/or a share of their income in lieu of better market access, round-the-clock shelter for their animals, utility services, access to veterinarian services, waste disposal and fodder. Local bodies, in return, would ensure quality checks on milk production, proper disposal of the generated waste which would ideally become compost rather than find its way to the sewage system. Migrants could preserve their social practice, earn extra money while local bodies could keep their cities clean, and create a new revenue source for their empty coffers. Local bodies, for their birth defects, were destined to miss this relationship between sanitation in cities and the artisanal existence of bovine breeding in urban households. Local bodies demonstrated similar brinkmanship for unregulated abattoirs, informal retail shops, real estate construction, automobile and electronics scrap dismantling, tea stalls, and roadside eateries. These issues simply demanded lateral thinking in urban design and operational muster, but turned out to be a tall task for the defective local civic bodies.

Bengaluru encapsulates the impact of the deformity of Indian local governance on sanitation delivery in its full glory – the lack of financial autonomy to internalize the cost of delivering sanitation, the compulsion to extrapolate the colonial approach to manage waste that has its genesis in societal bias, and the inability to sever the umbilical cord that ties the local bodies to their political masters. Nearly 40 percent of the 2015 annual budget of the municipal corporation of Bengaluru was made up of grants and aids from various state actors. Despite this support, the local body's estimated annual expenditure of ₹5,021 crores had a revenue spillover of ₹16 crores. The annual spend on solid waste management for the city was under 10 percent at ₹488 crores, but more than 80 percent of this expenditure went toward paying salaries of the city's sanitation workers, but the sanitation workers' strike over non-payment of salaries, almost a regular affair, crushes the city under the humungous weight of its own filth. The annual GDP of Bengaluru in 2015 surpassed ₹100,000 crores from a population of over 10 million. Any comparable city in a clean country would spend significantly more to handle the aftermaths of this consumption binge. In January 2016, sanitation workers in Delhi went on a nearly month-long strike over non-payment of salaries and dues. They began dumping the garbage in the streets, turning the city into a stinking hell. The incumbent chief minister had to divert over ₹500 crores from the budget meant for other purposes. Vizag and Hyderabad have also faced such strikes. Gurugram's tryst with this came in 2018, a situation that could only be diffused with the intervention of the state's incumbent chief minister.

Sanitation workers cannot be blamed, as they are merely manifesting a disabled local civic body that was set up to fail on sanitation delivery from the very start. The strikes represent an inadequate pricing of the cost of waste management. It explains the absence of any financial leeway after salaries are paid out, and the fractured organizational design of the local governance to deliver sanitation which only relies on the body count to clean up the city. The recurring nature of these strikes also suggests that flawed thinking leads to the symptom to be taken as the root cause and devise simplistic solutions: pay the workers and the cities will be clean again. This naivety is further vulnerable to political interpretations drowning out any possibility of the root causes coming to the surface for a bipartisan intervention. At the time of the work strike of sanitation workers in Delhi in 2016, the city's local governance was ruled by one political party and the legislative assembly of the 'state' of Delhi was ruled by another. After a few days of allegations and counter allegations between the two organs of the government, the incumbent chief minister announced an 'immediate' release of funds to pay the outstanding salaries. However, later he retracted from his commitment citing financial incapacity. Concurrently, the local governance threw in the towel also citing empty coffers, which was partly true, but mostly to corner the chief minister on the issue. The salaries were eventually paid through an abnormal intervention, but not before full political mileage was extracted. Should the sanitation challenge of Delhi then be blamed on its citizens for choosing different political representations for the local bodies and for state governance? Or is the city of Delhi retrofitted with an unwieldy structure that necessitates multiple state actors? Will it not be better to merge the functions of state government and the local bodies of the city and create an administrative response with strong technical and managerial abilities? Or should the city of Delhi do away with its legislative assembly and let it be managed under a single local civic body that can be piloted for brave new ideas on local governance? Not surprisingly, the issue of non-payment of salaries of sanitation workers returned to Delhi in 2018 with another bout of work strike for a month with an identical plot of dues, actors and partisanship. It is this brinkmanship that robs local governance in India of economic and intellectual leeway to pursue progressive (and right) ideas to overcome the sanitation challenge viz. waste segregation techniques, enforcement for sanitation, recycling, resource recovery technology, infrastructure & technology adoption, law enforcement, citizen outreach, training and community programs.

India needs a debate to critique the existence of local governance in the manner it exists today for its design to deliver sanitation. Its current position is drowned in the political and administrative hierarchy that makes it the wrong institution in its current avatar for the agenda of sanitation delivery. Should we abandon the 74th Amendment in lieu of a top-down administrative organization that reports to the people's will reposed in legislative assemblies and the national parliament on all matters that concern sanitation? If the existing local governance is the route to achieve the end goal of sanitation delivery as a matter of routine, how should this local governance be imagined in a manner that it can be injected with the stamina of empowerment and technical prowess? The chief minister of the state and the mayor/s of the city cannot both be looking at the deaths of the sanitation workers, stinking neighborhoods, or landfill fires at once, with each expecting the other to take the blame for these occurrences.

Part of the solution to the sanitation woes of India lies in seeking answers to these questions. The existing organizational design of local civic bodies needs a revamp. They sit at cross purposes with the rapidly evolving urban and rural areas they govern today. India not only comes up with the wrong answers for the sanitation challenges, it also ends up asking the wrong set of questions on the issue. In April

2016, the NGT issued notices to the local bodies of Delhi about a fire in one of the landfills in the city – an apt case of asking the wrong question and expecting the right answer. Waste management experts will concur that fires in open, unregulated landfills are natural, that all open landfills simmer with methane and other deadly gases. Precisely for this reason, open landfills were banned by clean countries decades ago. But, the NGT's notice was like asking an underage car driver as to why he jumped a traffic signal, whereas he should not be behind the wheel in the first place. The concerned local civic bodies responded to the NGT's questioning: citizens were blamed for not segregating waste, weather was blamed for the starting of the fire, even sabotage was not ruled out. While these are defendable causes of the fire, these are merely symptoms of a deeper malaise that resulted from the continuation of open landfills as an acceptable waste disposal method. The NGT instead should question the continuation of landfills in India and demand a migration roadmap toward environment-friendly waste disposal methods.

The 'birth defect' of the local bodies mutated them into helpless organizations, who were pasted with a mask of reformed exterior through the 74th constitutional amendment. Not surprisingly, local bodies couldn't do better than to make irrational or inadequate choices on sanitation delivery and public health became one of its obvious victims. Dirty neighborhoods created a cocktail of vector-borne diseases and the marginalized urban poor faced most of its brunt. They reconciled to the idea that cleanliness, like wealth, is a luxury that is accorded to a few and perhaps it is their destiny to live and die in the filth. Only when the diseases began to knock on the doors of the 'visible' habitants of the city did the local bodies swing into action with a troubleshooting plan. The well-endowed also started to buy 'cleanliness' and move to live in manicured surroundings of gated establishments or erect walls around their private clean oases, devoid of any expectation from the local bodies. The residual urban

Indians became children of a lesser God, who were compelled to live in the company of filth, diseases, stinking sewers and nauseating surroundings, impacting their collective psyche and making them grow immune to inadequate sanitation.

In the case of India, the administrative cerebral expertise was supplied to it rather than the local governance building it on its own. The state and union governments became the wholesale suppliers of this expertise and either played an overt role of supplying municipal commissioners, collectors, district magistrates, village development officers, and panchayat secretaries, or a covert role in monitoring and guiding the onboarding process of the administrative machinery in the local governance, which included sanitation workers, *patwaris*, engineers, and so on. Such an arrangement was perhaps well intentioned at the time of Independence, when states were devoid of resources, foresight, and strength to build such human capability from scratch. But this dependence on state and national governments for everything – from infrastructure development to financing, from political legitimacy to human talent – reduced local bodies to mere addicts, waiting for resources to be supplied. It seemed to be a tall order for the cerebral might of the bureaucracy to produce results from a deformed system that had been groomed to survive on doles and blessings. Neither was the bureaucracy allowed any intellectual leeway to make systemic changes, draft rules, or devise new ways to fill their empty coffers, nor question the existing operational systems for their costs, interdependencies, and logic. It was expected to deliver sanitation while working with a defective and structurally weak framework. Imagine a surgeon who is asked to perform a life-saving surgery on a patient but he is not allowed to use any tools like anesthesia or a scalpel. The surgeon, being mindful of the results expected from him, creates a pretense of the surgery and erects a façade of a complicated surgery in progress. Once his allotted time is over he is replaced by another surgeon who carries on with the same drill. The bureaucracy's engagement on sanitation delivery resembles such a surgery, fueling the false notion of normalcy while marching along the path of abyss.

Occasionally, this mediocrity conflicted with a rare few brave souls like T. Chandrasekhar. In the mid 1990s, Chandrasekhar, the municipal commissioner of the city of Thane, demonstrated that change is possible in spite of self-limiting conditions. He undertook some bold reforms in the city and instituted processes that transformed Thane from a dirty suburb of Mumbai to one of the cleanest cities in the country. In mid-2000s, he was appointed the joint commissioner in the municipal corporation of Mumbai. In November 2005, in an interview, he recorded his disgust and frustration with the structure of the local bodies that provides no leg room to the bureaucracy to undertake structural changes. He even compared this situation to a soldier who is asked to protect the country's borders, but is given no gun, not very different from our surgeon's dilemma.

S. A. Khadar Saheb also felt this conflict as joint director of municipal administration in Andhra Pradesh, and, on the suggestion of the citizens, executed the idea of a clean city championship on the lines of the Cricket League. G. Latha, municipal commissioner of Coimbatore, took the initiative to streamline waste collection and segregation processes in the city. These people ruffled the feathers of the establishment along the way and were forced to concede many a times, only to pick up their next battle with the same set of constraints. Tukaram Mundhe was allegedly transferred in 2017 from the post of municipal commissioner of Navi Mumbai for waging a war on illegal encroachments that has a direct bearing on sanitation; he landed in Nashik a few months later with the same resolve. Sriram Venkataraman, subcollector of Devikulam in Idukki district of Kerala, allegedly faced a similar fate in the same year when he took on an effective anti-encroachment drive against illegal construction in the ecologically sensitive zone of Munnar. These stories of individual brilliance highlight the extent of personal resolve needed to make any difference sans political sponsorship.

If Mumbai struggles to contain the fires on its landfills, if Bengaluru suffers from frothing lakes, if two out of three sewage treatment plants in Jammu city remain non-functional, if 87 percent of waste from toilets in urban Uttar Pradesh goes untreated into rivers and farmland disfiguring the soil's biodiversity and society's stamina to fight vector diseases and if Delhi faces perpetual strikes by its sanitation workers, blame the deformed local governance structure responsible for the delivery of sanitation in over 5,000 cities and 5 lakh villages across India. This realization will allow us to appreciate the severity of the gap that needs to be bridged with policy intervention in legislation, infrastructure, and implementation. But India's sanitation challenge is tricky: it lacks a vivid description of the desired state of a clean nation. From this unimaginative society on the issue emerge elected public representatives in civic bodies, legislative assemblies, and the national parliament. From this ignorance emerge prospective bureaucrats who fight it out in civil services examinations to devise policy and manage the daily affairs of municipal corporations. From this mediocrity emerge institutions like the Rajghat Samadhi Committee (RSC) that are tasked with sanitation delivery, which fail miserably to live up to the responsibility. The RSC, the institutional body responsible for the upkeep of the final resting place of Gandhi, was slammed by the High Court of Delhi in February 2018 over its failure to maintain sanitation of the area.

It is due to this limitation that the Indian state actors fail to interpret sanitation from the lens of policy, organization, legislation, enforcement, and infrastructure. They are unable to marry economics with it and are too blinkered to appreciate the explicit linkage of the myriad forms of human actions with the challenges of sanitation: real estate construction, electronics waste, biohazardous and medical waste, weddings and social functions in open areas, religious processions and festivals, dairies and abattoirs, informal retailing and living among others. They are incapacitated to be able to link the deaths of hundreds of children because of Japanese encephalitis in eastern Uttar Pradesh with the faulty urbanism in the region. An eatery on the pavement is a symbol of livelihood protection and not the sanitation mess it creates by disposing waste in the vicinity. Public representatives may compulsorily pay homage at a temple, but regulating the waste discharged from its premises will never become a priority for them. Booming construction activity will be interpreted as a sign of economic progress, but the disposal of the construction waste and the working conditions of construction workers will never be considered an essential sanitation issue that demands elaborate preventive measures. Private social functions will rarely be taken to symbolize conspicuous consumption and their apathy toward installing waste collection and disposal arrangements will never be condemned. Waste dumps on the outskirts are acceptable symbols of India's economic growth, as are leaking sewers, deaths of sanitation workers inside sewage pipes, and the informal waste recycling industry.

The question then is how can the governing body be the torchbearer for sanitation if it has itself emerged from a biased and an unimaginative society? It has failed to convey to the Indian society that a clean neighborhood is a basic need for all. With its meager resources to manage waste, local governance has perpetuated the notion of scarcity of sanitation that can only be delivered to a select few.

To perpetuate the attitude of troubleshooting under the guise of 'normalcy' is the momentous failure of Indian state actors on sanitation. Often, this failure becomes apparent subconsciously from their deeds. In 2017, when the union government sought donations from the Indian diaspora living abroad to clean the holy Ganges, the act reinforced the dependence of Indian state actors on such donations to fight the sanitation challenge. In the same year, a senior union minister requested the Bill & Melinda Gates Foundation, one of the largest philanthropic organizations in the world, to adopt 1,000 villages in regions affected by the Naxalite movement, and turn them into models of sanitation and hygiene. The minister's sincere plea conveys the 'addendum' view that the government holds on sanitation – one that does not have a vision of this clean model village, yet expects a development agency to define and deliver it without any reciprocal expectation. Let's say if these villages were sans electricity (a few may still be) would the minister use a similar pleading attitude to install electricity poles and an electricity generation plant without any consideration in return? On the contrary, he would proudly elucidate the government's role in shaping up policy, creating the requisite operational guidelines, and channeling capital (public or private) to light up homes in its villages. But in taking such a plea to the Gates foundation for sanitation delivery, the minister sub-consciously conveyed that in the Indian government's scheme of things, sanitation lies at the very periphery, never mind the hyperbole around it.

In 2017, the New Delhi Municipal Corporation (NDMC), which governs the cleaner parts of Delhi, proudly announced that a leading conglomerate in the consumer sector has won the contract to run waste management operations in its jurisdiction. For the private organization, waste management operations is not a core business, but the enterprise was willing to bankroll projects from the funds earmarked for corporate social responsibility initiatives. Though the organization is sincere and keen to be the responsible corporate citizen, the question to ask the NDMC is this: if its jurisdiction lacked access to water or electricity, would it have taken on a corporate player under a similar arrangement? Would it be willing to spare some cash from other business activities to invest in an infrastructure of water pipes and supply water without expecting anything in return? These citations demonstrate that the government is predisposed to viewing sanitation as a fringe affair and therefore cannot accord it the same exalted stature as issues like roads, water, and electricity.

Clean countries teach us that governance cannot position sanitation as an absolute right of the citizens and then scramble for doles in order to deliver it. The nation is the custodian of this responsibility on behalf of its citizens and arms the local governance to act as a facilitator. The citizens' payout for this service through waste management taxes and/or user fees symbolizes this relationship. Due to the fractured organizational design of the governance, India is unable to reconcile with this realization in its approach toward sanitation delivery. The more this realization is delayed, the closer India will have to travel to a point of no return, where the vulnerable would have died many silent deaths and the toxic rivers would have lost their ability to wash our sins.

A report released by the Government of India's Ministry of Environment, Forest and Climate Change in 2016 acknowledged that forty-one bustling towns in India suffered from the serious problem of air and water pollution, the key reasons being dumping of sewage in water bodies and improper disposal of garbage. In April 2016, the head of NITI Aayog, an advisory body of the Indian government on policy, acknowledged that the rapid pace of urbanization that is currently underway in India will pack 60 percent of Indians into urban areas in the next three decades. Juxtaposing these two pearls of knowledge highlights a startling truth: the current process and structure of local governance that is unable to manage the urban cesspool, and not capable of delivering sanitation in the foreseeable future, will only give rise to an even larger cesspool in the future.

Indian local civic bodies are tasked to solve the complex issue of sanitation, having been stripped of the tools and intellectual disposition to do so. In 2017, all current landfills in Delhi, to dispose of its 10,000 metric tons of daily garbage, were filled to the brim. They had reached the maximum height of forty-eight meters long ago. The best solution the local governance of the city could come up with was to find a new landfill site and continue with the same practice.

We must aim for a governance framework that can potentially change a society that has been wronged on the notion of sanitation for the past many centuries, and an organizational design which can create a reference point of a desired state of cleanliness in a society that is blind to it because of preexisting biases. But where do we start?

We first need to revive the spirit that sponsored the 74th Amendment of the Indian Constitution in 1992, explore the reasons that extinguished this spirit, and ask uncomfortable questions at the cost of usurping the status quo, allowing a new governance order to emerge for the delivery of sanitation.

Issues concerning waste management and sanitation are rarely solved solely by local municipal bodies. Clean countries realized that the complexity of waste management in the modern world was at odds with the simplistic design of local civic bodies. Effluent discharged into rivers impacted areas beyond the jurisdiction of the local body. The lack of civic sense of residents under the ambit of a particular local body flowed into other areas. Waste dumped in the open in one province polluted the air for everyone. They realized that the challenge demands cross-functional expertise on technology, research, social science, and legislation, which cannot be made a part of every local civic body. They also used this economically sound argument to determine the role of the different organs of governance in managing the value chain of sanitation rather than to make the local civic body the sole custodian of this responsibility. They took a segregated view and bifurcated the sanitation issue into two parts. The first entailed the development of a unified policy and codes regarding waste management, which became the responsibility of the national government by virtue of the universal applicability of this agenda. The second was the deployment of a sanitation policy which was intelligently forked into the two distinct heads of collection and disposal. The function of waste collection became the responsibility of the local bodies who were autonomous enough (surrogate for financial and enforcement independence) to purpose-build the infrastructure and operational systems. Concurrently, the clean countries appreciated that the waste should be treated as an energy resource, as precious as oil and coal. Just as every oil field cannot build an oil refinery and every coal mine, a thermal plant to process it, similarly every waste generating cluster (city, town or village) should not be expected to build infrastructure to process and dispose the waste, for the sake of economic optimization. It made sense to haul the generated waste to a central location for better resource recovery and superior environment protection standards. Toward this purpose, individual local bodies were rightly dissuaded from building their own waste disposal infrastructure for every waste type. If they were not expected to construct power generation plants to provide electricity to the city, they should not be expected to build waste disposal infrastructure. In other words, it was far more prudent to build a common waste disposal infrastructure and offer it to local civic bodies for a plug-and-play, rather than to expect every local civic body to hunt for its own landfill or scramble for money to build its own incinerator. These countries appreciated the advantages of grooming waste disposal as an industrial activity that requires capital and technical capabilities.

But what was so radical about this simple bifurcation? The national government responsibly defined a unified policy regarding waste management with legislative safeguards and freed it from partisanship, establishing a common minimum for one and all. Consequently, the issue received massive resource support of research, infrastructure, and technology to solve vexing problems that had no simple answers. The unified policy addressed wide-ranging issues, namely, acceptable waste disposal methods, workplace safety, productivity enhancements in collection, enforcement approach, emission norms, and so on.

Imagine defining the right method of disposing plastic waste in the 1950s, when everybody was so enamored with this new wonder material that the issue of disposing this kind of waste was farthest from the mind. How were the local civic bodies expected to individually solve this challenge? Similarly, the issue of making waste incinerators environment friendly was a challenge for technology. Local bodies neither had the budget nor the disposition to undertake such vague scientific projects with a long gestation period. Development of the appropriate policy for waste management therefore became a federal responsibility that involved a continuous process spanning decades. This demanded time, money, and human capital and went beyond the capabilities of the local civic bodies.

The pace of urbanization and the concurrent emergence of modern scientific marvels disrupted the consumption patterns in these societies, which became another challenge. There was not only a massive rise in the quantum of generated waste, but it also became tremendously complex. Policy intervention for waste management in these countries had to catch up with this challenge that proved to be beyond the intellectual capacity or administrative agenda of the local civic bodies. Here again the federal responsibility of a policy intervention on waste management ensured uniform deployment of the minimum threshold across the nation. There was flurry of dogmatic laws and legislation regarding sanitation and waste management between the 1960s and the 1990s in today's clean countries that created a minimum threshold for one and all. Denmark, for instance, banned the use of open landfills for waste disposal in the 1980s. This kind of an intervention made sure that the bad practices of waste management are not left as a discretionary choice of the individual local civic bodies. Otherwise, a local civic body could take a counterview that may seem beneficial to its human cluster in the short term, but adversely impact society as a whole in the long run. There were many short-term benefits and dissuasive factors for a local civic body to continue with the status, such as access to land, cheaper cost of waste disposal, a paucity of financial leverage to design new solutions, a high cost of migration to new methods, the disruption of the livelihoods of the people engaged in the existing methods of waste management, and the cost of educating citizens to migrate to the new methods, among others.

The federal responsibility toward a waste management policy in these countries also created a blueprint that incentivized the formalization of the sector, enhanced productivity, and brought economies of scale in waste collection and disposal systems. It put in safeguards and the necessary entry barriers that ensured compliance standards. Legislation like banning open landfills and emissions norms for various waste disposal methods compelled the existing value chain to replace prevalent approaches with formal alternatives.

The forking of waste management into collection and disposal, and the divesture of the responsibility of the local civic bodies from disposing waste, freed up their bandwidth. They could now improve the apparatus of collecting waste from within their respective jurisdiction and upgrade their enforcement methods to make their waste collection approach more productive. They no longer had to put their own systems of landfills, incineration plants, and recycling centers in place to dispose waste. They could offer the waste generated from their respective clusters to operators as raw material for resource extraction. In doing so, local civic bodies also became the process owners of pricing the cost of waste management with a mixed use of fees, fines, and taxes.

Waste disposal, on the other hand, turned into an infrastructure play that took the shape of a formal industry, deploying capital to create solutions able to withstand the benchmarks set by federal laws. Private capital sensed an economic opportunity in offering solutions to haul waste from different local bodies and aggregate it at central locations for recycling and processing. The waste management industry of the USA, which in 2017 generated

US$ 72 billion in annual revenues, emerged as a direct outcome of such realignment.

Federal ownership of waste management did the heavy lifting of the dogmatic legislation and accountability, and made such an outcome possible in the clean countries. The federal waste management policy was not merely a set of broad guidelines or vague laws that could run the risk of discretion. It was an exhaustive set of actions that triggered capital deployment, infrastructure upgrade, and operational efficiency to handle scale and complexity. Initially, federal legislation addressed the immediate issues of waste disposal at hand, but was able to improvise with the increasing complexity of the generated waste and put forth laws for every imaginable type of waste. The outcome of such dogma was the precision with which every aftermath of human consumption came under the ambit of such a waste management policy – solid municipal waste, pets' poop, soiled diapers, industrial waste, electronic waste, scrapped automobiles, construction waste, medical waste, etc.

In India's case whatever bravado was seen was primarily at the behest of its judiciary interpreting the existing vague environmental laws for sanitation. Public health crises in some extreme cases, as was with the plague outbreak of Surat in 1994, also witnessed this bravado. The result was a harangued judiciary seen nudging the executive to take actions ranging from enforcing bans on waste discharge into rivers to directing local municipal bodies to lift dumped garbage in neighborhoods. The judiciary demanded status report on all actions undertaken, issued fines, and reprimanded the bureaucracy at the risk of exposing itself to the criticism of the purists for judicial overreach. Therefore, the first call to action for the Indian state actors is to upstream the legislation from local governance to the national parliament on all matters that concern waste management and sanitation. Uncontained garbage affects the air, water, soil and the public health of the entire nation in unequivocal terms, is a defendable premise for this argument supported by a plethora of learning from the clean countries of today. It does not mean that New Delhi must monitor waste collection and disposal in over 5,000 cities and over 500,000 villages. It means that New Delhi will need to define an elaborate framework of a common minimum that is binding on all local civic bodies. Sikkim used the legislative powers of its legislative assembly to draft such laws and come out clean on the other side. But in this argument we forgo the possibility that precisely for this reason Sikkim stands out as a lone case if the interpretation of legislative urgency on waste management is left on the individual whims of the states. Many states chose to ignore Sikkim's wisdom in favor of other priorities, and upstreaming this agenda to the national executive provides a moat against such individual whims.

Clean countries also teach us that sanitation-related laws cannot be vague; they must be precise and comprehensive to cover all forms of human activities that generate waste. It needs to plug conditions that prompt the generation of waste and the inadequacies that lead to its improper collection and disposal. These laws will deter or serve to alter the daily practices that accentuate the problem of sanitation, and methods of waste disposal, like landfills, incineration, and recycling, need to be prescribed for appropriateness. Such progressive lawmaking is arduous and may need to address those social norms of Indian society that are contrarian to a clean nation. For instance, can the Indian state formulate laws to regulate the immersions of idols into water bodies during festivals? If the act of pilgrims abandoning their clothing in the Pampa river after paying homage at the Sabrimala temple in Kerala poses a sanitation (and pollution) hazard, then should not the onus be on the legislative intervention to educate society of the piety of protecting the river? Federal legislation on sanitation will need to be that guiding force if citizens as well as institutions are willing, and able, to bring about change. From such a legislative precision can emerge sanitation related laws that can mandate waste disposal approaches, define the balance between of sanitation workers and enforcement, provide framework to dismantle discarded automobile and mobile phones, to chop animal carcasses in abattoirs and to milk bovines in neighborhood dairies.

Suppose such precise laws do emerge from this upstreaming exercise, then it is the acceptance of Indian local civic bodies to implement these laws that one questions. If local bodies fight daily struggles to even pay salaries to their sanitation workers, they will surely lament their preexisting disabilities regarding financial leverage, intellectual incapacity, human resource constraints, and non-existent enforcement apparatus, and cite inability to implement such draconian mandates. Therefore, the second call to action is to concurrently price the cost of sanitation delivery for implementing the dogmatic federal laws on sanitation in letter and in spirit, and to make local governance responsible for it.

Upstreaming the process of lawmaking on waste management and the process of waste disposal in no way undermined the role of local governance in today's clean countries. Local bodies were the face of sanitation delivery. These divestures created the right setting for them to internalize the cost of delivering sanitation in its entirety, making them effective conductors of the orchestra of sanitation delivery. India's local governance will need to price all efforts in collecting waste from households and other generating units to enforce laws on sanitation and to safely dispose of, or recycle the waste, while implementing a system of recovering this financial cost from the citizens. It is here that the existing design of Indian local governance sits at odds with the demands for sanitation delivery, which is why the absence of any progress on the 74th constitutional amendment haunt us as a major cause for our failure on sanitation. The alternative is to completely disrobe local governance of this responsibility.

But this presents two concerns; first, India's umbrella approach toward taxation so far is yet to make a convincing argument about its efficacy to increase the share of taxation in the GDP, and any objective template for its deployment. But changing the nation's psyche against taxation is a long-haul operation. Therefore, bundling the cost of delivering sanitation with the vexed agenda of increasing the overall tax share runs the risk of extreme time delays that India can hardly afford. This pressure may also push the state actors to hurriedly attempt inadequate pricing of sanitation, as with the Swachh Bharat tax that was introduced in 2016, on services consumed across the nation. How will the money collected from this tax pool get apportioned across the value chain of waste management? Should it be assigned to the geographic area that generates the highest share of this tax? Or should it sponsor an infrastructure project in the dirtiest part of the country? What kind of infrastructure can be built from the money collected through this tax? Will the revenue collected through such a tax provide adequate financial support for the waste management infrastructure equally across the country, or will the money merely fill the gap that local civic bodies constantly face to pay up the salaries of the sanitation workers? Such intent is noble, but the specificity that a challenge like sanitation demands is compromised in an overarching attempt to pricing it. In November 2017, the state government of Delhi unwittingly found itself on the back foot when it was revealed that nearly ₹700 crores was collected in taxes as 'environment cess,' but hardly any money from this haul was put to good use. This revelation came at the time when the air pollution in the city was off the charts for days following Diwali, making Delhi a veritable gas chamber. The government's misconduct conveyed to the citizens that it has the resources, but is clueless about the ways to use them to improve the city's air.

Indian state actors will repeatedly fall into this trap if they continue to use such a generic taxation approach to the pricing challenge of sanitation, because it subsumes waste management into other generic services and fails to initiate specific actions necessary to overcome the challenge. It may be argued that the government has the capability to allocate its resources for specific use, but the existing arrangement does not provide any comfort that there exists a bipartisan template to administer such an allocation.

It is necessary to price the waste management cost so as also to correct the entitlement bias that exists in India on sanitation. The second concern is that subsuming the cost of sanitation delivery under a broad taxation framework will fail to correct this societal bias. It is inconceivable that local civic bodies of all 5,000 Indian cities and more than 5 lakh villages will be able to garner enough leverage to individually upgrade their respective waste management infrastructure to the desired minimum threshold from such a generic taxation pool without facing hurdles like incapacity and disbursal biases. A direct user fee method for waste management that puts local governance at the center better serves the purposes of appropriately pricing the cost of sanitation delivery and of correcting the biased social contract. In direct user fee or local taxes lies the opportunity for local governance to redeem itself and to capture its autonomy and truly imbibe the spirit of 74th constitutional amendment.

Sir Edwin Chadwick in England and Eugène-René Poubelle in France were early pioneers of understanding the role of enforcement in the context of sanitation in modern society, and that it had to be delivered by local governance. With the objective of improving the overall sanitation in nineteenth-century England, Sir Chadwick drafted the first set of sanitation laws under the Public Health Act of 1848. But he soon realized that the poor implementation of these laws would be their undoing. In response, he instituted a cadre of enforcement officers and named them 'inspectors of nuisance,' who were appointed across England's towns and cities to monitor and enforce every operational aspect of the Public Health Act, from installation of waste bins and deciding the size of these bins, to an adherence to waste collection methods and avoiding littering in public places. By virtue of their job, these inspectors also ended up as the best marketing investment to create awareness about sanitation laws among the franchise.

Today's clean countries eventually figured out that it made better economic sense to employ more sanitation inspectors as a preventive cost than sanitation workers as a post-facto cost, and this idea took root as a standard feature of sanitation delivery. Municipalities were reinforced with human capability to conduct regular surveillance and were armed with powers of enforcement to issue fines and reprimands. Beat plans to monitor garbage collection and littering were closely tied up with the quantum and frequency of waste generated in the area. Similarly, improper waste disposal, wrong effluent discharge, inadequate waste storage capacities, all came under the purview of this monitoring. By the time the clean countries emerged from World War II, the certainty of enforcement for sanitation had begun to bear the desired fruits. But by then, decades of enforcement by sanitation inspectors had disciplined them enough to handle this consumption responsibly and to instinctively abide by sanitation laws.

When the waste problem of these countries reached the level of nation-wide crises, the focus of enforcement was on retribution. Sustained focus on enforcement altered the society's motivations to comply with the laws from fear of punishment to a natural, instinctive response. With this altered behavior, the enforcement's focus shifted from retribution to deterrence that led to many local bodies replacing the enforcement apparatus with passive tools, technologies, and human resource, like outsourcing enforcement jobs to private contractors or deployment of surveillance cameras. Not surprisingly, inspectors of nuisance gave way to environment health officers (EHOs), which reflected the multipronged and progressive role of enforcement, one that was delivered through the local governance and covered all aspects of public health. Today EHOs go about doing their jobs in a fashion similar to a policeman guarding or supervising a neighborhood. Their enforcement approach may seem passive, but this was the intended consequence.

However, this does not mean that breaches regarding sanitation disappeared. As late as the 1970s, retired automobile tires were dumped into the ocean off the shore of Florida, destroying its sensitive marine life. In 2014, US organizations paid more than US$ 10 billion in environmental fines, settlements, and clean-up costs for such breaches. Local bodies in the UK collected nearly US$ 30 million (approximately ₹850 crores) in fines from littering-related offences between 2010 and 2016, at the rate of issuing nearly ten tickets every hour. But with over a hundred years of experience in active enforcement for sanitation behind them, the clean countries were content that it is a far better policy tool toward a clean nation than to invest in marketing campaigns to plead with citizens to comply with sanitation laws.

Sir Chadwick's contribution in this regard was path breaking in that he viewed enforcement for sanitation as a matter of citizens' right to a safe environment and that it was one of the key responsibilities of the state to deliver this right to them. The brilliance in the idea was to expand the definition of safety to include the notion of public health, and to nudge the society toward a desirable behavior, making local governance efficient and the city safer for everyone.

Indian local governance must absorb Chadwick's wisdom to make enforcement an integral part of sanitation delivery. But given India's overall attitude toward enforcement, it appears to be another steep hill to climb. In this context, the deployment of a single person as a sanitation inspector to supervise a ward of thousands on hygiene and to enforce sanitation laws stands to reason. Not surprisingly, Delhi could only manage to convict its first offender for improper industrial waste discharge in 2018, while breaches were rampant and evident. In 2016, Bhubaneswar employed a single food inspector to monitor all aspects of food safety in this city of nearly a million people. Neither can food safety and hygiene in the city's food outlets be a voluntary expectation nor can they be achieved without enforcement playing a proactive role to convey the desirable state. A similar plea is equally extendable to all other forms of human consumption that produce waste, be it hospitals, education, civil construction, automobile and electronic scrap, or weddings.

The journey of the clean countries regarding enforcement for sanitation can be synthesized into two key lessons for Indian local governance. The first is of effective enforcement to introduce a 'new normal' in the sanitation behavior of the society, deliverable by the local governance. The second lesson is that the financial cost of enforcement for sanitation should be priced and recouped from the citizens on actuals.

Indian state actors will also need to imbibe the clean countries' approach of forking the subject of waste management into two separate policy issues of collection and disposal as the final call to action. Say, a poultry farm produces 1,000 eggs every day, but the farmer has a lorry that can only take 100 eggs to the market. He has no choice but to leave the remaining 900 eggs to rot at the farm. The Indian local bodies' capacity for collecting waste is the lorry and the waste generated from their respective jurisdictions, the eggs produced by the poultry farm. One way to solve the problem is to adopt a frugal approach and reduce the production capacity of the farm to a 100 eggs a day to match the hauling capacity of the lorry. While the farm owner may take this approach, the growing aspiration of India cannot scale back its consumption binge that translates into a growing mountain of garbage every day. The civic bodies, therefore, are left with no option but to increase their installed capacity to collect the generated waste, akin to the poultry farmer buying nine more lorries to solve his problem. But unlike the simplistic solution that entails adding more lorries, increasing the installed capacity to collect waste will have to be modeled along the lines of a utility service, just as an electricity distribution company delivers electricity to homes, shops, and commercial establishments for a user fee. The function of electricity distribution is distinct from electricity generation: the former allows electricity distributors to supply electricity to users after buying it from companies that generate it. The approach to waste management is the same logic applied in reverse – a waste disposal infrastructure to provide a common destination for the collected waste. For this arrangement to work efficiently, local civic bodies will need to design the waste collection infrastructure as an elaborate grid that compulsorily plugs every waste generating unit. They will be required to install mechanisms so that this grid can collect all waste types generated in the city or village in an optimum and ecologically sane manner. It should be noted that the clean countries of today did not restrict the scope of waste collection to an operational system of infrastructure and processes to lift waste from generating sites.

The idea of dividing sanitation delivery into two distinct buckets and making the local civic bodies the primary custodian of only one, that is, waste collection, will take the pressure off the local bodies to dispose waste. Concurrently, local civic bodies, injected with enough autonomy, can install a comprehensive waste collection system including an enforcement apparatus to ensure compliance with sanitation laws. They will be transformed into facilitators of collecting all forms of waste in a segregated manner and hand it over to expert waste disposal entities on behalf of their citizens and emerge as efficient waste collectors. Just as the Indian state actors have deftly disarmed the local governance of many responsibilities in the past, they should play this act one more time and relieve them of the responsibility of disposing waste, like Germany and Denmark did in the 1970s. Waste disposal should become a concurrent subject of the union and state governments. Such joint responsibility will lift it out from its artisanal existence and make it a plug-and-play industrial function, available to the local civic bodies as a vendor.

While local municipal bodies take cues from the benchmarks and guidelines laid down by federal laws to devise tools most suitable to their clusters, central and state bodies will determine an appropriate infrastructure response to dispose the generated waste. Some states see the need for an aggressive industrial waste disposal policy and create a framework of contracts, guidelines, and operating models for infrastructure investments. Other states with simpler profiles of industrial activity and generated waste may adopt a cooperative or an indirect waste disposal intervention or pursue interstate treaties. All approaches are equally acceptable, provided they result in a formal infrastructure for waste disposal. For instance, a national prohibition on the use of open landfills for waste disposal will propel some states to opt for formal recycling and resource recovery as the only form of waste disposal and try to rapidly scale it up, while other states may opt for a hybrid approach of closed landfills and resource recovery centers. They could even decide to top-up the federal legislation with state-specific laws, as in the case of Sikkim, banning the use of chemical pesticides for agriculture, thereby demonstrating that agriculture is both feasible and sustainable without them.

In this forking exercise, local governance will act as facilitators for their two critical relationships: the first will be with the citizens, which will entail waste collection and enforcement for sanitation; the second relationship will be with the waste disposal entities to which local bodies will pay to dispose of the collected waste. The local civic bodies will reconcile all the cost incurred to uphold these two relationships and translate it into taxes and fees to be recovered from the franchise. This new organizational design for waste management should be viewed as a necessary tool to boost the autonomy of Indian local governance and as a catalyst to incentivize formal capital (private sector or public spending) to build a waste disposal infrastructure. This should also be viewed as an invitation for the creation of desirable capabilities, institutions, and human expertise, and as a natural deterrence for informality and artisanal existences, although nothing really stops state actors from getting confined to their role as assessors, regulators, or watchdogs. They can very well explore the opportunity to examine their role as an active equity investor and ride this excitement. Delhi Metro Rail Corporation (DMRC) emerged from this thought and brought the Delhi government and the development fund of Japan to create an asset that is among the very few financially sustainable metro rail corporations in the world. So did Titan Industries Limited, which emerged as a joint venture between the Tata Group and Tamil Nadu Industrial Development Corporation (TIDCO), owing to the Tamil Nadu government's keenness to boost local job creation through the development of local manufacturing in the state. It shook hands with the Tata Group in the 1980s and Titan was born, which today stands as a worthy example of a perfect marriage between private capital and vision-driven intent of a state actor.

In the 1980s, Maruti Suzuki triggered India's job growth in the automotive sector, driven by the rise in domestic demand and the indigenization of this industry. In the 1990s, India discovered the arbitrage potential in information technology and eventually emerged as a bellwether for white-collar jobs for the next two decades. In future, we are all poised to confront robotics and machine learning that will challenge the legacy-led businesses considered to be powerhouses of jobs in scores of sectors. Aging societies like Japan will suppress the domestic demand for many existing products and instead throw up new priorities of consumption, like rapid developments in adult care and hygiene such as diapers, funeral homes, and hospice living. Progressive nations constantly take stock of the impact of such forces and fine-tune their agenda of job creation. In the context of sanitation, India is confronted with the same need. If it is projected that by 2050 more than 60 percent of the country will have a strong urban character, it will need to answer the ensuing question about the generated waste that will compulsorily accompany it. India's economic trajectory leaves no doubts about this projected outcome, but also presents the compelling need for scores of jobs in myriad areas to manage its aftermath. Five thousand urban local bodies and nearly six lakh panchayats will require enforcement officers with skills of environmental sciences, administration, and technology, who can understand solid human and food waste, biohazardous and electronic waste, construction and non-biodegradable waste, alongside enforcement of sanitation laws. Indian towns will require urban planners that can suck out informality from Indian urbanism. Cities and villages will need last-mile waste collection experts who can run the apparatus to collect segregated waste from 250 million households and haul it safely to waste disposal centers. India will need resource recovery engineers, clean energy scientists, and experts in organic farming who can process and repurpose India's annually generated waste that currently stands at 100 million tons. Managing India's sewage and garbage is a necessary agenda for the Indian state actors, who restlessly search for the next big game of labor intensive, high economic growth opportunities.

This opportunity will likely be a colossal miss for the Indian state actors, however, if they fail to reconcile their individual stance on waste management. In 2017, the NGT banned any waste discharge into the Ganga out of exasperation and set a fine of ₹50,000 for every breach. The Delhi High Court, in the same year, directed various local civic bodies to submit an action plan toward garbage management in the city. Lawmakers are ignorant about the urgency and go about troubleshooting one crisis to the next. The local governance that should be facilitating sanitation delivery waits for a reprimand from the judiciary or for benefits from the executive. The judiciary which should ideally enforce the law on sanitation is constantly needled to draft one first. This gridlock among the state actors represents the brinkmanship of governance on sanitation. In the process, the judiciary is accused of overreach, while the governance secretly takes cues from these interventions to prioritize its meager and ill-equipped resources.

India's struggle with waste management starkly brings out the incompleteness of its democratic process. The state organs are yet to figure out the role each one must play in managing this issue. No clean country has ever got its way solely by the efforts of the local civic bodies, nor has any allowed its citizens to view sanitation as an absolute right. Also, no country got clean backed by vague legislation on sanitation, sans enforcement of these laws. Indian state actors should either drop the pretense of federal democracy or override the 74th constitutional amendment. There is nothing undemocratic about this stance, though it may be a tad less 'federal.' It will then be easy to upstream all aspects of sanitation delivery from local civic bodies to the state or central governments. Let the franchise elect members of the legislative assembly and national parliament, who in turn can take the onus of sanitation delivery across all towns and villages through a central command structure, administered from the capital headquarters. Administrative prowess through an appointed team of operational and technical experts will then be tasked to manage all daily affairs that concern sanitation, in every town and village, as is the case with few industrial towns like Jamshedpur.

The other option is to truly imbibe the spirit of the 74th Amendment and convert the organs of local governance into effective institutions to deliver sanitation, but without other state actors abandoning their responsibilities toward the issue. Local governance can then facilitate sanitation processes and correct its biased social contract, while the union and state governments take the onus to convert the collected waste into an economic opportunity. The city of Indore's rapid elevation on sanitation in a span of three years (2014–2017) is a direct result of this inference. When the commitment and operational capability of Manish Singh, the Commissioner of the city received sincere grass-root political sponsorship from the city's Mayor – Malini Gaud, the city managed to put together a sustainable framework to clean itself within a few years. 'Clean India' can either wait to emerge as a truly federal democracy, or it can spot a catalyst to strengthen its grass-root democracy as it makes efforts to surmount the sanitation challenge. The day India overcomes its sanitation challenges will also be the day India's democracy will truly be victorious, or vice versa.

3

URBAN PLANNING

'What is the difference between an architect and a city planner?'
'An architect gets to design only one building at a time, but a city planner can design many buildings in one go.'
'The Van Buren Boys,' *Seinfeld*, 14th Episode, Eighth Season, 1997

There are other reasons why urban planners score over architects. One can say, in many ways they get to play God: urban planners take decisions on behalf of citizens decades before they are even born. If people drive to work or use public transport, if the city gets waterlogged during the rainy season, if the motorways are choked in peak traffic hours, if you can have a picnic with your family in a neighborhood park or feel unsafe to even allow your children to play outdoors, if you can cycle or drive to work with equal ease or feel captive by your transportation choices, if the city's skyline is dotted with pretty houses or covered with unsightly slums; all are a direct outcome of urban planners' work decades ago. The inhabitants of today are merely the consumers of the fait accompli of that work.

But, a city planner's job is also the most unfortunate in the field of engineering. In all other fields of engineering, a prototype is first developed and then put to commercial use. A mechanical engineer first creates a model of a motor, tests it in a laboratory and only then puts it to human use. A computer engineer first designs a processor chip and tests it for performance before it finds its place inside a computing device. However, for an urban planner the inhabitation of cities almost always precedes any actual planning that happens to efficiently manage them.

The early man, with a realization of the advantages of living with others realized virtues of a community living. He learned to pool resources for better outcomes. For instance, it was no longer necessary for every family unit to dig its own well for water, one common water-well for the village was sufficient. Trade and commerce further facilitated his mobility beyond his village, and slowly, village tribes were replaced with kingdoms, which in turn were shaped into townships, as a means of a support system to sustain their lifestyle as well as governing their jurisdictions.

Kingdoms needed palaces, a support system to sustain their lifestyle and buildings to carry out governance of their jurisdictions. Monarchs needed administrators to collect taxes and armed soldiers to guard the borders. They needed noblemen, housekeepers, chefs, stable hands, and concubines to run the daily affairs of the palace. They were an integral part of the ecosystem of the palatial household and thus had to be provided living quarters. This need prompted housing and markets to come up near monarch's seat of power. Soldiers needed weapons, which created a need for smelters and furnaces to make weaponry and giving birth to the defense industry, another purpose for the town's existence. The hobbies of the monarchs also defined the inclinations of towns. If he appreciated art, the town housed painters and their schools. Fourteenth-century Europe saw the rise of the Renaissance period with artists like Da Vinci, Titian, Michelangelo and Botticelli and the art industry was a major urban activity across many towns that owes its emergence to the patronage received from the wealthy and the monarchy. Similarly, Lucknow owes its emergence to the patronage received from Nawab

Wajid Ali Shah, a man of fine taste. His creative pursuits for food, dance and music led to many artists, chefs, concubines and their families to move to Lucknow and make the city their home. The neighborhoods surrounding the Nawab's residential palace housed them to ensure that they were always accessible to attend to the needs of the Nawab. An entire town emerged solely on the recreational pursuits of its ruler.

In other words, cities in premodern times came into existence as an outcome of an immediate need of the respective kingdoms – armed conflicts, tax collection, administration, hobbies of the royalty. These towns housed people who were directly or indirectly involved in the smooth functioning of the kingdom. Rome in Europe, Kannuaj in South Asia, Nanjing in China are a few examples. Almost all major cities of Rajasthan were extensions of the Rajputs' seats of power. A fortress on a hill with clusters of human settlement on the planes surrounding it is a common sight in many cities in Rajasthan. Cities of Bijapur and Ahmadnagar in Deccan hosted political, security, recreational needs of Qutb Shah dynasty and so did Vijayanagar (present-day Hampi) that was an expression of the grandeur of the empire of the Sangama dynasty.

These cities held a magnetic attraction for commerce and scholarly pursuits by virtue of their proximity to the seat of power. It was easy for such opportunities to bloom under the direct shadow of the royal family. The city of Pataliputra (Patna of today), the capital of Magadha empire, is an apt example of this confluence. It was one of the largest cities at the time, a hub of trade, and the center for knowledge: it was home to Chanakya, the great thinker of the time. Under the Maurya dynasty, the city hosted the Greek ambassador Megasthenes, who wrote detailed accounts of the city's grandeur that goes on to suggest that Pataliputra received pampering attention. It was natural for dynasties to beautify their cities as they were symbols of the monarchs' strength and intelligence. However, such cities were small by modern standards. Today, a hamlet in India houses the same number of people as the ancient city of Pataliputra did centuries ago. Cities' primary purpose was restricted to its immediate need to attend to the monarchy. This purpose extended from the palace to the roads that lead to it and the human settlement surrounding the city. If the monarch was benevolent and had a vision about city planning, it was a stroke of luck. Otherwise the emergence of the city was left to the incremental need of the kingdom of that day.

Cross-border trade also gave birth to new cities. Though national borders were loosely defined and frequently changed form and shape, people traveled in search of markets for their produce, craft, or skills. Cities on the map of the silk routes owe their emergence to cross-border trade. Today's cities of Alleppo, Tehran, Tashkent, Almaty, Kabul, Quetta, Patna, and Urumqi, among others, were all part of the erstwhile Silk Route that extended from present-day China to the Middle East and Central Asia. Type of merchandise, trade intensity, and traders' profile determined the purpose of these cities. They bustled with lodgings and eateries to cater to the traveling tradesmen. Ancillary activities, such as warehouses, logistics and carriage services, and moneylending services, mushroomed, although the prosperity of these cities may have fluctuated with the vagaries in the commercial cycle and the stability of the kingdom that governed them.

Cities also emerged from the desire of humans to seek god and pursue knowledge. The city of Varanasi was born out of the human search for salvation and spirituality and does not owe its existence to a kingdom or trade. Temples and shops to support them defined the lanes and streets of Varanasi. People traveled here to lay to rest their dead. Cremation services and supporting infrastructure to deliver on that need became an integral part of this town. The old and terminally ill came here to prepare to meet their maker in the holy city, giving rise to many 'ashrams.' Varanasi's natural connect with god seemed almost contiguous and prompted many scholars or practitioners of music and religious studies to make it their home. Ashrams and religious and music schools started to define the landscape of this city. It is fascinating to imagine the process that determined the locations of temples, houses, shops, and streets in the city. It was not as though the banks of the river Ganga were given to a city planner at some point in time all those centuries ago, who then put temples, schools, houses, and shops in designated places with any predetermined thought and that the later expansion followed his plan. Since the recorded history of the city, people moved there and appropriated space for their pursuits and the holy city of Varanasi took shape.

The impact of industrialization drastically altered the purpose of cities in a short span of time. Within a decade, the city of Detroit in North America transformed from a sleepy hamlet into the largest ship-building center in the region in the nineteenth century. The population of Paris grew almost six times between 1800 and 1900, whereas it had just doubled between 1500 and 1800. Cities emerged from the new wave of human migration and acquired expansive overtones at explosive rates. Industrialization was also the time when the world saw drastic changes in the political establishments. Dynasties gave way to states that were perceptively based on peoples' voices and monarchs lost their right to treat their beloved capitals as a guinea pig for their individual expressions. More importantly, elitist governments began to make way for neoliberal thinking that put the common franchise at the core of its ideology.

City administrators thus saw the challenges of rapidly industrializing cities in a new light. Glaring institutional gaps in governing these cities became apparent. Municipal bodies headed by elected public representatives slowly started to emerge as viable operating models, and by the start of the seventeenth century this model of city governance caught the imagination of many Western cities. Paris appointed its first elected mayor in 1789. But this model of governance was yet to be stress-tested for the onslaught of urbanization in the post-industrial order, when the unplanned and chaotic migration that ensued snowballed into a massive hygiene and sanitation challenge in the First World. The degraded visuals and unbearable stench began to find mention in the writings of literary icons of the time. In 1835, Charles Dickens wrote about the city of London: '[S]treets and courts dart in all directions, until they are lost in the unwholesome vapour which hangs over the house-tops, and renders the dirty perspective uncertain and confined....' Noted British poet, T. S. Eliot, in the early 1920s wrote this about London: 'Unreal City,/ Under the brown fog of a winter dawn,/ A crowd flowed over London Bridge....'

Perhaps for the first time in the history of mankind the lifestyle of city people had started to become the thorn in the state's side. Until then peoples' lives in cities were an outcome of the monarchy's fancy. Never in the past had the local civic bodies been faced with the issue of providing housing to the increasing number of people in their cities. This pushed the cities to expand in a haphazard manner, relying largely on makeshift arrangements and extrapolated wisdom. Seattle, in its modern form, evolved from a congregation of local regions which were controlled by native Indian tribes in the nineteenth century. Early Western settlers in the city during that time came from the Midwest and usurped this arrangement. Once the case of dominance was settled in favor of the new settlers, they began to build the downtown areas of the city, commercial centers, and homes. But the city planning was based on ideas they were accustomed to in the plains back home. Everything from the choice of materials to the civil design approach that was undertaken to build Seattle was at odds with the topography of the city. For instance, Seattle perpetually struggled with the problems of disposing its sewage into the Washington lake for the flawed design of the sewer system. But the city pushed on with its dilapidated framework to accommodate the new arrivals at a fevered pace. And in 1889, a great fire razed the city to the ground.

Interestingly, fires in major cities were a recurring theme in the Western world in the nineteenth century, signifying their mediocre approach to expansion. The Great Chicago Fire in 1871 destroyed nine square kilometers of the city. The 1842 fire in Hamburg destroyed a quarter of its inner city and left many homeless. In 1827 the great fire of Turku destroyed three quarters of the Finnish city. In 1858, the fire in Auckland destroyed most of city's downtown area. The flawed city development exposed these cities to natural disasters as well. The great earthquake of San Francisco in 1906 razed the entire city to the ground. Its ramshackle infrastructure which collapsed like a house of cards was more to blame than the tremors. The floods of 1953 brought the city of Rotterdam to its knees and exposed its vulnerability to its surrounding water bodies.

The spectacular scale of these tragedies gave these cities a chance to contemplate and rebuild. The idea of a city as a thoughtful call was appealing at this stage. Peoples' squalid homes and their dirty surroundings ignited mass housing as a strong political movement, allowing political masters to take charge of the issue.

Europe tilted toward state-sponsored public housing, where local bodies could commission integrated urban redevelopment plans and plug holes that had emerged from the haphazard growth of their cities. This push toward mass formal housing had a direct impact on sanitation. One bold urban planning initiative that proved to be a game changer in sanitation was the 1919 Housing Act of the UK, the brainchild of David Lloyd George, the then prime minister. At the end of World War I, haphazard growth of homes of private landlords defined the urban landscape of UK that housed 80 percent of tenants in the UK. These cluttered cities applied little thought to the balance between public and private spaces, the need for space and transport, to the criticality of sewage systems and to the right design of industrial and commercial areas.

The Act exposed the relationship between bad urban design and sanitation. It provided subsidies to local bodies to build homes, called council homes, for the masses. New residential neighborhoods emerged that were designed to correct the inadequacy of the past, complete with spaces for gardens and markets, roads and pavements, sewage system, And access to public transport, schools, and clinics. Steadily, the urban landscape of the UK changed from squalid, cramped, and old to a modern one with a string of well-appointed neighborhoods.

However, the impact of public housing in cleaning the city was limited to residential neighborhoods or suburbs where these houses were built. The rest, like downtown, commercial establishments, harbors, and markets, still remained dirty due to the lack of a comprehensive urban plan that could set them up for the next five decades. This meant dislocation, discontinuity, and disruption. Such pressures lead to the realization that urban planning, besides being a technical subject, is also a political process. Cities needed a strong political narrative to undertake such a disruptive urban renewal intervention, but citizens were not exposed to the alternate reality it promised.

How could they have been? They had never seen anything besides the squalid cities they were born in, with the misery of urban life of commoners becoming more unbearable with every passing day. But, political leadership was preparing to bite the bullet and two telltale signs highlight the political convergence in the Western world for urban renewal during the time. First, the number of Western cities that concurrently underwent a comprehensive urban planning exercise during the period between the second half of the nineteenth century and the first half of the twentieth century is astounding. Georges-Eugène Haussmann was commissioned by Napoleon III in 1850 to redesign Paris and rid it of the medieval slums that dotted the city. Daniel Burnham developed the Burnham Plan for Chicago in 1909 and comprehensively imagined the city as a picture of mass transit systems, systematic patterns of roads, and space for civic institutions and parks. He also worked on such a plan for Cleveland and Washington, D.C. The second sign was the intellectual leadership on urban planning that blossomed at the start of the twentieth century elevated the subject to a stature of holistic reverence. In 1898, Sir Ebenezer Howard in the UK wrote a pathbreaking book *To-Morrow: A Peaceful Path to Real Reforms*, which initiated the garden city movement. He can perhaps be called the first theorist on urban planning, who imagined a utopian city where humans would live harmoniously with nature. His ideas became an integral part of urban development plans of the cities of Letchworth and Welwyn over the next two decades. Cities in Ohio, Wisconsin, and Maryland in the USA also adopted these ideas. His work laid the ground for the subject of urban planning to eventually evolve from an almost entirely technical exercise into a social movement. His ideas pushed town planners out of their slumber, and brought them the realization that they have been short selling their subject all this while. The underlying theme of Howard's spark was that economics, social contracts, people's rights and purpose, ecology, public health, and culture needed to be dovetailed into urban plans.

Essentially, three questions became the central theme to visions of these cities – the relationship between dirty surroundings and public health; the distance traveled by people from their place of work to their residence, which lead to informal living (slums); and the balance between urbanized humans and nature. These themes represented a significant departure from the pre-industrialized world, where cities were largely manifestations of the monarch's whims. These questions represented the common man's purpose in the city and became the lynchpin of future urban planning exercises. The common man became the central character to the urban plans and acquired a powerful political narrative at the start of the twentieth century, and urban planners received patronage from the political establishment. Cities, particularly in the US, became synonymous with their planners – George Kessler with Kansas City, Daniel Burnham with Chicago, John Nolen with Madison and San Diego, and Doc Maynard with Seattle. They also started to acquire a political stature of their own, one of the most famous being the Swiss-French architect Le Corbusier. This was a great triumph for urban planning and that set just the right tempo for Western cities to become symbols of cleanliness in the coming decades.

This is when World War II broke out. It is ironic that from the ruins of one of the greatest human tragedies of modern times has emerged one of the key reasons for today's clean First World. Following the War cities such as Paris, London, Berlin, Tokyo went through massive cycles of urban redevelopment. Urban planners got an opportunity to rebuild cities, and in turn homes for those who lost everything due to the War, almost from scratch, who, with their newly acquired political stature, lapped up this intellectual challenge, and in this way, past mistakes were corrected. New urban plans were transformational and envisaged cities five decades hence. Urban areas were experimented with formal mixed-use developments of shops, homes, and offices in the same neighborhoods thus optimizing space and convenience. Streets were widened for an anticipated increase in automobiles and public transport in the future. Public transport systems were given a massive boost. Sewage infrastructure was upgraded and redesigned as a grid that was modular and reached every consumption unit in the city. Smooth flow of electricity, water, and waste management services were kept in mind while redesigning spaces for public amenities.

There was political and social urgency to undertake rehabilitation of the people who lost their homes during World War II but urban planners did not deprioritize other goals. They did not buckle under this pressure and lose sight of the fact that the city's design should stand the test of time fifty years hence, rather than solely focus on the more immediate of putting a roof over the head of those rendered homeless at any cost. Sir Leslie Patrick Abercrombie's Greater London Plan of 1944, which later came to be known as the Abercrombie Plan, is a worthy example of this blueprint for the post-war replanning of London. Over seven decades ago he imagined the Heathrow airport in its current avatar, the complex web of London's public transport system, the open spaces that provide for a peaceful life, and the cross pollination of industry and housing that ensure a convenient existence. Such was the social and political impact of this exercise that Abercrombie featured in a film called *The Proud City*, wherein he is shown presenting the Plan to the public. The Plan became a prelude to the urban planning deluge in the post World War II cities of the Western world, South America, and even parts of Asia, and became one of the key contributing factors for these cities to remain clean till today. The Plan symbolized that the long-term goals of urban planning should never be compromised for short-term needs.

However, not all cities were planned the same way post World War II. Cities like Paris and Berlin were designed to preserve and promote their heritage in harmony with functionality, whereas cities like Seattle and Tokyo took a modern view. Beneath these different exteriors lay many commonalities. These cities were designed with a grand, long-term vision of several decades into the future and not solely to address the most pressing needs of that time. For instance, the Abercrombie plan for the city of London did not lose sight of the immediate need to redevelop London from the ruins of WW2 yet it had the foresight to re-imagine public housing, a mega airport and a public transport system that could stand the test of time. Patrick Abercrombie could have as well shunned air travel for it was still a discretionary choice for a few and paid little heed to the need for a giant airport in the future. But putting a giant airport in his scheme of things did not deprioritize public housing or public transport for the city. The Abercrombie Plan reflects a strong sense of purpose that occupied the minds of urban planners then. For instance, it acknowledged the criticality of mass (or public) housing to keep the cities clean and efficient. The concept of public housing was built into the city's plans at a time when the idea was just in its nascence. Similarly, public spaces like parks, museums, sport arenas in citys' plans were not a crying need of the public but were ideas that germinated from urban planners' imagination. The citizens were more concerned with survival, employment, and making their ends meet in the hard life of the city. But urban planners understood that clean and adequate public spaces would be central to a happy existence in the city. To take such decisions on behalf of people who would live in these cities much after the planners' lifespan presumably instilled a deep sense of purpose in them. This mind-set of urban planners ring-fenced urban plans from incremental thinking and shielded their plans from the vagaries of short-term considerations and temperamental tweaks.

By the time the World War II was over, the science of urban planning had gained nearly five decades of experience in designing and re-designing cities in the industrialized world. Urban planners by then didn't restrict themselves to being viewed as technocrats but considered themselves social scientists armed with the technical knowledge to design a city. They viewed themselves as guardians of the interests of the common man, philosophers or champions of equality. Philosophy, ecology, public health, economics and art constantly inspired them to think about the city in the present and in the future. They even took political stances to dovetail these views into their design plans. Concepts like libertinism, socialism, free-will, and environmental protection had started to make way into design plans of cities in the western world much before World War II. The initiation of the Garden City movement by Sir Howard dovetailed ecology with urban living in 1898. A few decades before the World War II, the community of urban planners came to a consensus that imagining the life in a city fifty to hundred years ahead should be the primary purpose of urban planning. Such intellectual maturity on the subject translated into ideas, research and fascinating results in First-World cities before the start of World War II. By the time the war was over, the thought leadership had created a strong shield around the idea of urban planning which did not allow it to fall prey to the unidimensional pressure of post-war re-habilitation priorities. Political activism of urban planners also ensured this protection. They took upon themselves to communicate the vision of the city to its people. They ran for public offices, held important posts that gave them direct supervision and control and raised the stature of urban planners to public heroes. Though not every famous urban planner was a purist. Many of them held polarizing views and led a controversial existence. But it was a small price to pay to protect the critical role of urban planning for the future sustainability of cities. The elevation of the job of urban planning in public perception allowed the injection of imagination, free thinking and a futuristic outlook into the job. This created a strong foundation and protected it from populist fascinations and blinkered tendencies.

Urban planning recognized the relationship between the city's sanitation levels and the adequacy of planned physical spaces (public and private) within cities. The rapid rise of slums in the city was a direct outcome of more people moving in for better economic prospects. Imagine a city that is designed for only a thousand homes. There are roads, shops, hospitals and schools to cater to them. They are also connected with underground sewer lines to haul solid human waste. The city has public spaces big enough to support these homes. There is just about enough economic activity that ensures a harmonious existence for them. Suddenly the city discovers gold. This brings nearly fifty thousand people from neighboring towns to the city in the hope to hit pay dirt. The new arrivals require another ten thousand new homes but there are none. They erect makeshift tents public places and on the outskirts. They cook and sleep in there, relieve themselves in the open space nearby and hitch rides to move around in the city in search for the promised gold. Another set of migrants comprising hundreds of shopkeepers and other service providers sense an economic opportunity of providing ancillary support to the newly arrived gold diggers in the city, as the news of the rush spreads. These new migrants also move in and erect make-shift businesses to sell merchandise and other services. In no time, retailing, transport, logistics, and other utilities for the new comers are tended to by a parallel informal infrastructure that runs concurrent with the formal infrastructure of the city. But the city's urban plan was designed for only a thousand homes. This meant that the roads, sewers, utilities, public spaces which were sufficient only for the inhabitants of these thousand homes, starts to crumble. Is, then, gold rush to be blamed for the crumbling infrastructure, or the urban planning of the city that failed to anticipate it?

The First-World cities understood the urgency to tackle human migration to cities. They needed adequate arrangements for public housing and transport, utility services, and commercial and public spaces to account for the human rush well in time. Vision documents of these cities imbibed this learning and offered design responses for all such anticipated human movements in future. What will be the economic drivers of a city? What kind of jobs will provide employment? Where will people live and work? How will people travel from their homes to their places of work? Where will the children play? How will people move around in the city? How will they consume products and buy merchandise? How will the children grow up, start their own families and move out of their parents' homes? In the post World War II scenario, these cities were armed with enough technical prowess and wisdom to deal with these questions well in advance and played a significant role in weeding out informal living from the urbanization discourse of their cities.

Kevin Lynch, regarded as one among the greatest American urban planners of the twenty-first century, further pushed urban planning's boundary when he wrote the pathbreaking book, *The Image of the City*, in 1960. The book, among its many pioneering ideas, talks about the relationship between city planning and the behavior (collective and individual) of its inhabitants. It provoked urban planners to think deeply about the factors that will influence peoples' actions in times to come, as core to their methodology on urban plans signifying the coming of age of urban planning in the clean countries of today and yielded spectacular results.

If an area in a city has the potential to become a hotspot of high public movement on foot then that area was accorded with wide footpaths, benches, resting places, and parks. The thrust on public housing was specifically intended to eradicate slum dwelling from urban living. Taking public transport facilities to each doorstep removed congestion and checked the emergence of illegal and unsafe means of transportation, and by design created convenient, safe, and clean surroundings. Formal public transport options removed non-desirable pedestrian or private vehicle movements from the road and created space for congestion-free, clean, and safe surrounding without compromising on the capacity of the city to handle the growing urban population. Harmony between public transport and roads created proportionate spaces for vehicular traffic and pedestrians. Pavements were designed in sync with access to public transport systems like buses and railways. They were conceived keeping in mind the high-density human movement on foot and had waste disposal bins at frequent intervals, walking paths covered with tiles, authorized entry and exit points to safely cross the road, and underpasses at road intersections at places where high human congregation was anticipated. Such measures were not by chance, but a result of philosophical thinking about urban planning that the likes of Kevin Lynch championed.

The First World's urban planners in the post World War II era also took the lead in shaping the behavior of their urban inhabitants, while the western countries urbanized at a rapid pace. These urban planners confronted an interesting question: What should be a model behavior of urban living? Can city designs play an active role to cultivate such a model behavior? But, urban planners were also humans with emotions and opinions. Expectedly, the subject of urban planning flirted with political thinking. Many urban planners emerged as strong political personalities and enjoyed tremendous clout. City planning decisions of many of them played a key role in shaping peoples' existence in an urban setting. Robert Moses, an American public official, was one such personality who held tremendous sway on the city of New York for nearly four decades before and after World War II. He played a significant role in the way the city looks today: the parks, public areas, bridges, and road designs owe their existence to Moses. But he was also one of the most polarizing and controversial public figures in North America. He was among the principal figures responsible for America's reliance on personal automobiles as the primary (and in many cases possibly the only) mode of transport today. He introduced the system of collecting toll taxes for the use of roads as a powerful tool to boost the financial autonomy of New York's local municipal body. His decision to build toll roads shaped the urban behavior of future American generations. He represents that breed of urban planners who combined the technical exercise of urban planning with political heft (though he never held an elected office) that converted these plans into reality. In other words, design calls made by powerful individuals played a key role in shaping the model behavior of urban living in the First World. Though many of these calls in retrospect can be argued for better or for worse.

But from the 1980s, the culture of personality-driven urban planning exercise in the First World made way to an institution-driven approach. Cults made way for partisan approach toward urban planning and participative processes replaced individual thinking. But eight decades of passionate leadership of strong individuals had added a tremendous reverence to the job. Their personalities, personal lives, and polarizing views notwithstanding, their immense contribution gave the profession the due importance well in time, which was critical for the cities of the First World to rise to the challenge of urbanization. For argument's sake, if these cities had started with a partisan approach to urban planning, they too would have turned out to be a case of too many cooks spoil the broth, like it happened in New Delhi as we shall see a little later. Strong individual leadership and intellectual capacity of urban planners at the start of the process of redeveloping or designing cities in the twentieth century created a strong foundation for the job of urban planning. This personality-centric leadership created blueprints that eventually went on to create efficient, clean, and beautiful cities. Their heft offered a strong reference point that created a filtrate of non-negotiable tenets upon which to build clean, sustainable cities. Therefore, by the end of the twentieth century the job of urban planning in the Western world became a well-oiled process in a plug-and-play mode, ready for an institutional response.

What were these non-negotiable tenets? The political statement of the city design notwithstanding, urban planners in the First World recognized the importance of public housing as an integral part of their city plans. Until public housing is at the heart of the urban plans, the city will remain a growing swath of slums, was the overpowering thought among urban planners. Planners also recognized important causation between public transportation (mass transit systems, footpaths included) and the city's ability to keep itself clean. Dovetailing economic activity (anticipated job generation source) with housing, provisioning for public places, and balancing ecology within the city were other important tenets recognized for their role in determining a city's clean or dirty future.

Modularity was also another important tenet incorporated in urban designs and championed by the planners, which allowed cities to be looked at as 'lego' blocks or an array of smaller sized units. Each smaller sized unit was designed as a mini city and provisioned for a few houses, shops, hotels, hospitals, schools, size of the road, type of public transport, parks, neighborhoods, and such. Modularity gave rise to suburbs in American cities and allowed rapid redevelopment to be incorporated as a key element in the urban plans.

Space in a city cannot be locked for purposeless activity because that adds stress on the city's land pool for its growing basket of needs. If any asset on a land parcel outlives its stated purpose, it should make way for a new asset that can serve a better purpose. The merit is in the purpose, not in the economic value. In a rational world, the two should essentially mean the same thing, but not in the asymmetrical world that confronts urban planning. A park, a lake, or a forest in a city has a purpose, so does a community center, a crèche, or a museum but their purpose cannot be evaluated in economic terms. If economic value is the sole criterion to choose a purpose in the city then a forest trail or a park will rarely make the cut and find space in any urban narrative. Vast stretches of land that house a cluster of badly designed under-occupied homes is purposeless, but possess high economic value. So does a thermal power plant that is no longer in use because the city switched over to a more sustainable form of electricity generation. It is the job of the urban planners to ensure that the importance of timely redevelopment and repurposing is not undermined. Urban planners in the First World effectively used the redevelopment tool to keep the city relevant with changing times and to ensure that it delivers on all its intended purposes, those of survival, ecological balance, and aspirations. The Tate Art Gallery in London, for instance, that opened in 2004 on the bank of the Thames was developed in a defunct thermal power plant, making a powerful modern statement for the future generations while preserving the industrial heritage of the city. The gallery receives 5 million visitors annually (compared to all of India that receives around 8 million tourists annually).

It is not as though urban planning in the First World managed to tick all the boxes or achieved utopian standards. One of the biggest misses of urban planning in the First World was the failure to appreciate the emergence of diversity in their societies in forthcoming decades. They accounted only for racially homogenous human groups, not the existing heterogeneity, and were ignorant about the inevitable social diversity that future generations would embrace.

The unfortunate trajectory of the city of Detroit that started from World War II and continuing till today failed to address the challenges of racial diversity that existed at the time. Today, Detroit is a case study on 'urban ruins.' Similarly, failure to appreciate the emergence of multicultural groups in the urban narrative led to the 'ghettoization' of neighborhoods in cities. Black, White, and Latino neighborhoods dot suburbs of many American cities. London, today, resembles chunks of ghettos stitched together. People from Turkish, Polish, Indian, Pakistani, Somalian, Nigerian, and Russian ghettoes rarely mingle for a multicultural living. The story of Paris is not very different from that of London, as it also failed to absorb ethnic people who migrated from erstwhile French colonies. Urban design crowded out native Indians from their lands in North America and reduced them to living on the fringes.

Despite these shortcomings, urban planning in the First World unanimously succeeded on two counts that contributed immensely toward its clean existence. The first success was to implement the mass housing agenda that sucked out all forms of informal living. Second, was to position itself as a holistic science with dogmatic procedures, guidelines and codes that governed all forms of human movement within the city. Every anticipated human action was responded to with an urban design intervention – a planning exercise that left no form of human movement to chance and individual whims. There were pavements where there were pedestrians, there were formal shops where retailing was anticipated and there were public spaces to address high human density. Urban planning's triumph in the First World was its ideological and operational transformation. Sanitation and cleanliness were among the many other fruits of this triumph.

The Indian urban planning journey, however, was not so fortunate. Colonial rulers developed Indian cities in the post-industrial world. Prior to this, cities were primarily an extension of the monarch's seat of power or were trading or religious hubs, as was the case in the rest of the world. Some monarchs were visionaries and had a penchant for town planning, like Sawai Man Singh II, who passionately designed and built Jaipur, and gave it broad roads, pavements, and public places. During the colonial rule, creation of cantonment areas birthed new cities like Bengaluru, Meerut, Ambala, Kanpur, Secunderabad, Trichy, and so on. Retail and commerce expanded the urban influence of these cities into neighboring rural areas. Cities then emerged as a direct outcome of being seats of power for the British, to rule over India's vast land mass. Kolkata, Chennai, and New Delhi acquired urban character by virtue of serving this purpose. Slowly these cities developed a character of their own and expanded during the colonial rule. By the start of the twentieth century, trading and commerce in textile and commodities grew and cities like Nagpur, Coimbatore, Ahmedabad, Ludhiana, and Mumbai emerged as important industrial hubs. Some cities also saw sporadic growth driven by migration under duress. For instance, rural distress caused by the Bengal famine of 1943 forced many people to move to cities for survival. Having said that, in the 1900s less than 5 percent of India's approximately 150 million people lived in cities. In other words, these needs were weak factors for urbanization and hardly made a dent in the predominantly rural character of India.

India inherited an infantile experience base to design and build cities unlike the First World, that had by now garnered decades of experience in this regard. India lay at such a juncture that even its independent existence was shrouded in doubt. The strong rural leanings of the political establishment also played its part in undermining the connect between urban planning and nation building. In the the 1940s and 1950s, planning cities was of much less importance than issues of communal harmony, integration of states into the Union, land reforms, farmer rights, and green revolution.

The first urbanization challenge hit India right at the time of Independence: the largest human mass migration in the recorded history of the world, of nearly 14 million, as a result of the Partition. People who migrated to India ended up in concentrated pockets on the outskirts of various cities of Punjab, Delhi, Rajasthan, Madhya Pradesh, Gujarat, West Bengal, Assam, and Maharashtra in makeshift camps, putting tremendous stress on the infrastructure of these cities. The union government created a Ministry of Rehabilitation to oversee permanent and immediate dwelling for the thousands of refugees in these camps. The obvious solution was to provide plots of land on urban outskirts. For the fortunate, colonies of independent houses sprang up on the outskirts of many Indian cities, whereas the less fortunate were packed in hastily built, cramped houses in other areas of the urban outskirts. This rehabilitation approach was not part of the grand urban plan of these cities and without precedence. Given the circumstances, the work done by public representatives was commendable, particularly that of Mehr Chand Khanna, a refugee himself, who served as the Minister for Rehabilitation in Nehru's cabinet from 1954 to 1962. However, in the process many Indian cities became unwittingly addicted to the plotted approach to city planning. It was the worst start urban India could make, right at the cusp of realizing its urban character.

Urban planning started to troubleshoot and landed in the short-term planning trap. City plans could only muster the foresight to envision formal spaces to cater to the immediate population which lived in the city in the present tense, as was the planning approach of the colonial masters. When faced with rehabilitation pressures, it created quick fixes only to confront the next set of pressure points. From the 1960s onwards, the thrust on refugee rehabilitation abated, but the experience of rehabilitation left Indian cities with some very bad habits. They could only imagine expanding the city by distributing new land parcels for migrants, while the supply of the relevant real estate was left to the individuals who owned the land. Under this free market approach, revenue earned through taxes from piecemeal transactions of land supply within the Indian cities became the single most important revenue source for Indian urban local bodies. We know that the infant Indian democracy rebooted local civic bodies and sucked out much of their autonomy. The local bodies savored tax revenues from land transactions because it was the only significant act to testify to their autonomous existence. But in this autonomy was mere lip service to the cause of the strong grass-root democratic leanings. The defectively designed local civic bodies quickly interpreted supply of real estate as a revenue-maximizing tool. Thus, the weakest member (local civic bodies) of the Indian state held the most sway over the urban planning agenda and suffocated the process of designing Indian cities effectively. Urban planning designed cities to serve this primary purpose so as to maximize revenue for local bodies. This unidimensional view misguided the urban planning exercise and restricted its scope. Unlike the First World, where urban planning became a champion of individual rights and of the state's duty toward the environment, urban planning in India became hostage to funding the existence of the weakest member of India's infant democratic set-up. This arrangement kept urban planners from imbibing and acting upon issues that were soon poised to cause trouble to urban India.

This unidimensional view about Indian cities was not totally unreasonable given the context of that time. Back then these cities were just big enough to house the 'privileged' who willingly lived there. Vehicular traffic on the roads was sparse, roads were good enough, drainage systems too were adequate and there were sanitation workers to keep the surroundings clean. To support the privileged – schoolteachers, doctors, traders, businessmen, journalists, lawyers, employees of government and public-sector enterprises – and ensure comfortable living, the not-so-privileged lot – gardeners, cooks, drives, sanitation workers – moved to the cities. Refugees from the Partition were rehabilitated, and life was simple and predictable with a 'Hindu' rate of economic growth. Compared to the 90 percent of rural Indians, these Indian urbanites were indeed a privileged lot. Electricity brightened their homes, and plumbing brought them running water. They bicycled and walked on tarred roads and lived comfortably in the knowledge that healthcare was never far. They sent their children to schools and talked to each other over telephones. The strong agrarian leanings of the political class were sincerely challenged to think about this urban living as anything but a privilege. How could parks, roads, broad pavements, museums and housing in the city take priority when the folks in villages were in distress, facing starvation and other existential threats? How could urban plans think about airports, when bullock carts and tongas were the primary mode of transportation to connect villages to cities? How could cities be planned for roads when owning a four-wheel vehicle was a far-fetched dream and Sanjay Gandhi's maverick idea to build a people's car was still a few decades away?

Urban planners, however, did not anticipate the future and wrongly deduced that this state of affairs would continue for perpetuity. What should be the state's approach to public housing in cities? How should cities respond to migrants? What is expected to drive the city's economy and what impact will it have on the profile of its inhabitants? What kind of spaces will be required to support diverse economic activities? How should commuters in Indian cities travel to their place of work and what should be India's approach to urban transport? How should cities allocate space to preserve their individual culture and create ecological balance? How should Indian cities deliver a healthy life to their habitants as a basic right? These seemingly operational questions needed a philosophical and moral rigor and missed the check list of Indian urban planning during that time.

A well-designed city becomes a basic civil right of an individual because as we shall see, the urban design plans have a direct bearing on public health. But, to live an ecologically balanced life in the city is also an explicit duty of an individual which translates into healthy living. What should be the urban planning approach to balance the two? Let's say a city comprises a natural water body. Conservation of the water body in its natural form is not only the duty of the citizens but through its preservation they are staking claim to their individual rights to a healthy life. A design response that can reconcile the two will mean that the immediate space around the water body should be planned in the form of walking and cycling trails, nature parks and no-go zones for any human activity. Spaces for any economic activity should not be ear marked within the primary and the secondary catchment area. Urban plans should make appropriate sewage systems and provisions for waste collection and disposal to ensure no waste is dumped in the water body. Residences in the vicinity should be designed so as not to be hazardous to the lake.

But, since the start of the twenty-first century, lakes in the city of Bengaluru have been witnessing a series of unusual events. Water bodies in the city have been frothing with foul smelling white form that envelopes the city every now and then. This is the result of the industrial and residential effluents discharged into these water bodies. This sorry state bears sad testimony to the fact that Bengaluru's urban planning a few decades ago was devoid of the intellectual bandwidth to critically examine its role in protecting civil rights and defining duties of citizens in the city. Planners could not even anticipate that this cantonment city with narrow roads and no pavements will be home to droves of migrants from all over the country by the turn of the century, and emerge as the silicon valley of the East. To expect farsightedness on the future of its lakes was a rather tall order. This is a moral dilemma for urban planners, one by way of rights, and the other by way of duty. But, the testosterone-driven development of the city of Bengaluru bull dozed this morality in a rush to accommodate its hordes of new comers, creating a new benchmark of urban mess instead. Real estate assets became a freely tradeable economic unit. The areas of the city which had sewage lines, parks, electricity and water connections and broad roads commanded a premium. Areas that lacked these went for cheaper rates. Property changed hands among urban residents and their extended families. For every real estate transaction, the local body earned revenue through taxes. Such piece meal real estate transactions fueled the addictive dependence of local bodies on real-estate monetization and constantly pushed planners to serve this purpose. Consequently, urban planning began to be viewed from the unidimensional lens of incremental real estate supply in the city and Bengaluru exemplifies it in full glory.

Some of the thrust of urbanization in the 1960s came about from Nehru's policy of 'modern temples' of India that saw the growth of higher education, industry, and trade. Industrial towns like Bhilai, Bokaro, and Kharagpur came into existence. Cities like Bhopal changed its character with the establishment of BHEL. Kolkata and Mumbai became home to automobile plants. New employment opportunities opened in these cities and prompted more people to move in for better prospects. This fueled the need for more homes in cities, but urban planners supplied them with empty plots to build houses on. From here arose the thought of mass housing projects as a more efficient means of creating housing than selling empty plots of land to individuals. The Delhi Development Authority (DDA) was formed in 1958, and Avas Vikas Nigam in Uttar Pradesh in 1965. On the other hand, cities like Mumbai allowed private real-estate players to create this supply and began to grow vertically. Even with all these efforts, urban planning was merely trying to catch up to the rapidly evolving urbanization of India because such responses were not a part of the grand urban vision but a reaction to the urgent need to address the rising migration to the cities. Such projects were not townships but a cluster of houses located in far flung areas. It took decades for a full array of utility services to reach these homes, not to mention the sheer inadequacy of the installed operational capability to meet the growing mass housing demand. To compound the misery, these 'mass housing' developments were exposed to free market economics without any caveats. Soon these homes were freely changing hands and going to the highest bidder, resulting in a widening chasm between the true need for these houses and their ownership, making them prohibitively unaffordable to the majority of the folk headed to the cities. Not only was the supply of mass housing short, whatever housing that was created could be freely traded and won by the highest bidder. But, in the process urban planning did well to serve its master – the local civic bodies by keeping the supply of real estate coming at full steam.

Urbanization has a unique ability to generate a multiplier effect. When a section of people moves to cities, they bring with them myriad needs. They need shops to buy groceries and clothes. They need drug stores and hospitals to take care of their health. They need schools and colleges to send their children to and they require taxis, rickshaws and buses to move around in the city. They need temples, churches and mosques to offer prayers. The affluent need a support system of domestic staff. The city requires sanitation workers to collect and dispose waste, policemen to provide security. These needs create their own ecosystem of infrastructure and open up opportunities for more people to move to cities to cater to these needs. Maids and gardeners come to the cities to find jobs in homes; priests, to manage places of worship. Shopkeepers open shop and sell merchandise.

When people move to the city to provide for the needs of urban citizens, they in turn need shelter and their own ecosystem that can cater to their daily needs of education, health, food and clothing. A cycle of such interdependencies eventually flows to the smallest actor in the chain. The presence of this last actor – a rag picker, a rickshaw puller, ensures a smooth and cost effective existence of other actors. Eventually every actor in the city starts to justify the existence of the others in this intertwined existence. But the simplistic approach of India urban planning to sell plots of lands for homes and to create overpriced 'mass housing' was woefully inadequate in addressing this complexity.

Urban planning was fixated with the assumption that Indian cities are homogenous clusters comprising people in formal occupations. These homes delivered through plotted, developed and 'public' housing programs were freely changing hands and going to the highest bidder, resulting in a widening chasm between need and ownership and did no more than to position housing as a speculative real estate asset in urban India. This is the point when Indian cities started to get sucked into an abyss of informality. The unequal economic chasm between different regions of the country, the heterogeneity of inhabitants who arrived in cities, and the rapid rise of cities as economic hotspots needed a segmented mass housing response on a massive scale. Think about a taxi driver who decides to move to the city because of his inextricable role in the city. But, where will he and his family live? Where will he park his taxi after hours? Is there an affordable home in the city he can buy? But, urban planning never appreciated the presence of such an interdependent diversity amongst the populace. Consequently, with every passing decade, Indian cities created more formal living spaces for a shrinking segment of urban population.

Assume for a moment a bazaar where every single shop only sells mithai – Indian sweets. No other shops are allowed in the bazaar.

Inhabitants only have access to this bazaar and are expected to buy mithai for all their needs. But, this excessive sweet binge is not tenable and neither is this weird arrangement. People need salt in their lives for sanity. They need clothes, toys and many other non-food products for daily living but the bazaar does not cater to these needs. Because it is impossible to override the bazaar's dictate, informal living comes to the rescue of the neighborhood and starts to cater to the other needs through shops in shanties. Their non-explicit existence allows them the safety cover to serve the neighborhood and to conduct brisk business with impunity. Soon, the entire neighborhood wakes up to the reality of its survival on the subaltern existence of informal commerce. India's urban planning is much like having only mithai shops. It created a housing supply that was no different, while what it needed was diverse mass houses, not unlike having different kinds of shops catering to various needs. The glaring gap marked the onset of uninterrupted growth of informal living (slums and shanties) in urban India as a parallel way of life, which thrives for the lack of state response. Everything from houses to shops, from schools to access to utility services gets created without a formal state response on a landmass that was demarcated by urban plans for some other use or with an undefined purpose.

Till the 1970s, there was hardly any attempt to acknowledge the existence of informal living in cities. Dharavi, in Mumbai, which is now an over-analyzed case study, resulted from this apathy. Dharavi came into existence in the 1890s, when the small village at the same place took up leather tanning. Mumbai was perhaps India's first city to keep up with the global urbanization trend driven by industrialization and saw the influx of the working class to the city at the turn of the twentieth century. But the supply of formal housing in the city (in spite of the chawls) was not sufficient to keep up to the housing demand. Living in slums became the next best alternative, and Dharavi changed from a tanning village to a slum dwelling. Until Independence, one can understand the British government's lax attitude to the expansion of the slums here. But in the period between 1947 and 1970 there was no political or administrative initiative that attempted to find a formal alternative to Dharavi or to understand the negative impact of its growth on the health, sanitation, and the environment of the city. By the mid-1970s, Dharavi started to expand at a rapid pace. But it was not before 1978 that the Government of Maharashtra recognized the urgent need of affordable housing in the cities and formed the Maharashtra Housing and Area Development Authority (MHADA). This body was primarily responsible to redevelop slums and create formal supply of affordable homes in the city. But the 2016 performance review of the MHADA's efficacy since its inception conveyed that the towering agenda of mass housing was way beyond its capability. In all, the MHADA managed to build 30,000 homes in Mumbai that could pack 150,000 people at best. During the same period, the population that lived in the Mumbai slums increased from nearly 1.5 million in 1980 to 6 million in 2016. Clearly, the policy that supervised the supply of affordable homes in Mumbai was woefully inadequate to meet the housing demand of the migrating population. In 2016, Mumbai recorded an unsold inventory of 0.3 million ready-to-move-in homes without any buyers. These houses were enough to provide decent permanent shelter to nearly 1.5 million citizens. But there were no takers for these homes because they were horrendously mis-priced for the masses. The role played by urban planning in imagining the profile of these homes – that of maximizing revenue for the local body through real-estate transaction than to incentivize a real estate industry that could become a reliable vendor of rightly priced mass housing units in the city – needs to be questioned.

How did the urban planners visualize the Mumbai of today, few decades ago, for this missed opportunity and colossal waste to have occurred? They should have thought about building formal solutions into the city's design plans, which could have been aplenty had the urban planners been of the right disposition to seek them out. For instance, slum living is not free living but tenants pay rent to non-state actors who have built these dwellings on encroached land or built these tenements without guidelines. It was easy to improvise upon the chawl system and develop it into formal affordable housing solution for the city. By way of the chawls, Mumbai created an efficient urban housing model that championed community living at the turn of the twentieth century and is arguably the first instance of creating formal working-class neighborhoods in the discourse of India's urbanism. Chawls created private spaces for individual pursuits and public spaces for shared resources. The urban planners should have modified the chawl into a smart community living concept as a sustainable solution for Mumbai's emerging needs. The state could have treated each chawl as one giant urban unit that can be plugged easily into the city's grid for utilities like water, electricity, and waste management services. Instead, the concept of chawls was shunned on the drawing board as some sort of a vestige of colonial past and with it mass affordable housing in Mumbai lost the only formal solution it had to fight the proliferation of informality.

Here is the thing with informality in a city: The more it proliferates the more it becomes indispensable to the formal part of the city. Its existence may fall flat on the barometer of human dignity, but human dignity be damned. The factor that contributed to the growth of slums in Mumbai was its economic value to the existence of the formal part of the city. The Mumbai slum metamorphosed into a self-sufficient set-up within a formal city. On the face, it may appear to be a filthy congregation of cheap labor force, but its very existence is the foundation upon which the formal city of Mumbai exists today. The informal city artificially suppresses labor costs, allows local government bodies to shun their responsibilities toward them and provide supporting infrastructure to the formal part of the city to thrive as an assisted economy.

Informality lives in city spaces that are invisible to urban plans. It is not entitled to receive anything from the formal city – access to waste management, parks, schools, clean water, roads, electricity. But urban plans cannot stop the forces of economics from manifesting themselves in physical forms. It offers support to the formal city's comfortable existence for an economic value that scores miserably on contracts but high on cost competitiveness. Mumbai's slums manifest low-cost labor force in informal jobs, such as masonry, handicraft, carpentry, that are paid without any tax to the state, job security or adherence to minimum standards of workplace safety to the employee – all proxies for fractured contracts. But, they encompass low-cost labor force – a maid at home, a security guard at the gate, a courier boy in a logistic company, a construction worker on a building site, a cook on a road side eatery and make the city living of formal inhabitants surprisingly comfortable and affordable.

Mumbai's slums magically make the waste disappear by absorbing discarded vehicles, water bottles, car batteries and old mobile phones in their narrow lanes and in dingy processing centers that engage in crude and dangerous processing techniques and host honest businesses like fabrication, masonry, handicraft, carpentry and many others. However, in discharging these roles, the slums silently pollute its surroundings, harbor myriad cottage industries of adulterated and spurious food trade, and unsafe transport.

But why should the state go after such informality when its presence in the city checked so many boxes? A cheap alternative to a more formal solution that the state failed to design, one which could challenge the cost competitiveness without compliance offered by informal living. Why should the formal inhabitants of the city rebel against the existence of informal living when it makes their lives in private spaces cheaper, more comfortable and less inconvenient? Informal living may be dirty, miserable and ugly but it provides efficient alternatives sans taxes, regulations, and dignity. So what if it has some unsavory side effects like undignified human existence without sewage, stress on environment, stink, child labor and lack of utilities.

Informal living in Mumbai became a conveniently acceptable equilibrium for all stakeholders. By the 1990s, Dharavi was counted among the world's largest slum clusters. With this disastrous achievement, Mumbai unknowingly provided a sort of undesirable template for other Indian cities that were rapidly getting urbanized. Mumbai gave these cities enough reasons not to view slums as a catastrophic outcome for sanitation, public health, and cleanliness.

A slum is an efficient response to an economic need of a locality. Every slum location thus denotes a failure of urban planning. Every formal living cluster in the city requires an ecosystem of support (markets, transport, waste collection and recycling, housekeeping, repairs, laundry). Either the city's design plan allows for this ecosystem or it will be catered to by informality. Indian urban planning never had a design response to these ubiquitous needs, thus no Indian city can claim to be slum free. Pick any formal living in any city in India and an informal living cluster will come as an essential addendum with it, in the vicinity.

The 2011 Census estimated that nearly one-quarter of the population in any Indian city lives in slums. This meant that while urban India provides economic opportunity, it does not provide for formal spaces that should essentially come with it. By the time the issue of affordable living entered the lexicon of the state, the formal and informal parts of Indian cities proceeded to create an interdependent and symbiotic existence. From here on, Indian urban planning was less about planning and more about troubleshooting. It missed the moot point about heterogeneity of the Indian urbanization discourse and failed to provision for it in housing and commercial spaces. It was a foregone conclusion that given the economic and caste inequality, urban India would remain an assisted economy for decades to come: that formal urban households of professionals, government employees, trades, businessman will be assisted by households of maids, drivers, guards, shopkeepers, cooks, taxi drivers to cater to their needs. But demand for this interdependent ecosystem was never part of urban planning's thought process. City designs failed to create formal spaces for these interdependencies in the vicinity and assumed a homogenous growth of the city. This gap was translated into economic opportunities that did not wait for a formal design response. Therefore, informal living mushroomed near formal neighborhoods to address the need of assisted living in response to this inadequacy, and unregulated eateries, quacks, retail stores selling spurious goods, shanty schools, illegal dairies and slaughterhouses came up as a result.

Beyond housing, urban planning needed to also imagine formal spaces for commercial purposes, such as for temporary markets. The concept of haats and melas that were integral to Indian villages and towns could have easily been extended to cities through farmers' markets or crafts bazaars. Instead urban planning designed cities without anticipating such needs, thereby compelling the unbridled growth of a hawking culture in the urban fabric of India, leading to the city's sanitation misery. The issue with Indian cities is not the act of hawking, but their failure to imbibe it in their design plans. How do these hawkers dispose the waste they generate? How do they maintain the hygiene of their merchandise and selling environment? Where do they live and handle the logistics? Clean cities acknowledge that hawking or temporary retail are an integral part of the urban narrative and are considered strong guardians of subcultures and local ethos, and thus imbibed them and created intelligent formal spaces for them. Singapore's food street, Seattle's Pike Place, Madrid's fresh markets, the night bazaars and flea markets of Thailand are all testimony of inspiring places both for customers and hawkers. Such formal spaces for temporary retailing created a sustainable revenue stream for the local bodies, while providing the customers a clean and hygienic surrounding.

Indian urban plans needed to think about vast formal spaces with common infrastructure and access that could make the hawking a clean and an inspiring experience for all stakeholders, and Dilli Haat, in the capital city, serves a reasonably good prototype. The venue's location, overall design, size of retail shops, and utility services were all provided for by the state. Crafts vendors from all over the country sell their products here and have made it among the top tourist destinations in Delhi. It was easy to extend the Dilli Haat template to formalize informal retailing and weed out bad retailing practices that accompany unauthorized hawking.

Success of this idea in clean countries teaches us two enabling factors. First, the relevance of the market for the catchment it serves, and second, the proliferation of such markets to be big enough to crowd out unregulated hawking from the city. If such markets are not housed in a convenient vicinity of the people they intend to serve, it will be a failure from the start. One location or one size or one type of market will also be just a flash in the pan to displace informal retailing.

The absence of urban designs compelled Indian local bodies to take a blinkered view to the problem of informal retailing in cities, although it is also true that the inherent problems of local bodies prevented them from thinking of such ideas in the first place. Irrespective of these causes, lack of formal alternatives disfigured the politics around hawking, while ignoring the challenges that it posed on public health and sanitation. In this tussle between local bodies and urban planning, unauthorized hawking grabbed Indian urbanism. In the eyes of the city administrators, the informal city took care of itself without bothering them for necessities, utilities, or clean surroundings. If informal living needed electricity, it stole from the nearby electricity poles. In the next elections, the political leader who promised regularization of this arrangement got the votes. The water body in the vicinity doubled up as the source of water and as a place to dump waste. Roads and pavements provided convenient real estate for informal markets. If one-third of the city's residents lived without bothering the city administrators, why should the city administrators disturb the status quo? Moreover, uprooting the marginalized from their homes and denying them a fair chance to earn a decent living neither makes for a good political statement nor does it pass the legal test. The duality of political and administrative advantages of informal urban living demonstrates a harmonious existence of the formal and informal actors in the city, in which both needed the other and neither party complained. Occasionally, city administrators went on anti-encroachment drives to fight informal living and uproot invisible inhabitants areas with minimal political risk.

A cluster of shanties surrounded by a perpetual rancid odor and filth, a series of roadside eateries cooking with adulterated ingredients, make-shift automobile repair shops that use spurious parts and spill out onto the roads, material recovery units banging out gold from mobile phones in precarious basements of slums, messy tea stalls that double up as drug disbursement points are the parasitic outcomes of this silent approval of informal living. These transform informal living into ground zero for child labor, sexual abuse, public health epidemics and malnutrition. They may not be spectacular catastrophes but they are silent killers. Few hundred deaths every year from vector diseases, and daily wage loss of a few hundred construction workers due to illness from water-borne diseases do not create any shock value outside of the affected households. The innocence of a few thousand children lost in an inhuman work environment is a problem far lower in the pecking order of social priorities. Open waste discharge from slums is hidden from the mainstream visuals of the city. But, silently these maladies grip the entire city forcing the administration to look for remedies that often leads to laughable solutions. Fumigation – an afterthought-cure to these vector diseases is one. Fumigation is a crisis response of the last resort often carried out as a disaster management tool in case of floods, earthquakes and fires. During such a catastrophe, the installed civic infrastructure is disrupted, which rapidly creates ripe conditions for the outbreak of vector-borne diseases and fumigation comes to the rescue to arrest the epidemic in the absence of infrastructure. Fumigation has its own set of challenges which have an adverse impact on water resources and build resistance in germs. Therefore, it is a tool of extreme discretion, rather than one to be used routinely for disease control, because it cannot eradicate the vectors but creates temporary relief. The more fumigation becomes routine the less it becomes effective.

But in 2017, the Delhi government indicated its 'steely' resolve to treat fumigation as a routine tool and perhaps to prove science wrong in the wake of the 2016 disastrous outbreak of vector-borne diseases. It proudly announced the over 300 fumigation machines it had procured at the onset of the rainy season, assuring citizens that the administration was ready to fight outbreaks of dengue, malaria, and chikungunya. It even submitted spirited affidavits in judicial courts about its readiness on fumigation. But every fumigation machine procured represents an urban planning failure. The root cause for these outbreaks lies in the fact that the city is ill-appointed to handle even a few millimeters of rain, and with its insignificant urban infrastructure has become hostage of its own consumption.

Sudden outbreaks of water-borne diseases are neither chance-based nor restricted to Delhi. At the onset of the monsoon in Kerala in 2017, one in every twenty-three citizens contracted a communicable disease. Between 2006 and 2010, Kerala cumulatively reported 6,400 cases of dengue, but in first half of 2017 alone the state reported more than 8,000 confirmed cases and at least 29,000 suspected cases of dengue. The 2017 outbreak also registered the highest number of viral fever cases at 871 from a dangerous strain of H1N1. Cuttack in Odisha was also on its toes the same year with repeated outbreaks of jaundice that saw more than a 100 people admitted to various hospitals across the city. The alleged culprit was a leaking water pipe close to a main drain in the city, which led to water contamination. Since 2014, Odisha has consistently seen a rising trend of jaundice cases. The dengue and chikungunya outbreaks in Kanpur in 2016 dissuaded people from watching the live test cricket match between India and New Zealand in the stadium. The fear was not unjustified because the city had 1,000 patients down with these diseases.

Cities conduct zealous campaigns to improve surroundings around homes. They fumigate neighborhoods and plead with the citizens to get rid of stagnant water, a spirited defense for actions that are set to fail because the root cause of our sanitation problem lies elsewhere: in the crumbling urban infrastructure that has finally fallen through trying to catch up with India's hyperbolic consumption growth. Without doubt, urban India needs a heavy dose of fumigation to survive a few more years, but soon it will need to direct its attention toward some sort of surgical intervention to correct the structural design of its cities. Otherwise, as the potency of fumigation reduces with every passing year, India will find itself scrambling for another crisis-management tool that is not yet in sight.

Many Indian municipal bodies, like the South Delhi Municipal Corporation, acknowledge this crisis. They concede that till the time the rapid rise of informal living is not curtailed in cities, this war cannot be won. In this wisdom lies the acceptance of the urgent need to redevelop Indian cities to overcome the public health crisis that stares them in the face. Consider the fact that the slum-dwelling population in urban India doubled between 2000 and 2015. The filthy surroundings in Deonar (Mumbai), Bhalswa (Delhi), Rajendra Nagar (Bengaluru), Saroj Nagar (Nagpur), Basanti (Kolkata), Indramma Nagar (Hyderabad), and Muhibullahpur (Lucknow) have broadly doubled in size since the start of this century. They are hellholes that create malnourished and mentally abused people with misplaced priorities. The Bhalswa slum on the banks of the Yamuna is a hub of child labor. The Indramma Nagar and Muhibullahpur slums are known waste-recycling centers that extract material from discarded items using bare hands and child labor in subhuman conditions, and release toxins into the air and water. How can then the residents in these slums be expected que up for amenities, when every day they must fight to fetch water from a water-tanker? How can they be expected to properly dispose garbage, when their very houses are built upon garbage pits? How can their personal appearance and speech be clean when congestion, noise and filth have shaped their visuals and played havoc with their dreams?

India naively sponsored the arrangement for political opportunism and administrative incapacity. Both viewed the arrangement as an intoxicatingly attractive opportunity not to be frittered away. This game of seduction overwhelmed urban planning and sapped from it the gumption to imagine formal solutions for this subaltern existence. Indian cities in the meantime continued their losing fight with poisonous air, polluted water, dirty surroundings, stunted growth, lost childhood, and zero self-esteem. But, as seen in the case of Dharavi, slum clusters are custodians of small enterprises that have grit and skills – band of musicians for a wedding procession, gardening tools and flower pots sold on a roadside, embroidered clothing sold in boutiques, cooks preparing food for social gatherings. The argument, thus, is in favor of protecting this spirit by hosting it in formal (right) ecosystems that can prevent it from drifting toward informal (wrong) ecosystems.

Hawking on busy city roads, a shack on the pavement, a barber underneath a tree, a ramshackle tyre repair shop in a dingy market, a plant nursery on encroached land, an eatery next to a drain, a mandir or a mazaar in the middle of the road or a juice corner near a taxi stand are all instances of informal behavior within a city. These are also failure points of urban planning to provide formal and clean spaces for such activities and to plug revenue loss for the state exchequer in the form of taxes or user fee in lieu of services and space. This leakage in state coffers outprice formal spaces in the city rendering them beyond the reach for the urban majority and eventually pushing it into an informal existence.

The interest of slums is better served if urban plans create legitimate spaces in the city and incentivize these businesses to operate away from informal settings. Creation of small and medium-sized enterprise (SME) clusters, which could house automobile recycling businesses, for instance, supported by housing access in the vicinity, would create a dignified existence for the human resource deployed therein. The space for such businesses could be purpose-built, and incorporate customized needs for logistics, tooling, warehousing, and utilities. The cost of creating such formal ecosystems would mean better overseeing of tax collection, environmental protection, waste management, working conditions of employees, and supervision to curtail exploitative practices like child labor. Businesses would reduce the transaction cost like bribes to non-state actors, improve productivity, and have access to utilities and formal banking systems. The idea is to crowd out informality and create the necessary entry barriers, while replacing chaos, dirt, and congestion in the city with serenity, cleanliness, and calm. The absence of such solutions in urban designs instead pushed the automobile recycling businesses to reside in slums and push them toward wrong business practices that artificially suppressed labor and other costs. This apathy toward proper planning allowed numerous such businesses to prosper on the wrong factors of value creation so much so that owners of such businesses now treat transition to formal ecosystem (improved working conditions and environment or tax compliance) as roadblocks to the status quo than an act which would be beneficial to the whole society. Why is it that what is good for the whole society is not perceived to be good for the individual?

In a way, is not Indian urban planning responsible for disfiguring our moral compass?

Till the 1970s, most cities in India had a simplistic existence. Over the next three decades, the sheer diversity of economic activities that started to define the character of Indian cities became mind boggling. Factory managers supervising a few hundred shop-floor employees working in a motorcycle manufacturing facility, doctors in hospitals supported by nursing and maintenance staff, warehousing & logistics units that engage lorry drivers for hauling goods, data analytics development centers employing hundreds of young professionals, religious centers supported by hundreds of employees and volunteers, housemaids working in homes, a team of cooks working at a popular restaurant, mechanics working in a service center of a car dealership, tutors working in an education coaching center, a sales office of a consumer durable company, college teachers, drivers of city transportation buses, freelance artists, journalists and reporters working for a local newspaper, real estate agents, administrative officers and food canteen staff of museums, traffic police force, wellness center therapists, corporate office management teams and so on became Indian urbanites.

Some cities had a strong skew toward industrial activities like Bokaro, while others had religious and educational overtones, like Varanasi. Cities like Murshidabad needed to preserve their history, while creating spaces to pack the new urbanites, whereas cities like Guntur amplified their existing purposes as agriculture trading hubs. Then, with a liberal sprinkling of religion, caste, regional diversity, gender, language, and beliefs, every city was a veritable kaleidoscope of people and activities. In this backdrop, the slip-up on informal living was not the only wrong step of urban planning. The planners imagined the urban Indian landscape from the lens of homogeneity and missed provisioning for complexity and dynamism. Local municipal bodies were the prime custodians of the urban planning exercise, but they themselves were struggling to get a foothold, and not having a strong foundation was a big reason for this miss. The structural deficiency of the local bodies sapped people who ran for their offices of any imagination and sense of purpose. Through urban planning, local bodies discovered an artisanal approach to create a supply of real estate which would be profitable. With this, the politics of cities discovered the perfect tool that could bankroll its existence, both within and outside the system, and ended up disfiguring the job of urban planning. It is this arrogance that allows Murshidabad to stomp its glorious legacy to make way for a mediocre future.

A city's design plan is the starting point to formalize its supply of commercial, institutional, and residential real estate for years to come. The process of urban planning determines areas and zones for future expansion of the city. This translates into a blueprint that effectively determines the supply of spaces for various uses within the city. Every time a plot of land, a shop, or a house changes hands for a commercial consideration, it generates revenue in the form of taxes for the concerned local civic body. The local body also charges property tax on all real-estate properties registered within its jurisdiction for perpetuity. For Indian local civic bodies, taxation on property is the only channel that they can lay their hands on to generate revenue and therefore the idea of merely creating a supply of real estate and earning their living from it fixated them. It also presented explicit opportunities for non-state actors to leverage the arbitrage and asymmetry in the system. This added incentive was the last nail in the coffin, so to speak, for urban planning, which lost its last remnants of sanity. Rather than the real-estate supply being the result of a comprehensive planning process, the main objective of which should have been to design the city for the larger benefit of its inhabitants, the creation of real estate became the primary purpose of urban planning in India.

Planners across India segregated urban spaces into residential and commercial boxes, and carved out real estate based on this broad categorization. As mentioned earlier, this real estate went to the highest bidder rather than to the deserving purposes or use. Soon Indian cities resembled mass congregation of chaotic clusters under a perpetual state of construction that fueled their haphazard expansion. Indian cities merely created spaces that were either not relevant or grossly inadequate to their various purposes. Separately, the supply of mass housing through various institutional responses was hardly adequate to fill the demand, given their sporadic and sparse efforts. This mismatch crowded out most of the inhabitants in Indian cities and cramped them in increasingly smaller spaces with every passing decade. But local bodies were addicted to this approach that sponsored their limited autonomy. Instead of critiquing it, they came up with the novel plan to further milk this productive cow.

The story of Delhi eloquently conveys this saga, one that spans decades. Delhi's urban planners first incentivized home owners in the city to build their houses on independent plots of land. To meet the growing housing need of the city, planning rules were redrafted to allow home owners to modify their homes to add additional floors for new home units. With this one change, the local bodies unlocked additional avenues for earning taxes on the new real-estate supply, while ticking the box to increase the supply of housing in the growing city. Everybody was happy. But how did this idea really impact the vistas of the city?

Imagine ten independent houses on a street, five on either side. Size notwithstanding, the infrastructure of the street around these houses was designed to support ten families. The width of the road, the kerb-side parking, the sewer line beneath these houses, the poles to support electric wires, the water pipes and waste collection points were all imagined to be sufficient for the ten families. Then all ten houses build two additional floors that are instantly bought by new families who soon move in. The street now has thirty families living there, while everything else remains the same. Soon, all families start to complain and fight for parking space, lack of water pressure, and cracked sewers that leak raw sewage onto the road. Residential colonies in Delhi may differ in names and locations, but today all of them offer a remarkably identical script on this count.

Building laws that allowed independent houses to reinvent themselves as four unit homes instead of one, from the ground to the third floor, created a real-estate developer out of many Delhizens. But just around the time Delhi's home owners were coming to grips with their new-found status of mini real-estate tycoons, and beginning to expand their dwellings into apartment blocks, Harpal Singh, was handed over the car keys of the first Maruti Suzuki car in 1983. This was a watershed event that eventually exposed Delhi's urban planning for its inadequacy and callousness. In the next three decades Delhi witnessed the growth of automobiles at an unprecedented scale. In 1990, there were nearly 4 lakh registered four wheelers in the city, which jumped more than four times to nearly 13 lakhs by 2003. By the end of 2015, registered cars in Delhi had more than doubled from 2003 and stood at more than 27 lakhs. The automobile density (defined as number of vehicles per thousand) of Delhi exploded from 192 automobiles for every 1,000 people in 1990 to 451 cars for every 1,000 people in 2015. This coincided with the rising prosperity of the city, which was set in motion with the landmark union budget of 1991. Cars became the ubiquitous means of transport in the city. At the same time, almost every independent house owner was erecting four units on his plot and soon every unit owned at least one car, if not two. The same plot of land now had to provide parking for eight or more cars. The fact that the residential plot of land and the surrounding space was not designed for the scenario of households owning motor vehicles reflects the urban planner's failure to sieve the plans through the filters of industrial policy and suffered from some sort of a rural hangover. Instead of showing foresight for the coming five decades and drawing future-ready city plans, urban planners imagined the inhabitants of

Delhi to either be a privileged lot or would forever use earlier means of transportation, such as tongas, cycles, rickshaws, and scooters.

Maruti Suzuki's advent in the 1980s proved to be a harbinger for the disruptive growth of the India automobile industry, and the landmark liberalization budget of 1991 were strong telltale signs of underlying shifts. These needed to be dovetailed into the design plans of the city. Instead, urban planning conveniently shifted the primary responsibility of creating a supply of new houses from state's shoulders to those of existing home owners without thinking about the consequences.

Even that would have been acceptable, had they thought about the consequences and created necessary caveats for their management. But, the mediocrity with which such re-development projects were pursued gave rise to the 'match-box school of architecture' that built homes stacked like houses of cards. Most of the residential colonies transformed from single homes to cramped and poorly ventilated four floor apartment blocks. Spaces in front which should have been reserved for pavements, underground drains, waste management and trees were encroached for parking of automobiles. Informal commerce to support these households occupied whatever was left of public space. Electric poles overstretched and exploded with legal and illegal connections. Sewer lines came under stress because they now had to carry four times the solid waste than they were designed for. The quantum of garbage disposed at the collection site increased manifold but the corresponding collection system was not upgraded to handle the manifold increase in load. Even if such an artisanal approach was the way to create a housing supply, a sensible urban planning approach would have been to compulsorily ban any housing unit on the ground floor and repurpose the ground floor space for car parking and utilities. The provision of cluster parking in the neighborhood should have been an essential pre-condition before builders/owners could embark on a real estate binge. This would have freed up precious space in front of the homes for essential functions and services. Such redevelopment projects should have been mandated to install a common garbage collection and segregation system for all the houses in the block, on the ground floor. This would have smoothened the implementation of a door-to-door garbage collection system. Electricity cables should have been taken under ground, which could have arrested transmission loss from theft and made the supply of electricity safe and efficient. Urban planners should have planned these colonies in clusters instead. Say, our street had ten houses. If urban planners wanted twenty more homes, they should have re-designed the street and come up with a re-development package for the ten house owners. Perhaps, razing all ten houses and instead constructing two buildings that with fifteen units each, supported by garden, common garbage collection point, under or over ground parking, convenience and utility shops, would have served the purpose much better. This would have still allowed the owners to have three houses each, if they so desired, yet be compelled to adhere to the minimum guidelines and pre-conditions for residential redevelopments. Delhi's urban planners finally woke up to this gross neglect in 2012 and made amends in the new building rules. But it was too little too late. Residential colonies of Delhi by then were choked with poor sewage, spilled out onto the streets, and their occupants fought daily wars for water, garbage, and parking.

Today, Delhi's residential colonies without exception cry for pavements and for adequate drainage. Either homes open right onto the roads or the space between the road and the house is perpetually blocked by parked vehicles. Rain water never finds an unchecked run-off and ends up waterlogging the roads. Water eventually pools at the lowest lying areas in these colonies, carrying along with it dirt, cow dung and garbage that is strewn on the roads, forcing residents to wade through floating filth during the wet months. Water on a tarred road is as corrosive as acid on human skin. If it is not given an immediate outlet through drains, it abrades the bitumen of the road, exposing the gravel beneath. It is for this reason that water logged residential colonies usually end up with badgered roads with loose dust flying all over the neighborhood when they are dry and Delhi-zens often wonder why even the slightest squall converts the roads to waterways. Logged water roads mixed with garbage usually strewn thereupon warms up in the sunlight making Delhi's neighborhoods a hotbed of vector-borne diseases. Local bodies scramble to fumigate neighborhoods and keep outbreaks in check. Journalists cry foul for the lack of preparedness of the city to tackle these diseases. Judiciary issue orders and demand explanations from local bodies. The city can do all this, yet there will be no respite because today's Delhi is a guinea pig of the urban planning lab that took these bad calls decades ago.

As if this blow was not enough, Delhi's urban planners came up with another ingenious idea to keep the gravy train on full steam. They figured the possibility that a residential plot can be converted into commercial use for more revenue.

The house owner will be more than happy to do so for it means a new source of income. Stakeholders lapped up the idea for it presented diverse arbitrage opportunities. But, it was impossible for every house to be given this permission without exposing the foolhardiness of the policy. So began the search for sound logic with which to identify some residences for such a play while rejecting others, so that the policy could be perceived as objective. They found it in the idea of 'change of land use.' This idea presented the argument that certain streets or neighborhoods over a period witnessed disproportionate increase in human movement. Such zones can no longer be confined to residential purposes and are therefore a fit case to build commercial real estate such as shops and offices. Property owners could build this commercial estate and sell or lease it to businesses. Urban planners thus took a flight of imagination way back to the walled city of Delhi that adopted a similar approach during the Mughal dynasty and built shops on busy streets and houses above or behind them.

Delhi's urban planners' 'cottage industry' mindset that spun this idea made it sound like a winning formula. It incentivized individual home owners into building shops on their residential properties and earn more revenue. They used a cleaver basis that was vague enough for arbitrage but sound enough on logic. Rather than think about the demographic human settlements in the city, their present and future consumption patterns, current and expected economic drivers of the city to determine the shape and quantum of commercial real estate, urban planners used the guise of human density to maximize commercial real estate supply in the individual interest of all stakeholders. The local body was satisfied because it funded its existence, as also the employees in DDA because the arrangement allowed them to exploit the arbitrage opportunities in the vagueness of the rule. It kept the house owners happy because it allowed them to fill their coffers. S. S. Safi, who was involved in urban planning of the city and with the DDA since its inception in 1956, went on record in 2003 to say that the 'DDA emerged as the largest real estate agency in the world, with over 50,000 acres of prime metropolitan land at its disposal.' Dunu Roy, an activist who works for the rights of urban poor, further asserted that 'the malpractices include regularization of unauthorized housing colonies, grant of approval for building plan alterations and land use pattern (converting residential areas into industrial or commercial zones) to serve the interests of a very strong mafia which comprises political leadership, land owners, affluent sections and the middle classes, and real estate sharks.' How does one comment on a policy that is individually good for all stakeholders, but detrimental to the health and sanity of the society collectively?

When a residential property was repurposed to commercial use, the plot of land and its surroundings were not redesigned to support this change. The front facade of a house was simply razed to make way for shops and multi-floored office spaces. This was free-market thinking at its best, without the onus to uphold the responsibility that comes with it, which urban planners abused to urbanize Delhi.

Successful champions of free market ideology spent enormous time and effort to define laws, lay down regulations and guidelines to ensure that the outcome of this philosophy is not at loggerheads with the principles of human dignity, public health and well-being of the society at large.

Consider the example of a highway construction project. A state (government) wants to build a motorway of 100 kilometers to connect two cities – X and Y. It invites private businesses to submit their quotes for the development and eventually chooses one. The state lays down minimum standards as prerequisites for the motorway in terms of the technology to be used, width, reinforcements, and passageways, road safety infrastructure, length, size of exit points, among others. These preconditions ensure that the expressway adheres to the minimum standards of performance and is thereby compliant to the argument of public good. The approach does not dilute free-market thinking. The state, instead of taking the onus of building the expressway upon itself, invites experts from private-sector organizations to undertake the construction. But in the process it never shuns the role of a regulator, custodian, and an assessor of the project. It defined the rules and guidelines that ensured two outcomes. First, it crowds out private-sector participants who lack expertise and skills to construct the expressway up to the desired standards. In effect, it raises the bar and puts up entry barriers for substandard participants. Second, it ensures that the output adheres to minimum basic standards needed for the safe and successful operation of the expressway. Defining guidelines and administering a regulatory framework to ensure compliance to these guidelines is the job of the state. Compliance to these guidelines is the job of the participants. The two work in tandem for the free-market approach to be successful.

What would have happened if such guidelines were not defined by the state before it invited private organizations to construct the expressway? The state expressed vague expectations that were open to interpretation, and the free-market approach in this case incentivized private participants to maximize economic gains. In the absence of any guidelines, there were no constraints on the participants to not take into consideration suboptimal building techniques, materials, and practices. The companies could prolong the project inordinately, reduce the width of the road, or construct haphazard entry and exit points on the expressway to maximize profits. In such a case, the free-market thinking produces a substandard product – a badly designed and unsafe expressway.

The DDA's artisanal approach to urbanize Delhi lacked any meaningful framework of guidelines, rules, and codes. There were no preconditions for different types of commercial activities that were poised to emerge. Once the land parcel received a green signal for change of land use, it was left up to the ability of its owner to imagine the nature of commercial activity and the eventual operator on the property. Sudden proliferation of commercial real estate in Delhi went way beyond the capacity of local bodies to supervise aspects related to utilities, parking spaces, structural and fire safety, waste water, and solid human waste collection and disposal systems.

Banquet halls (renting out space, with food and such services, for social celebrations, like weddings, birthdays, anniversaries) in Delhi best exemplify this shortcoming. Mid-1990s onwards, they sprang up in dingy lanes, next to main motorways, and in erstwhile residential streets that were now allowed to redevelop buildings for commercial use. Public infrastructure around these locations was never re-laid for large human gatherings. The sewer lines and drains were either absent or were not sufficient, and the garbage dumping sites in the neighborhood were small. A direct consequence of this proliferation was the manifold increase in the waste collected from these halls dumped in the open at the end of the street or in the nearby garbage bin. The width of the road in the area was too narrow to handle the high density and concentrated automobile movement. On 7 December 2015, Delhi hosted 25,000 weddings on one single day in these banquet halls, and streets witnessed massive jams. But, this was a small discomfort compared to the sole public car parking area that serves forty thousand shops in Karol Bagh area of the city that was also the creation of this approach.

This 'change of land use' approach to supply real estate for commerce in the city played havoc with Delhi's sanitation, ecology, and society's psyche. Commerce soon discovered the inadequacy of the space to cater to the booming demand and people soon discovered the ease to breach legal boundaries to create unauthorized solutions to fill this gap.

Offices needed parking spaces for their employees to park vehicles but the lack of it spilled unauthorized parking into residential neighborhoods. Permissions for use of building was taken for one type of commercial activity but they were used for another evading regulatory compliance. Restaurants needed buildings that could house their kitchens but structural design flaws resulted in these eateries choking sewers and creating smelly neighborhoods. Clinics needed a segregated approach to dispose their medical waste but they conveniently dumped it with the residential waste. In a sense a flawed urban planning approach ended up incentivizing a wrong model for commerce in the city of Delhi that never priced the actual cost of a formal parking space or a warehousing space or a well-appointed commercial kitchen or the apparatus to dispose medical waste. Businesses were happy for the lack of compliance cost and residents rarely rebelled presumably for their high tolerance levels or they were themselves milking the cow. But, the city was on a slow boil and in a matter of time it had to implode under the weight of this mother bomb of cross-purposes.

In early 2018, the judiciary 'suddenly' discovered rampant and blatant violation of the city's urban plan by city's trade and it reprimanded the local civic bodies. Shops were found to be built beyond their permissible limits, parking spaces were misused for storage purposes and commercial real estate was built in neighborhoods in the 'anticipation' of change of land use. The judiciary deemed these structures illegal and the city's bureaucracy went into an overdrive to 'seal' (Delhi's euphemism for closure) unauthorized spaces that violated building laws and permissions. People erupted with anger and the political class was found fumbling because the situation was a direct result of its naïve sponsorship all this while and sheepishly came out in support of the people who faced the axe of the 'sealing' drive. The Judiciary was in a spot of whether to rule in favour of citizens' livelihood protection or punish them for the breach of building laws. Amidst this slugfest, the union government intervened and tried to change the master city plan of Delhi to legalize countless instances of illegality so that all sections would be pacified. In this bravery, the union government had hoped to avert the crisis but it meant nothing to the existing structural designs of commerce and housing that spewed dirty neighborhoods, congestion and din round the clock. But in doing so, it attempted to cunningly bypass the judiciary's order that had deemed these structures illegal. It is like saying that a person is convicted of committing a murder by the judiciary but the executive legalizes the murder to save the convict's life. This brazen stance was confronted by a fuming judiciary who refused to play ball.

Congested neighborhoods and 'sealing' drives in the city are the product of decades of parochial urban design calls that pushed the city toward this explosion. Administrative incapacity, flawed political narrative and foxed judiciary are simply spectators of this misadventure. Every imaginable commercial activity was sucked up by this artisanal supply of real estate and this made a mess of the city's sanitation. Mosques built shops in their front façades that offered automobile repairs, thus robbing the area of the serenity and calm that precants yearn for. Corner houses leased out spaces to shops selling Indian sweets and snacks, who conveniently extended their kitchens to the pavements and dished out their savories on the road, leading to surroundings full of the generated food and dry waste. Road safety hazards from the shop's presence on the pavement notwithstanding steel, glass, wood and stone trading markets came up in small shops located on main intersections. The size of the shops in these markets were barely sufficient to house the goods and staff. Business owners never seemed to mind this shortage because the public space around the shop was free and liberally available to use as warehouses and showrooms. The encroachment extended to the logistics and transport activities which are critical for businesses. Pavements and other public spaces in the vicinity began to be occupied permanently for these purposes. Other such informal ecosystems of business emerged to support the commerce, forever stripping the neighborhood of sanitation and sanity. Changing the master plan as the solution was to simply dress up this arrangement in the bag of legality.

This brazen circus was not restricted to the change in land-use arrangement. There were erstwhile industrial zones located on the outskirts of Delhi not so long ago. These areas housed factories that ranged from fabrication units to food-processing plants and often operated with slack emission standards. Then the city expanded at breakneck speed driven by the plotted development approach to create real estate and soon reached the doorstep of these industrial zones. Industrial factories were no longer viable in the backyard of residential areas. Such a transition within cities is normal and sane urban planners take cognizance of these changes and plan for them. Cities like New York, London, Singapore, Paris, and Hong Kong also went through the same kind of transitions, but these were planned and anticipated by urban planners. But alas, not so in Delhi where urban planning remained inactive through this rapidly changing landscape as residential areas continued to grow unchecked and reached these industrial zones. Perhaps the intoxicating cottage-industry mindset had rendered them incapable of rational thinking. Instead of reconsidering the redevelopment approach, they merely overlooked the issue and its grave pitfalls. Then, when the supreme judiciary intervened in 2001, and nudged the local authorities to act, these polluting factories eventually moved out from these zones to the industrial zones of cities in neighboring states.

The Supreme Court's order in 2001 banned the continuation of industrial activity within the municipal limits of Delhi. This ban was much like the events of World War II and the great fires in First-World cities in the twentieth century (sans the mayhem and human sufferings) that gave the urban planners an opportunity to redevelop. Erstwhile industrial areas like Okhla, Hari Nagar, Naraina, and Badarpur offered ample space to redevelop as commercial zones. New-age commercial activities that were destined to drive the city's economic growth, such as delivery centers for outsourcing and technology industry, R&D centers and media studios, offices for consultancies and law firms, floors for trading businesses, integrated set-ups for logistics and warehousing operations, needed this kind of an infrastructure. These businesses required no machines and produced no emissions. They needed an efficient plugged-in ecosystem that could support their existence, thrived on ventilated spaces with liberal access to sunlight to minimize their utility bills, and required a complementary support of retail, services, and public transportation access for their employees. The DDA could have vacated and redeveloped these industrial zones to cater to such emerging needs, but this did not happen. Instead, the DDA's fixation with the creation of housing in the city, which had already wreaked havoc on the city plan, was extended to these industrial zones. The plot owners merely razed the earlier structures and erected poorly designed, dingy, uninspiring floors. The arterial roads within these zones could hardly withstand the load of the goods carriers and other vehicles that plied on them. Public areas were hardly redeveloped to tend to formal retail of food, conveniences, medicines, and communication, or public toilets and service amenities needed by those who worked here. Informal retail and commerce moved to fill these gaps. Inadequate parking spaces gave rise to informal parking lots in unassigned plots on the roadsides, sheds, or encroached land, plunging the whole area into a perpetual congestion mess. These much needed, however unplanned, features never allowed these zones to have proper sewage, water drainage, and pavements. Waste generated from these industrial zones landed up in uncontrolled disposal in surrounding areas. The unappetizing reality came fully to light during the monsoon season when the roads were replaced with vast stretches of black sludge and strewn garbage.

This approach to urban development was something like building a house without a toilet and kitchen. To compensate for their absence, imagine if the home owner builds a makeshift toilet at the entrance with rickety drain, and a temporary kitchen at the other corner of the house. The waste from the kitchen pools in a muddy puddle outside the house and stinks all day long. One can call the residents of the house foolish, but spare a rebuke for the intrinsic design flaws in the house. Without a toilet or kitchen, the house is destined to create dirty surroundings. Without correcting the basic design flaws, any effort to promote hygiene will be a futile. Similarly, Delhi's entire approach to urban planning created sub-optimal structures, spaces and localities that were set up to fail on sanitation from the word go. Any subsequent regulatory and monitoring interventions or the lack thereof were as ineffectual as taping up a leaky pipe. They made not a jot of difference. In 2012, the DDA made amendments in its building codes, making it mandatory for home owners to reserve the ground floor for utilities and parking. In 2017, it announced the land-pooling policy in the hope to create 25 lakh new dwellings within the coming decade, among other amendments. These policy decisions may have been right, but were a tad too late, which led to this mess in the first place.

The miserable urbanization story of Delhi resulted in a boom in the sleepy satellite town of Gurugram (earlier Gurgaon) in Haryana, at a stone's throw from Delhi. Gurugram sensed an opportunity in the paucity of real-estate supply in Delhi and rolled out development rights to developers at a pace never before seen in the history of India. They swiftly went ahead to create commercial and residential real estate that was required to bolster the brisk pace of India's economic growth at that time. But this also created a gold rush of opportunities which eventually blinkered the urban planners of Gurugram and set them up for failure in their own ways. The city solved only the first issue of creating the right kind of space for local economy, but went horribly wrong in backing them up with an integrated ecosystem to support and maintain the fragile ecology of the area. Gurugram built roads, but forgot to provide functional pavements. The city created islands of gated residential colonies and commercial units in a sea of garbage, poorly lit roads and informal living squatting on encroached land. Sewage connections and waste-collection systems took years to follow the human inhabitation and ended up delivering the city into the clutches of an informal industry for collecting garbage and dumping it.

Gurugram was an unassuming agricultural town flanked by muddy ravines and natural water bodies. These served a great purpose of channeling rainwater and building ground water reserves. Within a decade, Gurugram's myopic view to urban planning with the intent to leverage Delhi's need gaps ended up destroying 250 of the nearly 300 existing water bodies. Today, the city struggles with resources to let rainwater run off into drain pipes, which would otherwise have not been an issue had it accepted nature's apparatus and incorporated it into city plans. Consequently, the city cannot withstand even a few millimeters of continuous rain without all transport system and sanitation going for a toss. The administration gets into a huddle to troubleshoot and goes on a drain-building spree, which rarely delivers timely solution. The butterfly effect story of Chattarpur and Gurugram elegantly captures these sentiments. Chattarpur is a locality in Delhi that lies contiguous with Gurugram. The natural gradient between the two is almost ten meters, with Chattarpur being on a higher plain. Till the urbanization boom hit the area, rainwater drainage between the two clusters was channelized through bunds and natural ravines using a rainwater-management system that was installed during the colonial times. But the urban planning or the lack of it in the last three decades converted bunds into real-estate assets and *naalis* into prime targets for slums. Today, five millimeters of continuous rain in Chattarpur floods Gurugram and leaves the governance wondering for the cause and culprit.

The root cause of the urban mess in Gurugram lies in the urban planning of the past. The culprits are mediocre technical prowess and political brinkmanship on urban planning, a common theme witnessed in the urban planning discourse across India which set up to fail any and every person responsible. When our sense of nationalism attempts to self-congratulate the greatness in our past, it should temper its zeal to only pick perceived 'homegrown' greatness. The colonial, or for that matter, any other 'foreign' influences take away from the claim of absolute greatness of the homegrown past. Layering of biases for centuries distorted this past in its original form and devoid us of its precious wisdom. Consider this: despite the agenda of urbanization being on low priority for the colonial rule, a rainwater system for drainage and sanitation in Chattarpur was nevertheless put in place, and along with it came a convenient and scientific template for emulation. But when we took control of our destiny and made urbanization high priority, we lost the wisdom to preserve this structure. It is not as though the rainwater-harvesting technique was an invention of the colonial masters. It used to be a hallmark design feature practised by many Indian monarchies for centuries. The Agrasen dynasty of the fourteenth century, for instance, is almost synonymous with the stepwell for rainwater storage, and so were many kingdoms in Rajasthan. Why then did we lose this wisdom when we took the driver's seat? Thanks to the faultlines in our society, our glorious homegrown past never had an intellectual revival that could have contemporized it for modern-day living on many issues. Installation of the rainwater technique in Chattarpur signifies the colonial rule's attempt to augment our homegrown wisdom on water preservation and on the criticality of the system to recharge water bodies, given the subcontinent's intertwined fate on monsoons. But the first opportunity we got to urbanize ourselves, we thrashed it perhaps as an 'evil vestige' of the colonial past. The enemy is not the colonial rule, but our refusal to critique our biases that constantly make us overlook rationality in our homegrown past and cherry-pick blind belief from it. It exposes us as emotional fools and repeatedly holds us hostage to making wrong choices. Urban planners' abandonment of water preservation from its toolkit made Indian cities flood at a drop of rain and stare at parched existence for the rest of the year – a deserving outcome for this biased society.

Urbanization almost always comes at the cost of ecological shifts and environmental risks. Clean countries learned to create reinforcements to minimize this adversity through scientific research and careful planning. Gurugram had all the makings of one such great city as it had none of the baggage or legacy of the past. But the profiteering opportunity was so intense, political sponsorship so naive, and the technical prowess on urban planning so rudimentary that they drowned any chance there may have been for a clean, efficient, and inspiring city. Even the change of the city's name (from Gurgoan to Gurugram) could not save this mystical landmass of ravines and wild beauty from being turned into the most polluted cities on the planet within twenty short years. The travesty of Delhi and the hurried opportunism of Gurugram may be contrasting, yet both spewed an identical outcome of mediocre cities that represent Indian urbanism in totality.

The urban planners of the city of Bengaluru seem to have taken inspiration from Delhi and have ended up converting their beautiful garden city into an urban mess, in twenty short years. The commercial growth of banquet halls in the city replicated that of Delhi, almost identically. In 2016, it was estimated that the Bengaluru had nearly 2,100 function halls, almost 90 percent of which were operating without the required permissions. The planners created commercial real estate both through the cottage-industry mindset of Delhi and the industrial approach of Gurugram. The sheer demand for commercial spaces that unfolded in the city was unprecedented. It can be argued that the urban planners were not experienced enough to handle a demand explosion like this and jumped on any options of creating commercial real estate that came their way. The fact that the real estate in its new avatar was poised to attract human movement which would require enabling infrastructure for waste management, utilities, and transport was not heeded. Take an example of a takeaway Biryani joint that opens for business in one such street corner. Soon, the joint gains popularity among the locals and people start to throng the place. They park their scooters, motorbikes and cars randomly on the street. People stand outside the shop in the public area meant for commute and eat the biryani, discarding their empty plates and any leftovers on the pavement. The constant rush of customers creates traffic congestion in the area. Stray dogs sniff out the food garbage piled outside the shop and help themselves to any scraps they can find. By the end of the day, the street may be free from the beeps and honking of vehicles but now has a foul stench that bears testimony to the brisk business the shop did throughout the day. Neighborhoods of Bengaluru have many such holes in the wall, but its narrow streets were just not designed to handle their footprints. Is the Biryani shop owner to blame for selling his wares in a manner that they caused mayhem and a public hygiene crisis on the street? In doing so are we not curtailing an individual's right to live in the interest of keeping the streets and neighborhood clean? Or do we deserve this chaos because we really don't know how to handle economic development? It is here that the role of urban planners comes under scrutiny. If the shop was indeed the solution, then is the current format of the shop the best urban planning could visualize?

Inhabitants have needs and it is the job of the urban planners to anticipate them and create the most appropriate solutions for them. Some needs are explicit like a place to live and earn livelihoods. Some are implied like the need for a short commute time from home to office or the need for a safe and secure place for children to play and socialize or the need for a clean surrounding. The people can only react to good and bad urban designs through desirable and undesirable behavior. Informal living, which results in creating dirty surroundings in a city, is undesirable behavior that results from bad planning while an orderly commute back home is desirable. Urban planning is as much responsible for a choked drain in a congested commercial area as is the local body that has shown laxity in cleaning it in a timely manner.

The trajectory of urbanization of emerging towns like Bishnupur, Pandharpur, Maharajganj, and 2,000 others seem to be leading them toward the faulty urban planning which has disfigured the core of Delhi, Gurugram and Bengaluru among others. In May 2017, a 90-foot-long wall at a function hall collapsed in the town of Bharatpur in Rajasthan, killing twenty-four people on the spot. The cause was determined to be faulty design and poor-quality construction materials. Bharatpur, a town of nearly 300,000 inhabitants, is an infant town about five hours away from Delhi and is showing all signs of imbibing its banquet-hall business mania and the mess that comes with it. The water-harvesting system designed during the Mughal era to supply water to the town of Burhanpur in Madhya Pradesh used natural formations to channel water from the banks of the Tapti river. So ingenious was the system that it still quenches the city's thirst four centuries later, albeit on a much-reduced prowess. However, since the 1980s, the quality of urbanization injected its veins with garbage pushing the system into retirement, an uncanny resemblance to the case of Gurugram in the ability to disfigure its water preservation system. These instances imply that the failure of city planning to address well-acknowledged urbanization challenges in newly appointed towns will unfortunately ensure that within a few decades they will grow up to become hardened criminals, having learnt by example.

Urban planning is a profession of tremendous responsibility because all its actions or inaction have political and social repercussions in future tense. But the profession rarely offers credible tools to evaluate its efficacy in the present. Therefore, urban planning should be evaluated on its ability to discharge its moral responsibility to visualize future needs and prepare the city in response. Human needs change with time and the functionality of the city to address them should change accordingly. A hundred years ago, streets were designed to support horse carriages, but today in cities roads are purpose-built for automobiles. In the future these streets will have to accommodate driverless, electric transportation. Airports were hardly part of the urban-planning designs of cities, but today they are key economic drivers. Even changes in human values impact the functionality of personal spaces. Take, for instance, a bathtub, a symbol of luxury until only a few decades ago. Cinema of yesteryears immortalized the bubble-bath scene to depict seduction, beauty, and the notion of luxury. Fast forward to today and the issues of climate change, water conservation, and contamination have begun to dominate human values. The bathtub went from being a status symbol to one of avoidable indulgence and a source of water wastage. Digitally controlled fancy showers replaced the old bathtub, and hotels around the world went into an overdrive to replace them with the new symbols of luxury bathing, freeing up more space in the process. If only the urban planners of Delhi had imagined the economic growth that the city would experience in the coming decades, it would have been a far cleaner city than it is today.

Bad urban design decisions can go undiscovered for decades, and are rarely ascribed as the villains for human suffering or ecological imbalances of cities. If an urbanite fears for her life from vector-borne diseases, if she spends half of the day in commute, if she is forced to live near perpetual stench, if children yearn for open parks and fields to play in, if social functions are a bane rather than joyous occasions, if the family members are charred to death for getting trapped in a simple house fire and if bickering over sewage and parking issues ends up in a bloodbath within the family, perhaps the urban planning calls that the city's planners took on their behalf decades ago are to blame. Terrorists produce a measurable outcome of misery that creates mass shock. But, the sufferers of bad urban planning calls are no different from frogs that are put in a vessel of water, which is slowly put on the boil. Initially, they enjoy the warmth and become numb, but before they know it the water begins to boil and it is too late for the frogs to jump out alive. An Indian urbanite forced to breathe in foul air, live in perpetual filth or face chaotic traffic puts his mental health in question, wading through sludge and garbage on the way to work and silently praying that his undiagnosed fever is not a new strain of the virus. These are all 'slow boil' moments that are silently cooking him alive because Indian urban planners played the wrong kind of gods.

Urban planning is a technical exercise that needs a strong social conscience and therefore equally strong political backing, but Indian urban planning process missed this obvious link. At its root, it entails strong technical knowhow of civil engineering and design. But in the twentieth century, the act of building cities acquired a strong political backing in the clean countries of today. It led to a realization that urban planning ought to be more than mere drawings on paper for the city administrators, for them to also understand human behavior, economics and ecology. The political establishment sensed the importance of linking up with itself the expansive scope of urban planning for franchise dividends. Rolling out state-sponsored public-housing projects in the 1920s in the UK consolidated the political leadership of the then prime minister. Mass public spending projects like the Brooklyn Bridge in New York ensured mayorship. The common man's fascination with the process of building cities was not surprising. Mass migration and industrialization served a natural backdrop. Urban planning gave birth to a 'cult' of urban planners. The political establishment patronized them, sometimes to the extent that they became an authority in themselves. Politicians did not complain because they recognized the need for them to work with a free hand for optimal solutions. Moreover, there was no precedence to judge them. While cult planners designed future-ready cities with a free hand, they could do so because the agenda of building cities became important manifestos for the prevailing political establishment. By the end of the twentieth century, the 'hero' approach to urban planning made way for a non-personality-centric process approach. But the earlier syncing of creativity and technical knowledge with the political establishment afforded the clean countries a rigorous template to design their cities.

Up until the 1970s, the Indian political establishment failed to spot political dividends in the agenda of urbanization. Electricity and water, sanitation, housing and security in cities were hardly urgent matters over farm productivity, Green Revolution, agriculture subsidy, and external conflicts. India's approach toward urbanization became the immediate casualty of this neglect. Rural approaches were extrapolated to semi-urban towns which were in turn extended to cities. With the notable exception of Nehru's political sponsorship that created a mini-urbanization boom of industrial towns and commissioned the construction of Chandigarh, which captured the common man's imagination, no other example of political sponsorship for urban development during that time comes to mind. Both the political sponsorship to build cities and the technical process of creating urban plans suffered because of this lack of interaction. The technical process never had the chance to creatively explore responses for the challenges that Indian cities faced or were likely to face in future. Unlike in the clean countries where urban planning received unbridled political patronage to take an unconstrained flight of creativity and expression, in India it became bureaucratic and ended up in mediocrity before it could become technically sound. From this aridity emerges Indian urbanism's failure to harness the human brilliance of the architect Balkrishna Vithaldas Doshi, who designed some of the most inspiring urban ecosystems in affordable living in India (namely, Aranya, a low-cost housing project in Indore in 1989) and imagined buildings (such as the Indian Institute of Management Bangalore) that champion inclusion. It also does not matter that he ended up as the only Indian recipient of the Pritzker Architecture Prize in 2018. Rather than to extend him the same invitation that the Indian political order did to the likes of Dr Vikram Sarabhai for the Indian space program and to look up to him to plug capability holes in India's urban planning, Doshi's brilliance was ignored beyond a few isolated projects.

From the 1970s, political dividend from India's urbanism thrived on its challenges of informal living, land acquisition, and urban expansion. Instead of seeking the underlying reasons for these problems, delivering instant remedies became a more convenient form of quick wins. If a thousand families encroached upon a public land and started living on it, the political narrative was better served in 'regularizing' this arrangement rather than to seek the reasons for this informal settlement to come up and create formal residential alternatives for them. The latter was a long-haul approach that demanded research, policy intervention, and a wider consensus. Even if one section of the political establishment took a principled stand, it opened an arbitrage opportunity for a counter political narrative that promised instant gains. Therefore, political sponsorship on urban issues started to get centered around quick fixes: water-tanker supplies for colonies without access to water, instantly translating into votes. Political sponsorship also discovered the untapped potential of urban planning to pay rich dividends on space planning. The question of use of space in a city requires imagination to appreciate interdependent human behavior within the city, the knowhow to interpret the impact of technology on societal evolution, and the intellect to understand the deficits that plague the current urban setup and come up with the best solutions. In fact, the notion of 'best' is also nebulous. It is entirely possible that urban planners may interpret some solutions as best for the city today, but future generations may label them as villains. The same questions can also have quick fix responses – as opposed to the more painstaking deep solutions – which can create immediate relief. These may have short-term benefits, but are counterproductive in the long run. The Indian political narrative missed appreciating these nuanced differences and went with quick fixes, and this explains Doshi's missing invitation.

By 2016, nearly 750 shopping malls mushroomed across India. A mere 10 percent of these are deemed successful, the rest are abandoned due to bad designs or faulty business models. A similar fate rests for places of worships at odd places, empty structures housing educational institutes, and work places consuming half a day's commute.

Meanwhile, this suboptimal urban living also reached a critical mass with high political stakes. Small dingy residential colonies grew to bigger dingy colonies. Congested markets added rows of new streets of the same clutter. Illegal dairies in residential neighborhoods, unregulated factories in dark bylanes, and eateries dishing out food waste in narrow streets that severely eroded the health of urban neighborhoods became omnipresent. Salvation from this hellish scenario required an alternative solution focused on redevelopment of existing spaces. But this was a tall ask from urban planning, for it was never mentored to provide solutions that could pass the test of morality on public health, equality and dignity.

City planning in India is the job of a town planner. Depending on the city's jurisdiction, plans created by the town planner require executive approvals for subsequent implementation. Urban plans of big-stake cities like Delhi, Mumbai, and Chennai also require the 'blessings' of the entire political establishment. Political sponsorship ensures protection of the citizens' rights and curtails individual whims. But with India, its political urges run contrarian to the priorities of urban plans and leave them with no avenue but to slice and dice urban spaces.

Whenever purposeful urban planning was backed by political sponsorship, it created superior results. Whenever this sponsorship was diverted to contrarian needs, promising initiatives resulted in mediocre outcomes. The story of the creation of Navi Mumbai, a bustling city adjacent to Mumbai, and the life of late Charles Correa, India's fine and rare 'son of the soil' urban planner who went on to gain global recognition, eloquently captures this contradiction. Charles Correa was not merely a master architect restricted to designing buildings, but an artist who could imagine cites. In the mid-1960s, Correa reasoned that in the coming decades Mumbai will burst at the seams and that the city's geographical limitation to accommodate more human influx will accelerate this explosion. He conceived the idea of Navi (New) Mumbai on an empty land parcel in the neighboring districts of Mumbai and imagined it to become the administrative alternative to Mumbai and house the state assembly and secretariat. He envisioned the city as a global benchmark of sustainable public spaces. The idea caught the imagination of the state politics of Maharashtra, and in 1971 the City and Industrial Development Corporation (CIDCO) of Maharashtra was made responsible to put this vision into action. For the initial period, Correa received political sponsorship, but there was one little hitch: a vast supply of monetizable real estate was created. His plan proposed usages that made sense as regards the sustainability of the city and for the well-being of its prospective habitants, but perhaps lowered the monetizing potential. However, the political class of Maharashtra thought it was better to use the guise of the Navi Mumbai creation exercise and break the integrated plan into piecemeal and monetize it in parts.

The political sponsorship to Correa's vision was withdrawn and he moved out from the helm of affairs soon after. Administrative and government offices were never moved to the new city as he had suggested. Navi Mumbai was reduced to another suburb extension of Mumbai and remained isolated from the main city for years. By the start of new millennium, Correa's prophecy about Mumbai came true and Navi Mumbai came to stand out as a slightly better planned suburb that saw a vast upswing in human settlement. But the city was no different from any other urban settlement with its own woes of sanitation, congestion, and commute.

Undoubtedly, urban plans will be designed by technocrats who alone possess the knowledge and capability to take a holistic view of the future. But these urban plans cannot exclude the political supremacy that represents the people's rights. If not then the city is in danger of running into disastrous outcomes of a different nature and may be particularly visceral in nature, as we see in abundance in many cities in China today. Many megalomaniac Chinese cities that are strong on symbolism, but weak on sustainability, are outcomes of this autocratic approach where the vulnerable get crowded out per force to make way for posturing or excesses. The inhabitants fill up with anguish and their anger occasionally erupts, as was the case with Jia Jinglong. Jinglong and his parents were evicted from their ancestral home in an erstwhile village to make way for the planned expansion of the city of Shijiangzhuang near Beijing, without adequate compensation. Out of grudge, a year later, Jinglong shot the local party official, and later surrendered. He was executed in 2016. Vast stretches of ghost cities dot the urban landscape of China as a manifestation of this autocratic script of urban expansion. No one but architecture firms seem to have benefitted from this unrestrained symbolism of urbanization in China. Closer home, the ghost town of Lavasa near Pune stands as a towering symbol portraying the limitation of this approach.

All countries with half a decent universal franchise system require political consensus for urban space planning to produce superior results. For these countries, the technical process of urban planning and the political discourse on it are inextricably linked. It is also a fact that this convergence has never happened from the start. Most inspiring cities went through decades of suffering of informal living, public health crisis, bad sanitation, congestion, and foul air and water before political sponsorship matured to recognize urban planning's crucial role in the city's cleanliness and health. Then political sponsorship started to back holistic and sustainable future visions for cities instead of their earlier fascination with quick-fix approach in anticipation of instant political dividends. About a hundred years ago, London, Paris, Tokyo and New York were afflicted with the same problems that plague us today (foul air and water, slums and dirty public spaces), but in due course their political leadership matured and was able to see holistic urban plans as safe political bets. This is trickier than it sounds: the results of urban planning manifest decades after they are drawn on paper. But the citizen's woes from planning interventions are more immediate. Citizens never explicitly state the need for a holistic urban planning approach with such a long wait time for solutions. Moreover, they are unable to articulate the solution and merely highlight the woes. The maturity of political leadership needs to position such a planning process with a long gestation as a necessity for public good. The futuristic outcome of the process is dependent on the strong will of the political leadership to stay the course over long periods. This should essentially fulfill two preconditions in order to emerge triumphant – a strongly positive perception in the minds of the citizens, and a compelling case for economic gain. In First-World countries, urban plans were elevated to a grander vision than to merely relate it to clean roads and public hygiene. The importance of creating sustainable cities was interwoven with the ideology of building a strong nation. Roads and bridges were touted as symbols of superior engineering. Suburbs became the guardians of family values for baby boomers and public spaces were symbols of individual freedom. Such grand visions of future cities captured the minds of citizens and translated into votes.

In 1919, David Lloyd George, then prime minister of UK, brought in the Housing Act and laid down the foundation for the massive construction of public housing. This was followed by the Tudor Walters Report that formulated the design manual for these houses, specifying the size, number of rooms, design of colonies, and others. The Chamberlain Act of 1923 and the Wheatley Housing Act of 1924 modified provisions in the Act. In 1930, the Housing Act was amended to specifically stimulate slum clearance from the cities of the UK. The Housing Act of 1919 redefined the political sponsorship for urban planning. For the next two decades leading into World War II and immediately after it, public housing became one of the central themes of UK politics. The scope of council housing was expanded to address specific issues of urbanization like slums or informal living. Political sponsorship to public housing was constantly refined with the changing times. For instance, in the 1960s, UK politics revisited the standards of the council homes with respect to the changes in the living standards of society. The standards of the Parker Morris Committee, which defined new standards for these homes, like prefab material, smaller and smarter sizes in keeping with the paucity of urban space, were adopted. Superior vision to preempt changes in society and to interject it with an urban planning response at the right time was the key reason for the success of public housing in the UK that sucked out informal living from its urban narrative forever.

In 1914, Seki Hajime arrived in the city of Osaka, Japan, as its deputy mayor. Osaka was then a bustling industrial town that housed 3,000 factories and one million inhabitants, mostly factory workers living in squalid conditions. He immediately sensed the urgent need to undertake wide-scale redevelopment to address the issue of informal housing and arrest the haphazard development of the city. Redevelopment needed land, which was under the private ownership of a few individuals, and landowners were proving to be a hurdle. Hajime's efforts in Osaka grew into a pan-Japan movement as the country was getting rapidly industrialized with many of its cities having more than a million residents in their folds. In 1919, this led to the central urban planning act that served as the guiding principle for local bodies. Here again, the political narrative in Japan was shaped by the theme of urban planning. In 1910, voters in Seattle approved a grand redevelopment plan that came to be known as the Bogue Plan. Though the plan hit rough waters later, it conveys that great cities of today were talking about political narrative around urban planning a hundred years ago.

Public figures, who took upon themselves to back these visions, understood the gestation time needed to make these visions a reality may well be longer than their active political careers or even their lifespans. The key was to act upon these visions nonetheless for a constructive political response to end the misery of urban living, rather than to seek short-term solutions for quick gains. Until the Indian political narrative starts to hold urban planning in high reverence and demand visionary standards, cities will continue to be mediocre and bad sanitation will always be a natural outcome of this mediocrity. The failure of local bodies to fumigate a locality, lift garbage from a neighborhood, let car parking mushroom on a busy street, or remove illegal encroachments are merely failures to address symptoms of mediocre urban plans. The political sponsorship needs to own up and convey to the franchise that the roads in the city are bad because the urban planning of the city was messed up a few decades ago. It will need to announce that the repeated outbreaks of vector-borne diseases in the city are not because of the lack of fumigation but because of mediocre design plans that need an overhaul. It will need to make a statement that the daily struggles of urban citizens regarding commute, dirty surroundings and congested neighborhoods requires a redevelopment approach of the city that will add to the misery for the present generation but will ensure a healthy and inspired living for the future. The prospective local councilors will need to sell such visions when they seek support from voters who live hand to mouth and are not even sure if they will get the next day's water supply. The prospective mayor of the city will have to develop the financing plan for the funding of this vision. People who dream of becoming lawmakers will need to think about the kind of legislations required to make this vision a reality. The successful transition of the political establishment toward this narrative will determine whether or not Indian cities become clean in the future. How is that for a political challenge?

But political sponsorship alone will not deliver the desired result, because if a technically weak process were to receive it, the outcome would be comical. Like the flawed project of bicycle lanes in Lucknow. Akhilesh Yadav, the chief minister of Uttar Pradesh from 2012 to 2017, commissioned the building of dedicated bicycle lanes across the capital city of Lucknow. The city administration went on an overdrive and built these tracks at a fevered pace. The poor interpretation of the project as a civil engineering exercise in response to a political dictate made many parts of these tracks prone to encroachment or lie defunct. Yogi Adityanath, Yadav's successor and a member of the rival party, scraped the project due to alleged corruption and perhaps for the project's strongly symbolic link with the previous government. Once again, the weak technical capability of urban planning is to blame for its failure to defend the project with efficient execution, when it is accepted wisdom the world over that cycling tracks promote a clean, serene and healthy city, for example, like Amsterdam.

The history of urban planning teaches us that political sponsorship early-on allowed the build-up of technical capability to design cities. Had India received the right political sponsorship for urban planning right from Independence, like it did for the space research program, her technical capabilities to design cities would have been at par with the First World. But, the technical knowhow required to design cities cannot gather critical mass if for decades the subject has been shoved around.

Urban planning is not merely designing buildings in controlled spaces; it deals with designing systems that enable human living, movement and interactions within a society in a calm, efficient, healthy, environmentally friendly manner and protects human values of equality, dignity, and freedom.

Cities become filthy because certain urban human behavior was not accounted for by the city's planners. The rise of slums in urban India is a failure to envisage nature and volume of dwellings required in the city. Urban plans failed to recognize the correct locations within the city that have potential to become hotspots of economic activity and employment. Public transport which could ferry people to work at these locations was not provisioned. Consequently, informal means of transport sprang up that were not only unregulated, unsafe and polluting but also pushed their owners (rickshaw pullers and auto-rickshaw drivers) to live, eat, park their vehicles and defecate in unplanned surroundings. Urban plans failed to estimate the diversity in retailing needed to support the city's population, which led informal retailing to move in and bridge the gap. Stray cows on roads of Indian cities is a failure of urban planning to take into account certain aspects of human living in cities. India's urban planning was never exposed to these intricacies and was left with little choice but to extrapolate architects' methodology for designing buildings onto planning cities, thus confining itself to technical blueprints that spewed one ineffectual design after another.

Urban planners need to be social scientists who can understand human behavior in the city and predict its evolution in times to come. India is a young country, but by 2050 it will have more than 300 million senior citizens, as opposed to 100 million of today. What should be the urban planning response to tackle this challenge? Today, India is grossly underprepared for this challenge: Delhi boasts of only two old-age homes for its nearly two million senior citizens. The elderly face isolation and abandonment from their families many a times due to their incapacity or genuine lack of time, money and space in urban homes. Assisted living homes are well appointed spaces in clean countries, designed to offer a dignified and medically assisted living for old people. It is accepted behavior for grandparents to move into assisted living homes permanently, while affording them the freedom to visit their families whenever they desire. Indian urban planning will need to think about a segmented approach to assisted living as one way to address it. Urban plans can guide local bodies with operating and regulatory guidelines to democratize assisted living centers across income classes, and can even inspire them to operate such centers as part of state-sponsored welfare or explore them through fees charged from pensions, endowment support, or annuity income of any assets owned by users. Then rejuvenating the notion of growing old in India becomes a route for urban planning to deliver new purposes to India's urbanism.

Circular migration also characterizes India's urbanization. Typically, male members of a household move to cities for better economic prospects and leave their families behind in the villages. Issues like absence of child care and lack of affordable and safe housing for the family deters them from moving to the city as a cohesive unit. For them, home ownership in a city is a secondary need. They secretly long for similar economic opportunities being available back home. Urban planning in mega Indian cities will be better off thinking of housing as a pay-as-you-go concept rather than as an essential ownership asset for these circular migrants. It is the lack of formal temporary housing that leads to the rapid rise of informal living, slums, and unauthorized colonies, rather than the lack of affordable houses, which are assets of a more permanent nature.

Students moving to cities for better education is one such case of circular migration. At any point of time, Delhi has a floating population of 100,000 people, calling it their 'home,' solely to enroll in preparatory classes for various competitive examinations. They live in makeshift private hostels or as paying guests in dingy homes and move out of the city once their purpose is served. Agra, Nagpur, Lucknow and Jaipur house nearly 10,000 such circular migrants. Construction workers who move to cities to seek employment are also temporary residents. Once the ongoing project is over, they move on to the next site within the city or to a new city altogether. They live in makeshift housing in squalid conditions. Informal markets spring around them to support their needs dishing out everything from spurious liquor to quacks. The social consequences of this arrangement unfolds in unpleasant ways, such as sexual exploitation of children and women, domestic violence, deaths from vector-borne diseases and adulterated liquor, depression and suicide.

Should not then the absence of a formal urban planning response to the housing problem of construction workers be considered the root cause for such painful consequences?

Formal rental housing colonies appointed with amenities and access to public transportation can provide dwelling to temporary migrants in the city and can address these gaps effectively. Unlike leasing a house from an individual, the occupant can lease a unit in one of these rental colonies from an entity who has built its numerous units for this very purpose and operates them. The challenges of living in a city can catch up with the rental rates of independent formal housing units and make them unsuitable as affordable housing on two major counts: first, if the formal housing supply in a city has never so far quenched the purchasing appetite for affordable housing in urban India, logically the rentable housing, which invariably falls within this set, will also face a similar crunch. Temporary migrants can no longer afford to rent houses in the few well-appointed neighborhoods that offer conveniences as they tend to become greatly overpriced. This squeeze inevitably pushes them toward an informal existence to survive in the city. An informal setup becomes a preferred vendor for affordable rental living by avoiding cost on land ownership, non-compliance to building codes and civil construction norms and accessing utilities illegally. In other words, unauthorized colonies manage to provide affordable rents not because they have perfected a winning business model of renting, but because of all the legitimate costs they save due to non-compliance. This arrangement balloons the growth of unauthorized housing with more circular migrants arriving to the city, and aggravates the sanitation challenge.

This arrangement has a distressing tendency to produce macabre outcomes. The death of Ramesh Bisht in July 2017 in Gurugram highlights this. A migrant student, Bisht was enrolled in a catering school in the city and lived in a rented room in a building. The school had tied-up with the building's landlord to rent some rooms out as students' accommodation. Allegedly, the school paid only half the fee it charged its students to the landlord, without his knowledge. For the landlord, providing the school with affordable accommodation meant no costs associated with adherence to building codes or approvals from local authorities to construct the building. His rental housing also included installation of more than thirty air conditioners on a sanctioned electricity load of two, not to mention an erratic water supply. Formal waste collection from the building was farthest from his mind. Bisht and his friends, appalled at the terrible living conditions, protested. This incensed the landlord to the extent that he arranged a bunch of goons to beat up the students, so also venting his anger against the school when he also found out that school was shortchanging him. In the scuffle, Bisht was pushed to his death from the fifth floor of the building.

An industrial approach toward rental housing can become a strong counter to avoid this trap, offering formal ecosystems for the diverse inhabitants of the city. This solution would be much the same as public housing that is provided to families of policemen and armed forces personnel, or university hostels that house students for extended periods of time. Quite like the residential sprawls in industrial townships and the chawl system in Mumbai, formal rental housing colonies will provide a safe shelter to those who look up to the city for a temporary stay. It would also serve to normalize rent rates for all income groups and create a tacit check on migration to the city beyond its installed ability, while dis-incentivizing informal living. Circular migrants will favor such colonies over independent, outpriced rented accommodations or informal ghettos. These standalone giant formal units can be better supervised and regulated on quality of living, with access to utilities and services (banking, recreation, laundry, retail and others). Local bodies of cities can consider coinvesting in such facilities in partnership with private players and hope to fill up their parched coffers. The public areas of these units can be strengthened with libraries, digital technology, common storage spaces and open areas for sports and recreation.

On similar lines, formal shelter homes can be created for temporary migrants like maids, drivers, security guards, cooks, constructions workers, and factory workers. Designed using modular structures, these will have common toilets, with drainage and sewer lines, common waste-collection and segregation points, and electricity. Kitchens can be designed for common use, while the bedrooms can be secluded for privacy. Primary health care, crèche services and education can be integrated with housing as essential addendums. A combination of local infrastructure development charges, grants received from federal agencies, and revenue collection from the users can sustainably fund these shelters. Such places can become self-sufficient colonies, with clever and efficient design features, and offer a strong counter that will make a lot of sense when the cost of living in them is found to be lower than that incurred in informal ecosystems, which is a foregone conclusion if resources are pooled for common gain.

The discovery of fire taught our forefathers how to cook their food, which changed their eating habits forever. The industrial age exposed our ancestors to the magic of machines, which eased hard labor. We are now experiencing a similar shift driven by digital age. Digital technologies have opened new frontiers and started to challenge the existing norms of living on the planet.

India's urban planners will need to deeply think about the implications of this digital age on urban living and reconstruct the purpose of the city. The rapid commercialization of additive printing technology is poised to reduce the space required inside factories to produce the same quantum of output. Existing space ratios may not apply to future industrial zones. Electric cars will need fuel stations to be replaced by charge stations. Digitally networked teams are breaking down centralized offices into smaller shared spaces with work-from-home options, which is bound to recalibrate the space and human density norms in the future. Urban planners will need to interpret the digital evolution into design calls for the larger good in future. Toward this purpose, they may even need to take a moral audit of desirable and undesirable adaptation to the digital age. Being custodians of a reactive response alone will not do the trick.

Urban planning in clean countries played a powerful role in changing human behavior for the better and one way it did so was by championing public spaces over private ones – city centers, parks, sidewalks, and river fronts. Take the case of Seoul, which has become synonymous with cycling and walking trails and is championing 'pedestrian first' movement in its design plans and shaping its habitants toward sustainable living. Canada proposed 24,000 kilometers of walking and cycling trail, called the Great Trail or Trans Canada Trail, that will run through the majority of the country and connect the east and the west coasts.

Multipurpose public spaces and the spread of formal public housing symbolize the long way clean cities have come in the last two hundred years in the way they think about their designs. For them urban design is equally an issue of public health and human rights as it is of spatial planning, and is a serious and respected profession, such as the Academy of Neuroscience for Architecture (ANFA) in California that links neuroscience research to the understanding of human responses to the built environment, and symbolizes the triumph of urban planning that now sits at the intersection of humanities and science. What will be a person's state of mind if he encounters congested, stinking lanes on his daily commute to work, versus a one who walks through a park? Can the design response toward senior citizen housing cure patients suffering from dementia? Can better designed prisons reform prisoners? Can the layout of public spaces increase social interaction among the people? Today, practitioners in clean countries look up to urban spatial design to answer these questions precisely and offer a 'templatized' response for replication. Indian urban planners should take a cue from them to understand the role and responsibility in shaping our behavior for a cleaner outcome. Only through such progressive design calls, can many actions of urban Indians that give rise to dirty surroundings be addressed.

Repurposing projects in collaboration with Indian Railways on vast stretches of railway lines that pass through cities and currently present a filthy picture of India could be one unique approach that can crowd out the slums that hold our railway tracks hostage, and start to shape up urban public spaces for the better. Take the apparently benign practice of livestock breeding in many urban households. While families migrated to cities and moved away from farming, this practice hinges both on symbolic association and economic reasons. But urban homes, let alone neighborhoods, are not designed to breed livestock. Solid waste from the livestock chokes up sewage lines. Lack of open area limits air circulation and creates ripe conditions for growth of pathogens. Livestock are released on the streets, adding to the road safety hazard and congestion. They wander to nearby garbage dumps and ingest all sorts of inedible materials that contain toxins, passing them into the milk. The practice of livestock breeding cannot be assimilated into city life in the form it existed in the villages. Urban design response will need to create a community space owned by the local civic body that can be used by any households keen on livestock breeding. The space will provide for common sheds, milking booths, resting places, bio-gas plant for solid waste disposal and others. A progressive design that will take urban livestock away from roads and garbage dumps becomes a purposeful challenge for urban planning.

Disposal of automobiles is another behavior that breeds informality adds to the sanitation woes of cities. Nearly one million automobiles are discarded in Indian cities, annually. These vehicles are disposed of piecemeal, one vehicle or component at a time. It is not unusual to see a condemned automobile disposed through traders in shanties, lying abandoned on pavements or inside auto repair shops, spilling out onto the street and attracting scavengers. They harvest parts, modify and up-cycle them, and metals are sold as scarp. The mechanical and chemical treatment to salvage the spares and metals is done out in the open and releases dangerous toxins into the air, smothering the city in an invisible blanket of poison. Urban planning can change this behavior and imagine formal scrapyards that can either be owned by one big operator or can be shared by many operators for a user fee, on the similar principles as the livestock community. Such productive uses of urban spaces will boost revenue sources for cash strapped local bodies, create a clean environment, while doing away with the informality of the current arrangement.

But before such solutions can be conceived, urban planners will need to make a significant jump in their intellectual capability to absorb the interdependencies of these issues on the design plans of the city. Urban planners' call to action ought to be far more than to possess the mind of an architect. But, it will also be inadequate for Indian urban planners to copy-paste only the outcomes from the triumphs of the First World. The pursuit should instead be to learn the process and not necessarily chase the outcome. The extent of multi-ethnicity, multi-faith and economic diversity of Indian society almost stands out in the world order, which gives rise to unique urban human behavior and bound to produce different outcomes.

For instance, human congregation around religious beliefs is an important and uniquely essential part of Indian urban living. People carry out their search for God in myriad ways but leave a trail of garbage and pandemonium in their wake. An urban planning response for such an issue will have a limited global design precedent. Faith tourism drives the economies of many Indian cities, big and small – Ajmer, Varanasi, Ujjain, Nashik, Haridwar, Sabrimala, Mathura, Allahabad, Datia to name a few. An array of support system works round-the-clock to service floating population in these cities and define the character of these places – buses and taxis, inns and hotels, food stalls, retail selling religious merchandise and ritual services. The floating population enters and exits these cities in nonlinear peaks and troughs. Auspicious occasions draw a disproportionate share of people, often overwhelming the city's civic infrastructure. An urban planning design response similar to a metropolis or an industrial city will not work for these cities. Any planning for one of these places will have to include restricted zones for vehicular traffic, wide walking paths designed for dense human movement, retailing and non-retailing zones, hub and spoke system of public transport that favors smaller (and now energy efficient) vehicles over large ones, installation of sensors and cameras for monitoring and civic enforcement. Such cities will require smart, well-appointed temporary shelters with utility services, surveillance, access to internet and efficient waste collection systems.

Waste from the temples, human waste and the debris from the commercial ecosystem in these towns eventually find their way to the 'pious' water bodies that sit next to them. Intensive redevelopment to re-arrange the commercial ecosystem, free up space for human movement and create better utility services are urban design calls to solve this challenge. The allocation of private spaces near the water bodies like Ghats for instance can be completely done away with in favor of community spaces with better utilities, and provision for food and shelter. Areas can be segregated into paid and free zones, depending upon accessibility and services provided. Establishments with high waste output activities can be zoned up together, moved away from the Ghats and synced up with a common waste segregation and collection system. Portable waste collection systems can be designed and installed in all the religious structures that surround the Ghats. 'Holy' cities like Varanasi, that today attract millions of religious tourists are just not designed to handle a sudden flux of people seeking salvation and merely adds pressure on city administration to troubleshoot to manage this influx. Mostly, city administration manages to scrape through these gatherings, although with severely stretched resources. Sometimes, arrangements break down, which leads to disaster and chaos. Not surprisingly, Varanasi, Pullumedu, Haridwar, Allahabad were ground zero for some of the major stampedes that happened between 2011 and 2016 where human lives in hundreds were lost. Stampede aside, these cities also face an unprecedented challenge of managing the waste generated by the sudden dense human congregation for an extended period, characterized by discarded plastic bottles and food packets, open defecation and garbage discharge into water bodies. City administration cannot be blamed for 'lack of arrangements' if the design of these cities and faith tourism they attract are at cross purpose with each other. In the pre-industrialized era, faith tourism entailed people traveling hundreds of kilometers to these cities on foot, horseback or bullock carts, encountering insurmountable obstacles on the way. Many never made it alive on these journeys. So it came to be believed that only the 'chosen ones' could visit these religious spots, adding to the mystique and romantic attraction of these cities. They evolved to a size that was just enough to handle the number of people who made it there alive. The sheer effort and risk involved in getting there acted as a high entry barrier against huge human influx. But our progress removed these accessibility barriers. People could now take trains, buses, cars, planes and reach these cities in a jiffy. This changed people's view toward pilgrimage and visits to these places became more a matter of recreation than an act of salvation. One could wish for a dip in the holy river to cleanse your sins and be in that city the very next day. This change in thinking toward pilgrimages posed a structural challenge for these cities. The size of the cities and ancient holy installations within them cannot be expanded to accommodate more people. Neither can the size of temples or ghats be increased nor can their presence be distributed all over the city. Similarly, their proxies cannot be deployed elsewhere in the city to distribute the human footprint. The sites that earlier witnessed a few hundred people in a year, now have several thousand seekers thronging it every year. This is a challenge that can at best seek global reference in the Vatican for an urban planning response that witness throngs of religious tourists round the year. An optimum urban planning response would be to re-design the primary space around these religious pivots. Instead of the cramped streets with suffocating homes and shops, this space needs to be designed as a spacious area for the floating population with access to utilities within the primary perimeter, available through user fees. This would replace a free-for-all mind-set of the visiting population with a quid pro quo between the local body and the visitors. This would boost the coffers of the local body and allowed them the financial leeway to further improve the experience. Sadly though, none of this happened in these religious hotspots. Varanasi for instance expanded instead in the same out-of-control way as all other mediocre Indian cities. The city-style development of high rise flats and industrial zones in a city whose primary economic driver is faith tourism and handloom is sheer foolhardiness.

A formal space in a city means a space that is accounted for by the local authorities, with a stated purpose. Its usage is adequately monetized by local authorities which creates resource capability for the local body to ensure its sustainable existence in the foreseeable future. Formal environments are synced up by the local body and regulated for safety, productivity, cleanliness, and efficiency. Cities fail when urban planning fails to provide such formal environments, putting stress on their infrastructure and resources. Every incremental addition of an unplanned human life in the city adds to unplanned waste generation, public health threats, unplanned consumption of utilities and all subsequent interventions of city administration to address these issues are merely efforts to troubleshoot bad design decisions of the past.

The enormity of this challenge will require India to rapidly scale up the technical ability in urban planning. India needs urban planners who can speak of human behavior and civil engineering in the same breadth, who can appreciate the evolution of technology and realize the virtues of leveraging it, who grasp development economics and understand the advantages of sustainable space planning, who are liberal enough to imagine inclusive cities and conservative enough to monetize the city's assets for a financially secure future. It is no mean task to make the existing urban planners unlearn whatever they have learned and start afresh. And it is equally challenging to create a fresh talent pool overnight and expect them to churn out relevant design responses. When the Indian education policy figuratively scratches its heads about how to make its universities world class education centers, it should spare a similar thought for the subject of urban planning. Indian institutions for engineering, design, medicine and humanities will need to find ways to talk to each other to deliver on this multidisciplinary study area. From these juxtapositions will emerge centers of excellence (CoEs) on urban planning that can address the complex, unique and challenging issues that Indian urbanism faces today. Hopefully, these CoEs will nurture and incubate urban planners who will encapsulate the qualities of the likes of Laurie Baker who saw functionality, social conscience and respect for nature in the same line of sight, and Charles Correa, whose restless vision for urban India still lies unfulfilled.

Many questions in the context of urban planning are complex that require examination before convincing solutions can be found. Urban planning will need a segmented template for different city types. Its response for mega metropolises of Delhi and Mumbai will be useless for religious centers like Varanasi. Similarly, an industrial city like Kanpur that sits in a high population density state like Uttar Pradesh will need a different urban planning treatment, versus a city like Coimbatore in Tamil Naidu that shares a similar industrial inclination, but a far lower population density. Purely industrial suburbs like Hosur in Tamil Naidu and Dewas in Madhya Pradesh will need a different template compared to what a combination of industrial and agriculture towns like Aurangabad and Guntur will require. Cities that sit at the heart of tourism, heritage, and nature like Nainital, Munnar, and Shimla will need a separate set of urban planning rules that can keep them ecologically viable in times to come. Centre of Excellence (CoE) on urban planning will need to invest in research, collaboration, and investigation to develop technically feasible and comprehensive solutions to many such questions. As of now, the onus of finding answers to all these questions is on the urban planners, cash-strapped local bodies, and the bureaucracy, with time-bound responsibilities to troubleshoot.

Urban planning should be de-linked from the deformed local bodies and should be given an obstacle-free path for innovative and comprehensive city plans to emerge similar to the century-old approach adopted by Japan. This should be done by buffeting urban planning with national legislation that should define boundaries, guidelines, and codes for urban planning. Plans may then differ for different city types, but will comply to a common core underneath on affordable housing and commerce, scope for public spaces, ecology, and society's collective needs and responsibilities. Local bodies will then act as guardians of these plans and urban planning in turn will earn its rightful freedom from the subservient compulsions of slicing and dicing up urban land. This will also unbundle urban planning as a natural employment destination for the talent pool that the CoE academia will create for the agenda. If one considers the 5,000 Indian cities and that each city needs spirited participation from urban planners in various capacities, then whichever way we do the math, India will need urban planners in lakhs to redesign urban India. But freedom from operational constraints of local bodies does not mean autocracy. It implies autonomy that protects unconstrained thinking and an organization that continues to receive regular political sponsorship.

Toward this purpose, redevelopment of cities needs to supersede all other considerations. It would mean urgent emphasis on mass housing that can root out informal living. This can be achieved in a variety of ways, for instance rapidly executed redevelopment projects of existing residential colonies where residents can be incentivized to land-pool their houses in favor of efficient homes and free up space to create clean and inspiring surroundings. Rebuilding commercial and public spaces on similar lines to create adequate supply of the right kind of spaces that suck out informal commercial activities, yet score high on the monetizing factor for local bodies is the way to think about redevelopment. The existence of an informal footprint in the city serves a certain purpose, and that purpose needs to become an integral part of the redevelopment agenda to reduce stress on urban infrastructure. There is nothing novel about the crying need to prioritize redevelopment of Indian cities over their expansion. It has been feebly attempted for some time now, but ended up injecting uncertainty in people's lives and only aggravating the urban mess. It has been two decades since the redevelopment of Dharavi was conceived, but it still stands at the boundary of Mumbai international airport. It took four years to conceive a redevelopment plan for the dilapidated structures of walled city of Shahjahanabad in Delhi before it was tabled by the local civic body of Delhi for discussion in 2009. It took another six years to figure out the organizational structure needed within the governance framework to undertake this project and an additional two years to develop the first draft of the finance plan. Twelve years after the redevelopment plan of the walled city was first mooted, it is yet to break ground. These failures have essentially been on two counts. First, the redevelopment plans never took into account the time taken to make a transition from the existing to the redeveloped living, from the perspective of the inhabitants of the walled city. Essentially, the time taken for people to unplug and replug their lives needed to be the cornerstone of the redesign plans, and the complete absence of this factor and the consequent resistance made this project a non-starter. Second, these redevelopment plans lacked the text to convey to the inhabitants their incremental benefits over existing ecosystems. Redevelopment is not merely a civil engineering exercise to replace shanties with concrete boxes, but a social exercise that requires the political acumen to sense the votes in it and, therefore, the salesmanship to convince the beneficiaries to gain their support. Only streetlights and paved roads in the new plan would not cut ice with the inhabitants if it meant they would be displaced for a long time.

Take, for instance, the redevelopment plan for informal retailing like hawking that can significantly enrich the local bodies' revenue streams while eradicating chaos. But such a plan will need to fulfill the precondition of creating such spaces in sufficient numbers to successfully nudge informal retailing into the formal fold. Street markets can be designed with utilities, parking, and waste management support, which will dissuade hawking at any vulnerable place and add further stress to the local infrastructure. A hawker has no formal commercial contract with the local body. He pays no rent for the use of the space nor does he subscribe to any utility service. But he does pay protection money for hassle-free continuation of retail at his chosen site, which makes the cost of his business only marginally lower than that in a formal arrangement. The hawker uses the urban space that is provided for by the local body, but the local body does not get any monetary return, the local land mafia syndicate does. This asymmetric arrangement disturbs the level-playing field for retailers who own businesses in a formal environment like bazaars and malls. Formal retailers invest capital in shops, and pay utility bills and taxes on the merchandise they sell. Informal retailing conveniently escapes all these investments and ends up grooming non-state actors in the process, not to mention the perpetual stress this arrangement creates on the meager resources of local bodies, the garbage it generates, and the congestion it causes in public spaces. In a way, the inaction of urban planning penalized formal retail for good behavior and incentivizes informal retail for bad behavior. The hawker may be a well-intentioned entrepreneur who is keen to make an honest living, but informal retailing steers him toward illegality.

Farmers and fishermen need makeshift retail facilities for their produce and catches, respectively, as do small craftsmen. People also resort to makeshift retailing to supplement their household income, such as those selling festive merchandise like water guns and colors during the Holi, or rakhis for Rakshabandhan, as a quick way to earning additional income. City areas that are impractical for shops require makeshift retailing. For instance, construction sites or areas that are sparsely populated or road intersection points that see high movement of humans. Urban planners of clean cities recognize the importance of makeshift retailing and create viable formal solutions. They assign places for flea markets with utility and waste management support and hawking zones with user fees and detailed guidelines of use. They do not infringe upon individuals' rights, instead have designed adequate formal spaces to carry out temporary retail with dignity, at the same time keeping the city clean. Mercado San Miguel in central Madrid is a gastronomical delight that opened in 2009. It took six years to restore an old building into an iron-and-glass facade market that houses street-food stalls. A stunning place abuzz with small food stalls that sell everything from aromatic bread to delectable seafood defines Mercado San Miguel today. Planning for common utilities, arresting monetization leakages, and a superior yet inexpensive customer experience lie at the heart of this market's inspiring exteriors.

In the Indian context, the spirit of village fairs and haats can be remodeled as a formal response to informal retailing to sell home improvement goods, preowned goods, street food, and handicraft. Old buildings, industrial sheds of abandoned public enterprises, empty institutional grounds, and land repossessed from encroachment offer great possibilities to be reimagined as spaces for such formal temporary retailing, which will keep aside the trail of filth that these informal markets leave behind.

Reducing urban local bodies' dependence on real-estate transactions as the single most important source of financial sustenance needs to be urban planning's second tenet of its purpose. The more urban plans create freely traded real estate for homes and shops at the expense of a comprehensive urban-planning approach, the more this will create chaotic and dirty cities.

Indian cities need old age homes that can operate without biases, crèches that are safe, accessible and affordable for even a low wage earning housemaid to deposit her toddler on her way to work and pick up the child in the evening. They will need rental housing ecosystems or smart chawls that are prolifically sprinkled across the city and promote community living as a counter to the mirage of affordable housing that India chases today. They will need technology enabled kerbside parking systems, and stand-alone parking installations that can significantly enhance revenue from parking fees and arrest free use that leads to congestion. They will need sporting arenas and music schools in the low-income suburbs giving equal opportunity for everyone to explore individual talent. They will need more public spaces over private ones in the form of parks, community centers, walking and cycling trials that can be monetized in myriad ways. They will need automobile scrapyards and urban dairies in financially viable partnerships and that can provide formal solutions. Operational sustainability of these ideas will then become essential deliverables of urban design responses that will open many avenues for local civic bodies to monetize assets and services within their jurisdictions.

By 2030, the economic size of many Indian cities will individually be greater than that of many countries of the world, and the aspirational needs of these future mega Indian cities will not be restricted to basics like food, shelter, and work. Urban planning should aim and recognize the psychological make-up of these emerging cities to keep them clean and its citizens happy and healthy.

The story of informal transport hubs that operate on the fringes of India's urbanism is an interesting case that can bundle these ideas. These transport hubs act as convergence points for lorries that either transit through the city or halt here before entering the city due to traffic restrictions. More than three quarters of India's goods move through surface transport, which makes these transport hubs a critical microcosm of urban India. They act as vital transit points for movement of goods, as tax collection points, as automobile repair and retail zones to provide vehicle maintenance to the lorries and as lodging destination for truckers. Their location on the urban fringes also makes them important economic drivers for rural economies in the vicinity. But, the structural existence of these transport hubs hardly captures their importance. There are no parking places for the hundreds of lorries that throng there and spill out on the motorways, significantly increasing the road safety risks. Food stalls, eateries, automobile repair shops and washing centers that operate out of shacks open their doors onto the motorways. The bumpy mud surface at these hubs are sans any drainage and sewage lines. Human waste from lodges and hotels, food waste from the eateries and black sludge from washing centers converge into an open cesspool that can invariably be seen beside the motorway and becomes an unmissable welcome signage to most Indian cities. The lack of urban design response to create a formal space for this need, more than these transport hubs themselves, needs to shoulder the primary blame for this outcome. A better design response for these transport hubs has enormous potential: formal parking bays can be designed, for instance, to be used for a fee on either a pay-as-you-go model or a monthly pre-paid system. Digital technologies can be used easily to roll out such a system and arrest the practice of unauthorized parking on the highways. Zoning and space planning techniques can be used to provision for optimum number of automobile repair shops, restaurants and motels in the vicinity. Formal warehousing and logistics operations can be planned to support the functioning of the hub. Every activity in the informal eco-system of the hub can be formalized through an integrated design solution with the intent that every shop or commercial function is financially sustainable. Support system such as recreation and primary health centers can be planned, improving the working conditions of truckers and other employees associated with this sector. These informal, filthy, and unsafe working environments can easily be transformed to become clean and efficient, and bring dignity to the road transportation sector, while affording the local bodies incremental revenue through interesting monetization models. The design response will demand five thousand such transport hubs in different forms and sizes across India.

Reduction in the commute time between the home and place of work needs to be the third important tenet of Indian urban planning's purpose. Urban plans will need to push formal solutions to reduce unproductive human movement and to eliminate the stress that it puts on urban infrastructure. Take for instance an industrial zone that houses ten manufacturing units located on the fringes of the city. Each manufacturing unit employs one hundred workers, which means there are one thousand workers in the cluster. If this zone is not supported by formal affordable housing units with access to schools, hospitals and retail, then the needs of the labor pool will be met in two ways. First, workers will prefer to reside in various parts of the cities and undertake a grueling daily commute to work. Without formal transport systems, the transportation needs of the one thousand workers promotes informal (and unsafe) public transport options of polluting unregulated vehicles. This creates a domino effect, triggering an informal retail ecosystem of eateries and automobile repair shops to mushroom in the by-lanes of the industrial zone. Alternatively, one thousand workers in the industrial zone start to live in slums in the vicinity to cut out the grueling commute. This slum colony with no formal access to utilities, retailing and healthcare is the next best option for employees to avoid the grueling long commute. Dera Bassi on the outskirts of Mohali, slums in Noida and shanties in Kanpur signify that a well-meaning initiative to create an industrial zone and spur economic development in the city ends up creating informal living, congested roads and dirty surroundings. The culprit is not the intention but the urban planning response that failed to orchestrate the smooth conduct of this initiative.

Sensible solutions need to appreciate the nature of different ecosystems that drive various economic activities in the city. Retailing needs real estate and sales staff; commercial offices need security, housekeeping, transport; taxis need parking, repair and maintenance among others. For a productive and clean discharge of economic activities, urban plans will need to account for every component, big and small, of these ecosystems. It means design interpretations in keeping with the nature of various economic activities. In the case of building industrial zones, industrial development policy can easily mandate the factories to share the cost for building formal residences for its staff as a precondition. This can start to quantify affordable housing units, parks, schools, health centers, and markets near the industrial zone both for the currently employed workers and for the estimated future increase in human density. A simple pursuit to reduce commute time that requires a design response of interdependent solutions can yield cleaner outcomes.

Commute times are also reduced by democratizing transport choices – an idea fine-tuned by clean cities in the world in inspiring ways. Increasingly, more and more cities are jumping onto this bandwagon. Dedicated bicycle and walking paths are no more restricted to parks and jungle trails. These paths are designed for mainstream use and cut through the cities. Long sky walks for people to walk to work on top of city's highways are common sites in Tokyo (the city of Mumbai has had good success with this idea). Surface walking paths that are clean and safely intersect with motor roads are delightful to watch in the city of London. It is a visual treat to witness dedicated cycling lanes that allow hundreds in the city of Amsterdam to cycle to work in the lap of safety and calm. It is no wonder that there is a striking commonality between cleanliness in a city and its democratic approach to transport design for human movement. These cities think about transport options more as an issue of equality than merely as an infrastructure response. Increasingly city planners are drifting toward the idea that citizens should have optionality of transport choices. Every transport choice should be equally safe, secure, clean and not be provided for as an afterthought. Many cities use this template to increasingly make private transport more expensive than public transport, but ensure that all transport choices rate equally on comfort, safety and convenience. They make private transport expensive by levying congestion tax for the right to drive in certain areas of the city or by making permanent parking slots for cars as expensive as the cars themselves. But these cities were able to take such calls only after they built myriad transport systems as viable alternatives in adequate supply. They created convenient public transport systems and safe cycling and walking tracks for intra-city commute. Cities like London, Singapore, New York, Tokyo unabashedly sided with public transport and restricted private vehicle ownership as an aspirational purchase for those who could afford it. Other cities promoted equality by allowing inhabitants to choose all forms of transport will equal ease. For instance, in Seattle, one can choose to cycle, walk or drive to work with equal ease and safety. An elaborate network of exclusive trails for pedestrians and cyclists runs through the city and is fast mirroring the road network on reach and access. Clean cities established objective tradeoffs between different transport choices which contributed immensely in keeping their respective cites clean.

In 2017, a research by a consortium of leading academic institutions concluded that not so far in the future people in India will travel longer distances to work and their fuel expenses will rise by 35 percent from the present levels. This implies that urban transport in India fails to offer a similar trade-off. Let us say the local municipal body of an Indian city plans a bus service between points A and B. But the frequency of the bus is once every hour. However, the movement between these two points creates enough commuters to fill up one bus every fifteen minutes. This is when informal transport emerges to fill this gap for the same fare. The issue with informal transport is same as that with informal retail: it creates human movement that is not planned by the city. Informal transport ferries people from unscheduled bus stops and causes road safety hazards. Unplanned stops for commuters give rise to informal retail that increase human consumption points not accounted for by urban plans. Soon, the route between points A and B is a chaotic mess with informal public transport vehicles making road travel unsafe for one and all. Urban planning should be able to give an equal chance to all means of transport, if cost is not a factor. If a wellness enthusiast wants to cycle to work from Vashi to Bandra in Mumbai, she should be able to do so without the fear of getting run over by a speeding car. A family should be able to walk from Varanasi to Allahabad for holy pilgrimage without running the risk of getting robbed midway. A worker employed in a factory in NOIDA should feel safe enough taking a stroll back home through a park after work. Urban planning needs to create options for inhabitants to walk, cycle, or drive to their destinations or take public transport. One road cannot be the solution for all of these options. But sadly cows, bicycles, dogs, pedestrians, cars, scooters, bullock carts, scooters, motorbikes, buses, trailers, and dumper trucks all jostle for their glory on one single road.

In Hollywood, the chaotic Indian road has replaced snake charmers as the quintessentially stereotypical symbolism used to depict India. For Hollywood Inc., chaos on the road has an instantaneous connect with 'Indianness' on celluloid. Can we really blame Hollywood for this bias? Have we not rightly earned the mind-numbing bewilderment with which the First World views our cities? Why don't Indian roads have pavements for people to walk on? Even if they do, why are these pavements built as an afterthought or encroached upon by hawkers? Why are dedicated bicycle lanes absent when we have so many people cycling? Indian urban planners took half-baked inspiration from North America and made roads the primary transport platform for cities, keeping automobiles at the heart. In the 1950s, the USA opted for roads as a primary transport platform to support its growing automobile industry. The policy push rapidly developed an elaborate road infrastructure across the country and created enabling conditions that made it possible for every American to own a car. That is why American roads are designed in a manner that they serve the need of the American majority. India's case was different. Its economic disparity, its stage of economic lifecycle in relation to the world order, and its external dependence for energy needs never made for such a clear-cut choice, yet we ended up viewing the road as the only platform of urban transport. Not surprisingly, a few decades later chaos reigns on these roads. The world of today is very different from that of the 1950s. So much so that even the American narrative on transportation is expanding to include environmentally sustainable choices (with or without the ratification of the Paris climate change declaration), which is forcing urban planners to go back to their virtual-reality applications (erstwhile drawing boards) and take a fresh stab at designing cities.

The impact of current and expected economic activities and the kind of employment cities provide naturally has implications on human movements within the city. Indian urban planners need to appreciate such inextricable links to imagine urban transport to reduce commute times. Agriculture is at the fulcrum of the ecosystem in many cities like Jalgaon in Maharashtra and Guntur in Andhra Pradesh. State-spending drives the economic activities of capital cities such as Bhopal, Raipur, Patna, and Lucknow. A high share of remittance incomes from abroad in cities like Muzzaffarpur in Bihar or Trichy in Kerala will need to be accounted for urban design of these cities. Economic powerhouses like Pune and Hyderabad will act as hubs and pose their own set of challenges arising out of a diverse mix of exports, small-scale manufacturing, services, state spending, and so on. These cities have high and diverse human migration compared to a city like Jalgaon that sees migration from within the state. No doubt the recognition of these aspects should have far-reaching implications on city plans, provided urban planners pay heed to them.

The agenda of urban planning for Indian cities is comprehensive with multiple goals: environment and ecology, public and private health, effective local governance, equality, and commuting time. If urban planners were to choose only one unit to measure the progress on all of these goals, then the cleanliness of the city should be that unit because it symbolizes a triumph on all these parameters. A clean Indian city will have no informal living and has achieved inclusion through community living. It will have planned all human movement and created a safe environment for one and all. It will have vibrant public spaces that symbolize its preserved heritage and provide a healthy environment to its citizens. But it should begin with recognizing the unfortunate fact that the current urban planning approach is calibrated for failure. The default setting of the urban-design approach spews waste, informality, and congestion. It should also accept that the problem is humungous, resources scarce, and intellect meager.

There is also an increasing likelihood that the millennial generation will grow up to be very different from us. The evolution of a multicultural society, environmental degradation, and the role of technology will shape their worldview and expectations from cities, which may alter their notion of urbanism. They may shun private transport in favor of shared rides or public transport. Respect for the environment may see them embracing responsible living and opt for cozy, ecologically sustainable small homes in cities over big, resource guzzling sprawls in suburbs. The concept of suburbs as an addendum to cities may be replaced by compact cities with efficient living, vertical farms, short commutes and shared public spaces.

These outcomes may not purely result from willing choices, but also from compelling needs forced by factors beyond our control. For instance, technology that is rapidly changing the discourse on job creation in the First World through e-commerce, robotics, virtual reality and data science will have implication on the nature of real estate in the city. Many existing jobs will be replaced by robots. Centralized offices and large workforces will metamorphose into distributed office spaces and significantly nimbler human congregations. These will have implications on the labor markets in not-so-pleasant terms. Unemployment may become prolonged and underemployment more prolific, forcing societies to seek frugal living, championing public transport, sharing public resources, and sparse homes more as a matter of compulsion than choice. There is an increasing likelihood that the urban planning outcomes in the First World delivered in the last century will become redundant and get replaced with designs that today appear to be improbable.

Urban planners in the clean countries are acknowledging these trends and their implication on the future of the cities. They are adopting virtual reality and data science to visualize the cities of the future. Urban-space planning is now more about pixelated game-like apps that can promptly throw up 3D models of future cities than about laboriously drawing blueprints and technical drawings. Solutions like an app designed by Toolz, a French start-up, allows urban planners to design city projects in virtual reality today offer possibilities for Indian urban planners to imagine futuristic cities, lets them peek into the future for political sponsorship and sell it to the franchise.

Indian urban planning needs to unlearn, relearn, improvise, and deliver at the same time. If more than half of India's population are to live in cities by 2050, urban living will massively sway the social and economic landscape of India in the next century. It will be up to urban planning to ensure that the narrative of the coming century is held in reverence and not in disdain. The concept of 'space' in an urban setting is one of the hardest to define and will determine India's future. Our current urban mess is partly an outcome of consistently managing urban-space planning with a surprisingly simplistic toolkit. Once this is owned up to, there will emerge explicit chasms that can be bridged with intellectual rigor and holistic appreciation of the intertwined issues. Urban planning will need intellectual liberation to be able to create the right reference points. It will require well-meaning political sponsorship to take bold calls that can shape human behavior, and the financial fuel to stay the course and take them to their logical conclusions. In July 2017, the Chennai Metropolitan Development Authority (CMDA) announced the redevelopment plan of old contiguous buildings in the George Town area, in the hope to correct past mistakes – 1 percent of all structures here are built as per the development control rules. In 2018, Maharashtra also took a serious push toward redevelopment of dilapidated structures. But if the first instinct of Delhi in 2018 to redevelop a neighborhood on the pyre of 16,000 trees is anything to go by, informal living, illegal commerce, water wars, and agony over transportation will continue to spit out unpleasant outcome in urban India for quite some time.

4

INFORMAL LIVING

We the Invisible Citizens

Jaane Bhi Do Yaaron is a popular Indian feature film, a rare gem of satire on many themes of Indian urbanism – inequality, sordid real-estate alliances, trials and tribulations of the struggling masses, local governance, and the role of media, among others. The film's slapstick yet stinging humor is delivered from the viewpoint of the city's oppressed middle class in a manner that is seldom seen in Indian motion pictures. In one scene, a newly constructed overbridge is being inaugurated. During the ceremony, various stakeholders deliver speeches from the podium, including the owner of the construction company that built the bridge with inferior materials, and the municipal commissioner who he was hand-in-glove with. The owner unabashedly proclaims that the new bridge will not only reduce the commute time for motorists, but also be home to hundreds of people who will build their shanties in its underbelly. Formal spaces in Indian cities cannot exist without informal living in their vicinity, was the poignant message of the speech delivered by the shrewd real-estate magnate in this hilarious scene. This satirical take on informal living in India is as relevant today as it was at the time of the film's release in 1982.

Informal living stems from the illegitimate liaison between urban planning and state actors. The technical inaptitude of urban planning and the vulnerability of the state actors spawn this ill-begotten product, whose arrival spells adverse effects for public hygiene, cleanliness and sanitation, and disfigures the Indian urbanism on many counts. Therefore, India's best bet to partly solve the sanitation challenge would be to arrest this illegitimate consummation. But, a credible blueprint to manage excreta and other waste discharge of India's informal citizens will elude us as long as this cry of desperation falls on deaf ears; a cry for sure because the status quo is nothing short of a catastrophe that represents wholesale abandonment of the sanitation needs of India's invisible citizens.

To use expressions like 'jhuggis,' 'shanties,' and 'squatters' for informal living is to reduce its expansiveness. 'Slums' is a term often used for informal living, though this too seems limited in scope. Informal living is a curious case of an entire urban ecosystem existing where it should not have. Philosophically, informal living is a dichotomy of shattered dreams, on the one hand, and of unbridled hope, on the other. Socially, it is the first pit stop for urbanization in the modern world and no country can claim to have been free from it in its post-industrialization history. Economically, it is the flag-bearer of labor arbitrage that offers affordable convenience to the formal consuming class of the city in the form of maids, drivers, factory workers, security guards, gardeners, courier boys, spa therapists, and so on. Informal living may be an eyesore; its existence embodies the inability of the state actors to perform their duties, thus presenting a captive political opportunity which can be seized with minimal toil. A slum absorbs inconvenient truth and difficult questions.

Until the pre-industrialization era, explorers brought people as labor, farmers, and soldiers from their native lands to access precious raw material, fertile land, and resources that presented the single biggest source of wealth creation then. Such adventures led to the colonization of most of Latin American and the Caribbean cluster. This kind of human migration was, however, controlled and to that extent self-limiting. Industrialization at the start of the nineteenth century changed this discourse because it shifted the focus from land as the principal source of wealth creation to technology and markets, giving rise to factories. Lured by better pay, people migrated from farms to cities in Europe and North America during this period to work in the industries of automobiles, steel, transportation, consumer products, and financial services. People working in banks and factories needed a support system of schools, hospitals, markets, shops, local transportation, saloons, that further fuelled the migration of people to towns to run retail shops, drive carts and taxis, supply food through eateries, pubs, and operate hotels. Concurrently, mechanization in agriculture and advancements in food processing divided the society into food production and consumption hubs. Everybody did not need to till the land anymore to access decent food, prompting people to look to cities for greener pastures. Soon the demand for workers outstripped the supply causing a wage imbalance in favor of the labor force. This prompted more humans to migrate from farms to cities in Europe and North America in the industrial era – an uncontrolled migration that was based purely on demand and supply. Unlike previously, there were no checks and balances on the nature and quantum of movement by any authority. This uncontrolled migration was based purely on demand and supply – it could be seen that three-quarters of Stockholm's population at the start of the twentieth century, for instance, was not born in the city.

Such a human rush requires any city to rapidly scale up housing, healthcare services, streets and sewage systems to adequately support massive urbanization propelled by abrupt economic growth. Today, this insight may seem obvious, but during the nineteenth and early twentieth centuries, no historical precedence for such an event could be used for guidance. Therefore, it was an unprecedented phenomenon that caught these cities off guard and led to their unplanned growth and for the first time in their living memory, they began to grow beyond their walled limits or city centers. Shanties and ghettos became the mainstay of housing that stretched the installed sanitation and waste management infrastructure. Garbage and human waste was disposed in the open on streets more or less describes the Paris of 1880s, which was in the thick of such a social change. It is hard to imagine the city we know of today as fashionable and romantic, as an intolerable mess of sanitation at the turn of the twentieth century.

During this period, the structure of most cities in the First World was at odds with the rapid urbanization. This led to the mushrooming of informal living or inferior formal living characterized by deplorable conditions, 'tenement,' as it was called in the city of New York. In 1900, two-thirds of New York's population of over three million lived in these tenements. Houses were dingy, had limited or no plumbing, and dozens of people had to share one toilet. In 1890, author and photographer Jacob Riis captured the state of tenement housing in New York in his seminal work, *How the Other Half Lives*. His seminal work was equally relevant to London and many other cities in Europe, Japan, and North America at that time. For instance, in a survey conducted by Charles Booth between 1887 and 1902, one in three Londoners was affected by widespread poverty and informal living. Slums in London were overcrowded, with no access to sanitation and water, whereas the city's formal living was tasteful, indulgent, and clean.

The ill effects of informal living manifested in the form of public health crises. Infant deaths, low-life expectancy, and repeated outbreak of water-borne diseases began to weigh down on the citizens. The direct relationship between economic growth and informal housing was finally understood and the purpose of cities in the post-industrialized world underwent a rapid transformation thereafter. Public housing emerged as a strong political agenda that saw various acts, legislations, and government-sponsored initiatives in the First-World countries to eradicate informal living from their urban landscape. Today, the First World is nearing a century of a slum-free existence even though it took them half a century to figure out the problem and find a solution.

The democratization of technology and manufacturing, and lowered trade barriers in the post World War II order propagated a new wave of economic growth that further accelerated the pace of urbanization across the world and led to massive exodus of people to cities in the decades that followed. It happened at a magnitude that had no previous parallel. In 1950, nearly 30 percent of the world's 2.5 billion people lived in the new cities. By 2015, this urban population had increased to 54 percent of the nearly 7 billion people on the planet. To put it differently, cities in the world packed 3 billion new residents in sixty years, a number that was more than the entire world population in 1950.

The human migration to cities in the twentieth century in Europe and North America was nowhere near this magnitude. For instance, till 1950, nearly all the 700 million plus urban humans in the world and were concentrated in the First World. But, after the 1950s, the size and scale of urbanization witnessed a tectonic shift. A significant number of the new urbanites, who witnessed the first wave of economic growth in the post industrialized world, lived in the Third World: Korea, Philippines, Indonesia, the Indian subcontinent, and the Middle East cluster in Asia; Nigeria, Kenya, and Egypt in Africa; and Brazil, Chile, Argentina, and Columbia in South America. The urbanization wave in the Third World coincided with the time when many of these countries were discovering their political ideologies. Some were young democracies, while others were to end up as quasi-autocracies or absolute monarchies. Unlike the developed world that had a mature political order at the turn of the twentieth century (one that emerged from its own cycle of trials) so as to appreciate the agenda of urbanization and economic growth, the Third World was still discovering its political will. The institutional capability of their public institutions was weak, and the urban housing agenda seemed too far-fetched and ahead of its time. Moreover, the economic growth in these countries was not in lieu of the growth in the developed world, on the contrary, drivers in the First World (in the form of markets, demand, or technology) were the lynchpin of this growth, for instance, the demand for oil by the First World drove economic growth in the Middle East and South America. In many of these countries, the World War II hangover acted as a catalyst for economic growth, one that was skewed around industries, such as automobiles, engineering, aerospace, that had produced goods for the war and needed stable markets after it. Therefore, the economic growth in the Third World acquired a subservient attitude to the First World. This led to the de-coupling of the issues of economic growth and urbanization for a coordinated policy response. Issues relating to urbanization became a post-facto governance matter that failed to imbibe the learning of the First World, that economic growth and urbanization needed to go jointly for a cleaner outcome. Unregulated and free-for-all urbanization started to disfigure the cities of the Third World. The cities' lack of readiness to absorb the exodus of people from the rural provinces was a non-issue for the people because economic safety and anonymity in the city was unmatched, nor was there the constant threat of persecution in extreme cases. The rise of slums in the Tondo region of Manila is a case in point. Still recovering from the aftermath of the US occupation, this area known for its beach resorts was razed to ground during World War II and was immediately occupied by squatters to escape the poverty and exploitation in the villages. Today, Tondo is one of the most densely populated land masses and houses over 80,000 people per square mile in deplorable living conditions.

The reasons for the rise of slums in Nigeria, Kenya, Indonesia, and India were similar to that of Manila – abrupt economic growth coupled with abandonment of urbanization by policymakers, ignorance, institutional incapacity, a nascent political voice. Some countries, like South Korea, did succeed in addressing the urbanization issue in tandem with economic growth, although it did have an advantage of a relatively smaller population and a concentrated agenda of urbanization (60 percent of South Korea's population lives around Seoul). Countries in the Middle East had miniscule populations and the oil money allowed them to buy their way out of this problem. These exceptions, notwithstanding, the rise of slums in the Third World block had a few distinctive traits with respect to the rise of informal living in Europe and North America a century earlier. First, the sheer scale and pace of urbanization was significantly grander than what the First World experienced. Second, the rise of informal living in the Third World lacked resistance from the political order. For example, it is inconceivable for the political order in Kolkata to sniff dividend in the urgency to transfer the thousands of squatters living in shanties on the pavements to non-deplorable living conditions or in the push back to resist these squatters. This is unlike the inhuman living conditions of the slums of New York and Chicago that triggered a spate of laws against these conditions or the roll out of the public housing program in the 1920s in the UK to cull slums.

It will not be far-fetched, though, to say that political apathy toward informal living in the Third World was partially borne out of ignorance. For the lack of resources, institutional capacity, and lack of past references related to slum living, the political narrative lacked the tools to tackle this issue. Political maturity and institutional capability of the First-World countries recognized the adverse impact of the growth of informal living on civic and urban infrastructure, sanitation, public health, human rights, and individual dignity in a timely fashion. They recognized the urgency to create formal solutions to address factors that gave rise to informal living because they were quick to learn the inevitability of migration to the cities in the wake of industrialization and rapid economic growth. Therefore, instead of resisting human migration, these cities created formal living solutions. On the other hand, political order in the Third World first ignored the issue and later unwittingly began to seek dividends in sponsoring informal living. Slums were groomed as hunting grounds for political strength, which gave a free pass to the parallel economy, slowly blurring the lines between informality and illegality. By the twenty-first century, the Third World witnessed unhinged growth of informal living, and slums emerged as a picture of contradictions manifesting both despair and cause for child labor, spurious trade, and nefarious encroachment.

In the case of India, the scale of urban migration and the lack of political sponsorship on the issue translated into a nearly fourteen-fold growth of the slum-dwelling population between 1951 and 2016, whereas the overall population grew at less than half that rate during the same period. In 2016, India had over 100 million people living in slums, ghettoes, and shanties that dotted the urban landscape, a number that is more than the entire population of countries like the UK. India started to lose the plot on informal living in the wave of movement toward the cities that started in the late 1970s, and by the time of the economic reforms program in 1991 informal living in urban India was bustling, which grew manifold in the subsequent years with impeccable credentials.

Human migration to Indian cities was prompted by the disproportionate rise in the fortunes of urban India which motivated people to come here in search for a 'better' life. But the country's urbanism lacked policy response specifically on public housing to address this social change. This chasm served up informal living as a mouth-watering political dish on a platter. Informal living turned out to be a dish that yielded rich calories for the political machinery but ended up disfiguring the arteries of India's urbanism. The political narrative could not resist the seductive appeal of rising number of vulnerable habitants in the slums in urban India.

It was harder toil to make the state address their need of housing and commerce through formal responses and easier to harvest this insecure vote bank through non-state intervention. It was more lucrative for an aspiring politician to get positioned as the messiah of this vulnerable class than to allow the state to intervene with formal solutions. It would, however, be unfair to say that the state was pressured by the political narrative to vacate its role on the issue. The state willingly abdicated this role due to its inherent bias of viewing India solely through the rural lens. The state's failure to appreciate the full gravitas of the issue created an opportunity for non-state actors to seek arbitrage on informal living and take control, would be a fairer way to put it.

Informal living became a hotbed for political leverage; the bigger the ghetto, the greater its potential for patronage, in lieu of protection for their invisible existence (from abrupt eviction, access to utility services and others). A ghetto attained critical mass when it breached the threshold of tolerance on filth, congestion, crime, and public health risks. The foulness of the odors and the sights indicated the readiness of the ghetto as a politically relevant mass ready to be taken into its fold. Alas, the 'breach indicators' of the ghetto also became a qualification for a fit case to receive a stamp of legitimization or 'regularization.' Theoretically, regularization meant that habitants living in the ghetto would come into the fold of the formal space of the city, and enjoy utility services of the local governance, like water, waste collection, and electricity, notwithstanding the wherewithal of the concerned municipal body. It also meant that the ghetto's structural design would be assessed for its ability to deliver clean and healthy living, re-laying the civil infrastructure to allow for parks, community centers, pavements, and sewerage systems. How can the design of houses and shops be reimagined if so far it has been an amateur, knee-jerk response toward a stop-gap arrangement? The race to 'regularize' the ghetto to reap political dividends pushed questions about their 'post-regularization' existence out of the checklist forever. Squatters were satiated to receive the stamp of regularization and become 'visible citizens' as they could now be above board and transact and construct real estate in the ghetto. The local governance extended some semblance of utility services to the ghetto for pocket change worth of taxes in return, while the political order of the day smirked over the captive support base it gained in lieu of the regularization. No one had the time to go through the painful process of looking at the structural design of the ghetto for a cleaner and healthier outcome. The political narrative had to move on to the next one and the local governance could slyly look the other way after symbolically extending its presence to the ghetto. Such an allegorical regularization meant nothing to the structural design of the slum colony and to its waste management and sanitation systems. The streets within it remained deplorable with limited access to sewage system, while provisions for formal public spaces like parking, parks and pavements were not even part of the consideration set. This did not, however, prevent the newly legitimized home owners to monetize their real estate. They constructed shops and houses in the slums in the manner that defied all logic of sane living. In doing so they often went beyond the permissible construction limits and successfully tested the inability of the local governance to call out their misdemeanors. This further disfigured the 'regularized' living that continued to breed congestion and dirty surroundings by default. Dingy informal colonies became dingy formal colonies that in turn led to illegal spaces, a template that may have solved the informal living crisis on paper, but ended up with an even dirtier outcome. In 2012, more than 900 unauthorized residential colonies in Delhi were 'regularized' under this script. Seven years on, nothing in these neighborhoods has changed for the nearly four million residents, besides their 'formal' status on paper.

Informal living in India meant different things to different people. For, the political narrative, it was a cost-effective vote bank that could successfully launch political careers. Intermediaries saw opportunities in spurious trade and land encroachment for a quick buck. For the formal consuming class, it was a convenience that came without the paraphernalia. Urban India willingly accepted informal living despite the ugly truths, thus creating the endearing legacy of *Jaane Bhi Do Yaaron,* which is remembered decades on.

In 2015, the South Delhi Municipal Corporation (SDMC) and Public Works Department (PWD) hired a civil contractor to construct a bridge over a sewerage drain in south Delhi. Instead of providing formal accommodation to them, the contractor asked them to make temporary shelters over the stinky drain for the duration of the construction activity. The grave health and the sanitation risks such an arrangement posed were hardly paid heed to by the contractor. The run-off from all the daily chores of the labor force like cooking and toilet was allowed to navigate freely next to the open drain and litter the vicinity. In January 2017, the Delhi High Court reprimanded these state actors for such a callous approach of their contractor, owing to a PIL on this matter. But much to the chagrin of a rational-minded judiciary, the contractor's conduct on the matter is acceptable as per the state because the notion of informal living and the narrative of India's urbanism are so intertwined that state actors often unwittingly find themselves morally on the wrong side of this issue. The state fails to see anything wrong in such arrangements because it is conditioned to build and govern Indian cities that perpetuate inequality as a default outcome with slums and bungalows sitting in the comfortable company of each other. What, then, is the big deal if the contractor appointed by them followed the same drill?

The implicit benefits of informal living to different stakeholders allowed state actors to not take a hard stance against it. By the start of the twenty-first century, Indian cities could merely witness its swift rise without offering any resistance. The rapid economic growth of Indian cities presented the wage arbitrage between the rural and urban life prompting millions to move in to take up the jobs of drivers, security guards, cooks, factory and construction workers and such others. They, in turn, needed a supporting ecosystem for their existence, which triggered more people to head to cities to run informal groceries stores and meat shops, temples and mosques, eateries and dairies to support the burgeoning informal workforce. Slums, squatters, shanties, and ghettos slowly enveloped urban India. In the face of this mammoth scale of human influx, political discourse lost the gumption to build a contrarian viewpoint. Furthermore, it wrongly equated the opposition of informal living with objecting to the presence of its inhabitants, while in reality the objection should have been made not to the fact that they were coming to the city, but to the way they went about finding a place to live. This, undoubtedly, would have brought with it, the more uncomfortable responsibility of finding them decent shelter, upon the state actors. Instead they opted for the easy route and meekly surrendered to informal living at the first instance. They did not mind that millions of people lived in deplorable conditions, but took exception to any bold stand against this, for the risk of wrong posturing. Is not the state's dormancy on the issue the real culprit for society's immunity toward this inequality, one that needs an overburdened judiciary to show them the folly of their distorted thinking?

Formal habitants from hinterlands became informal habitants in cities. The economic benefits of their informality that were remitted to their domiciled villages kept the social order in check and were good enough to overlook lack of jobs, farming distress, healthcare access and infrastructure in the hinterlands. Informal habitants were a large chunk of vulnerable votes that could be traded for false hopes both in the cities and in their domicile. Why cull a hen that lays golden eggs? Yet late Sunderlal Patwa, chief minister of Madhya Pradesh from 1990 to 1992, launched mass slum-clearing programs in the state, as the first explicit case of political sponsorship against informal living above the Vindhyas (the Dravida Munnetra Kazhagam [DMK] initiated slum clearance and public housing in Tamil Nadu in the 1971). Though Patwa's views on slums cannot be disputed for righteousness, his demolition drives lacked the support of formal housing solutions, crucial for replacing informality. His unidimensional anti-encroachment approach lost political steam and prematurely ended his promising career. He remained active politically and went on to play a key role in his party and otherwise, roles that were not a patch on his potential and desires, while informal living continued its onward march.

In 2006, the Delhi government constituted a committee on housing and urbanization in the city. The committee's findings concluded that 40 percent of Delhi's population lived in slums, shanties, and ghettos implying that by the start of the twenty-first century India had successfully upgraded the stature of informal living from an addendum to an integral piece of its urbanism. This still does not answer the question: what has informal living got to do with India's sanitation mess? For this, informal living needs to be dissected to understand just how much at cross purposes is informal living with sanitation in urban India. Two centuries of post-industrialization economic growth had rendered people incapable of living an isolated existence. Be it in villages or cities, they needed a support system to carry on with their daily lives. This expectation reshaped their relationship with the state: they began to expect the state to provide water and electricity, affordable healthcare, education, transport, and the collection and disposal of all waste types.

In India, the organizational design of the state to deliver sanitation is flawed. That it delivers sanitation to the formal citizens, who live in spaces recognized by the local civic body – a direct outcome of the urban planning process – cannot be disputed. But because informal living is invisible to the state, it is not legally obligated to extend the services to the over 100 million informal habitants of the city.

The state had not planned for their existence in cities and there is no quid pro quo established between them and the state (in the form of user fees or taxes), and therefore they do not qualify to receive sanitation services, among a host of other utilities. Therefore, informal habitants cannot be granted a sewage system underneath their shelters and waste collection beat plans cannot pick up garbage from their squats. Moreover, the local body cannot be seen receiving any money from them even if they are willing to pay, because then it will legitimatize their informal existence, only for sanitation and not for other services, which may unnecessarily upset the apple cart. Formal citizens, on the other hand, live in spaces recognized by the local civic body as legitimate places of stay or work, which is a direct outcome of the urban planning process. It plans its revenues and costs to manage these areas and in doing so builds a fair argument that only such legitimate spaces are entitled to utilities like waste management. The waste generated from informal living falls outside this purview and in the eyes of the state, attains the status of invisibility. It does not matter if the informal habitants defecate in the open, burn trash or dig up authorized drains to dump their waste into it. These acts are invisible in the eyes of the state on legally sound grounds, but the human eye unlike the state's eye cannot practise selective blindness and must daily witness the unauthorised and unhygienic disposal of waste from one hundred million informal Indians.

Imagine an informal cluster of five hundred families on a small plot of land in an Indian metropolis. The ownership of the land is in dispute, which incentivizes the local mafia to encroach it. A lengthy arbitration for establishing ownership gives confidence to the mafia to stay put for a very long time, if not for eternity. Soon this land mass is transformed into a real estate venture at zero real estate cost. It offers residential shanties and space for commerce to a migrant workforce. By then, the frenzied growth of economic activity in the neighborhood has attracted future taxi drivers, construction workers, cooks, maids, dog-walkers and security guards to the neighborhood and the inventory of shelter-units is sold or leased out in a matter of days. For all governance intents and purposes of local civic body, this informal settlement is invisible, while for the legitimate citizens in the vicinity it is a lifeline that gives them the comforts of assisted living at affordable rates. The daily ablutions of this informal human congregation are no different from those of their counterparts in the formal colony nearby. They bathe, cook and relieve themselves just like formal folks. They consume aspirational merchandise like mobile phones, clothes, and sweets. They spend money on dowry, child birth, festivals and weddings and discharge solid, wet, dry and non-biodegradable waste. But the similarity ends here because theirs is an invisible existence in the eyes of the state. Their houses are neither connected to the central sewer line nor are their homes on the beat plan of municipal bodies to collect waste on regular basis. They steal electricity or pay exorbitant rates for it. They buy cooking gas cylinders from the grey market at twice the cost. They pool their resource to buy the services of a private water tanker once in a while or make a beeline in front of it provided for by the municipal body. They cook food and drain the wet waste in the open in front of their shanties and dump their non-biodegradable waste in the open drain nearby. They defecate in the open field, on the railway tracks or in privacy of the shrubs nearby. This squatter living prosper on the strength of its economic value to the neighborhood and slowly acquires virtues of permanency. In doing so colony's makeshift waste management approaches also deepen their tentacles. Sewage puddles in the front of the colony acquires the hue of a miniature open drain (*naali*) that becomes the eventual carrier of untreated solid waste from this informal settlements. Occasionally this naali finds its way to the main drainage system in miraculous ways, while resembling a black streak of stinking sludge that flows in the company of vector larvae and discarded wrappers. Often, the naali fails to locate the main sewer and attains adulthood in the form of clogged open drain. A thick composite of plastic bottles, plastic wrappers, construction waste and mud covers it like a face mask amply conveying the naali's long age. Patches of visible black sludge underneath its face mask remind of the naali's purpose though it is as still as silence and await a bout of good monsoon for an onward push. These face packed clogged swamps that resemble a stale espresso are unmissable symbols of informal settlements and showcase their prowess of not only carrying the human solid waste of 100 million plus informal Indians but also their heft to distort public health, environment and mental health of urban India.

Informal living's potency to reduce natural water bodies to a poisonous legacy is an apt reminder of this heft. These unprotected natural formations (in the form of lakes, reservoirs, ponds, rivers and even drains) become vulnerable targets of informal living for their inability to defend themselves against its ferocious march. They become attractive targets for the convenience they offer to absorb the waste from informality at zero cost and no inconvenience. Informal living quickly reduces the bank of these water bodies to garbage hill tops. Surreptitiously, the garbage from these stinky crests flows into the water body and slowly engulfs it forever. Within a few years, the water body changes its call sign from a reservoir to a stinking pile of sludge. Such a conquest ends up as a ticking time bomb that explodes at the opportune time with dire consequences.

It was a regular rainy day, on 28 July 2016, during the peak of the monsoons and Gurugram received slightly above-average rainfall for an hour. But the city came to a grinding halt for the next twenty-four hours: homes ran out of food, money, and electricity; children stayed back in schools; people were stuck at their workplace while others were stuck in monster traffic jams; ambulances could not attend to patients. In the post-facto analysis, it emerged that one of the main drains in the city that acted as the workhorse to clean the city of monsoon rains was clogged due to encroachment of informal settlements around it. Shanties built on the drain clogged it and scuttled its capacity to discharge the sudden rush of monsoon water in time. Consequently, the water that the city collected because of the rainfall and that the drain should have been pushed it out in normal course spilled across the city and reduced it to a watery hell hole.

In 2011–12, unauthorized encroachment also brought down Shimla to its knees albeit in a different manner. Land mass around the water bodies that served as sources of water supply to the city was encroached upon, thereby contaminating the drinking-water supply with sewage water causing a jaundice outbreak in the city. This man-made tragedy left two dozen people dead and affected 30,000 residents of Shimla.

Open defecation is another adverse result of the heft of informal living in urban India. Nearly 60% of the one billion plus people who defecate in the open in the world reside in India making the issue of open defecation and India inextricably linked with each other. That open defecation is a time bomb for cholera, diarrhoea, bacterial outbreaks, contamination and stunted growth is now a wisdom in open source. Though experts still debate this wisdom in parts, but organizations like Unicef puts children as the most vulnerable to the practice of open defecation and blame it as one of the principal reasons for their stunted growth that physically drags the kids behind their mental age and therefore it is hard to ignore that 40 percent of Indian kids are stunted. Open defecation is a practice rampant in rural India and that is to do with behavioral factors of people who are conditioned to relieve themselves in the open and see no incentives to sponsor an infrastructure for defecation behind closed doors. Therefore, policy response to correct this behavioral defect rightly involves a combination of financial, social, and infrastructure initiatives. Having said that the wonder of open defecation in the urban setting has nothing to do with behavioral factors and everything to do with urbanization policy that breeds informal living. A train ride in the morning from New Delhi to Agra or a quick rendezvous in local train service in Mumbai offer different itineraries but identical sights of open defecation in urban setting that has its roots in informal living. Open defecation in urban context is far more lethal than it is in rural setting. Lack of natural soil slows the bio-degradation process and chokes the surroundings. Closed spaces provide natural proximity between the excreta and humans that increases the risk of cross contamination by many folds. Food, water, air in such chocked surroundings become fertile carriers of germs that leads to water-borne diseases or to air-borne infections that saps out nutrients and immunity from human body. If humans are habitually disposed toward open defecation they can be cajoled away from this practice through a mix of tools involving incentives, coercion, awareness and advocacy. In rural India, all these tools are applicable to make the society build toilets at homes and to make it move away from this practice. Therefore, since 2002 there has been a formal push by the Indian state to nudge rural folks to move away from the practice of open defecation and in 2014, this policy push was re-booted to accelerate this journey. But, what happens to the folks who live in informal settlements in urban India? The anatomy of informal settlement does not allow them the structural elbow room to patronize toilets in the confines of their homes. The makeshift living area that jostle for space with other dwellings on pavements, near railway tracks or in the bylanes of markets and neighborhoods offers no feasible physical space for closed toilets because shanties unlike permanent housing in villages are temporary in nature and come up in places that are not envisaged for housing in the first place. The lost cause of the effort to retrofit a closed toilet with an enabling ecosystem in such a setting is anybody's guess. Moreover, lives on pavements and in makeshift tents do not offer access to municipal sewer lines or septic tanks that is a pre-requisite for a functional toilet in the first place. Even if such toilets do come up against all odds, the discharge from these toilets offers no guarantee that it will not navigate in the open nallis and raise the stink of the city. Therefore, the results of Delhi Urban Shelter Improvement Board (DUSIB) of the survey it conducted in 2016 are not surprising. The results of the DUSIB survey conducted in 2016 found 259 open defecation spots in Delhi. It also discovered that out of the 3.29 lakh slums in Delhi, 72 percent (2.37 lakhs) had no access to toilets, even when the DUSIB had constructed 10,000 community toilets in the last two years. During the same time the government of Delhi launched a spirited initiative to build community toilets for all informal clusters, with a target to make the city open-defecation-free within a year. Public representatives lapped up the initiative for its dividend-reaping opportunities and went into an overdrive to inaugurate these toilet complexes across the city. Had Delhi's over seventy-five lakh slum dwellers been formal citizens, they would have needed fifteen lakh toilets, that is, a toilet in every home of five people. How will a few thousand community toilet complexes do the trick to address the wide chasm for closed defecation? How will these complexes address peak demand? What will be the operating mechanism for these toilets to maintain decent functional standards to operate round-the-clock? Inadequacy on these counts reduces toilet complexes in informal living to a symbolic gesture, in spite of the sincerity of the purpose, as is the case with the toilet complexes in the slum cluster in Jahangirpuri in northwest Delhi. In February 2017, this slum colony had four toilet complexes (comprising 36 bathrooms) that catered to the needs of 10,000 homes (or roughly 50,000 people), that is, 1 bathroom for every 277 people. If this inadequacy is not enough, the local civic body around the same time put up notice on one of these toilet complexes stating that its structure is dilapidated, sewers choked, and that it is dangerous to use the facility. The quality of the civil structure notwithstanding, residents of the colony cite pathethic conditions of the complex that made it unusable anyway. Is it then wrong to infer that the challenge of open defecation in urban India is more an act borne out of compulsion than out of people's intent?

There is no rocket science here to appreciate that informal living and closed door defecation cannot see eye-to-eye and the union between the two is bound to create stress. Even if informal citizens of urban India have all the desire to move away from this practice, they cannot do so for the anatomy of informal living. It means that even if India nudges all its rural folks to stop open defecation, transitioning the invisible citizens in the cities to closed toilets will remain a challenge. The issue of open defecation in urban setting demands a separate view, one which is distinct from the view that addresses the same issue in the rural setting and one that needs to be looked at in tandem with informal living.

Informal living needs to be critiqued on two counts in order to solve urban India's sanitation puzzle. The first concerns surgical removal of informal living. The second count concerns the sanitation issue during the phase of transition from informal to formal existence. Till informal living is not sucked out from the Indian urban narrative, what should be the policy approach toward its sanitation and waste management? Answers to both these questions lie in many policy buckets involving multiple stakeholders. Therefore, it will be prudent to dive into them to seek answers before getting into an overdrive to install waste bins and community toilets in the neighborhoods or to hunt photo opportunities with brooms in hand to preach clean living to invisible urbanites.

Informal dwellings trigger an entire chain that ends up creating a parallel world – an existence within a city that operates below the radar and beyond the purview of any formal existence. The chaos, congestion, and dirt outside Anand Vihar railway station in Delhi is a good case in point. The train station was commissioned in 2009 with a view to decongest the main train station located in the central part of the city. Trains from Uttar Pradesh, Bihar, and West Bengal –

vendor states for Delhi's majority of the informal workforce – were diverted here, making it popular among the migrant informal dwellers in the city. Nearly 60 percent of the daily passenger footfall at this station was contributed by this segment. In 2017, the train station was enveloped by nearly eighty informal retail shanties and kiosks with a combined annual revenue estimated at nearly ₹10 to 15 crores. This informal retail ecosystem is not bound by any tax laws nor zoning laws, not compelled to follow food and product safety laws, and not under any obligation to manage the generated waste.

Two facts about this informal retailing are inarguable: that it conveys the lucrative market opportunity given that 60 percent of the traffic at the station consist of its customers; and that it is an outcome of the lack of formal retailing at and around the station that could cater to retailing demand posed by this customer segment. In other words, the dirty surroundings of the station is hardly to do with the lack of dustbins or people's civic sense, but more a result of skewed spatial planning response that crowds out retailing needs of informal habitants while creating formal retailing spaces. These retailing spaces should have been set up in kiosks and shops. For that to happen the spatial structure offered by the station enterprise should make financial sense to the shanty retailers outside the station. This means that the station's leasing approach needs a departure from a purely economic objective of maximizing returns while leasing commercial spaces, thereby creating a formal supply of retailing space, such as cafés, merchandise shops, and restaurants, that will be out of bounds for majority of the footfalls witnessed by the station. Instead the station enterprise will need to segregate the commercial space into zones that can house retailing shops proportionate to the economic strata of the footfalls witnessed by the station. A café selling hot espresso at ₹100 bucks will need to sit next to the food service vendor dishing out rajma chawal or Idli Sambhar at ₹10 a plate. The onus is on the station enterprise to work out the economics of such a heterogeneous tenant mix in order to make informal retailing outside the station premises untenable. Only then can the station premises provide the formal environment necessary for sanitation and clean surrounding. In the absence of such a narrative any coercive effort to uproot the shanties outside the station premises will perpetually miss the mark because informal shanties outside the station is a brutal response to the needs of millions of migrants who travel through the station every day. Congestion, clutter and the filth around the train station just happen to be collateral damages of this misalignment.

It is, however, wrong to assume that informal retail outside the train station is a cost-free existence. Instead of the state seeking the rent, it is the non-state actors who seek rent to protect the dilapidated existence of shanty retailing. Ideally, the rent should be going in the pockets of the station enterprise in lieu of a dignified shop inside the station's premises for a cleaner outcome but for an exclusionist approach of Indian railways in spatial planning approach that has given away this retail space to the non-state actors.

The default setting of India's urban planning approach that creates formal spaces (shops, markets, offices) at a price (rent, capital) is exclusionist. It can only create spaces that increasingly appeal to a smaller section of its urban population. Let us take the example of a salon in a formal commercial complex in a 'middle-class' neighborhood. The shop of 700 square feet is rented out at ₹50 square feet per month, that is, ₹35,000 per month. To make the economics of work, the salon owner needs to keep this rent outflow at under 10 percent of his monthly sales, implying a desirable monthly sales of ₹350,000. Now consider the cab driver, who lives in an informal cluster in the same neighborhood. He cannot afford to spare more than ₹50 on a haircut every month, unlike an executive working in a reputed company who can shell out ₹200 for the same. The salon owner can either give a haircut to 7,000 cab drivers to achieve his monthly target or to 1,700 people of the same economic strata as the executive. Of course he prefers the latter, where he can achieve the monthly target by approaching an even smaller number of middle-class heads by offering additional grooming services. The cab driver does not mind such services as long as he can get them for under ₹50 a month. A salon kiosk pops up on the planks, loosely covering an open drain flowing in the area, and starts to offer a haircut for ₹20 and a head massage or hair coloring for an extra 30. The waste is discharged into the open drain underneath this makeshift salon. Its presence may be visually disconcerting but this informal salon on top an open drain is a response to the grooming need of the cab driver that is beyond the scope of formal retail in the neighborhood. The barber on top of the drain represents informal retail that addresses the need of nearly 40 percent of Delhi's invisible population. It is for this mismatch a formal international fast food service outlet in a swanky mall co-exists with the food stall on the pavement next to it in the city because both address the same need of two different strata of consumers.

Anti-encroachment drives are often the simplistic tool adopted to get rid of this barber's makeshift saloon or its equivalent as juice corner, food stall, garment shop, electronic kiosk among others, but this only temporarily halts the unison of the informal retailing with its consumers. Till the time sixty percent of Anand Vihar station's traffic will comprise informal citizens of Delhi and the station premises will lack formal spaces to address their needs; any attempt to uproot the informal retail outside of it will be nothing more than a flatulence release. Anand Vihar train terminus station represents Indian state's tame retreat against informal commerce only for its focused efforts to make formal commerce out of bounds for the informal inhabitants of the city. Hawkers that line-up city streets selling everything from food to clothes, from shoes to electronics, from repair services to healthcare are responses to the need of informal living because formal retail is irrelevant to informal living for its out priced offer or access or both.

Waste management of this informal commerce is then not even an afterthought because the informality offers the convenience to not worry about any of its aftermath. Human hairs from a barber in a shanty, wet waste of food leftovers, rancid cooking oil and dirty water from an eatery on a roadside, packing material and trims from a hawker selling fashion have the luxury to get dumped or incinerated in the open. By the time the baton of this arrangement passes from one generation to the next little sewage puddles in the vicinity grow up to become open drains and miniature garbage dumps get transformed into mini landfills.

The impending influx of people to the Indian cities triggered by high-economic growth was a foregone conclusion as was the case with First-World countries a century ago. In spite of the plethora of historical references available on urbanization, mass migration, and challenges of informal living that these social changes ensued in the First World back then, India did not pay heed. The deformed birth of local governance and the incapacity of the Indian political narrative to appreciate urbanization led to this oversight. Consequently, proliferation of informal living in urban India had to become an unavoidable reality in the twenty-first century; every fourth urban Indian became a recipient of it. These factors also scuttled objective research and allowed policy toward informal living to get laced with perceptive response and ideological interpretations. This intellectual limitation to appreciate informal living from the lens of spatial planning and behavioral economics curtailed India's ability to craft a comprehensive policy response that could have appreciated nuanced challenges associated with the issue.

One ideological interpretation of informal living wrongly applies the libertarian argument to it as a matter of individual right. Any displacement or uprooting of informal colonies gets colored as an attack on individual freedom, although the genesis of this view is sincere in that it lies in the nature of informal living that signifies distress and dislocation. People live in makeshift arrangements when they confront extreme adversities caused by conflicts, wars, or natural disasters. People get displaced due to floods and earthquakes and bunk in makeshift tents. They escape persecution and genocide to live in temporary shelters. In these instances, informal living becomes a temporary response to address this misery where the state is expected to make a move toward permanency and restore normalcy in the lives of the affected. The extrapolation of this libertarian viewpoint to informal living that is caused by rapid urbanization wrongly interprets its discontinuation as an encroachment on the individual's right. Rapid urbanization is not crisis situation but social phenomenon that demands a constructive response from the state. This interpretation ends up as a strong tool at the hands of the weak state to justify its inaction. More potently, this viewpoint is hammered into a reliable vendor of political capital with minimum toil allowing informality to breach the barrier of legality and engulf the city under the nose of a helpless state. Not surprisingly armed with this twisted interpretation that has reliably supplied political capital for decades, Delhi willingly ignored the ominous implosion of the city under the weight of illegal living. Only when the issue was injected with rational arguments by the supreme judiciary in 2018, the city's well-informed apathy toward the issue was compelled to make way for their reluctant action armed with hammers and bulldozers to uproot or seal illegal structures within the city. This view point puritanical it may be, provides the state with an escape route and in doing so sponsors the status quo of informality. The state uses it to seek incremental changes in informal living rather than to think about its transformation. It views dole outs of a few mobile toilets and water tankers in a slum as effective solutions to informal living. It pitches such solutions as winning arguments in front of the judiciary that ends up dragging the continuation of subaltern living for decades masking permanency under the gab of temporary shelters. This viewpoint deflates the gumption to seek disruptive intervention that can change the game. Instead it focusses on making slums a little less miserable and more tolerable in daily lives.

Such a viewpoint eventually becomes a sitting duck for political arbitrage and paper legitimization of informal living eventually becomes its sole output. It demands no urgency to make structural changes to these newly 'formalized' settlements on sanitation, building plans, or access to utilities that were essential issues that demanded legitimization of the informal settlement in the first place. The political drowning of this viewpoint eventually pushes informal living toward sustenance of the status quo and saps the administrative machinery of any energy to confront this challenge with a transformative response, and Nagpur perfectly embodies this narrative. In 1971 the city had less than fifty slum colonies, but over the next forty years it grew to more than four hundred, hosting one-third of the city's population in 2011. Equally interesting is the fact that 65 percent of these slum colonies were notified, that is, the state's tacit approval of the status quo of informal living. In other words, not only did the city witness a tenfold increase in the number of slum colonies, the state display amazing alacrity to stamp them as legit at equal pace.Dignity in living was never a prerequisite for the notification and a sanitation mess was a foregone conclusion. The libertarian viewpoint it turns out was never the end goal. It was that nimble inexpensive cherry that brought the cake of informal living to Nagpur for everyone to share.

The disfigured libertarian argument becomes the mask beneath which lies the syndicate of all other considerations that gang up to procreate informal living. It sponsors a vote bank to tilt political fortunes for the non-state actors to exert a win over the state. The sacrifice of sanitation is a small price to pay for these juicy gains.

When civic authorities armed with enforcement support reached Metro Road in Ludhiana in April 2017 to clear illegal structures, they were chased away by a mob. Political representation from both sides grabbed this chance and assured the errant mob of a permanent solution. A complex fate awaited a similar demolition drive carried out in Gurugram in 2015, which left scores of people, including residents, injured whose houses were razed by the authorities and policemen – the aim was to clear thirteen acres of the state's land encroached by the slum colony. An elected member of the city's municipal corporation was also arrested for allegedly provoking the residents against the encroachment drive. The authorities' actions seem logical, but the brawl deflated their energy to pursue such drives in future. The elected representatives were not to miss this political opportunity in the protest against an alleged unilateral action of the state and convey to the squatters that encroachment for slum living is not only cost effective but also politically protected.

A fruit vendor parks on the side of the busy motorway in the hope that vehicles passing by will stop mid-way to buy fruits gets viewed as a means of honest living for this viewpoint. Though, the existence of this vendor on the road entices motorists to make un-scheduled stops adding serious risks to road safety. Its existence blocks lanes on the roads, slows the traffic and adds to congestion. It's existence leads to wrappers and food wastes to get littered on the road. This fruit vendor can also be a food stall at a traffic junction that dishes out food items in utensils that gets washed on the soiled ground nearby and dumps its garbage in the open land mass nearby or burned it at the end of the day. Should the food stall be encouraged to support the vendor's daily living or should the civic body relocate the food vendor to a formal urban space that can ensure hygiene, sanitation and food safety? In contrast, why should a fast food retailing shop in a nearby formal shopping complex that provides formal employment to a dozen people and pays taxes be viewed as a symbol of foreign culture? These issues expose the limitation of the perceived libertarian viewpoint toward informal living and solutions can only emerge if the issue of informal living is de-coupled from the misplaced extrapolation of libertarian ideology.

The conservative view toward informal living takes a condescending approach and stretches it to the other extreme. Its view toward informal living considers a unidimensional approach of administrative enforcement to 'clean' the city from informal living as an effective tool. The local machinery's 'anti-encroachment' drive emerges as an intuitive response for this view. The debris from these drives dotes the cleared spaces for a while, only for the informal living to crop up at these same spaces within a few months. From the political bravado of Patwa in Madhya Pradesh to the administrative righteousness of B. G. Khairnar in Mumbai in the 1990s, mass anti-encroachment drives have rarely solved the issue of informal living. It acknowledges the illegality of informal living and therefore the state ensures that the eyesore of informal living does not appear at the place it does. But, the stick of 'anti-encroachment' drive toward informal living cannot do anything more than to create a false notion that the state is at work. When squatters in Aliganj area of Lucknow were uprooted in one such anti-encroachment drive in 2017, the displaced dwellers placed their belongings on the road side and started to live under open skies further stressing the public infrastructure of the neighborhood causing sanitation mess and misery all around. Stories of such drives eventually become statistics that cry out the bluntness of this viewpoint. If 'anti-encroachment' drives were indeed successful in reducing slums in Indian cities then why is it that the growth in the number of Indians living in slums leapfrogs population growth? In the absence of formal alternatives to informal living, it is fool hardy to pin the hopes on enforcement drives to free Indian cities from informal living. These drives will always get exposed as a villain against human rights whenever they will attempt to uproot informality in isolation without addressing the economic need that seeded informality at the spot in the first place. Not surprisingly, the enforcement teams get chased away, hurdled, beaten up and are frequently abandoned by their political masters when they need them the most.

Why aren't slums present on pavements of the manicured roads that lead to the Rashtrapati Bhawan, the Governor Houses, the Parliament or the official residences of the public representatives? Why are these spaces in the city not surrounded by stream of hawkers and informal commerce? Why does absence of informal living in selective urban spaces in India almost stand out like a sanitized eye soar? The absence of informality in these spaces proves that there is clarity in the mind of the Indian state to extinguish informal living wherever it wants to and ignores its unbridled growth in other areas. It is naïve to harbor any false notion that political ideologies are polarized between the libertarian and conservative viewpoints on the issue of informal living. Same public representative (or same ideology) can take a diametrically different viewpoint on informal living on a case to case basis. Anti-encroachment and the authorization drives toward informal living are two sides of the same coin that are used intermittently and both are self-serving. Same political actor can been seen 'cherry picking' demolition drives against informal living in one instance and demanding legalization of informal living in the other. When the political stakes are high in swinging the pendulum of informal living from one end to the other there is no merit to politically sponsor the fact that informal living and sanitation are antithetical to each other. In this high stake game of binary swing, such a sponsorship can only deliver a premature political obituary to promising careers. On the other hand, swinging the pendulum keeps the issue vaguely stashed away making informal living as an abundant supplier of political fuel till eternity.

The rise and the fall of the Kathputli colony – an informal living cluster of street performers in the city of Delhi is nothing short of such a swing. When a group of street performers moved into makeshift tents on the then outskirts of Delhi in the 1950s, few in the city noticed their presence. These artistes regaled the city and the city paid in kind. Both the artistes and the city coexisted happily in their private spaces. Over the next six decades, it became the world's largest informal settlement of street performers and housed nearly 3,500 people. By then buildings, markets, flyovers, commercial spaces, and formal residential colonies encircled the colony exposing the real-estate potential of the land mass, and soon the settlement and all the hazards that came along with it started to pinch the formal city as an eyesore. In 2010, thus, the colony's redevelopment and relocation plan began, but the residents were against it. This redevelopment project resembled drama on a celluloid with an ensemble of a diverse star cast. One of the central characters in the script was the urban planning authority of Delhi that constructed formal housing for the residents of this colony (in the right earnest though). Another character was the group of colony's residents up in arms against this relocation plan for the far-flung location of these formal houses that the performers alleged will kill their livelihood. Local governance was another character in the script that was eager to raze the informal settlement but it was swiftly resisted by the judiciary – an actor who was forced to perform the central role in the script. The judiciary saw any premature demolition of the settlement not tenable in the court of law on many counts of individual rights. Then there were quite a few free loaders who wanted to ride on the redevelopment plan of the colony to get free housing though they were allegedly not staying in the colony. Eventually, these actors and their purposes reduced the colony's redevelopment plan into a swinging pendulum of political partisanship. By 2017 – seven years into the saga the script gained enough political steam to carry demolition of the colony in defiance of the judiciary's order. It took seven years and counting for a half-baked and semi-concocted solution to convert three thousand five hundred informal habitants into formal habitants of the city and India has one hundred million more informal habitants to go.

Kathputli colony's struggle to gain a formal status in the city reflects the intellectual drought on the issue of informal living. Public housing and other spaces in adequate supply at right places, legislation toward informal living and preventive enforcement are obvious solutions. But informal living fall into a perceptive bias born out of ideological standpoint converting it into a dangerous political fuel. In 2017, habitants of a slum colony in NOIDA, a bustling new-age suburb of Delhi, attacked a formal gated residential colony situated across the road. The slum dwellers alleged that one of the house owners in the gated colony assaulted their housemaid who lived in the slums, but the house owner counter-alleged that she was caught stealing red-handed and was being held back to be handed over to the police. Within the next forty-eight hours the case acquired political overtones. The demography of the slum dwellers ran counter to the political order of the day and did the undoing for the colony. The city administration 'deftly' and 'efficiently' uprooted the entire slum colony due to its illegal status built on an encroached land. Undoubtedly, the action of the city administration was based on legally sound logic, but why was this logic not applied to all other such slum structures in the city and demolished with the same zeal on the same day? Are slums that house people from one region or one demography less illegal than the slums of the people from other region or religion? Why was the slum colony allowed to come up in the first place under the 'able eyes' of the city's administration is a better question to pose? Perhaps the political and administrative circumstances at that time provided the needed window of opportunity for the slum colony to mushroom in the neighborhood. It is this vagueness that is thoroughly enjoyed by the political order that allows informal living to be conveniently argued both for encroachment and for demolition. Sanitation just happens to hapless spectator in this game. Informal dwellers are blamed for littering and unauthorized disposal of waste, but they cannot be blamed for being forced to become informal citizens. Municipal bodies should be blamed for not providing waste collection and disposal services to the colony, but not because the informal living does not exist in the city's administration records. Law-enforcement agencies should be blamed because they allowed these informal settlements to come up, but not because the enforcement apparatus is subservient to its masters and can be nudged, cajoled, threatened, and coaxed depending on the direction of the political wind and the extent of the identity doctrine.

Amidst this vagueness, informal living silently seeps into the realm of illegal living blurring the line between the two. If a land mass can be encroached upon for a perfectly functioning urban ecosystem to emerge and the state can ignore this, then the template offers exciting possibilities to create an unauthorized supply of new space for many non-state actors to share the extra dough. It means an opportunity to occupy defunct and disputed land parcels to run garages, eateries, paan shops, nurseries, warehouses, marriage halls, showrooms and temples. This impunity cannot be missed in the case of the 108-feet-high idol of Lord Hanuman that came up on an encroached government land at a busy intersection in Delhi's Karol Bagh area. The congestion that resulted from the believers visiting the structure was the foregone conclusion, not to underscore the safety risks it posed. No logic can imagine such a structure at the place it came up and perhaps that prompted the High Court of Delhi to make the following comment about this structure in December 2017, 'Will prayer reach God if you pray from illegal property?' From this it can be seen that illegal living also means evoking god and using spaces for purposes they are not meant for, thereby reducing urbanism into a precarious structure of a house of cards that perpetually envelopes sanitation mess under its fold and awaits a minor jolt to crumble.

Utsav Vihar in Delhi used to be a vast swath of green fields in the mid-1980s, until it was allotted to an ashram, but the plan ran into trouble with the sudden death of the spiritual head of the sect. The land mass began to be encroached upon in the 1990s, and over the next decade it transformed into a dingy and cramped housing colony with no sewage system and inferior civil infrastructure. In 2004, the

DDA challenged the residential status of the colony and dragged the residents to the judicial court. However, by then the real-estate agents who sold the colony to the naive owners had already moved on to erect another such colony elsewhere. After thirteen years of legal battle, in 2017, the Delhi High Court vindicated the DDA's stand and deemed Utsav Vihar as an unauthorized colony, paying no heed to the residents' pleas of being short-changed by the scrupulous agents. If the colony was indeed illegal then why was the colony plugged with the electricity and water facilities, however broken and antiquated it may be was another argument presented by the residents. All these post facto arguments appear logical but at the end of the day it all boils down to this – for two decades a thousand families in Utsav Vihar discharged unregulated solid municipal waste in the area only for the inability of the city to provide formal affordable housing solutions. If the formal affordable housing agenda of Delhi supplied decent homes in adequate numbers it would have culled the arbitrage opportunity for the unscrupulous real estate agents to create Utsav Vihar reiterating the hard fact that sanitation and formal public housing are inextricably linked to each other.

Unauthorized living is like a cunning vulture that waits to grab the opportunity because of the state's ineptitude to craft formal solutions. Illegal housing colonies are a response to the arbitrage that the state created for its inaction. Non-state actors – land sharks, wheeler dealers, government employees in private roles – were with no choice but to seize it to cater to the burgeoning housing demand for all kinds of migrants to the city, and ignored the chaotic streets, congested neighborhoods, broken sewage system, and stressed civil infrastructure. The building collapse in November 2010 in the Laxmi Nagar suburb of Delhi that killed seventy people – all migrants – is a testimony to this view. On the night of the tragedy these victims were sleeping in an assembly line arrangement on floors of the house that resembled more like a bare shell than a decent home. Investigation concluded that unauthorized construction of additional floors in the building stressed its foundation and water logging in the area during the monsoon season few months back further weakened it. The unauthorized expansion of the building by its owner in collusion with the local authorities masked its existence in the record keeping of the state appears to be the explicit reason for this heart wrenching tragedy. But, the lack of adequate formal housing solutions in the city incentivized the instincts of the owner to erect this dilapidated structure as a natural response. In the aftermath of the tragedy, the building owner can be prosecuted for criminal action and so can the concerned government officials for their collusion, but these are post facto actions to an individual occurrence. These actions cannot guarantee that such a tragedy will not happen in future and nor are these actions any solace to vulnerable migrants who are on a constant look out for shelter and employment in any form.

In January 2018, in Bawana, a dusty suburb in north Delhi, seventeen workers – again, all migrants – lost their lives while working in an unauthorized firecracker factory. The intense economic growth of the city demanded equally prolific supply of formal spaces for industrial activities in the city. But the supply was a trickle and that converted this dusty village into a supplier of a profitable business model that delivered industrialization by trapping invisible habitants for cheap labor cost and circumventing building laws for cost effective real estate under the able guidance of state actors in private capacity.

Six months after this disaster, nearly a dozen people lost their lives to an unauthorized housing building collapse in Shahberi village of Greater NOIDA. During the façade of investigation, the sole question that troubled the authorities was this – How the hell did the building get erected without any approvals or plans? Soni – a class VIII student in a government school would have never thought that at the start of 2019, she would loose her father and brother and leave her mother battling for life. All three were blue-collar workers and assembled ceiling fans in an unauthorized factory in Moti Nagar area of Delhi. When the dilapidated structure of the factory collapsed, all three including others came under the rumble as helpless guinea pigs. Barely two weeks before the tragedy, the factory owner was served notice by the state and asked him to close it down, but he had full faith in his brazenness to ignore the notice, given his experience with the state in the past. Soni is a helpless spectator that is destined to watch the macabre dance of crumble and sorrows sponsored by the state with unsurprising regularity – Laxmi Nagar, Bawana, Shahberi, Moti Nagar, and counting.

When Assistant Tower Planner – Shail Bala Sharma and her colleague – Gulab Singh were shot dead by Vijay Singh a hotel owner in the picturesque town of Kasauli in Himachal Pradesh in May 2018, it became clear that the state's depravity silently nurses the poisonous tentacles of illegal living that ultimately stands exposed as the culprit. The government in Himachal Pradesh flirted with the town's structural plans with liberal doses of discretion for decades to allow illegal construction to sprawl across the state. These bi-partisan discretions offered a template to people like Singh to invest their life's savings in this gravy train of urbanism as a perfectly acceptable norm and Singh expanded his hotel in Kasauli by constructing additional rooms defying existing building laws.

The government then attempted to legalize nearly 35,000 such acts of discretions across the state further reinforcing Vijay Singh's belief in the state's approach to urbanism and the safety of his investment in the unauthorized expansion of the hotel. The citizens received economic windfall from this action of the state in the form of extra development rights on land masses that could hardly withstand rains or earthquake tremors and lacked sewage systems. Never mind these trivial risks, Singh – the citizens willingly extended their support to this seemingly brazen action of the executive organ of the state. Singh's brazen action was fed with legitimacy from the state on mutually dependent desires of Singh and the political order of the day.

Only when the judiciary smelled the illegality of the state's brazen attempt to accommodate the desires of the nearly 170 such hotels across the state, did Singh invite the judiciary's scorn and prompted Sharma and Gulab Singh to supervise the demolition of his hotel's unauthorized expansion. Facing the prospect of losing his life's savings, Singh, a perfectly normal living soul till then got desperate, lost his moral compass and allegedly shot Mrs. Bala and Mr. Singh dead. Not surprisingly the judiciary thinks of illegal living as a ticking time bomb and it banned new construction in illegal colonies while hearing the case involving illegal construction in the city of Delhi in 2018. However, the executive did not mind submitting an affidavit justifying protection of unauthorized construction from demolition in the same case. After all, 'regularization' of more than 1,700 illegal colonies in the city was a major poll promise of elected government of Delhi in 2015.

The institutional prowess of the Indian state to seek proactive solutions for illegal living is so arid that it does not mind at the drop of the hat to become a helpless spectator of its menacing rise and later seek ways to legalize it. For the franchise the arrangement does not appear nefarious for the economic gains that the largess of legitimacy unleashes. Public representatives on the other hand lap up the bankable political capital of this gravy train with both hands. Ordinances, affidavits in the court of law, political manifestos that promise legality to informal living and the criticism of the judiciary for legislative overreach are then used as gabs to keep this gravy training running full steam. Under this façade, illegal living envelopes Indian urbanism one brick and one day at a time and numbs us with its slow poison. Late Mrs. Shail Bala and Mr. Gulab Singh should be accorded the status of a martyr who laid down their life to expose this poisoning and Vijay Singh Thakur should be treated as an actor of this state sponsored script.

People uproot themselves from their rural or semi-urban dwellings in the hope to permanently seek a future in the cities and they do so because of declined fortunes in agriculture, lack of employment opportunities, skills or wage arbitrage. They look up to the city to permanently host them and become errand boys in an office or get self-employed as taxi drivers and plumbers or start their own entrepreneurial venture as owners of eateries. For quite a few, the city is also a temporary zone of expectations and opportunities. For them migration to city is an economic opportunity that needs to be harnessed in hope for a better future for their families back home. They shun the investment of emotional equity in the city and the city too does not offer any incentives for its cockiness or its demographic barriers. Sans the economic opportunity, they so secretly wish to go back but stick around as janitors, security guards, construction workers, cooks and maids. Their needs from the city hinges on frugality and therefore they happily accept the cluster of makeshift shanties of tinned roofs, a small hole in the wall on a pavement, a makeshift humid room on the top floor of a dilapidated house built on an encroached land. Though, it is a slightly different matter that within a few years these circular migrants end up permanently extending their temporary expectations from the city.

It is then obvious that formal housing for both types of migrants will take the game away from informal living and fire the much-needed salvo to clean up the city. Though the salvo will miss its mark if formal housing is imagined as a mass supply of freely tradeable 'affordable homes' in isolation as has been the case till now. Informal living at the location it comes up performs a key role in the city's economic cycle. It exists near industrial units and high density commercial zones, next to train/bus stations, temples, formal housing colonies and other areas. The economic need of these places demand maids, retail shop executives, warehouse operators, drivers, mechanics, washer men, security guards, factory workers, courier boys, cooks in the vicinity. It is a complex existence. Formal citizens loath the ugly visual sight of informal habitant, the informal habitants loath the certainty in the life of the formal citizen. While, both may loath each other they cannot live without each other. But, India's affordable housing policy has always identified land on the fringes of the city to chase the mirage of affordable living in the hope that this informality will re-habilitate to such remote clusters. Hard mandates do force it to move to these remote corners but its eviction from the spot does not extinguish the economic need of the location, which was the trigger for the informal living to come up at that spot in the first place. Squatters merely manifested that need. If the first batch of these informal habitants get evicted, a second batch will promptly move in and fill the spot because informality has an uncanny vision to spot such an opportunity.

In the 2000s, urban development authority of the state of Haryana notified a housing initiative for the economically weaker section or EWS that required private real-estate developers to build affordable homes for every 10 percent of formal homes they built. The policy stated that if the developer builds 500 flats, he will also be required to build 50 affordable homes as part of the project. One decade into the policy, empty buildings of EWS housing attached to such private housing projects dot Gurugram's urban landscape, while informal living prospers in the slums in the vicinity. Expecting private real-estate operators to build affordable homes was done to create a supply of tradeable real estate that will always find ways to seek market prices for its meager supply making it attractive to everybody except for informal habitants or will remain inhabitable for tactical reasons. Gurugram's EWS housing cries out failure on both these counts.

Affordable housing was refreshed in 2014 by the national government and given an ambitious target of housing for all by 2022. But in February 2017, the union minister for housing and urban development admitted that between April 2015 and January 2017, the government rolled out 3,214 affordable housing projects comprising nearly 75,000 homes across 100 cities in India totaling ₹90,000 crores. But, this roll out was sans any private capital participation, thereby admitting a problem at hand. Ninety thousand crores of rupees is a significant opportunity to be ignored by private capital, but it argued that the affordable housing push by the government was primarily around the cost of land. If the price of the land is factored in, affordable housing no longer remains affordable, and that pushes it on the fringes of urbanism and defeats its purpose to eradicate slums that exist within the cities. The question then needs to be asked about the multiple false starts of India's affordable housing agenda. Affordable housing as a real-estate asset is at cross purposes with the heterogeneity of Indian cities. Alternatively, creating formal affordable living as an integral package of formal ecosystems of Indian cities needs to be the lynchpin to solve the housing challenge for informal habitants. Integrated complexes built on rental models in the heart of the city's economic hotspots are better solutions than to imagine homes as individual units to be sold as assets to their occupants. Homes for informal habitants need to be thought through more as an infrastructure play rather than as a real-estate asset play. The advocacy needs to be for an industrial rental-housing approach that should be imagined to deliver decent, dignified mass-housing solutions that cost not more than one-fourth of the household income of the informal habitants. Such mass rental-housing solutions can only be created when mass housing need is imagined as an economic activity and not essentially as a real asset delivered to every citizen. This will require allocation as done for hospitals, schools, and roads that are sprinkled across the city. Mass supply of rental houses that are tagged to all the economic purposes of the city will thus cull informal living. Rental housing as an economic opportunity will provide options for its supplier to think about revenue streams for sources beyond rents received from these housing units – an approach not very different from airport operators. Like airport operators don't earn their entire revenue from airlines who pay these airports for every use by their aircrafts, rents from rental housing supply will only contribute partially toward the financial sustainability of the rental housing project. If airport operators had indeed earned all their revenues from airlines for their landed aircrafts, it will be prohibitively expensive for the airlines and unviable for operators to sustain the airport project. Nearly half the revenue that airport operators earn comes from what is termed as 'non-aero' revenue and comprises fees / charges earned by monetizing the airport ecosystem. On similar lines manufacturers of mass rental housing solutions cannot be burdened with the expectation that the rent earned from these houses will be the sole income source. If that is the case then the workable rent rates for the tenant (the informal habitant) will not only be unaffordable for the intended habitants but the rental income thus earned may also not suffice the sustainability of rental housing project.

The occupants of industrial rental housing need to be viewed as users, not home buyers. An affordable housing model with annuity-based revenue streams that are not solely dependent on lease income, but also on the opportunity to monetize the larger ecosystem that such housing complexes provide, will inject affordability for the occupants and sustainability to rental housing projects. There are myriad possibilities, namely, opportunity to earn revenue from commercial and retail activities or the opportunity to play the role of carrier on behalf of the state to deliver welfare support, education, healthcare, sanitation, etc. Ownership rights to build and operate ecosystem of such services to cater to the tenants can be comfortably hosted in such colonies among many other options.

A variation of such a housing model is the industrial hostel. These can be built to provide temporary housing spaces with access to amenities and utilities in a manner that addresses the needs of the circular migrants. Their needs from the city are frugal and temporary though not without dignity, safety and cleanliness. To cater to such a demand Industrial Hostels can be imagined near industrial zones, construction sites and dense economic hotspot. Revenue model for such industrial hostels can be tied up with the employers of circular migrants. These hostels can be imagined as ecosystems to deliver healthcare, utilities, employment support, services (banking), food and such while simultaneously providing financial sustainability for their operators. Crèches, playing arenas, education, sanitation can all be built within such industrial hostels that can inject dignity and respect and can be championed as powerful assets to rejuvenate human development. For instance, employers of circular migrants can be proactively engaged to hire people residing in such industrial hostels and softly nudge formality in the employment contracts of these migrants or part of the wage payment by the employers can be directed as rents to industrial hostels incentivizing the adoption of such hostels within the city.

China's rapid industrialization at the turn of the twenty-first century saw overnight transformation of sleepy towns into industrial powerhouses that packed a vast number of migrants in cities. With its restrictions on labor movement between regions, China kept a tight leash both on the nature and the number of migrants that reached the cities. Consequently, many migrants to these newly industrialized cities were temporary, who landed up with jobs in various factories. China made it mandatory for factories to build industrial hostels along with the manufacturing plant to house their respective workforce; therefore, these cities rarely faced the issue of informal living.

But the model's implementation collapsesd due to its restrictive nature. Industrial hostels were inextricably linked with their respective factories in every sense. Every factory had its own industrial hostel within the same campus that perpetuated the sweatshop model and offered limited visibility on labor rights, wage rates, and working hours. But these flaws cannot undermine the efficacy of these hostels to provide housing, sanitation, and hygiene to the migrants. The China model of industrial hostels without its implementation approach offer interesting insights for the feasibility of independent industrial hostels for the Indian urban landscape. The question for India is that the concept will need to be crafted as a sustainable independent ecosystem that provides lodging, food, retail, utilities, education, and healthcare in a formal environment to circular migrants.

The rental housing and industrial hostel can instil a definitive purpose to the redevelopment agenda of Indian cities. Conversely, the success of these models will depend on their development as an integral part of the city's economic hotspots. Land-pooling policy, for instance, can help communities come together to take a cooperative or equity-based approach toward industrial supply of rental living or industrial hostels at right locations rather than to accommodate them on the fringes as an afterthought. Home and commercial space owners can come together and collectively seek redevelopment rights of their real estate to build them. Municipal bodies can become equity partners in mass rental-housing projects. If Maharashtra Police can build 9,000 affordable flats for its police force in Mumbai through active participation of the Maharashtra State Police Housing and Welfare Cooperative Ltd (MSPHC), then there is no reason for not extending the same argument to build formal ecosystems for informal living.

In the current industry of informal living the occupant is rarely an owner and more often a tenant who pays rent and transaction costs. These costs end up as revenue in the pockets of non-state actors who supply informal living under the state that chooses to be ignorant about its existence. Then the primary metric to define the success parameters of formal mass-housing models should measure their ability to replicate the economics of the informal living. Only then can the state divert informal living away from filth toward dignity and sanitation and score a win over non-state actors. Otherwise, scarce urban space will continue to sink further in the quicksand of informality, as has been the case till now. The might of informal living is so potent that it has even disfigured cities like Chandigarh that were constructed in the post-independent India with the hope that it will not fall in this trap. Today Chandigarh's markets, suburbs and satellite towns prolifically carry the badge of mediocrity that is identical to Indian urban narrative with nearly ten percent of its population living in the slums. A similar fate was bestowed on other cities built post Independence like Navi Mumbai, Gurugram and Noida but today host anywhere between ten and twenty percent of their population in slums.

For all the criticism, informal living is also the last line of defense for myriad skills and artisanal caliber of rapidly depleting art forms. Handcrafted jewelry is made in the slums of Kolkata; Dharavi absorbs zari and embroidery work and couture bridal wear; accessories get stitched up in the dingy colonies of Delhi. But beyond this nobility, informal living also attempts to address need gaps in the market by circumventing rules and established procedures, as is the case with Shiv Vihar colony in Delhi that spews denim jeans from makeshift dyeing and manufacturing units. These units may appear vibrant entrepreneurial ecosystems, but they cannot be absolved from the challenges of waste management and environmental safety that results from their operations. Industrial effluents gets dumped or burned in the open or mixed up with other waste types at no extra cost. The dyes blatantly discharged in the open has led to the unusual spike of cases of cancer in the colony labeling it as the Blue Poison neighborhood – living up to the blue color and poison that symbolize the Hindu deity, Lord Shiva, on whom the colony is named.

To expect artisinal industrial hot spots like Shiv Vihar to move out of informality without appending their lucrative cost structure that offer convenient bypasses on costs and compliance, never mind the slippages on sanitation is a perpetual barrier and one installed by the state. The solution then needs to offer at-par proposition of accessibility and cost without relenting on working conditions, compliance, and waste management approaches while hosting them. Shared access to utilities and other resources like logistics, water, electricity, and support functions is required, while the formality of the structure keeps a better visibility on working conditions, labor rights, and waste discharge.

Informal retail, as discussed earlier, is another aspect of informal living that appears benign, though its existence significantly stresses the civic infrastructure on sanitation and hygiene. Solution demands formal space in adequate supply in proportion to the customer segments and their needs that informal retail addresses in the city. We know that heterogeneity strongly underpins Indian urbanism and that urban planning has failed to appreciate this reality. Consequently, the free-market-based real-estate development chases the highest price creating a skew in favor of homogenous formal retail spaces. This happens for an increasingly small share of formal urbanites who are a small minority among an increasingly larger pool of unaddressed need of invisible urbanites. Therefore, ideas like rental housing and industrial hostels need to be thought through as expansive notions.

But formal space for commerce and trade to address informality need not be constricted to these ideas with gestation periods. Formal retailing in the form of temporary formal bazaars, pop-up markets, and haats can create equally compelling formal environment. Authorities can provide such solutions in lieu of user fees that are transparent and tenants can in turn rejoice in the arrangement because instead of paying up the non-state actors for informality, the money goes in the state coffers for being above board. But, a sparse or a sporadic attempt to supply such temporary spaces for commerce will be akin to putting a drop of cold water to cool down a hot cooking pan. Instead, a strong stream of cold water will be needed to do the trick.

Mass transition of invisible urbanites toward formal existence in rental housing, industrial hostels, or clusters that host small enterprise, community markets, haats, and temporary structures for commerce will deliver a cleaner India. This transition will also extinguish non-state actors and their rent-seeking behavior in favor of beefed-up coffers of local governance. For such a future, Indian cities will need to become imaginative about the approach to design and supply formal spaces and that can only happen if the state becomes both a proactive vendor to create such formal spaces and a progressive facilitator to manage these spaces for a cleaner (and healthier) urban living. From this altered thinking the supply of the right kind of formal urban spaces can be released in abundance and only then can the argument favoring enforcement to cull informal living will triumph. In the new reality formal spaces will exist in adequate supply to meet the diverse needs of the city.

A fruit seller on the road side in a non-prescribed zone will then be deemed illegal because the city provides formal hawking zone in the same neighborhood that sells the same merchandise to the same consumers at the same price. Enforcement will win here because now the fruit-seller's presence on the motorway under-cuts the fruit hawkers who sell in the prescribed hawking zone in the vicinity and they should not be left with the feeling of being short-changed. Emergence of a small unauthorized tea stall that operates from a shaded corner of a road traffic signal will then undermine the business of an authorized tea stall that exists a few meters ahead on the road. An enforcement drive against this unauthorized tea stall will then be both legally and politically viable. The synchronization of enforcement with the supply of adequate formal spaces will convert 'anti-encroachment drives' into pro-active administrative interventions. Enforcement can then nip the germination of informal living to protect formal equivalents. The prolific supply of the right kind of formal spaces will allow enforcement to undergo a much-needed makeover from being imagined as a brutal response to displace the vulnerable to taking small and timely steps to nip the emergence of one small shanty on the roadside at a time.

Today, technology offers immense possibilities to imagine enforcement as a proactive and a precise tool. Satellite imagery and circuit cameras can assist local governance to develop heat maps about informal existence in the city. Active data analytics can be deployed to proactively red flag sprouting of informal living in a neighborhood. These surveillance techniques can arm local civic authorities with tools to judiciously deploy human skills on the ground in a cost effective manner and nip informal living in the bud much before the innocuous presence of a shanty becomes a cluster of few hundred indispensable slums.

The question of sanitation delivery in informal living till such a transition remains unanswered. One cannot say there can be a sort of temporary solution that can tackle the sanitation woes of informal living till such time, because such intervention can also be interpreted as a stamp of legitimacy for the informality's status quo. The issue of informal living in South American countries dates back to the 1950s, especially Brazil with its favelas, immortalized by Michael Jackson's hit pop song 'They don't really care about us.' In Rio de Janeiro, one-third of its nearly 15 million people live in 200 favelas spread across the city, a reality not very different from the giant slums of Mumbai or Delhi. Given the extent of informality, these favelas are surprisingly clean – a feat achieved through community-development projects. One such program was trash-for-light program, where residents were encouraged to get the recyclable trash to the neighborhood electrician shop to get discounts on merchandise. In 2013, 80 percent of the residents had access to collective garbage-collection system that increased from 40 percent in 2002. Can Brazil's experience be used to institute waste management approaches for India's informal living clusters in transition?

Use of technology to profile informal clusters for customized responses is a good way to start the exploration. This would throw up the demographic profile of the cluster, number of residents, type of their economic activities or employment, and the nature of consumption practices. The intent is to get a reasonable estimate of the type and quantum of waste generated by such informal living clusters within the city. Such a profiling will allow segmentation of these informal clusters on the nature of the generated waste. Armed with such insights local civic bodies can define guidelines on waste collection and segregation from within these informal clusters and simultaneously extend invitation to corporations, cooperatives, individuals, and institutions to install and operate waste management services from within these informal clusters. This invitation can be sweetened through incentives under social responsibility programs. Work will be cut out for these entities, who will manage waste collection from their adopted cluster on daily basis. These entities will devise rules and issue fines to proactively engage the dwellers on the daily compliance of segregation and collection waste. It may mean distributing garbage collection bins or bags within their respective adopted cluster, charging fees for waste collection services, or engaging the representatives of dwellers and run the collection service as a community program. These entities will ensure that the collected waste from the adopted cluster is segregated, bagged, and ferried to the assigned collection hub for onward journey. They will also install mobile or portable toilets, common kitchens, and bathing or clothes washing centers in their adopted clusters as common and portable facilities for all activities that generate waste and safely collect it for disposal or recycling. These entities can be imagined as cooperatives of people who work informally in the waste management industry to come together to own and operate such an infrastructure. Proceeds from waste recycling and user fees collected from dwellings can define the revenue model of such entities, whereas state support in the form of seed capital, incubation, and grants to groom such cooperatives can become the raison d'etre for the state's investments on sanitation.

Such entities will be mandated to discharge two kinds of roles. First, they will manage the daily operations of waste management in their respective adopted clusters. This will ensure collection of waste at source in a secured setting and segregation of waste to inject efficiencies in the upstream value chain of waste disposal. Second, these entities will be expected to play the role of a change agent to bring the informal dwellers into the mainstream on waste management practices. They will do so through regular audits, mass outreach, user fees, fines, and incentive programs with the intention that with every passing day cost of managing waste in informal dwellings will be incrementally mitigated. These entities will become champions in ensuring that waste generated in informal dwellings is isolated, localized, and collected at source and not allowed to infiltrate open grounds or get dumped in a dangerous manner as has been the case so far.

Rapidly emerging applications for segregated and secured wet waste have started to challenge the conventional wisdom on the issue and that will pose exciting possibilities for such entities. Today, it is commercially viable to recover fat from the sewer waste and convert it into bio-fuel or to convert all forms of wet waste into Agri protein using flies. Such possibilities will demand an effective intermediator that can collect and segregate waste at source that these entities will do from the squatters, slums and shanties in urban India. For their ability to collect waste and segregate it, these entities will emerge as viable vendors for such possibilities and over time will get groomed as enterprises of India's municipal bodies for managing waste in informal dwellings and temporary shelters. For instance, an informal dwelling comes up as an outcome of a real estate construction project and houses construction workforce for a short duration (say a road project or a residential colony). In such a scenario, the real estate company will be required by laws of the local municipal body to hire such entities for a fee to manage garbage collection, mobile toilets and bathrooms for the construction workforce at the site for the duration of the project.

Informal living's resilience to emerge against all odds cries out the intensity of the economic need that it addresses. Informal living by the virtue of its invisibility may appear cheap, but it is not the case for its inhabitants. They pay upfront cost to access informality that finances the seed capital of 'the informal living industry.' The recurring expenses to fetch water from a water tanker or to illegally procure cooking gas cylinders and get them refilled at prohibitively inflated rates. Informal living symbolizes dirty arbitrage for the state's lack of imagination that is equally bad for its habitants, vendors, and customers. It robs values from human life and wreaks havoc to human dignity. It scars the city, disfigures its character, and reduces it to a stinking cesspool making sanitation delivery a collateral damage for the entire society and cannot be justified on any plank of intellectual debate. Extinguishing such a justification needs to be the starting point to seek any chance of escaping this rot and one way to do it is to appreciate the economics of informal living while imagining formal alternatives. Formal solutions are needed in a manner that the cost of informality to migrate to these solutions is lower than it costs to maintain the status quo. Then the transition of informality toward formal living becomes a plausible solution for a cleaner outcome. A cleaner India and the drive to make invisible urbanites visible are inextricably linked with each other. There is no point in issuing sermons to these informal citizens to change their behavior toward sanitation without creating enabling conditions for them to affect this change because infrastructure precedes compliance. Till now we have not really cared about this invisible segment and that partly explains the struggles of the country on the issue of sanitation.

5

WASTE COLLECTION

They Don't Really Care About Us

In his 2006 book titled *The Box,* Marc Levinson wrote a brilliant account about the invention of the shipping container and the disruptive role this big metal box played in the global logistics industry. Today, painted with colorful names and symbols, it roams on highways firmly planted on trailers and sails the seas on giant ships. But, before the arrival of this ubiquitous metal box, hauling cargo between nations and sorting and loading the cargo were labor-intensive and time-consuming activities. The floor of a cargo ship was chaos. Fish and spices sat next to chemicals. Inflammable cargo rubbed shoulders with boxes of fireworks. Space within a cargo ship was poorly managed and grossly under-utilized. Ships took months to unload the cargo at ports. Sorting and loading the cargo were time consuming activities and labor intensive. Issue of hauling volumetric cargo like cotton and heavy and fragile cargo like glass was incredibly tricky. In retrospect, we can dissect these problems with the advantage of hindsight wisdom. However, in the old days global commerce was designed around these bottlenecks. No one had experienced an alternate reality that was better than the status quo. Then came the metal box that defined new rules to haul cargo around the world.

This innocuous metal box changed the life of every stakeholder involved in the cargo industry for the better and spurred world trade. Every commodity traded across the border was converted into units that could be stored in this metal container. Cargo ships began to be called 'container ships.' Shipping companies started to use shipping containers as a standard unit to price their freight services that brought transparency in pricing. Ship builders could estimate precisely the amount of space needed based on the number containers a ship had to hold, and design them accordingly. Loading and unloading of the cargo became efficient and spurred automation in the logistics supply chain, thereby increasing productivity of ports. These containers proved efficient even for inland transport. Trucking companies quickly seized the idea and the world saw the advent of trailers which could effortlessly transport these containers.

The first shipping container sailed in 1956. It was the result of two ideas that had begun to fascinate the First World at the beginning of the twentieth century, which acquired cult status by the end of World War II. These were standardization and productivity. During the five decades leading up to World War II, the First World was making scientific innovations at an intense pace. The discovery of oil, development of the steel industry, invention of polymers, and advancement in the field of physics were major enablers that spurred the invention of aeroplanes, automobiles, telecommunications, and electricity, among others. By the end of World War II, science and capital started to look at these innovations as opportunities for monetization in the new world order. There was a rush to take them to the masses and capitalize on the juicy market opportunities presented by the liberal order of the post–World War II era. The aim was to make these scientific innovations affordable for masses, so as to maximize the opportunity. Plastic, for instance, had to find multiple applications so that its manufacturing economics would work at a large scale and thus it became ubiquitous. The twin ideas of productivity and standardization lead to improvements in tooling, machinery, and manufacturing processes, and many of these innovations permeated the daily lives of consumers across the First World, such as detergent powder, packaged juice and soups, candies, toys, electric oven, and automobiles.

Many of these products had been in practical use since the nineteenth century. But the thrust on productivity and standardization in the post–World War II order democratized their use. Productivity aimed at efficient utilization of resources like time, labor, and capital, while standardization took a stab at infusing dogmatic focus on repeatability of actions, with the idea of reducing variation and increasing the probability of the same output. This was complimented by a concurrent change in the wage rates in the First World. Industrialization created sustained periods of economic growth that spiked wage rates and brought prosperity to the common man. People started to choose jobs that paid higher wages, adversely affecting the supply of labor for lesser paying jobs. This created an additional urgency in the First World to better productivity, which in turn led to rapid advancements in automation and greater desirability of machinery over human resource.

Productivity and standardization began to profoundly impact human thinking in the First World during the period. These tenets began to be applied to solving chronic and perennial issues. Cargo movement was one such issue, others being production of cars, processing of food, and the seemingly trivial issue of waste collection from homes and streets.

On the one hand, rising wages during the time restricted the municipal bodies to hire more sanitation workers owing to their limited budgets. On the other hand, the fast-paced industrial activity in these societies had begun to disruptively increase the quantity and complexity of the waste they generated, forever. While city administrators like Sir Edwin Chadwick of the UK and Eugène-René Poubelle of France ensured that disposing waste in bins became a matter of habit in their respective cities, the daily collection and transfer from these bins to disposal sites was still a grossly inefficient affair. At the start of the twentieth century, sanitation departments were understaffed. Horse carriages were deployed to carry human solid waste from homes without sewage lines, and lorries or street sweepers collected garbage from the streets occasionally. In 1895, the newly elected mayor of New York City, William Strong, known as a no-nonsense man with a genuine desire for public good, was appalled at the state of the city's streets, filthy with strewn horse excreta, gunk, dead animals, and discarded food. Strong noted that in its fourteen years of existence, the Department of Street Cleaning – formed in 1881 and later renamed the Department of Sanitation in 1929 – had achieved nothing, and thereby appointed George Waring, a war veteran who called himself a 'sanitation engineer.' One of the first tasks he undertook upon his appointment was a massive clean-up exercise that saw hundreds of people sweeping the streets of New York. Waring encouraged the press to cover this event extensively to build public support toward sanitation and cleanliness of public places. His efforts exemplified the First World's struggles with waste at that time. But, at the end of this long journey, it understood that human progress also manifests itself as a complex trash problem. It is no surprise then that the seemingly trivial issue of waste collection extended a hearty invitation to concepts like productivity and standardization to solve its prevailing problems.

It was no coincidence that when the first shipping container sailed in 1956, waste collection bins (along with the system) underwent a scientific rebirth. City administrators quickly realized their pivotal role in solving the growing menace of waste. The simple garbage bin, introduced in the nineteenth century, was replaced by the galvanized metal can because bigger bins were now needed for the greater waste generated by households, shops, and offices. They also had to be of a standard size so as to act as a unit of measurement and allow local authorities to measure garbage output and help them to efficiently allocate resources.

Say 500 kilograms of mixed garbage scattered on the ground is to be collected. The primitive solution would be to have two men armed with shovels and buckets collect the garbage and load it on to the dump truck. Assuming it takes them thirty minutes to finish the job, the local civic body will need to deploy two people, one truck and one man-hour to haul this garbage. Now, imagine this 500 kgs of garbage is deposited in 25 garbage bins of 20 kgs each. The dump truck could simply be equipped with a fork lift to mechanically lift the bins, tilt and empty them, and put them back on the ground in a matter of seconds. The driver and one sanitation worker can safely accomplish the task in far lesser time than it takes two men with the earlier primitive approach. This idea of collecting waste at source in containers and standardizing the process facilitated massive improvements and efficiency of waste collection in today's clean countries.

Standardized bins were also used to shift the responsibility of waste collection from local bodies alone to the citizens. Every household now had to install standardized waste bins issued by local bodies. Such a regulated approach served two purposes. First, to ensure all kinds of consumption and waste generating units were converted into a standard and measurable unit for garbage collection; and, second, these bins articulated the role of every household toward a cleaner city. Households (and other consuming units) were mandated to install garbage bins on prescribed lines and deposit the garbage from their private spaces into these bins (and nowhere else). These were the only two things that the households needed to do in making their city clean. This 'dumbed down' the waste collection process for citizens and simplified its assimilation and aided its acceptability. Local bodies were now in the know of the total garbage bins issued to households, shops and offices in a city, the waste generation spots and the nature of waste generated from various parts of the city. They also got the hang of the frequency of waste generated and of its cyclical nature. All these insights lead to an immediate improvement in the resource planning process. Local bodies could design better route plans for waste collection. For instance, waste from some areas was collected more than once a day whereas in other areas, the truck came once a week. Concurrently, the act of collecting waste in a polybag and disposing it in the garbage bin metamorphosed into a household chore in the First World. Apart from walking the dog and doing the laundry, parents also expected their children to take responsibility of taking out the trash. This became such a quintessential slice of contemporary American life in the 1960s, that Hollywood's screen icons were often seen putting bagged garbage in the bin outside their homes in movies. Romances blossomed, murders were planned and conspiracies unfolded over this mundane chore. A country that struggled to clean its streets in 1890s, was now using an essential act of keeping the home an neighborhood clean to depict everyday American life. Such was the extent of social transformation that resulted from improvements in the so far unglamorous waste collection system. Clean countries successfully used the new systems to make waste management a shared responsibility of the citizen and the state, and drive home the point that this was not an arrangement of equals. It entailed heavy lifting by the citizens while the local authorities would play the role of an able facilitator. In other words, it was mandatory for the citizens to install garbage bins at home, put their garbage into it and hand it over the garbage collection truck sent by the state.

Around the same time when these countries managed to put a decent system of waste collection in place, they were confronted with another problem, that of the rapidly rising complexity of the generated waste. At the turn of the twentieth century, biodegradable waste such as ash, animal carcass, horse excrement, and food matter were dumped in landfills or in the ocean. The composition of waste changed to plastic, construction debris, industrial refuse, tires, glass, tin cans, durable goods, and diapers by the 1960s. This pushed for the next round of improvement: segregation of waste at source, because different types of waste required different methods of disposal. Therefore, the idea that waste should be segregated before collection sat at the heart of the success of waste disposal methods.

During the same time, a small development in Slough, a town in the UK, proved to be a game-changer in this effort. Frank Rotherham Mouldings invented the modern plastic wheelie bin in 1968, which replaced the galvanized cylindrical metal trash cans, to improve the efficiency of moving materials on the shop floors of his factory. However, a refuse collector took notice of these bins and immediately understood their practical applicability in waste collection, and the rest, as they say, is history. These bins were easy to maneuver and reduced the hazards of handling garbage while unloading. Local authorities started to issue color-coded bins: yellow or blue ones to collect wet waste or waste that would naturally decompose, such as food, dust, ash, liquids, paper, etc.; and green ones to collect waste that would not naturally decompose, such as plastic, glass, tin cans, etc. By the 1990s, the First World was successful in institutionalizing the principle of waste segregation across all its households and other waste-generating units. The advent of wheelie bins spearheaded better design innovations in refuse collecting vehicles. They were equipped with fork lifts to exactly fit the wheelie bins and empty them faster, improving the efficiency of waste collection. Further research into recycling of non-biodegradable wastes created pressure to improve the accuracy of waste segregation at source and further expanded the scope of the color coded wheelie bins.

Today, in countries like Germany, Japan among others waste must be segregated at source into seven different types of bins before it is touched by refuse-collecting trucks. Glass and plastic waste now go into separate bins rather than clubbed together. Electronic waste like batteries need to be disposed in a separate bin. If the waste needs to be disposed in an environmentally sustainable and safe manner, the collection system must ensure precision in its segregation was the logic behind this dogma that made circular economies out of Sweden and Denmark. The hundred-year journey of the First World, from Chadwick to the wheelie bins, saw the task of waste-collection system transition from menial labor to a subject of scientific thinking and engineering application. Through this transition, the First World was also successful in drafting an equality-based social contract between the local civic bodies and the citizens. This contract made citizens accountable for initiating waste collection for the overall success of the waste management and sanitation system.

Today, emerging technologies offer interesting possibilities to further refine waste-collection systems and the First World is wasting no time to imbibe them. They have begun taking steps to safeguard waste-collection systems by exploring automation, recycling, and modular solutions. Underground conveyor systems to automatically carry waste may well eliminate the use of trucks. They are increasingly championing re-cycling, re-processing and re-use over disposal to mitigate carbon emissions. Underground bins are being piloted to limit exposure of the garbage to the environment. RFID technology is being applied to tag bins so that they can proactively measure waste loads and types to better plan waste pick-up schedules and further improve productivity and recovery during recycling. In doing all of the above they have not forgotten the hard-learned lesson – for any waste disposal approach to succeed, an effective collection system must precede it. It is this symbiotic relationship that continually pushes them to improve and innovate refuse collection system and it all started with installing a garbage bin in every household more than one hundred and fifty years ago.

Let's take the example of a house with four rooms built in the middle of large area earmarked for human habitation. It is occupied by the owner, the spouse and a child. They hire a housekeeper to keep the house, clean it and to ensure that the house and its surroundings are well maintained. They give him a broom-stick and mop with which to sweep and swab, and a bucket to collect the rubbish and dirt. They also give him a rickshaw to haul the rubbish collected from the house and dump it in a nearby landfill. Over time, three more houses come up in the area. The new householders request the services of the housekeeper of the original house, as he is trained and knows his job well. They start to use his services but don't give him an additional broom, mop, bucket or rickshaw. The housekeeper doesn't mind because he gets an extra income. However, his original employer notices that the housekeeper's pace of work has slowed, he has begun to cut corners in his work and take liberties with the upkeep of the first house. Upon questioning, the housekeeper gives the justification that since he has taken up additional assignments, his schedule does not allow him enough time to do a proper job. After a few years, five more houses come up in the vicinity and the new residents also engage the services of the one housekeeper. They pay him but don't give him any extra equipment to clean their houses with. With the additional burden, the housekeeper's standard falls further and everyone is unhappy with his lowered efficiency and pace. Instead of cleaning the original house four times a day, he now cleans all the houses only once in two days. Not counting the fact that the cleaning equipment has suffered great wear and tear over the years but never been replaced or upgraded. The housekeeper himself appears exhausted piqued.

With the increase in the number of households, the housekeeper's capabilities were not upgraded. He should have been given bigger and more garbage bins to work with. The rickshaw should have been adequately upgraded to store and ferry more garbage. He should have had more brooms (at least one for every house) and taken on a few more hands to share the workload. None of this happened and the area turned into a mess in a few short years despite noble intentions. Suppose the residents of the colony get together and decide to address the handicaps of the housekeeper. They arm him with more brooms, mops, garbage pails, a bigger cart, and two helpers to share the workload. This helps to restore the status and everybody is happy. Now let's add some complexity to this fictional story. With time, the residents change their consumption pattern. Earlier these households would only generate food and solid human waste. Now their consumption habits generate waste that comprise plastic in the form of bottles, stationery, medicine and processed food wrappers; metals in the form of tin cans, batteries and aluminum foils; diapers, paper and such others. However, the housekeeper, who was never exposed to such complex waste before, doesn't know what to do with it. He looks to his employers for guidance but they pay no heed to him. After all, it is not their job to figure out the right way to collect and dispose waste but the housekeeper's. So the housekeeper decides to collect and dispose the new type of garbage in exactly the same manner as he used to dispose the wet and solid waste. He uses the broom to collect it, dumps it in the cart and makes his way to the landfill. He repeats the drill day after day. After a few months, residents see plastic bags floating across the settlement. They see fumes and smoke rising from the landfill. An odd smell permeates through the houses. When the residents wake up and decide to take stock of the situation, it turns out that the wind blew away the loose plastic bags from the landfill. Discarded food that remained trapped in plastic bags had begun to decompose, giving off a foul smell. Batteries, plastics and tin foil that were dumped in the landfill were emitting methane and other toxic gases. Residents decide that the housekeeper is to blame for this situation. They replace him with another equally clueless employee on the same terms, hoping for better results.

Extrapolate this story onto India and one gets to see the construct of India's challenges with waste collection and the gaping holes it represents in India's struggle for sanitation. Like in this fictional account, two problems confront the Indian waste-collection system. The first is the sheer inadequacy of the installed capacity for collecting garbage and the second is the antiquated nature of the installed capacity. Should the solutions to these problems not be simple, meaning, measure the right capacity and install the right systems? But the First World's history of waste collection and that of India's flawed social contract teaches us that these solutions are not as isolated as is the problem.

With rapid urbanization of the clean countries of today, people from the villages moved to the cities in search of jobs. But they also brought along their practices of waste disposal, such as dumping in the open. But cities comprised compact homes and streets. The roads and pavements were cobbled or tarred. Any garbage thrown in the cities therefore stood out like an eye-sore. Garbage disposal in the village was a simpler affair. The house would have an open pit in the backyard that would absorb food waste, dust and other tit-bits of waste that the house generated daily. When the pit was full, it would be covered and left dormant for the waste to decompose into manure. Cities had no such system and they slowly started to burst at the seams with garbage, which finally pushed the administrators to define a system for waste collection that put citizens at the heart of the problem. Garbage bins at homes or other establishments became the interface between the state and the citizens on the issue. Eventually, a system was perfected that allowed for further improvements and refinements involving waste segregation, recycling linkages and use of technology.

In contrast, India's story is more complex. Before the colonial rule, Indian villages were circular units, where the consumption and production cycles were balanced and they hardly relied on outside agencies for consumption needs. However, Indian villages relied on the cleaning caste for managing waste, and this remained the same for centuries. During the colonial rule, Indian rural folks witnessed the first mass-scale pressure to shun farming. The colonial rulers' home country went through an unprecedented wave of industrialization.

In this backdrop, the rule saw in India a consumption powerhouse of British industrial output. This commerce transformed many big trading centers across India, namely, Kolkata, Ahmedabad, Nagpur, Kanpur, Chennai into urban ecosystems with activities that India had never witnessed before – constructing houses in these emerging towns; laying a railway line; ferrying passengers within the city; running post offices, schools, hospitals; manning police stations; managing judiciary; or printing and distributing newspapers. Such ecosystems also became natural markets for cheap British import of textiles and other goods – a handloom kurta was more expensive than a shirt stitched at a loom in Manchester. This pressure suffocated the local skill-based cottage industries and more and more people left villages in search of 'urban' jobs.

The colonial rule absorbed some of these migrants within the fold of newly formed cities for these needed human labor in different hues. Simple manual labor to construct roads and pavements in the emerging administrative towns, educated labor force to discharge clerical roles in administrative jobs, technical skills to run locomotives and man railway stations along the way, to nurse patients in the hospitals and to teach in schools. While the canvas may seem overwhelming, the net movement of people toward towns during that time was small. At the time of independence in 1947, less than 10 percent of India's 200 million population lived in cities. These 20 million people were first, or at most, second-generation Indian urbanites. The circumference of the cities was miniscule compared to the massive Indian cities of today. Bombay of British India was 15 kilometers in length, whereas today Mumbai sprawls over 600 square kilometers. New Delhi, on becoming operational in 1915 was a mere 50 square kilometers that encompassed the administrative blocks, a few residential colonies, and markets. In 2015, Delhi spanned across 1,500 square kilometers. Cities like Chandigarh were not yet born, whereas cities like Bhopal were merely walled ghettos.

These cities generated waste in a setting and manner that was markedly different from that of villages and needed a waste collection response. The village system was a simple one that deployed 'lower' caste sweepers who would go from house to house collecting the waste and sweep the streets. Therefore, the ability of the village to keep itself clean was primarily dependent on the ability of its sweeper to collect garbage. The colonial rulers took this system and improvised it for the cities. The municipal bodies of these cities enrolled sweepers and tasked them with collecting waste from homes and cleaning the streets. The system was purpose built to keep those areas of the city clean that mattered to the colonial rule, like downtown markets and town halls, administrative buildings and residential colonies of the sahibs and their direct reports. Beyond these few square kilometres of area that the British considered 'urban,' everything else in the cities was merely a settlement – colonies of quasi-permanent shelters that hardly had any civic amenities connecting the individual units. These settlements housed people who had moved to the cities due to the economic stress in villages or had been displaced due to natural disasters or sectarian violence. The devastating famine of Bengal displaced thousands of families. The second World War moved a lot of people toward sea ports to support the colonial cause.

Local civic administration of these emerging Indian cities took a hub-and-spoke approach for waste collection. Households were expected to dump their garbage at a designated dumping place in the neighborhood. The civic authorities assigned sweepers to collect the garbage from this place, while the cleanliness of the public areas within the settlements was left to the whims of the people in the settlement. Civic bodies were designed to cater to the 'formal' areas of the city and so most sanitation resources like sweepers, garbage carts and other equipment, were restrictively earmarked to maintain public places of these 'desirable' areas of the city. This gave a false start to independent India's waste management journey. For one, the role of citizens toward waste collection was never defined in colonial times. People who moved to the cities then were never guided, coached or mandated on methods of disposing their waste, and city life was more complicated than what they had left behind in the villages. There were bustling bazaars, long commutes to work, small houses and congested lanes that impacted the frequency and place of waste generation. There were no Chadwicks or Poubellas to tell the new urban Indians to install garbage bins at home or guide the local civic bodies to take a more systematic and sustainable approach to waste collection.

Both, the new city-dwellers and the local civic bodies compensated for this lack of guidance with the rudimentary village system and retrofitted it on to their urban lives. Sanitation in the city was never viewed from any perspective other than that of the human count of number of sweepers. When open drains got choked to unbearable levels, neighbors would come together and request the local sweeper to clear it. He would clear the drain, load the raw sludge onto his rickety wheelbarrow and push the entire apparatus to the next colony and repeat the drill. Similarly, local civic authorities commissioned the sweepers to sweep the streets, pavements and markets at a fixed pre-determined frequency, notwithstanding the intensity of human movement in these areas that directly impacted the volume of waste generated. Consequently, some areas remained relatively clean by the time the next cleaning cycle was due whereas other areas were a stinking mess due to accumulated rubbish. No more than ~20 mn urban Indians lived with this arrangement and there seemed no urgency to reinvent the waste collection system because it didn't appear broken to the layman's eye. People's lives were not endangered by the dirty surroundings like they were by communal violence and famine. Society was still learning about the connection between poor sanitation and diseases.

The three decades that followed Independence were tumultuous – three wars, a crippling drought, the Green Revolution, creation of dams and engineering and steel companies, nationalization of banks, declaration of Emergency, and self-reliance on nuclear technology. In this backdrop, the polity hardly scoped out any appetite for 'mundane' issues like waste collection and a false sense of belief in this innately flawed sweeper system of waste collection that was conveniently carried forward in the twenty-first century.

Today households, shops, offices, eateries, tea stalls, garages, factories totalling to millions across India start their day with a daily clean-up, which earns the members of the lowest rung of the social ladder a meagre wage. Meanwhile, the cleaning of the home falls on the shoulders of the homemaker who discharges her duties without any commercial consideration. The arrangement cries out for help. If sweepers or housemaids collect waste from a household but the dump site is far away, they would resent hauling the waste all the way. They have other 'important' jobs to do than to engage in a long walk to dump garbage that eats into their productivity. It is here cognitive abilities of the human brain that allow us to improvise and seek convenient solutions come handy. An empty plot of land in the vicinity, an unfrequented cul-de-sac, a broken pavement, the areas next to drains and water bodies would serve as a convenient place to dump the waste and the neighborhood witnesses the birth of an unauthorized dumping site. On a lucky day, the waste collection truck comes to pick up waste from the assigned dump site. Sanitation workers in the truck have neither the time nor the tools to clean any other unassigned areas where the garbage is being conveniently dumped. Slowly, this unassigned area becomes a veritable garbage hill. The unbearable stench and / or an outbreak of vector diseases shakes up the neighborhood. The residents urge the local municipal body to clean-up the area. After some political manoeuvring the complaint gets attended to. An earth-moving vehicle moves around the neighborhood cleaning up the newly instituted garbage peaks and hillocks. Citizens breathe a sigh of relief and go back to their daily lives only for the peaks to re-appear not very long after, demanding the same drill.

The waste collection system in India has an intrinsic flaw: it seeks an adherence to the desired action on a voluntary basis. It expects households (or any other waste generating units) to transport the waste to a pre-appointed point for pick up (dump yards, dhaolas, and such). There are no barriers for non-compliance. It is easy for the citizens to deviate and try short-cuts or become non-compliant. Dump sites are not located in convenient places, and this compels people to dump the waste at unauthorized places that are more at hand. This voluntary arrangement also reinforces biases among Indian minds that garbage is an outsourced responsibility. Why bother to segregate waste if it is not part of the job? Why walk half a kilometer to dump the waste when it can be just as easily be disposed off on the vacant plot of land next door?

Clean countries understood the limitation of this approach for waste collection that lacks quid-pro-quo. It was not feasible for authorities to continue ramping up the human count with the rising quantum of complex waste. The system needed to put citizens at the center of the waste collection responsibility, while local administrators acted as facilitators, provided enabling infrastructure and processes. This ensured that the local administration's efforts are sharply directed toward waste collection rather than on sweeping neighborhoods. This insight gifted them with enormous productivity gains in the entire value chain of waste management. India, on the contrary, due to its biased social contract completely missed this point.

Millions of garbage generating households start their day by cleaning their areas and dumping the garbage in the open dump sites, on empty plots of lands, by the sides of streets or slyly pushing it in unauthorized spaces. This mixed garbage comprises vegetable peels, stale lentil curry, gnawed chicken bones, dried flowers and plastic wrappers, used insulin injections, sanitary napkins, broken glass and discarded batteries. This waste is exposed to sunlight and starts to emit gases, creating a nauseating smell, breeding vector-borne diseases and serving open invitation of buffet to scavenging birds, domesticated bovines, stray dogs and rodents. The crumbling old garbage truck, which emits a smell far worse than the unauthorized dump site, comes around to collect the rubbish, disturbing the scavenging-feast. A few men use their bare hands to lift the putrefying trash from the site, only to dump it in with the rest of the open garbage in the truck. They move on to the next site, spilling some of the garbage onto the road, in their wake, while commuters cover their noses in disgust. Some cities have graduated to closed top trucks, while others may have been able to provide protective gear to the sanitation workers or kept colored bins at garbage dump sites, but, as we shall see, that makes not a jot of a difference in India's growing challenge to pick up garbage from its neighborhoods.

Following Independence, India's urban population witnessed an exponential growth, which put ever-increasing stress on the waste-collection apparatus. Between 1961 and 1991, the population density (number of people per square kilometer) of Delhi increased from 1,729 to 6,352, a 370 percent growth. The per capita waste generated in the city also increased from 310 grams in 1981 to 472 grams in 1991. Not only was Delhi packing more people every square kilometer, these people were also generating more waste than those before them. View this change from the perspective of waste collection, and say a sweeper in 1981 is assigned to clean an area twice every day. He is fairly efficient and effectual in his duties. But, ten years on he struggles to keep it clean because not only has the population grown four times but his equipment and capabilities have not once been upgraded to handle the manifold increase in the generated waste. Is it then only the sweeper's fault to not be able to clean the city? But, the local bodies overlooked this intricacy and simply hired more sweepers as a response. Even this hiring was temperamental. Should it be based on number of households that need to be serviced, or on the quantum of waste generated? What should be the waste collection approach from informal settlements (invisible living in the eyes of local governance)? The job of waste collection was soon reduced to manage the deployment of sweepers across the city. Local governance of Delhi found itself troubleshooting as a standard template to prioritize its flawed capacity to collect garbage. The parts of the city that complained more received more attention, while informal neighborhoods were a stinking mess and sought political representation to get cleaned. Soon, municipal bodies had exhausted their financial bandwidth to hire sweepers owing to their meager financial coffers, and began outsourcing the job to private contractors, who in turn hired an army of sweepers in blatant violation of labor laws. At the end of the day, Delhi's waste collection approach was reduced to this: citizens viewed waste collection as a duty of the local civic bodies. Local bodies viewed it as the duty of contractors & sweepers. Contractors outsourced it to sweepers and illegally milked the labor cost arbitrage. Sweepers, the most condemned class for centuries, were expected to clean Delhi with their bare hands and beaten-up broomsticks.

Till 1991, this arrangement rarely troubled the mainstream for its out-of-the-ordinary existence. Since then, rapidly expanding urban India also grew in aspirations, choices and dreams which significantly altered its consumption patterns and Delhi was a poster boy of this shift. But, in the din of this new-found consumption binge, Delhi like the rest of India was also setting itself up for a massive failure on waste collection. Between 1991 and 2011, the daily waste generated in the city of Delhi alone increased from 4,000 metric tons to nearly 11,000 metric tons, a whopping 2.75 times increase in 20 years. But the city's antiquated sweeper system cracked under the sheer pressure and scale of the disruptive growth of the generated waste in the city. Mr. Pinto's story vividly captures this collapse.

Pinto, 28, is one of the nearly 1.1 million workers in India formally engaged in the job of cleaning and collecting garbage, almost equivalent to the number of employees in the Indian Railways, the third largest employer in the world. These sanitation workers are required to collect garbage daily from 250 million households and nearly 15 million shops, not counting all other waste-generating units like hospitals, schools, offices, factories, and so on. Thus, every sanitation worker must collect waste from 240 such establishments. Everyday Pinto loads the garbage onto a truck at the Janakpuri District Centre market in New Delhi, and ends up cleaning human excreta frequently found here. He is paid a monthly salary of ₹5,000. 'Toilets in this market are not easy to locate, so parents let their children defecate in the open. It is not the job of the sweepers, but I take personal responsibility. I am a sanitation worker here, but I am not allowed to use the toilets. The guards shoo me away. So I too defecate in the open near the garbage house,' he says. Pinto arrives at the market at 5 a.m. every day and goes about removing garbage till 3 p.m. 'My body begins to ache within a few hours and I feel very tired. When I request that my work be shared by one more person, I am told to quit the job.' When he calls for the garbage van to carry away the waste from the dumping place, the response he often receives is that the driver is either sleeping or drunk. 'What you see is two days of garbage rotting away because the van has not arrived,' Pinto points to the stinking heap spilling out onto the road. His employers have provided him with a cart – without a seat or tires – to remove the waste from the marketplace, so he prefers to use his own. He did not receive any money for its maintenance either, he says, struggling to control his cart on a slope. Mr. Pinto also lays bare India's severe limitations in collecting waste from all households if it continues to extrapolate the existing sweeper system.

From 1991, 'reformed' India saw an explosion of waste that was as complex as it was in the First World. By the end of 2014, Indians were consuming, annually, over 300 million disposable syringes, over 30 million condoms, over 90 million smartphones, over 400 million potato chips bags, over 2,000 million bottles of packaged drinking water. After serving its intended purpose, every single item on this list landed up in the garbage bin. None of these items had been in Indian's consumption basket in such volumes twenty years earlier. Till 1991, buying a bottle of packaged water while traveling was considered very posh and that became ubiquitous two decades later. But we continued to dispose the empty plastic bottle in the same way as the wet waste. It was tossed carelessly out of the car or bus window on a highway, or thrown from the train onto the tracks or by the way side on the railroad. At home, the bottle went under the kitchen sink and emptied out in the neighborhood open dump site the next day. If it wasn't eventually picked up by a rag picker, then it would be picked up during the regular sweeping plan of the area to land up in the city's open landfill.

India's antiquated system of waste collection was not only exposed for its inadequacy to handle the aftermath of India's rising consumption binge, but it also laid bare the deplorability of the arrangement as seen in an incident in a shopping mall in Delhi in 2017 that took the lives of two brothers, Jahangir and Izaz. The brothers assisted their father in his scrap trading business and collected waste from the mall. Occasionally, the mall management would ask them to clean the sewers located in the basement of the mall for a few extra bucks, without providing any safety. In August 2017, on one such 'work order,' the brothers descended into the sewer, and the deadly concoction of sulphur dioxide, carbon monoxide, and ammonia proved fatal. Around the same time, a similar fate awaited Maakandas and Amarjeet who descended into the sewer at the premises of an ashram located in the outskirts of Delhi. These deaths coincided with the deaths of three sanitation workers hired by Delhi's local civic body on contract to clean public sewers under an identical deplorable arrangement. It is fair to say that the Indian state lacked any lens to spot the mall and the ashram for the deplorable condition because these private entities merely mimicked an institutionalized action of the Indian state.

India has a standing army of 1.3 million soldiers in active duty. In reply to a query in the Lok Sabha in 2012, the Indian government acknowledged that between 2000 and 2012 nearly 4,000 Indian soldiers died in the line of duty. This makes the annual mortality rate of the armed forces at under 0.03 percent. On the other hand, officially, there are 1.1 million sanitation workers in the country, and nearly 23,000 lose their lives annually on duty, making the mortality rate of a sanitation worker at around 2 percent. Statistics show that compared to a soldier, therefore, being a sanitation worker in India is 66 times riskier. Indian society's wholesale abandonment of the job of waste collection and its refusal to see it as a specialized skill that needs technical and operational enrichment stands exposed as the glaring culprit for this reality. This abandonment forces the process of waste collection to seek refuge in antiquated system that pushes thousands of lives into the sewers in this one-way street to martyrdom. Circumstances demand a neutral examination of the waste collection approach both for its relevance and its adequacy to serve the needs of the post-independence India in the coming decades. But, biases have a unique ability to blur an obvious solution into an elusive mirage as is the case with the job of waste collection in India.

Freedom from colonial rule was never perceived as a fitting rebuttal to the caste system and the job of waste collection. In independent India, there was hardly any intellectual neutrality that could critique the sweeper system, which sat at cross purposes with India's challenges with waste management. For the political leadership of the time, this system worked well through a self-trained 'caste' of people, which gave a false sense of orderliness till the time India grew at the 'Hindu' rate of growth. But the economic reforms of 1991 revealed the fallacy of this system. The First World began to reduce its dependence on the labor-intensive system of waste collection when it faced a similar onslaught of consumption binge. An absence of earlier prejudices also allowed these countries to view the job from the standpoint of productivity and standardization. However, India, owing to the lack of adequate criticism as an outcome of both individual and institutional biases, hoped that someday the likes of Pinto would be able to collect waste from 260 houses every day without complaining.

A hardened human body that only knew hard labor (often with his bare hands), inseparable from dirt, pathogens and foul odors did not unsettle the local bodies that employed it. Why would it? This human body was an inexpensive and convenient tool that suppressed many difficult questions about the birth defects of local governance in India. These defects were responsible for their financial emaciation that increasingly pushed them into a corner with the rapidly rising complexity of generated waste. More sweepers under their direct fold meant more payroll cost that sucked up the entire budget allocated for waste management. Concurrently, the rising complexity of the generated waste was making sweepers grumpier and more cynical about their job. But the local bodies' dependence on the sweeper system was iron clad. Soon, they began outsourcing such jobs to contractors by packaging the cleaning job as a 'project.' The contractor's quote for the project was a fraction of the cost that the local civic bodies incurred by employing sweepers on their own rolls. The only way a contractor could do the same job at a much lower price was to exploit the labor cost arbitrage. The contractor hired sweepers at one-third the wage rates paid by the local civic bodies, and bypassing labor laws. They further exploited other margin-improvement opportunities by cutting corners on equipment, infrastructure, and safety gear. Pinto is the manifestation of this arrangement. He is on the rolls of the private contractor at ₹5,000 per month, while minimum wages demand that he be paid at least ₹20,000 per month. He works long hours without safety gear and with antiquated equipment. He is expected to clean and collect increasing quantities of waste littered on the street, without any complaints lest he be replaced by someone else at a cheaper cost. Under the Indian labor laws, an entity can hire a contract worker for no more than 240 days of employment. While the contractor's cleaning contracts with the local bodies are long term, the contractor terminates sanitation workers days before the mandatory 240 days and draws up a fresh contract with same or reduced wages. If a disgruntled employee leaves mid-way, his job is taken over by a person willing to work for lower wages and willingly accepts the exploitation on the platter.

But Mr. Pinto's silent suffering pales before the issues in the job of cleaning Indian sewers. The sewage system is like the nervous system of the body, and must remain free of clogs for a smooth flow of solid waste. Sewers need regular maintenance because they are prone to blockages resulting from a sudden surge of waste release during monsoons, festivals and other occasions. It is a common sight that a clogged sewer brings many Indian cities to their knees during the rainy season. Maintenance of sewer lines requires a person to descend into the man-holes to clean the drain pipes from the inside, among other mechanical solutions. It is not the most inspiring job, in fact it will not be entirely wrong to call it one of the toughest jobs in the world, because a closed sewer is quite like a poisonous gas chamber with trapped emissions from the flowing sludge. Clean countries treat it as a specialist's job which requires various safeguards, and recognize the importance of this work in keeping the surroundings clean and odour-free. They take it very seriously and this is reflected in the elaborate operating procedures, rules, regulations, safeguards and laws that are laid down for the job. In Hong Kong for instance, a sanitation worker requires fifteen different licenses before he can set foot inside a sewage pipe. He should be covered head-to-toe in such a manner that his skin should never come in direct contact with the refuse; this is only one of many safety requirements. Contrast this with the events at the recruitment drives conducted by the local civic bodies of Moradabad, Meerut and Agra in 2016 where prospective sanitation workers were asked to clean open sewers with their bare hands and uncovered bodies. Every day many under-clothed, under-nourished and under-equipped people make the descent into India's sewage pipe. Not surprisingly, a few thousands every year never come back alive.

Another unintended consequence of the administration's blind faith in the sweeper system was informality, which sucked most skill-based jobs including the job of waste collection. The hangover of structural decimation of skill-based livelihood triggered by the import of industrialization in the twentieth century continued unabated in independent India. This allowed the demon of informality to suck most skill-based jobs into it. In 2016, nine out of ten people were employed informally in India – a landless labor working in the fields, an errand boy working sixteen hours a day in a kirana store, a taxi driver doing forty sorties a day, a security guard in a residential colony doing twelve-hour shifts, a weaver weaving chanderi sarees, a chef cooking biryani at a takeaway joint, a maid cleaning six homes a day, and many more.

Such jobs are shrouded in insecurity and uncertainty because the contract that binds the relationship between the employee and the employer for such jobs is mostly verbal. It does not provide any safety or minimum wage clauses, or benefits and demands no binding commitments from the employers. A verbal contract also eliminates any incentive for either the employee or the employer to improve their skills. If the skills don't live up to the employers' expectations, they simply fire the employee and hire another in the hope that they would be better at the job. And employees rely on practices passed on to them in previously held jobs and the mistakes they made. A farmhand who harvest crops learnt from his parents and rarely looked at improvement opportunities through better tools. A lorry driver continues to drive on the wrong side of the road because that's what he picked up from his teacher – possibly another lorry driver who did the same. A construction labor working on a site continues to ferry bricks on his head, unquestioning and without safety gear because that is what brings home the bread at the end of the day. A weaver continues to weave the same old designs because he cannot afford to get off the loom to explore new trends and think about evolving consumer taste. A cook in an eatery will continue to cook in unhygienic conditions because that's what he learned from his predecessor. The verbal contract's intrinsic design has no room for job improvement, productivity and dignity. Employers were always flushed with next batch of possibly cheaper labor and the prospective employees hardly have the mind space to think about their job beyond a day or a week. Most informal jobs broadly fall into two categories: those that have existed for centuries before colonial times such as weaving, commercial cooking, retailing, farming labor among others. People gained the requisite skills by assisting family members. A father passed them on to his son, who in turn passed them on to his son and so on; and those that started with India's journey of industrialization, such as driving, masonry, plumbing and sanitation work in the cities.

Like nature plays a role in genetic mutation to trigger a biological evolution that allows the subject to adapt to the new circumstances, the state is expected to trigger desirable evolution in the human capability of the country. It does so by activating regulations that encourage equality in employment contracts. It defines minimum skill requirements, working environment and provides a job description that outlines acceptable and non-acceptable standards. The state further ensures that these guidelines are refreshed with the changing times. But, in the case of India, informal jobs provided livelihoods to millions without the state having to bother about such interventions. Bringing informal jobs into the formal fold meant governance response in the form of legislation and enforcement. But, informality gave livelihood without these added complications and the Indian state happily accepted its presence because the alternative meant a hard toil to manage the consequence of disturbing the status quo and any slip-up in it posed grave political risk. The design, quality and productivity of the job could never make a debut in the debate. And so these jobs could never evolve to deliver on the changing needs of independent India and the faulty gene continued to pass down to the next generation without interruption. Eventually, all these jobs found themselves trapped in the vicious cycles of low productivity, exploitation and isolation.

The informal job of waste collection was a little more unfortunate than the others. Prior to Independence, not only was it assigned the lowest place in the pecking order of caste, it was also bound by a skewed social contract. The sweeper's ability to earn was largely dependent on the society's willingness to pay because the job faced extreme isolation and condemnation. Other informal jobs not only figured higher up in the caste hierarchy but also their contracts were not as lopsided vis-à-vis mainstream society. A boatman, for instance, earned his fair wage to ferry people across the river. An ironsmith sold the goods he forged at the market rate for a livelihood. In other words, all these jobs delivered services in lieu of the price they demanded. On the contrary, the waste collection job faced a fractured economic contract. The sweeper's ability to earn was largely depended on the society's willingness to pay because the job of waste collection faced extreme isolation and condemnation. Therefore, collecting waste from homes was more an entitlement for the consuming class, whereas the same sense of entitlement didn't exist to fetch a ride on boats or to purchase cooking vessels from the ironsmith. Neither was the boatman underpaid for his service nor was the ironsmith expected to sell his products at below cost price. Institutional discrimination further disallowed the decoupling of the function of waste collection from the sweeper who executed the job and silently sponsored this informality. Individuals like Mr. Pinto, a high mortality rates while cleaning sewers and reliance on rag pickers to circumvent the institutional pitfalls are all expressions of this awry system. Post Independence, a poorly paid sweeper armed with rickety infrastructure was the sum total of the waste-collection methods, while what it needed was an objective design of the processes to haul the waste from households to disposal centers. This needed a scientific temperament to determine the resources and to design methods for productivity, a process response, and someone to act as an enabler. The response needed the imagination to 'future-proof' waste-collection processes to handle the rising complexity of generated waste.

India needed institutional sponsorship to bring waste collection into the formal fold and the story of Rai Bahadur M. S. Oberoi conveys both its possibilities and its advantages. Fascinated with the idea of an Indian luxury hotel, in the 1920s, at par with the colonial standards of fine living, Oberoi, the father of the Indian hospitality industry, founded the East India Hotel Co. (now EIH Ltd.). He started the first hotel in Shimla in 1925. The standards envisioned by him meant not only the very best of culinary and service experiences, but also hygiene and cleanliness to be delivered by housekeepers. But there was no other hotel in the city that had ever before cultivated such human capability, nor were there any set guidelines or procedures to carry the task out. He thus created a cadre of housekeepers who were no less important than any service staff of the hotel. This method-based approach freed-up the job of cleaning from the clutches of societal stigma and instilled dignity in the job. Cleaning thus moved into the realm of professional service, which was critical for the success of the hotels. He went on to build some of the most iconic hotels with a dogmatic focus on standard operating procedure, which governed all operations of the hotel including hygiene.

The Oberoi Centre for Learning and Development was founded to encapsulate this vision and with the purpose of creating a constant supply of best-in-class human capability for housekeeping, services, and culinary art to cater to the increasing footprint of the Oberoi Hotels. Today, cleaning toilets and rooms in star-rated hotels in India are specialized jobs that involve formal contracts and are not confined to specific caste groups, so much so that we often forget cleaning jobs outside the confines of these hotels remain an unresolved matter. If, from within the Indian ethos, such service excellence on sanitation could emerge, then replicating the enabling conditions that exist within these hotels in the whole of India should yield a clean nation. Rai Bahadur's story exemplifies the importance of viewing any job from the perspective of its purpose and not from a stereotypical fixation on the person who discharges the job. This change in paradigm lends itself to objective evaluation for improving productivity and efficacy. Imagine the plight of the first Oberoi hotel if Rai Bahadur had pinned his hopes on sweepers in Shimla to clean it, with Indian society being drenched in its mediocre hygiene standards and calcified biases.

Foremost, India needs to imbibe this learning and must let go of its current fixation of viewing this job in the measurement unit of human bodies. Only then can it appreciate the crucial role the waste collection function plays to get the garbage from generation points to disposal centers. It is not as much about the number of people engaged in the job as it is about the critical link in a chain which must be designed for an efficient and effective response. The story of the sharp contrast between the New Delhi International Airport and its neighboring suburb conveys both the possibilities this argument opens up and the deep chasms that need to be bridged. In less than a decade, the international airport at New Delhi went from a picture of stained carpets and chaos to one of neatness and order. It has since consistently ranked among the best airports in the world (presumably cleanliness is an important aspect) in its class. This airport's ecosystem represents cleanliness and well-ordered spaces that make the right statement, as any world-class airport should do. An institutional response that involved investment, an operating model and execution, one that also encapsulated cleanliness and sanitation within its fold was responsible for this change of image. Not very different from the story of the Oberoi Hotels.

But 3 kilometers away from this airport sits the chaotic suburb of Mahipalpur, which appears to have absorbed all that was discarded from the airport when it had its makeover. The suburb provides a shorter access route to certain parts of the city through its narrow road that is just wide enough to accommodate all forms of mechanical and motorized vehicles that jostle with each other to get ahead. Occasionally, they encounter nonchalant bovines on the tarmac. Till 2017, halfway down the road there used to be an open garbage dump, which sat in front of a school. It occupied part of this busy road and part of the pavement next to it. A casual glance at it gave a fair idea of the consumption preferences of the area: discarded bandages from the medical clinics, peels and juiced out sugarcane sticks from the juice shops, leftover food from various eateries, plastic bottles and food wrappers from the grocery shops and homes. Barring the few hours immediately following the daily waste collection beat, the place always carried this noxious concoction of garbage and was frequented by a variety of livestock in search of a tasty morsel. An open dump-site with unsegregated rubbish, on a busy road, posing health risks all around especially to the school it faces, welcomed guests from all over the world. The challenge India faces in extending its success with the airport to this neighboring suburb is sharply brought out by this juxtaposition. The quantity and type of waste dumped on the site far outpaced the ability of the local civic body to handle it. The makeover of the airport in the vicinity did little to change the arrangement in Mahipalpur. The problem with such a contrast lies in the confusing signals it gives to the society. Let's think about the young shop owner in the neighborhood who grew up assisting his father in the store. He sees the dilapidated airport replaced with a world class infrastructure and marvels at it, yet he continues to dump his garbage in the open like his father did for two decades before him. Occasionally he reads about the 'Clean India' campaign and struggles to make the connection and wonders how it applies to him and his neighborhood when nothing seems to have changed, save for the swanky new airport in the vicinity. Mahipalpur can easily be replaced with any other congested lane of Delhi and the storyline of contrasts will hardly change.

While India mirrors the First World on the complexity and quantum of generated waste, it continues to rely on waste-collection practices that lost their relevance in the clean world over a century ago. Armed with this antiquated sweeper system, the best of Indian cities like Pune, Indore, Bhopal, and Mysuru can lift three-quarters of the garbage they generate daily in their jurisdiction; the worse-off ones can only lift one-third. The unattended garbage is left to the mercy of the abandoned bovines, stray dogs, scavenging birds and rodents, or is most of the times set alight.

A rationed supply of clean space becomes a visible symptom of this challenge. The inadequacy of the waste-collection system to lift the entire garbage generated daily across India invariably compels the respective local civic bodies to perpetuate a policy of discrimination. They allocate their meager resources based on opaque considerations defined by personal biases and end up having to troubleshoot the problems. The proximity of the area to the governance apparatus and profile of people living in the neighborhood determine the allocation of waste collection resources. VIP or the important areas are always given priority. For the rest of the town, the incapacity of the respective body to collect garbage begins to pass off as the status quo and cauterizes the mind of ordinary citizens toward dirty surroundings. The ability to get garbage cleaned up from an area then emerges as strong political currency that can be cashed by advocating for a higher share of the paltry resources of the civic bodies. Political actors seek diversion of the woefully inadequate waste-collection apparatus toward the ignored area of the city only to get overshadowed by a more powerful lobby with a similar demand from another area of the city. The political currency misguidedly looks for instant gratification for their franchise by seeking a higher share of an antiquated waste collection system, rather than to think about structural improvements therein. Slyly, the notion of a clean surrounding becomes the entitlement of 'fortunate' physical spaces, owing to adjacencies and leverage rather than to the certainty of the state's response. Eventually, such a scarce clean space is packaged as aspirational merchandise going to the highest bidder, making clean living a discretionary choice for a fortunate few rather than a right of one and all. In this backdrop, to expect citizens to voluntarily haul the garbage to the dump sites cannot solve the problem because the state struggles with prerequisite infrastructure and processes that can pamper their volunteering act.

The first step must be a change in the core design of the process to collect waste. The allegory of the Lohar community serves as an apt inspiration to support this case. For centuries, the Lohars have lived as nomadic tribes in temporary settlements on the fringes of mainstream Indian society. The community gained acceptance for their skill to smelt and forge iron tools for daily use. Suppose at the time of Independence, India decided not to pursue any investment in modern steel plants, and instead decided to leverage the skills of the Lohar community to meet the growing need for steel and its modern applications. The Lohars' iron-smelting skills needed protection, reasoned the policy, and incentivized the community to deploy its proven artisan techniques to support the growing steel need. It expected the community to churn out steel for bridges, railway engines, buildings and to forge agricultural tools, cutlery, home utensils, containers for daily use, and so forth. How far would India have gone with this approach to fulfill its hunger for steel? How would the likes of Maruti and Hero Motors source the steel to produce the humongous volumes of automobiles they do today? Although India did not go down this artisanal path to cater to its need for steel, it fell into this trap when it came to the function of waste collection. India needed industrial design and a scientific approach to design the waste-collection function. Instead, it was trapped in an artisanal framework that reduced this job to informality, exploitative working conditions, under-installed capacity, and a rickety infrastructure. When cities like Jalgaon, Bulandshahr, Morena, Unnao, or Chikballapur race to mimic the bigger cities on consumption character, they also replicate this flawed waste-collection approach with equal speed. There is an urgency to assess the design of the process of waste collection itself.

Waste collection is the first crucial step toward an effective waste-management response. Long ago, the First-World countries struggled yet understood if the waste is segregated and collected at source, it makes disposal easier and effective. This relationship may seem obvious in the clean countries of today, but it was incredibly tricky to synchronize the two functions a hundred years ago, when they too loosely relied on the sweeper system to collect waste. Citizens under the new system were mandated to put sort their own garbage. With changing consumption patterns, laws were further modified to segregate the collected waste before bagging it for collection. Garbage bins were issued to households and shops alike. All waste-generating units were mandated to subscribe to the service in lieu of a service charge or a waste-collection tax. The next step was to build the infrastructure for a waste-collection service with support from the legislation. Local civic bodies went about doggedly issuing standard garbage bins to households and shops, bringing everyone into the fold, much like installing electricity meters to measure electricity consumption. Instead of a sanitation worker having to spend disproportionate time sweeping the streets and picking up littered garbage, he was now more productive by merely having to collect pre-bagged garbage from the waste generation source (homes, shops, offices etc.). This freed up the local bodies' capacity while making the cleaning jobs safer and faster.

The productive gains in waste collection allowed local authorities in the First World to focus on enforcement for Sanitation. Sanitation inspectors were tasked to survey assigned areas for compliance with these waste-collection rules and issued fines for deviations and non-compliance.Beat plans for the sanitation workers were designed to achieve maximum and frequent coverage. The quantum of fine was steep enough to act as deterrence for the future. The number of sanitation inspectors was synced with the density and spread of households in the area. With these in place, people started to graduate toward bagging rubbish in bins for a controlled and regulated release. Over time, the idea that the garbage at home would be collected the next morning became a natural extension of daily living.

This realignment moved the function of waste collection away from the custody of low skilled manual labor to the one that needed industrial design. Sweepers gave way to sanitation workers and inspectors. Rusty old wheelbarrows made way for motorized garbage trucks. Iron bins were replaced by 'wheelies' that were designed for swift and efficient interaction with the garbage trucks. This shift can be compared to the dramatic makeover of the defense forces at that time. Before the industrial revolution, war was a function of a soldier's skill in fighting with arms. An army's chances of success dramatically increased with more skilled soldiers. War was essentially a play of human skills and body count. After the industrial revolution, the nature of armed conflict changed. Aircrafts, ships, mortar guns, and artilleries were designed and deployed to fight wars. The job of a soldier changed significantly. He was no longer the sole reason for success in a war. He became an important facilitator of technology and equipment and so was the case with waste collection. The function became an interplay of mechanization, processes, and human skill. In 2016, New York and Mumbai, both multiethnic and urbane cities with a high share of migrant population, generated almost the same quantity of waste daily, that is, 10,000 to 12,000 metric tons. Mumbai deployed 29,000 sanitation workers and nearly 1,000 vehicles (dumpers, tippers, waste collection trucks, etc.) to collect it: 1 vehicle for every 30 sanitation workers. New York deployed nearly 12,000 sanitation workers and 5,000 vehicles to collect its garbage: 1 vehicle for every 3 sanitation workers. Increasingly, even the complexity of waste generated by Mumbai mirrors that of New York. While New York is rated among the best-managed cities on waste management, Mumbai struggles in the bottom quartile by global standards. Ironically, Mumbai deploys two and half times more people to clean and collect garbage than New York. By that logic Mumbai should be nearly as many times cleaner, but that is not the case.

The efficient system of New York and other clean cities was preceded by legislation on waste collection, a handbook of procedures that citizens must follow, unlike its Indian counterpart. For instance, recall Seattle's rule that spells out that a household is also responsible for keeping clean the public area that falls immediately outside, be it a pavement or a few meters of the peripheral area outside of the house. In Belgium, waste-collection laws have guided citizens to segregate waste into two bins until the 1990s, changed their reference point, and directed them to segregate it into six different bins (one each for glass, paper, plastic, electronic waste, batteries, and the rest) after the rules were modified in keeping with the changing nature of garbage. In contrast, the Indian legislative approach on waste collection has been vague and skewed more toward prohibition than guidance. Burning of trash was banned in India in 2001, but that hardly deterred people from the practice, or that the bio-medical waste rules of 1998 prohibit the disposal of medical waste containing bodily fluids with common garbage, but that has caused no reduction in the instances of such waste reaching landfills across India.

A mechanized unloading process by pick-up trucks equipped with fork-lifts designed to sync with the shapes of these standardized, color coded bins ensured that the waste collection from every household was completed in just a few seconds. Beat plans of collection trucks were defined and published for the sake of the citizens' information, who were mandated to subscribe to this paid service. However, they could call and place a special request for collection in case they missed the regular beat (sometimes paying a fine for it). This was akin to a water or electricity connection at home provided by a local utility company. The approach was simple to execute and easy to quantify and became a reference point for local bodies for taking operational decisions. The number of households in a ward or county could be translated into the number of bins to plan pick-ups. The quantum of waste generated from these households was easily converted into number and types of garbage bags. The segregation of waste at source efficiently segmented the waste into different forms. The capacity of different types of waste trucks was mapped to various parts of the city based on the nature of housing (condominiums, apartments, bungalows) and the garbage haul capacity of the truck. The time required for collecting waste from each household and the number of people required to do the job was also easy math. City administrators could quantify every activity on productivity parameters to determine the infrastructure and operational design required. The pieces of the puzzle started to fall into place and paint a picture of a well-oiled system that sweated the infrastructure and human resources in the most productive fashion possible. With the rising complexity of the generated waste, the First World had to constantly modify this modular approach which was easy because they had managed to create a strong baseline pivot. As a result citizens in Belgium could transition from segregating waste only into wet and dry, to segregating into half a dozen bins.

In the period immediately following World War II, the First World witnessed an explosive growth in generated waste. The yearly waste output in Japan, for instance, which doubled between 1955 and 1959, put severe stress on the existing waste-collection system. Fortunately, for these countries, the tool of 'enforcement for sanitation' had been under operation for more than five decades, thanks to the efforts of Chadwick and Poubelle at the turn of the twentieth century. The profound impact of Sir Chadwick's role on it could be gauged from his forming the Association of Sanitary Inspectors in the UK in 1883. While the First World was still dumping garbage in the sea and dead animals on the streets, the association trained people to be sanitation inspectors and framed guidelines on 'enforcement for sanitation.' The Association inspired establishment of similar institutions in other Western countries. In the next century, the Association was rechristened the Chartered Institute of Environmental Health, an institute that stands as a guardian of enforcement in sanitation. Owing to this early start, today's clean countries began to appreciate the role of enforcement in altering social behavior toward waste management. For instance, the 181,000 habitants of Toronto, Canada, generated 30 metric tons of waste every day in 1890, and 11 full-time sanitary inspectors were deployed to enforce sanitation laws here. In contrast, Bhubaneswar, Odisha, employed 11 sanitary inspectors that served the city's population of nearly a million and supervised nearly 400 metric tons of waste generated per day in 2015. Even if we take the 1890 employment norms of Toronto and extrapolate them to 2015, Bhubaneswar would need ten times more sanitary inspectors.

By the end of World War II, sanitation inspectors in the clean countries of today were going door-to-door monitoring people on good practices of hygiene and waste collection. The First World was well used to the sight of sanitation inspectors monitoring litter in public areas and issuing fines to anyone who was found breaking the rules. By now, First-World countries had amassed nearly seven decades of policy experience on the relationship between public hygiene and enforcement. They also learned that enforcement needed a simultaneous approach in three broad areas: on-the-spot violations, post-facto breaches and violations while collecting waste from households. This meant that casual littering in the streets, waste dumped in unauthorized spots and the bagged waste not segregated properly were equally likely to get reprimanded. This enforcement framework was intelligently juxtaposed with penalties. From the start, penalties were used both as an effective deterrent and as an enabler for the enforcement apparatus. Standard fines for littering violations were severe. Today for instance, in Denmark the standard littering fine is 90 Euros or ~₹6,000. There is also a laddered approach to fines to demonstrate that violations in some areas are graver than they are in others. For instance, littering in a national park in the United States attracts a fine as high as US$ 1,000 (nearly ~₹67,000) but lower for other public areas. In some instances, fines in the US can go as high as US$10,000 (nearly ~ ₹6,70,000). But, spotting errant behavior and earning revenues from fines were not the primary objectives. The goal instead was achieving a high probability of spotting an offence to curb the natural human instinct to discard waste at will. The thorn in the side of this enforcement agenda was not the human being but his instincts to discard generated waste in an unregulated manner. If the probability to spot any breaches had remained low then the instinctive behavior of the individual would take over. Therefore, a low probability of spotting waste and hygiene related breaches was as good as no enforcement at all. The focus of enforcement agencies was to increase the chances of spotting offences with the intention of curtailing the instincts. This persistent approach started to alter human behavior. Within three generations, these societies graduated from compliance with sanitation laws for fear of reprimand, to internalizing these laws as instinctive behavior. Enforcement enabled a user-fee based waste collection system, which quickly freed up the bandwidth of local civic bodies from physically cleaning vast tracts of land. The city administrators were no longer burdened with sweeping and picking up garbage because under the new arrangement this was either done by citizens who bagged the waste at source or by the enforcement apparatus which curtailed society's instinct to spontaneously release waste at will. Sanitation workers were no longer required to clean the streets or carry manual carts. They were now expected to drive vehicles, knock on doors to collect garbage bags, haul containerized waste and assist in enforcement to spot breaches. Like the waste collection system, the enforcement apparatus also kept itself current with the changing complexity of waste. The construct of New York Department of Sanitation offers some interesting clues in this regard. The Department in 2015 had a dedicated police force equipped with its own fleet of vehicles, fire arms, batons, pepper spray, and other safety equipment. It was divided into four specialized units comprising a uniformed sanitation police force, an illegal dumping task force, permit and inspection units, and an environmental police force. Not only did this team track acts of misconduct, it also conducted investigation and/or assisted regular police in serious crimes that resulted from breaches of sanitation and hygiene rules, namely, deaths and mass public health risks. In contrast, in 2012, the EDMC took a seemingly brave decision and announced that going forward, sanitation inspectors will be given motorcycles for the first time to travel into their respective city wards to conduct inspection.

The First World also extended the technical and operational rigour regarding waste collection to industrial and commercial waste. In the First-World countries, environmental laws were strengthened to make factories responsible for treating their generated waste and/or ensure its controlled release. The first phase of these laws was aimed at removing floating materials from the waste and treating it with disinfectants to kill pathogens. Concurrently, environment science increasingly started to establish the correlation between industrial effluents and environmental degradation, and the causal relationship between effluent discharge and public health. This led to the second phase, which was aimed at reducing toxins from the generated industrial waste. This created a fertile ground for legal activism that chased the connect between industrial waste disposal and environmental degradation. The activism of Erin Brockovich that led to the single largest class action suit settlement in US history involving the dumping of industrial waste and its adverse effects on public health is a case in point. Corporations, entities, and organizations started to factor in the legal risks involved in industrial waste disposal and cautiously redesigned and measured the steps of their operating value chain to eliminate all current and future breaches. Mitigation approaches and processes were designed and installed. Informal activities of the value chain across many industries were formalized.

All countries in the First World that succeeded in their fight with waste moved away from a sweeper system to collect waste through a system that involved citizens containerizing the waste and industrial units recycling them. It was a financially sustainable arrangement that engineered a chain reaction of improvement in the entire value chain of waste management. For instance, open landfills made way for closed ones and dumping made way for recycling and composting as a direct outcome of redesigned waste-collection system. This underpins the universality of the idea.

India will need to think about waste-collection system as a grid that needs to be developed across towns, villages, and cities. Every household (or any other consumption unit) will need to be installed with different types of tagged garbage bins of standard size issued by respective local bodies – one each for biodegradable waste, metal, electronics and batteries, glass, paper, and plastic and rubber. Under this grid system, households or other consumption units will need to be segmented on the number of occupants or on the nature of commercial activity, namely, office or food services, to enable the issuance of different types of bins to these units. An eatery dishing out home delivery meals will need a bigger food waste bin than that for a household, or a general provision store will need a bigger bin for paper and plastic waste, whereas a sweet shop will need a bigger bin for biodegradable waste. Each household or consumption unit will need to subscribe to this service for a user fee, requiring national legislation to ensure that they are plugged onto this grid. The legislation will also create a common minimum rules, guidelines, and processes for the waste collection covering different waste types and scenarios.

Currently, the journey of generated waste from the Indian households to the waste pick-up truck is fraught with vagaries, temperaments, and despair. The arrangement relies on the chance that a house owner will collect the waste, segregate it and deposit it on these dump sites in an orderly fashion. Instead, he may discard non-segregated waste on the dump site, or any other convenient place, inviting vulnerable rag pickers and scavenging bovines before it is manually put onto waste pick-up trucks. The waste generator is expected to behave in a certain manner, out of his own will and volition. A manual and unproductive collection process responds to the voluntary act and is forced to handle all its vagaries. This first wrong step creates a domino effect of a series of subsequent wrong steps. The user-fee-based system will free the citizens from this voluntary act, while putting on them the onus of bagging their waste in the prescribed manner if they wish for their surroundings to be free from garbage. This approach takes away any role of chance and individual discretion in the journey of the garage to the pick-up truck or to the sewer pipe, while freeing the bandwidth of the local bodies to upgrade their operating standards and infrastructure to collect waste.

The user fees will need to be designed in a manner that it funds the waste collection activity and the subsequent cost of disposal. It should also allow the local body to independently make an assessment of the trade-offs between in-house and outsourced choices to collect waste. It will be a first for India to undertake an intellectual exercise to discover the price for a waste-collection service. Past (mis)adventures in assigning a price to electricity and telecommunications offer ample wisdom. However, it will need to make a pricing distinction between entitlements like electricity and a responsibility like waste collection. Success will also depend on fee rates being realistic rather than being artificially suppressed. The premise is that waste collection is a duty of the citizen undertaken by the state on his behalf, and not his right. The argument that such a user fees will put additional financial burden on households should be negated with a counter that such a fee will compel households to re-align their expenditure and make space for waste collection costs in their new order of priorities. Households will perhaps be compelled to cut corners in their discretionary expenditure on gold, festivals, apparel, electronics among others to make space for this new category of household expenditure. The demand is not outrageous but one that requires a realization of the desired pecking order of household expenses. It is also normal for household expenditure to get re-jigged every decade or so. For instance, at the start of the twenty-first century Indian households did not incur any expenditure on internet and mobile services. In the next decade, this expenditure was among the top expenditure outflows in a typical household budget. It happened for the simple reason that mobile telephony and internet services became an essential part of daily living that enabled everything from train ticketing to filing tax returns. Waste management by the same logic is now to be a priority that requires a reassessment of the monthly expenditure of Indian households. The price discovery for waste collection services needs to be undertaken in a manner that it finds a space in the company of electricity bills and groceries in importance.

This will also create an equitable commercial contract between the waste generator and the local civic body, allowing the latter to respond with innovative models of collection that can deliver on effectiveness and social empowerment. The new approach will create strong enabling conditions for the cooperative organization model to bring informal waste-collection workers into the formal fold. The waste collection workers can view themselves as members of the co-operative organization that will undertake operational ownership of waste collection on behalf of the local civic body, using their infrastructure, guidelines and operational framework. The user fee will cover the cost and the benchmarked profit margin for the cooperative. The co-operative in turn will be mandated to define the guidelines for the use of the profits earned from the arrangement. These guidelines can outline avenues to deploy profits earned viz. deployment in operational training and safety, insurance of sanitation workers, family welfare support for healthcare and education. In 1993, the waste pickers in Pune formed a trade union to assert their rights, which later transformed into a full-fledged cooperative, SWaCH, that became India's first wholly owned cooperative of self-employed waste pickers. In 2016, its 2,300 members collected waste from the doorsteps of 400,000 households, offices, and shops. Cooperative members pay an annual fee to the committee, which guarantees insurance support, collective bargaining, and a safe working environment. Behind the success of SWaCH lie the waste-management rules of the Pune local body, revised in 2000, where waste segregation and door-to-door waste collection were made mandatory. SWaCH's onward survival was also an outcome of the support of the Pune Municipal Corporation (PMC) and mentoring from a few bureaucratic administrators that served within it. However, even SWaCH is yet to win its immunity from the flawed local governance model that exposes it to the challenges of building scale and drowns it in irritants like arrears and operational tussles with the PMC. Although chance worked in favor of Pune, they do not favor most other Indian cities. Uniform rules and implementation charter across over 5 lakh villages and over 5,000 towns in India with the sole objective of containerizing waste at source, and to collect it for effective and safe disposal seems like a very long list of tasks for a rather mundane outcome.

The user-fee-based system that espouses containerization and segregation at source during normal course of daily living will also need to branch out into multiple offshoots to address different scenarios of waste generation. One offshoot can incentivize the aggregation model for communities who can view themselves as a combined entity and subscribe to such a service, instead of individual households subscribing to it separately. For instance, dense colonies or housing complexes can be viewed as one entity for collection, provided rigid preconditions for bagging and segregation at source are ring-fenced.

Another offshoot may entail collection of construction and demolition waste. Before the commencement of any construction activity on a piece of real estate, the project owner should be required to install temporary waste bins and issue a user activation from the local civic authority. The local authority could charge a refundable security amount and a prepaid service fee to collect and process construction waste for the duration of construction period. This activation will ensure that the construction site becomes part of the beat plan of a pick-up vehicle that collects construction waste. At the end of the day's work, the construction waste at the site should either be bagged in the bin or left for daily pick up. The dustbins may be returned to the local civic body and the authority will return the security deposit once the construction activity gets over. For large-scale construction projects, local bodies may require the project owner to collect the waste from the site and haul it to a central collection facility (ideally, a waste processing center for construction waste owned and operated by the local body) or they will need to pay the local civic bodies for the same. Such projects should be required to register at the local authority prior to commencement to ensure such a water-tight arrangement. Local civic bodies can either exempt such projects from user fees for hauling the waste to the assigned centers, thereby squaring off the cost incurred by the project owner, or charge a fee for hauling the waste from the site on their behalf. Civic authorities can further think of jointly owning or subscribing to the services of expert entities, who may own and operate recycling centers to process and recycle construction waste. The output from these recycling or processing centers will be raw material for various other industries with a monetization potential. User fees from the waste generators will form the basis of the commercial contract between such entities and the local authorities. The monetization opportunity of the recycled resources recovered will serve as a complimentary revenue stream. In 2017, India generated 65 metric tons of construction waste which constituted 5 percent to the global output, and were disposed on the outskirts of the cities, delicate forest covers, open landfills, and across motorways and roads increasing the chances of contamination of the air and ground. Contrast this with Singapore that has managed to collect, recycle, and reuse 98 percent of its construction and demolition waste, or Hong Kong that has deployed a ladder approach to handle this waste, incentivizing on-site recycling and reuse. If the entire waste is consumed at the construction site, then the project owner is charged a nominal US$ 6 per ton. If more than 50 percent of the waste requires the local civic body to handle the disposal, then the project owner is charged nearly US$ 30 per ton.

In 2016, Indian union government legislated an act that for the first time defined the guidelines to handle construction and demolition waste and issued detailed operational rules for all concerned local authorities. But the act expects respective local authorities to pick up the cues and elaborate the operational mechanism for their respective cities, towns, and villages, and report progress. The act does not capture all scenarios that lead to the generation of construction and demolition waste and it is silent on the counter measures in case local authorities don't address the issue or procrastinate it. If Indian local bodies have never in past experienced legislative rigor on construction waste or they even fail to appreciate the its adverse impact on air quality, then national government's hope with the act of 2016, that local bodies will inject the needed operational specificity will sooner be dashed. When cities like Hong Kong have even managed to define the rates of the fees to be paid under different scenarios, it exposes the difference between the legislative approach of clean countries and India on the same issue. Also missing from the act is the nudge for real estate, engineering and project companies to re-use construction debirs and for the local bodies to define commercial and operational arrangements with such firms or individuals. Such omissions kill any chance for even half decent intervention to make an impact. The act lacks the commercial structure that binds the waste generator with the local civic bodies and that is crucial to operationalize it; therefore, it falls short on aspects of pricing, waste hauling infrastructure, and a monetization approach to recycled waste.

A third offshoot of the suggested approach will require a customized response to handle waste collection from temporary structures and activities that contribute a significant share of the daily waste generated across India. Political rallies, weddings and social functions, religious installations, temporary bazaars, and haats are among the prolific temporary activities that leave a strong garbage footprint. Under the current arrangement, the organizers of such temporary activities are expected to make 'suitable arrangements' to collect the garbage from the gathering and dump it at the assigned pick up point. But soon after such a gathering is over the venue becomes a giant litter of plastic cups, bottles, rotting food and wrappers. This mess is set afire in the open or, if not, puts enormous pressure on the sweepers to clean up the garbage heap the next day. These non-productive expectations eat into the already stretched bandwidth of the sanitation workers. Armed with rudimentary equipment, the sweeper pools the garbage and carries it to the nearby open dump-site. If the pile is too big and the distance too much, he might as well burn the heap in the open. If he does manage to pull the garbage to the site, the open garbage sits on there like an eye-soar till such time that it is picked up in the next beat plan. All this while, this orphaned stinking rubble releases harmful toxins into the air and offers a deadly meal to scavenging animals. For the paucity of time and tools, the cleaning team hauls this garbage onto to the truck without segregating it and moves on to the next site.

A user-fee-based system would be ideal for all such temporary activities of human congregation and can enable India's transition away from such a medieval and crude approach. Under the system, temporary gatherings will require a prior local body registration, issuance of a set of garbage bins, pay a security fee to the local body, and commit to bag the waste in these bins upon completion of the event. Once the bins are issued, the pre-tagged activation will bring the bins onto the beat plan of the collection vehicles in the area. The collection apparatus will receive bagged and segregated waste under safe conditions that otherwise would have taken up many man-hours of the bare handed 'safaai karamchaaris.'

However, while a user-fee-based system is propagated for most types of waste generated in towns and villages, solid human waste stands as an exception. Solid human waste requires sewer systems to work like a healthy nervous system of a human body that can carry sewage from the confines of the toilet to effluent treatment plants and compost pits.

Only 33 million of the nearly 100 million urban households are plugged to any form of underground sewer system and almost none of the 150 million rural households are plugged into to any such system. Differently put, only 33 percent of the 62,000 million litres daily (MLD) of the generated solid human waste in urban India has any chance of finding its way to the nearly 600 installed effluent treatment plants (ETPs) or other micro ETFs. The rest of it gets collected in closed toilets and pit latrines, or is dumped in the open and India has limited visibility on its onward journey. If solid human waste generated from 85 percent of Indian households (urban and rural put together) is dumped as untreated sewage, this waste becomes a contamination risk to 80 percent of India's surface water. Even the 15 percent of homes that are connected to closed sewer lines for solid waste discharge rely chance to safely dispose their sewage. They rely on the probability that the underground sewage system will remain clog free and on the sanitation workers for it to remain that way without they losing their lives.

This helplessness is believable because nearly a million toilets installed in urban India directly dump solid human waste into open drains. We can install a million toilets in homes, but without a functioning sewage system and accelerated investments in effluent treatment plants, urban India will increasingly face a shortage of potable water, while continuing to drown in sludge of untreated human waste. The missing piece of this puzzle is an infrastructure response that can facilitate the seamless flow of solid human waste from homes to the treatment plants. Until then, solid waste collection will always be vulnerable to manual intervention, individual disposition and unregulated discharge. Recall the brazen arrangement of Greater Faridabad that is compelled to dispose untreated sewage into the Yamuna for the lack of sewage infrastructure. In all the right earnest, citizens living in Greater Faridabad may be defecating in closed toilets inside swanky households or otherwise, but the onward journey of their poop is still disfiguring the soil and the water of Yamuna. Then how is their toilet behavior any different from the practice of open defecation of the informal citizens in their neighborhood. The theory that toilets in every household should extinguish unregulated discharge of untreated sewage and open defecation in isolation needs to be critiqued. Without a functional nervous system of sewers that reach every single toilet in urban India, the very best of toilets and treatment plants are no better than healthy limbs with defunct nerves. This lacuna lends credence to the scepticism of activists like Bezwada Wilson about the adrenaline rush to build more toilets. More toilets unilaterally will not solve the problem of untreated sewage ravaging India's flora and fauna. The seamless and covered journey of this waste from the toilet to a treatment plant is crucial for success. While 50 percent of the urban households rely on septic tanks to collect the toilet waste, urban design cannot accommodate the existence of a septic tank to function as a safe and an effective collection and disposal apparatus for human solid waste. Urban toilets need underground sewer connections which can either plug them to industrial effluent treatment plants or to modular ones that can treat raw sewage for processing and recycling. The zealous rush for more toilets without the essential addendum of sewer infrastructure and effluent plants is bound to only exacerbate the twin problems of human exploitation and of untreated raw sewage finding its way into the environment. Therefore, India's push to build more unplugged toilets at homes can only have two outcomes: the first may be that the incentives and social awareness elements of the policy succeeds to alter people's behavior to stop open defecation. They build toilets at home and start to use them. But, they continue to rely on either some form of manual intervention to collect the waste for its unregulated dumping, or plug these toilets with open drains through some makeshift arrangement. The second outcome may be that people build toilets but are unable to use them because they lack the resources to collect and manage the onward journey of the collected waste. Eventually, they revert to the practice of open defecation that is free of such hassles.

A sewer grid system is not a path-breaking idea. History shows instances of a sewer grid system, be it in the Indus Valley in 2500 BCE, or in Paris in 1855 built by Napoleon I, or the first modern sewage system in 1884 in Tokyo, or even the first wastewater treatment plant in Japan in 1922. The generated solid waste in India has witnessed a manifold increase but an incremental addition to the sewage infrastructure has not yet happened. For this reason India is only able to collect and treat around 30 percent of the cities' solid waste, not taking into account similar waste generated in rural India. The infrastructure response required to address this challenge must first pass the test of pricing and ownership within the governance framework, which should be tasked with the agenda of sewage infrastructure.

This challenge cannot be taken on with a mind-set of arranging funds by nibbling at corners of allocations meant for other purposes. The pecking order of the sewer grid system vis-à-vis other heads like education, healthcare and aviation needs to be clarified. A pot-holed road and a dengue-inflicted neighborhood sit next to each other, one for want of a highway and the other for want of a closed sewage system. This is a uniquely crucial question for India. Clean countries of today resolved this challenge when their investment choices were not torn between such priorities. The context then provided them the leeway to sequentially work on the agenda of a sewage system with undivided attention. But for India a smooth road and a closed sewage system are concurrently important. In other words, a sewer grid infrastructure needs to be elevated in priority in the comfortable company of other issues. But this convergence is a vexed issue because the cost to build and operate a sewage grid & treatment system across all five thousand plus cities in India, is pegged to be ₹84,000 crores by 2032. This amount can either be spent at one shot to build the infrastructure on a 'war footing,' or it can be crudely deployed at the rate of a few thousand crores every year, while our poop continue to poison the water and allow vectors to kill a few thousands every year for decades to come.

Is the current governance structure capable of absorbing this cost for an invisible infrastructure that will lie beneath the ground? More importantly, what should be the underlying thesis for India to build and operate such a sewer grid system; should it be installed because citizens are entitled to it, or as an act of responsibility discharged by India on behalf of its citizens? Citizens use the highways and trains as entitlements in lieu of the taxes they pay. Why, then, do they not want to pay for staking a similar claim for their solid waste to be collected from their homes? The wide chasm between the solid waste generated every day and India's inability to tax and to collect it through a straightforward solution indicate that the state feels obliged to create an underground sewage system for its entitled citizens, yet lacks the resources to do so. But taking a broad taxation approach aimed at a restricted pool of citizens and institutions to recover ₹84,000 crores would also be wrong. This cost is a little higher than India's annual expenditure on Education and more than double of its annual expenditure on Healthcare. It will be naive to believe that compulsions to prioritize expenditure on healthcare, education and defense will allow the sewage system to be evaluated on its own merit, more so for the tall financial ask it needs to climb. Political expediency can come to the rescue and garner whatever resources it could for sewers in star constituencies, which it has done till now and accord some form of a sewer system to two hundred out of the five thousand Indian cities. In this light, the sewage system that barely covers one third of the solid waste generated by urban India will be of no use. Solid human waste discharged from any human body needs to be tackled comprehensively because untreated raw sewage dumped into a river in an affluent city is as bad as the discharge of solid human waste into a pond in a village.

The cost of a sewer grid and related effluent treatment will be better served by charging a user fee or indirect taxation approach that can tax human footprint on consumption. It is here the delinking of waste collection and waste disposal functions and making local governance a responsible custodian of such a waste management user fee or tax model makes sense. Though local civic bodies will still need to reconcile with their masters on deficit support, legislative, and technical guidance, the approach can ensure that every city takes the ownership of sewer grid and related infrastructure with an unbiased and spirited mind. This unbundling is important because the current approach to seek resources for sewage infrastructure has managed to install nearly 600 public effluent treatment plants that are barely sufficient to treat 30 percent of all generated urban solid human waste. Differently put India will need capital to build treatment capability equivalent to 1,500 such new plants to treat all the solid human waste in urban India and this will not be the only drain on the resources. For the effluent treatment capacity to work effectively, India will also need a new sewage network of underground pipes and cables that can carry the solid human waste from every household across 5,000 cities to these treatment plants round the clock without operational downtimes. If nearly 15 percent of India's grossly inadequate installed effluent treatment capacity lies dormant at any time for maintenance or for the lack of financial lubrication, then the current arrangement does not inspire confidence to deliver on the exalted agenda even if India manages to find the magic wand to build sewage treatment plants in the desired numbers.

This chasm brings to forefront the pricing of waste management services. The state collects taxes to build utility and transportation infrastructure like electricity generation plants or railway network. But this does not imply that citizens can travel in the trains without buying tickets or use electricity for free. The efficient operations of the utility infrastructure require a commercial contract between these utilities and their users. Operations of sewage systems and ETPs are not very different from those of utilities and need a similar contract to exist, wherein the citizens must pay taxes for the infrastructure and user fee for the services rendered through it.

Local civic bodies must come to the forefront and extend a similar 'taxation and user fee principle' for sanitation infrastructure. Citizens will need to subscribe to the solid and other waste-management services that will render sewage collection through sewers and door-to-door waste collection service in exchange for a fee. Revenue collected from this subscription will provide the local civic bodies the leeway to mechanize, improve up-time, provide workplace safety, redesign the job profile of sanitation employees, and redesign the approach needed to fund the construction and operations of sewage and waste-collection infrastructure. They could evaluate whether to choose a blend of taxation and grants to fund the sewage-collection infrastructure and recover its operational cost through user fees from the citizens or fund it upfront through debt route and recover it later from users through user fees, as is the practice with toll roads. They could then decouple sewer grids and ETPs by inviting experts to own and operate these plants under a formal commercial contract. Expert organizations can optimize ETP operations by increasing the 'monetizability' of resources recovered from the treatment and processing of solid human waste, and allow the effluent treatment to emerge independently, not very different from electricity generation that is different from electricity transmission. This view will then open the door for cities to explore modular solutions in the form of miniature sewage grids and mini effluent treatment plants that can equally serve their purpose in an isolated existence and shorten the implementation cycle. Cities will then be at the liberty do a cost-benefit analysis, and in cases where it is prohibitively expensive to extend common sewage infrastructure to isolated human congregations (such as housing colonies on the outskirts or commercial operations) can opt for modular solutions.

Cities can then evaluate these modular projects on their efficacy to become zero-discharge communities by generating reusable water, energy, and organic manure. Local civic bodies can even push their autonomous existence and take calls for their cities on whether to side with industrial approach to sewage collection or toward a modular existence or a mix of both.

The lack of an equitable social contract between the waste generator (citizens) and the local civic body (authority) that underpins these waste collection ideas to enter the mainstream is the key reason for these simple ideas to be restricted to a few islands of excellence like Indore, Mysuru, or Pune. Even these islands that appreciate merits in the approach further need to evaluate the strength of this contract to drive meaningful change. Is the contract strong enough to mandate waste segregation to one and all? Have citizens subscribed to the service for a monetary consideration? Is the pricing of the service adequate to support social empowerment and productivity improvements in the waste collection apparatus? Is the waste collection system comprehensive enough to cover all forms of waste generation in the city or is it only limited to collecting waste of certain types? Has the waste collection system reduced the city's dependence on open landfills and spurred formal recycling industry? A dispassionate assessment of these questions will throw up courses of action and lay out the distance that purportedly even the 'cleaner' towns still need to travel before claiming victory and serve as an inspiration for those that are yet to initiate their respective journeys.

If the clean countries of today took several decades to fine tune such a system, we face the challenge of a shorter time to execute such a solution. But, fortunately, we confront this challenge at a time when technology, data measurability and capital allow ample leeway to install such a system at an accelerated pace. If India can roll out a unique identification number to nearly her entire population, activating a user fee-based waste collection system surely must be in the realm of possibility. Inspiration can also be drawn from the fact that India has managed to install standard sized LPG cylinders to deliver cooking gas to 50 million households. In the LPG story, India managed to containerize 'fuel' for its efficient distribution to users. Uniform sized tagged LPG cylinders allowed efficient refueling of cooking gas at the LPG plants and their efficient logistic movement to households through rail transport and all forms of surface transport (trucks, vans, cycles, and wagons), enabling ease in last mile delivery, while offering traceability of usage and demand. Tagged and standardized garbage bins and closed sewer lines, under the user-fee-based system are premised on similar lines – the explicit aim is to segregate the garbage at source, collect the garbage in closed bags and closed pipes – thereby eliminating exposure to the open air, and improve productivity of the local bodies to pick up the waste from their jurisdictions and to rapidly move toward environmentally safe waste disposal methods.

It will be a celebratory day indeed when Indian local civic bodies will be able to design efficient route plans for their waste-collection vehicles based on the data received from RFID chips embedded in the garbage bins. Equally laud-worthy will be when sanitation workers are discharged of their manual sweeping routine and their energy focused toward the mechanized tasks of picking bagged garbage and de-clogging sewers as well as toward technology-enabled tasks of surveillance. But implementing such a system is fraught with risks if the current enforcement (recall Bhubaneswar with its eleven sanitation inspectors) approach is relied on for results. Rarely countries overcome their struggles with garbage without layering the task of waste collection with enforcement and India will need to urgently break away from the existing notions on enforcement for sanitation and imbibe this insight. The agenda of 'enforcement for sanitation' needs to be built as an apparatus closely intertwined with waste collection, not different from a policing apparatus to maintain law and order. A cadre of sanitary inspectors and systems capable to monitor every ward of the town for litter, illegal dumping, open defecation, trash burning, and refuse discharge into water bodies will need to be cultivated. It will require ward stations similar to police stations, equipped with vehicles to conduct beats, the legal sanctity to issue fines, and special reinforcement to investigate major breaches on environment degradation in the area. These hubs will also double up as nodal points to store and disburse assets, register complaints, record violations, and monitor waste-collection-and-generation activities within their respective jurisdictions.

The First World realized that the objective of enforcement was to alter human behavior and deployed enforcement methods for maximum impact. But the First World took decades to become stable and achieve their current state of affairs. Contemporary enforcement norms in the First World may therefore be part-continuation of the past and part-optimized for the current cleanliness standards. For instance, toilets in every household in the First World are now plugged into an underground sewage system, and so their enforcement focus today is not surveillance of unregulated dumping of solid human waste. However, this will not be the case in India. Moreover, when the First World started its journey on enforcement, the size of their population and complexity of waste was very different from what it is today. India will be starting its enforcement journey at a time when the quantum and quality of its waste already mirrors many of the clean societies of today. Yet India has the advantage of dovetailing technology with human capability to enhance effectiveness of its enforcement approach to make up for the paucity of time. Local bodies can effectively use surveillance technology to record behavior of neighborhoods on garbage disposal, instead of physically deploying inspectors in the area. Areas that are susceptible to illegal dumping can be put under round-the-clock electronic surveillance. Drones and satellite imaging can be put to productive use to conduct dynamic surveillance of sensitive areas and to collect information to craft a preemptive response. Instead of installing a static human team to conduct vigils, technology and predictive data analysis can become effective enablers in enforcement. Technology can also be used to conduct passive enforcements: instead of issuing on-the-spot fines, challans can be sent to people's homes post-facto, along with electronic evidence of the offence. Surveillance feeds can also be used to monitor illegal hauling of garbage in dangerous and unhygienic conditions. A technology-enabled enforcement approach will provide rich data on the quantum and type of generated waste, which can be used to modify and formulate policies and plan efficient allocation of resources such as vehicles types and sanitation workers, among others.

Sanitation workers compelled to collect garbage manually, in debilitating and unproductive fashion cannot win the sanitation war for India. India will need to fight its war by elevating the stature of waste collection from condemned, hard labor to a technical and dignified job. India must install an overarching framework that can commercially bind the waste generators with local bodies, build infrastructure by making a sound case for capital returns, operate this infrastructure like an efficient asset, and imagine enforcement for sanitation. Until then, Indian towns will have to wait for their renaissance, while they maze through campaigns for request and rebuttals for neglect. The collective intelligentsia of Indian society will need to appreciate that the job of collecting waste is no different from that of a soldier guarding the border. We do not expect our soldiers to defend our national borders with their bare hands, then why do we expect our sanitation workers discharge their duties as such? Our disdain for the job makes the sanitation worker a fallen soldier long before he goes down the drain to clean it, so to speak.

6

WASTE DISPOSAL

Missing the Obvious

An independent, single storey house stands on a small plot of land in a non-descript town, somewhere in the semi-urban hinterlands of India. The occupants of the house include a man, the single bread earner, who earns enough to provide a 'decent' living to the family of four, by the standards of the town. His spouse is a committed home maker, whose world revolves around the comfort and happiness of her husband and two children. At the crack of the dawn, the lady of the house is the first one up. She runs a tight ship and takes great pride in making their ends meet comfortably with her sensible management of domestic economics. She hits the kitchen to cook packed meals for her children who will soon be leaving for school, and a cup of tea for her husband who might be browsing the newspaper, or practising some light yoga on their modest but utilitarian terrace. Soon, he too leaves for work armed with a lovingly packed lunch, a proud trophy of her devotion to him, and his to her domesticity. Shortly after, the arrival of the house maid signals the true start of the urban weekday, and the home maker heaves a sigh of relief. She begins her daily ritual of cleaning the house. She sweeps the floor, taking care to cover all the corners, and then swabs it with a wet mop. She finishes by dusting all the surfaces with a rag and collecting the garbage from the plastic bin that resides underneath the kitchen, which contains all the vegetable and fruit peels, egg shells, leftover morsels of food, milk packets, brewed tea leaves and chicken bones from the previous day's cooking and meals consumed. The maid tops up this garbage bag with all the dry waste she has accumulated from sweeping the floor, such as bits of paper from the children's room, toffee wrappers, discarded batteries, dust and the discreet newspaper-wrapped bundles of used sanitary napkins from the bathroom. In some time, she is through with her household duties. The lady of the house offers her a cup of tea, which she quickly drains as she has another three houses to attend to and repeat the drill. She takes her leave and on her way out she collects all the garbage from the house, shoves it in a discarded shopping bag, ties a knot on its mouth and chucks it on the empty plot of land in the neighborhood. Sometimes when she's running late, she omits tying a knot. This neighborhood site is where all her peers also throw plastic bags full of household waste they collect from the homes they clean. Once in a while this garbage is picked up by the waste collection team of the local municipal body, but until then, it remains strewn on the plot, raising a stink in the vicinity. Meanwhile the water waste from the bathing and cleaning of the bathroom, and the kitchen chores quietly drips out into the open drain near the entrance of the house.

The homemaker is not concerned about the disposal of her household garbage. Why should she be? After all, she employs a maid for this very purpose. The man of the house and the children never spare a thought, and it is a non-issue for them. Although once in a while they do witness burning garbage heaps, or bovines and dogs sniffing through the rubbish piled up on that neighborhood plot. Occasionally they even complain about the odd smell permeating the neighborhood.

This slice-of-life of a 'middle-class' Indian household sums up the waste disposal story of millions of Indian homes who can afford the services of a house maid. The story remains largely the same for the rest of the houses, except that the duties of the maid are performed by the homemaker, or the womenfolk. If the house in this story is substituted with an Indian city and the maid, or the lady of the house with the local governance, that also is India's story of waste disposal.

What is so disconcerting about India either dumping 80 percent of its garbage in open landfills without treatment or processing, or burning it in the open? What is the big deal if we go scuttling for a new landfill when one is full to capacity? In contrast, most clean countries of today hardly allow any of their generated waste to be dumped or incinerated in the open. Why can open landfills and trash burning not continue as waste disposal practices in tandem with superior sanitation standards? Then why is it that the burning of and dumping of waste in the open are punishable offences in the clean countries of today, both for the citizens and for the state?

Archeologists have concluded that in its glory the city of Rome housed 1 million inhabitants. Such urbanization created high population density areas where people were packed into smaller and more concentrated zones, where tossing garbage outside their homes created a perpetual stench. Open landfills located on the outskirts of human congregations thus made sense they gave the waste a resting place away from homes, neighborhoods and streets, and took it out of sight. Rome began the practice of collecting waste from their respective cities and dumping it in the landfills. Sites for new landfills were identified once the existing ones were filled and the process started all over again. But during the Middle Ages, the Roman wisdom of open landfills for waste disposal lost its relevance. Rapid urbanization altered the consumption pattern in a manner that they outpaced the capacity of European towns to dispose off the filth. Italian scholar Francesco Petrarch (1304–1374) coined the term 'the dark ages' for the period between 500 AD and 1500 AD (roughly a thousand years), which coincided with the fall of the Roman

Empire and the emergence of Italian Renaissance. The spread of the Roman Empire across a vast geography allowed an uninterrupted flow of capital, opportunities, and skills. With its decline and the ensuing fragmentation of the ruled area into many small kingdoms, the dominant cities of the Roman Empire swiftly fell in stature. New cities emerged in the backdrop of social and political shifts, and with it the issue of waste disposal went through major disruption. Historical accounts of cities from the Dark Ages up until the nineteenth century suggest that Europe struggled immensely with sanitation during this period. Affluent households disposed off their food and solid human waste in a septic tank (cess pits) in their backyards, but the common households dumped in nearby water bodies or out onto the streets. Shit Brook, a culverted water stream in England's Much Wenlock, Shropshire, received its name because it was used as an open sewer by the masses. Inhabitants of cities in Scotland, Italy, and France were in the habit of dumping their excreta on the streets, which were perpetually slicked with a sludge of human faecal matter, food waste and horse droppings.

The Dark Ages in Europe were known for sanitary woes and public health crises. Between the fourteenth and eighteenth centuries, Europe witnessed a series of plague outbreaks. The Black Death, or the Great Plague, in 1347 wiped out 60 percent of Europe's population. The plagues in Milan (1629–31), Seville (1647), London (1665–6), Vienna (1679), and Marseille (1720) killed thousands. The trigger for these outbreaks may be contested but there is a consensus today that bad sanitation and improper waste disposal was a catalyst in spreading the disease far and wide. Rodents, the primary carrier of the plague bacteria thrived on the fractured waste disposal methods and moved around without containment in these societies at that time. A chronicler wrote this macabre account of the Black Death that appears in Philip Ziegler's book *The Black Death*, highlighting the severity of the crisis:

> All the citizens did little else except to carry dead bodies to be buried.... At every church they dug deep pits down to the water-table; and thus those who were poor who died during the night were bundled up quickly and thrown into the pit. In the morning when a large number of bodies were found in the pit, they took some earth and shovelled it down on top of them; and later others were placed on top of them and then another layer of earth, just as one makes lasagne with layers of pasta and cheese.

Four hundred years (from the fourteenth to seventeenth century AD) of suffering that resulted from poor waste disposal created widespread realization in Europe about sanitation. Administrators began to understand the compelling need for better infrastructure and rules to improve sanitation, although this realization may not have been as synchronized as it seems. The public health crisis motivated medical research and prompted advances in medical science in the form of better pills, new research and vaccines. A major breakthrough was the discovery of the 'germ theory' which finally established a connection between disease and garbage – the understanding of the propagation of diseases was rudimentary at the time and the discovery of the theory was a significant step in this regard.

From the nineteenth century, systems and rules aimed at methodical garbage collection and disposal in cities came into active public discourse. New advances through industrialization and a system of waste disposal slowly began to emerge, allowing garbage to be collected from homes and sewage lines by horse-drawn carts for its eventual disposal in open landfills or into water bodies. Through this reconstruction, Europe managed to create a baseline system of waste disposal that was flexible toward innovation, improvisation, and improvement with the changing times. Open landfills were the first system of waste disposal that emerged or re-emerged. Concurrently, urbanization was becoming a disruptive social change. European cities were getting congested and soon began to feel constrained with open landfills as the only method of waste disposal. As mentioned earlier, cities either had a limited open area arising out of a high population density or their structural design made open spaces a scarce resource.

In some instances, as in the municipal enclave of Frederiksberg, Denmark, it was worse because both conditions, high density of population and a small municipality, were adverse. Administrators of such cities realized that they would soon run out of space and therefore have to move away from the practice of dumping in open landfills as the only method of waste disposal.

Confronted with such constrictions, Europe took a stab at controlled incineration for waste disposal. Waste was put in large furnaces and set afire. The residue of ashes, flue gas, and heat was channelized into the heating systems and boilers common in homes and buildings owing to the cold climatic conditions of Europe. The first waste incineration plant in the world, known as the Destructor, was built in Nottingham, UK, in 1874, whereas Denmark got its plant in 1903 and modern-day Czech Republic, in 1905. Within a span of forty years (1874–1914), incineration technology for waste disposal became a widely accepted method across Europe because it solved problems of space and foul-smelling fumes, not to mention the added advantage of recovering the energy to supply heat to homes and shops. But at the same time, the consumption trend in households in the First-World countries was dramatically changing. The arrival of Coca Cola in 1886 proliferated the use of glass bottles. Between 1888 and 1895, the concept of sanitary napkins gained wide acceptance. By the start of the twentieth century, tin cans became a common household good, from shoe polish to tea, paints, and even soup. In 1844, Good Year patented the vulcanization process for rubber, and introduced rubber into the daily consumption habits of households in the form of tires and rubber bands. These innovations altered the profile and chemistry of the generated household waste forever. By the start of the twentieth century garbage was no longer just human excreta and food waste. This complex garbage now included discarded glass, tin, rubber, which posed a tough challenge to incinerator technology. These furnaces were not designed to burn processed materials such as glass and tin together with human waste. These waste types burned at different temperatures, produced different types of emissions, altered the composition of the produced residual ash, and made the incineration process inefficient and dangerous. Untreated waste burned in the furnace posed life-threatening dangers to the operators. The technology was not leakproof and discharged heavy metals and toxins into the air through flue gas. The cleaning of the residue from incineration plant was a hazardous process but needed to be done more frequently with the change in composition of the waste.

For the first time human society was confronted with having to adapt its prevalent waste disposal methods, which were proving to be inadequate to the changing nature of household consumption, and this triggered the next wave of research in the trash science and policy agenda for the waste management. Enabling conditions that could optimize incineration technology and mitigate its impact on the environment and public safety were explored. Administrators realized the necessity of waste segregating at source and drafted rules to ensure that non-segregated waste does not find its way into incinerators. Emission norms for these incinerators were defined to ensure that the furnaces do not themselves become the demon.

Concurrently, scientists in the First World also looked at improving the technology of waste incineration with better resource and energy recovery capabilities. Waste-to-energy incinerator plants were soon perfected, which made them better than coal-fired plants to produce electricity both on emission norms and productivity. Mastering the incineration technology is fascinating on two counts. First, the changing character of the generated waste injected a scientific temperament into solving the problem of waste disposal in general. Aspects like emissions, recovery, safety and cost became important pillars in the debate to improve upon the existing solutions. An improved waste incineration technology also gave impetus to scientists to apply their minds to the other prevalent method of waste disposal, such as open landfills, and opened up the field of waste disposal to scientific rigor forever. Second, the challenge allowed waste-management experts to understand the importance of segregation at source in the success of disposal methods. Waste incineration worked fine as long as simple, homogenous waste was burned in the furnace. It became a challenge when it was forced to burned down different kinds of waste in one go. Thus, segregation at source became an important pre-condition for the success of any waste disposal method. It was a key insight that went a long way in changing both the upstream and downstream activities of waste management for the better. Both these outcomes were timely lessons that First-World countries learned just before the start of World War II.

Along with the unparalleled miseries and tragedy the second World War brought to the First World, came many man-made innovations: polyethylene, polyurethane, and nylon are three inventions that best exemplify the impact of the developments undertaken for the purpose of the War, but ended up making the garbage of modern society far more complex. Polyethylene was invented in 1935 and was used during the War for applications such as underwater cables and insulation of military hardware; thereafter, it found its way into Western households in the form of soda bottles, water containers, and poly bags. Polyurethane was invented in 1938 for making propeller blades and landing flaps of aircrafts during the War. It wound up in homes in the form of furniture padding, thermal insulation, and packaging. Today, polyurethane is a critical ingredient of lycra, used for making sportswear, stretch denim, and other performance apparels. Nylon was invented in 1937 for making parachutes, ropes, vests, tires, and combat uniforms. Post War, it acquired a cult status especially among women for its ease of use and comfort in intimate wear.

The emancipation of women and economic prosperity in the First World also emerged from the ruins of World War II. The role of women in the First World dramatically changed for the better. Their participation in the workforce and equality of rights defined the liberal order of the First World countries, post World War II. In simpler terms, it meant their liberation from the kitchen, which had a disruptive effect on the food processing, fast-moving consumer goods (FMCG), and consumer durable industries. Businesses responded with advancements in food processing and offered ready-to-cook meals and processed food options that were aimed to reduce women's time spent doing household chores. Women suddenly awakened to the pleasant fact that they need not worry about rising early to cook breakfast for their families because cereals and pasteurized milk were within just an arm-length away. They could put away the washboard because detergent powder and a washing machine could take care of tough laundry. Women began to demand goods to improve their quality of life and businesses and retailers obliged wholeheartedly, delivering convenience at to the doorstep triggering a prolonged cycle of economic growth in the First World. Concurrently, retailing in the First-World countries began to move away from neighborhood convenience stores to big box retail stores. They offered massive retail shelves for all kinds of merchandise ranging from fresh groceries to packaged food, new-age household goods of comfort to building materials. Consolidation in the retail industry continually improved the quality of merchandise on offer and opened up possibilities for consumer product companies to push more innovations and choices. The growth of organized retail companies fueled the growth of product innovation and vice versa. This was also the time of the great automobile boom in the First World, fueled by state expenditure on building motorways and road infrastructure. The automotive industry responded by making cars that could fit every domestic budget and space. This boom bolstered commerce, reduced distances, and served as the catalyst for the growth of many new industries, motels, tires, drive-inns, fuel stations that emerged as the new symbols of consumer convenience.

These disruptive social, economic, and technological changes transformed the western societies into consumption powerhouses almost overnight, from the 1950s, and created a new reference that had no past precedence. This had a deep impact on the waste generated from households, shops and factories. Neither was the garbage meagre in quantity, nor was it restricted to vegetables peels, meat bones, milk bottles, wooden slabs and tin cans. The baby boomers of the First World were discarding plastic wrappers, polyutherene, nylon, processed paper, alloys and so on in quantities never witnessed before. Generated garbage significantly increased in quantity and complexity in the post World War II era. The annual waste generated in Japan between 1955 and 1965 increased from 621 million to 1,625 million tonnes, 1.6 times that of what it generated annually till 1955. Around the same time, Japan's dramatic increase in the use of plastic is mindboggling: in 1950, the annual plastic production was 17,000 tonnes, which increased to 554,000 tonnes in 1960, an increase of more than 32 times in 10 years. As stated, the changing face of garbage in the decade following World War II began to put strain on the waste incinerators and landfills as viable waste-disposal methods. With the increasing complexity of garbage, the incinerators again started to spew out pollutants and suspended particulate matter into the air and emit bad odors. By the early 1960s, it was accepted that the then existing incineration approach was woefully insufficient to dispose garbage in a safe and environmentally friendly manner.

The first step toward a solution was to draft laws with the aim of defining a framework for waste disposal. The USA drafted the Solid

Waste Disposal Act in 1965, which extensively defined the guidelines for the incineration process. This was followed by the Resource Recovery Act in 1970, in the backdrop of heightened scrutiny of the rising air pollution. Activism in waste disposal translated into the 1976 Resource Conservation and Recovery Act (RCRA), which, for the first time, established the norms and standards for disposing hazardous waste and defined emission norms for waste incinerators. In the span of twelve short years (1965–77), the USA drafted four laws covering waste disposal in general and waste incineration in particular, signifying the heightened urgency for improving waste disposal methods, in the backdrop of disruptive consumption growth and the rapidly changing material complexity of generated effluents and garbage. The lawmaking continued with amendments to the 1990 Clean Air Act. These laws pressured experts to design waste incinerators that were capable of addressing the twin issues of emission and complexity of garbage.

The new generation of waste incinerators that followed allowed incineration to gain acceptance as viable alternatives for electricity and heating and successfully re-established themselves as an acceptable method of waste disposal in the First World. Though, till today, waste incinerators attract a fair share of criticism. Critics argue that it is a crude technology and is not fool proof. Yet, waste incineration technology has come a long way from its origin a hundred years ago. Today, waste incineration technology is a precision science that dovetails the principles of chemistry, thermodynamics, and nanotechnology, of which Denmark, Luxembourg, and Japan are world leaders (Japan burns 80 percent of its waste in furnaces). Faced with the challenge of the availability of land, these countries moved toward this technology.

Waste incinerators, however, did not do away with the need for landfills. Many countries adopted incinerators to make their landfills more productive and efficient and introduced it as an intermediate step before the garbage reached its final resting place in open landfills. When space for landfills became scarce, it dawned on the experts to reduce the volume of the generated garbage by burning it first. This reduced the volume of the waste by 80 percent and the administrators had to only dump the residual ash into the landfills. This intermediary function of incineration was the main reason incinerators became hugely popular in the first place; energy and heat extraction were an afterthought. Dumping of waste in a landfill is still the most cost effective way to dispose it, especially in countries like the USA, which are not constrained by the availability of land. The fascinating outcome is the manner in which these countries, particularly USA, have managed to convert the landfill method of waste disposal from a medieval practice to an engineering marvel.

Landfills proliferated across the First World and kept pace with its rapid pace of urbanization. This is not surprising, given the low cost and ease of operation. In fact, waste incinerators triumphed over open landfills only where land availability became an issue. However, with every passing decade, from the twentieth century, experts learned more about landfills and their limitations. The trigger was the research findings of Svante Arrhenius, a Swedish scientist, who claimed that there existed a connection between fossil fuel combustion (a planned human action) and global warming. Arrhenius is also sometimes credited for coining the term 'greenhouse effect' and his research largely pinned the source of the greenhouse effect on human actions. By the end of World War II, Arrhenius's findings had taken the shape of a conclusive understanding about greenhouse gases. The harm they cause to the earth due to their inability to escape the atmosphere thus heating it up if they breach the threshold of emission barriers, became an accepted fact. By then scientific advancement in spectroscopy immensely contributed to measuring radiation levels from various human activities to determine emissions of greenhouse gases. Until then human footprint was still believed to be too small to make any impact on the forces of nature. Methane, other than carbon dioxide, a direct result of human actions, emerged as a key culprit.

By the 1960s, advancement in environmental sciences established the adverse role of methane as a greenhouse gas and an air pollutant. This realization brought great criticism to open garbage landfills as a hazard to the environment because they were seen as active volcanoes of methane emissions. Garbage dumped in open landfills was subjected to anaerobic decomposition triggered by its own moisture and contact with air. This created an unhindered release of methane into the atmosphere that lasted decades, not to mention its highly inflammable properties, making them ticking time bombs. But methane was not the only villain. In 1868, scientists Wanklyn and Chapman delved into the adverse impact of heavy metals like arsenic, lead, copper, zinc, iron, and manganese on drinking water. Their speculations opened up a new area of research on the impact of the disproportionate discharge of heavy metals into the environment on public health and the environment. While small quantities of some heavy metals were desirable in humans, it was their abnormal release into the open that was cause for worry. Excessive exposure to heavy metals in any form was linked to cancers, scarring of lungs, deformity of the bones, stomach ailments, and skin disorders.

Lead was used extensively in petrol and diesel for the smooth running of automobiles and also used in paints and pigments to coat toys, household goods, and consumer durables to make them look glossy and attractive. Arsenic was used in coloring dyes, insecticides, and domestic rat poison. Cadmium and lead were powering batteries to make daily life convenient. Once these goods had served their intended purpose, they were hauled away to open landfills. The First World understood this issue in its entirety and its impact on the environment. For instance the moisture from the dumped garbage and rain water or melting snow accumulating on the open landfill formed a leachate which slowly seeped into the ground, contaminating the soil and groundwater. This exposed another limitation of open landfills, that is, their propensity to contaminate the environment with heavy metals, and made its continuation as a preferred method of waste disposal untenable. Moisture in landfills from any source works as a medium to form the leachate. So long as the garbage was biodegradable, the leachate was benign. But with the changing composition of garbage, it became toxic. From the 1920s to 1960s, the composition of garbage was undergoing change at such a rapid pace that landfill operators could do little else but get overwhelmed by it. The leachate was percolating harmful and dangerous toxins into the ground. In the new reality, it was composed of hazardous materials, inert substances and heavy metals. It leached out toxins from discarded injections, plastic bottles, battery cells, painted cans, condoms, tyres, plastics and carried with it heavy metals on its journey to the earth below. Groundwater contamination due to the leachate became a big environmental hazard and solutions were required both to reduce the quantum of leachate produced and to manage its production in open landfills.

This was also the period when the First World faced acid rain, bad air quality, smog, and adverse public health statistics. Backed by scientific discoveries, the agenda of environment protection generated a groundswell support of activism in the 1960s. It laid a strong foundation for the emergence of the climate change narrative in the 1980s. In this backdrop, the sanitary landfill came into focus as a viable alternative to open landfills. In a sanitary landfill, the garbage is compressed and compacted in the pit and then covered with several layers of soil to ready the pit for the next round of garbage dumping. The process is repeated many times over, just like making a layered sandwich. This covers the garbage with many layers of soil and mitigates the release of methane into the air. This idea was further developed with the intent of capturing the released methane and use it for energy, leading to the development of waste-to-energy methods which could extract methane from these landfills and put it to productive and safe use. This idea led to the development of waste-to-energy methods which could use this method to store and extract methane for productive and safe use. Interestingly, the sanitary landfill was invented in 1920 in England, but could not become an alternative to open landfills given the low cost and convenience of the latter. It was only when open landfills became untenable in the new-found wisdom of environmental sciences did the First World wake up to the virtues of sanitary landfills.

The design of sanitary landfills was improved to insulate them against the challenges associated with leachate. While regular sanitary landfills covered the garbage with soil, they did not prevent the formation of leachate and its eventual downward journey into the earth. An insulated landfill collects the garbage in a pit that has been coated with several layers of clay to prevent the leachate from seeping into the ground. Differently put, insulated landfills can be understood as giant bathtubs buried in the ground. Like a bathtub holds water and does not allow it to leak through its walls, an insulated landfill holds the garbage within the confined area of the pit. From smelly open pits, landfills were successfully repositioned as a gold mine for energy recovery, not very different from an underground natural gas well. But such landfills still had one severe limitation: apart from capturing methane from the residue, they were merely storing garbage. Then there was also the persistent issue of hazardous waste landing up at these landfills.

This challenge prompted the experts to conclude that it was imperative to segregate garbage and treat it through different waste-disposal methods, or send for recycling to prevent harmful materials getting into the sanitary landfills in order to improve the methane extraction capability of these landfills. This technical improvisation on waste disposal happened in the backdrop of another important realization in the clean countries of today. These countries appreciated that the rising complexity of generated waste posed serious environmental and public health risks, but addressing such a technical challenge was well beyond the capability of local governance. In Germany, for instance, the responsibility of waste disposal solely rested with local municipalities till the 1970s. But this soon became unsustainable and in 1972 its constitution was amended to bring the function under the wings of the federal governance through the Waste Disposal Act. The Netherlands also underwent a similar realization and made waste disposal a federal subject through the introduction of the Waste Substances Act in 1977. Even the USA, which prides itself on its federal structure with fiercely independent states, felt the need for federal ownership of waste disposal because the issue had become too complex to be left to local governance. The outcome was the Solid Waste Disposal Act of 1965.

Subsequent to the transfer of ownership of waste disposal from local governance to the federal state, the issue of waste disposal received injection of legislative frenzy in these countries to keep pace with the rapidly changing form of garbage. Japan best exemplifies this lawmaking journey. It enacted its first law in 1954 through the Public Cleansing Act, followed by an Act on Emergency Measures concerning the development of living environment facilities in 1963, and then addressed the issue of the rising industrial waste generation through the Waste Management Act (WMA) in 1970. Since then, the WMA has been amended seven times (in 1976, 1991, 1997, 2000, 2003, 2006, and 2010) to address the rising complexity of the generated garbage. The Wide Area Costal Environment Development Centre Act came in 1980 to promote the development of waste-management facilities, followed by the Private Sewerage System Act in 1983, aimed at defining the standards of environmental protection during waste management. Then came a series of Acts that specified waste-disposal approaches for different types of waste with baffling specificity: Japanese Basel Act 1992, Basic Environment Act 1993,

Container and Packaging Recycling Act 1995, Home Appliances Recycling Act in 1998, Act on special measures against Dioxins in 1999, Basic Act for establishing Sound Material-Cycle Society 2000, Construction Recycling Act 2000, Food Recycling Act 2000, Act for Proper Treatment of PCB Waste 2001, Automobile Recycling Act 2002, Small Home Appliances Recycling Act 2013. All laws and amendments put together, Japan drafted twenty-five Acts in fifty years to address the issue of waste disposal- that's roughly one act every two years to address the issue of waste disposal.

Two fascinating aspects of Japan's law-drafting journey on waste disposal stand out. First is the specificity of legislation. Its waste disposal laws literally imagined all scenarios of waste types and provided precise directions on standards, acceptable norms and prohibited actions. This specificity allowed these laws to transcend from merely a set of rules to specific guidelines that facilitated implementation. The laws defined detailed guidelines that served more as a manual for desirable action than a general directional goal. Second is its progressive outlook wherein existing laws underwent multiple amendments to keep pace with the changing nature of garbage. The Waste Management Act was enacted in 1970 but it was amended seven times to keep pace with the changing nature of garbage. As recently as 2013, Japan enacted laws for the disposal of small home appliances that included music systems, television sets for the simple but compelling reason that small home appliances constituted a miniscule portion of waste in 1970, but had become a big chunk of household expenditure by 2013. The laws were not an end in themselves, but were constantly subjected to iterations and amendments in order to keep them relevant and make waste disposal methods progressive and in keeping with the changing times.

A federal approach to legislation made the issue of waste disposal a national problem. These laws provided the framework, direction, and guidelines to the local bodies for proper collection of waste, and to the federal government to upgrade waste disposal as a national infrastructure industry. It provided a timely opportunity to the First World to convert waste disposal from smelly dump yards into assets of enormous national and economic importance. Concurrently, these laws created a desirable pressure on local civic governance to improve waste collection methods for their ability to segregate the waste at source – a prerequisite that was at the heart of any meaningful migration in waste disposal practices.

The effort to improve waste collection yielded an unexpected but a pleasant outcome. Recycling, which was meant to complement the disposal and reduce the load on landfills and incinerators, started to become the fulcrum of waste management in its own right. By the 1990s, preservation and reuse took precedence over disposal. Subsequent new laws and amendments were enacted giving a major boost to the recycling industry. Resource recovery, recycling, and reduction of use became central themes to waste disposal approaches. Waste was treated into biogas and compost. Glass was melted for reuse or pulverized to make sand. Plastic was converted into raw material for a variety of articles. Compost centers, recycling, and resource recovery plants for hazardous waste and next-generation incinerators took center stage in the field of waste disposal. Scandinavian countries embraced recycling with tremendous zeal. Sweden, particularly is a great example worthy every bit of emulation and reverence. In 1975, Sweden generated 2.3 million tonnes of annual household waste, nearly 30 percent of which was incinerated to produce energy for heating homes and the balance 70 percent was dumped in landfills. Four decades later, Sweden generated more than 4.3 million tonnes of household waste annually and recycled nearly all of it (part of it is still incinerated). In forty years, it has almost completely eliminated its dependence on landfills, while it generates nearly double the waste. Air and water contamination due to heavy metal emissions from the open landfills have been cut down by 99 percent since 1985. Today,

Sweden recovers energy for households from more than half of its generated waste and composts another 15 percent of the waste for use in agriculture. Everything else is recycled and reused. Germany, the Netherlands, Denmark, and Austria too have virtually eliminated the use of landfills for waste disposal. Today these countries are almost circular economies; a term loosely meaning whatever they consume is extracted as a resource for re-use. Arising out of resource and space constraints, centuries of misery and decades of trials and error, this is the pinnacle of human development.

In other cases, the recycling effort did not completely eliminate the use of landfills, but made them more scientific, safe, and efficient. For instance, in the USA, the recycling of generated waste increased from under 6 percent in the 1960s to around 34 percent in 2013. During the same time, while the number of landfills reduced by two-thirds, the average area of each landfill increased, suggesting upscaling and aggregation in landfill operations. Today, the installed capacities of operational landfills in the USA are synced with the waste left over from recycling leading to improvements in both these methods. Improved recycling abilities instilled confidence in landfill operators about the quality of input waste that reached the landfills, which was always a concern for them. The incoming garbage was evaluated for its decomposability and hazardous nature. The garbage that failed to meet these parameters not only posed unwarranted emission risks and a potentially high cost of compliance to the stringent environmental laws, but also occupied unproductive precious space in the landfill, which was one of its biggest constraints. Biodegradable waste decomposes and becomes smaller, making space for the next batch, while every ounce of non-biodegradable waste continues to retain the original state for the entire lifecycle of the landfill. It takes 500 to 700 years for discarded sanitary napkins and diapers to decompose in a landfill and 500 to 1,000 years for a plastic bag, while glass bottles take 1 to 2 million years to decompose. A formal recycling intervention gave certainty to the landfill operators that they would only receive the right kind of waste.

Improvements in waste collection and rise of formal recycling industry allowed landfills operators to gain this confidence and commit more and more capital. Their faith and backing succeeded in transforming the landfills into efficient and safe energy mines, which was a big departure from the open air 'garbage dump' of the nineteenth century. They were equipped with giant insulated pits that arrested the percolation of leachate into the ground and were armed with layering techniques that prevented exposure of waste to the air. Landfills finally emerged as harvesters of methane for energy purposes. As a result, they migrated from being plots of land on the outskirts of cities to gargantuan land parcels in remote locations that could last for hundreds of years, provided their operations were supported by efficient recycling and waste-collection ecosystems. A case in point is a landfill in Nevada, USA, that is spread across 2,200 acres. Given the existing daily rate of garbage arrival at the landfill, it will continue to be operational for the next 200 years.

Every landfill has a lifespan that runs into decades. Many a times they reach the end of their life much earlier for because of the increasing quantum of generated waste it is fed. But this was not an issue in these countries because due to the scientific advancement in the landfill technology, sanitary closed landfills were not viewed as mere waste collecting sites but as sources of energy. A landfill may run out of space to accommodate more trash, but it could continue to generate energy from the waste already collected for decades. Modern landfills in North America are designed to keep running long after they stop receiving waste. This was done by making sure that only bio-degradable trash hits the landfill and that it is managed, compressed and layered with fresh soil round the year. Over a period of time, a grid with layers is formed and each block of trash on the grid resembles an energy storage cell to be used for energy extraction in the future. It is like building a resource mine of waste for future needs. Converting trash into batches of stored energy is the reason why landfills are productive well beyond their 'trash input' life. Therefore, the second reason for the closure of a landfill is when it stops generated energy. This problem was overcome by converting them into public parks, golf courses and other real estate developments. For instance, in Broward County, Florida, retired landfills were converted into an elementary school and community soccer field. In Palm Beach and Hillsborough County in the same state, they were converted to toll plazas, mountain bike trails, community golf courses, office of the Chamber of Commerce and even residential buildings. In spite of this seemingly positive gains, the cost of managing the leachate and the paucity of space with the ever increasing waste heading to the landfills proved to be a constant challenge. The design of landfills was not fool proof enough to mitigate these risks. But the fact that the field of waste disposal had moved into the realm of scientific research and critical thinking, sanitary landfills were further engineered, and the next generation landfills were installed with bio-reactors. Bio-reactor infused landfills accelerated the decomposition of the waste and the production of methane gas, thereby reducing their operating costs and increasing their efficiency to manage leachate. These landfills created space at a faster rate and accommodated more waste per square inch, thereby increasing their active life. The Bioreactor landfills were not only storing the garbage but also disposing it by converting it into other forms.

Modern-day closed sanitary landfills in the First World are scientific marvels that showcase a beautiful synergy between different branches of science. But the credit does not go to technological innovation alone. Progressive legislation that up-streamed the function of waste disposal from the local bodies to a national responsibility, the capability infusion into the local civic infrastructure to collect segregated waste, and the formalization of the recycling and resource recovery industry to process all non-biodegradable waste also worked as an effective troika, enabling technological innovation to elevate the subject of waste disposal to one of science and economics. Today, modern landfills are no different from power plants that deploy modern tools and a technically skilled workforce to supervise and manage their daily operations. In the USA, landfill operations came under the federal purview of the Environment Protection Agency (EPA). The EPA defines exhaustive guidelines that cover all aspects of running a landfill – design, location, and operations. These guidelines also defined emission standards and stipulated regular monitoring of air, soil, and groundwater quality in neighboring areas. This elaborate regulatory framework evolved over decades, since the first scientific landfill in the USA came into operation in 1937 in Fresno, California.

While excessive regulation is often viewed with skepticism to institution-building, it had the opposite effect on waste disposal. Regulation created the requisite boundary conditions of processes, systems, infrastructure, and emissions. Overarching regulatory framework altered the thinking of administrators toward landfills to view it as an infrastructure play: haul the waste from towns and villages to these giant landfills, compress the trash, layer it with soil, and then extract energy to supply it to a common grid on a daily basis.

Once the waste disposal issue caught the fancy of infrastructure, the realization that waste disposal needs to be handled by experts and not as an administrative afterthought by the state followed suit. This accelerated the deployment of technology, scale, and scientific rigor in the waste disposal sector and opened it up for formal private capital. Stringent environmental regulation made any other substandard intervention untenable. This created a blueprint for capital and its accompanying expertise required in the sector, motivating private enterprises to invest.

The USA was particularly successful in developing a viable business model around landfill operations, which promoted widespread participation of the private sector and Waste Management Inc. aptly exemplifies the success of this idea. In 2014, there were about 850 active landfills in the USA. Waste Management Inc., a public limited company based out of Houston, Texas, managed and controlled the operations of about 250 of these and managed nearly 30 percent of the 145 million tonne annual waste of the country that made its way to these landfills. The company employed nearly 60,000 people and generated an annual turnover of US$ 13 billion (₹85,000 crores), with an operating margin of 70 percent. Waste Management Inc. generated nearly 70 percent of its revenue from the fees it earned from various local civic bodies to haul waste from their respective jurisdictions to its landfill sites. Around 15 percent of its revenue came from managing landfill operations and the balance 15 percent from sales of energy generated from waste and other allied activities.

US waste-disposal regulations defined the notion of customers, markets, and other governing principals to conduct the business of landfill operations as well as other waste-disposal methods, and succeeded to formalize revenue streams and operating costs of Waste Management Inc. The regulatory framework allowed landfill operations to be seen as integrated providers of waste-management services from collection and transport to processing. The fees earned from the local civic bodies to haul waste till landfills and process it was the major revenue share in the business model of the company. It also provided the right language to establish precise commercial contracts with local civic bodies that gave visibility on the revenue stream and enabled the company to commit capital. Had this not been the case, the waste disposal guidelines would have limited the scope of private capital to earn revenue solely through the sale of energy from the landfill. Then the business model would have fallen short of being commercially viable and struggled to meet the stringent environmental guidelines on waste disposal. Local civic bodies, in turn, passed this financial cost on to the citizens through taxes and users fees, under the justifiable premise of an equitable social contract. Other revenue streams of the company rightfully included revenue from the sale of energy and other resources. Managing modern-day landfills in the USA became a sustainable, value-creating business involving a network of engineering and supply chain operations. Waste Management Inc. depicts that it is not by chance that clean countries of today boast of a pragmatic waste-disposal policy which takes an industrial approach, allowing the successful deployment of private capital.

The ability of the waste-collection system to supply only pre-segregated waste was an imperative prerequisite for the waste disposal methods to be successful. This learning also contributed to the rise of the formal recycling industry that was premised on the belief that all kinds of waste can be repurposed for products or resources, only if the waste collection process ensured that the waste was segregated with precision. With improvements in the collection system this became a relatively easier task and private capital enthusiastically lapped up the opportunity in formal recycling industry that came along with it. Japan began segregating its waste into eight different groups that led to the success of incineration technology. The color coded dogma of waste segregation at source in Scandinavian countries ensured that their formal waste recycling industry took off in full glory. Viable business models were made out of waste disposal, recycling, incineration and landfill operations, and much revenue generated from fees and proceeds from the sale of recycled products and resources. This was further boosted with the recycling debate that started in Europe in the mid-1980s which gave a fillip to this operating model. There was a political consensus, regulatory push and social acceptance to move away from a disposing society, toward a more circular existence, and regulations and activism against dumping of waste in any form created the right enabling conditions for formal recycling to become the main waste disposal method in many clean countries of today.

There are a few important lessons about waste disposal that India can learn from the clean countries. The first is that waste disposal needs to be customized for different waste types. Solid waste can be completely recycled into compost and needs industrial or cooperative composting facilities to do so. Food and other biodegradable waste can produce energy and sanitary landfills can be used for this purpose. Plastic, glass, paper, metals, and similar waste must be segregated for reuse and need industrial and/or formal recycling facilities. Electronic waste needs to be isolated for resource recovery under controlled settings. This, however, requires technical capability, scientific temperament, and capital at a scale that is beyond the abilities of the local civic bodies. Instead of expecting every local civic body to build its own waste disposal infrastructure on desired lines, it is technically and economically prudent to build a common infrastructure that can service multiple cities, villages, and towns. Clean countries offer examples of this learning in abundance.

All methods of waste disposal are equally viable for providing environmentally safe and economically viable solutions. Japan still burns seventy percent of its generated waste, albeit in a controlled environment, whereas Sweden recycles most of the waste it produces. The USA, on the other hand, uses scientific landfills as the primary method to dispose its waste, in combination with other methods. All methods of waste disposal can come under severe criticism in no time if the enabling conditions and desired ecosystems required for their success are compromised. If the insulation in the landfills is not fool proof, then the leakage of leachate will pose a danger. If there are leakages in the incinerators' methods of extracting gases, then they will begin to pose a threat to the environment. If the compost pits are dumped with non-biodegradable waste, then they will become sink holes in no time. To create the right enabling conditions for each of these methods to become viable alternatives, in a manner that they are free from environmental and public health safety risks, is the other lesson that the clean countries of today teach us.

In order to apply these lessons, however, waste disposal requires federal legislation to create a common minimum for uniform implementation. Such a legislative intervention is also necessary to empower formal capital with the bite-force to suffocate the informality that dominates the waste-disposal sector, is perhaps the most important learning of all. Besides the three decades of legislative frenzy on environment laws in general and on waste management in particular that the clean countries experienced, it is difficult to imagine the creation of any alternative pressure point equally potent which could have accelerated these societies toward the desired state. After all, this legislative activism itself emerged in the backdrop of rapid industrialization and urbanization that had started to get submerged in smog, acid rains, premature deaths and putrefied air quality in the First World.

Although the clean countries have successfully improvised landfills and their waste-disposal practices, for India, it is happening at a fairly advanced stage of industrialization and urbanization. The linearity of industrialization and urbanization in the clean countries gave them the necessary breather that kept the cost of the learning low. The disruptive nature of these forces does not accord the same luxury to India.

This backdrop provides a good reference point against which to compare India's waste-disposal approach and to measure the chasm between the two. On 30 January 2016, Mumbai was engulfed in a thick blanket of smog and caused such a serious air pollution scare that city administration closed down nearly 70 schools in affected areas and instituted an urgent enquiry into the matter. The cause was discovered to be the fumes and smoke emitted from trash being burned at Deonar, one of the largest open landfills in the city. The incumbent chief minister ordered immediate action to bring the situation under control. Fire fighters swung into action at the site and it took three days to douse the fire. This kind of troubleshooting sums up India's approach to waste disposal – dousing one fire at a time.

The municipal corporation of Mumbai is touted as the 'richest' municipal civic body in India, with an annual turnover of US$ 4 billion (₹26,000 crores) in 2014–15. On this revenue, it made a marginal surplus over its expenditures, an exemplary performance by the financial yardstick of Indian local civic bodies. Even a city, whose local governance is not in the red is so helpless that it disposes its waste in open landfills like the one at Deonar and quietly dumps its sewage into the sea – practices banned by the clean countries decades ago. There are rules that mandate residents (at least in formal housing) in many parts of Mumbai to segregate their waste, a feat marked better than many other parts of the country. But the municipal corporation does not have any treatment centers to handle the segregated waste and eventually dumps it all in landfills or into the sea, frittering away the sincere efforts of the citizens.

The case of Delhi on the issue of waste disposal is even worse. The city disposes its waste in the three open landfills of Bhalswa, Okhla and Ghazipur – all exhausted their capacity long ago, yet the local bodies of the city continue to dump them with new truck loads of trash every day in blatant violation of judicial reprimands and under the guardianship of an incapacitated administration. It is a matter of grave concern when a state actor is found to breach the law of the land, not that there is any alternative in sight. Cities like Chennai and Kolkata are slightly better off. Kolkata undertakes a controlled dumping of waste, which is like a half-way between open dumping and an engineered landfill. In Chennai, waste is dumped on two dump sites that are virtually open dump yards, but the city does try to cover it with debris. But, the sum total of this story is that 80 percent of India's generated waste is dumped in open, unregulated landfills.

Thirty Indian cities generate nearly three-quarters of the total waste output of India. The composition of this waste can rival that of any First-World city. It comprises all materials that signify so called 'human progress' (plastic, polymers, lead, batteries, processed paper, plywood). India is among the top 20 plastic-consuming nations in the world. New Delhi and Mumbai generate around 11,000 tonnes of waste daily, almost equivalent to Hong Kong, which generates 13,000 tonnes of waste daily. India is also among the leading generators of hazardous waste, e-waste, construction waste, and medical waste. In the 1950s, half of India's generated waste comprised ash, sand, and grit, while the other half was organic. By 2011, nearly half of India's annually generated waste was non-biodegradable. In the good old days, when India put out food waste along with plates made of dried leaves and glasses made of clay and dumped it in a garbage pit on the outskirts, the arrangement was rarely questioned save for its unappetizing visuals and occasional foul smell. Today, India sends a deadly concoction of plastic, polymers, metals and chemicals to open landfills daily, which release fumes of carcinogens and toxins into the air and leachate that seeps into the soil and groundwater.

These simmering landfills turn into raging fires like the one in Deonar but this is not the last of its kind. Big and small, India will continue to witness many Deonars with the continuation of this status quo. This is not so much an emotional doomsday prophecy but an inference based on sound science. The union of open landfills and the complex profile of the present-day garbage generated in India is bound to produce an explosive and dangerous chemistry. This prediction did come true in 2017 when a part of one of Delhi's main open landfill sites at Ghazipur caved in with a loud explosion, instantly killing two people. Fifty tonnes of garbage spilled out on to the road and the drain skirting the landfill. It was common knowledge that the landfill was flirting with danger and defying the rules since 2005, when its towering height crossed the maximum mark. Since then the cave-in was more a question of 'when' than 'if.' For this reason, not surprisingly, one year later multiple fires erupted at Bhalswa landfill that took three days to extinguish.

Both the Ghazipur and Bhalswa incidents made the front page of leading newspaper, bringing into focus the ticking time bombs that open landfills really are for air, water and soil. Toxin release from these landfills goes undetected by the naked eye and the emissions silently dissipate into the surroundings till someday it explodes. By that time, the contaminants slyly enter people's lives and manifest tumors, birth deformities, stunted growth, reduced stamina and premature death. But, all of this is forgiven because the designated open landfills provide an inadvertent template for the convenience and negligible cost of disposing waste.

Rivers and seas have also always served free-of-cost disposal sites and Indian water bodies without exception stand testimony to it. Such alternatives may not be towering heaps of stinking rubbish, but a picture of disdain and contempt all the same, as is the case with Lawson's Bay Beach in Visakhapatnam where plastic waste is dumped into the ocean for years. The high tide creates the illusion of taking this non-biodegradable waste into the deep recesses of sea only until the next low tide siphons the filth back to the shores, meanwhile eating away at the intestines of endangered species of turtles and killing the natural sea weed, which is the staple diet of many indigenous fish. Many of Mumbai's beach fronts have also resigned to a similar reality, often witnessing litter and rancid odours. Blatant dumping of puja offering wrapped in plastic bags stagnates the flow of Musi river in Hyderabad and robs the river of aquatic life. City administrators are left with no choice but to push the garbage downstream and release the flow.

Hidden in such disposal methods is an unwitting template for smaller Indian cities and towns who now confront the changing complexity of generated waste and are quick to take inspiration from these examples to device a response. People in towns like Halol, Dholpur, Unnao, Jharsaguda and Bhilwara cut open sachets for oil, snacks, tobacco, shampoos; replace old electronic gadgets with new ones and buy cement in gunny bags to build homes. They eat food at weddings and social functions in plastic plates. The question to ask is this: How does the aftermath of this consumption get disposed in these town? Achrol village in Amber tehsil of Jaipur district supplies the answer. Achrol is located on Jaipur-Delhi highway, situated on the outskirts of Jaipur. Garbage collected from the shops and households flanking the highway is thrown in a common heap of biodegradable and non-biodegradable waste in the middle of the road. When the garbage pile is high enough and dried, it is set on fire to make way for more stinking, disease-causing rubbish. Achrol's method of disposing waste gets mirrored in Farah (Uttar Pradesh), Morena (Madhya Pradesh), Muzzaffanagar (Bihar), Sohna (Haryana), and thousands of other towns and villages. Heritage monuments and baolis (step wells), water bodies, parks and pavements, forests and isolated zones, public areas of markets, state-owned or disputed plots of land fall victim to dumping of waste, and the local governance turns a blind eye.

India has also undertaken brief stabs at incineration technology to dispose waste. Hyderabad was the first city to take the initiative to adopt it in 1986. Since then, a number of municipalities have warmed up to it a successful Indian case study on waste incineration, however, remains elusive. Located on the Gurugram–Faridabad motorway at the foothills of the Aravalli range, the Badwari incineration plant was commissioned by the Municipal Corporation of Faridabad in 2008 to process 1,000 tonnes of daily garbage produced by Gurugram and Faridabad. In right earnest, the contract for plant operations was awarded to an organization and the plant functioned fine for a while. However, in 2012, the plant closed down abruptly over cost and pricing disputes between the organization and local municipal bodies. The site of the incineration plant quickly turned into a dump yard with untreated waste heaped in the open. What was the blueprint of the plant for revenue and operating cost? How did the technology of the plant fair against global benchmarks? Why were the commercial contracts not stress tested for potential disputes? What were the checks and balances for its smooth functioning? These were obvious questions that an efficient waste incineration plant would have asked while the project was still at the drawing board. In 2017, the project was tamely revived by onboarding a Chinese company showcasing our helplessness to address these questions ourselves and not before a well-intentioned project was quickly reduced to an open landfill, causing irreparable damage to the ecology of the Aravallis.

Fifty kilometers away from Badwari lies another story of ineptitude. The Timarpur–Okhla waste incineration plant in southeast Delhi was conceived in 2005 under the public–private partnership model, but became operational only in 2011. From the start, the plant faced criticism about toxic emissions followed by legal scrutiny, with 28 hearings in the Delhi High Court and 21 in the NGT. The history of incineration technology teaches us that it was carefully nurtured with enabling conditions in the form of precise definitions, guidelines, regulations and operating standards to ensure its success. Regulations defined the rule of the game and established ownership of actions, emissions norms, the scope of scrutiny and mitigation measures. This preparatory work not only provided the operational safeguards but offered immense clarity to operators who would front the capital and run these plants. Why, then, did India display the helplessness, when the TOWMCL incineration plant was conceived in 2005, that the clean countries of today started to display a century ago? The enormous legal scrutiny that the plant faced implies that the regulations and guidelines needed to operate the plant were either weak or absent, exposing the plant's operations to different interpretations. Citizens living in the neighborhood viewed it as a health hazard, while the operator portrayed it as a picture of safety.

The incumbent government that conceived the plant was voted out of power, while the new government upped the scrutiny of the plant's operations, which brought its very existence into question.

It is ideal to be like Sweden which recycles 99 percent of its waste, rather than Japan which burns 80 percent of it. Having said that, waste incineration is a safe intermediate technology that has a history of successful deployment to replace open dump yards and prepare the society toward recycling. There are island nations, land-locked cities, and countries with limited resources that are primarily dependent on this technology for the last many decades and burn more than three quarters of their waste without much hue and cry. Why, then, has India not been able to come up with a half decent success story around this technology in the last thirty years? Incineration is dangerous, in that its operations are similar to a nuclear plant. A nuclear plant generates radioactive materials, while burning waste in an incinerator generates lethal and toxic emissions. It is unimaginable to build a nuclear plant without safeguards and guidelines. Once these safeguards are installed and adherence is assured, nuclear plants are as safe as any other factory. India has demonstrated great maturity in building nuclear plants, but not waste incinerators. The onus of implementing incineration technology for waste disposal rests solely on the weak local governance, as is the case with open landfills. Just as every local municipal body cannot be expected to build its own nuclear plant, it should not be expected to build and operate waste incinerators. But local governance with its misplaced priorities is burdened with this responsibility and ends up with suboptimal responses with remarkable precision to create a quagmire, where the operators of the incinerators argue that they are environment friendly. The citizens in neighboring areas present equally convincing arguments that such a facility is a health hazard and dangerously pollutes the air. The judiciary demands answers, but has not yet asked the right questions. Incineration technology in India thus has been more efficiently churning slugfests than burning the waste.

On the side-lines of this oscillation between open dump yards and ill-conceived waste incinerators that India has managed to collect, lies the method of trash burning that disposes waste that India is unable to collect and haul to a half decent resting place. The popularity of this method is not surprising given that it is the oldest, cheapest and most convenient. Yet, while the clean countries succeeded in making this method painfully inconvenient for its citizens, India helplessly resigned to it and became a hostage to it. The roots of this method lie in agriculture. Farmers needed to dispose the dried leaves and harvested remains of their produce for the next cropping cycle. They figured burning as the easiest, most time efficient and convenient way to get rid of it. It was indeed the best way to dispose of agricultural waste as the residual ash is perceived to be beneficial to soil health. Then, the practice extended to the village and people burned waste that was not collected at a common spot. The same practice extended to towns when communities acquired a more urban character.

In the pursuit of overall improvements in the waste management approach, this practice lost relevance and support in the clean countries of today. However, in the case of India, local governance largely saw the waste management value chain from the eyes of a sanitation worker. He swept the area, piled up the collected garbage into small heaps in the corner of the street and set them on fire before he called it a day. Neither was it in his job description to devise more efficient ways to dispose waste, nor was he ever reprimanded for burning the trash in the open. It was easy and convenient. Concurrently, local governance rarely paid any attention to its lack of ability to haul the generated garbage for safer disposal, rather than burning. It was only in 2001 that the practice was banned in India but by then it had made strong inroads into the Indian psyche. People saw sanitation workers burning garbage every morning and imbibed it as an acceptable practice into their daily lives. In the areas where municipal services barely held any sway, people swept the garbage into piles and burned it in the open, just like a sanitation worker would do at the end of his beat. The shutters of nearly fourteen millions shops opened every morning with owners diligently cleaning their premises, collecting the garbage into a small heap right outside and burning it. Thousands of tiny eateries across motorways, automobile repair shops on the city outskirts, informal tea stalls, convenience shops, wholesale cloth and general stores, electrical and electronic stores follow the same template to dispose waste – sweep the shop and its surrounding area, collect the garbage and burn it. Why bother to bag the trash, store it and wait for a regular collection van to pick it up when their shops are not connected to any formal garbage collection system? Even if these shops do have the access, the sheer effort of preparing the garbage for collection and storing it for a time far outweighs the simple task of collecting the garbage and setting it on fire. Communities deploy the services of sweepers to clean their neighborhoods for the lack of regular access to municipal services. These privately paid hands would collect, dump and burn the trash in exchange for their wages. The quintessential image of winter mornings in any Indian town has people sitting around a bonfire of garbage collected from the neighborhood, old tyres and all. Never have they been advised, reprimanded or guided for better alternatives for there are no alternatives to offer.

It mattered little if our grandparents burned the trash in the open or if the sanitation workers did. Then, the burning of trash was either benign or inconsequential or both. The human footprint was sparse enough to allow these emissions to dissipate into the air. But it matters profoundly today because of lethal emissions of toxins, carcinogens, heavy metals and various noxious gases into the air and disfigures everything that comes in its range. A roadside tea stall in the earlier era used to serve tea in clay cups and eatables in bowls made of dried leaves, but today they serve tea in disposable polystyrene cups and snacks in vacuum sealed plastic packaging. But, the tea stall owner continues to burn his garbage at the end of the day. He is hardly concerned about the dangerous aftermath of his actions for he has bigger battles to fight to eke out a living in his informal existence than to worry about the environment.

I may not be burning trash myself, but the trash I generate may eventually be getting incinerated in the open. Say, I throw a disposable tea cup and an empty packet of potato chips in the dustbin during a refreshment break on a highway restaurant during a road trip. The restaurant owner may be emptying the bin into an open pit in the backyard and combusting it at the end of the day. Trash burning may not appear to cause any visible discomfort to the existence of the mainstream but most of the trash that does not end up in an open landfill mutates into toxins and navigates its way into human wind pipes through the trash burning route. The pavements outside millions of shops and homes, dark by-lanes of countless busy streets, the garbage pits of thousands of road side eateries, the corners of many jhuggi clusters and the outskirts of lakhs of far-flung villages witness trash burning every day for the lack of alternatives. The cost-free nature and sheer ease of the practice offer unmatched convenience for everyone to resort to it at the drop of a hat. India despite prohibiting it since 2001 does not have a worthwhile alternative to counter it. Look at it any which way, open incineration of garbage is a perverse form of human behavior that wounds the environment just to get rid of the aftermaths of one's own consumption in the cheapest possible way.

There is, yet, a fair share of India's generated waste that escapes the clutches of open landfills and open incineration and lands up in a purpose-built recycling industry. Informality is the calling card of this industry that employs millions in exploitative, filthy, and dangerous working conditions. Large quantities of plastic and glass bottles, poly bags, and batteries, and almost all the old newspapers and magazines, are picked up by an estimated three million ragpickers before this waste is recycled and its residue is burned in the open or dumped in an open landfill. There is silent and unanimous acceptance of this informal recycling sector by the Indian mainstream, while ignoring two pitfalls of the arrangement.

The first is the technical inadequacy of the informal recycling sector to process the 100 million tonnes of waste that India generates annually. This arrangement adopts a simplistic approach of collecting the waste and extracting materials using crude and unsafe techniques. This artisanal set up is often taken on face value and is rarely critiqued for its technical prowess to address India's waste disposal need. The complexity and the quantum of India's generated waste needs the scale, capital, and the methods to pulverize, segregate, and process it. It needs the resource recovery capabilities to safely extract metals and gases from electronic waste; composting facilities spread across the country to convert solid human waste into organic fertilizer; and foam, plastic, concrete, metal, and glass-smelting facilities that can break down the construction, automobile, plastic waste, and process it for reuse. But this cannot be accomplished with ragpickers, nor through ubiquitous informal recycling facilities.

Second, the arrangement is informal and therefore unregulated, and operates sans supervision and guidelines making it illegal on many counts. The arrangement operates without any controls over the recycling processes and the output (recycled product). Untrained workers handle the discarded items with their bare hands and bodies, and without any protective masks. Shanties and makeshift arrangements serve as laboratories and processing centers, thus contributing to the informality of the recycling ecosystem in India. Low yields and substandard outcomes are the mainstay, as is the threat to the environment and public health due to the release of deadly emissions and hazardous residues. Plastic bottles are converted into substandard raw material. A discarded television set is manually hammered open to harvest metals while releasing toxins into the air. Metals from discarded automobiles are smelted and resins from old mattresses are burned in the open to extract value. Many a times the inconvenience of processing is bypassed and discarded plastic and glass bottles are simply reused with fresh labels to support spurious retail.

The acceptance of the informal recycling sector under the garb of livelihood support not only reinforces condescending biases toward waste disposal, but also exposes the vapidity of policymaking to offer a compelling alternative for India's waste-disposal woes. Both these factors create helplessness which compels stakeholders to seek incremental changes in the arrangement rather than to question the basic premise of the arrangement itself. The Indian recycling industry may appear to be a bastion for the marginalized to earn their livelihoods, but it lives a subaltern life of inefficiency, vulnerability, and exploitation. Rag-pickers are reduced to the lowest form of human existence and differ from scavenging birds only for their lack of flight. The same industry in the clean countries like Sweden has graduated to a specialized science that aims to safely recycle nearly all its generated waste. This means breaking down materials to convert them into interesting polymers and compounds that can be put to various productive uses; for example, bottles converted into raw material for insulation purposes, packaging bags into reinforcement products for the construction industry, and plastic casings into resins. Cleanliness in these countries is an outcome of the realization that effective waste disposal is a vital infrastructure play that cannot be left to the mercy of informality.

India, however, rests its hope on the vulnerable shoulders of manual labor to achieve this feat. It covers up the informality in the recycling industry with a protectionist attitude that it also extends to sectors like handicraft without recognizing the key difference between the two realities. Waste recycling is all about managing the aftermath of consumption and not a self-serving sector that celebrates human skills per se. Unlike, say, the handloom sector that has all the right ingredients to demand support for a level playing field to express human skills, the informal waste recycling industry does not. Yet, the cost of wrongly re-cycled waste affects everyone unlike a wrongly woven saree. It pollutes the air and the soil, and encourages spurious trade. The informality of recycling artificially deflates its cost and falsely perpetuates a sense of entitlement in the society. Profit in the recycling business is squeezed out by bypassing and abusing the operating factors in the value chain like meagre wages that are way below the minimum and discharge of the residual materials into water bodies free of cost from makeshift accommodation without paying rent. An exploitative value chain that poses grave risk to the environment and encourages child labor blesses this industry with profit margins. Then, what has the recycling industry to gain by being above board?

In 2015, the then union minister for Environment, Forest and Climate Change commented thus on ragpickers and the recycling industry, 'The informal sector has saved the country. They are doing a good job and I have decided to reward them.' In this comment lie the reasons for the mainstream society to continue accepting informality in the Indian waste recycling industry. More than the 'sympathetic' activism for livelihood protection delivered from a condescending ladder, it is the mainstream's dependence on the free of charge cleaning services of rag pickers that makes it look the other way and let the informal recycling industry be. This vulnerability of the mainstream compels it to deliver such patronizing sermons and overlook the rampant child labor and widespread financial and human exploitation prevalent in the arrangement. The anonymity and free-of-cost existence of informal waste recycling trade offers an unmatched template of ease, convenience and economics that trumps dignity and human values. The minister's comment smacks of helplessness and makes a meek attempt to pat the back of the informal ecosystem to keep up the good work, instead of raising a bugle against it.

Even though India only manages to recycle or process 20 percent of its generated waste, it can defend all its current antiquated waste-disposal methods for myriad reasons. Why worry when we still have open landfills yet to reach their capacity, or we have millions of unorganized recyclers to take care of the non-biodegradable waste? These arguments are logical, but they lack the luxury of time. The clean countries of today had time when they were trying to solve their waste-disposal problem. They sequentially built systems in response to the rising complexity of the generated waste. When waste was benign and biodegradable, they relied on landfills and slowly graduated to incineration. As the waste became more complex in nature, they were compelled to make further improvements in the landfill and incineration technologies and augment them with the formalization of a recycling industry. The sequential manner in which this came about allowed them the breather to improvise and improve upon their methods, and to unequivocally establish the relationship between the changing household consumption patterns and improvements in waste-disposal methods. Though, in retrospect, many of the earlier techniques may have been rudimentary or immature, they proved to be necessary and invaluable steps to test the boundaries of technology and human capability to devise better methods. In India, however, the stranglehold that the caste system had over waste management and the largely agrarian character of the country at the time of Independence created an illusion that waste disposal is a non-issue. Hence, India lost precious time in anticipating the onslaught the economic growth and urbanization would unleash.

Until the 1980s, the composition and quantum of India's waste were benign enough for open landfills, informal recycling, or open combustion. From the 1990s, however, Indian households leapfrogged on their consumption appetite; in 1991, 80 percent of the average urban consumption basket comprised five categories: food, apparel, jewelry, furnishing, and consumer durables. By 2014, seventeen categories made up this consumption basket, including smart electronics, large electrical devices, toys, education, personal grooming, and social event such as weddings, among others. This disruptive change had a direct bearing on the generated waste, making earlier methods of disposing waste irrelevant. The waste rapidly metamorphosed into a toxic composition of biodegradable and non-biodegradable materials in equal measure.

India literally caught up with the clean countries of today on the consumption march but left its waste disposal to open pits, bare-backed men and the trash burning skills of individuals. The generated waste rapidly metamorphosed from an innocuous mix of dust and food leftovers to a toxic composition of bio-degradable and non-biodegradable materials, in equal measure. India does not have the time to think about waste disposal approaches in a sequential manner and instead will need to jump to the present day wisdom of clean countries, bypassing many decades in between.

India is at the juncture where it has two choices. The first is to take a 100-year-long journey like the clean countries of today initiated a century ago and go through the churn of realizations, before we reach the final destination of exemplary waste disposal systems. In the process, we will suffer epidemics and many of us will die prematurely and our improvisations will make our land and water unfit for future generations. India seems to be moving in this direction, and should reach the final destination by 2100. The second choice is to wake up to the impending dangers of inadequate and rudimentary waste-disposal methods. With such an awakening a humble acceptance that we messed up, a refusal to undertake the century-long journey and a determination to imbibe the wisdom of the clean countries of today should come about.

Waste disposal is a challenge that transcends governance boundaries. Therefore, the challenge cannot be taken on by local civic bodies alone. Early attempts to address waste-disposal needs were undertaken within the ambit of the local governance framework in the clean countries of today. But they soon realized the merit to develop common frameworks, guidelines, and laws that should uniformly apply across the nation. This wisdom to upstream waste disposal as a federal subject, reiterated many times before, needs to become the lynchpin of India's approach on the matter.

Clean countries of today deftly used legislative tools to manage the successful transfer of the ownership of waste disposal to the federal purview. These legislative tools had two important hallmarks of specificity and enterprise development; India has no reason not to replicate this template. Federal laws of clean countries amply demonstrate the specificity in waste-disposal laws that mandated acceptable and non-acceptable disposal methods for all types of generated waste. These laws were uniformly applicable across all towns, counties, provinces, and regions within the country. For instance, the use of open landfill to dispose waste was made illegal in Germany in 1972. This meant that no local municipal civic body across Germany could resort to this method to dispose waste and if it did so it was liable to be punished. Similarly, acceptable emission norms, preventive mechanisms, and mitigation approaches to soil and air contamination for different waste-disposal methods were defined to provide enabling conditions for the installation of safe and efficient solutions. This meant that the success of an incineration plant could easily be gauged against these prescribed parameters to determine any breaches or deviations. India will need to subject its legislative agenda on waste disposal through a similar rigor to define laws and apply them uniformly across towns, cities, villages, districts, tehsils, and states.

Indian waste-management laws of 2016 made a significant departure from the EPA of 1986 in that they specifically talked about waste management, but still lacked specificity and operational guidelines demanded for waste disposal. The wisdom from clean countries conveys that such laws cannot merely be a laundry list of prohibited actions. They instead need to provide direction for actions. India's waste-management laws are still devoid of the desired specificity that could pack an operational punch. For instance, the newly minted waste management laws did not ban the use of open landfills or necessitate the use of desired waste-disposal methods. India's problem is that its waste is an exact replica of that of the clean countries of today and law-making, therefore, should also leapfrog to the present day. Until a few years ago, India's emission norms for automobiles used to be one or two generations behind those of the First World. But in 2015 India leapt ahead to be at par with legislations to that effect.

Specificity of the laws to make non-conformity inconvenient and create urgency for transitioning into formal methods will enable the development of enterprise in the Indian waste-disposal sector, as was the case in the clean countries of today. Waste disposal is an infrastructure play that requires capital, scale, and expertise, as also a legislative and policy nudge. The nature of capital or the enterprises that emerge is inconsequential: it can be a cooperative set-up, start-ups backed by venture capital, private-sector organization, micro-sized recyclers, or a public-sector intervention. But the value-creating potential of these enterprises remains subdued if they are compelled to hunt for solutions with meager capital, vague expectations, and opaque guidelines administered through local governance. In shifting the perspective, the sector can emerge as a lucrative destination for formal jobs and productive deployment of capital that can suck out informality, while it concurrently addresses the primary objective of safe disposal of waste.

Differently put, waste disposal methods are as good or as bad as the regulations and the policies that govern them. Take the case of recycling organic waste into compost. Urban India annually generates nearly 70 million tonnes of waste, nearly half of which is organic. At a 15 percent yield rate, this translates into an annual production of nearly 10 million tonnes of compost. In 2011–12, India's annual fertilizer consumption was 27 million tonnes. Theoretically, the compost potential of India can partially replace the dependence on fertilizers (technical differences, namely, yield per unit of use notwithstanding), saving the soil and water from excess nitrogen wastage (which can be as high as 50 percent), which the crops are unable to absorb from the fertilizer. Apart from putting city garbage to good use, this interdependent arrangement will arrest the declining soil and water health of the nation. This will need to be a policy response that can bring together the various stakeholders to make it work. In February 2016, the Government of India's Department of Fertilizers mooted a policy that incentivized the sale of compost under the Market Development Assistance (MDA) scheme in rural areas, through the retail channels of fertilizer companies. But, not surprisingly, the scheme was a non-starter due to its one-dimensional subsidy push that perpetuated entitlement, and without the federal agriculture policy being on board with urban sanitation. Sikkim demonstrated the potential of this reconciliation. The scale of the generated solid waste demands an industrial approach to compositing, which cannot emerge without the certainty of the market and clarity of economics at such a scale. It cannot then be left to the fertilizer company or on the farmers' discretion to use or not use organic manure. India's federal stance toward organic farming will determine the success or failure of compositing as the preferred method for solid human waste disposal. A coordinated policy push that mandates the use of Integrated Plant Nutrient Supply (IPNS), a system that advocates the use of fertilizer blended with organic manure, among farmers in the normal course is the answer. The game plan by the union or state government to provide the buffer required to absorb the financial cost, agricultural produce, and social shock during the transition is the answer. Can the high input cost of agriculture that currently favors fertilizer be replaced with the low input cost of compost, for the farmers? If so, what will happen to the installed capacities for fertilizer production? How can this transition be managed smoothly without any loss of farm productivity and loss of income? Can the agriculture policy transform fertilizer retail companies into active retail channels for compost products? How will the patience of agri-input companies to alter their business models to align with the new reality play out? These are the questions that India's agriculture policy needs to ask, in the hope that the answers would lead to the creation of a sustainable market for organic fertilizer, which in turn will trigger the disposal of urban organic waste powered by start-up capital, business enterprises, and cooperatives for economic returns in compost. Like food travels from farmlands to urban homes for economic value, compost & treated sewage will travel from urban homes to farmlands, an agricultural cycle in reverse that should make economic sense for the capital, customers, and vendors alike. The MDA's failure to make urban solid human waste reach agriculture farmlands as compost lies more in the lack of appreciation for this composite cycle than for the idea itself, or that an MDA-like operational response was out of its depth in addressing the magnitude of such a multifaceted issue. The teething troubles of KC Valley project – the first of its kind project piloted in India in 2018 also validates similar set of challenges that confronts the Government of Karnataka. A conceptually strong project on paper, KC Valley pipeline was built at the cost of ₹1,400 crores to haul water derived from 400 MLD treated sewage of Bengaluru city to the parched lakes and farmlands of Kolar district in Karnataka. Soon after its inauguration, the administration was fumbling with fundamental issues like untreated sewage getting pushed through the pipeline that did nothing more than adding to the misery of the farmers in Kolar or disagreement among stakeholders on acceptable standards of clean water that can be pushed through the pipeline. Here again more than issue of financial paucity, challenges faced by KC Valley project reeks of abandonment of responsibilities and tasks that are grey areas between the legislation, and the administration.

The experience of First-World countries has amply demonstrated the success of all available methods of waste disposal. We have examples of successful sanitary landfills in USA, waste incineration technology in Japan, and waste recycling to form compost in Sweden, and their quests continue. This journey continues because increasingly the challenge of waste disposal is now being viewed from the lens of recycling and re-use. The extolled virtues of all the waste disposal approaches in the First World notwithstanding, they are still inadequate to address the growing challenge of e-waste and plastic waste. Scientists are increasingly pushing the boundaries to seek more environmentally friendly solutions and pushing this challenge toward environment sustainability. Start-ups like Calysta Inc. in California and String Bio in Bengaluru are fine-tuning the technology that can convert methane into food on the premise that it is better to consume methane as a food than to use it as a fuel. Such a technology will again change the paradigm for sanitary landfills and waste incineration technology.

The larger issue is that for a sustainable enterprise development narrative to emerge, policy intervention will need to be imagined and customized for all waste types – plastics, construction, sewage, food, electronic, automobiles and industrial as is inferred in the coupling of agriculture policy with organic waste. Consider the policies of social justice and small and medium enterprises that can be fused with waste-disposal guidelines to formalize the recycling sector for non-biodegradable waste. This fusion should form entry barriers in a manner that ragpickers can graduate from being exploited life forms to dignified formal employees. Within this framework, a significant part of the recycling industry can be imagined as a cooperative movement that can harness the skills of ragpickers as resource recovery experts and make them owners of their operations. Entry barriers will also be in the form of emission norms, working conditions, and nature of assets needed that will require the state-sponsored enterprise to provide the seed capital. The fused policy will also protect this arrangement to secure raw materials (non-biodegradable waste) from the local governance of towns and cities that will subscribe to the services of such cooperatives, rather than allow informality to run amok in their respective jurisdiction. The policy will further need to secure markets for such cooperatives to channel their output (in the form of solids, liquids, and gases). In 2015, the surface transport ministry of the union government made an encouraging start that mandated the National Highway Authority of India (NHAI) to use recycled plastic as a resource to build roads. This is an idea that requires multiple disciplines to come together.

Here again, the activism is not for cooperative or private capital, but for the policy to create enabling conditions to incentivize formality over informality. Guidelines for contracts, emission norms, and working conditions are all methods to promote formality. There is also the possibility for multiple cooperatives to emerge across India that will compete with each other or with formal private sector in the spirit of healthy competition. Does Amul not compete with private dairy players as a worthy competitor?

Given India's immediate and mounting waste-disposal challenge, time does not allow India the luxury to seek waste-disposal methods solely from the lens of social development. The lead times for developing scale, expertise, and capacity through such cooperatives will run contrarian to the complexity of the challenge at hand. India will concurrently need to develop commerce and industrial policy to incentivize the participation of private capital and aspire to create enterprises like Shanks Group of the UK, a waste-to-product company that aptly embodies this narrative. In 2015, it generated revenue in excess of US$ 850 million and earned a net profit of US$ 30 million. In the same year, it processed more than 21,000 metric tonnes per day and recovered more than 17,500 metric tonnes of material and products for resale at an impressive 82 percent recovery rate. It was able to achieve this through horizontal integration that recycles multiple waste types under one roof, allowing it to cross-pollinate recycled products, assets, processes, and systems. It could handle all kinds of waste – hazardous, commercial, and municipal – and deploys diverse processing techniques, such as filtration, magnetic, chemical, and mechanical, in its sixty-one recycling and recovery centers to make in-demand products. Through this impressive arrangement, it made aggregates for the construction industry and compost for soil conditioning and animal bedding. It mixed recyclates to make glass, paper and cardboard, wood products for chipboards and medium-density fibreboard, and fuel for energy production. Only 5 percent of the waste that went into Shanks's machines and processes was unable to get recycled for reuse in any form and needed a landfill for disposal. Imagine one day, Delhi's open landfills receive only 250 metric tonnes of garbage instead of the 10,000 metric tonnes they currently receive every day because an entity half the size of Shanks was able to make it disappear. In 2017, Shanks acquired its Dutch rival and emerged as the largest waste-management company in the Benelux region in a new avatar, Renewi.

The vibrant existence of Renewi rests on long-term contracts from municipalities to manage waste processing in their respective zones. Additionally, it signs contracts with private colonies and construction companies to process the waste generated from their respective establishments. But this was made possible due to regulations and policies that mandated safe and efficient recycling over blatant dumping. This compelled local municipalities to internalize this cost through user fees (and/or taxes) and a superior waste-collection infrastructure, at one end, and gunning formal commercial arrangements with enterprises like Renewi for waste disposal, on the other.

The intention of Indian national policy should be to create choices for the states to pursue in a manner that neither is the immediate need compromised nor are the long-term social development benefits ignored. A status quo will be the only item that should not be considered. Stable cities or regions that are no longer at the cusp of urbanization witness a low growth rate of new households, host few migrants, and are devoid of informal living, and thus can be the perfect laboratories to experiment with a model that can concurrently pursue recycling and social development as one. Such cities should not be piloted for costly solutions and should instead aim for a circular existence on the lines of the state of Sikkim. In measurable terms, any Indian city or town that generates less than 500 tonnes of garbage per day can aspire to such a vision and accordingly build waste-disposal assets around it. For such a recycling approach to work, cities must create a web of sorting and recycling centers in every ward of the town to replace the current informal arrangement. These centers will collect, sort, and ready the waste for its onward journey to a centralized location and reduce both the cost and time of the recycling process. Biodegradable solid waste collected at recycling centers will be transported in semi-finished form to a central location for compost processing and packaging. Plastic, glass, metal, and paper waste can all be made ready as raw material for reuse. Wood, construction waste, automobile, and electronic waste can be routed through this infrastructure for a circular outcome. The nimble success of Mysuru in this regard offers hope in the merits of this approach.

For cities that generate a high volume of waste, however, say, above 1,500 tonnes per day, the time taken to build capability and capacity for such models will fall short in addressing the waste-disposal challenge. Such cities need industrial solutions that by definition are based on the economies of scale and aggregation. Therefore, an industrial model that can view waste generated from these cities as a precious resource to be processed through an integrated model of sanitary landfills, waste incineration plants, and resource recovery centers will be an effective remedy. States will require such a federal mandate to experiment with different ideas and possibilities.

Some states might take a hands-off approach and want that the waste of their respective cities should be processed by experts in a safe and efficient manner. They may invite private capital, but its representatives may demand the necessary enabling conditions to accept. For instance, private sector enterprises will surely expect to receive only segregated waste as a precondition for their economic viability and therefore may demand a greater role in controlling waste-collection systems. Such states can bundle the waste disposal and collection services in the cities in order to onboard private capital, as is the case with the Waste Management, Inc. in the USA. This enterprise emerged while addressing the challenge that waste disposal is only as good as the waste-collection system. Instead of the local governance underwriting the risk of unsegregated waste landing up at the doorstep of disposal facilities, it bundled the functions of waste collection and disposal into one scope of opportunity for the private capital. Licenses were issued to Waste Management, Inc., among other private companies, to manage this bundled offer. This allowed the company to collect segregated waste from doorsteps and dispose it through sanitary landfills and recycling plants. Federal regulations provided the framework to manage this bundle. This allowed the private companies to reposition themselves from waste-disposal operators to waste-management solutions providers, thus weeding out informality. In this manner, Waste Management, Inc. emerged as the largest player in the waste-management industry of the USA. Interestingly, its disposal infrastructure contributes only 30 percent of the company's revenue, earned through the sale of energy and materials recovered from waste-disposal operations. The company earns most of its revenue from collection, which is done through an elaborate waste-collection infrastructure supported by 300 waste transfer stations spread across the country. Federal and local laws mandate subscription to such a service allow the company to enter into service contracts to collect waste from residential colonies, municipalities, commercial centers, industrial units, and other such waste-generating establishments.

Few Indian states may take a contrarian view away from this approach and adopt a participatory approach toward enterprise development for waste disposal instead. These states may seek resource recovery and waste-disposal expertise through partnerships and alliances and in turn view themselves as incubators of such enterprises. These special purpose ventures can even build and operate waste-disposal assets like sanitary landfills, incinerators, recycling plants, e-waste management facilities, as shared resources for cities, towns, and villages of the state. This approach can allow state governments to build waste-disposal assets for scale and efficiency under one entity and offer them to the local governance.

In 2012, Kanpur, supported by funding from the central government, in private partnership built an integrated waste-processing plant under the public–private partnership framework. A private partner and the Kanpur Municipal Body were allotted 110 acres of land to build assets and conduct waste-disposal operations. Today, the facility processes 1,500 tonnes of solid municipal waste daily. Ninety kilometers away, the municipal corporation of Lucknow, generating the same amount of solid municipal waste daily, also attempted to build such assets on its own, albeit with limited success. Midway between Kanpur and Lucknow falls the city of Unnao that also produces a decent quantity of industrial and household waste. Only if the issue of waste disposal is upstreamed can the waste-disposal entity of Kanpur be scaled up as a common infrastructure for the cities of Lucknow, Kanpur, Unnao, and all the other towns situated in between. The existing resources and capabilities can be shared across for the efficient conversion of raw waste into segregated and semi-processed form. This waste can be transported as pallets by railway for final processing and recovery of energy or resources. Pune–Mumbai, Ajmer–Jaipur, Agra–Mathura, Indore–Dewas–Bhopal, Bhilai–Raipur, Chennai–Vellore, Cuttack–Bhubaneswar, Ahmedabad–Vadodara, and Ludhiana–Jallandhar are sister cities that represent low hanging fruits for an active approach by state governments to build common waste disposal infrastructure. The Renova Group, jointly owned by nine municipalities in western Sweden, offers a worthy template to emulate. Under its ownership are infrastructure and operations that dispose waste using a combination of waste-to-energy incineration technology and recycling methods. It also extends its services to other establishments, institutions, and local bodies. In 2016, it processed more than 3,100 metric tonnes of waste on a daily basis and generated US$ 150 million in revenues.

There is no reason for Indian states to stop short in determining the vision for such entities and to not offer their service to other states through inter-state treaties. States can view their geographic advantages and aspire to become formal centers for recycling and waste disposal for other states. Rajasthan, for instance, can enter into such an agreement with the land-stressed state like Delhi, where waste from the capital city can be sent for processing to pre-identified recycling centers in Rajasthan. Through similar treaties, a state like Madhya Pradesh can take advantage of its central location and offer its waste-disposal industry to neighboring states like Odisha, Maharashtra, and Andhra Pradesh. Moreover, using the railways network to fulfil such interstate agreements is a lucrative opportunity for the Indian Railways to improve its freight load factor.

Given India's humungous waste-disposal agenda, there are immense possibilities to seek interesting combinations. National waste-disposal guidelines should aim to create a modular menu of choices. For instance, guidelines can mandate a mix of waste-disposal approaches on the basis of the quantum of waste disposed in a city or a village. Cities that generate more than 2,000 tonnes of waste per day can be mandated to onboard entities that use a combination of sanitary landfills, waste-to-energy incinerators, and recycling plants. On similar lines, cities that generate 500–2,000 tonnes of waste per day may be nudged toward waste-to-energy plants and recycling methods, whereas cities that generate less than 500 tonnes must make a compulsory transition toward recycling by onboarding vendors that offer these services. This will save dumping in open landfills and informal recycling chains that attempt to make the waste disappear through crude, unregulated, and exploitative means.

In early 2016, Beirut, Lebanon, made global headlines for an infamous photograph entitled 'River of Garbage' – piles of garbage dumped in the open for months replaced the river water with garbage bags. Nearly thirty people lost their lives when a garbage landfill collapsed in Colombo, Sri Lanka, in April 2017 and more than a hundred people died in a similar tragedy in Addis Ababa, Ethiopia. In December 2015, a construction debris pile in Shenzhen, China, gave way, killing nearly seventy. There tragedies are unfortunate data point in this recurring theme of the waste-disposal challenge that uniformly grips emerging economies the world over. Countries in Asia and Africa are constantly taking a stab at piecemeal solutions to rid themselves of their rising mountains of garbage. Banning the use of plastic in Kenya and Sri Lanka is a direct result of these attempts. Some countries like Russia are increasingly toying with the idea of exporting waste to countries, just as Sweden that now seeks garbage from other countries to keep its infrastructure alive, or Turkish companies that have taken over the waste-disposal functions of cities like Karachi, or even Chinese resource recovery specialists that are increasingly enticing developing countries like India with their offerings.

In these pursuits is the silent rise of a global resource recovery industry that is poised to play an important role in the new wave of globalization and geopolitics. It will be a colossal miss if India does not participate actively to turn its own waste-disposal challenge on its head to emerge as global leader in resource recovery and waste recycling. Among the advocated state-sponsored enterprises, cooperatives, and private-capital-backed entities as solutions for India's waste disposal lies a unique opportunity to build a resource recovery industry bottom-up and position it as a viable destination for countries that struggle with this challenge. Other than the economic opportunity, it could make way for an enviable destination for formal, quality jobs. These factors together could command enough heft of their own and be a useful tool for soft diplomacy with exciting possibilities. Why can't the Indian state of Uttar Pradesh think of forming an entity like Renova and offer its services to Nepal, given their geographic proximity, and process Kathmandu's waste? Or states like Orissa and Andhra Pradesh entering into waste disposal partnerships with countries like Bangladesh, Vietnam or Myanmar and offer them formal waste recycling solutions via the sea route? The emergence of Alaan on the coast of Gujarat as an informal global ship junkyard and Panipat as a recycling hub for the world's discarded clothing proves the economic merit for India to pursue a leadership tag in global recycling and resource recovery. But that Panipat and Alaan exist as subaltern sweatshops without regulations and guidelines also signifies India's inability to connect industrial policy with lucrative economic opportunity. These opportunities require umbrella of incentives, a formal workforce, safe working conditions, technical expertise, processing norms, capital and land to seize the global opportunity. Instead, they receive child labor, antiquated infrastructure and dangerous working conditions. Underneath India's challenge to dispose waste lies this global opportunity that is currently up for grabs. Instead of handing it away on a platter or responding to it through an informal system, state sponsored solutions will need to travel beyond our shores to make this a game changer.

Upon his return from South Africa, Mahatma Gandhi traveled extensively across India and wrote about the villages and his vision for them. He recognized them as circular economic units that consumed only enough resources (land, labor, capital) to cater to the need of the entire village, plus a little extra. The availability of skills and labor here ensured equilibrium between production and the consumption cycle. Therefore, he championed the preservation – and development – of artisanal craft and skills in villages over industrialization. He perhaps despised the fact that man-made reasons like famine, de-forestation, industrialization and urbanization disrupt the self-sufficient nature of the villages and that may be why we find him sitting on the opposing side of the industrialization debate.

> I would say that if the village perishes, India will perish too. India will be no more India. Her own mission in the world will get lost. The revival of the village is possible only when it is no more exploited. Industrialization on a mass scale will necessarily lead to passive or active exploitation of the villagers as the problems of competition and marketing come in. Therefore, we have to concentrate on the village being self-contained, manufacturing mainly for use. Provided this character of the village industry is maintained, there would be no objection to villagers using even the modern machines and tools that they can make and can afford to use. Only they should not be used as a means of exploitation of others.

Industrialization entails the absorption of man-made inventions into daily living that permanently alters human behavior. The continuous desire to pursue 'bigger,' 'better,' and 'more' ran contrary to Gandhi's belief of living in harmony with nature. His anti-industrialization stance should be viewed as a resistance of a conservationist, rather contrary to the accepted norms of human evolution. The artisan and skill-driven cooperative living imagined by Gandhi definitely made for an idyllic setting. But had India taken an anti-industrialization stance and prioritized the development of villages on the lines prescribed by him, the idea of 'India' as we know it would have come under serious stress. A village-focused development would not have allowed the non-rural narrative to grow and the cottage industry approach would have prevented India from access to technology, knowledge, methods, and processes that defined the post–World War II order. The notion of such an India would have faced an existential threat, given its geographic vastness and the nature of the world order following the War: the world around India hardly provided the safety or comfort to build a country as a conglomeration of idyllic villages. Gandhi's anti-industrialization stance would have prevented timely investments in national security, electricity, higher education, and transportation. Major nations around the world would have taken a significantly different developmental trajectory, as they did, exposing the idea of India to vulnerability of isolation or possible mutation.

Gandhi's deep desire to correct the centuries-long structural flaws of Indian villages was a strong underlying reason for his vision. But the din of the then ideological and geopolitical debate wrongly interpreted it on the sole plank of anti-industrialization. There was no need for independent India to abandon Gandhi's desire while choosing industrialization. It is a different matter, though, that our path to industrialization was paved with false starts and missed opportunities, which would indeed have let Sir Mokshagundam Visvesvaraya's expectations down. It was possible for Gandhi's ideal villages to coexist in Visvesvaraya's industrialized India. The rural development narrative of independent India completely eclipsed the idea of invigorating the villages and correcting the structural flaws they had inherited, as was the Gandhian philosophy. Managing waste disposal in the villages was one of these flaws.

In a letter that Gandhi received in 1937 from a villager from Birbhum district in West Bengal, he was asked how he perceived an 'ideal village' and what problems he thought plagued it. Gandhi's response to the question, published in *Harijan*, a weekly publication that he edited since the 1930s, was as follows:

> An ideal village will be so constructed as to lend itself to perfect sanitation. The very first problem the village worker will solve is its sanitation.... If the worker became a voluntary scavenger, he would begin by collecting night soil and turning it into manure and sweeping village streets. He will tell people how and where they should perform daily functions and speak to them on the value of sanitation and the great injury caused by its neglect. The worker will continue to do the work whether the villagers listen to him or not.

This reflects Gandhi's dismay on two issues that concerned sanitation in Indian villages. First, the callous attitude toward cleanliness as depicted by villages; second, his abhorrence of the practice of manual scavenging for solid waste disposal. Gandhi's extreme criticism of sanitation in Indian villages was from the perspective of the universal values of human dignity, equality, and mutual respect. He thus viewed these shortcomings with remarkable clarity. The policy abandonment on these suggestions of Gandhi, however, exacerbated a sanitation mess few decades later.

The prevalence of manual scavenging in Indian villages partially addressed the disposal of solid human waste, and the practice continued unabated for many decades in independent India as well. Households that could afford toilets in their homes employed the services of the Dalit, who would haul night soil and other wet waste from the village and dump it in an open pit on the outskirts. For the majority, however, open defecation served as a convenient option and to that extent, manual scavenging was only part of the waste disposal solution.

The sewage and wet waste from the village households found its way to no-man's land through meandering open drains and formed stinky puddles here and there, or landed up in the water bodies that had been at the center of the very existence of the village for centuries. Occasionally, the Dalit was also detailed to unclog the open drains, when the stink went beyond tolerable. This arrangement rarely caused any discomfort to the consuming class of the village and this apathy was a major reason for Gandhi's dejection. There may have been a choked drain once in a while, or a puddle of black sludge in the center of the village. There was always a Dalit on call to fix all these, and the size of the villages and populations were small enough to hardly ever stress the arrangement. Other than Gandhi, perhaps, no one saw the deficiency of this orchestration. For the rest of the village folk, open defecation was the norm for its ease and convenience, as it eliminated the need for manual scavenging to dispose the solid waste, and because the act of waste generation, collection and disposal was all rolled into one. For this reason alone, open defecation remains a hardwired practice for 60 percent of rural households till date.

For all its limitations of the political narrative that emerged around Dalits in independent India, it showcased at least the political dividends to be had from affirmative action to bring the 'lower caste' in parity with the 'upper caste,' on many counts. This helped India to take legislative steps to reduce manual scavenging, so that by 2011, only a few hundred thousand people were engaged in the practice. This progress, though, was faulty on two major counts. First, it did not take away the convenience of open defecation for the majority of village folk as it did not require manual scavenging. The call against open defecation gained mainstream political sponsorship seventy years after independence, which created an aggressive policy push toward toilets inside every rural home. Undoubtedly, it was the right first step and began to change social behavior across rural India. Starting troubles notwithstanding, people saw the virtues of the dignity, health and comfort afforded by closed toilets at home and steadily began to opt for them. People began to augment the welfare scheme money with their own to build superior toilets. The final verdict on this initiative is awaited with anticipation and hope and will get delivered in the 2021 Census. (For reference, in 2011, more than four out of every ten households did not have a toilet at home.)

A victory on this count may not, however, ensure triumph over the larger issue of rural sanitation. People relieving themselves inside the toilets solved only one part of the problem, in that it ensured the discharge and collection of solid waste in a closed setting. Even so, the hauling and disposal (or recycle) of this waste in a safe manner was dependent on a sewage system, to which every toilet should be connected. This was the second fault. This part of the challenge remained a black hole and makes activists like Bezwada Wilson highly skeptical about the efficacy of this unidimensional policy push. The statistical decline in manual scavenging only means that there is no longer a need to collect and dispose night soil from households which can afford to install a toilet. But for every rural toilet to be connected to a safe and efficient sewage system, India must still cover some distance. Until such time, the efforts do not make a dent in the inextricable link between the 'lower caste' and the waste management in villages. Although manual scavenging was successfully stricken off the list, the absence of closed drainage and effluent treatment systems continue to put the caste system in play for manually cleaning open drains and carrying away waste, bare handed. So long as the 'toilet drive' is not bolstered with the enabling infrastructure and operational arrangement, kitchen, bathrooms, and cattle waste will continue to require hauling at one stage or another, perpetuating the indignity of the age old practices. The singular focus on building toilets will merely shift the scourge of manual scavenging from hauling night soil to cleaning open drains, septic tanks and clogged sewers, while waste shall continue being disposed into water bodies, strewn on open plots of land and burnt. At some point in the future the toilet policy will need to recognize this lacuna. This course correction will change perceived character of toilets at home from stand-alone constructions to an integrated system of closed drainage, septic tanks and effluent treatment plants.

Rural India traveled in bullock carts, lived in houses made of mud and clay, produced its own grains and cooked its own food, when Gandhi traveled across India. Almost all the waste that the villages generated during his time was biodegradable and was either dumped on the outskirts or combusted in the open by employing the services of the Dalits. But the Indian villages of the twenty-first century are an entirely different beast as regards consumption characteristics. In 2006, Unilever, India's largest FMCG company, initiated an ambitious plan to increase the penetration of its sales in rural India through 'Project Shakti,' with the aim to identify women (*amma*s) and appoint them as company representatives. They would aggregate the demand from their respective villages and sell the company's products. The company's distribution structure backed them with supply chain support. Within the next decade, Unilever appointed 72,000 ammas who sold its shampoos, detergents, toothpaste, and other products to more than 150,000 villages. On similar lines, Hero Motors, India's largest two-wheeler automobile company, has 3,000 dealers in rural India, who contributed 48 percent of its annual sales in 2016. The twenty-first century Indian village consumes shampoos, tobacco and oil packed in plastic sachets; food and water in disposable containers during social functions; potato chips and namkeens vacuum packed in plastic bags. Village folk wear shirts and trousers made of polyester and shoes made from teflon and rubber foam. They use cement to build their homes and sprinkle their crops with fertilizer from gunny bags. They buy pens, condoms, sanitary napkins; batteries for torches, transistors and inverters, mobile phones and DVDs; and tyres and engine oil for their tractors and motorbikes.

Although this consumption binge does not necessarily reflect rural prosperity. But this constriction could not halt the march of factors that alter their consumption. State welfare support and migration of family members to cities and better employment opportunities allowed many rural households to augment their farming income with remittances and this kept their consumption relevant with changing times. Many shun farming altogether and adopt an urban flavor while retaining their rural habits. Such clusters, given their proximity to urban centers, became half-towns and half-villages and came to be officially classified as 'census towns' in the 2011 Census, which counted their numbers to be more than 3,000 across India. These enabling factors altered the consumption character of rural India and had a direct bearing on the rapid rise of the generated non-biodegradable waste. Ironically, the villages raced ahead to generate both biodegradable and non-biodegradable waste in equal halves, while struggling with open defecation and a lack of toilets. Though, in the backdrop of the changing consumption pattern, waste management in rural areas is not a problem unique to India. It remains an unresolved matter in far-flung villages even in clean countries. Hooper Bay, a remote village of 1,200 residents in Alaska, is devoid of closed sewer connections and a waste-management infrastructure that can address their consumption profile. The residents dump all waste into open landfills or burn it in the open that release dangerous toxins into the environment. A connected waste-management infrastructure is yet to reach Hooper Bay due to its remote location and perhaps a high cost of accessibility. The USA's struggles with this village also suggest the inadequacy of a purely industrial approach to solve the waste management woes of far-flung rural communities, which perhaps need a different perspective. It is in exactly such a scenario that Gandhi's call for invigorating rural communities to address their sanitation challenge themselves begins to make sense.

An average Indian village comprises 2,000 to 10,000 people, or nearly 500 to 1,500 hamlets. Nearly six lakh such villages sit in the vast hinterlands of the country and access to the nearest town is usually measured in time, not in distance. Not counting the agricultural waste of crop residue, the quantum of waste generated per day in these villages is roughly the same as a medium-sized residential colony in an urban setting. Therefore, it will be wrong to superimpose industrial scale template of waste disposal onto these hamlets, both for cost and for relevance. In the waste-disposal challenge of rural India lies an opportunity to invigorate the villages toward self-sufficiency, a goal Gandhi defined a century ago. The key is to interpret his call as 'zero-waste-discharge-villages' through community engagement. Given the inherent nature of Indian villages, it is not inconceivable for them to become zero-discharges communities sans caste biases. Toward this purpose, waste-disposal methods need modular and micro-solutions that can imbibe recycling and reuse with zeal and sincerity. If we get it right for one village, we will get it right for six lakh correcting the flawed social structure in the process.

The starting point for this blueprint will need to be a drainage system that should be designed with three specifications. First, the drainage or sewage system should be a closed one. Second, every household in the village should be connected to this system. Third, the drainage system should collect the majority of the wet and solid human waste and haul it to a central effluent treatment plant or for processing into compost and water harvesting for irrigation. These miniaturized processing centers should be so designed that they are cost-effective enough to absorb the unit economics of the village, while diverting the open drainage from eventually being dumped into water bodies or pooling in the open.

In September 2017, the Indian Agriculture Research Institute (IARI), New Delhi, indigenously developed an effluent treatment plant, which was installed in Farah village of Mathura district, as a pilot project. It was to process 40,000 liters of sewage generated from about 1,500 households per day, which was normally dumped into the Yamuna. This plant was developed with a technology that reduced its operational and maintenance cost to fewer than 3 percent of that incurred in a conventional effluent plant, but eliminated more than 75 percent of the heavy metal pollution. It also required only a fraction of the capital (US$ 80,000 or ₹45 lakhs) for construction, compared to a conventional plant which costs many times this amount. Such a cost-effective indigenous solution is truly a commendable achievement, but at the same time highlights the financial scale of waste-disposal challenge in rural India. On a standalone basis, a capital outlay of more than ₹103,500 crores (US$ 15 billion) will be required if such a system were to be installed in only 50 percent of Indian villages. The frugal cost and capital claims of the effluent plant still needs financial sponsorship, which was provided by the central government and exceptional intervention like that of a trust body which agreed to operate it in Farah. The coming together of such extraordinary circumstances to bring this plant to life attracts criticism. How many boxes of the political and policy checklist will have to be ticked off for the government to front ₹45 lakhs by way of seed capital and operational support in every Indian village? What is the likelihood of a trust coming forward and agreeing to owning and running the asset in six lakh villages?

It will be equally interesting to track the trajectory of the plant's operational success in a village like Farah, which is located in a district where more than 90 percent of the households rely on open drainage or have no drainage at all. For the IARI's plant to deliver the intended results, the village panchayat will have to ensure that the direction of the drainage is diverted away from the Yamuna and toward the plant.

It will have to ensure that the drains that haul waste from all the 1,500 households and other commercial units in the village toward the plant are covered over a period of time. It will also have to develop an operational blueprint so that the plant does not meet the same fate as that of many others built in the state and operate at below than 25 percent of their installed capacity. Of what use is the effluent treatment plant if it is not synced up with a closed drainage system that carries segregated wet and solid human waste toward it round the year? The panchayat of Farah will have to battle numerous financial and operational issues to build a supporting infrastructure and operate it for unhindered continuity. The exceptional benevolence of the trust and the one-time seed capital of the union government cannot solve the problem in isolation and the project may well have to rely on a sustained supply of such timely interventions from an extraordinary source to save the situation. Then the repeatability of this model as a standard package for rural waste disposal will be called into question. The true quest is for an operational and financing framework that can democratize IARI's effluent treatment plant across six lakh villages in the normal course. Any out-of-the-ordinary initiative that cannot be replicated may work in the short term, but will fall miserably short in the long run.

A user fee that is premised to correct the skewed social contract should partially fund such a plant and be a key supplier of repeatable and replicable source to make this project a success in rural India. This model can dip into present and future incomes and place covenants on welfare disbursements. When the operational funding of the infrastructure is secured by such a normal customer–vendor arrangement, it immediately elevates the project to operational viability. It starts to serve as a magnet for state and private expenditure to support it and become a key component of sustainability. State-funded welfare expenditure aimed at different goals like rural sanitation and job creation can immediately sense the repeatability potential of such a blueprint. Expenditures from private enterprises and development bodies will also relish its measurability potential to evaluate the impact of their investments. Local panchayats can rise up to own and operate such an asset and use it a tool to assert their autonomy. This will require the panchayats to operate an integrated waste-collection system and to aggregate the recovery of resources from the effluent treatment plant. Toward this purpose, they will need to understand the human capital and organizational structure required to run an enabling ecosystem such as this. They will have to become formal employers for plant operators, waste collectors, and technicians of various skills. They may have to invite rural households to volunteer for waste-management jobs and perhaps facilitate the formation of the cooperative structure to run the project. But, as we know, panchayats have intrinsic 'birth defects' that make them no more than cauldrons of nepotism and partisanship, and this may indeed remain a pipe dream. Then, talk of reforms in rural local governance that argue for the rapid deployment of a social capital policy to improve the operational capability of the panchayats suddenly starts to make sense – there is a link between reforms in the panchayat raj system and clean India after all.

Panchayats will need to act as owners and operators of waste-collection and segregation systems from every rural household and to manage all waste types in order to ensure that only solid municipal waste land up at the effluent treatment plants. They will require stamina to mandate every household to bag and segregate other waste types and to facilitate a community task force that will haul this segregated waste to a central location for targeted action. Here, the biodegradable waste will go to the village compost plant, while non-biodegradables will be sorted and packed for their onwards journey. To enable this journey, panchayats must enter into contracts with waste disposal enterprises located in the nearest city, for a commercial consideration, which will mandate them to pick up the non-biodegradable waste from the village at a predetermined frequency. The money thus paid by the panchayat to the waste-disposal entity can be fully or partly recovered from the households. Some villages may even proactively decide to put restrictions on the use of certain non-biodegradable materials to reduce the outflow to the waste-disposal enterprise. Some may get inspired with the language of commerce to install their own micro-recycling centers that can cater to the needs of the neighboring villages as well as their own. Such a recycling infrastructure can be developed as an economic hotspot for the entire village under a cooperative model as a promising alternative.

This blueprint envisages effluent treatment and compost plants in villages installed with underground sewers and drains. There should be waste-sorting centers for non-biodegradable waste and a panchayat-owned organizational set up that runs this infrastructure with binding contracts with residents and disposal-service providers. Every village should be in a position to recycle and reuse all biodegradable waste and segregate all non-biodegradable waste, making it ready for safe disposal. Finally, panchayats will need to act as aggregators to collect recycled effluent (compost) and softly mandate the usage of it among the villagers on a predetermined logic, based either on the human footprint of each household, or on the size of the landholding, or on a combination of the two.

This model for village waste-disposal infrastructure that is premised on user fees to correct the skewed social contract will surely need financial supplementation which can be channeled from public- and private-sector possibilities. For instance, the adoption of villages by private institutions committed to expenditure under corporate social responsibility can be productively channeled for implementation sponsorship. On similar lines, welfare expenditure of the state can be sharpened for effective deployment to provide the seed capital for such an ecosystem. This corpus should be built in such a way that it takes care of the operational cost of the recycling plant, the transportation cost to haul the waste to processing centers, and the waste-collection service in the village. The last mile haul of the non-biodegradable waste from the village to nearest waste-processing center in the city should also be a smooth transit. It is this financial and operational tie-up that can convert waste-disposal challenge in rural India into an opportunity for job creation and all-round development.

Panchayats will still need an organizational structure for such an ecosystem to come to life, but the vision of rural invigoration will remain a pipe dream should they attempt to retrofit the caste system on this blueprint. Rural invigoration needs to be married with human capability so that the dependence of rural waste disposal on the caste system can be broken down. The panchayat's ownership and operational control of such a waste-management ecosystem should be interpreted as every resident of the village becoming its willing owner under a cooperative structure. This cooperative movement will become the lynchpin of the waste-management blueprint, with the panchayat acting as its custodian. Through such a cooperative structure, the village may offer its waste-management facilities to its neighboring villages. It will not be surprising, if such a co-operative movement could well fast track our villages out of the sanitation mess before urban India. Indian villages are at a juncture where they can still be maneuvered away from the wrong path urban India took on waste disposal. If India can eradicate polio, arrest child marriage, increase enrolment in the schools and put a mobile phone in the hands of every villager, it can surely also correct this social flaw that Gandhi so despised.

Early in their journeys, clean countries took an infrastructure view toward the issue of waste disposal. This changed the paradigm and the altered perspective allowed the governments to define the enablers needed to discharge the function more efficiently. Governments took on the role of facilitators and allowed capital participation to take ownership of expertise. Consequently, government, and more specifically local governance, could channelize its energy to legislate, build superior infrastructure, define guidelines and rules, monitor breeches, enforce laws, and act as a trusted mediator between the consumer (citizens) and the waste-disposal enterprises. The participation of capital in waste disposal was not imagined merely to ease the burden of waste disposal on the local governance, but acted as a proxy for expertise to improve productivity, efficiency, and effectiveness of waste-disposal processes. It was expected to dispose waste in adherence to environment and public health safeguards, install capacities to process the ever-rising volumes of waste and develop viable technologies which could handle the complexity of the changing nature of waste and root out informality. Not surprisingly, these countries were keen to deploy this capital and citizens were ready to pay for it. The Indian policy on waste disposal will need to transition toward this viewpoint. The mettle of this transition will be tested when India begins to think about waste disposal as a laboratory of scientific excellence, rather than a towering garbage heap. Young Indian minds should aspire to technical diplomas and degrees as waste recycling and resource recovery engineers, rather than underpaid sanitation workers stuck in unimaginative jobs and India's commerce policy can visualize the waste disposal industry as the new jewel of India's export basket.

By 2050, India will be among the top three nations in the world on the quantum of waste it will generate annually. This humungous agenda of waste disposal that stares at us in the near future cannot be left at the mercy of open combustion, dump yards and landfills, child labor, ragpickers, or shanties that double up as recycling centers. On the compass of human dignity and respect for the environment, these arrangements do not score any favorable arguments, whereas the technical incapability of these arrangements is the chief reason India dumps 80 percent of its colossal quantities of generated waste without any intervention or treatment. India will need to entice its ten million young minds that enter the job market every year with the waste disposal industry. Their skills, as varied as machine operators for waste disposal plants, waste sorting technologies, material science and manufacturing knowledge for re-cycled products can make the waste disposal industry the new destination for the talent pool. A new nomenclature of 'waste disposal' is perhaps in order as resource recovery will allow the Indian political order to tie up its perpetual hunt for new jobs and the 'sanitation challenge' at hand.

In the 1950s, Indian cities were waking up to the idea of electricity in homes. A localized market quickly emerged where small time operators generated electricity with diesel generators and supplied it to a few homes who could afford it. Imagine if the electricity sector had been left to such informality. Many sub-standard diesel generators would be electrifying our homes through a mess of entangled wires and polluting the air, instead of giant power transmission lines, silent turbines and sub-stations. In today's context, such a poor infrastructure is unimaginable for India's electricity needs. And yet, the Indian mind is conditioned to absorb such a subaltern arrangement for waste disposal, which continues thoughtlessly without any imagination or inventiveness. Conversely, waste disposal needs to be imagined just as the power industry in reverse, as argued throughout this narrative. There are plants (thermal, nuclear, hydro) that generate electricity and distribute it to homes through an elaborate formal infrastructure. Waste generated in homes needs to be hauled to processing centers and eventually to disposal plants for recycling and resource recovery. If not for our biases, how hard is it to imagine that?

Javed Akhtar, a prominent poet, gave an emotional farewell speech in Parliament, on the completion of his term in its upper house in March 2016.

> India's journey till date since Independence deserves a standing ovation because it has been on the bedrock of parliamentary

> democracy. Much more could have been done but whatever we have achieved is also no less of a feat. From here going forward, we have to think about who should we compare ourselves to? What kind of nations should become our benchmarks? If you learn from your mistakes, you are wise. If you learn from other people's mistakes, you are wiser.

For waste disposal, India needs to think about First-World nations and learn from their mistakes of the last century, their trials, tribulations, misery, struggles and their abundant wisdom in retrospect.

The quest is for a formal waste-disposal industry to emerge that can take over the job of disposing waste from local governance. The government will become a customer of this industry, which will in turn migrate existing open landfills to closed scientific landfills and/or many other non-landfill-based waste-disposal solutions. This industry will host cooperatives, public, and private enterprises that will build and operate waste-to-energy incinerators for organic waste, resource recovery centers for electronic and construction waste, processing plants for biohazardous waste, and energy plants and organic fertilizer pits for agriculture or biodegradable waste within its fold. Waste will be aggregated across towns and villages bringing in economies of scale, making the process of waste-disposal controlled, efficient, and effective. The controlled waste-disposal processing will abolish waste leakages into the environment, curbing air, water and soil pollution, and purging the waste disposal sector of informality, scoring a resounding victory over child labor, exploitation, and public health risks. It will free-up the precious bandwidth of local civic bodies to focus their energies on waste collection and enforcement. The desire is to significantly increase India's installed formal capacity to process generated waste by a factor of ten and to make it work round the clock for a cleaner and healthier outcome. Otherwise, the cesspool is growing and we are slowly drowning in it.

7

THE NEW AGE WASTE

The Silent Killer

The most recent type of waste that our planet finds itself battling with as a direct outcome of our 'smarter' existence' is e-waste. Products that have one or a combination of processor chips, an electrical circuitry, and an energy storage mechanism is classified as e-waste at the end of their lifecycle. This includes discarded mobile phones, batteries, laptops, computers, television sets, air conditioners, refrigerators, microwaves, tablets, music systems, and so on. It is a 'silent' waste because unlike stale food and rotting animal carcasses, e-waste does not play with our visual or olfactory senses, nor do they dirty our roads and neighborhoods.

We know that every incremental addition of garbage on this planet is a direct outcome of the insatiable human desire to progress. Plastic waste made way with the advent of industrialization, construction waste resulted from urbanization, and medical waste made a grand entry with the advançements in healthcare. Similarly, e-waste was a side effect of our desire to make smart machines that could bring 'convenience' and 'quality' into our daily lives. From this desire emerged gadgets packed with silicon, copper, gold, silver, lead, zinc, and polymers. These appliances came in all shapes and sizes – from giant TV sets to miniature computers; towering speaker stacks to mini music systems; tablets to wearable smart wristwatches. They did not guzzle electricity, were portable, had remarkable alacrity and presented limitless possibilities, making them an essential accessory to human living in no time. They too had a shelf life, as any other man-made goods, which was a function of usage and time. However, after the completion of their natural lifecycle, when these gadgets were discarded it was realized that they could be classified neither as wet waste nor as dry waste; they were neither plastic nor metals; hence, 'e-waste' seemed an appropriate nomenclature for it.

A categorization was, however, just the start of a very long and arduous waste-management saga that outsmarted all other waste-management challenges in the First World. A consistent economic growth in a relatively stable world post World War II created ripe conditions for consumer electronics to become objects of common need. TVs brought world into people's in a jiffy, microwaves dished out cooked meals within minutes and washing machines gave people freedom from their laundry woes. While the world marched into the twenty-first century, people bought increasingly more TVs, refrigerators, music system, microwaves, washing machines and mobile phones to make life more convenient and efficient. Then came an intelligent twist to this consumption binge – technology obsolescence. In order to keep this heady mix of convenience and choice relevant, the electronics industry spurred innovation and spewed out 'smarter' gadgets with surprising regularity and speed, leading to faster obsolescence of existing gadgets with every passing year. Pagers became obsolete; whereas the TVs changed their character from a picture tube based technology to an LCD technology. Computers became faster and leaner, while mobile phones raced ahead from being merely communication devices to personal companions. This disruptive reinterpretation of electronic gadgets enabled the growth of tertiary industries like semiconductors, processors, software and application development, and complemented the growth of telecommunications and the Internet. The ecosystem quickly emerged as an intricate mesh that crisscrossed countries and continents – processor chips were designed in the UK; semiconductors were tested in India; components were manufactured and assembled in Chain and Japan. With efficient logistics, this thriving global trade succeeded in putting these gadgets in the hands of consumers across the globe faster than ever before.

The electronics industry emerged as a bellwether of economic growth and jobs for countries like China, India, and Japan. In the case of India, a mobile-phone-led ecosystem supported a direct employment of 2.2 million people in 2014. Owing to the industry's concentrated efforts to make the world smarter and more connected, human beings gained access to the Internet at an unprecedented rate. In 2007, merely 20 percent of the world's households had access to the Internet, which increased to nearly 48 percent by 2017. These connected households not only represented units with internet access but were also manifestations of the premise that modern living was impossible without consumer electronics. Children were able to do their homework faster, without having to lift their pencils. People could access their money held at banks in remote locations without ever having to step out of their homes. Staying in touch with friends and family was never easier, and e-commerce presented many enticing opportunities for retail therapy. Consumer electronics were no longer a matter of discretion but an all-pervasive phenomenon. The logic for technology obsolescence was indeed elegant.

Faster obsolescence, however, artificially reduced the lifecycle of an electronic gadget. People replaced their gadgets faster for the next upgrade or a better alternative than they did before, thereby shortening the ownership period. Consumers were unable to resist the seductive appeal of an upgraded device much before the natural decay of their existing one. A laptop, for example, would hardly ever be owned for more than five years, even though its natural lifespan was twenty, because consumers would go for a sleek new model that was perceived to accomplish more. The electronic industry further ring-fenced this faster replacement cycle with proprietary software, hardware, and IP protection which made the reuse and even repairs of these products economically un-lucrative and out-of-bounds for consumers in the First World. It was economically more efficient for the consumer to go for an upgrade than to try and retro-fit existing gadgets.

Retro-fitted solutions never stood a chance against the lure of the upgrade at a fractional more. The story of the LCD television best captures this sentiment. When televisions were adapted to digital technology, everything from movie making to broadcast feed began to move toward the digital era. Analogue Cathode Ray Tube televisions which were the mainstay of the television industry until then were not designed for this digital era and became obsolete. Consumers swiftly discarded their CRT televisions in favor of digital ones, and so began the creation of television sets as e-waste. Consequently, the cathode ray tubes from these sets, which were packed with lead, mercury and phosphorus landed up in open landfills and in the informal trade. However, CRT televisions merely needed a small digital box to be attached to them in order to make them receive digital signals, was a fact that was cleverly concealed from the consumers, so as not to impede the potentially lucrative consumption glut that followed. Many CRT televisions prematurely became dangerous e-waste on the back of this crafty spin-doctoring.

In 2000, the USA generated 1.9 million metric tonnes of e-waste from CRT televisions. By 2017, this figure had increased to 6.3 million metric tones, an increase of more than 3.3 times in seventeen years. The disruptive shift in sales of consumer electronics in the same period is noteworthy: in 2000 there were hardly any smartphones sold in the USA. In 2017, however, smartphones in excess of US$ 50 billion were sold in the country. Before 2010, hardly any American adult owned a tablet computer, but by 2017 more than half of them owned at least one such device.

This binge led to increasingly higher volumes of electronics goods getting discarded with every passing year. These gadgets were smarter than ever before and were made up of a complex chemistry. Chemicals that are lethal in their naked form were packed in to make these 'smart' electronic gadgets and were manufactured in sanitized plants. But this 'smart' device was an unknown beast that had no precedence. It was part polymer and part metals. They had resins and polymers that could poison the air if incinerated in the open. Liquid crystal displays (LCDs) contained mercury. Batteries contained lead, nickel, cadmium, and mercury. Plastic casings contain brominated flame retardants (BFRs) and polychlorinated biphenyl (PCB), and the processor board was additionally packed with lead, beryllium, antimony, and organohalogen compounds. Consumer electronics made the world interconnected, supercharged, and on the move no doubt, but it was only a matter of time before the unbridled aftermath of this consumption binge hit the world. How do you dispose of a gadget that did not even exist in 2000? Do you burn it and risk the release of dangerous fumes and toxic metals into the air? Or do you dump it in a landfill and risk contaminating the soil with forever?

The disruptive dance of gadgets and technology soon became society agnostic and that added the dimension of scale to the issue. The innovation that the electronics industry spurred made the devices (and the accompanying ecosystem) affordable beyond the First World and it was only a matter of time before the unbridled aftermath of this consumption binge hit the rest of the world, which it did. By 2017, Asia and Africa alone were responsible for nearly half of the e-waste generated in the world. It took these regions less than twenty years to oust the First World as leading e-waste generators on the planet.

We can argue that the generation itself of e-waste, should not attract any criticism in isolation and neither should the human desire to go digital and become smarter. If the matter of waste management, especially in the First World, is resolved on many fronts like segregation, collection, and disposal, then the generated e-waste should simply be a modular addition to this existing framework should score a win for this argument at least in the First World. The criticism is the plunge of this optimistic premise. In 2017, the world generated nearly 45 million metric tonnes of e-waste, but only 20 percent could be traced to secured processing methods: the rest disappeared without any documented traceability. It was likely to have been dumped in open landfills or processed through informal channels be it in Europe, where non-traceability of e-waste stood at 65 percent, or in Asia where it is 85 percent, or the Americas where it is 83 percent, or Africa where nearly 100 percent of e-waste is untraceable. The unfortunate revelation in these numbers is the surprisingly low traceability rates in Europe when within its fold are countries that are benchmarks for circular existence. Then why is it that its existing waste-management infrastructure is unable to capture and process e-waste in a secured manner and show the way to the rest of the world?

The realization that the management of e-waste is poised to become a serious environmental hazard gathered momentum in Europe in the 1980s, when discarded refrigerators began to hit landfills in increasing numbers. A discarded refrigerator was a cocktail of toxic metals and gases that threatened to damage the earth's ozone layer. This created an urgency among European nations to draft laws banning the disposal of home appliances in landfills. E-waste is very different in its composition from other forms of waste forms and such a ban did not provide for a safer alternative. The capability of local municipal bodies in Europe was grossly inadequate to appreciate any other form of disposal method but landfills for these discarded appliances. The proliferation of mobile phones and computers were still some years in the future suppressing the decibels of the issue on the urgency barometer.

The economics of waste, for the lack of formal options, always finds an alternative course no matter how destructive the outcome. The landfill ban on e-waste in Europe prompted stakeholders to look for alternatives to pass on the task because it did not mandate them to seek solutions. When the aim is not to find a solution, one way to solve a problem is to make it someone else's and that is exactly what happened. Countries in Europe (followed by North America) started the practice of exporting e-waste to the Third World countries for discarding and disposal. These countries had a readily available solution, but one that was without the pangs of environmental protection, legislation, safe working conditions, labor rights, or public health risk safeguards. Dismantling of discarded electronic gadgets was simple enough – hammer them down to separate different components, give them a chemical bath to recover precious metals and sell them for money. All one needed was a hammer, an acid concoction, bare human hands and a shack, and voila, the processing of e-waste made a great deal of economic sense. Countries like Nigeria, Ghana, China, and Philippines rushed to seize the opportunity and an intricate global trade of supply chains, middlemen, agents, and recyclers sprung up. The adverse implication of its informality on public health and environment was of little consequence. There was a sane reason to ban the dumping of this waste into landfills in Europe. But the 'gold rush' to bathe discarded printed circuit boards with acid and strip them of their precious metals without any protective gear in make shift shanties outweighed those reasons in the third world. This trade was unperturbed about dumping the effluents of these baths in the open and permanently contaminating the vicinity with heavy metals like tin, lead, arsenic, cadmium and mercury. It was ignorant of the dangers that dioxins in the e-waste posed when released into the air and water and breach the food chain to enter the human body, and cause reproductive disorders, cancers, growth retardation, tumours and nervous diseases.

The electronic devices were manufactured in a controlled and sanitized environment. It therefore made no sense to dispose of them using medieval methods and crude tools, in an uncontrolled environment. It does not take much of an expertise in material science to understand this causation. But the global informal trade of processing the e-waste in the third world was more to do with the abandonment of the issue by the mainstream and less with its own nefarious intentions. The First-World countries, which were then the nerve center of the electronics binge, were complacent enough to note that the e-waste they were generating was getting processed far away from their shore and was thus legally defendable. They made the easier choice: feign ignorance of the informal recycling industry, knowing full well the ramifications of hammering out gold and silver from mother boards under the open sky.

The First World's selective exclusion of the problem of e-waste that prompted it to depend on third world countries for the processing and disposing of was a chief reason for the world at large to let down its guard against the rapid proliferation of e-waste. It was not until a little before the explosive growth of computers and mobile phones in 1989 that disposal of e-waste attracted the world's attention. The Basel Convention of 1992, ratified by 182 nations, including India, banned the First-World nations from exporting their hazardous waste to developing countries for disposal. Curiously, the USA signed the Convention, but abstained from ratifying it. For the advocates of the Convention, it may have seemed the right first step, but the gaping holes in retrospect point to the lack of the stakeholders' collective will to take the issue seriously. Until the start of the twenty-first century, the world was still taking in implications of the electronic devices that were slowly taking over peoples' lives and the fact that these have a shelf-life and need to be done away with, like any other consumable. The architects of the Convention lacked foresight because while it hoped to stop the global movement of e-waste, in return it offered no alternative to dispose of the obvious fall-out of the burgeoning demand for consumer electronics around the globe in the not-so-distant future under the gab of technology obsolescence.

The treaty hoped to stop the global movement of e-waste, but in return offered no alternative. The economics of e-waste soon figured that the Basel treaty was only a minor bump in the road. Some clever wordsmithing was all that was needed to figure a way around it. The treaty explicitly barred the cross-border movement of e-waste for disposal, but was silent on cross border trade of used electronics meant for refurbishment or re-use. A country was therefore well within its rights to export pre-owned electronic gadgets for refurbishment to another country. Once these gadgets landed at the ports of the importer, there was no teeth in the treaty to check if the preowned gadgets were indeed headed for repairs and re-use or were being stripped for material extraction informally. This interpretation of the Basel treaty gave a new lease of life to the global informal trade of e-waste processing. The treaty's wordsmithing incidentally coincided with the incremental growth of mobile phones and other 'smart' gadgets, as bulky electronics gave way to sleeker and faster devices, which were in-turn replaced with even more intuitive ones and so on and so forth. But, by virtue of being smarter, these new age devices were also packaged with even more complex chemistry than ever before.

When the world marched into the twenty-first century binging on these 'smarter' gadgets, this informal trade merely extrapolated itself to grab whatever of these smart devices in discarded state it could and miraculously made them disappear without a trace. By the twenty-first century, this trade was so entrenched that it merely extended its hold on the intense profiteering opportunity that the world's rising consumption of electronics presented for e-waste processing. In a matter of few years the global trade of e-waste recycling mushroomed with interconnected supply chains, shipment routes, networks, agents, and intermediaries, who efficiently hauled it from the consumption hubs to sites in the Third World for disposal without restrictions, regulations, or trade barriers. Disposal 'labs' in dilapidated shanties next to water bodies hammered out and washed discarded gadgets with acids to extract precious metals, while spewing heavy metals and dioxins into the environment. Guiyu in China and Lagos in Nigeria emerged as the largest informal disposers of e-waste in the world. It was not until the early 2000s that the USA and Europe drafted the first set of laws that specifically addressed the challenges of e-waste, and it was not until 2010 that data of any value, which could measure the quantum of e-waste generated in the world, began to surface. Though even until 2017, the world was still figuring out the definition of e-waste and the methodology to measure it.

By 2016, it was estimated that China alone informally processed 70 percent of the global e-waste. Its annual demand for consumer electronics at the time was way ahead of any other country. This domestic consumption propelled the rise of its informal e-waste processing sector as a ready base for the global trade to pivot toward it. Though other waste-processing centers also emerged in Ghana and Cote d'ivoire in Africa and Philippines, India, and Pakistan in Asia on the backs of arbitrage opportunities in logistics cost, or unhindered access to operations (a lack of state supervision). The world disposed 80 percent of the 44 metric tonnes of e-waste generated in 2017 by either anonymous dumping or informal trade. The rest of the 20 percent was done through traceable methods that were qualified as formal, safe, and secure. In value terms, US$ 44 billion (₹300,000 crores) worth of resources that reside within e-waste were either harvested through the informal global trade or were dumped anonymously.

In many ways, the script of global informal e-waste processing trade is a spitting image of the cocaine trade. Just as the EU and the

USA are key customer markets for the cocaine trade, the informal e-waste processing trade expanded on large volumes of discarded electronics from the US and EU. Like the cocaine trade that flourishes in spite of enforcement and legislative restrictions, the global informal E-waste recycling has grown exponentially right under the nose of the Basel treaty. Other than geographic advantage, the vendor base for the global drug trade pivots toward countries with a weak enforcement apparatus. The informal e-waste processing trade expanded on large volumes of discarded electronics from the USA and the European Union (EU). It gravitates toward countries with a weak legislative and administrative framework regarding environmental and labor laws, because compliance cost makes it prohibitively expensive for the First World to process e-waste domestically. After all, it is inconceivable for the First World to hand-tool the e-waste to recover materials in an uncontrolled manner, and thus they began to ship it to countries that were ready to do so.

The technology obsolescence race also put immense strain on the consumer of the electronics industry to dish out improved and differentiated products frequently. Television screens became thinner, mobile phones became lighter, and refrigerators started to resemble cupboards. Introducing something novel became incrementally harder with every passing year. This pressure pushed the industry toward consolidation across many product categories and in a few years defined the industry leaders that cornered most of the market share. The top ten brands of mobile phones, laptops, video games, televisions, and home appliances owned almost the entire global market share of these categories in 2016. Incidentally, these were all categories that produced nearly all of the world's e-waste. Instead of the consumption of electronics being spread out over thousands of brands, there were only a few hundred that consumers bought from across the different categories of gadgets. For instance, in the USA in 2016, 80 percent of the market for mobile phones was shared by only three brands. Similarly, in India in the same year, the top five mobile phone brands made up 75 percent of the market.

Such a consolidation was good news for the better management of e-waste. For one, based on the number of gadgets sold and their stated first-use life, it was possible to calculate with reasonable accuracy the quantum of e-waste expected to hit the garbage bins in a few years. This brings about the question of the logic for granting a free reign to the electronics and information technology industries to creating an addiction to smart devices, without the responsibility of handling its aftermath. If sending a memo faster, taking a clearer selfie, listening to high fidelity music, or living a paperless existence is poisoning our atmosphere, disfigures the environment and creates a threat of mass health crises, should not the mitigation of this consumption be a non-negotiable condition upon the growth of the consumer electronics industry?

Europe and Japan installed a legislative and operational framework for the formal management of e-waste. Although Japan was a little slow in waking up to the issue, it managed to set a template of excellence worthy of emulation. In 2001, Japan drafted the Home Appliance Recycling Law. This was based on the premise of extended producer responsibility (EPR) that was earlier propagated by European countries in the mid-1990s. EPR puts the onus on everyone – manufacturers of the electronics, retailers, and consumers – for the safe disposal of e-waste. The law made all existing practices of disposing, and informal processing of, e-waste illegal. Consumers were required to pay a recycling fee for every electronic item delivered at retail shops; retailers would in turn play the role of taking them back to the manufacturers– a sort of logistics process in reverse. The fees paid by the consumers would take care of the collection of the item at the retail point, hauling it back to the manufacturer, and recycling it. Under such an arrangement, the law mandated manufacturers to process e-waste equivalent of 60 percent of the volume of the sales each year. Unlike other legislative interventions, the Home Appliance Recycling Law provided a solution in lieu of the ban. This progressive legislative intervention displaced the informal options, particularly exports of gadgets to Third World countries under the garb of refurbishment and allowed the birth of a formal resource recovery industry. This law made it the responsibility of the electronics firms to safely dispose e-waste the responsibility of the electronics firms primarily, while consumers and the retailers were also made to play a key role in this task.

The Panasonic Eco Technology Center (PETEC), an e-waste processing plant based in Japan, owned and operated by Panasonic, came into existence as a result of this legislation. Its e-waste processing is designed to capture every solid, liquid, or gaseous particle that has gone into the making of the electronic item in a controlled and environmentally safe manner. The plant recovers aluminum, copper, steel, rare earth metals, noxious gases, and resins from plastic, and has a recovery rate of 85 percent. For example, if a mobile phone is made up of a 100 gms of total raw materials (resins, gold, silver, lead, cadmium etc.), the PETEC recovers 85 gms of these materials in their original form. There are forty-eight plants of PETEC across Japan, employing hundreds of qualified engineers and resource recovery specialists, who treat e-waste as a precious resource. It takes resource recovery so seriously that it works closely with the product manufacturers for feedback and collaboration so as to further improve the recovery rate. During one such collaboration, PETEC's engineers observed that if Panasonic laser-printed the logo on its air conditioners instead of pasting it as a plastic patch, the resource recovery rate during processing would go up. This anecdote not only sums up the mindset of the PETEC resource recovery specialists, but gives an insight into the progressive stance of Japan toward the management of e-waste. PETEC exemplifies Japan's endeavors to address the challenge of e-waste through a temperament of scientific excellence. Japan's pursuit was to scale up the share of formal recycling of e-waste from a negligible single digit number, to a respectable 30 percent in 2012. But a good 70 percent of it was still being exported to the Third World. But why is it that the likes of the PETEC could not manage to completely extinguish the export of e-waste, which continues to perpetuate the informal global trade? This is the other half of this story.

The scope of Japan's Home Appliance Recycling Law of 2001 covered only large electronics. It made consumers pay up for the cost of formally processing these discarded appliances. This included the cost of transporting the discarded appliances from their homes to recycling plants and of safely processing them. It furthermore made retailers responsible for collecting the discarded goods and bringing them to the recycling plants. It also made it mandatory for manufacturers to invest in resource recovery plants. Consumers would pay these costs upfront at the time of purchase. When consumers deposited the used appliances back with the retailers, they were issued receipts signifying the completion of the cycle. The law facilitated this operational framework and enabled Japan's electronics brands to develop formal resource recovery enterprises to process discarded appliances, hence the PETEC. However, the law did not extend to cover small electronic goods like mobile phones, laptops, computers, and tablets. One possible reason could be that unlike large home appliances that were all primarily manufactured domestically, smart appliances were chiefly non-Japanese and imported into the country. The operational challenge of mandating importers to set up resource recovery plants within the country may have played on the minds of the Japanese lawmakers. The result was that in spite of the existence of PETEC-like facilities, Japan continued to export discarded smart electronics to the Third World countries under the loophole of the Basel Convention. This helplessness also represents the limitation of all First-World countries, which were unable to extrapolate their domestic e-waste management laws on the global supply chain of smart electronic gadgets that spanned multiple continents, with IP ownership residing in one country, manufacturing set-up in another, and consumer demand elsewhere. Consideration for formal e-waste processing domestically conflicted with this complex global supply chain and compelled the First-World countries to knowingly overlook the informal global trade of e-waste processing for smart devices. Thus, the share of informal global trade of e-waste disposal continues to be very high, in spite of the Basel Convention and PETEC-like capabilities.

E-waste recycling underwent a paradigm shift in the EU, like it did in Japan, and worked on closing the loopholes in the Basel Convention. It took a different route, however, that ended up creating a second model of formal enterprise to solve the e-waste challenge. The Suez Environment, a French company, came into existence in 2008 as an outcome of mergers of multiple small entities. An independent waste management company with an annual turnover of nearly US$ 20 billion and 80,000 employees, Suez Environment viewed e-waste recycling as an independent business opportunity and created formal processing facilities in different countries. Two major conditions were in place in Europe for a company like Suez Environment to be able to offer formal solutions and emerge a leader in the sector. First, the legislative ban in Europe on informal processing of e-waste erected barriers for informal trade to operate in this space, coupled with strict enforcement of the law. This created urgency for the municipal civic bodies of cities in Europe to seek formal alternatives. Second, Europe had an organized and efficient system of waste collection in place that was dogmatic on segregation. Municipal bodies had to merely mandate their citizens to add one additional bin for e-waste, as they segregated for collection, which could be handed over to Suez Environment for safe disposal. If the e-waste was not segregated at source and collected from the generating units, then expecting the recycler to collect and segregate it would render the entire process unviable. This mandatory condition is not very different from that put on any other manufacturing business. Thermal power generation plants will not work if the incoming coal is contaminated. An automobile plant cannot produce cars if the steel supplied is of a wrong grade. For the success of formal waste processing business, the certainty of segregated waste provided by the collection service is an essential precondition that Europe met for Suez Environment to emerge as a viable solution for formal e-waste disposal.

It is essential to appreciate this global scenario of e-waste management on two counts before critiquing India's approach of handling it. First, e-waste is still an unresolved matter on many fronts. Unlike the management of other kinds of waste, for which India can rely on global trends for a great deal of post-facto wisdom, for this challenge homegrown insights need to be sought for a purpose-built solution. Second, in this challenge India has an opportunity to create a powerhouse of technology and jobs and to emerge as a dominant global player.

The legislative awakening on the issue of e-waste management in India took place in 2015, when the first draft of laws governing e-waste was floated, a good one-and-a-half decades after the First World had taken a similar step. By the time e-waste management law came into existence in 2016, India already had 150 million television sets, over 150 million smartphones, 50 million refrigerators, 25 million personal computers, and 10 million air conditioners. India also became the third largest e-waste generator in the world, after the USA and China. For 2017, the Global E-waste Monitor pegs the quantum that India generates annually at 2 metric tonnes, while other studies pegged it at a little over 1 metric tonne. Theoretically, an electronic gadget or component qualifies as e-waste once it completes its natural lifespan, which may range from ten to thirty years. But, technology obsolescence artificially reduces this lifespan and accelerates the frequency with which consumers discard a gadget.

For instance, a mobile phone can have a natural life for fifteen years but the changing technology and consumer preferences will make it obsolete in five years or less. Then, there is the issue of first ownership, second ownership and in some cases third ownership of gadgets, which extends its use – a behavior more pronounced in India than in the First World, given the fact that India offers diverse consumer price points and needs, within a single market.

In 2015, Technopak Advisors conducted a study on e-waste in India and mapped most of the gadgets and equipment that make up the profile of the e-waste sold in India since 1997. This quantity was filtered for lifespans and ownership of the gadgets before they were discarded. It concluded that India has generated 4.5 metric tonnes of e-waste since 1997, out of which 1.1 metric tonnes was generated only in 2014–15. In 2000, India had an installed base of nearly 65 million television sets, which grew to 160 million by 2016, which means 100 million new televisions were sold in India between 2000 and 2016. In 2005, on similar lines 32 million mobile handsets were sold in India, whereas 231 million were sold in 2012: in eight short years 989 million mobile handsets were sold in India. Now consider device penetration from the viewpoint of the lifespan of the device. Gadgets like mobile phones have a shorter replacement lifespan, unlike a television. There is a high probability that mobile phones sold in 2010, for instance, turned into e-waste by 2015, as was the case with televisions sold in 2005. With the disruptive rise in the consumption of mobile phones, the e-waste generated in 2015 will be significantly impacted by the increase of those sold between 2008 and 2010. Now consider the interplay of device ownership and technology obsolescence. While in 2000, no digitally enabled flat-panel televisions were sold in India, by 2016 more than 80 percent of such televisions were sold annually. For the 65 million households that already had a television set in 2000, there was great temptation to discard their existing CRT televisions much before their natural lifespan in favor of flatscreens. This means that in 2015 the generated e-waste not only comprised disproportionate quantities of discarded cathode ray tubes, but also flatscreen televisions with a more complex chemistry than that of the CRT ones.

In this backdrop, the Global E-waste Monitor's conclusion that India generated nearly 2 metric tonnes of e-waste in 2017 makes sense. But this statistic is essentially meaningless without profiling the onward journey of this generated e-waste. Extrapolating Technopak's study to 2017, it may be estimated that India can collect and process only 25 percent (0.5 metric tonne) of its generated e-waste (2 metric tonnes). The rest of the 1.5 metric tonnes cannot be traced. The informal processing of the e-waste should by no means offer the comfort that at least a quarter of India's annually generated e-waste has traceability of collection and processing. The global standard of traceability applies to only 0.05 metric tonnes of e-waste that India manages to collect and process annually through formal means in a safe and secure manner that translates to about 2.5 percent compared to 35 percent in the European Union. The informal trade that handles the balance 22.5 percent is a reflection of the global informal trade of e-waste disposal, while the rest of the generated e-waste in India is dumped, stored, or cannot be traced.

Interestingly though, India is mutely plugged into the global informal trade of e-waste recycling. The processing and recycling of electronic goods imported on the pretext of refurbishment contributes to a mere 10 percent of the total e-waste processed in India annually. The majority of the e-waste processed is what is generated from gadgets discarded domestically. Due to this all-pervasive informal trade in shanties and makeshift camps, this trade seems efficient enough to sniff out discarded gadgets before they could hit the garbage dumps. But this trade has a limited prowess to process only a little over one-fifth of India's annual e-waste is a disability that cannot be ignored. India's informal trade of e-waste recycling bears an uncanny resemblance to its global counterpart on all counts of labor exploitation, particularly child labor, unsafe working conditions, and non-existent emissions and effluent management systems. It successfully prevented large discarded gadgets from reaching the garbage dumps in their original form, but did not stop them from being hammered down in deplorable conditions. Its filters also could not prevent smaller components like used batteries, discarded PCBs, LCD screens, lamps, wires, etc., from being dumped in the landfills or burned in the open. It breaches boundaries of environmental protection, safe working condition, and labor laws for financial viability, employing rudimentary practices to harvest resources from old electronics out of dingy ghettos with bare hands. It is foolhardy to expect such a trade to solve the problem of India's e-waste when this informal trade is in fact itself a manifestation of the problem.

In India, one expects salvage value for discarded electronic gadgets. E-waste begins its journey from the household or any other waste-generating unit. For countless small electronic items like wires, batteries, and light bulbs, this journey leads them to a common dustbin or in the neighborhood dump, for the lack of wisdom to segregate them at source. The larger, more costly devices usually make their way to a *raddiwala*, a neighborhood electrical goods shop, or a scrap dealer who buys or trades these old used gadgets and acts as an aggregator, who further sells them to a scarp dealer at a mark-up for hauling the merchandise to his junkyard. This scrap dealer undertakes the first processing activity on this aggregated waste. He hammers out and separates the circuitry from other materials with his bare hands, which is melted in a makeshift furnace to extract tradeable raw materials. Though it is of little concern that every stroke of the hammer or drop of chemical applied to the discarded gadget in this way releases toxic compounds that disfigure the air, soil and life form in the vicinity. The meatiest part- the printed circuit board, which is packed with precious metal like gold, is beyond this scrap dealer's processing capability. He, therefore, pushes these boards onwards for a monetary consideration, which land up in one of the three major aggregation points of Bengaluru, Mumbai, and Delhi, where they are further beaten up and segregated in ghettoes and pushed along toward their final destination, Moradabad, a city located 150 kilometers from Delhi. Here, 200 odd units extract precious metals from nearly 80 percent of all discarded PCBs every year.

The ingenious nature of the economics of waste that manages to sniff out a business case in the most debilitating of circumstances provides the answer to the existence of Moradabad as a central character in India's story of e-waste. Until the turn of the twentieth century, Moradabad had a flourishing cottage industry of brassware that was renowned globally for its craftsmanship and quality. The town was dotted with many microenterprises involved in the craft. It was an art form because of its ability to create aesthetically pleasing statuettes, but was also a science because it involved a technical knowledge of extracting, melting, welding, and casting metals. Then business declined partly due to the rise of cheaper Chinese brassware because it was mass produced on an industrial scale. The state's indifferent attitude toward the craft, because of its crude manufacturing methods which were environmentally damaging, was another reason. As with many other artisanal skills in India, instead of handholding the trade to refine the manufacturing processes, the state regressively banned these units, drawing the curtains on many of them. While the art of brassware lost its sheen, the science of metal extraction could have been successfully redeployed for e-waste processing, an opportunity a progressive state could have cashed in on. Hundreds of units in the city shifted their focus to the informal extraction of precious metals from the circuit boards and clocked a revenue of nearly ₹1,200 crores in 2014. They were straining, stripping, and smelting gold, silver, aluminum, and copper from the e-waste and selling them to jewelers and small industrial units in the vicinity. The science behind the business was the use of acid baths to extract metals learned during the brassware trade, a recipe guarded with life.

Switching from brass trade to e-waste recycling was a bet that paid off handsomely due to its coincidence with the disruptive growth of the demand of consumer electronics in India. With every passing year, the Moradabad 'lab' solidified its hold on the trade by erecting aggregation outposts in key markets of Delhi (Gaffar Market, Nehru Palace, Seelampuri, Gokulpuri), Mumbai (Saki Naka, Kurla, Grant Road), and Bengaluru (Jolly Mohalla, Ghauripada) to collect e-waste from all over the country. Delhi became a conduit, receiving and partially processing all the e-waste that the informal trade managed to collect from all over the country and readying it for Moradabad, apart from its own and that of neighboring regions. About 0.36 million metric tonnes of e-waste entered and exited Delhi's shanties on its processing journey.

On the face of it, there seems nothing wrong with the arrangement. It is infused with the spirit of entrepreneurship, ingenuity, and economic growth. It was an efficient supply chain, preventing a certain proportion of the e-waste from being dumped in landfills, and provided livelihood to thousands of people in the process. The chief problem with this saga is its addition to informality. The zealous state intervention that banned brassware manufacturing in Moradabad ended spawning an informal trade of e-waste processing that exacerbated the problem of pollution and environmental degradation that it had aimed to solve in the first place. With its crude and hazardous methods without guidelines, rules, controls, and regulations, e-waste processing in India is vulnerable to abuse and exploitation, and poses grave risks to public health and environment. Its avoidance of rules, frameworks, infrastructure, and safe practices, however, gave it financial viability. Makeshift furnaces save the cost of controlled and secure manufacturing units. Underage youths eagerly use their bare hands to handle the acid baths, which saves the cost of protective gear. The toxic exhaust fumes from this process find their way into the open air saving the cost of an emission control apparatus. The residual effluent of lethal acids, dioxins, and heavy metals is conveniently discharged into the open, saving the cost of running an effluent treatment plant.

A closer examination of the use of just one compound – Polyclorinated biphenyls (PCBs) will reveal why this is a big deal. Delhi serves as a major aggregator and refurbishment point for discarded electronics from all over the country in makeshift arrangements in Nehru Place, Gaffar Market, Chandni Chowk, Gokulpuri, and Seelampur. Here, the scrap is hammered out to separate the circuit boards from the plastic before it proceeds to Moradabad, releasing heavy particles and toxins on the way. PCB is a colorless, odorless synthetic organic chemical. Due to its non-flammability, chemical stability, high boiling point, and insulating properties, it finds extensive application in hundreds of industrial purposes ranging from oil used in hydraulic motors to adhesive tapes and electrical switches. Electronic gadgets especially employ it widely for its insulating properties. Studies have established causation between PCBs and tumors in the brain, liver, and stomach and it is no wonder that its production was banned in the USA in 1979. But that did not stop its production in other countries and its use in the manufacturing of electronic gadgets that were eventually shipped to the USA. PCBs, however, do not pose a risk as long as the gadget or appliance is in active use, but its escape into the environment when the gadgets are discarded and dumped in open landfills, incinerated in the open or harvested for resources in an uncontrolled environment, makes it lethal. Delhi's status as a primary transit point for the processing and aggregation of India's rising mountains of e-waste and the crude methods adopted therein allow for PCBs to mingle freely with the environment, adversely affecting the city's air quality, which contains the highest levels of this compound in the country. In

2015, the Supreme Court of India admitted a plea on behalf of three children from Delhi, who demanded a reason for the deteriorating air quality in the city. They need to be told, perhaps, that the informal e-waste processing trade flourishing in the city is partially responsible and that the intellectually feeble state has been fooled into believing that this is a benign arrangement.

India's current appetite for electronic gadgets offers a reasonable cue to imagine the magnitude of the problem of e-waste at hand in the foreseeable future. The scale of the generated e-waste is an outcome of 110 million mobile phones sold annually on an average between 2004 and 2012. Added to it are another 50 million units on average of other consumer electronics like televisions, air conditioners, refrigerators, microwaves, laptop computers, etc. Overall, Indians purchased 160 million devices annually that were responsible for more than 80 percent of the generated e-waste in the country. Not only is this device consumption expected to continue its northward march, but the devices already sold till date are also expected to turn obsolete faster due to technology obsolescence. Thus, even though India generated 4.5 metric tonnes of e-waste in the seventeen years between 1997 and 2014, it will produce the same amount in the next six (2014–20). Untraceable e-waste dumped in the open that disfigures the environment in its own ways absorbs three-quarters of India's e-waste. Traceable processing through informal means that takes care of the majority of the balance quarter only compounds the risk of toxicity in Indian towns and cities. Both options spew toxic heavy metals, resins, and non-biodegradable polymers into the water, air, and soil. India's current choices for e-waste management lie between the devil and the deep sea. Between the two choices, India surely has tumrous despair in its not-so-distant future is the story of e-waste in India so far.

Why is it that India's response to a problem like e-waste management is a Moradabad lab, whereas Japan's and Europe's is PETEC and Suez Environment, respectively? The answer lies partly in India's faulty interpretation of Gandhi's dream for small-scale enterprises. The environmentalist in Gandhi saw India as a congregation of self-sustaining economic clusters comprising micro-enterprises of artisanal and agricultural skills that lived in perfect harmony with nature. But the world that emerged after World War II was destined to be impacted by advancement in technology, science, and machines. Nehru realized this impact and possibly reasoned that Gandhi's vision might be inadequate to prepare India for the next century. He imagined machines, large-scale enterprises, and advancement in science as new temples of modern India. Both viewpoints were right and a fine balancing act to reconcile the two to lay out India's approach toward industrialization was needed. It created instead a regressive framework that merely ended up extending a 'holy cow' status to small scale enterprises. Once an issue acquires such a stature, it is good only for reverence, losing its relevance for any other purpose, and a similar fate awaited small-scale enterprises in India. Instead of building on Gandhi's thought, the preservation of small-scale enterprises in their existing avatars became the policy's mainstay. It did not matter if the small-scale enterprise was inefficient, produced poor quality products, operated in an unsafe working environment, employed child labor, abused labor laws, used stolen utilities, and discharged effluents in the soil. It was an industry that provided livelihood to the masses taking the load away from the state. It was a manifestation of the Mahatma's dream no matter how disfigured was its representation.

Instead, proactive intervention was required to contemporize small-scale enterprises. They needed enabling conditions that could improve the value chain of their businesses in order to make them withstand the cost of compliance and of human values. They craved ideas that could bolster their wherewithal and help create conducive conditions to reduce their time and cost to access markets. The state instead shirked these responsibilities and was not inclined to interject to make them productive enterprises or to play an active role in bettering their lot. The state was fine for these enterprises to seek survivability in non-compliance. For this reason, hundreds of small enterprises engaged in the leather trade in Kanpur have continued to discharge effluents into the Ganga for decades, with the state turning a blind eye to the compelling need for infrastructure regarding the safe treatment of effluents that necessarily accompany this trade. Similarly, it took us six decades to figure that the mere tag of 'small-scale' industry for the food-processing sector was woefully inadequate for managing the longer distances food items had to travel from the farm to the dining table in the 'reformed' India. If obvious and visible trades like leather manufacturing and food processing failed to receive liberal dosages of a progressive outlook, it was a tall order indeed that a hidden trade like e-waste processing would figure on the radar of the policymakers. Hence, the Moradabad lab seemed a reasonable response to the Indian state.

There were then usual suspects who were responsible for this outcome. A flawed social contract and incapacitated state actors that have numbed society's collective mental faculties to acknowledge even visually distressing forms of waste like solid human waste, food, and medical waste from the standpoint of intellectual curiosity cannot be expected to spare any bandwidth to appreciate the challenges of a seemingly benign and invisible form like e-waste. In this backdrop, the birth of the Moradabad lab does not come as a surprise.

The PETEC and Suez Environment have demonstrated that e-waste processing demands capital investment to build human and technical capability in the science of resource recovery. Consumers, brand manufacturers and retailers were made responsible for and were willing to pay for the safe collection and disposal of e-waste. These responsibilities were converted into financial cost that allowed capital investment, and formal solutions like Suez Environment and

PETEC emerged. Consumers were required to deposit discarded gadgets with retailers at the end of their lifecycle without any monetary consideration in return. The end product liability to dispose the electronic gadgets on the brand manufacturers compelled manufacturers to realign their value chains that created a favorable environment for the birth of PETEC-like organizations in Japan. Alternatively, in Europe municipal corporations readjusted their existing waste collection systems that collected discarded gadgets from households and handed them over to independent e-waste processing companies like Suez Environment.

In India, one expects salvage value for discarded electronic gadgets – a mentality that is principally borne out of society's sense of entitlement toward waste management, the fruit of our flawed social contract. In order to extract salvage value from old electronics, society sees nothing wrong in the existence of an informal system to make e-waste magically disappear from the mainstream. The condemnation of this informality and its hazardous nature is hardly a matter of concern as it pays the salvage value demanded by the mainstream. Conversely, a formal system of safe and efficient disposal will not only ask that the gadget be given up for free, but also that the consumer bear a part of the cost incurred to dispose it. Small wonder then that the emerging solution is less of science as manifested by organizations like Suez Environment or PETEC, and more of an art form open to the fancies of its practitioners. This arrangement creates the right conditions for informal trade and dis-incentivizes formal solutions. While informality will beg, borrow and steal to eke out a living by merely selling recovered metals, formal methods need capital infusions to deliver safe and secured transportation, investment in environmentally controlled processing units, minimum wages and the treatment of effluent discharge. Why would a society so conditioned give away its asset and pay for its safe disposal, when it can just as easily sell it for a sum of money and never have to spare it another though?

Yet, there are a few formal waste-processing enterprises like Attero and Ramky in India that recognize the growing deficit in the area of e-waste disposal. But they continue to be on the fringes and take advantage of no more than 10 percent of the total e-waste processing opportunity. The flawed value chain of e-waste processing loads the dice against their success and their bravado can only attract sympathy because it incentivizes consumers who generate e-waste and penalizes those who process it. Waste disposal should be viewed as a responsibility of the society that needs to bear the cost of its safe and secure processing. This role reversal will allow much-needed financial leeway for the value chain to be reconstructed in a desirable way that favors formal processing, wherein India has a great opportunity to redeem itself on many fronts: human resource development, environmental protection, and social reform. The Moradabad lab needs a re-examination from the lens of intellectual curiosity. Within its subaltern existence lie many clues to create a reform push toward formalization, the first being that e-waste recycling is financially unviable on standalone basis if it is solely dependent on the monetization of extracted resources. The informal trade recycles e-waste, but does so in a manner that is destructive to the environment for the lack of financial leeway. Therefore, any formal solution for e-waste processing needs to envisage dual revenue streams: the service fee to process e-waste in a safe and secured manner, and the monetization of the extracted resources.

Moreover, the e-waste trade is a fairly consolidated play with efficient supply chains that crisscross state borders and beyond. Even the informal trade in India operates a fairly efficient supply chain to aggregate and haul e-waste from all over the country to a few centralized locations that process nearly 90 percent of it. This suggests that economies of scale are critical for any desirable formal solution and no more than a few players can coexist is this space.

The subject of e-waste processing needs to be a national responsibility given that it crosses boundaries. The formalization effort will need to be driven by the intervention of the union government, while states should be made an active party with defined expectations. In doing so, the union government should view itself as an active creator of guidelines for methods, capabilities, measures, and the working environment needed for a formal existence. It should play the role of a regulator much like the Reserve Bank of India (RBI) did in issuing licenses to payment banks in 2016. The RBI developed guidelines for the banks and invited applications from interested parties, which were evaluated on their individual merit before rolling out licenses to the selected candidates. It would be a good starting point for the government to emulate the same model and give out licenses to recyclers of e-waste.

Another compelling argument for e-waste recycling to be made the responsibility of the union is that it is as yet an unresolved global challenge. On the back of the world's unending romance with smart devices is an economic opportunity worth US$ 67 billion of embedded resources in e-waste in 2016, set to cross US$ 100 billion by 2022. Although the First World has taken on the challenge, a bulk of e-waste processing still resides in the clutches of the informal global trade. Based on the strength of India's own electronics consumption, it has the opportunity to tap into this need gap by developing a frugal formal solution and offering it as a viable alternative to other countries. Formal e-waste recycling has all the makings of an effective diplomatic tool and to become a new export powerhouse. Such an important global agenda with implications on foreign policy cannot be left on the shoulders of individual states.

The final clue that the Moradabad lab offers relates to the options at hand regarding the nature of formal enterprises for e-waste processing. Explicitly put, there is an opportunity for private capital to come on board, undertake risk, and build scale. The enterprise thus born will constantly seek new customers and avenues to grow, both in India and abroad. Inarguably, India will need a few such e-waste processing enterprises of scale and global repute which will foster a healthy competition and, thereby, a much-needed progressive outlook toward e-waste. This will allow a few existing formal enterprises to build on their scale and stature. But it will be wrong to assume that formal enterprises might only be private entities in nature. Enterprises too can be purpose-built through a cooperative structure. India can only do so, however, if it succeeds in breaking the myth that cooperatives and industrialization are at opposite ends of the spectrum.

Fonterra, a cooperative owned by 13,000 farmers in New Zealand, is the world's leading dairy enterprise. Cranberry and walnut growers in the USA successfully dominate the world stage through their respective cooperatives. Cap Siene and Ocealia use drone technology to improve precision in agriculture and can easily pass off as agri-tech companies, but are cooperatives that represent the interests of thousands of farmers in France. India's success with cooperatives, though, starts and ends with Amul. If a few hundred families in Moradabad can collectively emerge to dominate the informal trade, then why not channel their strength constructively? Instead of demolishing their synergy, they should be brought under a co-operative umbrella and mentored to remove all the flaws that currently plague them. In 2015, when the informal e-waste industry of Guiyu, the e-waste capital of the world, became an embarrassment for China, the government consolidated a thousand-odd workshop into twenty-nine big units and relocated them to a US$ 233 million industrial complex. For India to seize this opportunity is not whimsical or fantastical. Although the jury is still out on the efficacy of the Chinese intervention in reducing unregulated discharge and emissions into the environment, the Guiyu experiment does demonstrate great potential in formalizing small-scale enterprises to resolve the growing challenge of e-waste.

India should initiate this journey with the curtailment of society's expectation of a salvage value for discarded gadgets and appliances. Such a prohibition will append the existing economic argument in favor of e-waste recyclers and away from the consumers of electronics. One of the key reasons for the success of Suez Environment in Europe was the installed waste-collection capability of the local civic bodies and their equitable social contract with the society. Consequently, local bodies were able to collect segregated waste from all units within their jurisdiction for a price paid by the waste generators. They merely extended this formal contract to collect e-waste too. This took care of the logistics cost incurred in hauling it to the processing site and in processing it safely. On the other hand, the local bodies entered into a financial contract with waste-processing specialists like Suez Environment and handed them the segregated e-waste who in turn processed it for a fee. Additionally, Suez Environment also monetized resources harvested from the e-waste which contributed toward its financial sustainability. This model, however, still is some years away to entirely plug the gap of the non-traceability of e-waste in Europe.

The PETEC, on the other hand, emerged from the argument that the operational responsibility to haul and process e-waste should be that of the electronics brand, without diluting the financial responsibility of the consumer toward it safe processing. Therefore, Panasonic established the PETEC and began to charge the cost of processing e-waste from the consumers upfront. It also partnered with retailers to facilitate the reverse logistics of the e-waste to its premises. Japan's highly consolidated electronics industry manufactured and sold these gadgets domestically. So, it was easy for consumer electronics brands to imagine an organization like PETEC and plug it in to recover discarded gadgets and process them safely for resource extraction. However, the model runs out of steam when it comes to handling e-waste that emerges imported gadgets and appliances. Thus, in Japan, like in the EU, the quantum of non-traceable e-waste stands at a high 70 percent annually.

India can learn from the lessons offered by the EU and Japan to devise a homegrown model on e-waste management. But local bodies here are a still few decades away from installing Europe-like precision in collecting segregated waste from the doorstep of households, which facilitated the creation of Suez Environment. The construct of the Indian electronics industry, on the other hand, comprises a high share of imports, which does not bode well for economies of scale in e-waste processing needed to make a success story like Japan's PETEC. India needs an amalgamation of the two approaches to purpose-build a formal solution, which will entrust electronic brands with the responsibility of collecting discarded gadgets and hauling them to processing sites. Instead of expecting these brands to build and operate processing solutions like the PETEC, they should be encouraged to have financial contracts with independent e-waste processing specialists. Electronic brands, in turn, should collect the cost of transportation logistics and processing from the consumers at the time of purchase. The primary role of the brands should be to utilize their retail distribution network to manage the reverse logistics of discarded gadgets, the cost of which should borne by the consumers, making it difficult for the brands to shirk the responsibility. The brands can discharge this duty in a variety of ways: they can install collection centers for e-waste by tapping into various consumer touch points like post offices, banks, retailers, even schools. Electronic brands can even imagine a consortium of sorts, or a third party who can offer reverse logistics to all the brands, a similar approach to a common tower network offered to multiple mobile operators. Indian technical institutions and universities that were endowed with the tag of eminence in 2018 or those who hold the grudge for having missed out to achieve one or those who face perennial struggle to break the clutches of mediocrity can think about e-waste micro factories in their campuses on the lines of the world's first e-waste micro factory that went live in 2018 on the campus of University of New South Wales in Sydney, Australia and emerge as worthy vendors to consumer electronics industry to serve this objective. Such micro factories will be part progressive laboratories for research and part commercial enterprises can perhaps even demolish the assumption that industrial scale is the only way to go to process this new age waste and may go a long way in democratizing scientific temperament that is needed to address this challenge in India.

The other part of the cost paid by the consumer to the brand at the time of purchase will involve the processing cost of e-waste. The electronics brand will pay this cost to an e-waste processing specialist on behalf of the consumers. The revenue earned by the e-waste recycler from this arrangement will become its basis for a formal existence, while the revenue it will earn by monetizing resources recovered from the processing of e-waste will provide the profit. With these two revenue streams, e-waste recycling will move away from its current avatar of the Moradabad lab toward a viable technical formal resource recovery industry. The two-sided financial contract of the electronics brand with the consumer to recover the cost and the recycler to process e-waste will act as the guardian to oversee the transition and compliance.

India's laws on the management of e-waste makes consumer electronics brands operationally responsible for its processing. But it fails to shift the economics of e-waste in favor of the recyclers. It gives broad guidelines that are very expressive about the desired state, but is vague on the actions needed to achieve it. Take, for instance, the broad brushstroke used to define the responsibility of urban local bodies. These rules state that local bodies should ensure that e-waste, if found mixed with municipal solid waste, must be isolated, and orphaned products need to be handed over to authorized recyclers. But they lack progressive arguments to ensure their adherence to these rules, especially in the backdrop of the fact that eighty percent of e-waste generated in India disappears without a trace.

These laws painstakingly outline the documentary process for waste recyclers to seek authorization to do the job, but throw no light on how informal recyclers may become formal resource recovery specialists, nor on the trigger points for the informality to transition toward formality. For instance, the rules could mandate electronics and consumer durables brands to use materials recovered from recycled e-waste from authorized recyclers as raw material for new products. They could mandate jewellery retailers to increase the share of recycled gold and silver from formal e-waste recyclers in their annual sourcing. Given the increasing consensus to make consumer electronics brands transition toward reusing resources harvested from e-waste, India has an opportunity to emerge as a thought leader and legislatively push its discretionary consumption toward a more circular existence. From this perspective, a legislative sponsorship is all that is needed to trigger the recalibration of the e-waste processing value chain toward formality.

It is possible that the current Indian e-waste management rules may yield the desired results eventually. But the rules give enough hints that smack of our past biases on waste management and it is equally possible that these rules may shift the informality of the trade to other cities to enforce these rules. Japan and Europe teach us that the legislation necessarily needs an implementation framework to accompany prohibited actions which can propel the transition toward a desired state. They will need state-sponsored vigilantism to prevent even a single discarded gadget from getting hammered out in the open or being dumped in a landfill. We will run out of time if we assume that the Moradabad lab, Jolly Mohalla, Ghauripada, Saki Naka, Kurla and Seelampur will circumvent the rule book and make our mountains for e-waste magically dematerialize, as has been the case so far. Confronting the stark reality that our consumption of electronic gadgetry is conspicuous, but its disposal rests on a crude infrastructure should humble. If we do not bridge this chasm, India will continue to be fooled by the silent nature of this waste, sending us on a wild goose chase while it surreptitiously robs us of our lives and health. And so far we have not even taken into account discarded automobile, construction waste from buildings we and the impending arrival of discarded solar panels in near future.

8

CLEAN INDIA

Capturing the Chimera

A country being clean or not is not accidental, nor is it due to genetic superiority or inferiority. The sequence of events a country experiences and its economic growth, coupled with the societal changes it brings about, puts pressure on society to pool their resources on all issues concerning sanitation. Had it not been for population growth, rapid urbanization, and industrial development, inhabitants in the clean countries would not have had the motivation to seek a change in their lifestyle. A sparse population would have happily lived in the countryside, and a small garbage pit on the outskirts of the village would have served well as an environment-friendly waste-disposal method. An occasional stench would hardly have created enough of a flutter for the villagers to look for a better waste-management approach. Only when people left the countryside to live in squalid cities in the hope of hitting pay dirt did they realize that problems surrounding garbage were unbearable. This was good enough for these societies to acknowledge the challenges of sanitation in their entirety and set out in search of lasting solutions.

India stands at the same crossroads a century later, but in circumstances that are more unforgiving than they are fortunate. India can use the journey of clean countries of today as an operational guide about sanitation. But India also confronts this challenge at a time where it can bypass the long trajectory of the First World by using technology on myriad fronts – for effective enforcement, resource planning, and operations in sanitation delivery. Advancements in resource recovery and material science can be used to accelerate the growth of the formal recycling industry. Digitization of the economy, data science, and fabrication technology can be effectively used to design future cities that minimize the generation of waste. The clean countries did not have such powerful tools at their disposal when they started their respective journeys. In this, India is fortunate.

A century ago when the clean countries of today were busy putting their house in order, plastic was yet to enter their daily lives. There was no e-waste, and garbage largely comprised solid human waste and animal droppings on the streets. While the problem was loathsome and unsightly, a series of simple and timely steps did the trick. Regulations backed by diligent enforcement overcame society's illiteracy about public hygiene. Investment in an infrastructure for waste collection removed the offence of any alibi for non-compliance. The wisdom to appreciate the economics of waste management created economic value and allowed local civic bodies to function effectively. These societies also learned that tidy surroundings were a direct outcome of urban planning, the methods of which were improved to design cities for cleaner outcomes. All said and done, the waste-management challenge in these countries was linear and allowed them the bandwidth to put in place a decent working system to overcome the challenge.

Today, the composition of India's garbage bins and landfills is identical to that of the clean countries, in both complexity and quantity, with plastics, medical waste, toxic effluents, e-waste, metals, and solid waste being the chief components. But India's response toward addressing this challenge lags behind that of the clean countries by at least half a century, a reality exposed by our legislative journey on waste management. Until 2016, littering in the open attracted a paltry fine of ₹50 to 500; it was then increased to ₹10,000. The clean countries, however, introduced steep fines as a form of deterrence as early as the 1950s. Similarly, they started to reduce the use of open landfills from the 1960s, while India is yet to wake up to the dangers of this arrangement. Burning trash in the open was banned in India as recently as 2001, a good fifty years after the clean countries did so. Finally, India's centuries-old challenge of caste biases in waste management yet remains unaddressed.

This makes India's starting point to tackle the sanitation problem significantly harder. Although the solution will entail multiple actions that are identical to those undertaken by the clean countries decades ago, the complexity of the generated waste makes sequencing and prioritizing these actions a web of intricacies. The architects of the solutions will need to appreciate the dual challenge of the complexity of consumption and society's mind-numbing bias. On the one hand, they will need to imagine technological and application-based solutions, and, on the other, have enough bravado to make habit-changing interventions that can drill through the calcified mind-set. 'Architects' would perhaps be the most appropriate way to describe these providers of a solution that must span regulations, enforcement, urban planning, infrastructure, reforms in local governance, the state's contract with the society and influencing the very human psyche, for achieving a clean nation. Then there is the sequencing of these actions. Not to mention the vast scope of these actions: it is, after all, a question of collecting and processing over 100 million tonnes of the waste India generates annually, the third highest in the world. We are referring to 210 million households that need to be connected to closed sewage lines and effluent treatment plants.

The architects should be nothing short of super heroes to come on board to tackle India's naïveté on the issue. Sadly though, superheroes do not exist beyond celluloid. We must thus settle for lesser mortals in the form of institutions, and arm them with legislation, human capability and infrastructure. This war need not be grueling if we can put aside psychological inferiority, cultural apathy and prejudice. It can even turn out to be a beautiful symphony if every stakeholder plays his part well and in tune with the others.

In the 1940s and 1950s, Japan witnessed a surge in the quality movement that propelled the country toward industrial development, economic growth, and social progress. Concepts of total quality management, envisaged in the 1920s, gained wide acceptance and transformed the country's image from a producer of cheap, poor quality products to a haven for the world's best. The starting point of this quality improvement was the understanding that people have a tendency to think of symptoms of problems as problems themselves, and then try to find solutions for the symptoms. Sakichi Toyoda, founder of Toyota Motor Corporation, conceived this thought, which is simple to articulate, but hard to practice. A broken exhaust in a car is not a problem but a symptom. A screening of the board problem statement with multiple levels of 'why' revealed that the exhaust pipe was broken at the time of installation. The laxity of the quality assurance department in inspecting the incoming consignment of exhaust pipes was the root cause of a defective piece of equipment being fitted into a car. The problem: 'broken exhaust in car' was rephrased as 'lack of inspection system in quality assurance department.' This made the statement precise and gave clarity on a set of corrective actions. In 1968, Kaoru Ishikawa, a Japanese organizational theorist, further expanded on this thought. His fishbone methodology aimed to not only define the root cause, but to also figure out its nature: whether it was the result of human error, the lack of tools available to discharge the task, or the methods to carry out the task effectively. These ideas reflected the objective and unbiased thinking of Japanese society and their commitment to improve the status quo. Japan's pursuit for quality may have had its beginnings in the automobile sector, but its universality made it travel far and wide. Today's practitioners can vouch for its contribution in myriad fields, including sanitation delivery to citizens.

India's meek defense against waste has a propensity to hide behind the simplistic statement that 'India is dirty,' and so every stakeholder expects the next one down the pecking order to pick up a broom and clean. But the fact that India is dirty is more a symptom of a number of mini problems than the problem itself. Without bringing these problems to surface and critiquing them, any effort to clean the country will be futile. India's script for the symphony of a clean nation will thus be more intricate, for which it may have to take inspiration and recourse in Japan's quality management approach.

An omen of the trap into which the Indian state falls repeatedly, treating symptoms of problem as the problem itself, is its failure to clean its rivers, especially the sacred river Ganga. The phrase 'Dirty Ganga' throws up a convenient problem statement because rivers in India represent the ownership of everyone and the responsibility of no one. Disputes between Tamil Nadu and Karnataka for the Kavery waters, Madhya Pradesh and Uttar Pradesh for the Ken Betwa, between Punjab and Haryana for the waters of the Sutlej, and between Haryana and Delhi for the Yamuna reflect the aridity of our attitude toward taking advantage of rivers, but none of the accountability of their rapidly deteriorating health.

'Dirty Ganga' began to receive political sponsorship in 1986. Yet a few thousand crores of rupees and thirty years of efforts later, the Ganga was adjudged the fifth most polluted river in the world in 2007. In 2014, it received reinvigorated political sponsorship, so much so that the union government installed a dedicated ministry to solve the problem. Efforts continue in the hope they will yield results in the next few years, but in the Dirty Ganga problem definition the Indian state fell into the symptom trap. The naïve statement that the 'Ganga is dirty' misleads one into recognizing it as a problem instead of a mere symptom of a series of problems, and is at the heart of this criticism. It begets a shallow defense – 'clean the Ganga.' But, 'cleaning the Ganga' is nothing more than an articulation of the aspiration or desire, much like 'becoming rich' or 'feeling happy.' Toyoda developed Root Cause Analysis precisely to avoid falling into this trap, but India's 'dirty Ganga' agenda was snagged for the lack of such imagination or tools. Therefore, all the efforts and money that made their way to treat the symptom cascaded away with the flow of the river.

'Dirty Ganga' also encapsulates within it all the reasons that plague 'Dirty India' and serves as a good proxy for all the problems that are the road blocks toward a clean nation. The Ganga passes through five states, dozens of cities and hundreds of villages as it makes its 2,500 kilometers way to the Bay of Bengal. The river crosses state boundaries, cuts through the municipal corporations and traverses many panchayats. If a local leather factory in Kanpur dumps its effluent into the river, does the Municipal Corporation of the city have the administrative wherewithal and motivation to take the factory to task, once the effluents are released into the river and flow downstream. For this incapacity, municipal body may be all to relieved for passing this headache to the next jurisdiction. If the factories, commercial establishments and households located on the banks of the river in all the cities it passes through in Uttar Pradesh dump solid waste into it, and the river then crosses the state boundary to enter the state of Bihar, can Bihar pull up Uttar Pradesh for tainting the waters of the holy river?

Water bodies are sponges that can soak up waste without additional effort or cost. Due to this vulnerability, mankind world over has relied on water bodies as reliable receptacles of human waste, for centuries. Therefore, the same treatment meted out to the Ganga should not come as a surprise. But, today, the clean countries are wiser on acceptable and unacceptable waste management approaches. Abusing water bodies to dump the aftermaths of human consumption now falls into the bucket of unacceptable practices, while the abuse of the Ganga's exposes the severe gap in the intelligence and judgment of our society.

Our comfort with using the Ganga for waste disposal stands at odds with the religious significance of the river. The holy water from the Ganga is inextricably tied up with rituals and is believed to have a purifying effect on everything it touches. Indians revere the Ganga as a demigod, but are also at ease with their fecal matter contaminating its pious waters. We abominate fecal and dead matter, but when the same comes in contact with the purity of the Ganga, it becomes acceptable. Shouldn't then the river be revered as a symbol of convenience rather than of holiness? If we take away the religious symbolism of the Ganga from the argument, the arrangement seems more palatable because most modern societies started their waste management journeys with dumping their waste into rivers for the sheer convenience. India, however, is yet to embark on its journey, hence the status quo.

If the society is hard-wired to prioritize convenience over all other considerations, even piety, any attempt to clean the Ganga, premised on a collective 'awakening,' is downright foolishness. In 2017, the treatment plants of Mirzapur in Uttar Pradesh could only process a little over 60 percent of the 28.8 million liters of sewage the city generated. The remaining 10 million liters of untreated sewage became an unholy offering to the Ganga daily. The municipal body of Mirzapur, on receiving a reprimand from the judiciary for this brazen practice, submitted an affidavit citing delays on the part of the private contractor who was tasked with increasing the installed capacity of the treatment plants. Suppose the delay in question was to do with arresting a leak in a nuclear power plant. What if the nuclear plant operator decided to run the plant anyway? What is the difference between running a nuclear plant that is leaking radioactive material, and dumping untreated sewage into the Ganga? The shock value of nuclear contamination that immediately leads to horrendous deaths is perhaps the only difference, because sewage discharge into rivers carries comparable prolonged misery, albeit a few years into the future.

The acceptance of this ludicrous arrangement is a direct outcome of Indian society's apathy toward garbage, an issue which is perceived as operational and is mentally outsourced to the caste system. Consequently, unlike the clean countries, society mistakenly began to equate the management of rubbish with the rubbish itself. In caste-afflicted India, though, this technical problem swiftly became an avoidable social evil. This challenge is unique to Dirty India and Dirty Ganga.

From the apathy of the Indian society emerged the brazenness of the Indian state. Public representative rarely feared losing their jobs if the Ganga absorbed a few extra million liters of raw sewage because they took comfort in the society's lassitude. For the franchise, a clean Ganga was a nebulous aspiration, featuring way down in the order of importance. Public representatives faced zero threat of losing their political luster in the eyes of the franchise for not being able to clean the river because the franchise was just fine with the duality of their arrangement with the holy river – one of reverence and the other as a receptacle of sewage. Meanwhile, the waters of the Ganga and its tributaries changed from a beautiful translucent to an opaque sludge. The union government did not legislate against the dumping of untreated waste into the Ganga, or any other river for that matter, and neither did the state-concerned governments. The futility of such a legislative intervention was not lost on them because neither did the franchise care, nor were their waste-disposal methods efficient enough to take of all the sewage without raising a stink. The Ganga, however, did not mind or complain and forgivingly went down its course absorbing the biases of people, as it had done for ages. It was this helplessness of the Ganga that fueled the anguish of Late Professor G. D. Agarwal – an accomplished engineer, teacher and environmentalist. He channeled his pain into a Satyagragha of fast unto death demanding proactive legislation against illegal dumping into the Ganga, but it was too much of an ask from the state. His passing away came first in 2018, while the legislation is still awaited.

Society has the disposition to either discriminate against or adulate a particular job, depending on the nature of the contract between the one who discharges it and the one who is its beneficiary. If the contract accords equal status the both parties, then the job itself protects the principle of equality while delivering the intended output. Take a transaction between a shopkeeper and a customer, where the customer values the shopkeeper's role because it provides him access to the merchandise he needs. A commercial transaction between the two establishes this equality. If, however, the person who discharges the job is considered a messiah, a protector, a guide, or fulfills aspirational need of the beneficiary, the job tends to receive reverence. Ideally, a teacher is held in reverence because he is a source of knowledge, as are priests because people seek solace and guidance on their respective faiths from them.

There are reasons for these social contracts to be skewed for some jobs and not for others. A part of the answer can be found in neo-classical economics because wage rate is a good measure of equality of social contracts. The availability of labor for a certain job determines the wage rate. If a job commands a high wage, it will have monetary safeguards against societal discrimination because the labor pool is most likely in short supply, thus mitigating the risk of exploitation. If the labor pool is prolific then the supply outstrips the demand and the wage rates drop, exposing the job to exploitation. When the supply of labor is abundant, certain jobs assume a master-servant relationship between the one who pays the wage and one who carries out the duty. The jobs of drivers, housekeepers and cooks are often viewed in this light. Inadvertently or by design, this causation was understood centuries ago in India. The caste system was an approach to stratify the society based on the nature of jobs, and ensured that labor migration between different jobs was restricted, ensuring the availability of a labor pool for all types of jobs. A farmer always remained a farmer and sold his produce for an economic value. His son grew up to be a farmer. A cobbler always remained a cobbler and repaired footwear for an economic consideration. His son grew up and became a cobbler. A carpenter remained a carpenter, and so on and so forth. In all these jobs, a fair economic consideration in lieu of the services rendered protected the principle of equality between the customer and the vendor.

Yet, the same caste system prevented the discovery of a fair economic value for the job of waste management. The nature of cleaning jobs was such that they were always to be conducted in abject filth accompanied by nauseating smells. Therefore, perhaps, they always ran the risk of the labor pool abandoning the job and refusing to do it. The conjuncture is that the caste system was used as an effective tool to mitigate this flight risk. It not only erected rigid boundaries around the people who were engaged in sanitation jobs but also prevented the discovery of a fair economic value for the job. In a sense, it was the best of both the worlds. On one hand, the society did not have to pay fair market value for cleaning jobs and on the other, there was no shortage of labor: most cogent way to hold an entire class of people hostage to their profession and make them toe the line.

The existence of a skewed social order over a prolonged period pushed the notion of sanitation as an entitlement in India, not as a service to be availed for a fair economic consideration. The social contract for waste management jobs ended up becoming a master-servant-master relationship with non-reciprocal expectation. It then stands to reason that a service that a society has consumed nearly free of cost for centuries will always be neglected for its methods, design and approaches. The effluent discharge from the Kanpur factories, the blatant affidavit of the Mirzapur municipal body citing delays in constructing effluent treatment plant and other such occurrences suddenly start to make sense when viewed in this light.

The absence of an economic transaction to establish equality in sanitation-related jobs prevented the cost of waste management from getting priced by the Indian society. Capital is required to maintain an infrastructure for collecting and disposing waste from households. There are also operational costs like salaries and maintenance of equipment, etc. The entitlement bias, however, had seeped so deep into the governance apparatus of post-independence India that it pushed the state further into becoming a silent sponsor of this flawed social contract. India's waste-management apparatus thus ended up a severely under-funded and anemic structure. The problem statement for the symptom Dirty Ganga therefore should be the antiquated waste-management infrastructure of the local municipal bodies of the cities on the banks of the river that relies on a recruitment drive to select sanitation workers based on their ability to lift untreated sewage with their bare hands. A direct outcome of this blow was the continuation of the quagmire of informality that engulfed all activities concerning sanitation. Informality perpetuated unregulated working environments, exploitative employee-employer contracts, inefficient work flows, unproductive economic conditions. Yet, informality had all the lure of a no-strings-attached affair, whereas formality was that unyielding commitment that had 'chaotic transition' written all over it. Informality was the easy way out, giving employment to millions without job security, or ever having to ensure a safe working environment. Formality, on the other hand, would have kept them on their toes with guidelines, riders and disclaimers. Informality enveloped the waste-management value chain in its entirety, resulting in archaic waste-collection and disposal practices and the exploitation of caste groups working in the sector; and received the stamp of approval both from society and from the state.

One way to remedy this is to change the perception of cleanliness in the minds of its beneficiaries, from entitlement to a sense of duty. This shift will allow cleanliness to have an economic value, which should be bankrolled by the society for more desirable and superior waste-management interventions. This will necessitate internalizing the cost of waste management by mandating the society to pay, which will in turn fund the capital and operational expenditure of a superior waste-management system. For the mainstream, this will be added as a head on the list of monthly expenses like water and electricity, and they will re-jig their discretionary expenditure to make room for it. There may be initial dissenting, but they will have to be made to understand that the onward march of their consumption cannot proceed without sorting out the disposal of things already consumed. The acceptance by Indian households that waste management must be a paid utility service will transition it toward industrial development and uncork a tax-paying economic opportunity that currently lies tethered and serves as a ground zero for casteism and condemnation. In this backdrop, the existence of the flawed social contract between the society and the state on sanitation delivery is one of the minor problems that contribute to Dirty Ganga, and its solution is to make sanitation a service available at a cost, monetized by a fee payable by the inhabitants of the cities, towns, tehsils, kasbahs, and villages along the banks of the river.

But the affidavit submitted by the municipal body of Mirzapur to the NGT casts serious doubts about their stamina to deliver this solution. All that the local body of Mirzapur could do was to take the umbrage of helplessness when the private contractor tasked with the construction of the effluent treatment plant failed to erect it in time and dump the city's raw sewage into the Ganga. The anemia of the local governance of Mirzapur is widespread and rampant in that it afflicts the local governance of all the towns and villages that host the Ganga. The submission of the affidavit does not show any explicit willful mal-intention but it is an admission of this illness. It reflects the local body's powerlessness that is a result of its lack of autonomy to draft laws, undertake enforcement and raise revenue – the enablers essential for crafting customized solutions to manage the generated waste in cities.

The defective birth of Indian local governance and its systematic bullying by other organs of the Indian state resulted in its anemic existence. The 'big brother' state actors supplied them with doles and political legitimacy bundled as dictates. Consequently, they did not foster the perspective to marry costs, investments, and returns. They had a limited drive to pursue monetization as an essential ingredient to design superior public utility services. Out of desperation and limited leeway, their misguided steps on waste management became a recurring theme, as was the case when Mirzapur's local civic body hurriedly on-boarded private capital through vague contract terms for its sewage treatment plant. This slavery of Indian local bodies hardly allows them any institutional capacity to think about the waste-management infrastructure from a perspective to tie it with the capital and processes needed to run the show. One of the reasons for the non-existence of an underground sewage infrastructure and effluent treatment plants is this very slavery, which does not allow the capital to reach the waste management agenda, among others.

Rescuing the local governance of towns and villages on the banks of the Ganga from this quagmire can ratify India's claim of true cooperative federalism. India will need to view the Dirty Ganga as an opportunity to stamp its credentials on federal democracy. Such a challenge can only be overcome with unraveling the knots one at a time and this can perhaps create a template for successful cooperative federalism on other issues as well. The first step is decoupling of the functions of waste collection and waste disposal. Waste collection entails all activities and efforts needed to collect waste from all waste-generating units and haul it to a preordained destination for disposal.

Waste disposal involves methods and infrastructure for recycling, reducing, or disposing this waste in a safe and environment-friendly manner. The local municipal bodies of towns and villages on the banks of the Ganga should be made primarily responsible for the collection of waste from all households and establishments within their respective jurisdictions. This responsibility will require an infrastructure response from the civic bodies to install a collection system and an operational response to manage the daily drill of collecting bagged and segregated waste from every unit and through the underground sewage connection. The civic bodies will have to become the custodian of the entire chain by acting as the interlocutors between the franchise and the state to determine a fair economic value service and to recover it from the franchise through user fees and/or indirect taxes.

We now know that disposing waste safely is learned behavior that is contrarian to human instinct. The act of waste generation is a burden on the state, thus disposing it cannot be an entitlement of the citizens, but a duty that needs to be imbibed by society, not just by pleas, requests and calling upon morality. An enforcement apparatus needs to become an integral part of the waste-collection responsibility of the civic bodies on the banks of the Ganga, which is designed with the broader intentions of deterrence, conditioning people's mind toward a new reference point, and rounding up the society toward the desired behavior. This apparatus will need to be purpose-built to make the act of collecting waste efficient and effective. The economic rationale for such an argument is simple: it costs far more to collect unregulated littered waste than to reduce its occurrence in the first instance. Construction waste getting dumped on the banks of the Ganga will require the services of sanitation workers and a loading truck to make an unscheduled visit to the area to clean it up. It is cheaper and far more effective to install an electronic surveillance camera in the area to act as deterrence and make illegal dumping prohibitively expensive for potential offenders. This enforcement apparatus for sanitation will be responsible for all legislative compliance that concerns waste management. It will need a cross-functional disposition on issues like public health, environment and material science, data and analytics, and surveillance technology. The release of industrial effluents into the river, processing of toxic waste in unauthorized operating units, households dumping waste in open fields, households not subscribing to waste collection services, and social gatherings dumping waste are instances that will then appear as crimes in the rule book of this enforcement apparatus and reduce the probability of these elements finding their way into the holy river.

Current advancements in technology have removed the initial constraints that clean countries of today faced when they started their journey on enforcement for sanitation. It will be a colossal waste of an opportunity if this perspective is missed by local civic bodies on the banks of the Ganga when they attempt to build such an enforcement apparatus. Data science can now be used to predict human behavior and accordingly position the surveillance apparatus. For instance, the manufacturing durations of various industrial goods can be mapped to predict their production cycles and in turn their effluent discharges. Enforcement teams can delegate their resources to apprehend such offenders red-handed. Illegal dumping in public places during festivals can be predicted and checked using surveillance technology solving perennial this challenge that cities like Varanasi and Prayaagraj often face.

Armed with user-funded model and enforcement apparatus to collect waste, segregated waste thus collected on the banks of the Ganga will convert the region's local civic bodies into vendors of black gold – resource-rich waste ready to be harvested for energy and reuse in a safe and secure manner. But the waste on the banks of the Ganga is complex concoction of waste which cannot be bundled into one waste bin or sewage pipe for any decent disposal effort to be successful.

A recycling plant that processes plastic cannot be fed metals and glass waste or the machinery will run the risk of seizure. Similarly, food waste cannot be treated for organic manure if mixed with plastic. Thus, it is necessary for the local civic bodies of all human clusters that host the Ganga to collect segregated waste before attempting any effort to dispose it in a safe manner, and then offer it as raw material to the resource recovery industry. Once having achieved this objective, it should not be the job of the local civic bodies on the banks of the river to scout around for land-fills and scramble for resources to put up mediocre effluent treatment or recycling plants. Upstreaming this responsibility will trigger a much-needed formal infrastructure response and spur the upgradation of the existing waste disposal approaches to the status of a resource recovery industry. Their certitude of collecting all the generated garbage from their respective jurisdictions on the banks of the Ganga in segregated form will be the biggest incentive for specialists in waste disposal to buy or barter with them. The disposal specialists will employ infrastructure that can absorb all the wet waste to make India's agriculture lucrative and pesticide-free again. They can deploy closed scientific landfills with methane harvesters that can put the gas to safe use, deploy paper and plastic recycling capabilities to churn raw material for reuse, processing facilities to convert construction waste into pre-fabricated bricks, and formal resource recovery factories to extract gold from discarded gadgets. This will require economies of scale and capital to build machinery, assets, supply chains, and markets for the recovered resources. The joint sponsorship of the union and the concerned state governments will need to facilitate such independent entities.

De-delinking the activity of waste disposal from the local municipal bodies and unlocking its intrinsic value to facilitate the birth of a formal resource recovery industry is the key to a cleaner Ganga. The forking of waste collection and disposal is no different from the separate functions of electricity generation and distribution.

Electricity distribution companies focus on creating an efficient grid network to distribute electricity to homes and shops. They do not aspire to generate electricity (although a few keep toying with the idea), which requires a different set of expertise and capital investment appetite. Instead, they buy electricity from entities that specialize in its generation, like nuclear power plants, hydro generation facilities or wind energy operators and solar plants. Intuitively, the dual existence of customers on both ends of the proposed waste-disposal spectrum defies logic. A classic value chain has a vendor at one end and a customer on the other and the financial payout at every step of the chain takes a linear path from one end to the other, with a mark-up at each step. The question that arises is why should the waste-disposal industry charge money from the local bodies to procure segregated waste. Two arguments negate this criticism. The first is that the safe and efficient processing of waste requires technology, risk mitigation, logistic and operational assets, etc., that have costs which cannot be recovered solely from the salvage value of the processed waste. Benchmarks from clean countries suggest that only one-third of the costs and margins are funded by the salvage value of the processed waste, while two-thirds are borne by the commercial contracts with local bodies. It is the absence of this duality that holds waste disposal hostage to a subaltern existence in India. The second is the moral argument in favor of the duality, that waste disposal is not an entitlement of society, but a shared responsibility toward the sustainable existence of human beings. Such a duality will also demand a new outlook toward law-making and regulation. For example, mandating a user-fee based waste-collection system and issuing pricing guidelines to ensure that the price of sanitation delivery covers the cost of waste collection, disposal, and the enforcement apparatus. A national body must define waste-segregation codes and collection apparatus, prohibit archaic methods, employment norms, punitive actions for violations, moratorium period to manage transition, and so on, which will offer local civic bodies to install the operating framework. These tenets will also serve as a reference guide for the state governments to determine their role in the industrialization of the waste-disposal process.

A legislative awakening of the Indian union on all matters that concerns sanitation will have a direct bearing on the color of the Ganga. The emphasis here is all matters, not just matters that are perceived to have explicit linkages to sanitation, and there are many issues that fall in this implied bucket, but they face policy abandonment for the lack of a perceived correlation with sanitation. India's sugar policy is one example that has contributed immensely toward the Dirty Ganga problem. In 2015, the Central Pollution Control Board (CPCB) directed its counterpart in Uttar Pradesh to prevent the 120 odd sugar mills situated on the banks of the Ganga from discharging effluents into the river. This seemingly well-intentioned directive offers revealing insights about India's failure to reconcile the industrial development policy with waste management. When the fact that the processing of sugarcane for the production of sugar is among the worst industrial polluters is well known, then why was the matter of effluent discharge from the sugar mills not addressed in India's sugar policy? Although the same policy was proactive enough to control the prices of sugar across the value chain to demonstrate a moral high ground to the farmers and was overzealous to proliferate suboptimal sugar mills, the same promptness was missing when it came to controlling the pollution of the Ganga as a direct aftermath of this largess. The low priority accorded to environmental protection in favor of other pressing issues can be argued for this oversight given the fact that it was not until 1986 that India drafted its first set of comprehensive laws on the subject. If the cost of installing and operating an effluent treatment plant at each of these 120 sugar mills was prohibitive, given their suboptimal scale and price control mechanism sugar was subject to, why was the logic of manufacturing consolidation and price control for a discretionary commodity like sugar not presented to the franchise for choice? They could either choose a clean Ganga or enjoy cheap sugar, but not both. The cost of the subsidy on sugar was thus borne dearly by the environment.

Sugar, unlike wheat or rice is a discretionary commodity, one that is extracted from a water-intensive crop that poses severe water-distress risks. It has come under a lot of scrutiny and criticism both for its adverse impact on human health and for the ecological imbalances caused by its agriculture. Yuval Noah Harari, author of the popular book *Sapiens*, labels sugar as more dangerous than gunpowder. Perhaps the policy should have evaluated the trade off of its import and incentivized domestic farming to migrate to other equally economically viable crops. It was also equally possible to examine the viability of a grid-based approach to treating the effluent discharged from these sugar mills to neutralize the cost to some extent. Instead, the sugar policy dealt with import duties to protect the domestic sugar industry without addressing its chronic issues like delays in payment to farmers for the procurement of crops, the depleting water tables, the value chain that disproportionally rewards its traders than its farmers, and not to mention its inefficient manufacturing that spews effluent discharge in the Ganga.

Every commercial activity generates waste, as does every seemingly innocuous human imprint in modern society. If the sugar policy failed to address effluents from a hundred overtly visible and giant-sized sugar mills, it is a foregone conclusion that the waste generated from thousands of other commercial units that dot the banks of the Ganga are undoubtedly being silently absorbed by its waters. India's sugar policy reflects a larger malaise of India's policy approach toward industrial development that does not treat the management of waste as its essential core. If only the sugar policy had allowed for the sugar mills to treat the effluent, the water thus recovered could be ploughed back to the sugarcane fields for irrigation instead of coursing through our towns and getting immersed in the Ganga.

The plight of the city of Kanpur due to the explosive growth in the automobile density is another case that highlights this failure. Kanpur's vehicular density stood at 89 vehicles per 1,000 residents in 2001 and increased to 219 in 2011, a 140 percent growth, while it is estimated that the road network of the city grew at less than half this rate during the same decade. Policy intervention was absent for retiring old automobiles (a part of the waste disposal exercise), prompting the informal commerce of roadside garages and repair shops to fill in the need gap. This informal industry dismantled automobiles and harvested their parts, disposing any waste into the drainage system, allowing it to eventually merge with the Ganga. It was easy for a city like Kanpur to rollout guidelines and licenses for such formal junkyards and prevent their waste from being disposed in the Ganga. It could prevent substandard vehicles from polluting the air and free up precious, illegally occupied urban space, thereby preventing informal resource harvesting of components from discarded automobiles through environmentally abusive means. Even such a policy may fall flat on its face if it is not buttressed with the revamp of steel policy to incentivize mini-mills that use scrap metal to produce steel – an approach quite popular in many clean countries of today, for instance, Singapore.

In 2016, the Motor Vehicles Act was amended, making it mandatory for all diesel vehicles to be discarded after ten years. In 2018, the vehicle-scrapping policy was announced amidst much fanfare to promote formal dismantling units. But it still needs to pass the litmus test for its ability to divert all the discarded automobiles on the banks of the Ganga toward the premises of these formal dismantling units. The policy's test will also be on the funding model of these dismantling units of whether they will beat the haggard drum of doles and limp ahead or the policy will show teeth to retrieve their cost from the consumers by revisiting the taxation on registering new and old vehicles.

All these solutions will still be ineffectual in cleaning the Ganga if cities and towns on its banks refuse to confront the issues of their fractured approach to urban planning. Even if we forgo the exclusionist approach to urbanism in British-occupied India, cities in independent India were designed without political sponsorship and with a strong rural hangover. Up until motorways, metro train projects and river sidewalks began to make their way in the political manifestoes, more than one-third of India's population was living in mediocre cities designed to spew dirt and filth, and a sizeable few landed on the banks of the Ganga.

To imagine a use for a particular piece of land in an urban setting is tremendously tricky. The nature of households, the drivers of the economic development of the city, the model behavior of the citizens, and how the plans of the city should respond to instill this behavior, are all questions that must be taken into consideration. Urban planning is a complex agenda that requires the autonomy to make tough design calls in the present context and to ensure a better future. Urban plans may ration space for some undesirable outcomes or create restrictive designs to alter behavior of the city's habitants in the interest of a better collective future. For instance, it may promote shared living over exclusive space for individuals. It may curtail private spaces to extinguish informal living. It may envisage solutions that require citizens to pay more taxes to yield cleaner and safer outcomes. All these considerations require creativity, bravado, and a scientific temperament. Sadly, a dirty Ganga is a direct outcome of these qualities missing in action for urban planning on the banks of the river.

Urban planners in the clean countries were allowed unbridled expression of creativity and scientific temperament. They took bold decisions, envisioned future populations, and developed detailed city codes, guidelines, and rule books. The institutional response that emerged subsequently preserved their brilliance in the form of frameworks, methods, references, and vision documents. In these countries, urban planning first achieved greatness and was then preserved though institutionalization. For India, and for the cities on the bank of the river, the subject of urban planning suddenly went from non-existence to a bureaucratic set-up sans political patronage post Independence. This rendered the urban planning process impotent to face the impending urbanization challenges, which encouraged proliferation of informal living. It comes as no surprise that if 30 percent of Patna's population today lives in shanties without access to a sewage system, urban designs calls taken decades ago are to be squarely blamed, for failing to provide for formal, affordable spaces for commerce and living. No matter what efforts we make to correct sanitation delivery for formal human clusters on the banks of the Ganga, informal living in the region will continue to discolor the river.

Today, urban planners of towns on the banks of the Ganga must think of solar powered walkways, higher share of public spaces, urban designs that prioritize pedestrians over others, smarter sewage grids, recycling centers & formal junkyards, rental housing, formal temporary markets, integrated surveillance systems, parks and museums, old age homes and day care centers, shared spaces for commerce, charging stations for electric public transport vehicles, eco-friendly temples and river fronts in the same breadth. Today, cities on the banks of the Ganga will need to take inspiration from cities like Seoul and Seattle that are rapidly executing these ideas for a sustainable future. In an inclusive, multifaceted, and inquisitive urban planning approach lies another key to a cleaner Ganga, but city drawings on the drafting table in the confines of the district headquarters will miss spotting it. India's urban planning was pushed into this abyss due to the congenital defect of the local civic bodies that reduced them to antiquate cost centers with only the discretion to earn revenue from real-estate supply in cities. Urban planning became an operational exercise of slicing up city spaces to fund the existence of the local civic body and urban spaces were viewed as individual parts and not as pieces of a larger puzzle. Changing the purpose of land use impulsively, legitimizing informal living, brokering deals to allocate space for commercial use, and political brawling over allocation of spaces for memorials, colleges, marriage halls and associations in towns and cities on the bank of the Ganga have played an overt part in changing her color. Therefore, part of the solution to clean the Ganga lies in reforming the local civic bodies to reduce their addiction to real-estate monetization and free urban planning from this captivity. Cities on the banks of the Ganga must take the congenital defects of their respective local bodies and the antiquated urban planning as a bundled problem statement for the 'dirty Ganga.' They will then need to temper this statement with freedom to explore their higher purpose and customize urban design responses accordingly – a Kanpur, a Varanasi and a Patna cannot have identical outcomes. The Ganga's color will be a lot different in the next two decades should such a bundled problem statement gets taken up as an inspiring challenge.

In February 2017, when the NGT pulled up the National Mission for Clean Ganga (NMCG) for wasting public resources and not doing a proper job of cleaning the river, the irony was hard to miss. The NGT pointed to the lack of coordination among different state agencies and their inaction on preventive measure. But the creation of the NMCG itself manifests India's misguided approach toward sanitation. The template to clean the Ganga encompasses precise legislation, enforcement for sanitation that proactively conditions society's behavior toward a new normal, urban planning that celebrates the spirit of humanity, state actors with bifurcated roles, local civic bodies rejuvenated with the autonomy to face the challenge of sanitation delivery, and a resource recovery industry birthed by state intervention and infused with responsible capital. The NMCG will always be a misguided expenditure and any of its efforts to tackle the issue will amount to troubleshooting, masquerading as work in progress, while the franchise may bask in the false-comfort that the magic pill is working. But, it is equally possible that NMCG demolishes this inference. By the end of 2018, this program did manage to divert nearly 300 MLD of untreated sewage away from the Ganga toward secured STPs and remained committed to delivering a Clean Ganga by 2020. But, in doing so NMCG will manifest a solution that will force us to concede that India can only clean one river at a time and it can only do so by allocating exceptional resources and nibbling finances from other priorities. If we do get a clean Ganga by 2020, the next five years should then see another 'National Mission for Clean next river' in waiting and then the next and so on and so forth. It will then take a century to clean the tenth Indian river assuming an uninterrupted supply of political sponsorship for the cause till then.

The call instead is for a bipartisan template for a Clean India that delivers a Clean Ganga and clean all other rivers as a default output. Clean countries of today demonstrate the success of this template. Take the USA for instance, which generates 300 million tonnes of trash annually. It recycles 60 percent without burning a single gram in the open. The USA's waste management industry in 2016 was estimated to clock a turnover in excess of US$ 70 billion annually, generating profits for entities (public, private, or quasi government bodies) in the waste-management value chain. In doing so, the sector provides dignified employment to thousands. This outcome was not a miraculous bestowing, but an achievement that took decades of toil and turmoil to accomplish. It was able to position the notion of waste as a duty of the society and used legislation and contracts to formalize this expectation. This laid a strong foundation to build a superior waste-management infrastructure that was modular enough to improve with the changing times. Concurrently, the country revised its institutional responses to build cities designed for a cleaner existence and capable of sucking out informal living. The

USA's solution for waste management is also the solution of western Europe, Japan, and Scandinavian countries and many countries in South America and South East Asia. In this light, if the 300 million tonnes of the USA's waste translates into a US$ 70 billion industry, one can only gauge the scale of industry India's 100 million tonnes of waste can give rise to.

The Ganga is not the only misadventure that embodies all that is wrong with India's approach to sanitation delivery. The high ammonia levels in the Yamuna, the pollution of the Periyar, the disposal of solid waste in Narmada, the reduction of Mithi in Mumbai into a floating sewage, the frothing lakes of Bengaluru, the release of toxic waste by Kalamkari units in Krishna district, the reduction of the entrance of the Golconda fort into a garbage dump due to illegal encroachment, the pathetic state of the Taj and the hopeless cause to preserve it, the untreated discharge of 87 percent solid human waste of urban Uttar Pradesh into rivers and water bodies, the political order that attempts to side both with the demand for cleaner air in Delhi and with the illegal status quo of the scrap units in Mayapuri that pollutes the city's air in the first place for its failure to imagine an industrial policy that can transform these units as formal resource recovery enterprises, the silent sponsorship of the local governance of Gurugram for the brazen dumping of garbage in the open in the city's downtown area and setting it on fire, the repeated strikes and on-duty deaths of sanitation workers across India, the medieval practices used to onboard them, the crisis calls by the judiciary and its frequent reprimands to state actors, the rampant child labor in waste collection and processing activities ... the list can go on.

The tools to address these grave issues are the same ones to clean the Ganga with, if only India can transform the patriarchal, abusive marriage between society and the state that is the notion of waste management, where the society behaves like the quintessential demanding husband and the state the dutiful wife fulfilling all his whims, into a partnership based on the principles of equality. If the dastardly ideas of child labor and emaciated workers slithering down chocked sewage pipes to clear sewage with their bare hands are acceptable norms under the charade of livelihood protection, then any attempt to transition toward a better reality will be nothing more than intellectual fantasy, with the occasional release of the flatulence of debates and gimmicks. India's prognosis is not good if a new open landfill is the answer to one that is full and contracted sweepers in lieu of sanitation workers who are perpetually on strike. Installing more bins and pleading with the franchise to use them to throw rubbish will not clean our public spaces. We seek solutions to our trash problem with a mindset that has been corrupted by centuries of misfortune, prejudice and poor decisions. It has resulted into a form of sanitation delivery that breaches the equality tenets of our fundamental rights and duties, respect and concern for environment, and constantly falls short on the yardstick of judicial scrutiny.

An issue like poverty alleviation has a veil of nebulosity about it that concedes varied interpretations. It is still debated, for instance, whether the baseline for defining poverty is the money spent on food daily, or a state of mind born out of social structures. Sanitation, on the other hand, is a ruthlessly unforgiving binary. Dirty surroundings visually expose a failed policy. A perpetual stench is an indictment of a careless society. Illegal scarp units in the middle of the city that are more seen as vote banks than as voracious emitters of pollutants is a sign of an impoverished political argument. Contaminated rivers incriminate misplaced priorities. These overt cues cannot hide behind intellectual deliberation, nor can they offer a false counter argument of hope, except that in India, they do. We can chest thump our credentials to assert our place in the changing global order, but as long as we fail to get the trash to the bin, such a claim gets exposed for its hollowness. If a society that claims to be deeply entrenched in history and culture refuses to critique this very heritage, wherein lies the genesis of the social prejudice that created the sanitation mess, it proves itself unworthy of such lofty attainments. Our constant denial to own and examine our heritage for the reasons that twisted our psyche on sanitation smacks of a guilty conscience.

Centuries of prejudice that has made Indian society biased toward the notion of cleanliness has no parallel in the world. Dirty homes are not acceptable but dirty public places are fine. The inner sanctum of temples should be clean but the filth and garbage piled up outside do not bother the priests and the followers alike. We seek out God in the remotest of places but we do not mind littering the path we travel to meet that God. People traverse miles to take a holy dip in the dirty Ganga but will not protest the dumping of effluents into the river. We get incensed when sanitation workers go on strike but never spare a thought to their pitiable working conditions. We can get aggravated by inter-caste love marriages, lose our civility to protect a nebulous understanding of 'Indian' culture, blindly follow ritualistic sermons of self-styled evangelists and satiate our egos to re-interpret history to our liking, but our fervor runs remarkably thin in the face of the filth in our neighborhoods that stuns us into silent acquiescence. We fervently protest against 'sealing' drives but can wait an eternity for garbage to be picked up from the neighborhood dump. We see the enemy in flesh and blood across the border but refuse to accord the same animosity to the filth that kills thousands of sanitation workers every year and silently eats into our cities, countryside and the environment. The sanitation challenge exposes our tall claims of equality, which refuse to uplift waste-management jobs and bring them up to the stature of the perceived 'superior' jobs. It exposes our democratic credentials that supposedly champion cooperative federalism, but assign the job of disposing the aftermath of the consumption binge of our aspiring nation to the weakest member of the Indian state.

Indian society will never come to full boil over this fractured response toward sanitation delivery. On the contrary, it will simmer perpetually in remote corners and hidden alleys ways, one death or one failure at a time. Contaminated water and soil will cull a few thousand vulnerable human lives every year. The rancid air will weaken the respiratory systems of millions. Methane emissions will alter the weather patterns over decades. A few thousand sanitation workers losing their lives cleaning sewers will create dissenting murmurs and occasional outbursts, but do not have the shock value of a mob protesting a piece of art or expression, presumably due to their inability to create mass angst, hurt collective sentiments and offend the pride a sizeable populace. A reverse engineered protest that seeks to ban a motion picture re-boots political careers and concurrently offers explicit dividends to many. But sanitation delivery does not have any such superior references in the minds of people, nor offers milking opportunities. Generations have lived their entire conscious lives in the company of dirt and thus their minds are conditioned to accept dirty surrounding as the status quo. Such a society cannot fight for a superior reference point on sanitation when none exist in its mind in the first place. Such a society cannot be reasoned with to feel dogmatic about cleanliness, above the basic needs of healthcare, food and employment. It is wishful thinking to wait for an awakening of Indian society to fix the broken waste-management system. Cleaner societies of today were nudged toward a clean living rather than citizens expressing their demands for a clean living and the state working toward it. An awakened society as a prelude to clean living is even more of a far-fetched dream in the case of India because the notion of sanitation is burdened with the unique challenge of social prejudice.

India cannot leave the issue of waste management to its society's will and volition, nor can it wait for society to get responsible toward sanitation as the starting point. On the contrary, the issue will require political bravado backed by dogged policymaking to make a 180-degree shift on the relationship between the Indian state and its citizens. It will require the congregation of stakeholders to pool their collective solutions, many of whom do not even know that their jobs have a direct bearing on the nation's cleanliness, because the solutions are masked in the dark recesses of unexplored perspectives. The anemia of Indian local governance has a direct bearing on sanitation. The failure of Dalit politics and social empowerment to champion industrialization of the sanitation sector as a tool for the social mobility of Dalit castes has resulted in filthy neighborhoods. The inability of urban planning to suck out informality from India's urban narrative has given birth to dirty cities. The incapacity of the political and policy discourse to reconcile cow – the deity with cow – the economic asset has not only twisted the moral compass of the society but it has also resulted in chaotic streets, insecure farmlands and clogged drains. The inaptitude of the industrial policy to appreciate recycling and environment protection as a powerhouse of industrial growth rather than a much delayed or often missed afterthought has given a convenient escape route to toxins and effluents. India will triumph over waste management when it wins over casteism that makes us blind to the unconscious discrimination we commit every day, over informality that wrecks more havoc to human dignity than good to put food on the table, over impoverished state institutions that need a dose of energy to strengthen the credentials of the federal democracy of our country, and over a society with misplaced priorities that need to be dismantled and reordered.

Therefore, India's barometer to measure its cleanliness standards will need to be zero mortality in sanitation jobs, complete eradication of child labor from the waste management sector in letter and spirit, 100 percent recycling of waste water and making it portable to reduce water distress, piped sewage connection in every home, expenditure on enforcement for sanitation as the new head in the annual budgeting exercise, complete shift of bi-partisan political sponsorship from nurturing ghettoes and informality to urban planning and execution that champions formal living and inclusion, recharged water tables and clean water bodies that harnesses our indigenous knowledge and community participation and emergence of a formal resource recovery and recycling industry that not only supplies organic manure and composites to energy, but proudly displays itself as the newest export from India and an engine of economic growth.

The effort to clean India will take a little more than to simply pick up the broom and start sweeping.

REFERENCES

References for Introduction

1. Judgement of Nation Green Tribunal, April 13, 2017 for Original Application No. 596 of 2016 in the matter of Tapes Bhardwaj versus UP State Pollution Control Board, Mathura Cantonment Board, District Magistrate Mathura, Central Pollution Control Board
2. Patrick Suskind, Penguin, Perfume: The Story of a Murderer
3. India Consumption and Retail 2015, Research by Technopak Advisors Pvt. Ltd.
4. India Brand Equity Foundation (www.ibef.org) Flexible Packaging: Changing Dynamics of Indian Packaging Market
5. Gill Plimmer, Financial Times, March 22, 2017, Thames Water fined record GBP 20 m for sewage dump
6. The Economist, March 18–24 2018, Dutch Elections, Domino theory
7. The Economist, March 18–24 2018, Dutch Elections, The centre holds

References for Chapter 1: We the People

1. K. A. Nilakanta Sastri, Oxford, 1958, *A History of South India from Pre-Historic Times to the Fall of Vijaynagar*,.
2. R. C. Majumdar, Motilal Banarsidass (henceforth, MLBD), First Edition 1952, Reprint 1994, *Ancient India*.

3. Radha Kumud Mookerjee, First Edition 1973, Reprint 2017, MLBD, *The Gupta Empire,*.
4. L. N. Rangarajan, Penguin, 1992, *Kautilya: The Arthashastra.*
5. M. S. Nateson, Forgetten Books, First Print 1917, Reprint 2018, *Pre-Mussalman India – A History of the Motherland Prior to the Sultanate of Delhi*
6. Edwin Greaves, FB& Co. Ltd. (www.forgottenbooks.com), The Brahmo Samaj.
7. Mahatma Munshi Ram, Published in Arya Patrika, Lahore (An English Organ of The Arya Pratinidhi Sabha Punjab) Lecture on Arya Samaj and Politics.
8. Colin Spencer, *Fourth Estate* 1993, *The Heretic's Feast, A History of Vegetarianism*
9. J. N. Farquhar, The Macmillan Company, 1915, *Modern Religious Movements in India.*
10. http://www.gandhi-manibhavan.org/gandhiphilosophy/philosophy_environment_sanitation.htm Gandhi's views on environment – sanitation and hygiene (web link last accessed on March 13, 2019).
11. http://www.gandhi-manibhavan.org/gandhicomesalive/speech2.htm Famous speeches of Gandhiji, Banaras Hindu University speech, February 04, 1916 (web link last accessed on March 13, 2019).
12. Vincent Sheean, 1951, Council of Foreign Relations, The Buddhism that was India https://www.foreignaffairs.com/articles/india/1951-01-01/buddhism-was-india (web link last accessed on March 13, 2019).
13. http://savarkar.org/en//Encyc/2017/5/23/Cow-protection-and-cow-worship.html, Cow protection and cow worship, English translation of Savarkar's assorted views on cow protection and cow worship (web link last accessed on March 13, 2019).
14. Prof. Eleanor Zelliot, Dr. Ambedkar and America, *A Talk at the Columbia University Ambedkar Centenary,* 1991.
15. Jawaharlal Nehru, Penguin Books, 2004, *The Discovery of India,*
16. Premchand, Star Publication, 2017, Maansarovar 4.

17. Tathagata Roy, Penguin 2012 & 2018, *Shyama Prasad Mookerjee, Life and Times.*
18. Dr. B. R. Ambedkar, Kalpaz Publications, First Published in 1948, Reprint 2017, *The Untouchables, Who Were They and Why They Became Untouchables.*
19. Bhalchandra Mungekar, Rupa 2017, *The Essential Ambedkar.*
20. http://twocircles.net/2017apr07/407472.html, *Remembering Fatima Sheikh, the First Muslim Teacher Who Laid the Foundation of Dalit-Muslim Unity* (web link last accessed on March 13, 2019).
21. Uma Chakravarti, Conceptualising brahmanical patriarchy in early India: Gender, class, caste and state, *Economic & Political Weekly*, April 03, 1993.
22. Shankar Narayan, 38th IVU World Vegetarian Congress, August 01, 2008, Speech on Origin & History of Vegetarianism in India.
23. Ashok Yadav, modernrationalist.com, November 2010, Periyar remembered in Patna.
24. B. S. Satish Kumar, *The Hindu*, November 30, 2012, Entire Sikkim to take to organic farming by 2015.
25. Manu S. Pillai, Juggernaut 2018, *Rebel Sultans: The Deccan from Khilji to Shivaji.*
26. Malini Narir, *Scroll.in*, Why the rest of India should read Wayanad adivsasis' retelling of Ramayana.
27. Suryakant Waghmore and Hugo Gorringe, *Scroll.in*, By Diluting SC/ST Atrocities Act, Supreme Court undermines Dalit and Adivasi Struggles for Dignity.
28. Sandali Thakur, *Scroll.in*, Obituary, Rajni Tilak (1958–2018) was an activist and poet who fought tirelessly against caste and patriarchy.
29. Ramachandar Guha, *Hindustan Times*, April 13, 2014, Our leaders are not asking hard questions.
30. Karthik Shashidhar, *The Mint*, August 15, 2015, Narendra Modi still a popular PM – Mint-Instavaani Poll.
31. Avinash Kumar, *The Hindu*, November 22, 2015, Our waste, our responsibility.
32. Harsh Mander, *The Hindu*, November 29, 2015, Schools of dishonor.

33. Mohit Sharma and Ritam Halder, *Hindustan Times,* December 08, 2015 Residents must pick cleanliness tab.
34. Saurabh Chauhan, *Hindustan Times,* January 03, 2016, Revellers leave Shimla in a shamble.
35. Rachel Feltman, *The Washington Post,* January 09, 2016, How Roman toilets (any fish sauce) may have helped spread parasites across Europe.
36. Soutik Biswas, *BBC,* May 10, 2016, Why are many Indian Muslims seen as untouchable?
37. Anuja, *The Mint,* June 08, 2016, Kamat's exit a big blow to Congress.
38. Sneha Mary Koshy, *NDTV.com,* June 23, 2016, Actor Mohanlal flags Kerala's 'biggest terror' to Chief Minister Vijayan.
39. Himadri Ghosh, *The Wire,* July 03, 2016, Soldier's funeral reveals India's outsize, outcaste problem, https://thewire.in/rights/discrimination-soldiers-funeral-reveals-indias-outsize-outcaste-problem/amp/?__twitter_impression=true (web link last accessed on February 16, 2019)
40. Manish Kumar and Suparna Singh, *NDTV.com,* July 27, 2016, Sitting cross-legged, he ate a Dalit widow's lunch, rescued her job.
41. Roli Srivastava, *The Hindu,* July 29, 2016, Pokhari is swachh village on the app, but then it's not.
42. The *Scroll.in,* August 02, 2016, Book Excerpt of B.R. Ambedkar's 1948 work *The Untouchables: Who They Were and Why They Became Untouchables.*
43. Mallica Joshi and Soumya Pillai, *Hindustan Times,* August 11, 2016, Nobody's problem: Delhi has no time for its cows.
44. Adita Iyer, *Hindustan Times,* August 11, 2016, TN Dalits fight for a day with God.
45. S. Raju, *Hindustan Times,* August 11, 2016, Priest stops Dalit girl from drinking water in temple.
46. Amulya Gopalkrishnan and Vaibhav Ganjapure, *The Times of India,* September 28, 2016, Khairlanji shows how caste crimes fester.
47. Rohit Bhan, *NDTV.com,* August 20, 2016, Dalit boy thrashed in Gujarat after family refuses to pick up carcasses.

48. Shantanu Nandan Sharma, *The Economic Times,* September 25, 2016, How Sikkim became the cleanest state, an is working towards becoming poverty-free in four years.
49. Rachel Lopez, *Hindustan Times,* September 25, 2016, A spotless record.
50. Ishan Marvel, *The Caravan Magazine,* September 01, 2016, In the name of the mother.
51. A. R. Venkatachalapathy, *The Hindu,* September 16, 2016, The atheist and the saint.
52. Brinda Karat, *Indian Express,* September 29, 2016, Khairlanji, then and now.
53. D. Shyam Babu, Swarajmag.com, October 2016, Re-assessing Gandhi – Gandhi and the Dalits.
54. Akanksha Jain, *The Hindu,* October 06, 2016, Entire Delhi is your drawing room, keep it clean, says High Court.
55. Niranjan Rajadhyaksha, *The Mint,* October 10, 2016, Why the 2016 Economics Nobel for Contract Theory really matters.
56. Gulam Jeelani, *Hindustan Times,* November 25, 2016, Troubled waters of hindon carry waste, sickness.
57. *Indian Express,* December 16, 2016, Church & caste.
58. Ritu Sharma, *Indian Express,* February 28, 2017, Citizen (riot refugee) Nagar: After 15 years, no government school, no hospital, no piped water.
59. Visvak, *The Hindu,* February 19, 2017, 60 minutes: With Hartman De Souza.
60. Abhishek Angad, *Indian Express,* March 13, 2017, The dirty truth.
61. G.T. Sathish, *The Hindu,* March 20, 2017, Dalits refuse to take part in Sidi ritual: It is a reality show entertainment at the cost of our pain, say families.
62. Dhruv Munjal, *Business Standard,* March 25, 2017, The ascetic's Playground.
63. Siddhant Mohan, April 07, 2017, Twocircles.net, Remembering Fatima Sheikh, the first Muslim teacher who laid the foundation of Dalit-Muslim unity.

64. Mrinal Pande, *Scroll.in,* April 10, 2017, From Ramayana to the scriptures, it's clear India has a long history of eating meat.
65. *Indian Express,* April 12, 2017, Where Indian buffalo meat exports go?
66. Gaurav Tyagi, *Hindustan Times,* April 16, 2017, Hundreds of factories dumping garbage in Yamuna at Mommalnath.
67. *Indian Express,* April 20, 2017, NGT pulls up "Art of Living" for slamming tribunal.
68. Pramod Carpenter, *Hindustan Times,* April 29, 2017, Upper caste members pour kerosene in Dalit's well in revenge in MP village.
69. Tony Joseph, *The Hindu,* May 11, 2017, Substance over sound bites.
70. Nistula Hebbar, *The Hindu,* May 12, 2017, Passmandas will engage with BJP.
71. Udit Raj, *Hindustan,* May 15, 2017, Sanitation means fight against age old mindset.
72. Sudhir Kumar Suthar, *Indian Express,* September 22, 2017, What ails rural Rajasthan.
73. Manish Sahu, *Indian Express,* May 05, 2017, Thakurs vs Dalits in Saharanpur: One killed, 25 houses set ablaze.
74. *Press Trust of India,* May 08, 2017, Famished cows left ot die on streets by owners.
75. Anjuli Bhargava, *Business Standard,* May 16, 2017, What rubbish is this?
76. Editorial, May 16, 2017, Know your river.
77. *The Hindu* Hyderabad, May 27, 2017, Man kills son-in-law for honour.
78. *Hindustan Times,* June 01, 2017, Jat Sikh man discovers wife's mother is Dalit, kills himself days after marriage.
79. Vikas Vasudeva, *The Hindu,* June 18, 2017, Haryana Dalit groups plan stir.
80. Omar Rashid, *The Hindu,* June 19, 2017, Interview: Keshav Prasad Maurya, We want to instill fear in those who kill the cow.
81. Soumya Pillai, *The Hindu,* June 19, 2017, Bhim Army calls for Azad's release.
82. *The Hindu,* June 20, 2017, Dalits on Kerala border live in fear of caste clash.

83. Shaju Philip, *Indian Express*, June 23, 2017, A marriage sharpens caste divide in Kerala village.
84. Rajesh Komath, *Economic & Political Weekly*, June 24, 2017, Ambedkar will teach the nation from his statues.
85. *The Hindu*, July 20, 2017, Buffalo meat exports fall 4.35% in April–May.
86. Ashwaq Masoodi, *The Mint*, July 13, 2017, From manual scavenger to professor, the journey of Kaushal Panwar.
87. Javed M. Ansari, NDTV, July 19, 2017, Mayawati's resignation gives away her decline as dalit leader.
88. Shubhomoy Sikdar, *The Hindu*, July 19, 2017, Buffalo meat traders cowed down by attacks.
89. Milin Ghatwai, *Indian Express*, July 23, 2017, Villager to take dip in Ganga after killing cow in MP.
90. Milind Ghatwai, *Indian Express*, August 06, 2017, Now the cows are home.
91. Rishikesh Bahadur Desai, *The Hindu*, August 06, 2017, Amid clamour over cows, who will save the Deoni?
92. Santosh K Singh, *Economic and Political Weekly*, August 26, 2017, The Caste Question and Songs of Protest in Punjab
93. V. V. Krishnan, *The Hindu*, August 07, 2017, Mo(o)vers and Shakers, Taking it easy: Cows rest on a carpet left to dry by a tent house in Dwarka
94. Maulshree Seth, *Indian Express*, September 02, 2017, How UP's cattle crackdown makes a village call its wealth a curse.
95. Manash Gohain, *The Times of India*, September 04, 2017, This is why you may not want to believe anything your future leaders promise.
96. *Press Trust of India*, September 07, 2017, Rusticate students found sticking posters on DU walls.
97. Krishnadas Rajagopal, *The Hindu*, September 07, 2017, Attacks by cow vigilantes must stop, SC tells States.
98. Avijit Pathak, *Indian Express*, October 02, 2017, Gandhi, the subversive.
99. Ritu Sharma and Ritesh Gohil, *Indian Express*, October 03, 2017, Day after Dalit youth's murder: "They banged his head against wall, they kept kicking him".

100. *The Hindu*, October 03, 2017, Dalit killed for watching garba.

101. Pratap Bhanu Mehta, *Indian Express*, October 03, 2017, Lingayat leap of faith.

102. Rahamath Tarikere, *Economic and Political Weekly*, October 28, 2017, Inter-caste marriage and Shakta Myths of Karnataka.

103. Abantika Ghosh, *Indian Express*, January 07, 2018, Mission 90%.

104. Surendra Kishore, *Hindustan*, January 08, 2018, A leader who could not become a messiah.

105. Amrita Dutta, *Indian Express*, January 21, 2018, On a wing and a prayer, interview with Bama Faustina Soosairaj on 25 years of Karukku.

106. Rahul Govind, *Economic and Political Weekly*, January 27, 2018, Ambedkar's Lessons, Ambedkar's Challenges.

107. Karthikeyan Damodaran and Hugo Gorringe, *Economic and Political Weekly*, January 27, 2018, From superstar to CM.

108. *The Economic Times*, February 13, 2018, Abandoning cows after they stop giving milk will cost you ₹5,100 in Haryan.a

109. Narayan Hegde, Indian Express, March 15, 2018, Desi breed conservation should not be at expense of farmers, milk output.

110. Harish Damodaran, *Indian Express*, March 15, 2018, A not-so-white vision.

111. Omar Rashid, *The Hindu*, March 26, 2018, As bulls have a field day in U.P., farmers scurry to save their crops.

112. Khalid Anis Ansari, *Indian Express*, March 29, 2018, It's not just religion, it's also caste.

113. Gopal Kateshiya, *Indian Express*, March 31, 2018, For riding horse upper caste men kill Dalit youth.

114. *Hindustan*, April 05, 2018, Municipal Corporation in Gurugram seals 24 butchery shops.

115. Ravish Tiwari, *Indian Express*, April 15, 2018, The discovery of Ambedkar.

116. Shoib Daniyal, April 18, 2018, *Scroll.in*, https://scroll.in/article/875815/ambedkar-was-vilified-by-his-contemporaries-what-explains-his-popularity-today, Ambedkar was vilified by his

contemporaries when he was alive, what explains his popularity today? (web link last accessed on March 13, 2019).

117. Rajan Kurai Krishnan, *Economic and Political Weekly*, April 21, 2018, Tamil Politics without Caste.
118. Harsha Kumari Singh, NDTV, May 01, 2018, In Rajasthan, 7 Arrested for forcing Dalit groom to dismount his horse.
119. Deep Mukherjee, *Indian Express*, May 01, 2018, Dalits attacked in Rajasthan after groom rides horseback.
120. Manish Sahu, *Indian Express*, May 01, 2018, Dalit man says he was beaten, made to drink urine; 4 held.
121. Aditi Phadnis, *Business Standard*, May 05, 2018, Will Chamling's charm work in 2019?
122. Milind Ghatwai, *Indian Express*, May 05, 2018, Ujjain's Dalits must give baraat notice: official order.
123. Milind Ghatwai, *Indian Express*, May 06, 2018, Ujjain admin revokes Dalit baraat circular.
124. Bhasker Tripathi and Shreya Khaitan, *Business Standard*, April 29, 2018, How Dalit bridegrooms are changing caste status quo.
125. Amrita Dutta, *Indian Express*, May 12, 2018, On Basava turf, Lingayats question Congress move to win them over.
126. Partha Sarathi Biswas, *Indian Express*, May 17, 2018, For these farmers, dairying is not just about milk, but also dung.
127. Debjani Chatterjee, NDTV, May 20, 2018, Man beaten to death in Madhya Pradesh by mob that suspected cow slaughter.
128. Megha Aggarwal, *The Hindu*, June 04, 2018, Harbingers of a green future.
129. Kiran Stacey, *The Financial Times*, June 11, 2018, India's cleanest village is a distant model in a polluted nation.
130. Murad Ali Baig, *Business Standard*, June 15, 2018, India's endangered bulls.
131. Prashant Pandey, *Indian Express*, June 16, 2018, Villagers cite cattle thefts, kin says victims traders.
132. Editorial, *Indian Express*, June 18, 2018, Parched or polluted: Urgent reforms are needed to deal with the acute water stress in most of India.

133. G. Ramakrishna, *The Hindu*, July 01, 2018, Photo Feature: Life in plastic, not fodder: The call may be for cow protection, but in Hyderabad they plunge into garbage to consume plastic.
134. G. Samptah, *The Hindu*, July 14, 2018, The Congress's OBC outreach.
135. *Press Trust of India*, July 17, 2018, "Didn't join Railways to service seniors" employee tells Piyush Goyal.
136. AM Faruqui, *The Hindu*, July 23, 2018, Photo Feature: Roadblock: People drive around stray cattle as they occupy a road in Bhopal
137. *Press Trust of India*, August 05, 2018, 18 Cows locked in Room suffocate to death in Chattisgarh.
138. Ashok Kumar, *The Hindu*, August 06, 2018, What else do you expect when robbers strike?
139. Vaasanthi, *Indian Express*, August 08, 2018, Democrat and patriarch.
140. *The Times of India*, August 09, 2018, FIR against 124 polluting units on Hindon banks, other rivers.
141. Narayan Lakshman, *The Hindu*, August 09, 2018, The last anchor.
142. V. Geeta, *Indian Express*, August 10, 2018, A mirror of his time.
143. Christophe Jaffrelot, *Indian Express*, August 11, 2018, Hindu Rashtra, de facto.
144. ANI, DNA, August 11, 2018, Dalit Lawyers purity Ambedkar statue in UP after BJP leader garlands it.
145. Amar Maurya, *Hindustan*, August 11, 2018, Land meant for cow shed sold for private residential colonies.
146. *The Statesman*, August 22, 2018, Gurudas Kamat | Lawyer-turned-politician and 5-term Lok Sabha MP.
147. Brijesh Singh, *Hindustan*, August 23, 2018, Cows dies because of eating polythene and drinking dirty water.
148. Aditi Singh, *Bar and Bench*, August 24, 2018, Atrocities against Scheduled Castes have shown no signs of abating, Delhi High Court on Mirchpur violence.
149. Order Copy of the Judgement of Delhi High Court, CRL.A. 129/2012 & connected matters, August 24, 2018, www.barandbench.com.
150. Pritam Pal Singh, *Indian Express*, August 25, 2018, Delhi HC convicts 20: Grim reminder of absence of equality, fraternity in society.

151. Avishek G. Dastidar, *Indian Express,* August 25, 2018, Cattle dying on tracks: numbers double in one year.
152. *Press Trust of India,* September 11, 2018, Scheduled Caste leaders allegedly scalped for "wearing turban".
153. Sreenivas Janyala, *Indian Express,* September 19, 2018, We dreamt of bringing up our child without caste prejudices.
154. Esha Roy, *Indian Express,* September 25, 2018, I have been called a sweeper, it hurts... this is a temple, I am doing God's work.
155. Ashok Kumar, *The Hindu,* October 11, 2018, Meat shops forced to close in Gurugram, as Navratri begins, right-wing outfits say they are taking action against illegal shops; police vow action.
156. *The Hindu,* October 04, 2018, Kejriwal, Gupta trade verbal blows over gaushalas in city.
157. Abdul Khaliq, *Indian Express,* October 29, 2018, Glass ceiling, caste wall.
158. Anshuman Kumar, *The Economic Times,* December 27, 2018, Protesting Aligarh farmers lock up stray cattle in schools, hospitals.
159. *Hindustan,* January 05, 2019, Farmers in Agra turn into night watchmen.
160. Omar Rashid, *The Hindu,* January 06, 2019, As cattle market collapses stray cows raid UP farms.
161. Omar Rashid, *The Hindu,* January 05, 2019, Yogi's fresh fiat to District Magistrates on stray cattle.
162. Sourav Roy Barman, *Indian Express,* January 06, 2019, UP's animal farm.
163. *Press Trust of India,* January 30, 2019, UP to barcode stray cows.
164. Manish Sahu, *Indian Express,* February 07, 2019, UP stray cattle crisis: Police start closing cases against angry farmers.
165. Suhas Palshikar, *Indian Express,* February 13, 2019, Psedo-social justice – Policy is not based on assessments of deprivation – it merely addresses specific groups.
166. *Hindustan,* February 04, 2019, Gurugram is free of abandoned cows only on paper.
167. Shruti Jain, *The Wire,* February 15, 2019, With Jaipur gaushala in fund crunch, hundreds of cows starve to death, https://thewire.

in/government/with-jaipur-gaushala-in-fund-crunch-hundreds-of-cows-starve-to-death/amp/?__twitter_impression=true (web link last accessed on March 06, 2019).

168. Sakshi Dayal, *Indian Express*, April 12, 2019, Murder accused among 2 more held for shutting meat shops.

References for Chapter 2: State Actors

1. Central Pollution Control Board, Ministry of Environment, Forests & Climate Change, Delhi, May 2017, Consolidated Annual Review Report on Implementation of Solid Waste Management Rules, 2016 prepared in compliance to the provision 24(4) of the SWM Rules, 2016
2. Order of the National Green Tribunal, February 27, 2017, Original Application No. 134 of 2017 In the matter of: Court on its own Motion Vs. State of West Bengal, http://www.indiaenvironmentportal.org.in/files/Mahananda%20river%20pollution%20NGT%20Order.pdf (web link last accessed on March 13, 2019)
3. The National Green Tribunal, Easter Zone Bench, Kolkata, M.A 1199/2016/EZ & O.A 136/2015/EZ ARK Nirman Pvt. Ltd. Vs. Subhas Datta and Ors.
4. Introduction and Historical Background (http://shodhganga.inflibnet.ac.in/bitstream/10603/4262/10/10_chapter%201.pdf)
5. C. R. Mohanty, U. Mishra, P. R. Beuria, *International Journal of Latest Trends in Engineering and Technology*, Volume 3, Issue 3, January 03, 2014, Municipal solid waste management in Bhubneshwar, India – A review.
6. Indian Public Finance Statistics, 2014–2015, Ministry of Finance, Department of Economic Affairs, Economic Division, July 2015, https://dea.gov.in/indian-public-finance-statistics (web link last accessed March 4, 2019).
7. Bruhat Bengaluru Mahanagara Palike, Budget Analysis 2015–2016 (bbmp.gov.in).

8. Janagraha Centre for Citizenship and Democracy, Jana Urban Space Foundation (India), Annual Survey of India's City-Systems, 2015 & 2017 (www.janaagraha.org).
9. Rakesh Gir, D. Rastogi and Sanjay Tiwari, *International Journal of Research in Engineering and Technology*, Volume 03, Issue 02, February 2014, Through managing municipal waste public-private partnership in Gwalior (http://www.ijret.org)
10. Centre for Civil Society (www.ccs.in), 2016, Delhi's Citizens' Handbook, *Perspective on Local Governance in Delhi.*
11. Centre for Civil Society (www.ccs.in), 2017, Delhi's Citizens' Handbook, *Government to Citizen Services.*
12. Brahim Djemaci, Working Paper 2009, International Centre of Research and Information on the Public, Social and Cooperative Economy, Public waste management services in France: National analysis and case studies of Paris, Rouen and Besancon (http://www.ciriec.ulg.ac.be)
13. Local Government, India.gov.in/Archive
14. http://www.chennaicorporation.gov.in/about-chennai-corporation/aboutCOC.htm (web link last accessed on March 13, 2019)
15. www.mumbai.org.uk/history.html (web link last accessed on March 04, 2019)
16. Srobona Roy Choudhury, *Frontline*, Volume 19, Issue 05, March 02, 2002, A struggle in Bangalore (https://frontline.thehindu.com/static/html/fl1905/19050380.htm) (web link last accessed on March 04, 2019),
17. V. Sriram, *The Hindu*, September 29, 2013, Chennai – the 2nd oldest corporation in the world.
18. Dhananjay Jha, *Hindustan Times*, May 01, 2014, Bandhwari contract is for 30 years, so it can't be terminated now.
19. The New Indian Express, October 05, 2014, Clean is a dirty word for India's municipal bodies.
20. The News Minute, Sunday July 12, 2015, Hyderabad sits on garbage as municipal workers continue strike. https://www.thenewsminute.

com/article/hyderabad-sits-garbage-municipal-workers-continue-strike-32143 (web link last accessed on March 04, 2019)

21. *The Times of India*, December 30, 2015, 1 food inspector for city of 10 lakhs.
22. Mohit Sharma, *Hindustan Times*, January 05, 2016, City stares at civic shutdown as 1.5 lakh staff threaten stir.
23. *Hindustan Times*, January 31, 2016, Delhi government starts clean-up, tells MCDs to show books, Corporation strike day.
24. Satish Nandgaonkar and Swapnasaurabha Kulshreshtha, *The Hindu*, January 31, 2016, Smoke from Mumbai dump forces closure of schools.
25. *Hindustan Times*, January 31, 2016, Deonar fire under control but toxic smoke refuses to wane.
26. *The Times of India*, February 22, 2016, Why the Mysuru model wins the Swachh sweepstakes.
27. *The Times of India*, March 15, 2016, Manpower shortages, inadequate revenue crippling municipal bodies: Survey.
28. Pretika Khanna, Rihan Najib and Seema Chowdhury, *The Mint*, March 15, 2016, Survey highlights urban India's band-aid mindset.
29. *Press Trust of India*, April 07, 2016, Why can't government pay MCD salaries.
30. Satya Prakash, *Hindustan Times*, April 2016, Supreme Court pulls up states for 'ostrich-like attitude' on drought.
31. *The Hindu*, April 22, 2016, Landfill fire ignites AAP-BJP fight.
32. *The Times of India*, May 1, 2016, Dalit Sarpanch "beaten" for sharing dais with MP CM.
33. *Press Trust of India*, June 07, 2016, People turn to courts only when executive fails: CJI.
34. Prashant Jha, *Hindustan Times*, July 12, 2016, In a chaotic city, a state at loss.
35. Akriti Arora and Vasundhara Dudeja, *The Hindu*, July 27, 2016, Pothole, waterlogging complaints flood PWD.
36. Akansha Jain, *The Hindu*, August 20, 2016, Give Najafgarh Zone modern equipment for waste disposal.

37. Shruti Tomar, *Hindustan Times,* August 21, 2016, Ex-sarpanch awaits CM to keep word on Dalit right.
38. *The Hindu,* August 29, 2016, Civic bodies downsize plantation drive targets.
39. Jacob Koshy, *The Hindu,* August 29, 2018, India's most polluted: 30% have no clean-up plan.
40. Krishnadas Rajagopal, *Indian Express,* September 14, 2016, Approved strength of judges enough to end backlog: Law panel head.
41. *Hindustan Times,* September 14, 2016, Swachh funds lying unused with civic bodies, says study
42. Soumya Pillai and Vidha Sharma, *Hindustan Times,* September 14, 2016, Locals don't allow civic workers to enter houses.
43. Maria Akram, *The Hindu,* September 17, 2016, MLAs, councilors ignored civic problems, says report.
44. Richa Pinto, *The Times of India,* September 29, 2016, BMC to return open spaces to citizens for maintenance.
45. Faizan Haidar, *Hindustan Times,* November 26, 2016, Eye of civic polls, CM to open 12 toilet centres.
46. Damini Rath, *The Hindu,* December 06, 2016, Over ₹3,600 crores deficit expected in North Delhi Municipal Corporation.
47. Ajit Ranade, *The Mint,* December 28, 2016, A fair tax for long-term capital gains.
48. *Hindustan Times,* January 09, 2017, Government okays ₹119 crores for civic workers but strike to go on.
49. *The Hindu,* January 09, 2017, EDMC to get "advance" funds.
50. *The Times of India,* January 23, 2017, Lack of Infrastructure crippling lower judiciary: Report.
51. *Hindustan,* February 01, 2017, High Court scold the government and the civic body over lack of cleanliness.
52. *The Times of India,* February 20, 2017, ₹350 crores for use by Mohalla sabhas unspent in Delhi.
53. Mayank Manohar, *The Times of India,* February 22, 2017, Shahdara Lake revival dries up due to financial woes.

54. Paras Singh, *The Times of India*, February 22, 2017, ₹1 crores cleared for Naini Lake redevelopment.
55. Dhananjay Mahapatra, *The Times of India*, February 23, 2017, Apex court threatens to shut polluting industries.
56. B. R. Rohit, *The Times of India*, February 23, 2017, Short-staffed and ill-equipped, forest department faces a formidable task.
57. Pradeep Thakur, *The Times of India*, March 02, 2017, Police, I-T & customers to get lion's share of manpower.
58. Citizen Reporters, *Nav Bharat Times*, March 13, 2017, Photo Feature.
59. R. K. Raghavan, *The Hindu*, May 29, 2017, Mapping out the police overhaul in UP.
60. Paras Singh, *The Times of India*, April 03, 2017, No running away from ugly truth in Badli.
61. *The Hindu*, April 17, 2017, Abolishing house tax was part of BJP's 2007 manifesto.
62. *The Hindu*, April 17, 2017, BJP cheated vendors, hawkers: AAP.
63. Ashok Kumar, *The Hindu*, April 17, 2017, Residents accuse government of delaying setting up of Gurugram authority.
64. Kaunain Sheriff M. and Sowmiya Ashok, *Indian Express*, April 17, 2017, A civic mess.
65. Jatin Anand, *The Hindu*, April 17, 2017, Will transform Delhi into Smart City: BJP manifesto, protection extended to stray cows, no new taxes and scheme for hawkers.
66. *Hindustan*, April 21, 2017, All residential colonies will come under the jurisdiction of the municipal corporation in Gurugram.
67. Isher Judge Ahluwalia, *Indian Express*, April 26, 2017, Starving the municipality.
68. *Indian Express*, May 05, 2017 Gujarat and MP dominate Swachh rankings, Indore is "cleanest" city.
69. Shalini Nair, *Indian Express*, May 05, 2017, Bulk of scores from urban bodies rating themselves.
70. Bhanu Joshi, *The Hindu*, May 08, 2017, Blurring the lines on what is local.

71. Dhiraj Nayyar, *The Hindu,* May 16, 2017, The Modi Paradigm – the force multiplier will come from embracing cooperative and competitive federalism.
72. *Press Trust of India,* May 18, 2017, ITC bags NDMC mandate for zero waste management programme.
73. Shoumojit Banerjee, *The Hindu,* May 18, 2017, Fadnavis ends Pune garbage stalemate.
74. Bindu Shajan Perappadan, *The Hindu,* May 20, 2017, Polluting floodplains to invite ₹5000 fine.
75. *Hindustan,* June 17, 2017, Only when someone is send to jail, will the kusak drain be cleaned asked the High Court.
76. *Hindustan,* June 22, 2017, Municipal corporation is misleading the court on the issue of cleanliness.
77. Manish Raj, *Indian Express,* June 22, 2017, High Court slams civic bodies on garbage: Let's move government colonies to Seelampur or Kotla.
78. *Nav Bharat Times,* June 23, 2018, 7000 people will assemble to clean Gomti River.
79. Damini Nath, *The Hindu,* June 24, 2017, 30 more cities win contest, make the smart cut.
80. *Indian Express,* June 25, 2017, States' fiscal deficit may widen to ₹4,49,520 crores in 2016–17, say RBI data.
81. Rashmi Bansal, *Business Today,* July 02, 2017, The Curious Case of Clean Clean Indore.
82. Sanjukkta Bhaduri, *The Hindu,* July 08, 2017, Redraw the lines for better planning.
83. *Indian Express,* July 08, 2017, Officials who leases out part to lose salaries, Commerical use of Park led to damage: EDMC.
84. *The Hindu,* July 08, 2017, 52 booked for handing out bizarre punishment to man, His wife had cast a vote against a naib sarpanch candidate.
85. Sahil Gandhi and Abhay Pethe, *Economic and Political Weekly,* July 08, 2017, Emerging Challenges of Metropolitan Governance in India.

86. Manish Raj, *Indian Express*, July 13, 2017, Let citizens monitor sanitation workers: Delhi High Court's suggestion.
87. *Hindustan*, July 13, 2017, Committee needed to supervise cleanliness.
88. Bindu Shajan Perappadan, *The Hindu*, July 14, 2017, Tribunal prohibits dumping of waste near Ganga banks, Green Tribunal for "No Development Zone" close to river.
89. Naveed Iqbal, *Indian Express*, July 14, 2017, Delay in notifying civic zones stalls work in MCDs.
90. *Hindustan*, July 20, 2017, Corruption in the collection of property tax in Gurugram.
91. *Hindustan*, July 20, 2017, High Court scold municipal corporation for illegal construction in its jurisdiction.
92. Alok Prasanna Kumar, *Economic and Political Weekly*, July 22, 2017, Rethinking India's Federalism.
93. Yashwant Singh, *NDTV.com*, August 01, 2016, Chief Justice of India broke down, what's going wrong.
94. Alok Mishra, *The Times of India*, August 04, 2017, 3 municipal corporations lose nearly ₹100 crores to illegal hoardings annually.
95. Vinay Gidwani and Julia Corwin, *Economic and Political Weekly*, August 5, 2017, Governance of Waste.
96. *Press Trust of India*, August 08, 2017, Sewer deaths: Jal Board denies awarding contract to any agency.
97. *Hindustan*, August 08, 2017, People suffer from the fight between the government and the civic body.
98. *Hindustan*, August 08, 2017, Four residential colonies will soon come under the purview of municipal body.
99. *The Hindu*, August 11, 2017, NGT bans use, sale of plastic bags less than 50 microns.
100. Sahil Makkar, *Business Standard*, August 14, 2017, Gorakhpur Live: VIPs come and go, garbage remains.
101. Omar Rashid, *The Hindu*, August 16, 2017, Yogi blames lack of hygiene for Gorakhpur deaths.
102. *Hindustan*, September 08, 2017, MCG elections 2017 coverage, Ward 5 in Gurugram needs better roads and sewer systems.

103. *Hindustan,* September 08, 2017, MCG elections 2017 coverage, Ward 31 in Gurugram: People struggle with lack of hygiene and encroachment.

104. D. Shyam Babu, *The Hindu,* September 12, 2017, Reappraising the Raj – Can India continue to ignore Macaulay's foundational contributions?

105. Bloomberg, September 12, 2017, How a 39-year-old Indian woman is trying to stop a $ 10 bn mega theft.

106. *Press Trust of India,* September 19, 2017, Poisonous emissions worse than genocide: High Court.

107. Leena Dhankhar, September 22, 2017, Gurgaon's ward 12: Residents unite in fight against civic apathy.

108. *Hindustan,* October 02, 2017, Delhi should become clean like other cities in the world – Hardeep Puri.

109. Mansi Mishra, *Hindustan,* October 02, 2017, No respite from the stink even after a month.

110. Sahil Gandhi and Vaidehi Tandel, *The Hindu,* October 03, 2017, Urban upgrade to smart governance.

111. Richa Banka, DNA, November 14, 2017, Filthy pond makes teen moves High Court.

112. *Press Trust of India,* November 14, 2017, Girl moves High Court over hygiene near school, Seeks direction to civic body to remove garbage from pond in south Delhi.

113. *Outlook,* November 15, 2017, After criticism over ₹700 crore unused environmental cess, Delhi government moves to buy electric buses.

114. Vijaita Singh, *The Hindu,* November 17, 2017, Rajnath asks Gates to adopt 1,000 Maoist-hit villages.

115. *The Hindu,* November 17, 2017, UP bans garbage burning in urban areas to tackle pollution.

116. Omar Rashid, *The Hindu,* November 26, 2017, In the heart of Lucknow, a ward cries for civic attention.

117. Sushil Kumar Verma, *The Hindu,* December 06, 2017, Photo Feature: Covering the problem, Man-made mess: Firefighters spray foam over piles of garbage at the Bhalswa landfill. The site often sees fires caused

by gases emitting from the garbage. The North Delhi Municipal Corporation Commissioner has said that garbage dumping at the site will be stopped in a few years and the area will be covered with a "green membrane".

118. *The Hindu,* December 10, 2017, L-G orders facelift of Red Fort.
119. Swagata Yadavar, *Business Standard,* December 17, 2017, What Surat can teach other cities about public health.
120. Prakash Singh, *Indian Express,* January 08, 2018, Give polices its dues – To enable the force, revisit the constitutional arrangement.
121. Afshan Yasmeen, *The Hindu,* January 08, 2018, Food poisoning, a common outbreak in 2017.
122. William J. Glover, *Economic and Political Weekly,* January 13, 2018, Living in a category – A history of India's census town' problem from Colonial Punjab.
123. David Sadoway, Govind Gopakumar, Vinay Baindur, and Madhav G. Badami, *Economic and Political Weekly,* Volume 53, Issue 2, January 13, 2018, JNNURM as a window on Urban Governance.
124. *The Times of India,* January 17, 2018, ₹500 crore civic funds to power up GMDA, is MCG left with enough?
125. *Press Trust of India,* January 30, 2018, HC flags "pathetic state" of Rajghat Gandhi memorial.
126. Anand Mohan J., *Indian Express,* January 31, 2018, Dead men still running factories, one inspector for entire industrial area.
127. *Press Trust of India,* February 01, 2018, Singrauli pollution: Plea in NGT against inaction.
128. Faisal Malik, *Hindustan Times,* February 09, 2018, Three transfers in two years: Story of an upright IAS officer.
129. *The Hindu,* February 16, 2018, HC slams Rajghat Samadhi Committee: Can places of worship be treated in such an unhealthy, unhygienic condition?
130. *Hindustan,* February 20, 2018, Municipal corporation will make a proposal and submit to the state government to solve sewer problem in Aayudh depot area in Gurugram.

131. Abhinav Saha, February 28, 2018, Photo Feature: Deep dive: Thirty-six-year-old Rajeev cleans sewers on Aruna Asif Ali Road Rajeev is not sure which agency he is working for, and only knows he has to collect ₹250 from the contractor at the end of the day.
132. Shanker Chakravarty, *The Hindu*, March 01, 2018, Photo Feature: Right under their nose: A heap of garbage lies in front of a municipal corporation-run primary school in east Delhi's Trilokpuri.
133. Chaitanya Marpakwar, Mumbai Mirror, March 08, 2018, Corporator's sneaky plan to sell off open spaces scuttled.
134. Chaitanya Marpakwar, Mumbai Mirror, March 08, 2018, Garbage contracts: Tainted contractors get a lifeline.
135. Achlendra Katiyaar, *Hindustan*, March 27, 2018, State Minister reviews progress of municipal corporation with officers in Mayor's absence.
136. Achlendra Katiyaar, *Hindustan*, April 08, 2018, Councilors could not even protest errors in the proposed budget of the municipal corporation.
137. *Press Trust of India*, April 08, 2018, Delhi: East Delhi Municipal Corporation fails to check illegal dairy in Shakarpur.
138. Editorial, *Indian Express*, April 25, 2018, The Third Tier – As Panchayati Raj Act turns 25, country must debate why grassroots churn has not found express in politics above.
139. *Hindustan*, April 25, 2018, Municipal commissioner issues order – dumping of sewer waste in the open with attract penalty and jail term.
140. Mani Shankar Iyer, *Indian Express*, April 25, 2018, Panchayati raj at 25.
141. *Hindustan*, April 28, 2018, Take steps to restore the reputation of Raj Ghat.
142. Aanchal Magazine and Anil Sasi, *Indian Express*, April 30, 2018, Tax net widens as individuals fuel the surge.
143. *The Hindu*, May 5, 2018, Response sought on Azadpur encroachments, National Green Tribunal directs North MCD to file its response within a week.
144. *Indian Express*, May 25, 2018, Demanding jobs, NDMC staff dump garbage in Lutyen's zone.

145. *Hindustan*, May 26, 2018, Factory owner jailed for causing ground water pollution, First conviction in Delhi involving the issue.
146. Wajahat Habibullah, *Indian Express*, May 31, 2018, A bureaucracy for our times.
147. M. A. Oommen, *The Hindu*, June 04, 2018, Federalism that's not cooperative: Indian public finance.
148. Sampad Patnaik, *Indian Express*, June 14, 2018, Daan dakshina: why an SC order has triggered disquiet in the Lord's home.
149. Mathew Idiculla, *The Hindu*, June 14, 2018, The missing tiers.
150. Amrith Lal, *Indian Express*, June 18, 2018, The dark knight.
151. Mallica Joshi and Sourav Roy Barman, *Indian Express*, June 18, 2018, State of play.
152. Ashok Kumar, *Hindustan*, June 19, 2018, Sewage from Greater Faridabad will spew poison into the Yamuna.
153. *The Hindu*, June 22, 2018, Should Delhi be given statehood?
154. *Hindustan*, June 26, 2018, Ministers made responsible to remove water clogging in the city.
155. *The Hindu*, July 06, 2018, Act against protestors who dump trash on road, stall metro services.
156. *The Hindu*, July 07, 2018, Agra civic body fined.
157. *Hindustan*, July 09, 2018, Councilor and waste management company fight over waste collection in Gurugram.
158. *The Hindu*, July 10, 2018, CM orders suspension of PWD officials for lax attitude.
159. *Indian Express*, July 12, 2018, L-G thinks he is superman, passes the buck on garbage disposal: SC.
160. Anindita Sanyal, NDTV, July 12, 2018, On Delhi garbage, Supreme Court's "Superman" snub to Lt. Governor.
161. *The Hindu*, July 13, 2018, SC pulls up "superman" L-G for garbage pile-up in city.
162. *Hindustan*, Gurugram, July 21, 2018, Responsibility of Eco-green company to be fixed: Rao Inderjit, Minister reviews the contract with the company.

163. Manish Raj, August 03, 2018, *Indian Express*, High Court wants waste management draft in 2 weeks.

164. *Indian Express*, August 07, 2018, Try dumping garbage outside Raj Niwas: SC, Court slams EDMC trash dumping plan.

165. Krishnadas Rajagopal, *The Hindu*, August 07, 2018, Why cannot waste management start at home, asks apex court.

166. Pritam Pal Singh, *Indian Express*, August 07, 2018, Temple can't encroach on land meant for hospital: High Court.

167. *Hindustan*, August 07, 2018, Civic body seeks report on waste collection company.

168. Swati Ramanathan and Ramesh Ramanathan, *Indian Express*, August 09, 2018 Paradox of the vote.

169. Somdutt Sharma, *Hindustan*, August 19, 2018, 5000 thousand complaints pending in Gurugram Municipal Corporation.

170. *Hindustan*, August 30, 2018, We are ashamed for water logging in the city: Rao Inderjeet.

171. *The Hindu*, September 07, 2018, Major push for cleanliness initiatives in Noida.

172. Vivek Tripathi, *The Hindu*, September 12, 2018, Photo Feature: Road not taken: A board thanking Okhla MLA Amanatullah Khan for getting the road from Jamia police station to Shaheen Bagh done at a cost of ₹1.66 crore stands on the street that remains in disrepair.

173. *The Hindu*, September 26, 2018, You want your pound of flesh, HC tells Delhi government, Pulls up authorities for not disbursing funds to civic bodies.

174. R. V. Moorthy, *The Hindu*, September 25, 2018, Photo Feature: The day after, Left out: Idols of Ganesha and puja materials floating in the Yamuna river in New Delhi on Monday after their immersion on Sunday at the end of the Ganesh Chaturthi festival.

175. P. S. Rohit, *The Hindu*, September 25, 2018, Making the most of immersion waste.

176. *The Hindu*, September 25, 2018, Idol immersion: NGT tells States to follow CPCB guidelines.

177. Praveen Khanna, *Indian Express*, September 25, 2018, Photo Feature: For God's sake: Workers remove idols of Lord Ganesha, immersed as part of Ganesh Chaturthi, from the Yamuna. The Delhi Pollution Control Committee has undertaken a water quality analysis. A report is expected in 10 days.
178. *The Hindu*, September 25, 2018, Manual scavenging law not implemented effectively.
179. Sidharth Ravi, *The Hindu*, October 01, 2018, No end in sight to east Delhi's trash woes, EDMC safai karamcharis demand arrears among other things; garbage piling up on streets since September 12.
180. *The Hindu*, October 09, 2018, "Cannot spend ₹500 cr on back wages of sanitation workers".
181. *Indian Express*, October 10, 2018, 28 days on sanitation workers agree to end strike; East Body Promises Regularisation.
182. Vijaita Singh, *The Hindu*, October 10, 2018, AAP government not doing charity by pledging ₹500 crores.
183. Nidhi Jamwal, India Spend, November 13, 2018, Sources Contaminated: Jammu Represents Swachh Bharat Sewage Crisis: 94% Untreated, Drinking Water Sources Contaminated.
184. Shinjini Ghosh, *The Hindu*, December 07, 2018, Karnataka must set aside ₹500 crs. For Bengaluru lakes.
185. Star of Mysore, January 20, 2019, https://swarajyamag.com/ideas/neighbour-issues-karnataka-cries-foul-as-kerala-dumps-garbage-on-outskirts-of-mysuru, Neighbour Issues: Karnataka Cries Foul As Kerala Dumps Garbage on Outskirts of Mysuru (web link last accessed on March 06, 2019).
186. *The Hindu*, January 30, 2019, 139 polluted cities not on clean air plan: report.
187. K P Shankaran, *Indian Express*, January 30, 2019, Tyranny of the majority, In many ways, Gandhi's skepticism about representative democracy resonates.
188. Narendra Pani, *The Hindu*, February 15, 2019, The Karanataka model of politics.
189. Arun Kumar, *Indian Express*, February 14, 2019, Who will pay for sops?

190. Abhishek Mishra, *Indian Express*, February 13, 2019, The Confession: Government's resort to populism in budget indicates failure to address critical issues.
191. Rathin Roy, *Business Standard*, February 07, 2019, Government's shrinking fiscal space.
192. Pulapre Balakrishnan, *The Hindu*, February 08, 2019, Governing India's many spaces.
193. *Hindustan*, February 26, 2019, Gurugram Municipal Corporation passes 12th annual budget of ₹2150 crores of annual expenditure, sanitation services to receive five percent of this budget.
194. Isher Judge Ahluwalia and Almitra Patel, *Indian Express*, February 27, 2019, Small town, cleaner future.
195. Damini Nath, *The Hindu*, February 27, 2019, In its last budget, Kejriwal government targets ₹60,000 crore spending, Highest-ever budget for the Capital: Education gets maximum share.

References for Chapter 3: Urban Planning

1. Ebenezer Howard, Kalpaz Publiciations, *Garden Cities of To-Morrow*, Second Edition of *To-Morrow: A Peaceful Path to Real Reform*.
2. William C. Speidel, Nettle Creek, 34th Printing, May 2017, Sons of the Profits – The Seattle Story 1851–1901.
3. Thomas J. Sugrue, Princeton University Press, 1996, *The Origins of the Urban Crisis – Race and Inequality in Postwar Detroit*
4. Stephen Inwood, Carroll & Graf Publishers Inc. 1998, *A History of London*.
5. Kevin Lynch, The MIT Press, 1960, *The Image of the City*.
6. Ministry of Housing and Urban Poverty Alleviation, Government of India, India Habitat III National Report 2016 (www.mhupa.gov.in).
7. Mila Freire – Senior Advisor, Sustainable Development Vice-Presidency, The World Bank, International Congress on Human Development Madrid 2006, Urban Planning: Challenges in Developing Countries.

8. Lalit Batra, Centre for the Study of Law and Governance, Jawaharlal Nehru University, New Delhi, 2009, A Review of Urbanisation and Urban Policy in Post-Independent India.
9. Ashish Verma, S.Velmurugan, Sanjay Singh, Anjula Gurtoo, T. V. Ramanayya, Raja Kambhampati, World Conference on Transport Research – WCTR 2016 Shanghai 10–15 July 2016, Transportation Research Procedia.(www.elsevier.com/locate/procedia) www.sciencedirect.com, Indian auto-mobility 2020: A Perceptive picture.
10. Donald Winchester, www.vision.org, 2012, "I Will Arise": Charles Dickens and the City.
11. https://www.britannica.com/biography/Ebenezer-Howard (web link last accessed on March 13, 2019).
12. www.lauriebaker.net (web link last accessed on March 13, 2019).
13. Bryan Nelson, June 17, 2013, mnn.com, 10 of the worst wildfire in US history.
14. 10 August 1958, Great Fire of Auckland, https://trove.nla.gov.au/newspaper/article/13011941.
15. https://archive.nytimes.com/www.nytimes.com/learning/general/onthisday/big/0418.html#article (web link last accessed on March 13, 2019).
16. https://dutchreview.com/featured/65-years-ago-today-1953-flood-watersnoodramp (web link last accessed on March 13, 2019).
17. A dreadful catastrophe visits Santa Rosa http://content.cdlib.org/ark:/13030/hb809nb5z5/?order=2&brand=eqf (web link last accessed on March 13, 2019).
18. Tinder for Cities: How Tech is making urban planning more inclusive (https://www.theguardian.com/cities/2017/jan/24/tinder-cities-technology-making-urban-planning-interactive?CMP=share_btn_link).
19. *The Times of India*, January 24, 2010, Delhi, a city of refugee enterprise.
20. Rebecca Dalzell, Smithsonia.com, June 05, 2011, How Charles Dickens Saw London.
21. Anant Prakash (https://huesofasoul.wordpress.com/2015/06/21/story-of-a-development-project-in-kanpur/) June 21, 2015, Words That

Couldn't Get Space Elesewhere, Ohh! CM Promised? But who cares your land is so valuable (web link last accessed on March 13, 2019).

22. Haryana Government, Town and Country Planning Department, Notification Affordable Housing Policy, No. PF-27/48921, August 19, 2013.
23. Agewell Foundation (http://www.agewellfoundation.org) Changing Patterns of Income & Expenditure of Older People in India: An Assessment April, 2018.
24. Anumita Roychowdhury and Gaurav Dubey 2018. The Urban Commute: And how it contributes to pollution and energy consumption, Centre for Science and Environment, New Delhi.
25. Kate Allen, *Financial Times,* October 03, 2014, The man who created London – and other urban master planners.
26. Vandana Ramnani, *Hindustan Times,* May 28, 2015, Wanted: Town planners for smart cities.
27. *Firstpost,* June 18, 2015, Navi Mumbai was Charles Correa's dream: Here's how it turned into a nightmare.
28. Kartik Kumar, *Hindustan Times,* July 14, 2016, Municipal building bylaws to apply in Lal Dora villages in Gurugram, In "Lal Dora" areas, villagers can build houses and set up establishments without adhering to rules until now.
29. Ananya Panda, *The Tribune,* August 05, 2015, NDMC- like civic body for walled city re-development.
30. Kailash Babar, *The Economic Times,* September 21, 2015, Two-third of Mumbai's unsold homes over ₹1 crore, beyond most home-buyers' reach.
31. A Sarwar Borah, *Hindustan Times,* December 07, 2015, Another day of crazy traffic? Delhi to witness 25,000 weddings today.
32. Chitra V. Ramani, *The Hindu,* November 2, 2015, 90% of marriage halls in city not licensed.
33. *The Times of India,* April 27, 2016, India's urbanization likely to be 60% in 3 decades: Panagariya.
34. *IANS,* Max Martin, July 12, 2016, How India's concretising cities are becoming heat islands.

35. Abhishek Behl, *Hindustan Times*, July 14, 2016, City drowns as natural drains missing.
36. Ashok Kumar, *The Hindu*, July 30, 2016, Gurgaon drowning under unplanned urbanisation.
37. Sanjeev K. Ahuja, *Hindustan Times*, August 01, 2016, With ₹23,000 crores builders' dues pending, city infra suffers.
38. Vibha Sharma, *Hindustan Times*, September 14, 2016, Authorities clueless about origin of 50% of cases.
39. Soumya Pillai and Vibha Sharma, *Hindustan Times*, September 14, 2016, Tajpur Pahadi among worst-affected areas.
40. Vibha Sharma and Soumya Pillai, *Hindustan Times*, September 14, 2016, Death toll will double in 5 years if agencies don't act together: Experts.
41. Editorial, *The Hindu*, September 15, 2016, Sapping India's vitality.
42. *Hindustan Times*, September 22, 2016, What were you doing for two months, why didn't you plan, ask green court.
43. Abhishek Behl, *Hindustan Times*, September 22, 2016, Huda drops plan to acquire land for green spaces.
44. Sharad Deep, *Hindustan Times*, September 22, 2016, India vs. New Zealand: Mosquitoes, filth keeps fans away from Green Park.
45. Parvez Sultan, *Hindustan Times*, September 22, 2016, Official apathy, shortage of funds put Old Delhi revamp project in limbo.
46. John Brownlee, Fast Company (www.fastcompany.com), September 23, 2016, Atlanta wants to cover a major highway with this high line-style garden.
47. *The Times of India*, September 29, 2016, Dharavi sub-cluster revamp plan gets in-principle nod.
48. Sweta Goswami, *Hindustan Times*, October 06, 2016, Residents wait for nod to Lutyen's redrawing plan.
49. Parvez Sultan, *Hindustan Times*, January 16, 2017, Government to review ADB funding proposal for redevelopment of Walled City.
50. Soumya Pillai, *The Hindu*, February 07, 2017, 80% of city markets are prone to fire.

51. Shiny Varghese, *Indian Express,* February 19, 2017, Architecture is larger than life, it outlives you.
52. Express News Service, February 25, 2017, Jaundice puts Cuttack administration on toes.
53. Subhomoy Bhattacharjee, *Business Standard,* February 27, 2017, Why cheaper housing is the elephant in the room.
54. Judhajit Chakraborty, *Economic and Political Weekly,* March 04, 2017, An unequal process of Urbanisation.
55. Purusharth Aradhak, *The Hindu,* April 22, 2017, Congested Noida roads held up fire tenders, says fire department.
56. Purusharth Aradhak, *The Hindu,* April 21, 2017, Noida Blaze: "building had no fire clearance".
57. Lalitha Sridhar, *The Hindu,* April 30, 2017, Puducherry reaches into its past for a smart future.
58. M. Venkaiah Naidu, *Indian Express,* May 19, 2017, How to build the new city.
59. *Hindustan,* June 12, 2018, Hospital wards filled with patients of Diarrhea in Gurugram.
60. Shalini Nair, *Indian Express,* June 26, 2017, The Too Smart City.
61. *The Hindu* / Thomson Reuters Foundation, April 21, 2017, Deafening power looms muffle desperation in textile hub.
62. Rahul Devulapalli, S. Harpal Singh, and R. Avadhani, *The Hindu,* May 03, 2017, Summer of dry lakes and dry throats.
63. Naveed Iqbal, *Indian Express,* June 22, 2017, Running out of space, government gaushalas turn away cattle.
64. *The Times of India,* June 27, 2017, Hyderabad lake goes Bengaluru way, spills toxic foam.
65. *Hindustan Times,* June 28, 2017, Family recalls fire horror: Joy turned to tragedy in seconds.
66. Sweta Goswami, *The Hindu,* June 29, 2017, The ugly truth about old age in India.
67. *Hindustan,* July 22, 2017, Why are coaching centres running in residential colonies in the city, asks High Court of Delhi.

68. *The Times of India,* Chennai, July 4, 2017, A remodelled Chennai in the pipeline.
69. *The Economist,* July 04, 2017, Obituary: Jia Jinglong died on November 15th.
70. *The Times of India,* July 10, 2017, Infragaps, layout violations in Sushant Lok-1, says report.
71. Sahil Makkar & Ishan Bakshi, *Business Standard,* July 13, 2017, After two years, smart cities crawl.
72. Diana Budds, Co.Design, July 20, 2017, This California Ghost City is a monument to bad planning, one of California's largest cities is also its emptiest.
73. *Hindustan,* July 20, 2017, Illegal parking slows pace in Gurugram.
74. Meg Miller, *Fastcompany.com,* August 24, 2017, Branding matters in local government, and Atlanta is leading the way.
75. Manshi Asher, *Economic and Political Weekly,* Volume 52, Issue 36, September 09, 2017, Is there no place for the poor in Dharamshala "Smart City".
76. *The Hindu,* September 20, 2018, Supreme Court issues contempt notice to "defiant" Delhi BJP chief – Directs him to appear before it on September 25 for allegedly breaking seal of premises being run in violation of the Delhi Master Plan.
77. Pooja Pillai, *Indian Express,* September 29, 2016, In the city: The urban space is a crucible for the banal and the fantastic in Schon Mendes' vivid, crowded paintings.
78. Damini Nath, *Indian Express,* October 02, 2016, Foggy impact of fumigation on dengue, chikungunya.
79. Dipak Dash, *The Times of India,* October 04, 2016, Small towns hurtling towards infra hellhole.
80. *The Hindu,* October 06, 2016, Need to adopt prefab technology to provide housing for all: Naidu.
81. Daniel Stacey, *Business Standard / Wall Street Journal,* October 19, 2017, New 'Smart City' hatches solutions to urban chaos.
82. Dipti Jain, *The Mint,* November 23, 2016, Circular migration is holding back India's urbanization.

83. *Hindustan*, December 05, 2018, Survey of illegal paying guest accommodations operating in Gurugram couldn't be completed even after eight months.
84. Shivani Singh, *Hindustan Times*, January 09, 2017, Decongesting never easy but gains worth the pain.
85. Soumya Pillai, *Hindustan Times*, January 09, 2017, Plan for car-free CP sparks fresh hope in evicted vendors.
86. Ritam Halder, *Hindustan Times*, January 09, 2017, Experiment will work, look at other cities: Experts' message for traders.
87. *Hindustan*, January 09, 2019, Union Minister Hardeep Puri admits there is corruption in DDA.
88. Shiny Varghese, *Indian Express*, February 04, 2017, His was a way of living than just a way of building.
89. *Hindustan*, February 09, 2017, India is the third largest market for spurious medical drugs in the world.
90. Shalini Nair, *Indian Express*, February 18, 2017, Adding portability to benefits: Social welfare of migrant workforce.
91. *The Hindu*, February 28, 2017, Cuttack civic body slammed for jaundice outbreak.
92. Damini Nath, *The Hindu*, February 28, 2017, 891 unauthorised colonies await sanction.
93. Pragya Kaushika, *Indian Express*, March 11, 2017, Government, MCDs wasted money on sprays that didn't work.
94. Subhomoy Bhattacharjee, *Business Standard*, March 19, 2017, Land acquisition may not be a zero-sum game, two new studies show.
95. Josh Artus, *Quartz.com*, March 21, 2017, The surprising ways neuroscience can help design smarter, more intuitive cities.
96. Shubashree Desikan, *The Hindu*, April 26, 2017, Amaravati could become the prototype for building cities.
97. *Hindustan*, April 21, 2017, 6 people die in a factory fire in Noida Sector-11, The factory was running without NOC, case registered.
98. Ritika Chopra, *Indian Express*, April 23, 2017, Delhi SPA chief to PM: Don't move us to Urban Development.

99. Pranav Mukul, *Indian Express*, May 05, 2017, Smart standards needed for better city planning.
100. Aniruddha Ghoshal, *Indian Express*, May 16, 2017, Even as city retains top spot, over 17 lakhs are BPL.
101. Manish Raj, *Indian Express*, May 17, 2017, Vector-borne diseases: HC slams "lack of measures".
102. *Hindustan*, May 18, 2015, Action against illegal parking on roads in Delhi.
103. Shalini Nair, *Indian Express*, May 20, 2017, Not-so-strong foundation for rental housing.
104. Shaju Philip, *Indian Express*, June 22, 2017, Fever panic in Kerala: numbers and the reasons.
105. K. C. Deepika, *The Hindu*, June 27, 2017, Motorisation costs to soar in 3 years, says study.
106. *Hindustan*, July 01, 2017, DDA launches a new project of 12,000 houses.
107. *The Hindu*, Bengaluru, June 27, 2017 People will prefer public transport, cycles.
108. *Hindustan*, July 03, 2017, Roads submerge in water and manholes overflow in Gurugram.
109. *The Hindu*, July 03, 2017, Five hurt as four-storey building collapses in Laxmi Nagar.
110. *The Hindu*, June 27, 2017, Kerala posts its worst dengue figures.
111. *Hindustan*, July 07, 2017, Students tortured for 45 mins at midnight.
112. Sourabh Singh, *Hindustan*, July 07, 2017, Had the management institute taken cognizance of the complaint, Ramesh's life would have been saved.
113. *Hindustan*, July 07, 2017, 500 PG accommodations running without facilities.
114. Editorial, *Indian Express*, July 08, 2017, Off Track.
115. Omar Rashid, *The Hindu*, July 08, 2017, A spike in the footprints of time.
116. Sowmiya Ashok, *Indian Express*, July 14, 2017, Tanneries must follow orders or face closure.

117. *Press Trust of India*, July 25, 2017, High Court angry over Hauz Khas village eateries.

118. Dipak Dash, *The Times of India*, August 04, 2017, Farmers can now turn land along National Highways into 'highway nests'.

119. Citizen Reporter – Suraj Kumar, *Navbharat Times*, Lucknow, August 13, 2017, Photo Feature: Illegal dairy operational in Indira Nagar.

120. *Navbharat Times*, Lucknow, August 13, 2017, 500 homes in residential colonies face regular water logging for the lack of STP pump.

121. *The Economist*, August 31, 2017, Rent collective: Co-living is for hipsters not hippies, Pricey housing markets mean co-living buildings are on the rise.

122. *Press Trust of India*, September 09, 2017, Few smart cities will not make a big difference: VP Venkaiah Naidu.

123. Katharine Schwab, Co.Design, September 12, 2017, How the chief architect of 21st Century New York envisions the future of cities.

124. Shiv Visvanathan, *The Hindu*, September 25, 2017, The idea that used to be Bangalore.

125. *Indian Express*, September 28, 2017, State government announces slew of measures for police force.

126. Dipti Singh, *Indian Express*, October 24, 2017, Illegal hawkers: A problem Mumbai city has been battling for decades.

127. Krishna Kant, *Business Standard*, December 10, 2017 Realty firms struggle with record ₹99,000 crores unsold inventory.

128. Jamies Smyth, *Financial Times*, December 09, 2017, New Zealand looks to ban foreigners from buying houses.

129. Ravik Bhattacharya, *Indian Express*, December 17, 2017, In Afrazul's wake.

130. Ram Singh, *The Hindu*, January 08, 2018, The problem of land hoarding.

131. Soumya Pillai, *The Hindu*, January 08, 2018, 80% of Delhi's markets are death traps.

132. Shiny Varghese, *Indian Express*, January 14, 2018, Unto the Earth.

133. Anjuli Bhargava, Business Standard, January 21, 2018, A new lesson in affordable education.

134. Gautam Bhatia, *The Hindu,* January29, 2018, Rebuilding our cities.
135. *The Hindu,* January 31, 2018, Government will move Supreme Court for stay on sealing drive: Kejriwal.
136. Anand Mohan J, *Indian Express,* January 31, 2018, Bawana Republic: Fire trap Bawana, why majority of units take no precautions, fly under radar.
137. Damini Nath, *The Hindu,* February 01, 2018, Assembly committee grills municipal officials.
138. *The Hindu,* February 01, 2018, L-G assured me of immediate solution to sealing issue: CM.
139. *Indian Express,* February 01, 2018, As trader fury rises, Puri proposes amending Master Plan: Lower conversion charges, business in basement on table.
140. Abhinav Rajput, *Indian Express,* February 03, 2018, Relief for city's traders as DDA approves changes to Master Plan.
141. Shinjini Ghosh, *The Hindu,* February 03, 2018, In a relief to traders, DDA to introduce uniform FAR.
142. *Hindustan,* February 19, 2018, High Court concerned about the master plan of Delhi.
143. Nardeep Singh Dahiya, *Hindustan Times,* July 30, 2018, It was far better in good Gaon days.
144. Aakar Patel, Business Standard, February 24, 2018, Understanding your city.
145. *Hindustan,* February 24, 2018, Cycles tracks blatantly converted into car parking sites in Gurugram.
146. *The Times of India,* Gurugram, February 19, 2018, 76 banquet halls owe MCG ₹9.5 crore as property tax.
147. Hina Rohtaki, *Indian Express,* February 20, 2019, Municipal commissioner puts brakes on paver work in Chandigarh.
148. *Indian Express,* March 07, 2018, Fuming Supreme Court puts Master Plan changes on hold.
149. *Indian Express,* March 07, 2018, Court pulls up BJP MLA: CM has nothing to do with sealing.

150. Pankaj Chaturvedi, *Hindustan*, March 05, 2018, Source of traditional wisdom is in danger.

151. Chidanand Rajghatta, *The Times of India*, March 08, 2018, BV Doshi first Indian to win architecture "Nobel", Doshi is also known as an institution builder.

152. Hardeep Puri and Jagan Shah, *Indian Express*, March 15, 2018, Moving to the city.

153. *The Times of India*, March 22, 2018 PM Awas Yojana: Only 8% target met under urban housing scheme.

154. Malini Krishnankutty, *Economic and Political Weekly*, March 24, 2018, Fragmentary planning and spaces of opportunity in peri-urban Mumbai.

155. *Hindustan*, March 27, 2018, Relief planned for 351 roads in Delhi through mixed use development rights.

156. *Hindustan*, April 14, 2018, Fire alarm saved 19 people in Kohaat Enclave.

157. Divya Shekhar, *ET Bureau*, April 22, 2018, Chickpet: Bengaluru's original business district is congested, dirty.

158. Prabhat Kumar, *Hindustan*, April 23, 2018, Colonies cannot be regularized by tweaking master plan directs High Court of Delhi.

159. Sandeep Saxena, *The Hindu*, April 24, 2018, Photo Feature: Up in Smoke, A six-year-old was killed in a fire that broke out in the shanties of Shahdara's Mansorovar Park. About 250 jhuggis were reduced to ashes in the blaze.

160. Sagar Hugar, *The Hindu*, April 25, 2018, Redevelopment of Kathputli Colony begins.

161. Isher Judge Ahluwalia, *Indian Express*, April 25, 2018, Bring back the lakes.

162. Hemani Bhandari, *The Hindu*, April 28, 2018, Three of family dead after dispute over parking space.

163. *Hindustan*, April 28, 2018, Minor scuffle ended in blood bath.

164. Raghvendra Kamath, April 30, 2018, One year after, RERA remains a work in progress.

165. A. G. Krishna Menon, *Indian Express,* May 01, 2018, Big city blues.

166. Praveen Khanna, *Indian Express,* May 06, 2018, Photo Feature: Razed, Illegal structures on pavements being demolished by the North MCD near Delhi Gate on Saturday, as part of a drive to clear pavements and no-parking zones.

167. *Hindustan,* May 09, 2018, Posinous water supplied in new residential colonies in Gurugram.

168. Pronab Sen, *Economic and Political Weekly,* May 12, 2018, Puzzles of Indian urbanization.

169. *Hindustan,* May 12, 2018, One parking zone among 40000 shops in Karol Bagh.

170. Alexandra Staub, *Fast Company,* May 16, 2018, The hidden cost of our obsession with luxury living.

171. *Hindustan,* May 16, 2018, Main road in Lajpat Nagar becomes a parking zone.

172. *Hindustan,* May 18, 2018, Experts will search for affordable housing solutions in the city.

173. Shailin Nair, *Indian Express,* May 29, 2018, Master Plan should shift with ground reality: Draft.

174. Achilendra Katiyaar, *Hindustan,* June 05, 2018, Gurugram will get Chandigarh's Sukhna like lake.

175. Hemani Bhandari, *The Hindu,* June 13, 2018, Deplorable living conditions inside de-addiction centre.

176. Megha Manchanda, *Business Standard,* June 14, 2018, Varanasi's freight village seen to be game changer.

177. *The Times of India,* Gurugram, June 14, 2018, How half of Gurugram's water bodies vanished in 40 years.

178. Vikas Vasudeva, *The Hindu,* June 16, 2018, When Shimla queued up for water.

179. *The Hindu,* June 16, 2018, Man shot dead by neighbor after brawl over water connection.

180. Justice Ilevbare, The Nation, Nigeria, June 16, 2018, From slums to affordable green homes.

181. Anto Antony and Dhwani Pandya, Bloomberg, June 19, 2018, Lavasa, A Billionaire's Dream City Near Mumbai, Turns Into Ghost Town.
182. *Hindustan*, June 20, 2018, Notices served to 12 illegal banquet halls in Gurugram.
183. *Navbharat Times*, Lucknow, June 22, 2018, Widen road intersection points, identify hawking zones: CM Yogi.
184. *Navbharat Times*, Lucknow, June 22, 2018, Administration to Hotel Owners: Do the impossible possible in 15 days.
185. Mallica Joshi, *Indian Express*, June 22, 2018, Trees to be felled for housing project despite NGT order saying replant first.
186. Somdutt Sharma, *Hindustan*, June 25, 2018, 85% of public lakes in the city encroached.
187. *Indian Express*, June 25, 2018, Can Delhi afford to cut down so many trees for housing project, High Court asks NBCC.
188. *Hindustan*, July 03, 2018, Next four days not good for Banquet Halls in Ghaziabad.
189. Bindu Shajan Perappadan, *The Hindu*, July 07, 2018, Elders compromise for sake of care from family: study.
190. *Hindustan*, July 10, 2018, Water connections to be given in Illegal housing colonies.
191. *Hindustan*, July 13, 2018, India will need to build a new Chicago every year – Mr. Hardeep Puri.
192. Somdutt Sharma, *Hindustan*, July 13, 2018, Plan underway to regularize unauthorized construction in Gurugram.
193. AFP, July 15, 2018, Chinese officials halt show on tainted water.
194. Arif Hasan, *The Dawn*, July 15, 2018, Houses or housing?
195. *Hindustan*, July 21, 2018, Six illegally constructed buildings sealed in Gurugram.
196. Deepak Sirohi, *Hindustan*, July 23, 2018, Narrow lanes poses challenge for rescue and relief work.
197. R. Krishna Kumar, *The Hindu*, August 01, 2018, Redesigning Brindavan Gardens not a good idea.

198. *The Times of India*, August 02, 2018, Delhi houses 25% of all "fake" engineering colleges of India.

199. *Press Trust of India*, August 10, 2018, India's elderly population will Cross 340 Million by 2050.

200. *The Economist*, August 10, 2018, Where are the people? How Tianjin, once China's fastest-growing region, became its slowest.

201. Andrew Small, https://www.citylab.com/transportation/2018/08/is-it-time-to-rethink-what-a-bike-lane-is/568483/?utm_source=twb August 24, 2018 (web link last accessed on March 06, 2019).

202. *Press Trust of India*, August 26, 2018, 51,837 industries in Delhi under NGT scanner.

203. Sakshi Dayal, *Indian Express*, August 29, 2018, Gurgaon grinds to a halt after highest rainfall in 8 years.

204. Mallica Joshi, *Indian Express*, August 29, 2018, Interview: NBCC chief Anoop Kumar Mittal, 'Redevelopment cannot happen without either cutting or transplanting trees. Do we want people to live in slums?

205. Manju Menon and Vidya Viswanathan, *The Hindu*, August 30, 2018, How not to do an environmental assessment.

206. Rahul Srivastava and Matias Echanove, *The Hindu*, September 01, 2018, Shenzen's unfortunate urban turn.

207. Ashok Kumar, *The Hindu*, September 12, 2018, Kant Enclave dwellers face uncertainty after SC judgement.

208. *The Hindu*, September 27, 2018 Seven, including four kids, killed in building collapse in Ashok Vihar, Delhi.

209. Saurabh Trivedi, *The Hindu*, September 27, 2018, I built the fourth floor and it took the life of my two sons.

210. *Hindustan*, September 25, 2018, Water logging in Gurugram due to Monsoons, Commuters on Sohna Road braved traffic jams for hours.

211. *Hindustan*, September 25, 2018, Incomplete residential housing projects in Noida will be completed in three years.

212. *Hindustan*, September 25, 2018, High Court of Delhi bans culling of chickens in Ghazipur Murga Mandi.

213. Visvak, *The Hindu*, September 30, 2018, From Manipur to Madras.

214. *The Hindu,* October 1, 2018, Parties lock horns over sealing in the capital – The Aam Aadmi Party, the Congress and the BJP, which is in power in all three civic bodies speak against the drive being held across the city.

215. *The Hindu,* October 12, 2018, Land pooling policy gets Centre's nod.

216. Cheryl Gladu, https://www.inverse.com/article/50943-cohousing-builds-better-smart-cities?refresh=74, November 18, 2018, What is Cohousing? How to build a smarter city without tech? (web link last accessed on March 13, 2019).

217. Hina Rohtaki, *Indian Express,* November 15, 2018, Chandigarh: Place where Nehru envisaged "modern city" now a shamble.

218. Sama Khan, *Indian Express,* November 21, 2018, Urban only in name.

219. Maria Crawford, *The Financial Times,* December 14, 2018, How we lost our ambitions for the tech-enabled home.

220. Bishwanath Ghosh, *The Hindu,* December 10, 2018, Beautification plan destroys oldest neighbourhoods in Varanasi.

221. Sakshi Dayal, *Indian Express,* January 21, 2019, Road to nowhere – Once expected to boost the Delhi-Gurgaon link, the Dwarka expressway now stands delayed by over a decade.

222. Radheshyam Jadhav, *The Hindu* Business Line, February 06, 2019, Just 20% completed under "Housing for All".

223. Surabh Trivedi, Shinjini Ghosh, *The Hindu,* February 14, 2019, Mahipalpur's wait for fire station continues.

224. *Indian Express,* February 28, 2019, Bill passed in Haryana Assembly opens Aravallis to construction, opposition objects and alleges that the move is to benefit builders, real estate developers, land mafia.

225. 6 Thoughts on materials and construction: Decisions that improve people's quality of life, https://www.archdaily.com/909823/6-thoughts-on-materials-and-construction-decisions-that-improve-peoples-quality-of-life?utm_campaign=trueAnthem%3A+Trending+Content&utm_content=5c78cdfa1adf640001b93700&utm_medium=trueAnthem&utm_source=facebook (web link last accessed on 28 February 2019).

226. Eric Baldwin, https://www.archdaily.com/912445/unstudio-designs-worlds-smartest-neighborhood-in-the-netherlands?utm_medium=email&utm_source=ArchDaily%20List&kth=4,185,966 (web link last accessed on March 01, 2019).

227. Michelle Jamrisko, *Bloomberg*, March 05, 2019, Gurugram world's most polluted city, 6 others in India in Top 10: Study.

Reference for Chapter 4: Informal Living

1. Junio M Ragragio, Understanding slums: Case studies for the Global Report on Human Settlements 2003, The case of Metro Manila, Philippines.
2. Report of the Tejendra Khanna Committee of Experts set up by Government of India to look into various aspects of Constructions & Misuse of Premises in Delhi, New Delhi, May 13, 2006, http://delhi-masterplan.com/wp-content/uploads/2009/09/Tejinder-khanna-comittee-report.pdf (web link last accessed on March 13, 2019).
3. *Rediff.com*, November 18, 2010, Delhi collapse: Death toll rises to 70, 38 building declared unsafe.
4. *History.com* Staff, 2010, Tenements, http://www.history.com/topics/tenements (web link last accessed on March 13, 2019).
5. Dr. C Chandramouli, Registrar General & Census Commissioner India, Housing Stock, Amenities and Assets in Slums – Census 2011.
6. *The Times of India*, June 27, 2011, 36% population lives in 446 slums in city.
7. *The Times of India*, December 4, 2011, Nagpur has a whopping 447 slums!
8. Dipak Kumar Dash, *The Times of India*, August 20, 2013, By 2017, India's slum population will rise to 105 million.
9. S Rukmini, *The Hindu*, October 01, 2013, 65 million people live in slums in India, says census data.
10. United Nations Department of Economic and Social Affairs, July 10, 2014, New York, World's population increasingly urban with more than half living in urban areas.

11. You tube channel – rtaylorsmith, October 14, 2014, City slums – Megacity Problems, https://www.youtube.com/watch?v=6fcDF3PESXI (web link last accessed on March 13, 2019).
12. Research done by Technopak Advisors on Space Planning for commercial development to enhance Revenue Maximization and provide superior Customer Convenience for Anand Vihar Railway Station, December 28, 2016.
13. Slums, Exploring 20th Century London, http://www.20thcenturylondon.org.uk/slums (web link last accessed on March 13, 2019).
14. Charles Booth's London Poverty maps and police notebooks, https://booth.lse.ac.uk/learn-more/who-was-charles-booth (web link last accessed on March 13, 2019).
15. Paul Roy, *NewStatesman*, September 18, 2014, In the slums of Manila, inequality is so bad that the worst off have no chance to protest (www.newstatesman.com).
16. Rashpal Singh, *Hindustan Times*, July 30, 2016, Badshapur drain neglect proves costly.
17. *The Times of India*, August 29, 2016 Slum-free city, a distant dream.
18. Sweta Goswami, *The Hindu*, August 29, 2016, Development promises in illegal colonies ring hollow.
19. Soibham Rocky Singh, *Hindustan Times*, January 04, 2016, Illegal colonies cause traffic chaos, environmental degradation, says HC.
20. Paras Singh & Abhinav Mittra, *The Times of India*, January 05, 2017, HC order leaves illegal Utsav Vihar helpless.
21. Shiv Sunny, *The Hindu*, January 9, 2017, Kathputli Colony residents "slum" it for a better future.
22. *Hindustan*, February 08, 2017, HUDA removes encroachment and reclaims 40 acres of its own land.
23. Akanskha Jain, *Indian Express*, February 2017, Civic agencies create slum over drain.
24. Abhishek Angad, *Indian Express*, February 08, 2017, 4 Toilet complexes for 10,000 homes: Jahangirpuri wakes up to daily struggle.
25. *The Times of India*, April 22, 2017, Mob chases away Ludhiana civic body demolition team.

26. Shaju Philip, *Indian Express,* April 23, 2017, Removal of cross halts anti-encroachment drive.
27. T. Nandakumar, *The Hindu,* April 23, 2017, Kerala's high ranges sit on powder keg.
28. *The Times of India,* May 17, 2017, Is blue the colour of death in Delhi's cancer colony?
29. *The Hindu,* June 23, 2017, All slums to be open defecation-free by April 2018: CM.
30. *Hindustan,* June 28, 2017, Temporary colonies spreading garbage: MCD.
31. *The Times of India,* July 25, 2017, Displaced slum-dwellers continue to haunt Aliganj residents.
32. *The Times of India,* August 04, 2017, Vendors vent anger over crackdown.
33. Gajendra Yadav, *Indian Express,* August 09, 2017, Photo Feature: Despite the Rain: A barber at work at a waterlogged stretch in Nodia's Sector 63.
34. Ipsita Pati, *Hindustan* Times, September 25, 2016, MCG maps water bodies to remove encroachments.
35. Rohit Bhan, *NDTV.com,* October 03, 2017, Gujarat councillor tied to tree, beaten up amid anger over demolition.
36. *Hindustan Times,* October 06, 2017, 800 illegal structures razed in Ghata village.
37. *Indian Express,* October 6, 2017, Unauthorised buildings before December 2016 to be made legal: North body.
38. Nirnimesh Kumar, *The Hindu,* October 27, 2017, Rebuild demolished Sainik Farms home, court tells SDMC.
39. *Hindustan,* October 27, 2017, 32 illegal restaurants to be closed in Hauz Khaas.
40. *The Hindu,* October 31, 2017, Hawker standoff: Congress plans rally in Dadar.
41. Somya Lakhani, *Indian Express,* November 3, 2017, Kathputli Colony demolition. Homeless overnight, residents say streets are not safe at night.

42. Linah Baligha, *Mumbai Mirror,* November 29, 2017, BMC official faces ₹6L fine.
43. *The Hindu,* November 30, 2017, 40 families left homeless after CPWD demolition drive.
44. *Hindustan,* December 1, 2017, NGT seeks report from the government on hotels in Mahipalpur.
45. Soibam Rocky Singh, *The Hindu,* December 13, 2017, Will prayer reach God if you pray from illegal property: High Court.
46. K. C. Smitha and Barun Deb Pal, *Economic and Political Weekly,* January 20, 2018, Spatial reproduction of urban poverty in global city – Gender, informality and mobility in Bengaluru.
47. Press Trust of India, February 16, 2018, Centre to file reply justifying law protecting illegal colonies.
48. *The Hindu,* March 15, 2018, Encroachments in Asola village demolished.
49. Amar Maurya, *Hindustan,* March 31, 2018, Three days after sealing drive, Jacobpura Furniture Market encroached again.
50. *The Hindu,* March 31, 2018, 15 colonies to be regularized in Gurugram.
51. *Hindustan,* April 05, 2018, Illegal construction inside Kamla Nehru's haveli stayed.
52. *Hindustan,* April 08, 2018, Heritage buildings converted into flats and shops.
53. Laura B. Nolan, David E Bloom, Ramnath Subbaraman, *Economic and Political Weekly,* April 14, 2018, Legal Status and Deprivation in Urban Slums over Two Decades.
54. *Hindustan,* April 15, 2018, Encroachments will be removed in Anand Vihaar and made free of traffic jams.
55. *Hindustan,* April 22, 2018, 155 Jhuggies and one factory gutted in fire in Gurugram.
56. *Hindustan,* April 23, 2018, Illegal school buildings demolished in Delhi.
57. Pritam Pal Singh, *Indian Express,* April 25, 2018, Unauthorised construction a time bomb says High Court.
58. *The Hindu,* April 25, 2018, 500 shanties gutted; no casualties.

59. *Hindustan*, April 25, 2018, Supreme Court refuses to vacate the stay on modifications of Delhi Master Plan – 2021, No construction in illegal colonies.
60. *Hindustan*, April 28, 2018, Illegal construction goes on blatantly in temporary colonies in West Delhi.
61. Damini Nath, *The Hindu*, April 28, 2018, Survey of illegal colonies may miss September deadline, only 62 out of 1797 colonies authenticated.
62. Sourav Roy Barman, *Indian Express*, April 29, 2018, City's unauthorised colonies: Surveys hit by pending bills.
63. *Hindustan*, May 01, 2018, Business of illegally filling cooking gas cylinders going on at 26 places in Ghaziabad.
64. *Hindustan*, May 01, 2018, Illegal construction in five colonies in Gurgaon demolished.
65. *Hindustan Times*, May 02, 2018, Woman town planner shot dead by Kasauli hotel owner during demolition drive ordered by SC.
66. Navjeevan Gopal, *Indian Express*, May 02, 2018, 3 hours after this photo, she was shot dead doing her job as per SC order.
67. *Hindustan*, May 05, 2018, From Sadar to Saket, illegal constructions razed to ground.
68. PTI, May 05, 2018, Son behind bars, mother picks up pieces of her life from debris.
69. Sowmiya Ashok and Navjeevan Gopal, *Indian Express*, May 13, 2018, Once there was a hill.
70. Vikas Vasudeva, *The Hindu*, May 14, 2018, One more Kasauli shooting victim dies.
71. *Hindustan*, June 04, 2018, Special task force to be constituted to stop illegal construction in Delhi.
72. *Hindustan*, June 25, 2018, Gurugram will be free of encroachment within two months.
73. *The Times of India*, July 4, 2018, Illegal extensions of 200 homes on protected Jharsa dam land razed.
74. Srinath Rao, *Indian Express*, July 15, 2018, Baby's Days Out – The rise, fall and possible resurrection of a Mumbai drug queen.

75. Abhishek Angad, *Indian Express,* July 20, 2018, Three left farming for chance at a better life in the capital.
76. Aditi Vatsa, *Indian Express,* July 20, 2018, Question everyone is asking: Who gave approval?
77. Abhishek Angad and Sukrita Baruah, *Indian Express,* July 20, 2018, 9 dead in greater Noida building collapse: No building plans meant NDRF went in blindsided.
78. *Hindustan,* July 23, 2018, 21 buildings in Shahberi to be demolished.
79. Abhishek Behl, *Hindustan Times,* July 30, 2018, The crisis is far from over for Gurgaon.
80. *The Times of India,* July 31, 2018, 179 illegal colonies in Delhi to get drains.
81. *Indian Express,* August 07, 2018, Ahmedabad Municipal Corporation demolishes illegal structure near NH 08.
82. *The Hindu,* August 27, 2018, EWS houses with illegal floors in Gurugram to face the heat.
83. *Hindustan,* September 07, 2018, Illegal shops near Valley View Society in Gurugram demolished.
84. Express News Service, *Indian Express,* September 12, 2018, Kant Enclave constructions after 1992 will have to go, says Supreme Court.
85. *Hindustan,* September 19, 2018, Illegal construction in 72 colonies in Gurugram to be legalized.
86. *Hindustan,* September 20, 2018, Street vendors throng roads of Sadar Bazaar few months after the encroachment drive in Gurugram.
87. *Hindustan,* September 26, 2018, 130 acres of illegal encroachment removed in Bhatti Village of South Delhi, Many illegal. structures were "posh" farm houses, authorities mulling offices in them instead of demolishing them.
88. Hindustan, September 26, 2018, Supreme Court hauls up Delhi State BJP President for entering a sealed property – You can't take law in your own hands, even if you are a Member of Parliament.
89. *The Hindu,* November 30, 2018, "Jain being targeted for legalising illegal colonies", AAP cries foul after Centre gives CBI permission to prosecute Minister in DA case.

90. *Hindustan,* November 28, 2018, Eviction from the Marble market in Gurugram stayed by the High Court.
91. Ajay Jadhav, *Indian Express,* September 30, 2018, 20-yr-long saga behind 4th canal breach in Pune: Water thefts, encroachment and unfinished civic plans.
92. Anand Mohan J, Abhinav Rajput, and Abhishek Angad, *Indian Express,* January 05, 2019, Seven dead in Moti Nagar Building Collapse; Another collapse, another red flag ignored.
93. Hemani Bhandari, *The Hindu,* January 04, 2019, 06 killed in Moti Nagar factory collapse.
94. Hemani Bhandari, *The Hindu,* January 04, 2019, Officials only sealed factory's toilet two days ago; Locals claimed the unit was supposed to be sealed as its condition was terrible and the walls had cracks; rescue operations under way.
95. Chief Correspondent, *Hindustan,* January 08, 2019, NGT issues directives, gets tough on factories operating in residential areas, Factories running in Daryaganj need to stop.
96. *The Times of India,* January 11, 2019, Gurugram MLA stands before excavator demolition of illegal houses.
97. Sakshi Dayal, *Indian Express,* January 25, 2019, Gurugram's Ullahwas village: 7 dead in building collapse, area had "no bylaws".
98. *Hindustan,* February 04, 2019, Police firing during anti-encroachment drive in Gurugram, six injured.
99. Sidharth Ravi, *The Hindu,* February 04, 2019, Slum dwellers reside amid debris after High Court stay, Most of the 90-odd shanties below the Safdarjung flyover have been demolished by the Railways.
100. *Indian Express,* February 16, 2019, Bawana again: 9 workers injured in factory fire, unit had no clearance.
101. Abhinav Rajput, *Indian Express,* February 14, 2019, Hotel Nightmare Karol Bagh, When Act prevents action.
102. *The Hindu,* February 22, 2019, 155 waterbodies across Capital encroached upon, panel tells NGT.
103. Sourav Roy Burman, *Indian Express,* February 27, 2019, Drone to map unauthorized colonies? Government says okay.

104. *Hindustan*, March 01, 2019, Footpaths at Subhash Chowk and Sohna Road in Gurugram converted into parking zones for bikes and retail kiosks respectively.

105. Prabhat Kumar, *Hindustan*, March 04, 2019, Jeans manufacturing units running illegally in residential areas need to be shut down.

References for Chapter 5: Waste Collection

1. Marc Levinson, Princeton University Press 2006, *The Box*.
2. Census of India, 1961, 1971, 1981 and 1991, Density of Delhi's Population.
3. SWaCH, https://swachcoop.com (web link last accessed on March 13, 2019).
4. Centre for Science and Environment, New Delhi (www.cseindia.org), 2014, Construction and demolition waste.
5. Complied by Doerte Peters, Sustainable sanitation and water management (www.sswm.info), Strengthening enforcement bodies.
6. Central Pollution Control Board (Ministry of Environment and Forest, Government of India), March 2015, A report on Inventorization of Sewage Treatment Plants under Control of Urban Pollution Series.
7. R. Kaur (Water Technology Centre, Indian Agricultural Research Institute, New Delhi), S. P. Wani (International Crops Research Institute for the Semi-Arid Tropics, Hyderabad), K. Lal (Indian Council of Agricultural Research, New Delhi India), Wastewater production, treatment and use in India, Water Aid India, January 20, 2016, Fecal Sludge Management Report (http://wateraidindia.in/wp-content/uploads/2016/01/Faecal-Sludge-Management-Report.pdf).
8. Tarun Sharma, Nagrika, April 06, 2018, Presented at Centre for Policy Research, FSM Operations case studies from 3 cities: Findings and insights Dehradun, Jaipur, Bhubaneshwar.
9. Anindita Mukherjee, Prashant Arya, and Shubhagato Dasgupta, Centre for Policy Research, April 06, 2018, Presentation on Understanding Small Scale Business of Informal De-Sludging Operators.

10. Naomi Radke, Seecon international GmbH Sustainable Sanitation and Water Management (www.sswm.info), Strengthening Enforcement Bodies.
11. Aashish Gupta, Nazar Khalid, Devashish Despande, Payal Hathi, Avani Kapur, Nikhil Srivastav, Sangita Vyas, Dean Spears, and Diana Coffey, Rice Institute, January 4, 2019, Changes in open defecation in rural north India: 2014–2018 (https://riceinstitute.org/research/changes-in-open-defecation-in-rural-north-india-2014-2018-2/) hyperlink last accessed January 05, 2019.
12. Aarefa Johari, *Scroll.in*, December 06, 2014, How Indian firms use dirty tricks to deny sanitation workers their rights.
13. Water and Sanitation Program, World Bank Group, March 2016, Financial Requirements of Urban Sanitation in India – An Exploratory Analysis www.wsp.org, www.worldbank.org/water.
14. Mari Marcel Thekaikara, Dying for living, https://www.quora.com/How-many-cleaning-workers-die-in-India-every-year-What-to-do-about-it.
15. (https://www.collectorsweekly.com/articles/when-new-yorkers-lived-knee-deep-in-trash).
16. www.indiaspend.com /cover-story/70-of-urban-indias-sewage-is-untreated-54844 70% of Urban India's sewage is untreated
17. *The Times of India*, September 1, 2017, Sewer deaths rampant, states refuse to report.
18. The current methodology to record major and minor accidents during waste collection / sewer cleaning / sewage treatment is non-binding upon the respective process owners. Many states in India don't compile this data. A few states that do report numbers barely exceeds a few hundreds. The premise is that if 70 percent of solid human waste in India is untreated (www.indiaspend.com /cover-story/70%-of-urban-indias-sewage-is-untreated-54844) and that if urban India alone comprises 4000+ recognized cities and 3500 + census towns (http://mohua.gov.in/cms/number-of-cities--towns-by-city-size-class.php), it is inconceivable that

the accidents and fatalities that occur annually are limited to a few hundreds. Given the non-binding framework to record and report accidents of sanitation workers, independent research largely rely on deaths of sanitation workers reported in the media to collate Pan India view. Given this limitation, the author has therefore referenced the estimation analysis of S. Anand reported in 2007 with inputs from Shalini Singh in Mumbai Reprinted from *Tehelka* magazine, Volume 4, Issue 47, Dated December 08, 2007 in (https://www.quora.com/How-many-cleaning-workers-die-in-India-every-year-What-to-do-about-it) as estimated number of fatalities that occur in India annually on the account of waste collection (web links last accessed on March 13, 2019).

19. Government of India, Ministry of Home Affairs, Lok Sabha, response on July 26, 2016 to the Unstarred Question No. 1509 asked by Shri Rajan Vichare and Shri C. R. Patil: (a) whether there is shortage of Police personnel in the country; (b) if so, the details thereof and the reasons therefor; (c) the existing strength and requirement of Police officers separately, Statewise including Delhi Police; (d) the present ratio of police to population and the steps taken to increase the ratio between police force and the population in the country; and (e) whether the government has any proposal to increase the strength of Police personnel in the country and if so, the details thereof along with the details of advisories issued to states and police department to fill all the vacant posts?
20. *Tehelka*, Volume 4, Issue 47, December 08, 2007.
21. Mari Marcel Thekaekara, Infochange News & Features, February 2009, Dying for a living.
22 *Press Trust of India*, November 26, 2012, 4000 Army soldiers killed, 390 suicides since Kargil.
23. *Heather Horn*, April 1, 2013, The Atlantic, The secret world of Garbagemen.
24. Hunter Oatman-Stanford, *Collectors Weekly*, June 24, 2013, A filthy history: When New Yorkers lived knee-deep in trash.

25. *The Hindu,* October 01, 2013, Kozhikode, local bodies fail to enforce sanitation rules.
26. Vidha Sharma, *Hindustan Times,* May 01, 2014, Greenbelts in pathetic condition: Most of them are being used for dumping construction waste and garbage.
27. Dhananjay Jha and Snehil Sinha, *Hindustan* Times, August 07, 2015, Construction debris to go from Golf Course Road in two days.
28. Vijetha SN, *The Hindu,* August 19, 2015, Colonised by garbage.
29. *The Hindu,* August 17, 2015, I end up cleaning human excreta.
30. Snehil Sinha and Vinod Rajput, *Hindustan Times,* October 25, 2015, Choking on dust.
31. Ritam Halder, *Hindustan Times,* December 07, 2015, Delhi trapped under concrete debris.
32. Barbara Harriss-White, *The Hindu,* October 07, 2015, The politics of waste management.
33. Mohit Sharma, *Hindustan Times,* December 01, 2015, Mountains of waste a threat to health.
34. Mohit Sharma, *Hindustan Times,* December 04, 2015, Public apathy stalls segregation project.
35. Ritam Halder, *Hindustan Times,* December 04, 2015, Ensure that no waste goes waste.
36. Mohit Sharma, *Hindustan Times,* December 04, 2015, Organize rag-pickers to help clean Delhi.
37. Ritam Halder, *Hindustan Times,* December 04, 2015, Government seeks police help to stop waste burning.
38. Kritika Sharma Sebastian, *The Hindu,* December 11, 2015, More number of child labourers turning into rag pickers: Survey.
39. Saurabh Chauhan, *Hindustan Times,* January 03, 2016, Revellers leave Shimla in a shamble.
40. *Live Mint,* March 05, 2016, The martyr who cleans your drains.
41. *The Times of India,* March 29, 2016, Civil hospital dumps bio-medical waste in own campus.
42. *The Times of India,* April 16, 2016, Inspector shortage affects sanitation work in city wards.

43. Larisa Brown, *The Daily Mail,* May 02, 2016, Litter fines soar as councils hand out nine an hour: More than GBP 20 mn raised from fixed-penalty notices since 2010.
44. Anvit Srivastava, *The Economic Times,* May 02, 2016, How IGI Airport moved from 101 rank to world's best.
45. Rohit P.S, *The Hindu,* August 02, 2016, More toilets only mean more scavengers, says Bezwada Wilson.
46. Soumay Pillai and Mallica Joshi, *Hindustan* Times, August 11, 2016, With no gazing space, cows left to feed on plastic, medical waste.
47. Sidhartha Roy, *The Hindu,* September 05, 2016, The not-so-swachh life of the Railways' cleaners.
48. Vibha Sharma, *Hindustan Times,* November 26, 2016, Sanitation staff to get anti-pollution masks in S Delhi.
49. *Dainik Jagaran,* Lucknow, December 25, 2016, Candidates made to lift garbage and sewage with bare hands as part of the recruitment process.
50. *Dainik Jagaran,* Lucknow, December 25, 2016, All is not well in Lucknow Development Authority.
51. V. Sudershan, *The Hindu,* February 19, 2017, Photo Feature: Dirty picture, Not pretty: A canal in Dallupura, East Delhi, is choked with polythene bags and other waste, making a mockery of concerns expressed by environmentalists over rising pollution in Delhi.
52. *The Hindu,* February 28, 2017, Despite awareness, sanitation, toilet access lacking in city: Adequate sewer lines must for improving hygiene indicate study.
53. Hemvati Nandan Rajoura, *Hindustan,* April 23, 2017, Jamia University requests UP government to clean garbage near its campus.
54. Sushil Kumar Verma, *The Hindu,* May 02, 2017, Photo Feature: So much for sanitation.
55. Rajanya Bose and Anirban Bhattacharya, *Business Standard,* May 14, 2017, Why ragpickers, unrecoginsed and unpaid, are critical for waste management.
56. Nauzer Bharucha, *The Times of India,* May 15, 2017, Mumbai dumps 2100 mn liters of human waste in sea daily.

57. Manish Raj, *Indian Express*, June 28, 2017, Why should we suffer dengue when MCDs can't clear garbage, asks court.
58. Naveed Iqbal, *Indian Express*, June 28 2017, Assured salaries, EDMC staffers call off strike
59. Jatin Anand, *The Hindu*, July 19, 2017, PWD to double its mechanized vacuum cleaning capacity.
60. Sushil Kumar Verma, *The Hindu*, July 27, 2017, Photo Feature: Ugly truth.
61. Mohit M. Rao, *The Hindu*, July 27, 2017, Post-GST, heavy sacks and small change.
62. *The Hindu*, Delhi Metro, July 25, 2017, Out for a walk, man falls to death in open drain.
63. Abhishek Angad, *Indian Express*, August 07, 2017, Cleaning Lajpat Nagar sewer, 3 labourers die of "suffocation".
64. *Hindustan*, August 07, 2017, Sanitation workers compelled to descend into a 15 feet deep sewer without security gear.
65. *Hindustan*, August 07, 2017, Manual labour instead of machines used for cleaning.
66. *Hindustan*, August 07, 2017, Municipal Corporation of South Delhi dismisses 400 sanitation workers from their jobs.
67. Abhishek Angad, *Indian Express*, August 8, 2017, Sewer survivor tells police "DJB contractor" gave him work, was supposed to make ₹300.
68. Shubhomoy Sikdar, *The Hindu*, August 08, 2017, Can't clean sewer again.
69. *Hindustan*, August 08, 2017, White Paper demanded on challenges faced by Sanitation Workers.
70. Aniruddha Ghosal, *Indian Express*, August 9, 2017, Contractor was not doing his job for charity, who asked him to do it, Kejriwal asks DJB chief.
71. Anand Mohan J, *Indian Express*, August 13, 2017, Two brothers die cleaning sewage tank in east Delhi mall.
72. Photo Feature: *Navbharat Times*, Lucknow, August 14, 2017.

73. *Navbharat Times*, Lucknow, August 16, 2017, All India Shri Valmiki Navyug Sangh raises demand of the use of masks and machines during cleaning sewers.
74. Subhodh Ghildiyal, *The Times of India*, August 30, 2017, Contractors to face music for sewer deaths.
75. *The Times of India*, September 05, 2017, India has 5 times more private guards than police personnel.
76. Somya Lakhani, *Indian Express*, September 06, 2017, With no alternate site to dump garbage, trucks come and go despite LG orders.
77. Aniruddha Ghosal and Anand Mohan J, *Indian Express*, September 8, 2017, Segregating trash: A tale of two colonies.
78. *Hindustan*, 18 September 2017, Two people die while cleaning sewer in Satlok Ashram.
79. Ajaz Ashraj, *Scroll.in*, September 12, 2017, More Indians die cleaning sewers than fighting terrorist in Kashmir.
80. Aditi Vatsa, *Indian Express*, September 22, 2017, Three daily wagers, "inspecting" a sewer line in Noida, found dead.
81. Sushil Kumar Verma, *The Hindu*, September 27, 2017, Photo Feature: Burden of waste; Business as usual- a rag picker existing Pragati Maidan in New Delhi.
82. V. V. Krishnan, *The Hindu*, September 27, 2017, Photo Feature: No reason to chair; Single seater: A man carts away old and broken chairs in the Capital.
83. Sidharth Bhardwaj, *The Times of India*, September 29, 2017, 25-yr-old cleaning tank inhales toxic gases, dies.
84. Sushil Kumar Verma, *The Hindu*, October 03, 2017, Dirty Picture, Piling up: An open drain full of garbage at Bhalswa village in Delhi.
85. Perumal Murugan, *The Hindu*, December 24, 2017, 60 minutes: With Bezwada Wilson, Look at my hands, look at my life.
86. Isher Judge Ahluwalia, *Indian Express*, December 27, 2017, Segregation must being at home.
87. G. T. Sathish, *The Hindu*, January 28, 2018, Shravanabelagola latrines run afoul of manual scavenging law.

88. Somdutt Sharma, *Hindustan*, February 20, 2018, Walk carefully, Drains and manholes are open.
89. Shanker Chakravarty, *The Hindu*, March 01, 2018, Photo Feature: Right under their nose: A heap of garbage lies in front of a municipal corporation-run primary school in east Delhi's Trilokpuri.
90. Praveen Khanna, *Indian Express*, March 07, 2018, Photo Feature: Wasteland, a biker crosses a stretch in Burari, where waste is collected and kept for recycling.
91. V. V. Krishnan, *The Hindu*, March 15, 2018, Photo Feature: Cycle and recycle – A boy ferries a load of empty cartons in New Delhi.
92. Sandeep Saxena, *The Hindu*, March 31, 2018, Towering waste: Man-made mountain, the Ghazipur landfill in Delhi continues to grow, despite warnings by the Supreme Court and the NGT to the authorities. It has touched 60 meters, double the permissible limit.
93. *Hindustan*, April 16, 2018, Debris stops the flow of the canal in Faridabad.
94. *Hindustan*, May 16, 2018, Sanitation workers surround minister's home.
95. C. S. Sharada Prasad and Isha Ray, *Economic and Political Weekly*, May 26, 2018, It has to be done only at night, human waste disposal in Bengaluru.
96. *Hindustan*, June 04, 2018, Neither is waste getting picked up from home nor from the roads.
97. Akhilesh Kumar, *The Hindu*, June 05, 2018, Photo Feature: Digging through.
98. Megha Shenoy, *The Hindu*, June 13, 2018, A plastic charter.
99. Shalini Nair, *Indian Express*, June 15, 2018, 53,000 manual scavengers in 12 states, four fold rise from last official count.
100. *Hindustan*, June 22, 2018, Waste and Water clogging at Madangir poses risks to the National Capital.
101. *Navbharat Times*, Lucknow, June 23, 2018, Photo feature of waste not getting picked up from Sarojini Nagar and Indira Nagar.
102. V. Kalyan Shankar and Rohini Sahni, *Economic and Political Weekly*, Volume 53, Issue 26–27, June 30, 2018, How demonetisation affected informal labour, waste chains in a city.

103. Daliya Banerjee, *The Hindu*, July 1, 2018, Photo Feature: Eyesoar, Garbage left unattended near Majnu ka Tilla in New Delhi.
104. Sukrita Baruah, *Indian Express*, July 09, 2018, Under shadow of death, sewage plant remains shut.
105. Sukrita Baruah, *Indian Express*, July 09, 2018, Ghaziabad sewage plant cleaning takes fatal turn, three men dead.
106. Sidharth Ravi, *The Hindu*, July 09, 2018, Colonies flooded in Kirari, but not due to rain.
107. *The Hindu*, July 09, 2018, Three suffocate inside sewer tank.
108. Akhilesh Kumar, *The Hindu*, August 05, 2018, An unending pile; digging through.
109. Alok Singh, *Indian Express*, August 10, 2018, Men who died at petrol pump weren't given masks, sub-contractor arrested.
110. Sourav Roy Barman, *Indian Express*, August 13, 2018, Manual scavenging a reality in capital: Delhi government survey.
111. *The Times of India*, August 16, 2018, Cleaner loses fingers in sewage tank accident in Delhi.
112. Abhinav Rajput and Mallica Joshi, *Indian Express*, August 27, 2018, Raising a stink.
113. *NDTV.com*, September 10, 2018, 5 Men suffocate while cleaning sewer in Delhi.
114. *The Times of India*, September 17, 2018, Delhi: A week on another man dies inside sewer.
115. Shalini Nair, *Indian Express*, September 18, 2018, Official data shows 1 manual scavenging death every five days.
116. Sourav Roy Barman, *Indian Express*, September 19, 2018, DLF STP ran without a licence: Government report.
117. Apurva, *Indian Express*, September 27, 2018, I am just a safai karamchari here but this police station depends on me.
118. Sidharth Ravi, *The Hindu*, September 26, 2018, "Stop killing us": hundreds protest against sewer deaths – Kin of victims gather at Jantar Mantar to demand that government come up with solution.
119. *The Hindu*, September 25, 2018, Drains overflow as rain lashes Bengaluru.

120. Priscilla Jebaraj, *The Hindu*, September 30, 2018, Four years after Swachh: Cleaning excreta for roti.
121. *The Hindu*, October 1, 2018, "No waste segregation at transfer stations" Allege members of citizen's collective in Gurugram.
122. *The Hindu*, October 4, 2018, City government proposes to release ₹500 cr to end garbage crisis.
123. *The Hindu*, October 23, 2018, In urban UP, 87% of waste from toilets goes to rivers, farmlands.
124. Shiv Sahay Singh, *The Hindu*, December 07, 2018, Tourists bring a wave of trash to beaches.
125. Neha Bhatt, *The Hindu*, December 16, 2018, It takes an army – An experiment at the New Delhi railway station is proving rather effective in keeping it clean.
126. *The Hindu*, January 05, 2019, Open defecation continues unabated.
127. *Hindustan*, January 29, 2019, Drainage system in Badshahpur, Gurugram will get ready in two months.
128. *Hindustan*, February 03, 2019, On the lines of Lucknow city, Gurugram to install underground waste collection system, Municipal Corporations ties up with a Chinese company.
129. PTI, February 08, 2019, After UP, NGT lens on Bihar hospitals that generate biomedical waste.
130. *Hindustan*, February 23, 2019, House and water pipeline pose problems for the construction of drainage pipeline in Badshahpur, Gurugram.
131. *The Hindu*, February 26, 2019, Sanitation workers slam Modi government, Demand end to manual scavenging, regularization of contract jobs.
132. Sushil Kumar Verma, *The Hindu*, March 13, 2019, Photo Feature: Litter matters: Cows feed on a heap of garbage in Ram Nagar, New Delhi.
133. *The Hindu*, March 27, 2019, Six choke to death after entering septic tank in Tamil Nadu.

References for Chapter 6: Waste Disposal

1. Timeline – World History Documentaries, https://www.youtube.com/watch?v=M4o1dc41r28, The Dark Ages: An Age of Light (web link last accessed on March 13, 2019).
2. http://greenrisks.blogspot.com/feeds/posts/default.
3. https://www.revolvy.com/page/Shit-Brook (web link last accessed on March 13, 2019).
4. History of materials, http://www.petrochemistry.eu/about-petrochemistry/discovery-timeline.html (web link last accessed on March 13, 2019).
5. The Dark Ages http://study.com/academy/lesson/the-dark-ages-definition-history-timeline.html (web link last accessed on March 13, 2019).
6. *The Black Death by Philip Ziegler: A Review*, https://aprilmunday.wordpress.com/2015/07/19/the-black-death-by-philip-ziegler-a-review/ (web link last accessed February 04, 2019).
7. S. M. Enzler MSc, *History of Greenhouse Effect and Global Warming* https://www.lenntech.com/greenhouse-effect/global-warming-history.htm (web link last accessed on March 13, 2019).
8. Adam Johnson, Eastern Metropolitan Regional Council (www.emrc.org.au), Belmont, WA 6983, Australia, The Development of Waste Management Law.
9. Goldstein Brownfield Group, The making of a new brownfield redevelopment market: Regulators, local governments & the public sector discovering and perfecting landfill reuse to unlock intrinsic real estate value, create new neighborhoods and usable places and amplify sustainability.
10. Evridiki Bersi-Kathimerini, Landfills a thing of the past in Germany where advances waste management rules.
11. Dan Morrison and Chris Tyree, Orbmedia (www.OrbMedia.org), Invisibles, The plastic inside us.

12. Neil Tangri, Global Anti-Incinerator Alliance or GAIA (www.no-burn.org), July 14, 2003, Waste incineration: A dying technology.
13. Nepra, http://www.nepra.co.in/index.html (web link last accessed on March 13, 2019).
14. Kenneth Barbalace, EnvironmentalChemistry.com, August 2003, The history of waste. https://EnvironmentalChemistry.com/yogi/environmental/wastehistory.html (web link last accessed on March 13, 2019).
15. Norimitsu Onishi, *The New York Times,* May 12, 2005, How do Japanese dump trash? Let us count the myriad ways.
16. David S. Barnes, The Johns Hopkins University Press, 2006, *The Great Stink of Paris and the Nineteenth-Century Struggle against Filth and Germs.*
17. P. U. Asnani, India Infrastructure Report, 2006, Solid Waste Management – Chapter 8.
18. Municipal Solid Waste in the United States: 2007 Facts and Figures. USA EPA Publication. (http://www.epa.gov/waste/nonhaz/municipal/pubs/msw07-rpt.pdf).
19. Lewis Herbert, The Chartered Institution of Wastes Management (www.ciwm.co.uk) 2007, Centenary History of Waste & Waste Managers in London and South East England.
20. European Environment Agency (EEA) (www.eea.europa.eu) 2009, A report on Diverting waste from landfill – Effectiveness of waste-management policies in the European Union.
21. Earthscan, United Nations Human Settlement Programme (UN-Habitat) Solid Waste Management in World's Cities 2010.
22. Seattle Public Utilities, www.seattle.gov, 2011, Seattle Solid Waste Plan, Administrative and Financing Plan (web link last accessed on March 04, 2019).
23. Seattle Public Utilities, www.seattle.gov, 2011, Seattle Solid Waste Plan, Revising the Solid Waste Management Plan (web link last accessed on March 04, 2019).
24. Seattle Public Utilities, www.seattle.gov, 2011, Seattle Solid Waste Plan, Waste Prevention (web link last accessed on March 04, 2019).

25. Seattle Public Utilities, www.seattle.gov, 2011, Seattle Solid Waste Plan, Seattle MSW System: Managing Discards (web link last accessed on March 04, 2019).

26. Department of Environmental Protection, Florida, USA Solid Waste Section, February 03, 2011, Guidance for disturbance and use of old closed landfills or waste disposal areas in Florida.

27. Dr. Helmut Schnurer, Section Head at the Federal Environment Ministry, Germany (www.bmu.de), 2012, at the workshop organised by the Alexander von Humboldt Foundation at the International Institute for Advanced Studies (IIAS) in Kyoto/Japan, German Waste Legislation and Sustainable Development: Development of waste legislation in Germany towards a sustainable closed substance cycle.

28. Department for Environment, Food and Rural Affairs, UK (www.defra.gov.uk), February 2013, Incineration of Municipal Solid Waste.

29. Emmanuel C. Gentil, Copenhagen Resource Institute (http://www.cri.dk/), February 2013, Municipal waste management in Belgium.

30. Seattle Public Utilities, www.seattle.gov, June 2013, Seattle solid waste trends (web link last accessed on March 04, 2019).

31. Seattle Public Utilities, www.seattle.gov, 2013, Seattle solid waste plan, other Seattle solid waste programs (web link last accessed on March 04, 2019).

32. Department for Environment Food and Rural Affairs, November 7, 2013 (https://www.gov.uk/government/organisations/department-for-environment-food-rural-affairs) Statistics on waste managed by local authorities in England in 2012/13 (web link last accessed on March 04, 2019).

33. A. K. Agnihotri, The Energy and Resources Institute (TERI), New Delhi, 2014, Paper presentation titled "Current scenario of Indian Landfill and its solution through Biotechnological approaches" in 2nd International Congress on Green Urban Futures.

34. Dr. Anjali Acharya1, Dr. Vasudha Ashutosh Gokhale 2, Deepa Joshi 3 1(Institute for Excellence in Higher Education Bhopal. M.P. India) 2(B.N. College of Architecture, University of Pune,

India) 3(Institute for Excellence in Higher Education Bhopal M.P. India), *IOSR Journal of Applied Chemistry*, www.iosrjournals.org, January 2014, Impact of bio-medical waste on city environment: Case study of Pune, India.

35. Japan Environmental Sanitation Centre (http://www.jesc.or.jp), Ministry of the Environment Minister's Secretariat, Waste Management and Recycling Department Policy Planning Division, Office of Sound Material-Cycle Society, February 2014, History and Current State of Waste Management in Japan.
36. Citizens Budget Commission, New York February 2015, A better way to pay for solid waste management.
37. http://www.umweltbundesamt.de/en/topics/waste-resources/wastemanagement, December 27, 2015, Waste management in Germany.
38. Waste Management Inc. (www.wm.com), Annual Reports 2014, 2016.
39. Shanks Group Plc. Annual Report 2014. The company acquired Dutch Recycler van Gansweinkel Groep in 2017. The merged entity was renamed Renewi (http://www.renewiplc.com).
40. Renewi (http://www.renewiplc.com) Annual Report 2017.
41. Renowa Group, Sweden https://www.renova.se/in-english/about-us/ (web link last accessed on March 13, 2019).
42. Hindustan Unilever Limited, Annual Report 2016–17.
43. National Sample Survey Office, Ministry of Statistics and Programme Implementation, GOI, 2016, Swachhta Status Report
44. Seattle Public Utilities, www.seattle.gov, July 2018, Seattle recycling rate report 2017 (web link last accessed on March 13, 2019).
45. David Azoulay (CIEL), Priscilla Villa (Earthworks), Yvette Arellano (TEJAS), Miriam Gordon (UPSTREAM), Doun Moon (GAIA), and Kathryn Miller and Kristen Thompson (Exeter University). Edited by Amanda Kistler (CIEL), February 2019, Plastic & Health: The Hidden Costs of a Plastic Planet, https://www.ciel.org/plasticandhealth/, web link last accessed on March 06, 2019.
46. Mahesh Nayak, Business Today, June 09, 2013, New Age Alchemists (http://www.businesstoday.in/magazine/features/companies-that-

are-making-wealth-from-waste/story/195163.html (web link last accessed on March 13, 2019).

47. Ajita Shashidhar, June 19, 2013, Project Shakti has helped thousands of women – and also men.
48. Kota Sriraj, *The Pioneer*, July 04, 2013, Handle waste with seriousness.
49. *The Times of India* July 14, 2013, STP's project cost vary in different schemes.
50. Mallica Joshi, *Hindustan Times*, August 07, 2015, Incinerator told to stop dumping fly ash.
51. Umesh Isalkar, *The Times of India*, Pune, October 30, 2013, 4500 clinics avoid waste disposal facility.
52. *The Times of India*, December 01, 2013, Burning of garbage in open a major problem.
53. Dhananjay Jha and Mohit Sharma, *Hindustan Times*, May 01, 2014, City's garbage spills over to the Aravallis.
54. Garrett Hering, *The Guardian*, December 27, 2014, The eight costliest US environmental transgressions of 2014.
55. Chaitanya Mallapur, *Indiaspend.org*, Mid-Day.com, January 31, 2015, India's real trash problem: 3 million truckloads of untreated garbage disposed daily.
56. *Hindustan Times*, July 01, 2015, Auditor junks civic bodies' waste plan.
57. *The Times of India*, July 31, 2015, Export hub turns into dumping yard.
58. Manoj Sharma, *Hindustan Times*, August 02, 2015, A mountain of trash, fetid fumes and French dreams: Ghazipur Landfill.
59. Akanksha Jain, *The Hindu*, November 19, 2015, Segregate trash before burning at Okhla Plant.
60. Snehil Sinha, *Hindustan Times*, November 20, 2015, Waste dumping in seasonal water body goes unchecked.
61. Ashok Kumar, *The Hindu*, November 26, 2015, Gurgaon identifies 16 dumping sites.
62. Ritam Halder, *Hindustan Times*, November 27, 2015, Government calls review meeting on steps to curb garbage burning.
63. Sharad Akavoor, *Hindustan Times*, December 07, 2015, Dharampura pit: Once a pond, today a dumping ground for waste.

64. Arshad Khan, *Business World*, April 06, 2016, Hero faces challenging times in two-wheeler market.
65. Sunny Sen, *Hindustan Times*, May 24, 2016, Honda bets big on rural market to take on Hero.
66. *Press Trust of India*, August 08, 2016, Three strains of fungi to help recycle rechargeable batteries.
67. Kartik Kumar, *Hindustan Times*, August 26, 2016, Leachate cleaning at Bandhwari plant to begin next week.
68. Damini Nath, October 2, 2016, 2 years on, Swachh Bharat yet to reach Bhalswa.
69. Jayashree Nandi and Mayank Manohar, *The Times of India*, October 4, 2016, Bhalswa landfill emits toxic fumes but there's no quick fix.
70. Mayank Manohar, *The Times of India*, October 14, 2016, Civic bodies prepare landfill-free plan.
71. Prashant K. Nanda, *The Mint*, October 17, 2016, Government wants IITs, IIMs to go multidisciplinary for world-class institutions tag.
72. *The Hindu*, October 18, 2016, New waste-to-energy plant at Bhalswa.
73. *Hindustan Times*, October 18, 2016, People dying, act on proper waste disposal, says Supreme Court.
74. *The Hindu*, February 09, 2017, Leachate let into Bengaluru lake again.
75. Serena Josephine M., *The Hindu*, February 18, 2017, The groundwater beneath their feet.
76. Kushagra Dixit, *The Economic Times*, April 11, 2016, Tale of an untapped $13 billion waste management industry.
77. Himal Kotelawala, *The New York Times*, April 17, 2017, Sri Lanka death toll rises in garbage dump collapse.
78. Bradley Dunseith, Dezan Shira, and Associates, April 19, 2017 The waste management industry in India: Investment opportunities, www.india-briefing.com (web link last accessed on March 13, 2019).
79. Mallica Joshi and Mohit Sharma, *Hindustan Times*, May 05, 2016, Landfill sites or pollution bombs?
80. Satyasundar Barik, *The Hindu*, May 09, 2017, Odisha village swears by gram swaraj.

81. ENS Economic Buerau, *Indian Express,* May 15, 2017, Swachh Bharat an opportunity to turn waste into energy: PM.
82. Nauzer Bharucha, *The Times of India,* May 17, 2017, Mumbai dumps 2,100 mn litres of human waste in sea daily.
83. V. Sudarshan, *The Hindu,* May 20, 2017, The mane entrepreneurs.
84. Isher Judge Ahluwalia and Almitra Patel, *Indian Express* June 28, 2017, A city laid waste: A new rapid bioremediation process that can remove garbage hills and end their ill effects promises a low-cost solution to waste management and disposal.
85. *The Hindu,* July 01, 2017, Curb sewage flow into Ganga tributary: NGT.
86. *Hindustan,* August 15, 2017, MOU between municipal corporation and the company for Bhadwari garbage plant.
87. Shubhomoy Sikdar, *The Hindu,* September 02, 2017, Two killed in Ghazipur landfill collapse, five hurt.
88. *The Times of India,* September 02, 2017, Two killed as 50 tonnes of waste hurtles down Ghazipur landfill.
89. *Hindustan,* September 03, 2017, Simmering landfills of Bhalswa.
90. Soumya Pillai, *The Hindu,* September 02, 2017, Experts had warned of such a disaster.
91. Somya Lakhani, *Indian Express,* September 6, 2017, With no alternate site to dump garbage, trucks come and go despite LG orders.
92. Aniruddha Ghosal, *Indian Express,* September 07, 2017, What lies buried part II: Okhla shut, no new options open, http://indianexpress.com/article/cities/delhi/what-lies-buried-part-ii-okhla-shut-no-new-options-open-4832153/ (web link last accessed on March 13, 2019).
93. *The Economist,* September 07, 2017, Panipat, the global centre for recycling textiles is fading – The industry's decline is a missed opportunity for India.
94. *The Economist,* September 07, 2017, Alaska's remote villages have a trashy problem.
95. *The Times of India,* September 08, 2017 Leachate effect: Groundwater in Mangar, Bandhwari not fit for drinking says CPCB.

96. *Press Trust of India*, September 22, 2017, Sewage plant unveiled at RSS icon Deendayal Upadhyaya village.
97. Ann Koh, Bloomberg, September 27, 2017, Landfill gas for dinner? Scientists cooking food from waste.
98. Soumya Pillai, *The Hindu*, September 28, 2017, More waste dumping sites to come up in north Delhi.
99. Ashok Kumar, *The Hindu*, October 12, 2017, Biodiversity Park turns dumping ground.
100. Isher Judge Ahluwalia and Almitra Patel, *Indian Express*, October 25, 2017, Cities at crossroads: Don't waste the possibilities
101. *Hindustan*, February 26, 2018, Rampant burning of trash in the open in Gurugram.
102. Sanchit Waray and Arunabha Ghosh, *Business Standard*, June 26, 2018, Clean energy can boost rural economy.
103. Mallica Joshi, *Indian Express*, March 15, 2018, Okhla waste plant has no takers for tonnes of compost.
104. *Deccan Herald*, March 22, 2018, Residents of Kanakapura Road to don surgical masks to protest against air pollution in Bengaluru.
105. Mallica Joshi, *Indian Express*, April 15, 2018, Water at eight of 22 sewage plants fails test.
106. Bard Wilkinson, *CNN*, April 17, 2018, Scientists hope that new enzyme will "eat" plastic pollution.
107. *Hindustan*, April 23, 2018, Delhi sinking under the weight of plastic waste.
108. *Hindustan*, April 23, 2018, Compost made from garbage will increase greenery of parks and schools.
109. *The Times of India*, April 24, 2018, Trash set on fire in Gurugram Sector 23 green belt, residents choke on fumes.
110. Saurabh Trivedi, *The Hindu*, May 28, 2018, Gone in 60 seconds.
111. *The Hindu*, May 30, 2018, NGT stays dumping of waste in Noida Sector 54.
112. Sushil Kumar Verma, *The Hindu*, June 03, 2018, Eyesore: A polluted canal joins the Yamuna at Wazirabad.

113. Dinesh Mishra, *Hindustan*, June 04, 2018, We ignore the problem of increasing silt in our rivers.

114. Kanak Mani Dixit, *The Hindu*, June 05, 2018 To be an environmental world power – Cross border environmentalism is crucial for South Asia, but India is not inclined to take the lead.

115. Shiv Kumar Pushpakar, *The Hindu*, 06 June 2018, Photo Feature: Sea of garbage; a boy walks across plastic refuse dumped at south Delhi's Taimoor Nagar drain on June 5 – a day marked by the United Nations as World Environment Day.

116. Jacob Koshy, *The Hindu*, June 23, 2018, States' claim on fighting plastic only strong on paper.

117. Nirmalya Behera, *Business Standard*, July 02, 2018, A business beyond trash.

118. Krishnadas Rajagopal, *The Hindu*, July 07, 2018, A six-decade legacy of garbage mounds ails Capital: L-G tells SC that lack of land to establish new landfill sites has choked the city.

119. *Press Trust of India*, August 06, 2018, Dump Garbage Near Governor's House – Supreme Court's Outburst.

120. Vinayak Chatterjee, *Business Standard*, August 06, 2018, Water: The next frontier.

121. Isher Judge Ahluwalia and Almitra Patel, *Indian Express*, August 29, 2018, No more cover-ups, Municipal authorities are opting for capping as a solution to the problem of mixed waste at dumpsites. Bio-remediation and bio-mining may be more desirable.

122. Mohit M. Rao, *The Hindu*, October 13, 2018, A parched land, in a sea of sewage.

123. *The Hindu*, October 25, 2018, Air quality dips due to Bhalswa landfill fire.

124. Sidharth Ravi, *The Hindu*, October 23, 2018, Bhalswa landfill fire yet to be put out fully – Blaze broke out over the weekend; new fires keep breaking out at the site: official.

125. *The Times of India*, October 23, 2018, Bhalswa landfill continues to simmer as Delhi battles poor air.

126. Jacob Koshy, *The Hindu,* October 28, 2018, 5 lakh tonnes of waste dumped in the open in Delhi – Study says quantity 62 times more than solid waste generated per day in the city.
127. *Hindustan,* January 30, 2019, Protest against illegal dumping of waste in Sector 47 in Gurugram.
128. Jacob Koshy, *The Hindu,* February 15, 2019, Wasted effort: Half of India's waste-to-energy plants defunct.
129. *The Hindu,* March 01, 2019, Illegal dumping of waste takes a toll on Gurugram residents' health.

References for Chapter 7: E-waste

1. Census of India 2001, 2011, http://censusindia.gov.in (web link last accessed on March 13, 2019).
2. Technopak Advisors Research Reports 2012, 2014, and 2016 on Indian Retail and Indian Private Consumption; Indian Mobile Phone Market.
3. India's mobile phone market, Telecom Regulatory Authority of India (TRAI), http://www.trai.gov.in (web link last accessed on March 13, 2019).
4. Panasonic Eco Technology Center PETEC, https://panasonic.net/eco/petec/ (web link last accessed on March 13, 2019).
5. Attero (http://www.attero.in) Electronics Asset Management Company (web link last accessed on March 13, 2019).
6. United States Environment Protection Agency (EPA), https://www.epa.gov/pcbs/learn-about-polychlorinated-biphenyls-pcbs, Learn about Polychlorinated Biphenyls (PCBs) (web link last accessed on March 13, 2019).
7. Greenpeace, https://www.greenpeace.org/archive-international/en/campaigns/detox/electronics/the-e-waste-problem/where-does-e-waste-end-up/, February 24, 2009; Where does E-Waste end up? (web link last accessed on March 13, 2019).
8. Statista 2018 (https://www.statista.com); Smartphones sold to end users worldwide from 2007 to 2016.

9. Lucy McAllister, Population reference bureau, the human and environmental effects of e-waste.
10. Bi Bo, Kayoko Yamamoto, World Academy of Science, Engineering and Technology, Vol. 4, February 23, 2010, Characteristics of E-waste Recycling Systems in Japan and China.
11. Research Unit (Larrdis) Rajya Sabha Secretariat New Delhi June 2011; E-Waste in India.
12. International Telecommunication Union GSR 2011 Discussion Paper on E-Waste.
13. E-Waste Generation and Recycling 2000-2012 in USA, Environment Protection Agency (EPA), USA data from "Municipal Solid Waste Generation, Recycling and Disposal in the United States, 2012".
14. Suez Environment, Annual Report 2014 (https://www.suez.com/en).
15. S. O. Obaje, *International Journal of Engineering Science Invention*, ISSN (Online): 2319 – 6734, ISSN (Print): 2319 – 6726 www.ijesi.org Volume 2, Issue 11, November 2013 PP. 31–36, Electronic Waste Scenario in Nigeria: Issues, Problems and Solutions.
16. Technopak Advisors Pvt. Ltd, 2014; Market Assessment and Value Chain Economics of E-Waste in India.
17. Secretariat of the Basel Convention UNEP/SBC, http://www.basel.int/Portals/4/Basel%20Convention/docs/convention/bc_glance.pdf (web link last accessed on March 13, 2019).
18. C. P. Baldé, F. Wang, R. Kuehr, and J. Huisman, 2015, The Global E-waste Monitor – 2014, United Nations, University, IAS – SCYCLE, Bonn, Germany.
19. The Mobile Economy India, 2015, GSM Association (www.gsma.com).
20. Government of India, Ministry of Environment, Forest and Climate Change 23 March 2016; EWM Rules 2016 Published in The Gazette of India, Extraordinary Part – II Section 3, Sub Section (1).
21. Electronics Take Back Coalition, www.electronicstakeback.com, Facts and figures on e-waste and recycling, January 13, 2016 (web link last accessed on March 13, 2019).

22. A joint report by Internet and Mobile Association of India (IMAI) & Enixta Innovations, 2016; Indian Mobile Phone Market: Emerging Opportunities for fulfilling India's digital economy dream.
23. C. P Baldé, V. Forti, V. Gray, R. Kuehr, and P. Stegmann, The Global E-waste Monitor – 2017, United Nations University (UNU), International Telecommunication Union (ITU) & International Solid Waste Association (ISWA), Bonn/Geneva/Vienna.
24. Liz Carney, BBC, http://news.bbc.co.uk/2/hi/africa/6193625.stm, 19 December 2006; Nigeria fears E-Waste toxic legacy (web link last accessed on March 13, 2019).
25. Agiimaa Kruchkin, IBIS World Industry Report OD4510, February 2013; Electronics Goods Recycling in the US.
26. Arun Prabhudesai, October 20, 2014, trak.in http://trak.in/tags/business/2007/06/19/indian-telecommunication-story-from-10-million-to-150-million-mobile-subscribers-in-5-years), Indian Telecom Growth Story: From 10M to 900M Subscribers In 10Yrs (web link last accessed on March 13, 2019).
27. *Live Mint*, June 03, 2015, 76% of e-waste workers in India suffering from respiratory ailments https://www.livemint.com/Politics/tt0SWNyPcg7lqbwugF2VCK/76-of-ewaste-workers-in-India-suffering-from-respiratory-a.html?facet=print (web link last accessed on March 13, 2019).
28. Arnika Thakur, Fortune India, June 05, 2015, Lift cover for your next ring: Why urban mining is sustainability's latest battleground.
29. Arnab Dutta, *Business Standard*, June 28, 2015, Flat panel TV sales to overtake CRT sets.
30. *Hindustan Times*, May 03, 2016, Illegal battery recycling adding lead to Delhi air, says study.
31. *Hindustan Times*, May 06, 2016, Shut illegal scrap recovery units on boarder, UP told.
32. Jacob Koshy, *The Hindu*, May 09, 2016, Grey clouds loom over formal e-waste recyclers.
33. Michael Smith and Isabella Cota, *Bloomberg Businessweek*, November 14, 2016; We found your last smartphone, next to your old VCR.

34. Atul Aneja, *The Hindu,* September 24, 2017; Battling E-waste in China's industrial hub.
35. Partho Dasgupta, *The Economic Times,* March 03, 2017, How Indian TV universe expanded.
36. ET Bureau, February 13, 2018; "Clean to Green" campaign of Reverse Logistics to promote responsible e-waste disposal in India
37. *The Hindu,* March 15, 2018, High Court quizzes authorities on e-waste disposal.
38. UNSW Media, University of New South Wales, Sydney Australia, April 04, 2018, World-first e-waste microfactory launched at UNSW.
39. *Press Trust of India,* May 31, 2018, Contaminants founds in food-contact items shows new study.
40. Jacob Koshy, *The Hindu,* September 27, 2018, Recyclers storing electronic waste hazardously: Environment Ministry.
41. Sarath Babu George, *The Hindu,* November 05, 2018, E-waste management, Kerala's worry – Lack of dismantling and recycling mechanism has led to crisis in State.
42. *Hindustan,* January 08, 2019, With this approach it will take fifty years to remove Old Automobiles.
43. Jacob Koshy, *The Hindu,* April 12, 2019, India stares at a pile of solar e-waste.

References for Chapter 8: Capturing the Chimera

1. Census of India 2011 (www.cencus2011.co.in).
2. Centre for Study of Science Technology and Policy (CSTEP) and Institute of Urban Transport (India), 2011, Review of Urban Transport in India.
3. Urban Mass Transit Company Limited, Comprehensive Mobility Plan for Kanpur.
4. Transport Research Wing, Ministry of Road Transport and Highways, Government of India New Delhi Road Transport Yearbook, 2011–12.
5. Ministry of Road Transport and Highways, Government of India, 2012, Total registered motor vehicles in million plus cities.

6. Report of the Task Force on Waste to Energy (Volume I), Planning Commission of India (now Niti Aayog), May 2014.
7. Basin Planning and Management Organization, Central Water Commission, New Delhi October 2017, Reassessment of water availability in India using Space inputs.
8. The unknown US$ 75 billion Industry, August 2014, www.gridwaste.com (web link last accessed on March 13, 2019).
9. Status and challenges of municipal solid waste management in India: A review, by Rajkumar Joshi and Sirajuddin Ahmed, *Cogent Environmental Science* (2016), 2: 1139434.
10. Order issued dated March 07, 2017 on Ganga Pollution by The National Green Tribunal Principal Bench, New Delhi in the matter of M.C. Mehta Vs. Union of India & Ors. and Anil Kumar Singhal Vs. Union of India & Ors. and Society for Protection of Environment & Biodiversity & Anr. Vs. Union of India & Ors. and Confederation of Delhi Industries & CETP Societies (An Organisation of CETP Societies) Vs. D.P.C.C. & Ors. and J.K. Srivastava Vs. Central Pollution Control Board & Ors. and Swami Gyan Swarop Sanand Vs. Ministry of Home Affairs & Ors.
11. IFC (www.ifc.org), 2017, Climate Investment Opportunities in South Asia, An Analysis.
12. www.indiaspend.com May 30, 2017, India's Traffic Nightmare: Road Grows 4%, Vehicles Grow 11%.
13. Akanksha Jain, *The Hindu*, November 25, 2015, NGT summons over unclean Ganga.
14. Pretika Khanna, *The Mint*, December 09, 2015, Nirmal Bharat Abhiyan failed to achieve its desired targets: CAG.
15. Deeptiman Tiwary, *Indian Express*, February 17, 2016, Clean Ganga project hurts livelihoods, divides communities.
16. Prachi Salve, *Firstpost.com*, April 28, 2016, Dude where's the cleanliness? Swacch mission fails to meet urban trash targets.
17. Chelsea Harvey, *The Washington Post*, May 12, 2016, Air pollution in India is so bad that it kills half a million people every year.

18. Damini Nath, *Indian Express,* May 06, 2016, A new plan to clean up Yamuna.
19. Shivani Singh, *Hindustan Times,* June 06, 2016, Beyond green tokenism, what each of us can do.
20. Shubhangi Khapre, *Indian Express,* September 28, 2016, Rural and restless.
21. *The Hindu,* October 1, 2016, 10 MLD waste dumped in Ganga daily at Mirzapur, NGT told.
22. *The Hindu,* October 17, 2016, Burning of municipal waste discolouring Taj Mahal.
23. Dhrubo Jyoti and Umesh Raghuvanshi, *Hindustan Times,* November 23, 2016, Ganga is a marginal constituency in UP.
24. Somesh Jha, *Business Standard,* January 14, 2017, Government pushes to ease industrial pollution norms.
25. Bhadra Sinha, *Hindustan Times,* January 24, 2017 IITs to adopt five villages near Ganga, 10 ministries on the job.
26. *Hindustan,* February 08, 2017, Ganga safaai maamle mein NMCG ko phatkaar.
27. *Press Trust of India,* February 22, 2017, Shut shop if you can't treat effluents, SC warns polluting industries.
28. Anubhuti Vishnoi, *The Economic Times,* February 22, 2017, Ganga promise: Walk the ghats but don't take dip.
29. Jayashree Nandi and Neha Lalchandani, *The Times of India,* February 22, 2017, ₹2000 cr down Yamuna drain.
30. Vimukt Dave, *Business Standard,* April 15, 2017, Alang ship breaking shrinks 50% in March quarter.
31. Sowmiya Ashok, *Indian Express,* April 22, 2017, Hurdle in dust surveys: Violators who refuse to cough up fines.
32. Amitabh Sinha, *Indian Express,* May 20, 2017, Survey: Ganga-polluting industries have shot up.
33. R. Srinivasan, *The Hindu,* June 18, 2017, The spectre of unemployment – Sans quality jobs, "aspirational young India" will become "angry young India".

34. *Hindustan*, July 14, 2017, All attempts to clean the Ganga fail.
35. *Hindustan*, July 03, 2017, Come monsoons and Yamuna starts to emit white froth due to pollution.
36. Sumit Bhattacharjee, *The Hindu*, September, 2017, A safe beach turns an eyesore.
37. Agence France Presse, 02 September 2017, Sri Lanka bans plastic after garbage crisis.
38. Anand Mishra, The *Indian Express*, September 14, 2017, Swach campaign: Ministers to be roped in for Shramdaan.
39. T. Appala Naidu, *The Hindu*, September 18, 2017, Pigment effluents pose threat to water table.
40. Mallica Joshi, *Indian Express*, September 26, 2017, Toilets make for study in contrast in this tale of two Ganga villages.
41. Aditi Vatsa, *Indian Express*, October 11, 2017, 60 schoolkids fall ill, emission from sugar mill suspected.
42. Aniruddha Ghosal, *Indian Express*, October 19, 2017, What's fouling Delhi's air: 4 studies, 4 conclusions.
43. Jacob Koshy, *The Hindu*, November 23, 2017, Mass bathing in Ganga aggravates antimicrobial resistance woes.
44. Jyoti Mukul, *Business Standard*, December 1, 2017, IFC sees US$3.1-trillion business opportunity in green ventures.
45. *Press Trust of India*, February 05, 2018, Food ministry proposes hike in sugar import duty to 100%.
46. *Press Trust of India*, February 06, 2018, We are not garbage collectors, Supreme Court tells Centre.
47. *Hindustan*, February 09, 2018, Data on industrial units situated on the banks of Ganga not same across different government agencies.
48. *Indian Express*, February 13, 2018, Ammonia levels in water up, Jal Board dials Green Tribunal.
49. *The Hindu*, February 23, 2018, Waste is a greater contributor to air pollution than we realise.
50. *Indian Express*, February 13, 2018, Ammonia levels in water up, Jal Board dials Green Tribunal.

51. B. R. Rohit, *The Times of India*, March 22, 2018, Kaggalipura residents up in arms over toxic fumes.
52. *The Times of India*, March 28, 2018, Gurugram: Students wade through sewage pool to reach school for exams.
53. Vaishnavi Chandrashekar, *Scroll.in*, March 29, 2018, As India struggles to clean up its polluted urban rivers, ecological and economic costs are mounting.
54. Aditi Veena and Vikram Soni, *The Hindu*, March 31, 2018, Rivers, floodplains, cities and farmers.
55. Masoom Gupte, ET Bureau, April 02, 2018 Sugar is a greater danger than gunpowder, says "Sapiens" author Yuval Noah Harari.
56. Toufiq Rashid, *Hindustan* Times, April 03, 2018, India not water deficient, yet mismanagement a challenge.
57. Anisha Bhatia, April 06, 2018, www.ndtv.com, World Health Day 2018: In *Inefficient Management of Waste Is a Cause of Deadly Diseases.*
58. Meenakshi Kapoor and Krithika Dinesh, *Scroll.in*, April 9, 2018, Tourism scores over ecology, livelihoods as India's coastal law is amended yet again.
59. Virendra Singh Rawat, *Business Standard*, April 17, 2018, UP looks beyond sugar mills with khandsari, gur units.
60. Kunal Bose, *Business Standard*, April 18, 2018, A sugar-coated crisis.
61. Rajalakshmi Nirmal, *The Hindu*, May 06, 2018, Not so sweet.
62. Rajalakshmi Nirmal, *The Hindu*, May 06, 2018, Interview with M Manickam (Executive Chairman, Sakthi Sugars), The government should keep out of cane pricing.
63. Megha Manchanda, *Business Standard*, May 17, 2018, Vehicle scrapping policy will lead to 20 dismantling units.
64. Alnoor Peermohamed, *Business Standard*, May 21, 2018 Bengaluru's crumbling infrastructure – The urban nightmare.
65. Praveen Khanna, *Indian Express*, June 05, 2018, Photo Feature: Keeping clean: A man takes a bath amid piles of garbage and plastic waste, near Shaheen Bagh.

66. Interview with Heather Koldewey – Environmentalist by S Ravi, *The Hindu*, June 05, 2018, There is a strong link between plastic and poverty.
67. Editorial, *Indian Express*, June 8, 2018, Right price of Sugar.
68. Partha Sarathi Biswas, *Indian Express*, June 14, 2018, Govt's scheme for cane farmers benefits traders.
69. Virendra Singh Rawat, Jayajit Dash, Satyavrat Mishra, and Sanjeeb Mukherjee, *Business Standard*, June 29, 2018, Nation stares at water crisis, high-risk states ill-prepared.
70. Krishnadas Rajagopal, *The Hindu*, July 12, 2018, SC decries pathetic state of Taj.
71. Serish Nanisetti, *The Hindu*, July 19, 2018, Surge of trash lays siege to Golconda.
72. Shinjini Ghosh, *The Hindu*, July 20, 2018, NGT says no effective steps taken to clean river Ganga.
73. Virendra Singh Rawat, *Business Standard*, August 04, 2018, UP sugar millers knock at Yogi door for bailout.
74. Editorial, *Business Standard*, August 10, 2018, Sugar Muddle.
75. Jacob Koshy, *The Hindu*, August 29, 2018, India's most polluted: 30% have no clean-up plan.
76. *The Hindu*, September 07, 2018, Swachh Bharat progress key to UN SDG on open defecation.
77. Jacob Koshy, *The Hindu*, September 15, 2018, Shapoorji Pallonji bags major project to clean Ganga.
78. Ashok Gulati and Siraj Hussain, *Indian Express*, September 18, 2018, Drowning in sweetness.
79. Editorial, *The Hindu*, September 18, 2018, Saving rivers.
80. V. Sreenivasa Murthy, *The Hindu*, September 26, 2018, Photo Feature: Frothing trouble: The bellandur lake in Bengaluru started frothing again on Tuesday following rain since Sunday. In some places, the thick and smelly froth rose to a height of 10 ft. The phenomenon is caused by chemicals and pollutants in the lake.
81. Jacob Koshy, *The Hindu*, October 12, 2018, "Save Ganga" crusader Agarwal dead, he was on a fast to save the river; died of heart attack.

82. Sanjay Parikh, *Hindustan*, October 12, 2018, Professor GD Agarwal; One voice that was not heard.
83. Satyavrat Mishra, *Business Standard*, October 16, 2018, Despite ₹50-bn allocation, Bihar still far from the dream of clean Ganga.
84. Jacob Koshy, *The Hindu*, October 31, 2018, India among nations that face grave danger to soil biodiversity.
85. *The Hindu*, November 28, 2018, Most people unaware of true cost of pollution, said Michael Greenstone, Economist & Director, Energy Policy Institute, University of Chicago.
86. Sanjay Pandey, *Hindustan*, November 28, 2018, Ganga gets freedom from Asia's largest drain.
87. TCA Sharad Raghavan, *The Hindu*, December 5, 2018, The Wednesday Interview with Sanjeev Sanyal: Our calorie-oriented approach to agriculture in no longer sustainable.
88. Damini Nath, *The Hindu*, December 06, 2018, Government plans to store Yamuna's monsoon excess in reservoirs.
89. *The Hindu*, December 07, 2018, Air pollution case of 1 in 8 deaths.
90. *Hindustan*, December 10, 2018, 76% of Yamuna is dirty from Wazirabad to Okhla.
91. Jason Horowitz, *The New York Times*, December 24, 2018, Rome in ruins.
92. Partha Sarathi Biswas and Harish Damodaran, *Indian Express*, January 07, 2019, Cane arrears up to ₹11,000 crores set to mount before polls; in UP, Maharashtra, sugar mill owners fail to pay farmers government-fixed prices.
93. Gyanendra Rawat, *Hindustan*, January 09, 2019, Why did we forget pollution in the Yamuna River?
94. https://swarajyamag.com/infrastructure/namami-gange-how-modis-grand-project-in-progressing-in-these-seven-cities January 11, 2019 (web link last accessed) Namami Gange: How Modi's grand project is progressing in these seven cities.
95. Jacob Koshy, *The Hindu*, January 22, 2019, Plastic waste imports to India go up, Influx of PET bottles quadrupled from 2017 to 2018, according to green body.

96. *Hindustan*, January 30, 2019, Government of Haryana pulled up for high ammonia levels in Yamuna River.
97. *The Hindu*, January 30, 2019, Yamuna cleaning: NGT directs 3 States to furnish ₹10 crore each as performance guarantee; Delhi, Haryana, UP given 1 month.
98. Harish Gilai, *The Hindu*, February 04, 2019, Plan to ban water sachets in Araku Valley.
99. *The Hindu*, February 06, 2019, NGT imposes ₹25 lakhs fine on UP government of failing to stop dumping of sewage and untreated water in the Upper Ganga Canal.
100. *Swaraj* magazine, https://swarajyamag.com (web link last accessed on March 3, 2019), Zero Sewer Discharge in Ganga in Varanasi by November.
101. G. Ravi Prasad, *Indian Express*, February 21, 2019, How much urea does India really require?
102. Jacob Koshy, *The Hindu*, February 24, 2019, Ganga basin States stare at three-fold rise in crop failures by 2040, as flows decline and pollution worsens, there will be less irrigation and drinking water available in Uttar Pradesh and Madhya Pradesh.
103. Santosh Mehrotra, *The Hindu*, February 13, 2019, The shape of the jobs crisis: India has no industrial policy or employment strategy to ride the wave of its demographic dividend.
104. Sune Haugbolle, https://foreignpolicy.com/2019/02/20/lebanon-is-facing-an-environmental-and-economic-disaster-hezbollah-hariri-aoun/ web link last accessed on February 20, 2019, Lebanon is facing an economic and environmental disaster (web link last accessed on March 13, 2019).
105. Paul Salopek, *National Geographic*, In a land of many rivers, clean water is out of reach; for nearly half of India's population, water is scarce or polluted, https://www.nationalgeographic.com/magazine/2019/03/paul-salopek-out-of-eden-walk-india-water/ (web link last accessed on March 06, 2019).
106. *Hindustan*, April 12, 2019, Garbage burned whole night in the centre of Gurugram city.

107. *Hindustan*, April 13, 2019, Notice served to the municipal corporation of Gurugram for burning garbage in the centre of the city.

108. Hemani Bhandari and Sidharth Ravi, *The Hindu*, April 14, 2019, Sealing drive turns violent, officials hurt – Scrap dealers at Mayapuri market throw stones at sealing team, forcing police to resort to lathicharge.

109. Sidharth Ravi, *The Hindu*, April 15, 2019, Mayapuri traders given 48 hours to comply with sealing orders.

INDEX

ACKNOWLEDGEMENTS

Someone wise once told me that life should be enjoyed for the journey and not spent in waiting to arrive at the destination. Throughout my time writing this book, I have learnt many things about my own character and chief amongst them is that this teaching is deceptively hard to put into practice. Yet I have tried my best to enjoy this rocky journey and no official record of these thoughts will ever be complete without giving my gratitude to those who helped along the way.

The pivotal role played by Late Mr. Kripal Singh Dhillon begs mentioning foremost, because he was the first reviewer of the book's synopsis and it was his early guidance that made this project see the light of day. He is dearly missed today.

Preeti Gill's unwavering support and steadfast faith in the book helped me navigate the vagaries of the book's publication process. She has my sincerest gratitude.

This project was not possible without Technopak Advisors Pvt. Ltd. The unparalleled exposure and the experience of working on myriad consulting projects at Technopak proved invaluable for my research that went into this book.

I also extend my gratitude to friends and family, seniors and colleagues, new and old: Arvind Singhal, Saloni Nangia, Sanjoy Hazarika, Puneet Davar, Patu Keswani, Tulika Srivastava, Dinesh

Sharma, Priya and Siddharth Raja, Prof. Ashwani Kumar and dearest Parul Tyagi.

Shashi Bisen and Dr. Prakash Singh Bisen, my mother and father have my deepest gratitude for always standing by me and guiding me when the going was tough during this project. As does my brother Anand Bisen for being a friend, critic and a valuable sounding board throughout this journey. I fondly recall the urban trails we took in the scenic vistas of Seattle which were not only cleansing for my thoughts but also a treasure trove of information and fresh perspectives.

I thank Pan Macmillan India and specially Dr. Prasun Chatterjee – Editorial Director for believing in this project and for putting up with the endless queries and anxious e-mails of this first-time author. You folks have been great!

And now I must mention my staunchest critic and most brutal sergeant who also happens to be my co-passenger in this journey – my wife Sonia Rao. She edited the first draft of the book alongside her entrepreneurship and duties as a mother to our adolescent son and daughter who was then still an infant. The book owes its title to her. She chiseled the book into the form it is now in and it would not be an overstatement to say that many a times she put words to my thoughts more beautifully that I ever could. We make a great team and I feel the deeply grateful for everything she is to me.

Finally, to Angad (the adolescent) and Maya (the now-toddler) who are my sanctuary.

Millennium City: the pace of development outpacing the city's ability to handle the aftermath

Innocence lost: dismantling of e-waste in the by-lanes of Delhi by bare, young hands

The Moradabad Lab: India's predominant defence against e-waste

India's age old wisdom:
A rag-picker crosses a railway track;
'Sweepers' carrying off collected
garbage in an open truck

Invoking the Divine in India
at all costs

An organized flea market and
formal street retail in Madrid,
Spain

Informal living grows irrespective of the train tracks in an Indian city

A shopping street in Amsterdam

The cow as the deity, and the cow as the industrial asset meet at this neighborhood dump in an Indian city

Muzzafarpur, Bihar: the sides of a state highway seen piled up with rubbish

Chikkballapur, Karnataka: the underside of a fly-over serves as a convenient garbage dump

A high-tech sanitation van repairs and maintains a closed sewage line in Seattle, USA

Wade through waste: filthy water from an open sewage line floods a street in front of a school in Lucknow

The disfiguring of Delhi: three decades of irresponsible development

Cans of segregated waste lined up neatly awaiting collection in a Boston back-lane

A dilapidated 'dhaloa' or waste collection point in Dwarka, Delhi, and a sanitation worker

A beautiful, organized paved street meant only for pedestrians in Paris, France